THE HUMAN BUDDHA

The Human Buddha

Enlightenment for the New Millennium

AZIZ KRISTOF

MOTILAL BANARSIDASS PUBLISHERS
PRIVATE LIMITED • DELHI

First Edition: Delhi, 2000

www.azizkristof.org
email: grace@azizkristof.org

ISBN: 81-208-1753-2 (Cloth)
ISBN: 81-208-1754-0 (Paper)

Also available at:

MOTILAL BANARSIDASS

236, 9th Main III Block, Jayanagar, Bangalore 560 011
41 U.A. Bungalow Road, Jawahar Nagar, Delhi 110 007
8 Mahalaxmi Chamber, Warden Road, Mumbai 400 026
120 Royapettah High Road, Mylapore, Chennai 600 004
Sanas Plaza, 1302 Baji Rao Road, Pune 411 002
8 Camac Street, Calcutta 700 017
Ashok Rajpath, Patna 800 004
Chowk, Varanasi 221 001

Printed in India

BY JAINENDRA PRAKASH JAIN AT SHRI JAINENDRA PRESS,
A-45 NARAINA, PHASE-I, NEW DELHI 110 028
AND PUBLISHED BY NARENDRA PRAKASH JAIN FOR
MOTILAL BANARSIDASS PUBLISHERS PRIVATE LIMITED,
BUNGALOW ROAD, DELHI 110 007

DEDICATED TO THE SPIRIT OF GUIDANCE, THE SOURCE OF GRACE AND OUR ETERNAL PARENT WHICH HAS REVEALED HERSELF THROUGH MY UNITY WITH THE SOUL OF HOUMAN

Acknowledgement

We would like to express deep gratitude to beloved Antar Amira who dedicated her whole time for the editing work and inspired deeply the final shape of the book. Her enthusiasm, clear mind, passion and ability to sacrifice - truly made this book possible. We want also to express deep thanks to beloved Anna Gordon, Daniel Oz, Dharanasri, Elida, Alan and others for preparing the material from recorded Transmissions, and to beloved Tanmayo for her inspiring help in designing the cover.

Contents

Acknowledgement	vii
Preface	xiii
Introduction	xv
Enlightenment Beyond Traditions	xix
Meeting the Master	xxi
The Human Buddha	xxvii
Teaching for the New Millennium	xxxi
Guidance	xxxix
Model of Existence	xli
Model of Awakening	xliii
PART ONE: Transmission of Awakening	**1**
1. Seeking Freedom from the Collective Mind	3
2. Unfolding the Now through the Non-dual Path	11
3. Dispelling the Myth of Enlightenment	25
4. The Original Question	39
5. Awakening Points to the Now	53
6. The Garden of the Beloved	69
7. Beyond Forgetfulness	75
8. Becoming One Again	83
9. Discovering the Light of Creation	87
10. Doorway to the Timeless	93
PART TWO: Awakening to the Question	**99**
I. Transcending Ignorance	101
Entering the Path	103
The Art of Meditation	139
II. Dimension of I Am	161
Awakening of Awareness	163
Surrender into Being	185
Enlightenment of the Heart	209
The Inner State	227
III. Dimension of the Soul	253
Enlightenment to Me	255

Life as a Human 281
Facing the Unknown 331

IV. Dimension of Intelligence 357

The Wisdom of Clarity 359
The Nature of the Mind 387

V. Dimension of the Creator 409

The Beloved 411
The Presence of Grace 425
The World of Creation 433

VI. Dimension of Enlightenment 479

The Self Realised 481
Secrets of Teaching 523

VII. Upon Completion 547

The Human Buddha 549

PART THREE: Autobiography of Awakening **569**

I Have Been Blessed... 571
Explanation of Terms 597

TRANSMISSION FROM THE DIMENSION OF UNDERSTANDING

Preface

The book that we present has been compiled from the teachings of Aziz in the latter part of 1999. It is an immense amount of material which summarises the Teaching of Guidance - a revolutionary vision of Awakening channelled for the New Millennium from the Dimension of Pure Intelligence. This book cannot simply be read - it needs to be deeply contemplated. A seeker who wants to passively absorb this teaching will become quickly frustrated because it is not a presentation of intellectual knowledge but a Transmission of direct understanding. This transmission can be received only if one makes an extraordinary effort both from the mind and heart to actually enter the Inner Dimension, the truth of I AM.

Dear reader, in reading this book may you be one with deep meditation and an intense inner quest for clarity. This book is not a ready made dish, but a challenge, a mountain to be climbed in order to gain the whole panorama of Understanding.

Aziz mostly teaches in the third person. That is because he does not merely represent his individual consciousness but also the dimension of Guidance. This 'we' to which Aziz refers is not plural. Neither it is collective, nor is it individual. It is a vast space of Intelligence and Love, the realm of the Beloved. It is from that mysterious place that the Transmission of Awakening flows into the time-dimension where forgetfulness and the sorrow of separation abide.

A reader who is familiar with the teaching of Nisargadatta Maharaj should be aware that Aziz gives different meanings to terms like 'Beingness' and 'I Am.' The translators of Maharaj were using both these terms as synonyms for 'consciousness' or 'sense of existing.' For Aziz, I Am is more than consciousness as it includes the quality of Being and Heart. From the other side, Beingness (Being) is beyond consciousness and represents the energy of Rest, that which gravitates towards the Absolute. The Absolute represents the very ground of Beingness, where the manifested reality is transcended. The recognition of the Absolute, which was not elaborated by Maharaj, signifies the meeting of consciousness with Beingness. Because of this meeting, the

Absolute State, though beyond consciousness, can become consciously recognised.

Certain terms found in the text which may be unknown to the reader can be found in the explanation. Aziz often uses the pronouns 'she' or 'her' for terms like the Beloved, Divine, Heart, Soul or Me. This is because from the perspective of human psychology, these dimensions of existence and experience reflect closer that which we would consider feminine qualities. The term 'Me' is an equivalent to the Soul, but carries a slightly different flavour as it refers more directly to how the Soul experiences herself. When we refer to awareness in general - we use a small letter. When we refer to the awareness aspect of I Am - it is capitalised. The reader should take special notice of capitalised words, as they are terms relevant to the unique teaching of Aziz. In addition, they are not meant to de-emphasise other important concepts like 'universe,' for instance. These terms are not capitalised simply because they don't refer directly to the Transmission of Awakening.

This book is a continuation of the previous teachings presented in the books Enlightenment Beyond Traditions and Transmission of Awakening. Hence, it is highly recommendable to read these books to gain a more comprehensive understanding of the whole Teaching.

Introduction

'You always ask such impossible questions' a friend said to me, laughing and shaking her head. It was true. Since I was a child I had been asking these questions and nowhere could I find real answers. Parents and friends teased me and said: 'wait until you are old enough to go to University. Then you will be happy...you will stay up all night discussing these things.' Later, I went to Oxford and Cambridge Universities but still there were no answers. So, I sat with the questions inside and waited. One day I met Aziz and, to my amazement, he answered every question to my satisfaction. Since then more and more questions arise. I have books of questions and Aziz is endlessly patient in closing his eyes and transmitting a subtle and penetrating response.

Many spiritual teachers ask one simply to be in their presence. This may be temporarily uplifting, but it rarely brings about a complete and permanent transformation. Aziz draws to him those who crave understanding; those who wish to grow not only in awakening but also in intelligence. Without understanding, appreciation and clarity, awakening is only partial. I have seen a student ask: 'Why do I have no questions?' After a month of guided meditation with Aziz, the questions came. Asking the right question is as important as finding the answer. I hope this book will stimulate you, dear reader, to bring any latent questions you may secretly explore in your daily lives into consciousness and expression. Question and answer give birth to each other in a dynamic process and it is from this process that this book is being created. It is a living book, a living truth, not petrified by time into a fixed tradition.

There are souls who are lead by intuition or guidance to go inside and glimpse the awakened states but who lack the conceptual tools and the clarity to go deeper. Without a rigorous training in understanding, both experiential and conceptual, there is usually no clarity, no confidence, no consistency. Not finding any reflection in the outer world or any language in which to express a shift so subtle and profound, the person may not understand what has happened. Unless one knows that the State of Presence needs to be deliberately cultivated, the mechanical mind keeps pulling one back into collective consciousness or amnesia. Those with common sense may be further confused because they know that their humanness: their personal, time-bound self, coexists with their eternal identity. While they may merge with that which is beyond them, the unique, individual experiencer of the inner states remains. Most established spiritual traditions tell us that after Enlightenment there is no ME, no one relative, flawed or human. The standard image of an enlightened person is of a kind of superman with no human desires, no human attachments and no human ego. This image is unrealistic and unattainable and so many remain perpetual seekers instead of finders. Unless one has the courage and the insight to challenge the spiritual status quo, the mechanical mind may be left doubting what the soul doubtlessly knows.

What I am trying to say is that understanding is crucial and I have never met a catalyst for understanding like Aziz. On behalf of his students I would like to thank him for the most valuable of gifts. This is an important and revolutionary book because it addresses a crucial issue which has often been neglected: the human face of the Buddha. How do our human nature and our eternal nature interact? What happens where imperfection and perfection meet, where time and timelessness meet, where the human and the Buddha meet? Who are we and how can we integrate all aspects of our true selves? How can we find completion here and beyond? This book is, at last, a response to these vital questions and I hope that contemplating the answers prompts us to find our own understanding, our own nourishment, our own completion.

Who is Aziz? He is a Self-realised spiritual Master who demystifies the phenomenon of Enlightenment and shows one how to reach it directly. The Satsangs are beyond meditative techniques and beyond traditions. Beginning with the question: Who am I? Aziz guides his students inside to discover their true identity. Satsang consists of guided meditation or silent sitting followed by questions and answers. The guided meditation focuses on three gateways to the inner realm: Being, Awareness and Heart. We locate, activate and explore these centres to bring about a complete and radical shift in the inner experience. The effect is cumulative. It is hard to put the experience of being in Satsang or in the presence of Aziz into words. One feels thrown back on oneself, in a space beyond the mind. One finds oneself just sitting (Shikantaza), resting in the Now, one with God. Sometimes one feels neutrality, stillness, absolute rest; sometimes one feels moved, touched by Grace, Beauty and infinite Love. There is a new experience of oneself, a new depth. To be in the presence of Truth is always a relief and the energy of Guidance channelled by Aziz is nourishing, bringing balance, clarity, sanity, peace... After Satsang one feels renewed. Something extraordinary is happening: one is seen by the Beyond, by the Mystery and, like a child, one is embraced.

Aziz is not a Master who is posing as a guru. Those who are looking for guru worship are quickly forced to reconsider their attitude to the Spiritual Path, for Aziz is intensely and tirelessly testing their practice and level of awakening, not allowing them just to sit passively in his presence. The role of the spiritual master is extremely important for he is a channel of transformation, but a real master never emphasises his own presence. He remains in the shadow of the Truth humbly representing the Ultimate. Aziz is a true spiritual teacher who deeply dislikes spiritual slogans and a simplistic understanding of Enlightenment. He frees us from our crystallised and conditioned concepts about the Awakened State. If we are Buddhists, he takes us beyond the concept of no-self, beyond the concept of non-suffering, beyond the linear concept of liberation. If we are Advaita students, he frees us from the idealistic concept of Enlightenment, from the linear concept of not being a doer, from the static concept of non-duality. He clearly demonstrates the necessity of a methodical process in cultivating the Inner States in order to reach the Self. Aziz challenges many of the conclusions created by the past traditions in order to reveal a multidimensional reality of Awakening.

To seekers who ask the question: 'Am I That?' Aziz gives a surprising answer: 'You are not and you will never be and you are not even yourself yet, but you can become your Real Me and you can become one with God. Do not be fooled, thinking that you are the Ultimate Reality while you are living in the sorrow of ignorance. If you wish to find your way back home you must be honest with yourself and ready to go beyond slogans; it is here that you enter the Spiritual Path.'

Anna Gordon

Enlightenment Beyond Traditions

Aziz is a living, spiritual Master, who reached complete, multidimensional awakening after many years of tremendously intense inner work and desperate search for freedom. His journey to awakening was rich, complex, magical and full of surprises. From his first awakening as a five-year-old child, he was continuously yearning for spiritual completion. From contemplating spiritual matters in complete solitude, living in a small Polish village, he continued his awakening process in Zen monasteries in Korea and Japan, as well as studying deeply the Advaita tradition in India. However, it was the intervention of Guidance, Higher Intelligence or Grace which brought his Soul to the realisation of radical Wholeness.

After stabilising in December 1993 in the state of Pure Consciousness, he still continued his inner quest for the deeper experience of the Self. For the subtle matter of transcending consciousness, he could not find support from any living Masters or traditions. It was at that time that he met his beloved spiritual brother, Houman. These two souls became deeply connected because of their unquenchable yearning for Truth and their passion for Understanding. The unity of their souls, from the depth of their Hearts, manifested the appearance of Guidance, the presence of the Over-soul: their eternal parent. For the first time, they were encountered by the presence of this infinite Intelligence who could answer all their questions and appease their deepest longing. It was at that time that their lives were brought to a radical change. They had been seen by the Beloved. No longer was their evolution and destiny in their hands. They had surrendered their lives to the higher Intelligence, to the non-human source of pure Understanding, which is Love. For the first time they could see their lives from the universal perspective, beyond the limitations of human consciousness. There is no other word for what happened to them but Grace and no other reason can be found why this Grace entered into their particular existence but by the absolute sincerity of their Hearts.

Guidance directed Aziz to the retreat in which he received instructions about how to reach the Absolute. The shift into the Absolute State beyond Consciousness took place on 31 December 1996. After reaching the Absolute State, Aziz was further guided in America to awaken his Heart which culminated in Enlightenment to the Heart one year later.

Because of the gradual and methodical nature of his Awakening, as well as Revelation from the Beyond, Aziz was able to fully comprehend the subtleties of the Awakening process. He created in unity with Houman a revolutionary Teaching and system of Complete Meditation, a powerful tool for transformation which reflects the principles of the Non-dual Path to Self-realisation.

Meeting the Master

A Student's Perspective

There has been no time in history parallel to the Now. I speak not of the timeless present but this very opening in time whereby Truth is again breaking its silence. That which lies deepest in our being can no longer be held below a whisper.

This place we abide is utterly vast and the consciousness which permeates its every cell has been little understood. The language we have to describe this infinity of ours - in its humility, can only point to the suchness of its essence. It is no surprise that this suchness has never been grasped by the human mind. The linear and often mechanical nature of the mind can only make itself available to a conceptual understanding of reality. Unfortunately, Truth is free from concepts and as such, the mind which understands it through concepts must be transcended. Very few souls have reached this transcendence and among them even fewer have brought their experience into the light - wherefore others could delight in its wisdom.

Spiritual masters past and present have long struggled with the teaching work as it requires the externalisation of a deeply non-communicable inner state. This work is made particularly difficult, as it is not an ordinary subject matter: the transmission of Truth and the process of awakening to it. The subject matter is extremely sensitive and requires a great deal of precision, accuracy and wholeness in its delivery, so as to bring about clarity. But clarity in truth cannot be aroused unless the understanding of the master is absolutely crystallised.

While a master can be considered someone who has attained to the Inner State, not every master may have gained insight into all the subtle steps involved. This point especially pertains to those who attained a higher state solely through the effort of their own master who transmitted it. Here, an energetic exchange takes place but this does not necessarily include the related understanding. And though the clarity of a master may be indisputable, he/she may not possess the skill to make the teaching conversable, or the charisma to probe the wonder, intelligence and necessary perseverance of the student. And though it may be that all those qualities are intact, the slight differences between one master and another, could be for the student, the difference between awakening and not awakening at all.

As I have come to know, one of the most challenging aspects of being in the position of a master is to minimise the tempting bloating effect of the ego. Apparently, one of the biggest triumphs of the master lies in the learning of a deeper and deeper humility. A master without humility normally means a teaching based on the honorary master and his/her egoistic projections. On the other hand, a master with humility will emphasise the teaching while he himself remains in the background as a mere representation of its truth.

Aziz is one such master who represents the truth of his teaching. He upholds the integrity of the teaching work by maintaining the teaching itself as the central focus. But here the balance is delicate because he does not stand apart from his teaching. As there is a natural space between a master and his work, Aziz seems to have closed this gap in so far as possible. He is very much a living embodiment of the teaching, which means he lives what he teaches. In this respect, you could say Aziz is his teaching. This is critical because the master represents the potentiality of the teaching and for the student, this must be foremost when selecting a master. For Western students, it has been on the whole, not much more than a concept - to meet a teacher who actually believes in what he/she teaches. Actually, modern education systems in general are a true disgrace to the integrity of their students. In this sense, our times demand more than ever real teachers with real teachings. So it is the task of the student, to not only desire but actually search for a real master - for an incompetent master necessarily relays an incompetent teaching.

To meet him, to perceive his eyes - one is immediately overwhelmed with the absolute clarity which he so strongly emanates. His absolute presence to the Now, like a bald flame of attention - drops you hard into the immediate reality. Your personal world just dissolves into the nakedness of the moment. His presence seems to transport you into that very space beyond the mind, prior to all thought and emotion. In these moments, you feel a transmission of energy, understanding and wakefulness. It is clear there is an exchange being made on all levels. It is also clear that you are not only encountering him but the presence of Grace.

Aziz lives in the Now - in absolute presence to the present. He resides in a non-conceptual space, as it simply cannot be fathomed by the mind. This space is the most fundamental in truth, as it is the unmanifested, the source from which all apparent realities arise. This is indeed profound as most people dwell not in the source but rather in the world of appearances as rectified by the senses. I have felt him to be like a living essence, perhaps even like the Tao personified. Although his beingness penetrates you, you simply cannot grasp him - at least not within the frame of the known.

Often in the most face-to-face teachings, beyond all pretensions of separation - I felt myself briefly encountering the crest of life, the spirit of that which existed prior to Me and will maintain when I pass. I feel blessed by virtue of his multi-dimensional nature, that is, by his ability to abide in the Absolute space and yet be right here right now with us. It is actually a bit sad that our level of consciousness is so low that we cannot wholly appreciate a being such as Aziz. In a sense, he is left to his own experience, as we can only make gestures of understanding towards his inner state.

It seems he has always been very much alone on his life path. From his first awakening as a child of 5 up to now, his search for the inner Truth has actually been full of sacrifice. To want what is real in such unconscious and often superficial reality, meant always to make some degree of compromise. As a youth, he always had a difficult time conforming to the conventions of society and later on to the traditions of spiritual institutions. At a young age, he could perceive the poverty of western style education but yet had to undergo it. Similarly, he was forced to take part in the Army as a male citizen of Poland, something which was clearly against his nature. When he left his home to seek out spiritual guidance in monasteries in the East, he continually came across masters attached more to the confines of their religion than to Truth beyond traditions. He had to mostly make his own way and direct himself into each successive step on the path. It was his intense longing, fiery persistence and Grace that eventually led to his awakening. But far be it that his work is done.

Now, he is constantly giving his whole energy and attention to the teaching work. Each Satsang is incredibly intense and students often take as much as they can get, oblivious to the amount of energy this type of teaching demands. Even among seekers, there is much ignorance regarding enlightenment and so it is falsely regarded that Aziz is like a superhuman, never to be depleted and can just go on and on like some kind of machine. Not to say that this work is thankless, but often, little appreciation is extended. Still, Aziz asserts that Satsang is a sacred gathering through which the process of transformation is radically accelerated. When he is not teaching, he is busy writing literature to aid the philosophical aspect of the teaching. This is also quite demanding as so much is involved in putting across such a complicated and abstract subject matter as awakening.

Still, despite all the sufferings met in this dimension, Aziz is like a light full of shine and good humour. He honestly admits his difficulties and doesn't project himself as an untouchable. In this way, the human nature of his Buddhahood is openly respected. When I see his posters (regarding the place and time of his teaching) being purposely torn and removed - I feel deeply hurt on his behalf because of the truth of his dedication and sincerity in the service of others. For this, there is no animosity or negativity on his side, he simply replaces the poster and accepts that it is a part of the teaching work. It is even a sort of confirmation for him, because to do this type of work well - one will naturally be confronted with dark forces. He maintains his equanimity and perspective, neutrally asserting that it is just happening.

The spiritual path ultimately is your own but I know positively that the real steps, in my progress at least, have been made in his presence and under his guidance. The gift of awakening is most precious and entirely rare as no one before Aziz has offered such a precise technology on how to actually become awakened. As a seeker, I have had the chance to attend a number of different Satsangs being given by all sorts of personalities. I have found most masters, to be quite unable to give a holistic teaching, let alone offer clear and solid answers to the inquiry of seekers. There are even masters around that create a circus type atmosphere performing tricks such as swallowing scorpions and offering buffet meals before and after Satsang. This is actually offensive and even degrading to a true seeker, but I agree with Aziz in that most seekers aren't really seeking anything much more than seeking itself. Anyways, it is these seekers that give rise to the deformity of Satsang culture. Unfortunately, the buck doesn't stop there because these pseudo-masters create an atmosphere of understanding that reflect badly on masters who are genuinely working for the betterment of people.

Aziz is truly disappointed with the quality of masters around. For this, he has had to work extra hard not only to make contemporary the process of awakening but also to undo all the myths and misunderstandings being perpetuated by other masters in the present. All in all, it is clear that a master like Aziz is without a doubt, very rare. He must be characterised by his absolutely crystallised clarity, like a diamond of pure understanding pushing forth, through not only the clouds of the collective unconscious but also through the clouds of the spiritual collective ignorance.

Aziz has fulfilled his destiny, he has reached inner completion. By virtue of Grace, he has been delivered more space within which to evolve. He has been offered more depth, more angles from which the truth can be known. For this, he stays with us. His expansion is like the light of a star, spilling into all conceivable directions filling the horizon with glimmer, melting even the possibility of perceiving it. He washes us over and over with rays of consciousness, bringing us back to that intimate space - One with ourselves, One with the Beloved. Like a mirror, the Human Buddha in him simply reflects the one that lies dormant in us. This is the beauty and inspiration of his presence. He has not just reached enlightenment, that is a mistake - he is enlightenment and that has to be seen. To the seeker, I hope you can rest here.

Antar Amira

The Human Buddha

Returning to the Natural Perspective of Human Awakening

In ancient times, a few thousands years ago, the first awakened beings made an attempt to explain the truth of Enlightenment within the context of human life. It was a difficult task because the basic conceptual tools which could build the frame of understanding, were not yet created. It took the effort of many generations to crystallise a fundamental structure of philosophical, ethical and mystical models for spiritual realisation, which could reflect in a satisfactory way the reality of Enlightenment. There was, however, a danger that the natural reality of awakening could become distorted by the intervention of the human mind, which always has a tendency to impose on reality a certain linear and simplistic logic, a tendency to be extreme and dogmatic. And this is what has happened: the myth of Enlightenment replaced the reality of Enlightenment.

A long time ago, the concept of liberation was created: the vision of a free man, god-like, beyond suffering, beyond imperfection, an immaculate being. This idea, promising the ultimate freedom from the human condition, was not incorrect but extreme in casting off human nature and negating a certain essential human sensitivity. The price we pay for following this model to the very end is disconnection from our humanness, closing down, negating our essential vulnerability, the child-like quality of the Soul. The Soul cannot become awakened unless she acknowledges her inherent gentleness and innocence.

A liberated being is not automatically awakened to the Soul. Enlightenment, as is traditionally understood, may disconnect one even further from the reality of Pure Me. Why? Because one becomes stuck in the impersonal experience, not being able to make the final step, which is awakening to the personal experiencer.

Just as, at one stage of evolution, a human needs to become a Buddha, in order to transcend ignorance, so the Buddha has to go beyond Enlightenment in order to become human and reach the true Natural State. The complete understanding of the

Natural State goes beyond seeing it merely as consciousness free from thoughts or the non-abiding condition of pure being. The Natural State is total existence, radical wholeness, where human sensitivity, intelligence and emotion, are contained unconditionally in the universal space of isness, which is the unity of Being and Love. To become human again has a different flavour from the Zen idea of returning to the 'market place.' Here, we speak about the ultimate Suchness, where human sensitivity is acknowledged and the presence of the Soul fully manifested.

Who is the Human Buddha? He or she is simply a complete human being, who is one with the light of Creation. It is true that Enlightenment takes us beyond the human realm, but, paradoxically, it is being realised and experienced through human consciousness and within the basic limitations of the human dimension. Our wish is to bring back to the reality of Self-realisation, a truly human perspective. We call it compassion for our human nature.

Many awakened beings have suffered, trying unsuccessfully to fit themselves to the model of a spiritual hero or superman. When one is not awakened, one tends to project many unreal expectations and ideas onto the reality of Self-realisation. But when one reaches Enlightenment, one sees that there is no way to escape from the human destiny. Nevertheless, an enlightened being may not understand it, for he or she may be too conditioned by past concepts. For this reason, we see how important the role of intelligence and understanding is, which adds a new type of awakening to the Self-realised State.

When we look at the life of the historical Buddha Shakyamuni, we can feel that he experienced suffering as well; he had human problems and sorrows. This must be seen clearly, for this understanding liberates from the false. A Buddha is not invincible. A Self-realised being can be even more vulnerable to the difficulties of this insensitive dimension than ordinary people. This is particularly true when the Heart is awakened as well.

Not only is it true that Enlightenment frees us from suffering and gives enormous strength, the opposite is also true. Enlightenment makes us much more sensitive and conscious of difficulties. What this means is that Enlightenment creates a new type of suffering. We call it Pure Suffering. Pure Suffering is not caused by the neurotic tendencies of the mind but reflects the reality of being human.

The Human Buddha is beyond humanness as well as beyond Buddhahood. He or she is beyond these polarities, living the true natural life of an awakened human being. The Human Buddha has not stopped evolving and growing, for his or her last breath has not yet been taken. He or she sees the necessity for never-ending maturation on all levels. He or she fully accepts and honestly acknowledges the reality of human life, including the difficult parts of it as well. The Human Buddha acknowledges his or her human desires and needs, including emotional longing. The Human Buddha does, indeed, have desires and needs and experiences the various conflicts and contradictions of human life.

The difference between an ordinary human being and the Human Buddha is, however, enormous. It is not how they experience the human reality, which make them different, but from which place or perspective. The Human Buddha lives the human destiny, being rooted in the invisible dimension of the Beyond. He or she is one with the Divine. His or her mind is silent and free and the Heart, at all times, is immersed in the tranquil ecstasy, experiencing the constant joy of unity with the Beloved.

Oh yes, Buddha can be sad; yes, Buddha can cry; yes, Buddha can have a bad day; yes, Buddha, may experience frustration and become angry; yes, Buddha can make a wrong decision; yes, Buddha can drop a glass on the floor and spill tea on the carpet; yes, Buddha can be late or forget to come for a meeting; yes, Buddha can have desires and needs; yes, of course Buddha may want to experience human love, and not just compassion; yes, sometimes it is difficult for a Buddha to be a human; yes, Buddha still must learn how to be a human.

Buddha is free to be human. Buddha is free to be beyond freedom. The Human Buddha is Free and beyond Freedom.

Teaching for the New Millennium

The multidimensional vision of spiritual awakening which Aziz expresses and channels into this stage of human evolution is profound and, indeed, subtle. One is unable to receive the gift of new understanding, unless one is ready to let go of the shadow of crystallised concepts created by traditions of the past. The new vision of awakening, certainly, does not contradict the inheritance of the great past traditions with all their precious discoveries. This vision embraces the past teachings and transcends them within a sublime and holistic insight into the Truth. This vision is beyond duality and non-duality, embracing the paradoxical existence of the individual Soul and her evolution within the ocean of Universal Intelligence.

The New Map of Awakening

Many seekers, in their innocence, are misled by the notion of Enlightenment, assuming that it refers to one generic type of realisation. This view is very dangerous and absolutely incorrect. Enlightenment is not one. Unless a seeker has the basic clarity regarding different stages of Self-realisation and understands the map of awakening, he or she will be groping in darkness and confusion. Not everyone who speaks about Enlightenment represents the same state of Self-realisation and certainly not the same depth of understanding. Very few are in the Complete State. To bring clarity into this area, we present here a short version of the inner map of awakening.

1. Enlightenment to State of Presence or pure awareness

This awakening takes place in the third eye centre. Here, one reaches the state of self-awareness. The state of self-awareness represents the real centre of intelligence and is responsible for the continuity of our presence. When the state is stabilised, Awareness is permanently free from thinking, even though it includes the reality of the mind, as its natural extension.

2. Enlightenment to the Absolute State: Tradition of Nisargadatta Maharaj

The Absolute State takes us beyond consciousness. It is realised through the Being quality of I Am. The centre responsible for this shift is located in the lower belly (Hara). This state is quite rare and is not destined for most Souls. Here, the Soul becomes one with the Uncreated, reaching the condition of Pure Rest. The Absolute is the empty aspect of the Ultimate; it is the Being of God. Reaching this state one is in the permanent natural Samadhi, beyond any movement of energy.

3. Enlightenment to the Heart

This Enlightenment refers to the final expansion of the heart centre. Here, the Divine aspect of the Ultimate is realised. It is possible to awaken the Heart before Awareness and Being. More or less, this type of awakening is the destiny for most Souls, as it is in the Heart that the Beloved and Divinity are met.

4. Enlightenment to Me

We call it Soul-realisation. Here, the essence of our individual existence is met. Paradoxically, the Soul can be fully recognised or reflected only when the inner state of I Am is present. Only when one is free from the mind and resting in Being, with the Heart open, can the recognition of Pure Me take place. In some respect realisation of Me is even more subtle and mysterious than the awakening to the Self, for she is the Nearest to us.

5. Beyond Polarities

Before the shift Beyond Polarities, Being and the Heart are in the unconditional Samadhi. However, Awareness, even though free from the mind, still is not fully absorbed into the realm of Beingness. After the shift Beyond Polarities, Awareness also reaches the condition of unconditional Samadhi. Awareness, Being and Heart create one motionless field of pure energy, one with the Beloved: the Diamond Mountain.

Complete Meditation

Aziz in unity with Houman discovered a new technology of Awakening to the complete Inner State. This new technology is based on the very simple but revolutionary discovery that the energetic field of I Am is made of three distinct qualities or aspects: Awareness, Being and the Heart. The centre of I Am in the consciousness or intelligence is the State of Presence, otherwise called the witnessing consciousness of self-awareness. It is energetically located in the middle of the brain, in the third eye. The quality through which one experiences inner rest, stillness, absorption and motionless dwelling within the vertical reality of the Now, is called Being and is energetically located in the lower belly or Hara. When one is in a state of conscious rest, the energy, by law, gravitates toward the Hara. However, the experience of Being itself is not located in the lower belly but is felt all-over and beyond the body. Unless the Heart is awakened, even though one abides in the state of unconditional peace, free from the mind, still one is not complete. The Heart is the esoteric gateway to the Divine Dimension and the source of profound sensitivity and beauty. It is in the Heart that the Soul is met and the Beloved recognised.

Absolute Meditation, on which the Transmissions are based, awakens all aspects of our wholeness, leading us to the multidimensional experience of the unconditional state beyond personality. It is hard to believe that until now, the distinction between Awareness and Being, which is of utmost importance, has not been made by any of the past Traditions or masters. Here, we can, for the first time, clearly understand the inner dynamic of I Am.

Awakening to Me: Dual-non-duality

The biggest misconception repeated for centuries by many schools of Enlightenment, has been the negation of Me. No one has been able to appreciate and comprehend this very Me which reaches through its own presence awakening to the Totality. This Me has not been seen at all. It is about time to return to the reality of Me.

Perhaps, one of the greatest gifts of the New Understanding is the clear differentiation between awakening to the Self and the Soul-realisation. The Soul is not merely the illusion of separation which must be dissolved within Reality. The Soul is herself the perceiver and experiencer of the Ultimate as well as of her own existence within the Ultimate. This realisation is both, dual and non-dual. It is dual because Me is still present; it is non-dual because the Soul abides within the Ultimate in the state free from any movement and separation. Pure non-duality designates an absence of experiencer, which, in truth, is death.

New Psychology of Enlightenment

In order to express precisely the nature of Awakening and the complexity of the Spiritual Path, a new psychology must be created that takes us beyond certain linear conclusions from past teachings. Aziz explains in a very scientific way, the nature of the mind, the role of intelligence in the awakening process and the simultaneous presence of many different elements constituting our wholeness. Different aspects of I Am co-exist and relate to each other affecting the quality of the Inner State. It is intelligence which awakens the state beyond the mind, transcending its own movement. The centre of awareness 'witnesses' the mind. But the intelligence of the mind refers back to this very centre giving it meaning and creating understanding.

Role of the Ego

For the first time, there is a spiritual teaching which describes clearly the positive role of the ego. The traditional concept that the ego represents only ignorance and should be eliminated as such, has truly damaged a number of seekers. This misconception has created a real guilt complex in the minds and hearts of all those who, for centuries, tried to eliminate this ego which they were. How can one annihilate who one is? The ego, in truth, represents itself a highly evolved state of consciousness, where the mind is able to create a self-referral. This is essential for further evolution as well as for spiritual awakening. The ego is not Pure Me itself, but an expression of Me in the mind. It is ego which allows us to evolve and survive in the reality of time.

Enlightenment does not, at all, eliminate ego, but puts it in the right perspective, as an indivisible part of our multidimensional wholeness. The ego, which is disconnected from the real centre of I Am, is certainly ignorant, but ego, as an expression of I Am, is itself a part of the Natural State.

Co-existence of I Am and Me

When one is awakened, two parallel realities are experienced simultaneously - the unconditional reality of I Am and the dynamic reality of the personal self. Personal self or psyche evolves in its own dimension within its emotional body, mind and intelligence.

Apart from its own evolution, as if in separation from the I Am, it awakens and refers back to this very I Am. Here, personality finds its inner refuge, resting in I Am and deepening through it its very existence. Who, however, uses personality and rests in the I Am? It is neither the I Am nor the personal self. It is the Soul, the individual essence of divinity.

Multidimensional Human Being

One of the most frequent illusions in collective spiritual consciousness, is an idea that there is only one real essence within us, and everything else pertains to ignorance and should be discarded. It is true that there is an essential core of our eternal Soul's identity: the existence of Pure Me beyond body and mind. But it does not eliminate the validity of all the other aspects of our being. Me is multidimensional and exists on many levels at the same time.

Pure Me has a centre in the Heart and abides in a unified energetic field created by Awareness and Being. It is the very foundation of our awakened reality. However, this experience cannot be taken out of the context of our inherent human qualities. Me co-exists with a physical form, movement of feelings, conscious or subconscious thinking and creativity of intelligence. Me is one with the sensitivity of the Soul which responds in each moment to the fact of being alive in the world. As Me exists in this multidimensional way, she continuously encounters the reality of Universal Intelligence and Love, meeting and dissolving into the light of Creation, while remaining present as a part of this transcendental experience.

Non-dual Path

Aziz teaches a Non-dual or Sudden Path to awakening. The Non-dual Path is a reflection of the insight into the paradoxical nature of Awakening.. The Non-dual Path is not the same as the Non-dual philosophy. The Non-dual philosophy is not a path but a vision of awakening pointing directly to the Now. The Non-dual Path, however, sees the necessity of evolution and reflects, in a more dynamic way, the reality of Awakening. The concept of the Path involves movement-evolution in time, the becoming of Awakening. Awakening unfolds in time, reaching deeper and deeper into the reality of the Now. Enlightenment is not merely an insight into reality; it is a process of meeting this reality.

The fundamental understanding behind the vision of the Non-dual Path, refers to the co-existence of the already present reality of I Am with the complex process of reaching it. The dual Path sees only the element of reaching, pointing to the future realisation; the Non-dual philosophy emphasises only the immediate presence of that which should be reached. The Non-dual Path sees the unity of these apparently exclusive elements.

The Non-dual Path ultimately points to the reality of the Now. In this process, we are meeting from moment to moment the light of our existence and the transcendental reality of the Beyond. However, we understand the necessity of training, the need for effort and cultivation of the inner states.

Even though the Non-dual Path may have a paradoxical nature, it nevertheless reflects the reality of human awakening. This new vision liberates us from spiritual idealism and simplifications, as well as from the frustration which is caused by a search which bypasses the 'alive' meeting with the Now.

The Non-traditional Satsang

Aziz teaches a non-traditional Satsang. He Transmits Awakening not only through his own presence, but through the presence of Guidance or Universal Intelligence, which exists beyond the field of human traditions. Another important element which makes his Satsangs non-traditional, is the element of practice and the discipline of meditation. He introduces an element of Zen discipline and practice as a part of the Transmission. In this way Transmission does not only take place from the outside but from inside as well. It not only flows from the outside to the inside but awakens the Self from within the student's intelligence and being. During the Transmission, the technology of Complete Meditation is supported by intelligent teaching, clarifying the most subtle and complex spiritual matters. The whole meeting is embraced by the presence of the Other Dimension for it takes place in the womb of Universal I AM.

Grace

It must be seen with the utmost clarity that without Grace, no one has ever reached Transformation and Awakening. Grace is the very presence of the Over-soul, Higher Intelligence, which enters into our dimension of slow evolution and suffering, at the right time, bringing help and accelerating our growth on all levels. What Aziz represent is this Grace, the power of Guidance, the intelligence of the Beyond. A true master is a mouthpiece of the Other Dimension, a channel of transformation. A true master is teaching from a space beyond individuality, even though it is his or her creative intelligence which bridges the Inner Realm with the human dimension, finally manifesting - Transmission of Awakening.

Guidance

Guidance is the name given to the Divine Intelligence, which leads our Soul to the completion of evolution in time in manifold ways. It entered suddenly into the life of two Souls: Aziz and Houman, bringing about radical change in their spiritual evolution. They experienced Grace; they met their eternal parent. What happened to them, could not be foreseen or even wished for in their deepest yearnings... They were blessed by the conscious encounter with this mysterious force. They were seen and touched by the hands of the Divine. This force led them to the radical realisation of Wholeness, and brought to them the supreme understanding, beyond the totality of human knowledge.

What is Guidance? It is not a being or entity. It is the very presence of the Over-soul, which has no form. Its only form is the movement of intelligence, which can answer all questions, bringing understanding and transformation into the reality of an individual Soul. Guidance is the personal aspect of God, the manifestation of her intelligence and love in time. It is our eternal parent, abiding in the timeless heart of the Beloved. Guidance is not separate from the Soul; it is the Soul's deeper reality, linking her with the Light and Love of Creation.

Aziz represents not himself, not his own intelligence, but the dimension of Guidance. He has been completely transformed by the force of Guidance and now through his creative intelligence and Heart, he channels the Divine Presence into the evolution of other Souls. If we go deeper with complete sensitivity, with the whole of our intelligence and Heart into the teaching contained in this book, we will truly enter the light of the New. This teaching, apart from revealing the revolutionary insights into the multidimensional process of human awakening, so needed at this stage of human evolution, channels a completely different type of transforming energy. This energy is from the Beyond, from the Divine Dimension. It is not possible to speak about it, but you are invited to experience it directly in your own Heart.

The mind cannot transmit and communicate the truth about Guidance. It is only the Heart which can know it. One, who has met this Divine intelligence face to face, is a blessed being. Such a being is given an experience which is beyond human destiny. This knowledge cannot be fully shared. Even the highest experiences of Awakening, on some level, can and are shared; this is the function and skill of this Teaching. But the sacred meeting with Guidance cannot be shared. That which is the most precious in this ultimate encounter with the intelligence of God, the Divine presence of the Over-soul, cannot, by any means, be communicated. When the Soul is Seen, met directly by the Dimension of Understanding and Love, by the Beloved herself, that is the highest experience of all for a human being.

May Guidance become a living experience and transforming force in life of all those Souls, who submit their evolution to this Divine Presence of Universal Intelligence, which is, in truth, Love.

Model of Existence

Manifestation of Consciousness
From God to Creation

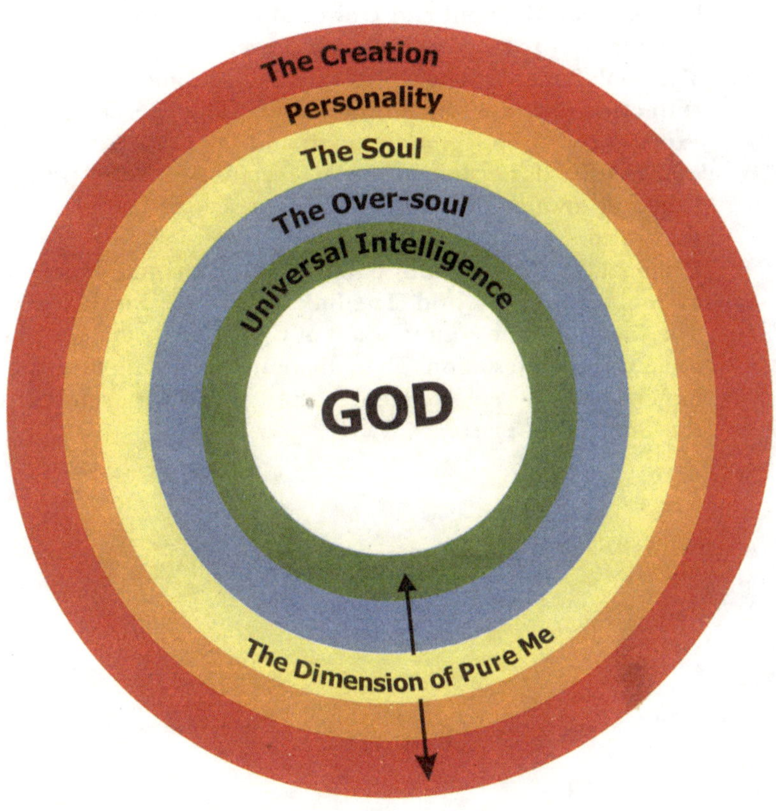

Legend:

1. **God:** The unity of the Absolute and the Divine. The unity of Emptiness and Love. The source of Existence including the Heart of the Creator and her Inconceivable Intelligence.
2. **Universal Intelligence:** The fathomless wisdom of God. The movement of Universal Spirit through which the Creator embraces her Creation.
3. **The Over-soul:** Grace. The eternal parent of the Soul. The link between the Soul and Universal Intelligence. The loving guidance of the Higher Intelligence over the Soul's evolution.
4. **The Soul:** Pure Me. The child of the Beloved and her foremost reflection in the time-dimension. The perceiver and experiencer of both, the Creation and the Creator. The Soul evolves towards her Inner Destiny, reaching the unity with the God and towards her Outer Destiny, reaching completion in the world.
5. **Personality:** The physical, emotional and mental expression of Soul within the world. The link of Pure Me with Creation.
6. **The Creation:** The cosmic vision of God. The Divine Play. The totality of manifestation. The apparent reality. The time-space dimension. The environment within which the evolution of the Soul takes place.

Model of Awakening

From Ignorance to Completion

The Human Buddha

Transcendence

Completion in The World

Emotional Completion

Purification of Personality

God-realisation

Soul-realisation

Enlightenment to the Heart

Absolute State

Awakening of I Am

Heart

Being

Awareness

Entering the Path

Collective Mind

Universal Unconsciousness

Legend:

1. Universal Unconsciousness: The state before to development of human consciousness.
2. Collective Mind: The state of consciousness prior to the awakening of the Soul.
3. Awakening to I Am: Transcending the mind and reaching the Inner State. The unity of Awareness, Being and Heart.
4. Absolute State: Reaching the Unmanifested. Oneness with the Source or with Emptiness.
5. Enlightenment to the Heart: Full expansion of the heart centre. Oneness with the Divine or with the Heart of God.
6. Soul-realisation: Enlightenment to Me. Awakening to our eternal subjective identity.
7. God-realisation: Complete meeting with the Beloved. Pure Rest in the Other Dimension.
8. Purification of personality: Cleansing of the subconscious mind in order to align personality with the purity of the Soul.
9. Emotional Completion: Reaching full maturation of the emotional body.
10. Completion in the World: Fulfilling the Soul's blueprint in the outer reality. Accomplishing the Outer Destiny.
11. Transcendence: Letting go inwardly of the time-dimension. Complete Surrender to the Beyond.
12. The Human Buddha: The profound unity of the transcendental state with the human nature. Living openly and fully the life of the human including all its difficulties and challenges, while abiding in the Unconditional State.

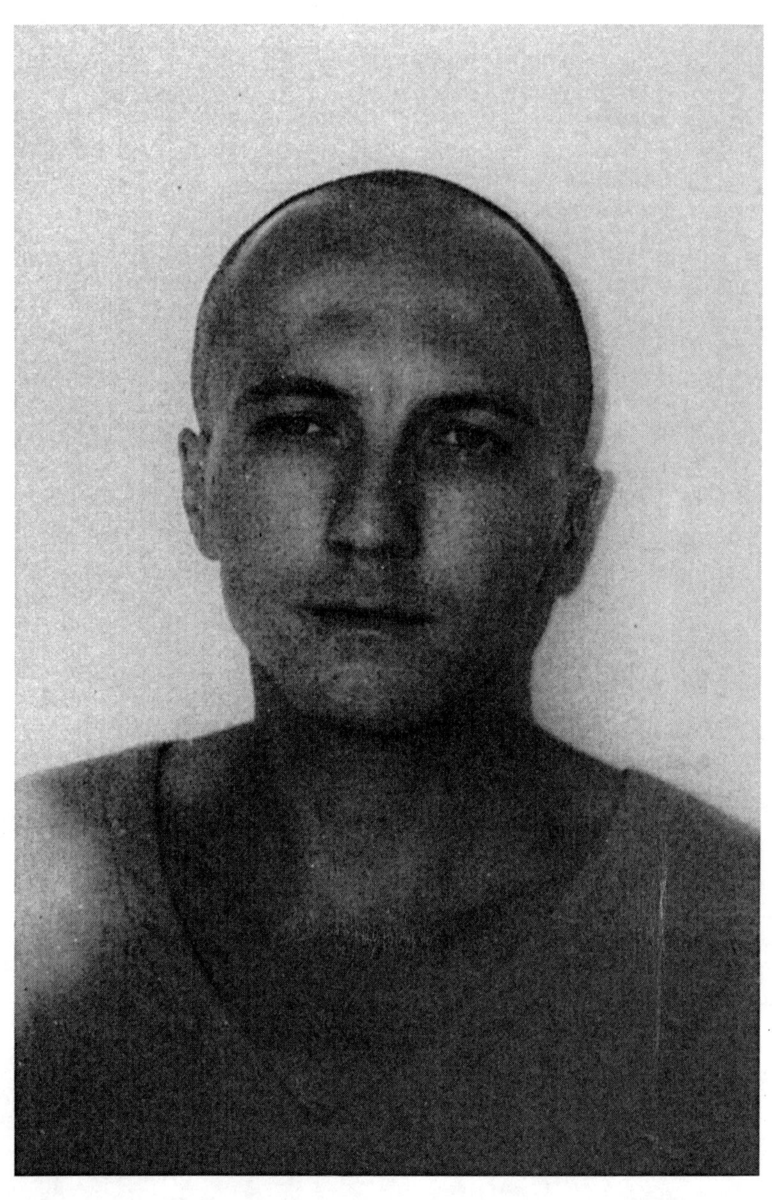

PART ONE

TRANSMISSION OF AWAKENING

SATSANG

Satsang with Aziz is beyond traditions; can be seen as a meeting of Advaita with Zen. In this space something new and extraordinary is born - the presence of Guidance. Aziz tirelessly points to the Awakening Now, however, within the proper context of intelligent effort and precise training. Unlike the traditional Satsang, here we are actually being given clear tools to realise the Self. Understanding alone is not enough; even self-knowledge is not enough. We have to respect the fundamental laws of the Awakening Process.

During Satsang Aziz sits Zazen in unison with the students guiding them clearly through the process of Complete Meditation, focusing on the three gates of the Inner Realm: Awareness, Being and Heart.

It is hard to put the experience of being in Satsang or in the presence of Aziz into words. One feels thrown back on oneself, in a space beyond the mind. One finds oneself just sitting (Shikantaza), resting in the Now, one with God. Sometimes one feels neutrality, stillness, absolute rest; sometimes one feels moved, touched by Grace, Beauty and infinite Love. There is a new experience of oneself, a new depth. To be in the presence of Truth is always a relief and the energy of Guidance channelled by Aziz is nourishing, bringing balance, clarity, sanity, peace... After Satsang one feels renewed. Something extraordinary is happening: one is seen by the Beyond, by the Mystery and, like a child, one is embraced.

Transmission 1

31 May 1999 Dharamsala, India

Seeking Freedom From the Collective Mind

Beloved friends, welcome to our next Transmission. As you are listening, you are tuning into your inner silence, because the words that are coming through can only be truly heard from the place of silence. It is not the mind that is speaking to the mind, but the silence that is speaking to the silence. The silence we speak about is not an absence of sound. It is, we can say, the ultimate intimacy. It is the most intimate place in you, where you are meeting yourself, where you become one with your own existence. Here, you do not need to translate your own isness through thought, perception or emotion. Your isness is direct, and you know it, there is no doubt. This direct experience of pure isness we call I Am. It is the primal recognition of your own existence. Not I am this, I am that, but I Am.

As you are born into the human dimension, you are born into a belief system, which you translate as common sense. You perceive reality in a certain way, where you have a certain set of ideas and concepts about what life is. You think that you know what you are doing here, what you want, what you should avoid and what you should like and what you should crave for. Even spirituality is a part of this belief system, a part of collective consciousness. But as you are coming closer to the inner light or truth, you move out of it. This belief system, your own mind which is a part of collective consciousness, becomes less and less important. The structure of your crystallised ideas about life dissolves more and more, and you find yourself more and more in a state of not knowing, where you directly encounter something which is real. But you have no way to know what it is.

There is the known and there is the unknown. The known is a belief system. The known is how your mind, being identified with collective consciousness, comprehends the apparent reality. The Unknown is this vast space which cannot be touched by the mind. It cannot be touched even by the science of Enlightenment, for it is completely beyond anything that one can imagine. The Unknown, is the place from which you have emerged originally and where you are returning to. It is your future and your very beginning. Now you are in the middle, between your very beginning and your very end, which is completion.

All of that, even this Satsang, this transmission, is happening in a dream. It is your dream, in which you are trying to find the way out of it. Or most likely you are trying to find a certain comfort, a better way of experiencing this illusion. You may be just looking for a peace of mind. But where the spiritual search, the true spiritual search is leading you to, is beyond the dream. Here, the time dimension becomes radically transcended and what remains is the original space. You still exist, your Soul is still a part of this experience, but you are Beyond. No longer are you Here, no longer do you play the role of an insignificant part of collective consciousness. You are completely alone and completely whole.

The main reason why most spiritual seekers, ninety nine percent of spiritual seekers do not reach Awakening is their insincerity. They are looking for Awakening within the frame of collective consciousness. It is not an individual search; it is a collective, unconscious search. That's why, spirituality from higher viewpoint represents unconsciousness. It is this kind of unconsciousness that speaks of consciousness and liberation, but, in truth, it is still unconscious. Within this unconsciousness that is called spirituality, one is trying to find a way out. And how one translates this way out is still within the unconsciousness. Those who truly succeed on the Spiritual Path are called individuals. The individual is the one who is searching alone. One is using certainly the inheritance of collective consciousness but from the place of freedom. One is applying various spiritual teachings, but never becoming a part of any system or a member of some spiritual club. Any system in the mind is limited by the past and blocked from the direct perception of Truth. The search is alone; it is the ultimate intimacy, where you are meeting the inner void, the place or state of being without any reference. That dimension just is, and in this moment you disappear, you die.

It is not difficult to become enlightened, to become Self-realised. What is difficult is to convince your intelligence that the spiritual search points not to vague ideas about Enlightenment, but to You. This very intelligence, in combination with the sincerity of the Heart, is our only security on the Path. It is our only assurance to transcend the dimension of darkness and to reach Light.

Meditation 1

As you sit, breathe into the belly, simply relaxing into the Now. When you relax into the Now, you relax into not-knowing; you relax into your own nothingness. Your mind or your ego, when it undertakes the Spiritual Path has certain expectations of reaching something, whether it's satisfaction, happiness or some status within the spiritual scene. But what takes place truly is that you disappear. This very you that is trying to enlarge oneself, is being swallowed by the light of the inner truth. You begin the process of dissolving into Totality.

As you sit, just like this, observe how your mind translates your existence. Your mind is like a very fast computer, very fast. It is translating your existence into something crystallised continuously. There is a continuous play of ego-images, which are referring to you and to your position in the world. But when you relax more and more into the Now, you see how unreal the mind is. You see that who you are is not an entity, it is not a thing, it has no crystallised identity. It is a space of Being which cannot be pinpointed, but which is completely real. Here, you are entering the Unknown. The Unknown is known as an experience but it is unknown to the mind. The mind cannot understand it, but your Soul knows it directly. There is an immediate confirmation from your Soul that your experience refers to reality.

So, just allow yourself to sit in this opening. Be very focussed in order to keep the mind in the present moment. And be very relaxed, letting go into the depth of this moment.

When you dwell just like this within the Now, you are beyond any belief system. No longer are you a part of any spiritual club or collective consciousness - you experience reality. To really understand it, to really long for it and to really appreciate it, is a function of maturity. This growth, this evolution into the Inner Realm, is not a matter of technique or hard practice. You must have this urge, this inner passion, this fire of intense longing to become One. Only this intelligent intensity can allow you to return back to your origin. You are not the human! That must be clear to you. You are expressing yourself temporarily as human consciousness, but your Soul is God-like.

* * *

You are breathing into your belly and letting go into Being. You are very attentive. If you are not attentive, how can you rest in your no-thingness; how can you rest when the mind is constantly crystallising your illusory ego-image? Only clear attention allows you to transcend the mind. Pure attention represents your real 'I.' Only when you reach your real 'I' can you relax into non-I, which is the vastness of Beingness, the timeless space of the Absolute.

Meditation 2

We come back to the centre of the Now. There has to be this strong will to be in the Now, to be fully present in the Now. Why to be Now? The mind does not understand why we should be Now. And there is no reason to be Now, for being Now has no reason.

As you sit, you experience yourself. You cannot escape from it. The only thing that you experience is yourself, plus the environment. The way you experience yourself is your only reality. It is precisely this experience of yourself we are deepening. If you are in a state of forgetfulness, completely identified with the mind, you don't really exist. The way you experience yourself is just a mess. There is nothing stable inside, nothing you can rely upon. There is just the fluctuation of thoughts, emotions and energy. This type of existing is called suffering. You are not suffering because of your desires or attachments. The primal reason you are suffering is because of the way you experience yourself, your own isness. That is the basic neurosis. For this neurosis no one is responsible, no one is to be blamed. It is simply a level of human evolution; a passage from animal consciousness to the noble remembrance of our eternal identity.

This passage is called human consciousness. Human consciousness is just a bridge, a bridge to your remembrance. This remembrance is not intellectual, it is a shift within your energy body, within your consciousness - a shift from darkness into light. Darkness is just a certain frequency of energy, which is low and retarded. Light is a sublime, sacred frequency of energy, which is the unity of pure understanding and Love.

So, what you are trying to do is to create stability in the way you experience yourself, a certain inner solidity. When the solidity is there, you are simply resting in a state which is comfortable, which has continuity from moment to moment. There is the continuity of your I Am, which means you have an abiding place beyond the mind, an inner refuge.

Everyone wants to escape from the mind; everyone wants to disidentify with the mind, but where to go? To go beyond the mind does not mean to stop the mind but to find a new location within your existence. This new location is called I Am. From the viewpoint of I Am, it does not matter if you think or not think. Here, you are beyond thinking by your very presence. So how do we create this inner refuge, this inner solidity? By developing attention and by deepening the energy within Being. There is nothing else, in truth, only Awareness and Being. When attention is crystallised, this very attention which is Awareness, is located beyond the movement of thoughts, in the third eye. When Being is deepened, you simply rest within. When you abide in Being, you recognise this experience directly. You know that you are abiding within something deeper than thought, you know it directly, even though you may not comprehend it fully. If you wish to follow the Path of Awakening, know that it points to this direct experience of reality, that is, to your very existence. Anything which doesn't bring you to the realisation of I Am, is just a deception. What is truly there is only: Awareness and Being.

Silence

For a few moments we will breathe in a special way. Through this breathing we initiate you into the practice of non-dual meditation. With each inhalation, we breathe into the third eye and stay there as long as possible. And with each exhalation, we relax into Being fully. When you keep your breath in the third eye, there is a particular energy experience and you will recognise it. Feel that the one who recognises this energy experience is you, and it is located in the third eye, in the middle of the brain. You are yourself this energy. That is the essence of attention.

Silence

That is enough. Still keep energy in the head but in a relaxed way. Now repeat a thought like the mantra: 'I Am.' Very slowly, in a very focussed and contemplative way, 'I Am,' with full awareness. The moment you finish saying 'I Am,' before you say the next 'I Am,' feel what remains. This that remains is I Am, which is not a thought but your own presence behind the thought. So after saying 'I Am,' stop for a while. Feel your own presence, that which remains and again say 'I Am.' The one who is aware of the mantra 'I Am' is awareness. The one who remains when you are not saying anymore 'I Am', is awareness itself. Simply recognise this fact that the pure light of awareness is beyond thinking.

Silence

Letting go of the mantra, keep your presence in the head area, in a relaxed way with a gentle focus. And from that place you let go into Being, breathing into the belly, deeply relaxing into non-doing. Awareness is reached by turning attention back to itself. There is certain self-referral in the mind where the centre is recognised. It is a very strong energy experience in the third eye, the essence of intelligence, the centre of consciousness.

Awareness can be recognised directly by turning attention back or can be slowly developed by paying attention, for example to the breath. When you breathe into your belly, when you remember, when you focus, Awareness grows indirectly.

Being is reached through non-doing. When you are not doing, energy drops into Being. But you co-operate for a certain subtle surrender to happen. You allow yourself to drop, and with the help of breath, which deepens your energy in the Hara, the experience of Being is reached deeper and deeper. It becomes more and more expansive, until the point that you simply rest fully in the unconditional Samadhi of Being. Gently breathing and relaxing... remaining in the centre. This awareness has to be like a laser inside you, penetrating your whole body. Just Being, even though you are not doing anything, you are. What is it? That which is called Being.

Meditation 3

Let us make an effort to be focussed, to be present, to be dedicated to this moment. To be dedicated to this moment, is to be dedicated to our nothingness. And our nothingness is our freedom.

How does evolution happen? It is difficult to understand it. Evolution is universal, all-pervasive. What the human being aspires to is right effort, right practice, keeping the Heart open and the mind intelligently alert. The mind has to be inspired, to be curious. And the Heart has to be sincere, in touch with the Soul. Evolution happens from within and from without. From within it depends on our own effort, in our mind and our Heart. From without it is called Grace, which means the intervention of Higher Intelligence. Evolution cannot be stopped, but it can be helped through our own effort, through our own co-operation.

That is precisely what we are doing here - co-operating with the evolution of our own Soul. Even though you may not know where you are ultimately heading to, you can know the next step. It is enough to know the next step. When you know the next step, after making this step you will know the following step, until you reach the place of completion.

We remain in a state of Being. When you are abiding in Being, you are real.

Silence

As usual, at this stage, we bring our energies to the Heart centre. Feeling our Heart, putting our hands on the middle of the chest, breathing to this area, warming it up. We become sensitive to the very presence of our Soul. She dwells inside the chest, the spiritual centre of the Heart.

As we feel our Heart, we try to find a connection with the force of love who has created and contained our Soul in its timeless presence. We feel the power of the mystery, which has bought us into this dimension of time, into life. We try to feel, to rediscover our eternal Parent, the mystery behind Creation.

PEACE LOVE GRACE

Transmission 2

30 September 1999, Pune, India

Unfolding the Now Through the Non-dual Path

Beloved Friends, welcome to our next Transmission of Awakening. This Transmission takes place in the heart of the Now, which is I AM. As you enter Satsang, you enter the Other Dimension. Welcome home!

The moment you incarnated, you forgot who you were and the place of your origin. You became lost in the reality of appearances, like a kid in a toyshop. You started to live in a dream world, disconnected from the universal Truth. Is it reality? Your world is just a shadow pretending to be real. It has no substance, no meaning and no depth. You live in a trance-state, hardly being alive. That's why, you are here. You feel that something is fundamentally lacking and you are painfully incomplete.

So, you enter the Spiritual Path hoping to fill this empty hole in your Heart. You wish to transcend your limited perception of reality and again become a part of Wholeness. You cannot know what kind of completion you are searching for; neither are you clear what it is that you are lacking, but your Soul knows and inspires you to evolve towards the Light and to enter the Unknown.

The Spiritual Path is a desperate search for completeness. One tries many things. One does many meditations, many therapies to improve one's own existence. One tries to go beyond the basic limitation, which is one's identification with the mind. It is all to reach a deeper and more meaningful experience of the Self.

The purpose of our work is to reach the state of Wholeness. This wholeness is not psychological but existential. It exists in the dimension of Being, free from psychological movement. In this dimension you still exist but in a new way. You are rooted in the Beyond. You give birth to a fundamentally new experience of yourself. This new identity is not made of thoughts, but of the pure light of I Am. This is your original face, the face-less face.

That is your face prior to any incarnation, prior to the acquisition of any ego-image

We are returning home. This process of returning home is itself the science of Awakening. It is a precise science and not based on miracles or accidents. We are not giving you slogans or hypnotising you with a romantic vision of sudden Enlightenment. There are certain laws on the Spiritual Path that must be understood and respected. The process of Awakening is real for it reflects the evolutionary blueprint of the Soul. It is the gradual dissolution of your sense of separation into the Totality.

It is not true that one needs to eliminate the ego in order to awaken. The ego is, by nature, a positive expression of human consciousness. It is the ego which takes you beyond the ego. It is true that one goes ultimately beyond the ego but the ego still remains a part of the Soul's existence. It is thanks to the ego that the Soul has the ability to refer to herself in the mind. Without this ability there would not be any possibility for evolution.

Therefore, there is the complete acceptance of yourself with the mind included. We are expanding into What Is. You accept fully who you are, not intellectually, but existentially with full presence. The moment you do it, you already experience a certain expansion and connection to What Is. A part of you simply merges into the reality of the Now which is deeper than your personal self. To accept is to Be and to be is to abide beyond the mind.

Our meetings are based on meditation. During meditation, you are being guided into the inner experience. The combination of guidance and your own effort allows you to go beyond the mind. You receive a lot of information to clarify the notion of Enlightenment and clarify the true meaning of the Spiritual Path. We want to free your psyche from all the wrong views, false ideas and superstitions relating to the phenomenon of Self-realisation. We describe precisely the process of Awakening, the different stages of the inner evolution. We want you to find your own place, your own point of reference in the Path to Enlightenment. Enlightenment is in your hands and indeed you can co-operate creatively with your own Awakening. You can become responsible in a true sense for reaching the Completion of your Soul.

The problem is that most seekers refuse to practice. They come for energy experiences or for the social reasons. They want to have a sense of being 'spiritual' without doing any real work. True seekers are rare! The masters of Old use to say that it is easy to find a master but very difficult to find a real seeker. That is the sad truth. Most seekers are either unintelligent or simply lazy. In the environment of 'Satsang,' the majority of seekers hide themselves behind pseudo-Advaita slogans about destiny and get stuck in some kind of intellectual Enlightenment.

Simply speaking, the purpose of meditation is to radically transcend the mind. The aim of the Spiritual Path is to create an ability to live, to be, to exist beyond thinking. It is not to 'space out.' Many translate the experience of being spaced-out as the 'no-mind.' The spaced-out state is the dark-negative side of no-mind. The true no-mind is grounded in the Self, in the reality of I Am. In this state, there is strength of energy, clear awareness and depth of Being. Here, one is solidly rooted in Reality.

Meditation is not a technique. The technique alone will not do. The State of Meditation is a condition of Being in which you don't do anything. In this state, you rest within Totality becoming absorbed into the Universal Presence. The State of Meditation is the state of surrender. This profound surrender unites you with the Beyond.

The state of mind which all human beings share is quite miserable. This mind is fragmented, chaotic and completely confused. In this mind, there is hardly a clear sense of identity and awareness. That's why, there is serious work to be done. Look at the nature of the mind. Do you see how it controls your psyche and suffocates you with unconscious thinking? There is no peace in such a reality, no silence and no love. In this constant flow of information, perceptions and mental impressions - there is no you! Knowing this, will you continue to live like this? Unless you see the whole pain in this situation, how can you rebel against it? How can you find the necessary strength and dedication to face all those challenges and difficulties on the Spiritual Path? Only thanks to clarity can you devote yourself to the task of liberation.

The true Spiritual Path is not an effort of the ego but from the Soul. It is not that you become someone special. You disappear...you become annihilated and only Truth remains. The one who wants to use spirituality as a commodity - will vanish, eventually becoming absorbed into the Vastness of Truth.

Let us repeat the basic teaching for those attending our

meeting for the first time. In order to experience the complete inner state, the three qualities of I Am need to be awakened. They are: Awareness, Being and Heart. Awareness is freedom from the mind; Being is the condition of Pure Rest - freedom itself; and the Heart represents the experience of divinity. When these three centres merge into one, you are whole. In this state, nothing is lacking and you can rest in the light of Truth.

* * *

We shall begin our meditation. The teaching will continue for it is a guided meditation. We not only bring you into the experience of the Inner, we open your Heart and activate you mind. The intelligence of most seekers is fast asleep. Their mind is utterly unclear in its vague search for its own absence. A certain amount of intelligence and clarity is essential, otherwise you will be simply lost, stagnated in darkness, wasting your whole lifetime. This lifetime is precious. It has been given to you so you can reach your own light. That is the main reason why you are alive. If you are not doing anything to become whole, you are living in the shadow of forgetfulness. In this way, you are not in touch with your Soul's evolution. The end result is suffering...

Please, sit in a comfortable posture. Sit in a solid and firm way. Most of you are young and to keep the spine straight should not be a problem. It is good if you sit on a high pillow with your knees firmly placed on the floor. We introduce here an element of Zen. This meeting is happening in the space of Love and not rigid discipline. Sill, a degree of discipline is essential to create some fundamental concentration in the mind. When you keep on moving, indulging in restlessness - how can you transcend the mind? There is simply not enough focus. The only way to conquer the mind is by awakening attention. Attention is your only security, the only weapon against unconsciousness. Therefore, keep this inner sword firm and high. Do not allow it to become dropped down, for you will get lost again!

* * *

We always begin with a short bow. It is an expression of respect and gratitude towards Truth. It is the ego bowing in front of I Am.

When your eyes are closed, what you encounter is your own existence. This very experience already points to reality. But to have the complete experience of the self, you need to dive inside and enlarge the frontiers of your Me. When you psyche is fully identified with the mind, you have no way to experience the depth of your being. Unless you transcend the mind, you will forever remain disconnected and fragmented.

We begin from the space of complete acceptance. We teach the Non-dual Path. The principle of this Path is that you are not looking for any future realisation. You are meeting the truth of the Now.

We are breathing slowly and deeply into the belly. This type of breathing activates the centre of energy in the Hara. This centre of energy is responsible for the experience of Being. If you are disconnected from this centre, you simply cannot rest as your energy is too high. Breathing into the belly is a very powerful tool to balance you energetically and re-connect with Being.

As you breathe, become one with the breath. You are not 'watching' the breath. You are the breath and you are attention. You are total and not seeking for anything. You have already found...this moment! You simply relax into What Is. As you inhale, your attention is burning like a fire inside you. As you exhale, you surrender, letting go into Being...just being.

It is not necessary to stop thinking. The purpose of meditation is not to switch off the mind but to go beyond the mind. That's why, we fully accept arising thoughts, but we don't get lost in them. Neither feed them nor fight with them - simply ignore them. Allow the mind to be as it is. In this allowance, use your breath and surrender into Being. In this non-conflicting way, you expand beyond the mind.

* * *

Being is attained through Non-doing, letting go. The moment you let go, energy gravitates down. It moves in the direction of your lower belly. As your energy becomes absorbed into Being, you come closer to the Absolute. The Absolute is the centre of gravity, the foundation of Beingness. You cannot grasp that which you are resting in, for it is beyond you. This experience represents your absence. You cannot grasp it but you can live it and you can know it directly beyond concepts. When you are at rest, something embraces and contains your Soul. It is as if you were in the cocoon of complete tranquillity. You abide in the womb of Beingness.

Meditation has two wings, two energies which co-exist and complement each other. One is attention which is the male energy of focus, clarity and concentration. The second is surrender which represents a feminine quality. In the beginning, you have to utilise more the masculine quality of attention. The reason for this is that the mind is too fragmented and unable to surrender. Before you submit yourself to the realm of Being, you must be first present. Before that, there is no one to surrender - there is just the mind. Attention gives you a sense of self. Through attention you are. And when you are, you can let go vertically, dropping into the depth of the Now.

Be attentive. Try not to move. Imagine that you don't care about the pain and discomfort in your body. Just be inside, unmoved like a mountain - a diamond mountain of awareness.

* * *

From certain perspectives, the Spiritual Path is based on the lack of self-acceptance. The moment you have a goal, you create conflict. This conflict is the split between the Now and the future. Therefore, a very important question needs to be asked: 'how can one journey towards a deeper, more holistic experience of the Self and still retain a degree of self-acceptance as we are?' The answer to this apparently unsolvable contradiction is the Non-dual Path. The Non-dual Path is still a 'Path.' It is not the non-dual philosophy, but the Non-dual Path. It means that there is somewhere to go, there is a certain process. However, even though there is a process, it is Non-dual. Why? Because it always refers to the Now. It is the constant meeting with This Moment and your own existence Now. In this meeting, there is a constant appreciation of reality. It is because the light of I Am is already present. Even though the experience lacks completeness, it is already the divine light of the Self.

One needs to practice. It is common sense. One has to subject oneself to the process of Awakening. The misconception of what is traditionally regarded as a non-dual philosophy is the negation of evolution. According to such a view, either one is Self-realised or one is not. Nothing in-between can be possible. This type of logic is far too simplistic and linear. This view doesn't at all reflect reality. Enlightenment is not one event, but a complex process of merging with the Ultimate, in steps. Awakening is a process of the deepening and unfoldment of I Am.

We initiate you into the Non-dual Path. Because you are on this Path, you are not seeking for the second head. One head is enough and it is already in the right place. You are not seeking for any future realisations but rather you dive into the Now. Your search refers to you, to your present existence and truth. You are continuously meeting your very Soul, the presence which lives inside you. You are intimately discovering your own existence, from moment to moment. That is the skill, the art of the Non-dual Path of Awakening. It is not a path 'to' Awakening, but the Path 'of' Awakening. This means that Awakening is already happening to You!

> *Once Rinzai was asked by another Self-realised master: 'What are your monks doing in this monastery, sitting Zazen the whole day?' 'They are trying to become Buddhas,' Rinzai replied. 'Is that so?' the other master said. 'Gold is very precious but when golden dust drops into your eye, it causes much pain!' Rinzai acknowledged his comment fully.*

The aspiration to become a Buddha is precious, but when it becomes a dualistic projection into the future, it turns into a poison. In this way, one becomes a beggar missing the truth of the Now.

Be wise and honour your own light, respect your own Soul and revere the Now. Honour your present experience of Existence, for it is where the eternal light lives. From the other side, be wise and understand the need for evolution. Acknowledge the process of deepening, growth and maturation. You are Becoming Awakened! Two sides, two polarised energies in the Awakening process need to become contained in a non-linear vision of Enlightenment. In this moment, the truth of spiritual evolution can be seen fully. The Non-dual Path is the unfoldment of the Now, a reflection of reality.

Silence

You are sitting and breathing. At times, you can let go of conscious breathing. Just Be. You are already experiencing yourself. What is missing here? What is lacking? Nothing! But still, your experience of the Now is being deepened.

In our second meditation, we focus on awareness. Being and Awareness are like the earth and sun. Being is the earth and Awareness is the sun - which makes this earth visible. Being without Awareness cannot be recognised. Similarly the earth without the light cannot be seen. From the other side, Awareness without Being is restless because it lacks any roots. Being is deeper and more significant for within Being you can transcend yourself. Through Awareness you transcend the mind and through Being you transcend Awareness. You cannot really transcend yourself through Awareness. Why? Because Awareness is You! Within Being this 'you' can disappear. When awareness is present, you are very much there - not as the ego but as the Real Me. The moment you drop into Being, you become absorbed into the Universal Presence. Being is the goal of our surrender, while awareness is your presence and the means to become free from the mind.

The centre of awareness is located in the third eye, one and half inches inside your brain, behind the forehead. When the centre is not activated, you are simply not aware of its existence. In such a case, awareness functions minimally, just operating within the phenomenal reality. When the wakefulness centre is awakened, the fourth state of consciousness (turiya) is born. Here, consciousness is just present to itself, in an objectless way. For the first time, you have a real centre, a stable sense of identity. For the first time, you can say 'I Am.' You can say, 'I am not the mind but this very presence which makes the mind conscious.' That's why, the state of self-awareness is so important.

We start to breathe. With each inhalation, bring energy to the head becoming fully present inside. And with each exhalation, relax into Being and rest at the bottom of the breath. When you bring the breath inside your head, what is it that which is present? Feel it! Who is present inside your own head? Of course, it is you who is present, but what is this you? Experience it directly!

The element of practice is essential but without self-knowledge, it lacks any transforming quality. Practice without understanding is dull and sleepy. For that reason, we emphasise so much the need for self-knowledge. With this clarity as a base, you will understand more what you are doing and what you are aiming towards. We initiate you from the very start to the knowledge of Real Me. But your intelligence has to fully imbibe this knowledge. And through the practice of self-remembrance, you must become one with this knowledge.

Silence

At this stage, please start to observe your mind. Become sensitive to the illusory nature of thoughts. When you are aware, a natural distance from the mind arises. You feel yourself as if somewhere behind. Thoughts arise and disappear into the nothingness from which they have come. You cannot find anything substantial in them. They are empty and made of nothing. If you don't give them the energy of attention, they have no way to survive.

Where does the observation of the mind come from? Who is observing the mind? Please, remain very focussed. The knowledge which we impart to you is extremely precious and difficult to obtain! In the past, one had to be ready to give one's life to receive this understanding. Nowadays, everybody is spoiled with the accessibility of this knowledge and consequently takes this knowledge for granted...

Observe the mind and see that, indeed this observation begins from a certain place. Who is the observer of the mind? How can you discover it? By turning attention back, making one step back in the mind. It is a radical change of focus that brings you to Awakening. When you turn attention in, what you meet is yourself! Yes, it is your own presence. What is it this 'you'? It is something completely new. It is not your past ego-image, the sense of being 'somebody.' It has no form, no age; it is neither male nor female; it does not belong to any country or human family; it is not even human... It is made of the pure light of awareness.

In this moment, instead of observing the mind, we repeat one thought. For many it is difficult to observe the mind, for its condition is too chaotic. There is not enough concentration. When you focus on one thought, it is easier to reach one-pointedness. It does not matter whether you passively observe the arising of thoughts or whether you actively think. It is the subject behind which matters; how you relate to the thinking is secondary. The observer and the thinker are the same, only their functions are different.

Please, repeat in your mind the thought 'I.' Repeat it like a mantra but with a different purpose. You are repeating it very slowly, in a contemplative way being intensely present. 'I...I...I...' What is the thought 'I'? It is merely a mental object in your mind which helps you to concentrate. As you repeat the thought 'I' in a focussed way, feel the subject behind. Feel that there is a real

'I' which is present at the back of the thought 'I.' There are two types of 'I' here. One is the thought and the second is the real subject, the sense of Me. Try to recognise your Real Me, to separate your sense of Me from the thought 'I.' When you are attentive, focussed in the mind, you are naturally present. The next thing to do is to discern the Real Me which is attentive, from the object of your focus.

Please be concentrated, for this is an important work. We are trying to repair the computer which is called the mind. Your computer lacks its own subjectivity, it lacks any clear sense of Me; and not having a real centre of identity in the mind is in a neurotic state. It is an abnormal normality which must be transcended. Isn't it an embarrassing situation not to have any Real Me?

The moment you have recognised the sense of Me which is present behind the thought of your focus, stay with this experience. Attach yourself to the sense of Me as your own centre and let go of thinking. Stay with this feeling, keep it firmly. It is the direct experience of 'I' inside your head. In the case that you don't recognise it, be present inside your head as much as possible.

Silence

Because you have activated the centre of wakefulness in your third eye, you naturally become more present. That's why, when you let go into Being, there is more clarity and more continuity. Stay in Being, resting within and not doing anything.

Silence

Please centre yourself. Make a last effort to be at the centre of your own existence, whatever it means to you now. You are the centre of your universe but you need to recognise it fully. Your consciousness has to go inside in order to discover its own subjective presence. In this way, your Me frees itself from being lost in the world of objects, infinite dreams...

Before we begin our third meditation, let us tell you one more Zen story. This story refers to today's subject - the Non-dual Path.

There was a monk called Basho who was a very tall and athletic man. He was sitting Zazen all day and was extremely dedicated. His master Nansen was, however, concerned about the quality of his practice. One day, he tapped Basho on the shoulder asking, 'what are you doing here?' 'I am practicing to become the Buddha!' Basho replied. In return, his master took a piece of brick and started to polish it. Basho got very puzzled and asked, 'what are you doing master?' 'I am making a mirror out of it!' 'Even if you polish this brick for a hundred years, it will not become the mirror,' said Basho. 'Similarly, replied Nansen, you can sit Zazen for the whole of eternity and you will not become the Buddha! When the cart does not move, you should hit the horse and not the cart itself!'

The meaning of this story is very profound. It is a Zen understanding that 'just sitting' is itself, the Buddha Mind. The non-seeking mind is the Buddha. Just Being, non-doing represents the original face of the Buddha. But it is intelligence which has to recognise it. When the mind is asleep, Zazen is like the cart which cannot move. It is true that the body is just sitting, but your being is unconscious. You can sit like that for a hundred years and nothing will fundamentally change. One has to hit the horse, which is intelligence, and not torture the cart (the physical posture). This intelligence has to wake up to truly understand the whole meaning of this situation. Otherwise, your practice will not have any force, for you are not alive!

When you put a dead man into a proper full-lotus posture, he will sit a perfect 'Shikantaza'! But, unfortunately, he is dead. That's why, he is unable to know it. Zazen without understanding is like sitting in a pitch-black room without any light. That is certainly not the Buddha State. You are not merely sitting to realise the Buddha State through non-doing. You have to meet yourself! You have to recognise the light of the Self. Sit without searching for future Enlightenment, but within non-seeking - wake up to the reality of What Is. Uphold the miracle, the splendour of I Am!

Silence

At this time, we will do special breathing. With inhalation, your belly expands. Next, your chest expands and you bring the breath to the head. You are fully present, retaining the breath. With exhalation, your chest falls down, your belly becomes flat and you rest. Breathe like this for some time...

And now relax, let go. See, what is taking place when you let go, Your energy naturally and effortlessly gravitates down. It moves towards the Uncreated, to the ocean of Beingness. It is the

Absolute upon which you are resting. It is the centre of gravity of all living beings and all universes. You are not sitting on the earth but on this ocean of pure energy. Your body is placed on the floor but your Soul is located in the dimension beyond the physical reality.

When your experience of Being deepens, you are at rest, a constant rest within the Beyond. You become free from yourself, from your sense of separation. You are free from this constant need to sustain your sense of identity. You rest in the Timeless. You merge with the transcendental unity of Being and Love, which is I AM. This primordial presence of I AM has created you. And now you are returning back home, to the domain of the Beloved.

We bring energy to the centre of the Heart, taking a few deep breaths to the chest. Feel your Heart in the middle of the chest. We put our hands on this area, feeling it in a sensitive way. In order to begin the work with the Heart, in a real sense, we have to drop all the conditionings attached to this area. We have to forget all concepts about love and compassion, and so forth. We have to become free from the moral and emotional idiosyncrasies we have carried throughout life.

Try to experience the Heart as she is and not as she should be! Meet yourself directly within the sacred space of the Heart. Become intimate with that space. In your Heart you always carry the seed of divinity. Even when you are completely lost, this divine spark always remains. This spark in your Heart carries the ancient memory of where you have originally come from. When you go into the Heart, don't feel her merely as an emotion but as the essence of the subjective reality of I Am. Your Heart is your Soul, your very Me in her most intimate experience.

Without the Heart, all is meaningless. Awareness has no more significance and Being is merely neutral. It is the Heart which brings meaning and value to any state. She brings the inner beauty, sensitivity, love and appreciation...for it is from the Soul.

You are the Soul! What is the Soul? She is the first and foremost expression of the Beloved. This very Me which you experience is the primary manifestation of the Creator, the spark from the fire of God. This Me journeys in time to discover herself and through herself, she recognises the Source of Creation. Me originates from the Divine Dimension. That is the place to which you are returning.

Awareness frees you from the mind; it brings the light of clarity and pure presence. Being allows you to rest within the Now. And the Heart is the final fruit, the blossoming of your existence. The Heart is your meeting place with the Divine.

Feel your Heart. Be with your Heart and rest in Being. Be intimately one with What Is. Know that What Is responds sensitively to your Awakening. She reveals herself to you as you submit yourself to this Divine Presence. It is like a flower opening its petals - revealing its innermost beauty and fragrance.

GRACE PEACE LOVE

Transmission 3

1 October 1999, Pune, India

Dispelling the Myth of Enlightenment

Beloved Friends, we welcome you to the next Transmission of Awakening. This Transmission comes from the Other Dimension. It flows from the Inner Dimension of absolute stillness, intelligence and love, into this dimension of forgetfulness, separation and sorrow. This Transmission is a bridge between the state of separation and the Source of Creation. And the true goal of our work is the experience of unity with the Universal Presence. It is a meeting between the experiencer of separation, the one who has forgotten its origin and the light of Creation. This very meeting is the purpose of Creation, the goal of evolution in time, the ultimate meaning of life.

We invite you to the Inner Realm. And we hope that you will be able to make a necessary and noble effort to reach the Truth. Awaken the passion in your intelligence, in your Heart and in your very being to come back to our dimension. Help us in your own Awakening! Help us in guiding you into the discovery of your eternal light of I AM. Without your co-operation this Transmission cannot be received, for the receiver is not ready for Awakening. The Transmission if a communication between the Uncreated and the manifested intelligence. It is a dialogue between Guidance and your very Me returning to the state of unity. That's why, how you respond is indivisible from the voice that you hear...

* * *

Once upon a time, the first human being had been awakened. It was not done through conscious effort, but through the intervention of Grace. The first human being had been reached by the transforming presence of Light. Immediately, as it happened, the 'devil' appeared. He did not want to allow this light to become distributed in a natural way to the whole of humanity.

The devil is a personification of ignorance and represents the intelligence of unconsciousness. Ignorance has its own limited intelligence or rather cleverness which is used to perpetuate its very shadow-like existence. Ignorance has its way to protect itself against the Light. It is the power of inertia, the power of the lower nature. This power never serves evolution but prefers to stay on the dark side of reality, in the mud of unconsciousness.

It was not the devil's desire to spread the news of Awakening, for it would end his neurotic existence. Because the devil was unable to face Light directly, he tried from the behind, in a malicious way, to hinder the positive evolution of light. Not being able to hide the news of Enlightenment, the devil found a very clever device to undermine the reality of Awakening. He decided to convince humanity that Enlightenment was unattainable, simply impossible to be reached by an ordinary human being. What he did was hypnotise the collective consciousness of seekers. In the hypnotised mind of seekers, he imprinted the idea that Enlightenment is something super-natural. He convinced everybody that Enlightenment is something absolutely special and possible to be reached only by extraordinary, charismatic individuals. He convinced humanity that the proof of Enlightenment must be found in psychic powers. That one has to show special behaviour, absolute moral purity, powerful energy, and so forth. He simply convinced everyone that Enlightenment is nearly impossible!

He has very successfully programmed the collective mind of seekers into an unreal and vulgar understanding-perception of Awakening. He could not win by criticising and insulting awakened beings but he managed to win by over-praising them. A strong ego-image has been projected, superimposed, on the natural reality of Awakening. It was a very clever strategy. In this way, the natural human perspective of Self-realisation had been lost.

This situation continues until our times. Seekers are truly hypnotised by the idea of Enlightenment which prevents them from being able to realise the simple, even though profound and subtle, reality behind this notion. Most Satsangs, as they are usually performed, unfortunately continue this hypnotic work. Many masters project a strong ego-image and use Enlightenment for their personal ego-upliftment.

Our work here has precisely the opposite purpose. Instead of hypnotising you with the idea of Enlightenment, we de-hypnotise you, bringing clarity and understanding into the reality of true

Awakening. Here, Awakening relates to you and you can relate to it fully, doubtlessly. When you become successfully de-hypnotised, you may stop even to use term 'Enlightenment.' You will return to the simple reality of the Self, beginning to live directly and innocently in the reality of I Am. You will start to live in the real world of What Is.

Enlightenment is 'nothing special' and it does not make you into anything special. That which you will reach is inner silence, humility and innocence. It does not give you anything apart from yourself. Therefore, if you hope to attain something other than yourself, you may choose a different Path, but not the Path of Awakening. In this way, you will avoid disappointment. Only a mature and sensitive being can receive the Awakened State and live this reality in a dignified manner.

In Buddhism, another term for the Buddha Mind is the 'Natural State.' It is a beautiful term. One is not aiming at the 'super-natural' state but at that which is simple and natural. This Natural State is present beyond the neurotic and unconscious mind, beyond the unconscious identification with the reality of appearances. It is as it is, simple but profound. The Natural State represents pure abiding in the Inner Realm, beyond movement and time. It is the unity of silence, calmness, clarity, intelligence and Love. Nothing special...

The purpose of our work is not to eliminate anything as such. We begin from the place of Complete Acceptance. We do not wish to stop the mind, to eliminate emotions or our human needs. Neither do we want to eliminate ego-consciousness which is positive in its essence. All is right as it is but what is missing is a deeper experience of the Self. That's why, what we need to do is rather to add the lacking part of our wholeness. We must add to you the invisible, that which dwells beneath the phenomenal reality. We need to add the experience of inner silence, the centre of awareness and the expansiveness of the Heart. And we need to add also the understanding and clarity of intelligence. We are enlarging your experience and perception of Me, until it becomes universal and re-aligned with the source and light of Creation.

After reaching the inner expansion, your human nature is not annihilated. The relative part of you, the psyche or personality continues to exist. Your personality remains always a part of your multidimensional existence. Your relative Me is not extinguished but embraced from the depth of Being. What it means is that you remain as you have always been - an ordinary human being, but the experience of yourself is rooted in the Beyond, in the transcendental state.

* * *

Today we would like to speak about the phrase: 'watching the mind.' We find that it is very important to clarify this term, as there are many wrong views attached to it. Watching the mind, from the higher perspective is an unnatural behaviour. Watching the mind creates a split within the conscious mind, a certain excessive dual experience in the mind. This type of practice is very useful in the beginning of the Path. It is a teaching device to create a distance between the 'observer' and the mind. It helps to free Me from being lost in unconscious thinking activity.

The ignorant state refers to the situation where consciousness, your sense of Me, is fully lost in the virtual reality of the mind. In such a situation, your Me simply does not exist. In this state, you are not - only the mind is. What remains is the unconscious or subconscious movement of thoughts. It itself is a neurotic state. It is the basic limitation of human consciousness and must be at one stage radically transcended. This is of course - if you wish to be alive!

In order to disidentify from the movement of thoughts, one creates firstly, an attitude of observation. One becomes attentively detached from the mind. The presence of attention in the mind expands reaching a new strength. A certain depth is added, a distance between the observer and the observed. The true purpose of observing the mind, however, is more than to become disidentified. It is to recognise, at one stage, this very Me which is present behind thinking. Attention, which is 'watching' the mind eventually needs to turn around back to itself. Awareness must discover its own presence, the centre of itself. This is how Awakening takes place. The intelligence of the mind, using the light of attention discovers its own centre. The centre of intelligence is the essence of consciousness. We call it the first Awakening.

When the centre of awareness is awakened, watching the mind is no longer necessary. It would be against the natural way of the natural mind. Why to watch the mind? After the State of Presence is awakened, the artificial separation from the mind has to be transcended itself; you again become the mind. When you are lost in the mind, we say 'you are not the mind,' to let you regain your true identity beyond thinking. When you awaken, your presence is energetically placed in the dimension free from thinking. When you stabilise in this state, it is constantly witnessing, so to speak, the mind. In that moment, one has to make the next step, which is going beyond the artificial separation from the mind. Paradoxically, you again 'become' the mind, but now from the place of no-mind - which is freedom. Here, freedom and spontaneity meet. The State of Presence is your freedom, thinking is your conscious or subconscious spontaneity. The thought-free state and the mind create one movement of reality. Watching the mind is an important tool but must be dropped at the end. One should not become addicted to it for it would disturb the natural spontaneity of intelligence.

* * *

Witnessing and observing are not the same. Observing is done from a deeper place of the mind and uses the personal energy of intention. Witnessing is not of the mind. 'Witnessing' is not a very accurate term for it implies duality. The term witnessing is a metaphor reflecting the motionlessness of pure presence. This Presence remains passive and uninvolved behind the activity of the mind. This non-dual Presence is not 'doing' witnessing - witnessing is being done. This Presence represents the Real Me. It always remains at the background, as the primal vibration of consciousness. We choose to use the term 'State of Presence' because it has no dual connotation. Presence not only remains at the background but also embraces the reality of the mind. This term is more inclusive. Witnessing is at the back of the scene, while the State of Presence encompasses all.

The complete human mind is not merely the centre of awareness. The complete human mind thinks, uses its intelligence and at the same time, is rooted in the State of Presence. The human being is multidimensional, we keep on repeating it. We are not only the witness but the witnessed as well. We are all. All that you experience within your psycho-somatic existence constitutes your reality. But through our work, we are adding to you more of yourself, letting you become whole. We give you the depth within, rooting you in Reality.

* * *

Let us repeat the basic teaching. The Inner State, that we are aiming at, is the complete experience of who you are, beyond the mind. We have named this state, the I Am. I Am itself is multidimensional for it is composed of three qualities. The first quality is awareness, the centre of consciousness. Awakening of it and recognition takes place in the spiritual centre of the third eye, inside your head. This particular quality takes you beyond the mind, giving birth to the experience of the Real Me. But still one has to deepen oneself. The next quality of I Am is Being. The energetic centre responsible for the experience of Beingness is located in the lower belly. The Being quality of I Am allows you to rest within, to be still. Thanks to Being you can abide in the condition of Non-doing. Even though the energetic centre of Being is located in Hara, the experience of it cannot be located in the body. It is beyond the body. The experience of Being is all-over you, so to speak. It cannot be located for it represents the absence of yourself. In Being you dwell in the Beyond. The third quality of I Am is the Heart. The Heart adds to Awareness and Being the energy of sensitivity, beauty and the flavour of divinity. In the Heart dwells our Soul, which is the essence of our individual creation. When these qualities of I Am are awakened and integrated, they become one. They create one energetic field of the Inner State which is united with the Other Dimension. Here, I Am merges with the Universal Presence of God.

We are transcending the mind not to negate it but to embrace it from a deeper perspective. The mind without I Am represents a very limited state of consciousness. But the mind within I Am represents the presence of true intelligence.

* * *

Let us begin our first meditation. Our practice is not too hard, but requires some essential discipline and dedication. Please sit in a comfortable but solid posture, keeping the spine straight. We sit with the intention not to move, unless it is really necessary. Sit like a mountain, a mountain of consciousness which cannot be disturbed by the mosquitoes of the mind. This mountain is rooted in the dimension of Beingness and is present to itself through the power of attention. The right posture of the body simply helps you go inside. Even though the I Am is beyond the body, it is being reached through the body. Because the body is not separated from the mind, the right attitude towards the body helps the mind to reach higher states of consciousness.

We begin with slow and deep breathing to the belly. We breathe with the intention to be fully present and letting go of the mind as it arises in each moment. We are breathing slowly and deeply, connecting to the Now, having the strength to drop the mind which is an insecurity. Having the basic trust allows you to Be without protections. Surrendering into the vastness of Existence, into the universal void. Let go of your self-protective mechanism which keeps you on the surface of your limited sense of self. Through this letting go, you reach the Universal Protection, which is Totality itself.

Meditation is beyond thinking and not thinking. Meditation is a state beyond the mind. What it means is that the presence and absence of thinking cannot touch the state of meditation. The state of meditation exists in a deeper dimension than the mind. Attempting to cancel the mind, to arrest the flow of thoughts is a dualistic approach. In Zen, it is called 'the heretic view.' However, you may find in Buddhism and Hinduism, they speak about destroying the mind and eradicating any form of thinking. This view is ignorant and against the nature of human consciousness. Meditation is the art of Being beyond conflict. It is based on the full acceptance of What Is and the mind is a part of What Is. Hui Neng, the great Zen master once said:

> *'There are teachers who propagate the view that the mind should be stopped completely. They bring only confusion and pull students into deeper ignorance. They are very dangerous!' Similarly, master Lin Chi expressed the same understanding, but in a more radical way. 'There are some bold-headed idiots who sit Zazen trying to eliminate thinking. They hate noise and are addicted to inner silence, and so forth.' Another master, Bankei, used to say that attempting to eliminate thinking is like washing blood stains with blood. It simply becomes more dirty.*

The goal of meditation is not to make the mind blank. The aim is to dwell clearly beyond the mind. Therefore, you simply accept the mind as it is. Through this very acceptance, you find yourself already beyond the mind. Even though you accept the mind, you are not giving it energy. To accept the mind is not getting lost in thinking. To accept it is to be beyond the mind. This point is very important. You are neither fighting with the mind nor indulging in it. It is the middle Path. When you keep this middle point, the mind will soon become silent without any conflict.

Silence

Breathing and Being. With each breath you relax, dropping into the mystery of the Now. You are letting go into that which cannot be grasped but which can receive your presence in its infinite depth.

You are doing three things. You are breathing into the belly without any special focus, becoming one with the breath. Second, you are paying attention, re-awakening attention from moment to moment. Attention is the link between you and the Now, between intelligence and Beingness. Being is already Now, while the mind is never Now. Attention creates the bridge between these two. The third thing that you do is to consciously surrender. Apart from breathing and being attentive, you let yourself go into Non-doing. This letting go, by the force of gravity pulls your energy into the direction of Beingness. Particularly, with each exhalation you are letting go, dropping down... On some level, to inhale is to become manifested and to exhale is to return to the Source of Creation. That's why, the first breath at the moment of our birth is inhalation; and the last, at the moment of death is exhalation.

* * *

We begin our second meditation. Please, centre yourself in your sitting posture, becoming fully present to your own existence. Our meetings are designed to provoke and accelerate the Awakening process. We offer you not just a teaching but an intelligent teaching. We present a very high and precise technology of transformation. We do not meet here out of social reasons, neither do you come here for spiritual slogans about Enlightenment. We give you clear tools by the power of which you can transcend the lower states of consciousness, reaching the inner wholeness. But it is up to your relative free will whether you choose to help yourself. You may choose to remain a pseudo-seeker, the 'eternal' seeker who never reaches anywhere.

As you sit, you must have a passion inside yourself. You need to have a passion 'to be' and to discover the Truth of this very moment. It is not the passion to become enlightened in the future, that we speak about. We speak about being alive in every moment of your existence. If you want to become enlightened in the future, you are not alive. If you want to reach Enlightenment by manipulating, for instance, with your kundalini energy this means that you are not alive. This means that you don't have the passion to enter the fire of the Now. The gradual Path is for those who are not ready to encounter the Now, who are not ready to live the reality of the Self. In such a case, one is not discovering What Is, but rather that which will be.

Reality is nothing special and you keep overlooking it searching for a fairyland, an utopia. You are more interested in ideas than meeting the existing Truth. Enlightenment, from the higher perspective is not an acquisition. You gain nothing but rather discover What Is. You gain reality and reality is simple. By becoming enlightened you don't gain anything but rather you lose your illusions. For that reason, one has to be sensitive and truly intelligent to see and appreciate the profound simplicity of Truth. Truth is so simple that the ego refuses to accept it! The mind looks only for entertainment and gets bored by the Truth. The ego, pursuing the spiritual goal, is seeking ecstasy and bliss. It simply turns from looking for the outer pleasures in order to search for the inner pleasure. It is precisely, this ego which must surrender and dissolve into the fire of Truth. The highest ecstasy is Nothing Special. It is the ego-less space of just being. Being no-one, having nothing, aiming at nothing... These are the characteristics of the Natural State: having nothing, being nothing, knowing nothing, wanting nothing.

* * *

We relax into What Is, meeting the alive Truth, the direct and profound reality of pure isness. Beingness is the essence of the transcendental state. But who is experiencing Being? Is it Being which is experiencing Being? If one is not sensitive enough and conditioned by non-dual concepts, one may think like that. But if you look inside, don't you feel that there is someone knowing and appreciating the experience of Being? Who is that one? It is You! It is your own Soul, the essence of your individual existence. She experiences all and rests in Being. Your Soul is alive, she feels and knows. She can be in pain and can experience the joy of becoming whole. It is this Soul which strives to reach completion, in order to realise the purpose of her existence. The essence of the Soul is in the Heart. You are primarily located in the Heart, but you need to use the mind to understand the fact of being alive and your evolutionary blueprint.

Being is our final goal. When the Soul is lost in the mind, the one who could rest in Being is simply absent and unconscious. For that reason, we have to activate the quality of attention and awaken awareness. In this way we free ourselves from certain unconscious tendencies of the mind. We become present to our existence. Attention is the tool used to become free from the mind. Awareness is in the mind, it is generated in the brain. It is the light of attention, of knowing, which is present behind all experiences. It is the light which makes possible all perception, recognition...and so forth. Awareness, when lost in the mind, still exists but as the mind only. In such a case, awareness knows itself only as thinking, becoming fully identified with the reality of appearances. The awakening of awareness refers to the fact that consciousness is able to recognise its own light. It recognises its own presence apart from that which is perceived, thought or felt. This awakening happens in the spiritual eye, inside the brain, in the centre of attention and wakefulness.

* * *

To bring more energy to the area of the third eye, we will do a breathing practice. With each inhalation, your belly expands and you bring the breath up to the head, keeping energy inside your head, as long as you can. With each exhalation, you are letting go, simply relaxing into Being.

Relax please, but still keep energy in the head. Imagine, that you exist only in your headspace. What is the mind? It is the movement of consciousness and information. Without your mind nothing exists for you, for you as a consciousness are actually absent. Centring yourself in the mind, become aware of arising thoughts. Be present inside the headspace. Put yourself in an observing position.

Watching is not a Natural State for you direct attention towards mental activity using your will and intention, which are the ego's qualities. In the Natural State, attention rests without direction. But for the moment we will observe the mind for the purpose of Awakening. You are observing the mind with the intention of being detached from arising thoughts, allowing them to arise and to disappear. Watching is an effort of attention-intelligence to be somehow present behind thinking, keeping the distance of disidentification.

As you observe the mind, notice that it feels as if thinking occurs on the periphery of consciousness. What it means is that thoughts are external from the viewpoint of your subjective existence. They are merely mental appearances, merely objects on the screen of consciousness.

The question, the master question, is: 'who is observing the mind? And the complementary question is: 'where is your sense of Me located within the observation?' In order to observe the mind, you need to have a location in the mind. In order to observe a tree, for instance, you must stand outside of it. If you are too close, you are unable to see the whole of the tree. So, what is this location from which the observation of the mind takes place? You may have difficulties in locating yourself, for you are yourself this location! Your very Me is this location.

You are being initiated here into the experience of 'I.' We are giving you back your very 'I.' This recognition is beyond any technique. Either you recognise it or not. Is it so difficult to recognise you own Me which is present behind the mind? You recognise it by paying attention to it, turning attention back to itself. You meet it by creating within yourself this profound Stop, through which You Are. Instantaneously, you encounter your own presence! No time is needed - just do it!

If you have recognised your 'I,' there is no longer any need to watch the mind. Watching is replaced by Being Present. Presence is higher than watching, for it is beyond any modifications of the mind. Presence abides in its own light, beyond personal will, beyond the ego. You are entering the dimension of true meditation, which is Non-doing, which is pure and effortless abiding in Reality itself.

When you have recognised the centre of awareness, hold onto it with full determination as it is your own centre. You are keeping this experience from moment to moment. In the case that you have not recognised it, stay with a certain amount of attention in the mind, being present and mindful.

How to Be with the State of Presence, retaining mindfulness without object? It is the art of keeping it and letting go, relaxing with this experience. If you hold it too much, the energy becomes too crystallised, too intense. On the other hand, if you let go too much, you will simply lose the state. As you relax with the experience, energy fills up the whole of your head and beyond, becoming all-pervading. Relax, but remain centred, being absolutely present. Be present and be absent at the same time.

* * *

We are entering again the inner shrine, the temple of I Am. We are entering the dimension of silence, the secret, the mystery. We take your hands, leading you to the inner realm, showing you around. We are teaching you how to live the reality of I Am.

Rest within and know that I AM. We are I AM. We are both the voice that you hear and the place from which this voice arises. We are the dimension into which you are invited. In order to enter our dimension, you have to make two offerings. One is to become present; and the second is to surrender. Your presence frees you from your negative absence in unconsciousness. In this way, for the first time you become your Real Me. You become a being which has a continuity of awareness. Such a being has the right to say, 'I exist, I am present.'

From the place of pure and clear presence, you let go vertically into the depth of the Now. You dive into the ocean of Beingness, which is the Mystery. In this way, you find yourself in the inner kingdom of I AM. You become a part of the infinite space of isness, intelligence and love, which is the Beloved. She is the Creator of All, the Only Reality. Rest within and know that I AM!

Silence

With each inhalation, your belly expands, your chest expands and you feel your Heart. Next you are bringing energy to the head becoming fully present. With each exhalation, you relax; your chest contracts, your belly becomes flat and you rest... Breathe like this for some time. You are feeling yourself from inside, as the Heart within the chest, as Presence inside your head and as Pure Being when you let go into non-doing.

Silence

At this stage, make a few deep breaths into the chest only. You are feeling deeply this area where the spiritual Heart is located. Put your hands on the Heart feeling her sensitively. With each inhalation, feel your Heart; with each exhalation let go into Being, resting within. You are resting in the unity of Being and Heart. In a very sensitive and empathetic way, discover your Heart. Allow her to reveal to you her depth and mysteries.

When you say 'I am in the Heart,' what does it mean? What is this primal feeling in your Heart before the mind can register it? This very first, pure feeling in your Heart is nothing but the ancient presence of your own Soul. It is precisely here that you meet yourself in the most profound way. This meeting is even deeper than Awareness, even deeper than Being. This very recognition in the Heart of your I Am is itself the original light of your Soul.

When listening to the music being played feel how your Heart responds. Feel how the energy behind this music is touching your being, touching something which is beyond words. Something which is most sensitive and most precious is being moved. What does it mean to be moved by music? Who is being moved? To whom is it pointing? It is this very subject, your Me which is touched by this extraordinary beauty. Isn't it?

With the presence in the Heart, you are resting within. You are experiencing What Is, as if for the first time you are experiencing What Is; as if you are being born in this very moment. And you are being given a chance, a precious chance to experience Reality. Awaken to That Which Is.

PEACE GRACE LOVE

Transmission 4

2 October 1999, Pune, India

The Original Question

Beloved Friends, welcome to the dimension of Perfection. Welcome to the place of Inner Wholeness where Understanding, Love and Being create one field of Reality, one movement in the Now. Entering into the Here and taking the form of manifested beings, by the design of Creation, you have forgotten your origin. You have forgotten the place from which you came, that is, the other side of the Now - the Divine Dimension of the Universal I AM.

As a pillow cover has two sides: the inside and the outside, so does the Now. One side of the Now is the universe, the phenomenal reality, with all dreams included. The other side of the Now is the Other Dimension - that which does not change, that which is pure Perfection.

The Soul, the mysterious experiencer of the Creator and her Creation is in-between the outer and the inner. Like a window: one side is looking at the outer, the other side is pointing to the inner. The Soul is in-between the Perfection of God and the imperfection of Creation.

When the Soul is lost in the phenomenal reality, she forgets that the Inner exists and begins to live in complete illusion, drunk with ignorance. She becomes disconnected from the heart of Reality, which is the dimension of silence, wholeness and Love. There is no change and movement in the plane of Eternal Perfection. The Spiritual Path is designed to reverse this process and allow the Soul to come back home. She must discover her inherent connection with the original state of I AM.

It is I AM speaking, that which created you. This I AM is not individual, it is the space, the womb of Existence. It is absolutely intelligent and knows you, your life and your destination. It knows even your forgetfulness as well as your illusions. You are invited to the domain of the Beloved which is your eternal parent. She gave birth to your Soul in the beginning and is your destination as well.

The Spiritual Path is designed for you to transcend the fundamental limitation: identification with the outer. It is created to go beyond the identification with the mind, the dream-like state of consciousness which is disconnected from the depth of Truth. In order to transcend this limitation, certain important work has to be done. Before we can speak about the positive experience of Truth, Awareness must awaken. Apart from illuminating Awareness, we must reconnect with the depth of Being; and finally, we enter the sweet dimension of the Heart.

The inner state, the I Am represents the complete, holistic experience of who you are before any thought, before any emotion, before any perception... This complete state of I Am is made of three colours of the inner rainbow: Awareness, Being and Heart. The essence of awareness is the state of self-awareness, which is the presence of the Real Me. The awakening of Awareness liberates us from unconsciousness. Beingness is your link with the unmanifested energy - it is the Soul's rootedness within the Source of Creation. And the Heart is the gateway to the experience of Divinity and the seat of the Soul. The complete human being is one with Awareness, resting absolutely in Being, and is one with the profound sensitivity of the Heart. The absolutely complete human being is one with the Beloved.

Silence

Today, we would like to contemplate the fundamental question of the Awakening process: 'Who Am I?' This question has been a very important tool in the technology of Awakening used by great spiritual traditions like Hinduism and Buddhism. In the East they discovered that before we know anything about God or the universe, first we must know ourselves. Before we discover any answer, we need to know who is the very questioner, who is the seeker. The seeker, the questioner cannot be taken for granted. He is himself a mystery. Paradoxically, the gateway to the experience of Oneness, of unity with Creation, is this very 'I.' That's why, the process of self-discovery and the process of merging with Wholeness, are parallel. They are two sides of the same awakening phenomenon.

One of the main misconceptions regarding the question 'Who am I?' is the assumption that we are seeking for one thing. Many are under the illusion that there is only one object of the spiritual search, namely the Self. But it is important to understand that the answer to this question is multidimensional. When our intelligence is faced with the question 'who am I?', we immediately look inside. The aim of this question is nothing else but to direct the energy of attention in. It is not an intellectual question but a teaching device used to direct attention to its source, to the centre behind the mind.

We can answer this question a few different ways, depending on which aspect of I Am we emphasise. From the viewpoint of the mind, the answer to the question 'who am I?' is the 'witness.' It has been given various names like: awareness free from thoughts, the centre of consciousness, self-attention or the State of Presence...and so forth. However, from the viewpoint of the feeling centre which is the Heart, the answer is in the Heart. In the Heart we meet our Soul face to face, awakening to the ultimate sensitivity of our divine identity. And finally from the viewpoint of non-reference, pure Being, letting go, the answer to the question 'who am I?' is: 'just being.' Just being is where the question 'who am I' is transcended in surrender to What Is.

Which answer is correct? These three answers are correct! The complete human being is composed of Awareness, Heart and Being. These three qualities create the whole experience of I Am... And that is not all, for when we go further, answering the question 'who am I?' we go even beyond I Am. We discover that we are the mind as well, we are the movement of intelligence and emotions... We are the creativity of the spirit which runs through the mind and adventures in life. The human being is multidimensional.

Originally, the question 'who am I?' was designed to negate the mind... 'I am the witness, I am not the mind, the mind is the witnessed.' However, it is not the complete truth, for the mind is not only the witnessed, the mind is also the subject and belongs to the Soul's multidimensional wholeness. We are simply everything. There is nothing in us of which we experience, that is not us. Everything is Me. This body is Me, this mind is Me, these emotions are Me. But there is something more, which is I Am - that which does not change, that which is founded on the Inner Reality of the Self.

Therefore, we do not negate anything. We are instead adding to you the forgotten depth of your eternal truth, so you can become whole again. In this way you experience your mind, your emotions and your human nature from a deeper place. You experience the difficulties and contradictions of human life from the depth of Inner Silence and Love. And when you discover the unconditional truth within, you will see that you still remain a human being. You cannot escape from this destiny. You cannot escape from suffering... you cannot escape from being caught in the contradictions of living in this dimension. But within this imperfection you are free. You abide in the Beyond.

Enlightenment does not eliminate suffering... Enlightenment allows you to experience Pure Suffering. Suffering which has the dignity of your own presence, which dwells beyond time.

Silence

We will begin our meditation. You'll sit in a straight posture, in a concentrated way. As usual, our first meditation is directed towards the 'Being quality' of I Am. We are learning how to Be. We begin with slow and deep breathing into the belly, with the intention of surrender, letting go into Now, into Non-doing, letting go, simply letting go the mind and letting go into Being.

What is Being? It is a very mysterious state. Being is not present unless it is awakened. Even though, some amount of Being energy is always present, it is very fragmented, lacking the quality of restfulness.

When you flow in time, you are becoming from moment to moment. Your mind is becoming, your emotions are becoming...all elements in your psycho-somatic reality and energy system are arising and passing away in the movement of time. Everything is becoming; perceptions are changing constantly. You are time; you yourself are time. You are not only the experiencer of time, but you are that time. Can you separate your existence from time? You are the river of time...

But where does this time arise from? It arises from the Now. Time is not flowing from past to future, but arises from the Now and passes back into Now. That is because the source of time is the Timeless and the very concept of past and future is contained within the Now. The movement of time takes place within the no-time dimension. The Here is not Here but Now! And the Now is not Here but Here is Now.

The Soul is both: the movement of time and the experiencer

of this movement as well. When the Soul is tired of becoming, when she is tired of being identified with the restlessness of the Here, she rebels against time. The moment the Soul opposes the fluctuation of this dimension, she awakens the wish to surrender into the Now. But how can she surrender into the Now? Through non-doing. Non-doing is the bridge which links the movement of time with the Timeless.

When you let go, your energy drops into the direction of the Timeless. And, suddenly, you discover that there is something which does not move. Everything moves around, but your Being is still. It is precisely that which we call the 'inner expansion.' Part of you becomes connected with the Timeless even though you still continue to live in the dimension of time.

Silence

We are breathing and letting go into Now. We are experiencing what it means to Be, how it feels to Be and growing in the appreciation of this experience. What does it mean to Be? As you are letting go of the mind, from moment to moment, with the intention to surrender into Being, you become absorbed. You meet a certain opening within yourself, as if the inner space has opened. You cannot grasp it but you can live it. This open space has no reference to anything. In Buddhism they call it Non-abidance, for one does not abide upon anything. There is no reference... there is nothing behind, nothing in front. Non-abiding is to dwell upon nothing - this is another definition of Being.

You're breathing. You're very attentive and there is a complete acceptance of everything. Absolutely everything! You do not create any desire to reach or experience any particular state. There is a complete acceptance, which is contained in the space of your own presence... and you are letting go into nothing.

Silence

In order to reach the dimension of the Self, one has to pass the Inner Gate. In Zen it is called the 'Gate-less Gate,' You are passing the inner gate, but there is no gate! Nothing separates you from the internal reality of the Self! However, there is a gate! What is the gate? It is nothing but the lacking ability to surrender to it That which keeps you on the surface is a combination of the unconscious mind and restless energy which constantly pop up. That is why, we are breathing and we are attentive. Breathing deepens our energy system, attention gives us the continuity of Presence and finally letting go into the internal space of the Now absorbs our sense of identity with Reality.

Silence

We are very attentive, and from the place of attention, we let go into Being.

Silence

We'll have a short break, relaxing and stretching the legs, but remaining however silent and mindful inside.

Silence

When you close your eyes, there is nothing to do, nothing to think about... The question arises: 'how to live in this inner state, how to live within the reality of I Am?' All that you see is an illusion, from the ultimate perspective. All that you think is meaningless, from a higher perspective. All that you experience is unreal... Only the One inside matters, the one who sits, the one who is present. That one is beyond any kind of experience. That one simply remains always, beyond bliss, beyond pain, existing deeper than time. That one cannot be named, for it has no form...it's only quality is that it is Real.

If you search for experiences, you're missing reality. But if you search for the experiencer, you're going into the right direction. Meditation is a state of Non-doing and it is nothing special. It is perhaps one of the best definitions of meditation - 'nothing special.' If you experience a special meditation, it is not real. Nothing special is the key, and nothing special is pure acceptance and complete surrender. That one who wants to experience 'something special' has to surrender into 'nothing special.' And when we surrender into 'nothing special,' we discover another beauty, the extraordinariness of being no one. We discover the beauty of simplicity, the profound beauty of calmness. In this dimension, our mind is absent but something else is present. And what is it? It is God.

There was a master in Japan who used to say that Zazen is useless. And he was adding: 'unless you understand that Zazen is useless, your Zazen really will be useless.' We are speaking about the 'true uselessness.' You cannot use it. The ego cannot make anything out of it. It is simply nothing special, but this nothing special is Existence; it is life itself. It cannot be used because everything is One. If you are ready to surrender to that which is useless, it shows that your Soul is mature enough to experience Reality. She does not use meditation as a commodity, anymore.

The key to meditation is your own absence. The aim is not to get something, or to develop a super-ego or to become 'enlightened.' The purpose is not to develop psychic powers or experience ecstasy. These are all the ego's products, the ego's fabrications. True meditation is useless, because There Is No-one To Use It.

We begin with a breathing practice. With each inhalation your belly expands. Next you bring energy inside your head, being fully present. Become a hundred percent attentive, totally present inside your own head. And retaining the breath as long as you can. When you exhale, let go into Being fully; your belly becomes flat and you rest. And again: inhalation, your belly expands, you bring energy to the head, becoming fully present. Repeat this process for some time.

Silence

Now, we relax the breath, but still keeping energy in the head. In our first meditation, we have been learning what it means to Be. To Be is one answer to the question 'Who Am I?' Let us discover the second answer. The presence to which the question 'who am I?' refers, has intelligence and it has the mind. Who is behind the mind? Who is thinking? Being is not thinking, the thinker is thinking, the observer is observing. These functions are in the mind, located in the head. The mind has a few layers. The more gross layer of the mind is the 'inner dialogue' or the constant thinking. We call it the 'subconscious Me,' the subconscious mind. On top of the subconscious mind occurs the movement of conscious intelligence, which is the ego. Intelligence represents the positive ego. The one who discovers oneself, the one who gives birth to understanding.

It is not merely the mind which is listening here. It is intelligence which is listening, the deeper part of the mind. We can call it the 'subtle mind.' To whom does this subtle mind belong?

At the centre of intelligence lives the King of the mind, which is your Real Me. It has also been called the host of the mind, pure I, atman, witness...and so on. In our terminology we call it 'State of Presence.'

The State of Presence is discovered when attention-awareness recognises its own centre, without referring to any object - the 'I-I' state. Because of the chaotic condition of the average human mind, it is difficult to discover this centre. That's why, a certain work with Being and attention is absolutely required in the beginning. However, a mature Soul can recognise the centre of awareness immediately, when the right teaching is given.

First, become aware of the space in the mind, being fully present. You can experience in this space a certain movement of thoughts or energy within the mind. We would like to ask you a very important question: do you experience anything, which you could identify as Me? Is there any sense of Me, something which is very familiar? It is so close to you that you keep on missing it, for it is you! What is this sense of Me behind thoughts?

We will ring the bell. When the sound stops, you will experience a moment of complete presence, full awareness. This experience of pure attention is no visual, it is beyond darkness and light, it has no form, it is objectless.

The bell...and stop!

This what you are experiencing in this very moment is Reality. Reality can be seen only in the light of pure attention. Wake up and recognise it!

Gently open your eyes, half-open, half closed. Looking just in front of yourself, on the floor, one meter in front of yourself. Through your eyes, consciousness is looking. Consciousness is making the floor visible and your mind using its memory, translates the picture into a name and form. Consciousness is looking outside through the eyes. And what you attempt to do is to recognise this very consciousness, by pulling energy back inside your head. Your head is like a camera, it makes things visible, but it is not aware of itself. You are aware of everything but your own head! Where is your head? Can you become aware of your head?

Your eyes are gently looking at the floor, but without any focus. There is no focus at all. It is like looking at the sky, in a completely open way, in a relaxed manner. And now you become aware of the back of your skull, feeling the sensation at the back of your skull. You may even imagine that you are looking behind your head.

Your eyes are open. When you are aware of the back of your skull, the energy naturally is directed in. You feel vibrating energy inside your skull. And at this stage, be simultaneously aware of this vibrating energy inside your skull and see the floor. Part of you is aware of this place inside your head and part of you is aware of the floor. And they become one.

Silence

Now you close your eyes being fully present inside your head and within this presence, you relax inside your head - vertically relax. We say vertically relax, which means that there is a centre, a vortex of presence inside you. You are not merely relaxing, spacing out. You are fully in. Vertically relaxing; as if within you there is a pillar of light. This pillar is made of attention, from the ray of awareness.

When you relax with this awareness inside your head, the state of attention expands. The energetic experience of awareness is felt not only inside your head, but around it as well. It has no borders: vast, infinite, brilliant, luminous, splendid. It is an infinite sky of pure awareness, which contains the whole universe...

Silence

The only capital that you have is the very experience of your existence. And you have no way to escape from this situation, for you have only yourself. At the end of the day, whatever you do, you came back to yourself. You come back to this simple experience of yourself which has nothing to do with your own ego-image, with your acquisitions, with your success or failures. The reality of Me, Pure Me.

What is this Pure Me, when emptied from its relative content, when all veils and masks are taken away? Who am I directly? Who am I? This inquiry is not intellectual, it is a beautiful adventure of the Soul, which is discovering her intimate inner light, the light of her own presence. She is returning back to the root. For that reason, we call it 'Awakening' for it feels like waking up from a dream.

One may say: 'I am just Me,' and stop there. But there is also another understanding which reveals to us that the experience of Me itself evolves, until it reaches its final depth. This final depth we have named the 'Complete Me.' That Me is complete from the bottom up to the top, she is whole. Your Me is already present... you are not looking for something outside of what you are. You are looking for that which is present in the heart of your very existence. You are deepening this experience through right understanding, right cultivation and right effort. The element of effort is indispensable as a part of our evolutionary journey, even though you have the support from Existence, support from the esoteric dimensions, support from below and above. It is your destiny, it is your responsibility to co-create your own Awakening. If you will not co-create, we assure you that you will remain in a state of painful separation. You will be forever stagnated in a state of limitation, remaining fragmented and sorrowful. In this way you will waste a whole lifetime.

Silence

Awareness and Being... Awareness is the light which makes this universe and everything visible. Without Awareness, no universe can be perceived or experienced. If there is no Me, there is nothing - only the original state prior to consciousness. Awareness is the building block of the Creation.

Who is experiencing awareness? Awareness, in truth, needs Me in order to experience the universe. To make the universe an object of experience, the Me is required. That's why, this universe is not something objective in a clinical sense. It is not a block of matter suspended in infinite space but a multidimensional composition of infinite angles of perception. There are infinite numbers of Me's which perceive this universe, mutually creating what we call the 'objective universe.' We call it 'objective' only in a conventional sense, for it is not objective as such. This universe it is relatively objective, in relation to a particular Me or a number of Me's. The Awakening of awareness occurs within Me and through this Me only. It does not happen in cosmic space but by the presence of this very Me which is the perceiver of the universe. It happens to the Me which discovering herself, discovers the building block from which perception is made - that is pure awareness. The essence of awareness is 'I.' The mistake that most seekers seem to share is looking for 'non-I' in order to discover consciousness. It does not work like that because without Me, there is no consciousness. Me is the only vehicle through which consciousness can become conscious. Awareness is freedom from the unaware Me which is simply awareness without any real centre.

However, deeper than Awareness is Being. Why? Because Being links Awareness with the un-manifested energy. Being is closer to the Source. Awareness is manifested, it is an expression of the Source. When you as awareness, when you as the mind, simply surrender into Being - you 'gravitate' towards the Source. Your energy is being pulled, sucked into the direction of the Uncreated. You cannot see this dimension, but you can live it... As you surrender, you are resting more and more within that which is beneath the surface of phenomenal reality, the Absolute.

* * *

In our third meditation we are going to find the third answer to the question 'Who am I?' which lies in the Heart. The Heart for the human being is the final, most profound answer to the question 'Who am I?' The reason is that the Heart is the centre of the Soul. In the Heart, the Soul experiences herself in her purest, most original, most direct and intimate way.

Awareness is the function of clarity. It is the centre of intelligence, while Being connects the Soul with uncreated energy. However, who is the Soul herself who is experiencing uncreated energy? Who is resting in Being? This has been hardly understood, so far by any tradition. And it is nothing but Me. And what is this Me? This Real Me is not the ego. It is not the ego-image but the pure experience of the Soul. This recognition can take place only in the Heart. In the Heart you meet your true identity face to face. There finally, you become yourself. You become that which you have always been, the child of the Creator.

The Soul is absolutely innocent. She is made of the pure light of sensitivity; she is completely intimate with the Beloved. But when she loses herself in the mind, in the ego-reality, she forgets. And now she is remembering, coming back to her senses. 'Yes, I am one with the Beloved, I am one with That which created Me.' The Beloved represents divine maternity, the womb of Existence.

Silence

We take a few deep breaths into the chest area to activate it and feel it more. The spiritual heart centre is an energy centre; we do not refer to the physical organ. Even though she is located in the chest, she exists beyond physicality. The Heart centre is the energy gateway to the Divine Dimension. In order to find the way back to our ultimate abode, we have to find the right entrances, the right doors. The Heart is one of them.

We feel the area in the middle of the chest. We put our hands on the Heart. It is important. The moment we put our hands on the Heart centre, not only do we awaken to the Heart's sensitivity but we heal her as well.

Who is putting their hands on the Heart? It is the Soul which is putting her own hands on her-self in order to discover herself, to feel herself and to heal herself. She has to heal herself from all those energies which the insensitive dimension of earth has imprinted in her. She has been hurt deeply within the delicate presence of her Heart.

As we are discovering our Heart, we are healing her as well. If the Heart is not healed, we cannot access her depth. It is otherwise closed within certain neurotic tendencies. Our Heart, being wounded from the very childhood, for protection surrounded herself with the energy of insensitivity. This insensitivity is like a thick skin, which does not allow us to feel the delicate touch of the Divine anymore. The Heart is afraid, she does not want to become vulnerable and to open herself. She has been hurt too many times. That's why, she prefers to live in the shadow of insensitivity, which is a false security. Another name for this type of false security is death.

Silence

As you feel your Heart, you become very tender inside. In a very gentle way, we are coming closer to the space of the Heart. With great sensitivity, as if we are discovering the child inside our Heart. It is like a child who is afraid and yet wants to be found, but at the same time is shy and uncertain. We are re-discovering the Heart herself, forgetting about all our ideas about love and compassion. We drop all those conditionings regarding how we should feel. We experience the Heart not as she should be but as she is and what she is.

When you discover your Heart, do it with the conviction that it is your Pure Me in her space which is being felt. You are discovering not an objective Heart but purely subjective Heart. Here, you discover the One who is behind everything. Behind the spiritual search, behind the search for love, behind the search for security, behind the search for completion, behind everything... It is that one who lives in the cave of the Heart and is not aware of herself until awakened. That One is You! You stay with this one inside the Heart, in silence. Being fully present and intimate with WHAT IS.

GRACE PEACE LOVE

Transmission 5

4 October 1999, Pune, India

Awakening Points to the Now

Beloved friends, we welcome you to our next Transmission of Awakening. This Transmission takes place in the womb of the Now, which is the unconditional space of I AM. I AM is the infinite domain of Beingness, Love and Intelligence which contains the whole of Creation within itself. The I AM is the light of Creation which gave rise in the beginning to the phenomenal universe. This beginning is Now.

From the Now arises an infinite number of angles of perception which reflect the multitude of subjective realities and perceivers. This is represented by your own Soul. Who is the Soul? She is the essence of your individual existence. She discovers wholeness and recognises the truth of Totality from her own unique perspective. She discovers Truth through her understanding, evolution and expansion. You are the Soul.

The essence of the Soul is in the Heart. It is in the Heart that you meet your true, ancient identity in the most direct and intimate way. But the Soul, in order to live in the world, needs to move out of her original form to the reality of Creation. She has to use awareness, intelligence and a physical form as well as many other elements. The true goal of the Spiritual Path is not at all to negate individuality. The aim is rather to re-awaken the state of unity with Existence, from the perspective of an individual reality.

Enlightenment is not the absence of Me, but the presence of unity. Here, Me and Existence create one unified field beyond individuality and beyond universality. In this experience, the unity of pure love, understanding and intelligence create the very life of the individual Soul merged with Totality. The Spiritual Path is the science of reaching the state of unity, from the place of relative separation.

We are taking you from the island of the separate Me to the Other Shore, to the motherland which is both your origin and your destination. The sailing ship which takes you to the Other Shore is Guidance. The wind which allows you to sail the ship effortlessly is the power of Grace. The right direction which you take, not to become lost in the vast ocean, is true Understanding. And the efforts which you make in order to help your ship reach its destination - is your co-operation and power of will. Your co-operation is responsible for your destiny, dedication, ability to overcome difficulties, as well as trust in difficult moments. In this way, you are not merely waiting passively for the wind to push the ship in the unknown direction. You aim at the right direction and sometimes you have to use the oars as well!

This island which is the separate Me and the continent are, in truth, already one underneath the ocean. They are however, relatively separated, for the infinite ocean lies between them. That is the amazing paradox of being a Soul. Even though we are One with the Source of Creation, still, we are reaching towards a state of unity. We have no choice but to start sailing.

The gate-less gate which leads to unity is within and not without. The experience of unity does not occur in the field of perception but in the dimension of Being. That which links one with the Source of Creation is the very sense of Me. Me is the foremost and ultimate expression of the Source. This sense of Me is mysteriously present behind all the experiences we have. This sense of Me links us with our origin. Our work takes place in the dimension of Me. We are deepening your very sense of Me, enlarging it to the point of its ultimate expansion, thereby returning to the state of unity.

Awakening is not a miracle but the fruit of evolution - the evolution of understanding, consciousness and energy. This evolution includes many lifetimes; it is a process taking place in time. In order to return to the state of unity, in a conscious way, awareness must be awakened. The way awareness operates in an ordinary person is very limited and fragmented. One is fully identified with arising thoughts and the psychosomatic flow of outer perceptions. No centre or clear sense of Me can be found in such a reality. This type of semi-awareness is flat, lacking any depth. For this reason, we emphasis work with attention. It is to free awareness from its shadow-like existence. Awareness is the light of knowingness which makes everything visible. When awareness is shallow, only the perceived is recognised, the perceiver is overlooked. Only when awareness becomes conscious of its own light, in separation from the perceived, does the perceiver awaken to its own existence. That is the birth of the Real Me. Here, consciousness for the first time refers to itself instead of to the outer.

Consciousness is not the Ultimate. The Ultimate is the realm of Beingness which is present prior to consciousness. Consciousness itself arises from Beingness. Beingness represents pure isness, the timeless Source of Creation. Beingness is the uncreated energy, the source of all and the centre of gravity for total Existence. In the State of Presence, consciousness is liberated from unconsciousness, from all its lower forms and subdivisions. Next, through its own presence, consciousness is ready to surrender vertically into the dimension of Beingness. At this point, consciousness and Beingness meet. The primordial presence of the Unborn and pure awareness create one field of I Am.

Apart from the awakening of Awareness and Being, we emphasis Enlightenment to the Heart. This realisation takes us beyond peace and beyond clarity into the experience of Divinity. Divinity is not a state but a profound sensitivity, linking us with the dimension of love and beauty. This realm of ultimate sensitivity gives the highest meaning to Creation. Therefore, it is the Heart which is the final flowering of Self-realisation.

The Path which we teach is multidimensional and is founded on new insights into the Awakening process. It is essential to understand that the Inner State, the Self-realised state is composed of three aspects. They are Awareness, Being and the Heart. Each one of these aspects can be activated to a different degree. They can once again be awakened separately from the support of the other ones. It all depends on a particular Soul's evolution and blueprint. Various Souls have different predominant centres.

The centre of awareness which frees us from the mind and gives continuity to intelligence is located in the third eye. In the lower belly is located the energy centre which is responsible for the experience of rest, absorption, stillness and rootedness within the Now. This centre refers to the quality of Being. And finally, the spiritual Heart is situated in the middle of the chest. These three centres are the esoteric gateways leading to the re-union with the Ultimate. A being who is fully Self-realised is one with pure consciousness; he or she rests absolutely within the Uncreated and is united with the Divine, or the Heart of the Beloved.

In our meetings many teachings are being given in order to stimulate intelligence. We find that intelligence, in the case of most seekers, lacks basic clarity about Enlightenment. Very few have any basic idea about the true meaning of Awakening. And without the clarity in your mind, evolution is slow and dull, without any transforming power. The understanding to which we point is not intellectual but intuitive. This understanding pertains to the subtle mind and is verified directly by the Heart.

Our meetings are based on sitting meditations and guidance. At the end, there is a time for questions. We encourage you to ask your questions, for it reflects the curiosity of the mind. Asking questions enlarges the capacity of intelligence for reaching new understanding. Through questioning, intelligence becomes able to grasp its own evolution in time. This intelligence belongs to the Soul, that is, it serves something higher than itself. Understanding is the only bridge leading to completion. A new insight allows one to go beyond one's present perception of truth. It is as if through a quantum leap, one is moved to a qualitatively higher state of consciousness-intelligence.

* * *

We begin our meditation. We emphasise some discipline. Please, sit with the spine straight, trying not to move. Put into your practice a lot of dedication and strong concentration. Be passionate in your self-discovery and search for Truth.

India is the place of Grace where the Transmission of energy from the master to the disciple happens much easier. However, there exists a certain extreme view regarding the phenomenon of Awakening. According to this view, it is enough to be in the presence of a Self-realised being in order to get transmitted the enlightened state. Unfortunately, reality is not so simple and more elements are required in order to reach Awakening. Evolution is a co-creation between the subjective and objective polarities of Existence. It is absolutely true that you always receive help. This help descends from the Divine Dimension or through the medium of a human master. But the birth of I Am takes place from within. It is your Awakening, it is your responsibility. Therefore, your intelligence must be engaged and your heart dedicated. Awakening is not a mechanical happening. It is not that you plug yourself into some source of energy and magically you experience transformation.

There are many pseudo-masters who surprisingly emphasise only their presence. They say: 'stay with me and it will happen to you one day!' They lack the basic understanding of the Awakening process. In India, there are many teachers (foreign also) who take the authority of representing the Buddha State after having some partial experience of Self-realisation. It is rather a joke. Masters who are fully awakened are extremely rare and difficult to be found, like precious pearls. Beware of guru-projections which are based on hypnosis and the seeker's inferiority complex. Always examine carefully the nature and sincerity of the spiritual teacher. True masters always give you tools through which you can awaken and be a light onto yourself. False masters speak only about their presence and the miraculous nature of Enlightenment.

We are entering the inner shrine, the dimension of meditation. The State of Meditation is beyond the ego but includes the ego. It includes the sensitivity of your Heart and the multidimensionality of Me. We are entering the vast, infinite domain of Beingness - into that which Just Is.

Meditation as such is a state of non-doing, Pure Being. However, in order to reach the state of non-doing, a certain doing is necessary in the beginning. It is the art of practice, the art of reaching the non-doing. It may sound like a paradox, but the non-doing must be attained. Similarly, the Now is always present but must be realised. As you arise in each moment of time from the mystery of the Now, so you surrender back into the depth of the Timeless. If you have not attained the Now, it does not exist for you. And what exists is time only, the moment of becoming.

* * *

We begin with slow and deep breathing into the belly. We breathe with the intention of letting go of the mind and surrendering into Being. We are dropping into non-doing. When you drop the mind, while with the breath letting go into Being, you are entering a new Dimension. In that dimension, you still exist but beyond thinking. Here, you are coming closer to Reality.

The basic principle in meditation is not trying to attain anything; it is complete acceptance. If you had in the past a deep meditative experience, naturally you want to repeat it. This is precisely the pitfall which you must avoid! If you crave for past experiences, you miss the present moment, you bypass the Now. To avoid the danger of overlooking What Is, we do not create a desire to reach any state, any experience. But at the same time, being fully present, we relax into What Is. We make ourselves available to the mystery of the Now.

As you are breathing, your breath is slow and deep. You become one with breathing. You are not watching the breath, but you are the breath. Watching is a mistaken concept, which create a split in the internal reality of I Am.

Please sit still, keeping the spine straight, not allowing the mind to disturb you. Keep constant attention and surrender, maintain a precise focus and let go. The mind is so unconscious. It does not have any centre; it is restless and discontinuous. The mind has to be conquered. The weapon which you use is the sword of attention, clear mindfulness and one-pointedness. If you don't have the essential will to crystallise your attention, how do you imagine getting out of this mind? There is no way. You will remain forever stuck in this prison of unconsciousness, wasting your whole lifetime. Do not wait for a miracle. Your effort, your co-operation is the noble sacrifice which you have to make on the altar of evolution. This is your true dignity, to become responsible for your own Awakening.

Just breathing and Being. If the mind disturbs you, count your breath from one to seven. Each inhalation and exhalation you count as one; do this from one to seven. You cannot give up. You must have some centre or focus - the quality of one-pointedness. You are One with the breath, becoming the breath.

At this stage, you can drop the awareness of breathing. Just being, resting in the soft energy of Being, non-doing, letting go... There is nothing to reach apart from the connection to What Is. But before you experience What Is, you must be fully present. Otherwise, What Is cannot be seen, as it remains hidden behind the thick cloud of the mind.

There is a famous poem written by someone who reached peace. 'Many steps have been taken to arrive at the simplicity of Truth. Wouldn't it be better to be deaf and blind from the very beginning?' How foolish is the spiritual search, for it leads us to the discovery of What Is and what has been always present! Isn't it foolish? In Zen it is said that before Awakening, 'the tree is green, the river is flowing and the mountain is high.' After

Enlightenment, there is no tree, no more river and the mountain disappears. But at the end, when Enlightenment is transcended, the tree again is green, the river is flowing and the mountain is high. It is the same reality, before Enlightenment and after Enlightenment. Reality is as it is, nothing can be added to it. You may think that being enlightened you will walk in constant bliss and ecstasy. It is foolish, for Enlightenment is nothing special. Reality is as it is, simple and ordinary. The mountain is high and the tree is green... all is clearly reflected in the mirror of pure consciousness.

However, there is another understanding, a more subtle understanding. Even though the Spiritual Path seems to be foolish, it is real and noble at the same time. We are reaching What Is, from the place of 'what is not,' that is, from the place of separation and forgetfulness. The Spiritual Path is real. It reflects the process of Awakening and the deepening of this very experience of What Is. It is the adventure of consciousness which discovers its own isness, always in a new way.

Before Enlightenment and after Enlightenment, there is the same tree and the same mountain, but the perceiver has changed. Before it was only the mind which was looking at the mountain. It was the dream world of no-Me. Now the mountain is seen from the place of silence, complete presence and love. For the first time Reality is seen As It Is.

We teach the non-dual or sudden Path. The Non-dual Path is very subtle and the linear mind is unable to grasp it. This is because the linear mind sees always only one side of truth and cannot comprehend the paradoxical nature of reality. One extreme view regarding the concept of Enlightenment assumes that because the Self is the only reality, there is no place for reaching it. Here, the very concept of a Spiritual Path is self-contradictory. According to this view, either you see Truth or you don't. And when you do have an insight into the Self, it is equal to complete Self-realisation. According to this view, Enlightenment is one, as there cannot be any degrees in the Self. Here, even the Path to Enlightenment is denied for it implies duality and the presence of time. The very process of reaching the Self takes place in ignorance and ignorance can give rise only to deeper ignorance - never to Awakening. If we followed this line of thinking to the very end, even Awakening must be negated. Recognition of the

Self is an event in time and implies the absence of Self-realisation in the past. The logical difficulty with this concept is based on the lack of differentiation between the Self and Enlightenment. The Self always is present, but the recognition of it takes place in time. Enlightenment refers to the recognition of Truth. Of course, it requires an element of duality. Without duality there is no place for any movement of intelligence. That's why, extreme non-duality cannot reflect the nature of truth. Dual-non-duality is the proper term for the truth of Creation.

Another extreme view speaks about the goal of Enlightenment projected into future realisations. In this way, our present practice or spiritual training is merely a means of reaching the future Awakening. This Path is dualistic and based on the promise of Enlightenment. These two views reflect partially the spiritual understanding, but are too extreme. The first view presents the unconditional truth, but misses the relative reality. The second view presents the relative truth, but misses the unconditional reality, lacking the insight into the Now.

The Non-dual Path goes beyond these extreme views, embracing them and melting into a qualitatively higher understanding. The Non-dual Path is not a man-made philosophy, but a pure reflection of the reality of Awakening. The Sudden Path emphasises the experience of the Now and does not anticipate any future goal. We constantly point to that which is the closest, most direct and immediate experience of the Self. We are awakening from moment to moment the recognition of that which is already present. We are facing reality through the instantaneous encounter with I Am. That's why, it is a non-dual approach. But it is still a Path for it involves the process of Awakening. We are not only discovering What Is, but evolving towards a deeper, more meaningful experience of Truth. We are in the process of discovering this very Now, until we reach the final depth of reality, dissolving into the Universal Presence. Because this Path is non-dual, we practice in the space of an absolute acceptance of What Is. At the same time, we see the limitations of the mind and our basic lack of completeness. For that reason, we understand the fundamental need for practice and cultivation of the Inner State. Here, there is the place for the right effort, discipline and conscious evolution.

It is true that there is only the Self, but by whom is this Self reached? The Self is not reached by the Self, for the Self is already One. Why would the Self need to reach the Self? There is no Two-ness in the Ultimate! The Self is reached by its foremost creation,' which you recognise as your sense of Me. Pure Me is the primordial expression of the Source and the perceiver of all.

If there is no duality, there is no experience. In non-duality, there is neither ignorance nor Enlightenment. Therefore, duality is meaningful and divine in this essence, for it allows Creation to happen. But duality without unity, that is, non-duality, is sheer ignorance. Duality, extracted from the context of Total Existence, represents the fragmented state of existence. From the other side, non-duality without duality is the absence of consciousness or simply death! It is only when duality and non-duality meet, that the complete Understanding is born. It is the ultimate meeting of time with timelessness; it is the ultimate reality of the Soul and the Beloved.

The mind has to intuitively grasp the subtle meaning of the Non-dual Path. If one does not practice according to this understanding - one is not honest to one's own Soul. Either one lives in the illusion of a pseudo-Advaita intellectual 'Enlightenment,' or one lives in an anticipated future, overlooking the truth of the Now. If you negate the Spiritual Path and the necessity of the inner work, you are being dishonest with yourself. If you keep on saying that the Self is all there is and there is no need to practice, you simply deceive yourself. In such a case, you simply refuse to see how fragmented your mind is and how painfully you are disconnected from the light of Creation. Wouldn't it be sheer hypocrisy? Many Krishnamurti's and Advaita followers are stuck in this incomplete understanding. Here, denying the need for practice, one tries to realise the Self immediately. But one is unable to! The Spiritual Path is a reflection of the basic necessity to evolve, a reflection of common sense and wisdom.

* * *

In our first meditation we will discover the quality of Being. When you breathe - letting go into the Now, what you encounter is the realm of Beingness. In the beginning, you are entering this new dimension in a very shy, uncertain way. You do not know how to behave, how to Be within Being. You don't know how to abide in this vast, infinite, bottomless space of pure isness. Nothing can be grasped, nothing can be seen, all you can do is Be. Beingness is existence without self-referral, the universal space of non-abidance.

But who is experiencing this reality of non-reference? Who submits oneself into Being? It is your very Me, which is so subtle that the mind cannot crystallise her existence - and yet she has been present all along. Me primarily is placed in the Heart. It is from the Heart that the instinctive desire for happiness and evolutionary fulfilment comes. The mind is the first expression of the Heart. Without the mind, the Heart cannot exist, for it is the mind which brings awareness to the Soul. If the mind is ignorant, fragmented and lacks continuity, such a mind cannot be used by the Soul to attain the condition of Being.

Therefore, in our second meditation, we work with the extension of the Heart which is the mind. Awareness is generated in the mind, within the head area. Without the brain there is no awareness, at least in our particular dimension. In our reality, consciousness requires the vehicle of a physical body and a brain in order to manifest itself. The centre of awareness, the centre of wakefulness, is located in the middle of the brain, in the third eye. When awareness is unconscious or rather semi-conscious, it becomes lost in the subconscious activity of the mind. This constant thinking which turns a human being into a living computer is caused by the absence of essential awareness. We are not speaking here about the awareness of thinking but about awareness as such.

In the awakening of awareness, we differentiate two basic stages. First is the ability to go beyond the mind by the act of observation or mindfulness. Here, through the general growth of awareness, you create a certain distance from the mind. The second stage, which in truth already represents Awakening, is the direct recognition of pure awareness. This state of self-awareness, objectless consciousness, we call mindfulness without object.

We begin with a breathing practice. As you inhale, your belly expands and you bring the breath into your head. Becoming fully present, you recognise clearly the One who is present. That which is present is pure attention. That which is You! Upon exhalation you relax into Being.

Silence

Please now become aware of the thoughts in your mind. The moment you are aware of thinking, it feels as if it was located on the periphery of the mind. Feel as if thinking itself was outside of you. Why does it feel like that? Because the observing intelligence is very close to the centre of awareness, while thinking is energetically removed from the centre. When the observing intelligence is active, attention is present automatically. When you observe you mind, you discover the subject or 'I' which is just behind the observing intelligence. See it!

We are entering into a very subtle area, the heart of consciousness, the essence of the mind. You can bypass the mind through expansion into Being, but the mind will be intact. To transform the mind, you have to enter it directly. It is like entering a camp of enemies and putting a bomb there. This bomb is your attention and the explosion of this bomb is self-awareness. And that which makes this explosion possible is your intelligence - the power of recognition which turns attention back to itself.

Now you are facing your own mind which is the main problem. And it is about the time to face it! Isn't it? You are observing the mind with the utmost focus. You are becoming conscious of the fact that this observing is coming from a certain place. It is not merely the mind aware of its activity. There is a certain place from which you observe. That which is observing is the subtle mind; it is your intelligence. But what is this very attention behind the observing intelligence. Where are you located in this observation? Where is your sense of Me? Look inside and find out!

There are two questions. One is: who is doing the observing? The second is: from which place does observing arise? That which is observing is intelligence. And the place from which intelligence is able to observe is the source of awareness. When that which is observing becomes aware of itself, the real centre of awareness is born. The centre of awareness is another name given to your very Me. Your Me represents the presence of the subject behind the mind. It is all very simple, elementary even. But because of the fragmented quality of the human mind, most experience serious difficulties in grasping the matter. But it is simple. It is not this subject which is complicated, but the ignorant mind.

Again, with the breath, bring energy up to the inside of your head while being completely present. Stop! Stop your breath, keeping it inside the head and discover, recognise the one who is present. Who is present? Recognise yourself! It is you, who is present, see it!

Unless you know who you are, all these talks about meditation and Enlightenment are completely meaningless. Be serious and wake up at last to yourself!

Now, simply be present inside your head breathing naturally. As you are present, various thoughts may come and pass, still there is something which remains in the background. That which does not change is the light of awareness. With this feeling, with this presence, you relax into Being. Let go into non-doing, into What Is and just Be.

In meditation, two elements are present. One is doing and the second is non-doing. Abide in a space that is comfortable, self-contained, still and calm; just stay there. There is no need to do anything, just be. But if your mind is restless, if your energy is not rooted and fluctuates, then concentrate. You must use your attention and create the necessary focus.

From moment to moment, you are one with the breath. Breathing, breathing, breathing.... You are concentrated and dedicated to the task of being present within the movement of thoughts and emotions. You have to crystallise the sense of your identity. Otherwise, you are like a ghost, a dream character lost in the dream world...

Silence

To discover oneself, one has to have passion. This passion comes from a divine intuition which links the state of forgetfulness with Awakening. There is no other connection between ignorance and Light - separation and unity. This intuition, the divine instinct of evolution is the only link. When this intuition is awakened, she gives rise to passion and passion brings determination, dedication and understanding. This ancient longing for returning home to our origin is the engine of evolution. Why otherwise, evolve at all?

> *Once upon a time, to a great master in China came a monk to inquire about the matter of Enlightenment. Before he even opened his mouth, the master Hui Neng asked: 'what is this thing which is standing in front of me?' Can there be a higher instruction? Can there be a higher*

question? The monk, dumb-founded, understood that that great matter of Enlightenment points to his own subjective existence. He went with his great question into the mountains, meditating for eight years! And one day he understood his true self. He went back to Hui Neng and said: 'If you called it a thing, you would miss the mark!' The answer was approved. By the way, Hui Neng had rather a good memory to remember this question after eight years!

In meditation, there are moments when one is tired and energy feels stuck or restless. In such moments, one wants to evade the whole situation and escape. But one does not escape. One keeps going! One stays Here and Now, at the centre. If we practice meditation only when we feel good or experience deep states - it is not real! You should precisely meditate when it is difficult to go inside and the mind is disturbing. It is a work against ignorance. When it is difficult, you need to meditate with even greater dedication. This is real! Ultimately practice is simply done irrespective of whether you feel good or bad. It is simply your responsibility to the truth of I Am.

We relax into the vast, infinite ocean of Beingness which underlies everything. The gateway to the Kingdom of God is Being, the Gate-less Gate. This Gate you cannot see, but you can enter! When you surrender, the energy drops. It is the law of energy - that when you are not doing, energy gravitates down towards the Hara. But in order not-to-do, you have to be present, attentive. What you are doing is mindfulness and what you are not doing is Being. Non-doing is the foundation and doing is the means to attain this foundation.

Spiritual expansion relates to the fact that your energy system is a part of Universal Energy. Your sense of identity experienced within your individual existence is merging into the Universal I AM. You become One with the ocean of God. Here, you are unable to separate yourself from this ocean anymore. Even though you remain on some level separated, you are fully merged with the Beyond. They are one and two, two and one - two within One. When we say that there is only unity, something is not fully expressed for it is Me who experiences this unity. When we say there is duality, again it is not correct, for you are in a state of Oneness...

Silence

With each inhalation, your belly expands; next your chest expands and you feel the Heart inside. Direct energy into the head, keeping it there for one moment and become fully present. And with exhalation, your chest falls down, the belly becomes flat and you rest before the next inhalation. You repeat this circular breathing for some time.

Silence

Now, you breathe only to the chest activating the Heart centre. You put your hand on this area, feeling it in a intimate way. Let the music which you hear become a part of this experience. This music is coming from the Heart of the one who created it. It is not coming from the outside but from within. Feel your Heart and recognise that there is someone inside your Heart which is being felt. Is it not? You are touching your Soul. Your consciousness is meeting its own Heart, which is the Soul.

Imagine please, that you do not exist on the earth, that you have no physical body. Imagine that you have no memories, no future and no past. But in that space, you do still experience your own Heart. Within the timeless dimension of the Divine, you meet your Soul face to face. How does it feel? Be like a child discovering your innocent Heart. What is it that does not change? Who am I?

With inhalation, you are feeling your Heart, with each exhalation you are letting go, resting within... Know who you are, be who you are.

PEACE GRACE LOVE

Transmission 6

1 November 1999, Arambol, India

The Garden of the Beloved

Beloved friends. We invite you to the continuation of the process of Awakening. Awakening to a deeper sense of identity represents your eternal essence beyond the mind. It is an awakening to the light of the Self, to the light of I Am. We reveal to you a reality which cannot be touched by the movement of thoughts, which is timelessly present and one with the Divine. We invite you to the garden within, the garden inside you. Enter the garden of the Beloved.

The purpose of the Spiritual Path, the purpose of meditation, is the dimensional shift from the mind to the depth of Being. In this timeless space you are still present but not as the ego-mind. You are present as the Soul, which is the original light of Me.

In order to experience this shift, your awareness has to be awakened. Otherwise you have no way to transcend the unconscious movements of the mind. Apart from the awakening of awareness, you need to develop Samadhi. Samadhi represents your connection with the dimension of Beingness, the rootedness within. And finally, you have to open your Heart and discover your divine quality.

As you enter the Path, you gradually leave the collective mind behind. You are becoming a different being, becoming free from your past. You are becoming an autonomous, independent being who belongs to the family of light. You are becoming a divine being.

We are entering the dimension of meditation, the inner garden of silence and beauty which is beyond the mind. How to enter this inner garden is the skill of meditation and it is the function of Awakening. The Path, the way to this garden has been lost long ago. No one remembers how to get there, no one even knows the direction to this garden. The knowledge about the existence of this garden is secret and many dis-believe in its reality. The direction to the inner garden is IN and the Path which leads you there is your own presence.

* * *

Again, we begin with breathing. Simply breathe into the belly, being one with the breath. Be one with the intention of being present to the Now, to the experience of life. Life is not thinking; Life is Being.

There is a full acceptance of the mind, the acceptance of everything. But, at the same time, you are fully present. You do not allow yourself to get lost in the mind. Drop deep down, deeper and deeper to the simple act of breathing and to the experience of Being. You are returning to who you are before thought, the forgotten world of I Am.

Just breathe, being very disciplined and focussed. Being fully present and attentive, you relax into Being, into non-doing... from moment to moment.

Silence

Who is that one sitting inside this body? Is this one alive or dead? What is this very Soul that lives inside? What is it made of? Who are you? As you are letting go of the mind, you are entering the way of Being. This new way of existing is not touched by thought and has no reference to your memories and personal life. Can you see the value, the importance of it? It is not just to be free from the mind but to meet face to face your Soul. This meeting takes place after an infinite time of separation.

Awaken this wonder, this amazement, this surprise, this curiosity for self-discovery. Awaken this passion through which you can meet yourself in a new way, not in the dull and passive way of the past. You are meeting your beloved, which is your own Soul. You may practice meditation for years and even have deep experiences, but still not know the significance of what you are doing. It is because your intelligence is asleep and your Heart insensitive. So, awaken your intelligence, awaken your Heart and meet yourself in a true way. It is time to wake up from dead, from life in the mind. And forgetting oneself is nothing but death, death of the Soul.

Breathing and Being. Being and discovering the one who is present inside. You are becoming a new human being, which has the dignity of I Am. The Soul of such a being is alive and not dead. The problem is that most meditators do not have any passion for truth. And it is this passion alone that matters, for it reflects the aliveness and intensity of evolution. When you meet someone whom you truly love, you are all excited. Why aren't you excited by going inside and meeting your own Soul?

* * *

This time with each inhalation, your belly expands and you bring energy inside the head, being fully present inside the head area. You are keeping the breath inside the head, in the middle of the brain as long as you can. And after exhalation, you simply relax into Being and rest. Repeat this type of breathing for some time.

At this moment, you relax the breath but still keep energy in the mind. You are keeping a clear presence inside the head. Who is present inside the head? Recognise this very 'I' which is present. It is your very centre of identity behind the mind.

Become aware of thinking, seeing that thinking is arising and passing outside of you. Recognise the centre behind thoughts. This sense of identity behind the mind never changes, it remains always the same. When you recognise the State of Presence, the centre in the mind, something very significant takes place. Suddenly, you see that you are not who you thought you were. You discover that you are made from the light of awareness. You have no form, you have no memory; you have no colour, no sex, no nationality, no name... Can you see the significance of this recognition? If you truly see... if you truly see that you have no form - you will be in a state of shock! If you are not in a state of shock, it indicates that you have not seen your true face yet. You are still identified with the form, you are still on the subconscious level, identified with your former ego-image.

Recognise clearly the State of Presence, the centre behind thoughts and stay with this experience. Abide in the state of pure awareness. Imagine that you do not have any form, you have no memories, no past and no future... You do not know what was yesterday and what will be tomorrow. You have no knowledge, you know nothing... But you are! And when you feel it clearly, you have a glimpse of eternity. You can have an insight into what it truly means to be eternal. It is not merely a poetic expression. Eternity is real. Wake up to your eternal identity!

It is not enough to have the experience of I Am. Intelligence also has to awaken to the understanding of this experience. Your intelligence has to fully recognise the utmost significance of the inner state. We can call it the second Awakening, the awakening of intelligence and recognition.

Silence

Keeping the State of Presence, you relax it inside the head. You allow it to stay in its natural condition. And next, you relax even more so the state expands into Being. Awareness becomes absorbed into non-doing, just sitting. You are just sitting in this inner garden, experiencing beautiful peace and resting in infinite bliss. But try to again discover the significance of this experience. See that it is your own Soul who is just sitting within the Universal space of I AM. Imagine once more that you have no form, no memory, no physical body; imagine that you are no more a human...but you just Are.

Silence

At this time, we will begin the next breathing practice. With inhalation your belly expands, next your chest expands, and you feel the Heart inside your chest. Next, you bring energy inside your head being fully present. And as you exhale, your chest becomes flat, your belly becomes flat and you rest.

A few times breathing to the chest, feeling the Heart. Now we put our hands on the Heart in the middle of the chest. We are experiencing the part of Me which is called the Heart. The Heart is the feeling centre, the centre of sensitivity and the doorway to the Divine Dimension. It is for these reasons why mystics who have been pointing for centuries to the Beloved, always spoke about the Heart. They didn't speak about Awareness or Being, but about the Heart. The Heart represents the sensitivity of the Creator. The infinite sensitivity of the Beloved is the Divine Dimension. The infinite rest, peacefulness and motionlessness of the Creator is called Beingness. Another name for Beingness is the Absolute.

To enter the dimension of the Creator is to enter Being and to enter the Heart. From the ultimate perspective, Being and Heart are one and they cannot be separated. However, the human being from the standpoint of relative separation can experience

Being without Heart or Heart without Being. For that reason, we have this task of reaching the inner wholeness.

As you are feeling your Heart, you are feeling the most sensitive part of your Me. Through the presence of your Soul, you are tuning into the Other Side of the Heart. In the depth of the Heart is the Realm of the Divine. You are tuning into the space of the Heart. But in order to fully enter the Heart, this very centre has to be activated and awakened. The golden key to open the Heart is cultivating clear intention, sensitivity and surrender. You need to be attentive to your own Heart, with the intention to feel this which is so delicate in you. The moment you fully surrender your mind to the Heart, the inner door opens and you discover that there is no gate, in truth, no door - there is only the Divine Presence.

Meeting the Divine and discovering your own Soul are the two sides of the same phenomenon. You cannot separate your Soul from the Divine. Unless you are awakened to your Soul, you cannot experience her Creator. For in truth, the Golden Gate, the Gate-less Gate to the Divine Dimension is your own Soul. That's why, Jesus said: 'I am the Gate.' He meant that the Soul is both the experiencer of the Divine and the entrance to reach it.

When you are present, your intelligence has continuity and solidity. You are not just spaced out and unconscious. That's why, you can surrender into I Am in a real way. No longer are you like a leaf floating in the air. You become like a tree rooted in the earth of the Now. When you have this inner solidity, you can enter the essence of I Am, which is the Heart. Here, you are not simply emotional. You have the solidity of presence and the depth of Being.

Entering into the internal space of the Heart is an amazing phenomenon. It is the whole world. Not only are you feeling the Heart but you are entering a dimension which exists beyond earth. You are entering a dimension which is infinitely vast and has many secrets to offer to you. It is an adventure of the Soul for she discovers her home again. The prodigal son or daughter returns.

GRACE PEACE LOVE

Transmission 7

3 November 1999, Arambol, India

Beyond Forgetfulness

Beloved friends, we welcome you to our next Satsang. As you are listening, please tune into your own presence and inner silence. Connect to the breath in the belly and courageously let go of the mind. Let go of your anxieties, fears and insecurities. In a disciplined way, experience the purity and austerity of the Now.

This meeting is taking place beyond master to disciple projections. This Transmission does not concern guru worship and is beyond spiritual slogans about Enlightenment. We present a clear Path to Awakening. And it is in your hands whether you want to use these tools to promote your own Self-realisation. Awakening is your destiny which you cannot avoid but have the freedom to postpone. It is your freedom to follow your lower nature and forgetful instinct. But the longer you delay your Awakening, the more you prolong your suffering.

To transcend the dimension of forgetfulness and ignorance, one has to free oneself from the addiction to unconsciousness. Most Souls do not have the desire for Awakening, at all, because they are addicted to ignorance. They still enjoy their nightmares! Awakening is the desire of very few Souls. That's why, there are hardly any seekers on the spiritual scene. Some masters seem to attract many disciples. But what is the quality of these people? And what kind of seduction takes place as masters basically gather unconscious individuals? Is it in the name of Enlightenment? It is all one big nonsense!

It is a real gift for a master to meet a real seeker. It does not happen every day or every month...it happens rarely. A real seeker is one who is ready to meet one's own light and face the naked reality of I Am. It is the light of aloneness that we speak about, the light of the Ultimate. Awakening does not take place within collective consciousness. When you hear about Enlightenment, it is just one more concept in the collective mind. It is just another idea translated in a vulgar way by the ego. The ego gets so excited by the concept of Enlightenment. Most seekers look for Enlightenment because they think that something amazing is going to happen to them. They are bored with their old life so they hope to change it through something more interesting. They don't want to discover their Soul, but rather to find a new way of escape.

One of the many aims of our meetings is to de-hypnotise you from the concept of Enlightenment, so you can see clearly the truth of spiritual evolution. For what is Enlightenment? It is just an idea unless you reach it. And when you reach it, it is always a big surprise, something you would never expect! Enlightenment is nothing special. If you knew that it is nothing special, would you make such an effort to attain it? Why would you like to reach nothing special? The ego always wants something special and is never satisfied. But it is your Soul's wish to reach nothing special. The Soul is not seeking excitement but rather she is seeking Truth! Truth is simple. It is not ecstasy, it is not bliss, it is not some amazing happiness...it is just what it is. And that is a surprise!

There are Two Paths to Enlightenment. One is the path of will, which is Zen and the second is the path of Grace, with is Advaita. Even though Advaita is called the path of Self-knowledge, it is not. Buddhism is the path of Self-knowledge. Advaita is the path of Grace and the Transmission of Awakening on the energy level. From the other side, Zen is the Path of discipline and a methodical cultivation of the Inner State. In our teaching we combine these two approaches. Without Grace, without help from the Beyond, the human being cannot get out of ignorance. But without the inner effort, discipline, self-remembrance, enquiry... Grace cannot enter either. Self-realisation is always a combination of our effort, the intensity of our search and the intervention from Beyond, that is Grace. When those two elements meet, they create the spark of Awakening.

One of the biggest misconceptions about Enlightenment is the belief that it refers just to one state, just to one type of realisation. In such a case, either one is enlightened or one is not. It is however very much incorrect. There are levels of Self-realisation and not every master represents the same state. In order to understand it, one has to know the Inner Map of Awakening. This map is subtle and still remains a secret, not available to the collective spiritual consciousness.

In the book written by Muktananda, he observed that some masters seemed to abide in various states. He felt that he himself experienced a different state than his own master, Nityananda. Using his knowledge of kundalini Yoga, he couldn't explain this problem because the science of this Path had not elaborated a clear Inner Map of Awakening. No one actually can, as the teachings of the past are too simplistic. They usually speak about Enlightenment as reaching a state beyond the mind. But the problem is that there are many such states!

The first enlightened state refers to the awakening of pure consciousness, the State of Presence. This Awakening takes place in the third eye centre, in the middle of the brain. When it is activated, you are in the permanent state of self-attention. The second Enlightenment is the Absolute State, which takes us beyond consciousness. The Absolute is realised through the Being quality of I Am. When the bottom of Being is pierced through, one moves to the Other Side becoming one with the Source. No movement can be found in that state. The third Enlightenment takes place in the Heart. Here, the Divine is realised. That is the basic skeleton of the inner map of Awakening. The evolution continues but knowing about these three types of Enlightenment will give you a lot of clarity. And you will be able to see that there is a big difference in Self-realisation, in regard to different masters.

We spoke many times about the complete vision of I Am. This complete vision relates to the work with three different qualities: Awareness, Being and Heart. It is a new technology of Awakening which allows you to understand the entire dynamic of the Inner State. You can easily verify the truth of this vision with your own intelligence. But first, you need to have some experience.

* * *

We begin our first meditation. We begin with slow breathing into the belly becoming one with the breath...surrendering into Being. Our first meditation is learning the art of Being and expanding the experience of it. As you know, meditation is a state of Being. It is not a technique but a State. The state of Being is present when experience of energy is restful and absorbed.

You are breathing, being very attentive, because only attention can free you from the mind. Attention is your only security in the realm of unconsciousness. You are breathing...being very attentive. In each moment, particularly with exhalation, letting go into Being.

What happens when you let go into Being is very profound, even though you may not recognise the whole depth of the experience. The moment you let go, your energy gravitates; there is a pull from the source of gravity, which is the Uncreated. The Absolute is the foundation of all universes. It is the underlying presence of the Source...the pure isness of existence. We are all resting upon the Absolute: trees, mountains, all living beings... However, the question is: how to reconnect with the dimension of Beingness? How to come closer to the Source? It is through surrender. This surrender is not emotional but energetic. The moment you let go, your energy merges with the universal space of Being. You become rooted in something which you cannot know... but you can it clearly experience.

Remain for some time like this. Breathing, being very attentive, focussed and letting go...letting go; dropping...dropping down like a dewdrop from a leaf falling into the earth of Beingness.

* * *

We return to the sitting position, bringing consciousness into focus. The sitting position is very symbolic, for it represents the stillness of our true nature. That's why, keeping the body still and not moving helps you to reach the stillness of Being. It is not to torture you, but to channel your energy into the right experience.

Meditation has no end and no beginning. But, being human and coming from the place of separation, you divide meditation. You create the distinction between being in meditation and being out of it. But it is only for the time being. As you evolve, becoming one with I Am, you gradually become the State of Meditation. No longer will it be 'an experience' but it will become your permanent state. You become contained in the State of Meditation which is constantly present in the background of your personality. It is a gradual process of expansion.

We emphasise Understanding because it is missing strongly in the case of most seekers. Most refuse to use their mind. They don't want to understand anything for they only want a peace of the mind. But how can you have this peace if you don't understand what your problem is? The difference between this Satsang and most other Satsangs is that there is actually a teaching given here! So, seekers come and become really perplexed. 'What? Teaching? We don't what any teaching. We want to be in the presence of an alive master who will tell us that there is nothing to do! We are tired of learning. We just want to relax...' They refuse to activate their intelligence. And because of that they stagnate to the end of their lives in incomplete meditative experiences. They miss the precious chance to reach Awakening. It is a real waste!

Understanding is your security, your only clarity on the Path. It is not about having lots of information, but about knowing what you are doing. It is to be clear about who you are as a multidimensional being.

* * *

In our second meditation we explore the dimension of Awareness. It is perhaps the most difficult and unclear area for an average meditator. Awareness is generated in the brain. If you take off your head, there is no more awareness. Awareness makes all recognition possible. Even the Heart cannot be experienced without consciousness. This is how different parts of your being complement each other.

In order to activate the centre of awareness, we will do some special breathing. With each inhalation your belly fully expands and you bring the breath up to the head. You are keeping it inside the head for some time. You are fully present inside the head and you recognise Who is present. Who is that one? With exhalation you relax, letting go into Being. You do this circular movement between crystallising presence in your head and letting go into Being. Please, feel the one who is present inside your head...who is present? What does it mean to be present? When you are not breathing, you are just present. This presence has no object, for it is the subject itself.

* * *

You can relax now, remaining fully present. You need to realise that most human beings have no any centre in the mind. What it means is that there is nobody inside; there is just the mind. People here want to celebrate, but there is no reason to celebrate. The situation is very serious. They should cry; as there is no one inside. There is just unconsciousness that reigns here. To break through this feast of unconsciousness, to stop this crazy dance of ignorance, you have to awaken the centre in your mind. In Zen it is called the host of the mind. Who is the host of your mind? Thoughts are coming and going but who remains?

Gently, become aware of the arising thoughts inside your mind. It is a very important process we are going through and very subtle. We are entering the reality of the mind, which is quite complex. Because you are so identified with thinking, you don't know how to separate your very Me from this jungle of thoughts. But on some level, you already know that you are just Me.

You are aware of arising thoughts, as they come and go. There is a feeling that the one who is aware of thinking, is itself deeper than the arising thoughts. Watching the mind is just a preparation for Awakening. Awakening takes place when the watcher becomes self-aware. It means that the observing consciousness turns back to itself and recognises its own subjectivity... It is Atman, 'I', the Real Me. As you are observing the mind, become sensitive to the one who is observing. Who is observing the mind? It is you!

Silence

We are again entering the inner shrine, the domain of I Am; that which does not change and always remains present beyond time. This is a mysterious realm, the secret which can be revealed to you but only when you are ready.

As your eyes are closed, you are experiencing yourself. That is YOU. But it is not the complete Me yet. Often there are just fragments, chaotic movement of energy thoughts and emotions. Such a reality has no depth and no continuity. That is ignorance. Ignorance indicates a fragmented state where your sense of identity is completely distorted...your Me is falling apart. It is an impersonal and collective reality. You are just a particular, pseudo-individual version of the collective mind. Even though you may feel yourself as being distinct and unique, in truth - you are just a part of the collective.

At this stage you are just the mind and the mind is not the Real Me. There is no Soul present. The Soul must become born in order to become present. When you are born from your mother, it is only the body and mind which are born. When you are born into this dimension, you become pregnant with the Soul.

And it is you who has to give birth to the Soul. But most never give birth to their Soul. They die still remaining pregnant. A master with the help of Guidance represents the midwife who is helping you to give birth to the Soul. But you have to co-operate; similar to the mother who is giving birth, there must be some co-operation. You cannot merely wait for something to happen, because it will never happen! Most seekers wait for Enlightenment; it is like waiting for Godot; it never comes. In the famous play of Becket, the main character is waiting the whole performance for the mysterious 'Godot' - but he never arrives!

Silence

We relax into this moment...into our absence. When you are completely silent, humble in the way you experience the Now, the other force enters - the Beyond. The Beyond embraces you becoming contained in the totality of Truth.

Please, become aware of the Heart, putting your hand on the middle of the chest. Breathing to this area, feeling it in a sensitive way...

We spoke about the three types of Self-realisation: the State of Presence, the Absolute State and Enlightenment to the Heart. In the State of Presence, the Soul reaches the essence of consciousness and freedom from the mind. In the Absolute State, the Soul becomes united with the Uncreated, merged with the energy of the Source. And, finally, in the Heart, the Soul enters the domain of the Divine. Here, she discovers the Heart of the Creator and meets the Beloved.

Many are confused about the question 'Who am I?' The reason is because, as there are three types of Enlightenment, there are also three answers. The first answer is: 'I am the witness, pure awareness.' The second answer is: 'I am not, for only Being is.' And the third answer is: 'I am the Heart.' All these answers are correct. However, it is the Heart that is the closest to us. It is because in the Heart, the Soul is energetically located.

What is the Soul? She is the essence of our individual manifestation. She is that which is nearest to our existence as Me. It is in the Heart that you meet yourself in the most intimate and direct way. It is not in Awareness and not even in Being, but in the Heart. For that reason, Ramana Maharishi thought that the Self can be found in the Heart. But what he called 'Self' was, in truth, his own Soul.

Feeling your Heart, you embrace your existence as the Soul. You ask yourself: 'who am I behind all my roles and masks?' As you sit here, who has come to this Satsang? Who is that one looking for happiness and peace? Who is trying to avoid suffering? Where does this instinct to be happy come from and to whom does it refer? It belongs to your Soul and you can recognise your Soul in the Heart.

But before you can meet your Soul fully, you must first become free from the mind. When Awareness is present and you rest in Being, in that moment you are free to enter the Heart. The experience of the Heart is beyond emotion. Love is not an emotion; Love is the pure energy of sensitivity. Love is the presence of the Heart which is directed neither in nor out. Love simply IS.

Breathing to the chest, we connect to the Heart, as if meeting our own Heart after a long separation. Meet yourself directly and go beyond all ego-images...beyond self-love, beyond even the need for self-love...

GRACE PEACE LOVE

Transmission 8

5 November 1999, Arambol, India

Becoming One Again

Beloved friends, we welcome you again to the Now. Our meeting always takes place Now, because we can meet you only within Reality. During our meetings we guide you into the understanding and experience of your own self. We are helping you to recollect this part of yourself which is eternal, beyond change, beyond personality and beyond the mind. You are regaining your connection with who you have always been, beyond any incarnation, beyond any dream...

The goal of our meetings is to shift the basic sense of identity, from the mind to I Am. We are awakening a new state of being; a new way of existing in which you become fully present as the Real Me which is untouched by the movement of the mind. You become One, united with your ancient Soul's identity. You are made of pure light and have always been.

However, this ancient identity has been totally forgotten. All humans have forgotten it. Your friends, your family, the society you live in - they have all forgotten. They live in a trance-state, having lost their Soul. They are all on drugs. And the drug they have taken, is the very birth into the body and into this dimension of forgetfulness. This dimension attracts Souls who are addicted to forgetfulness, addicted to ignorance. It is their adventure: to pretend that there is no God and only the apparent reality of appearances is real. It may be seen as 'fascinating' to live in a god-less reality when All is God. But now, as you awaken the ancient intuition, you begin the process of sobering up. Slowly, you are waking up from the trance. The effect of the drug is being removed from your blood stream, as you come back to our Dimension.

That which you have always been is your Me in her original form. When you come to Satsang, you come as a part of the collective mind. Most of you come as some kind of a personal version of the impersonal collective consciousness. But when you enter this process, one day you leave as an individual. That is our hope. As you awaken, you become an autonomous being which lives by the power of her own light, generated from within.

Meditation is the art of entering an unconditional state beyond the mind. Here, your sense of existence is beyond the movement of thoughts. You are not trying to stop the mind, not at all. You are re-locating your sense of Me - from being lost in the mind to the state of I Am. When this experience is stabilised, you will never lose it; it remains irrespective of your life situation. Spiritual expansion aims not at a temporary relief of the mind but at the permanent state beyond the mind.

Most human beings agreed to live in ignorance with their consciousness lost in the mind. They accepted to live in forgetfulness. But with this agreement, they have died. A person who is not free from the mind is a ghost and not a being. Freedom from the mind is your dignity as the divine being, which you are. A being has to be born. It is not born from another, it is born from within. When your are born in the body, it means that the body becomes pregnant with the Soul. The Soul is not released until you give birth to her. One day she will be born.

* * *

Please tune in, breathing to the belly and becoming one with the breath. From moment to moment, you let go of the mind. If you are not the mind, who are you? How can you experience yourself beyond the mind? These are important questions. If they have not been asked - one has not entered the Spiritual Path yet. What type of questions you are asking, reflects your level of evolution.

The first way of experiencing oneself outside the mind is Being. Being is the essence of meditation. Meditation can be called 'just being,' 'non-doing,' 'non-thinking.' But how can we reach the state of just being? The answer is: through just being. Being is attained through Being. In order to reach Being, one has to surrender...

In each moment that you breathe, you are one with the breath. You are letting go into the simple, fundamental experience of Being. Meditation is not a technique. It is not to repeat a mantra or to do visualisations. Meditation is a state of non-activity, a profound condition of just being. That is the only meditation. In order to reach this state, sometimes you need to use techniques. But you must understand that just being is the foundation. A technique is merely a tool to be dropped at one stage.

We are breathing, just being. There is a full acceptance of whatever you experience, including the fluctuating mind. The goal of meditation is not to stop the mind, but to go beyond thinking. It means that whether you think or not think, it truly does not matter. Meditation is beyond thinking and beyond not thinking. Thinking cannot touch it, but even though you are beyond thinking - you can also think.

With this full acceptance, we are breathing. We are absolutely attentive. As if the fire was surrounding you and you are going to die any moment. In this way, you attentively sit on the edge of life and death. Only with this attitude will you transcend unconsciousness, otherwise you fall asleep. Just being, breathing, remaining fully present... Let it all be as it is.

GRACE PEACE LOVE

Transmission 9

8 November 1999, Arambol, India

Discovering the Light of Creation

Beloved friends, welcome to our next Transmission of Awakening. This Transmission takes place in the eternal space of the Now which is present beyond time and space. Such a dimension does exist beyond the manifested reality; it represents, in truth the Only Reality. All else is merely a play of appearances, a play of dreams.

When you incarnate into the body, you forget your origin... you forget all. You mind is blank like an empty page. You are in a trance state. The only source of information which is accessible to you is collective consciousness, the human collective knowledge and belief system. Because you start being completely blank, you have no choice but to learn from humanity. In order to fit yourself into the plane of forgetfulness, you fill your blank mind with all kinds of trash. You accumulate knowledge from your apparent parents, school and surroundings. Soon, you become a perfectly collective robot.

Even though collective consciousness is quite sophisticated within its ignorance, it is simply unaware of the Divine Dimension. The collective mind is disconnected from the light of Creation, living in a virtual and arrogant ego-world. That's why, in order for you to regain a connection with your eternal home, you must become free. You must go beyond all the knowledge through which the collective mind has shaped your illusory perception of reality. You have to rebel against collective ignorance by virtue of your own individual evolution. At that stage, your evolution becomes individual and splits from the collective.

The meeting with your Eternal Parent can happen only in the internal space of aloneness in your Heart and in your Being. When you reach a certain existential impasse, you simply become frustrated with what the collective mind has to offer to you. Here, you may enter the noble path of self-discovery. That which links your collective past with your awakened future is divine intuition.

It is the inner voice of Guidance which continuously whispers to you the truth the Awakening.

Our work is to help you remember your ancient identity, to wake you up on many levels, not just one. Fundamentally, we aim at the energy expansion through which you merge with totality. Enlightenment, the experience of Oneness is an energy phenomenon. What you are is an energy system and inherent to you is intelligence. Through spiritual expansion, you go beyond the limitation of your individual self and become one with the Source of Creation. Our work, the work with Awareness, Being and Heart aims at this type of energetic expansion.

Another level of Awakening is the one of intelligence and sensitivity. If there is no intelligence, one cannot see the sublime depth and subtlety of the internal world of I AM. Thanks to intelligence, you can attain a real clarity about the process of Awakening. You can understand who you are and what your connection to the Other Dimension is. It is intelligence united with the Heart which allows the real meaning of your individual Creation to be understood. This understanding is not intellectual but direct.

Part of you does not believe in the truth of Awakening. Even when you are deeply connected to the Path, you still don't believe. Even when you already experience some level of Awakening, you still paradoxically don't believe it. The reason is that on the subconscious level, you are identified with your collective past. You are simply unable to believe that the Here does not represent Reality. Reality is made of the invisible light of I AM, which is Love in truth. You cannot believe this, for your subconscious computer program is designed to trust only the apparent reality of time and space. You are programmed like this by the collective consciousness and by the very design of your DNA.

But the Soul which grows within you moves slowly out of the womb of the collective mind and transcends the limitations of the program. Subconscious conditionings prevent you from being able to reflect the true universal understanding. In order to free your psyche from its own past, a certain cleansing of the subconscious mind has to take place. You cannot do it by will. But it is being done by the work of Guidance which is, in truth, the work of Grace. When certain essential elements in your subconscious mind get cleansed, suddenly something becomes free. Suddenly, you can see clearly and your distrust is transformed into absolute clarity. Here, you become free from your past and the past of humanity. To be free is not to negate the past but to transcend it within a qualitatively new perspective. To conclude, there are three elements of our work: the awakening to I Am, the awakening of intelligence and the cleansing of the subconscious mind which tries to prevent any shift of perception.

Our basic work is to create within you the ability through which you can experience your sense of identity, your very Me in complete separation from your psycho-somatic reality. Only when you awaken this ability, you can say 'I Am,' for only then is your Soul present. For the first time, you become freed from forgetfulness, giving birth to the Real Me. That is the purpose of evolution. To become a new being, an awakened being. It is not merely to improve yourself or to become a better person. It is to experience a dimensional shift, to return home. This new being which we are awakening, exists fully outside the mind. Such a being uses the mind but is placed beyond the field of thinking. He or she is rooted firmly and unconditionally in that which does not move, merged with the inner silence. This is your future which you are already experiencing. But staying with the process takes you to a new depth.

* * *

You are breathing, being one with the breath, being one with this moment. You relax into Existence. There is no need to reach anything. You practice within the space of complete acceptance. Whatever this moment is offering you is the truth of your reality. And to be with this truth is meditation.

When you are unconscious, each thought, each emotion creates your sense of identity. In this way, you are made from the movement of the mind. Now, you are learning something fundamental - how to exist before the mind. You are learning how to be present before a thought arises on the screen of consciousness. You are discovering the zero point of your being and becoming one with this reality. We speak about something much deeper than mindfulness of the environment. We speak about being present prior to perception, about being present to the subject. We speak about mindfulness without object. The zero point of experience is the experiencer. The zero point is the gateway to the reality of the Soul, the dimension of Me.

An ordinary person has no Me. You can ask such a person: 'who are you without memory? Who are you without thinking?' This person would probably answer: 'I am nothing.' Unfortunately it is true for most people, for they are nothing without the mind. No one is inside, the mind alone reigns.

In Buddhism they meditate on the absence of 'I' in order to discover emptiness. But not finding any 'I' is true only for unconscious individuals. Of course, the ego as such has no substance. But we are not speaking about the ego. We are pointing to the Real Me. We are giving birth to the one inside, to the one who exists without the mind. To the one who does not need to translate its existence through thinking because the dignity of its own presence is realised.

Silence

We are breathing and we are Being. Letting go of the mind, moment by moment. Neither are we fighting with the mind nor are we indulging in thinking. We ignore the mind, allowing it to be as it is. Just remain attentive enough not to become unconsciously lost in thinking. As you are breathing and letting go into Being, you find yourself energetically located deeper than the mind. You become rooted in the inner stillness. You are expanding.

Your subconscious mind re-creates, from moment to moment, your sense of identity as a particular person. It is very fast. You may not be aware of it, for you experience already the result which is the ego-image. You experience constantly a recreated image of the person you think you are. This image allows you relate to your situation in the world. This image revolves around your wellbeing, sense of pride, fears and hopes, your security and happiness. That is how you are being recreated from your subconscious computer program. That is fine, but is it really you? Is this image through which you identify yourself really you? You are not this which you think you are! You are that which you don't think you are! The ego image is just an outer layer, a superficial shell, a shadow of your real self.

But as you meditate, as you breathe you expand into something deeper. As you are relaxing into the space of non-reference, you move away from your ego-image. You are dissolving into the openness of Being. Within this space of non-reference, you still remain but beyond any crystallised ego-image. Here, you exist in a new way. That's why you don't know who you are anymore, for you are unable to translate this experience through your past concepts. You are in a state of not knowing.

You may even experience fear of entering this void because you have the feeling of losing yourself. But in truth, you are not losing yourself. On the contrary - you are gaining yourself. The unreal dies so the real can be born. The unreal does not want to die, that's why it holds onto its past sense of identity. But when you see clearly how unreal this past sense of identity is, you let it go. It is not even a matter of courage but rather understanding. If you wish to be afraid of something, it is only this ego-image to be feared. That void into which you surrender is absolutely safe, for it is made from peace and love. It is the original womb of life, the domain of Truth.

Holding onto the ego image is the cause of suffering, incompleteness and isolation. One lives in a cage, locked in the mind. If someone lives in a prison all their life, one does not want to leave this prison. One holds desperately onto a false sense of security; this is death. When a bird is born in a cage, it will not fly out even when you leave the door open. One gets easily addicted to bondage and slavery. We are the race of slaves, slaves of the mind. That is what we are. Now we rebel, breaking away from the inner prison. In esoteric Christianity, there were some schools propagating that the body is the prison of the spirit. However, it is not the body which is the prison, but the mind. Even if you are out of this body, you remain a slave of the mind. How to get out of the mind? That is our work.

* * *

We relax into that which is beyond the mind. The cage itself is an illusion. Ultimately the bird (the Soul) does not even need to fly out, for it is already out! It is like a Zen koan. A little goose has been put inside of a bottle. It has grown up and cannot leave the bottle. The question is 'how to let the goose out without breaking the bottle?' What is the answer? The goose is already out! Do you understand? You are already free! Just be and live this freedom. There is no cage, for the mind is empty and illusory.

But when you are unconscious, an illusory cage suddenly surrounds you and you find yourself being locked inside of it!

* * *

Breathing, being fully present and letting go into the void of the Now. The void is not that something is empty. The void is the state of non-reference, the ungraspable dimension of Beingness. It is a void for the mind and it is the fullness for the Soul - the fullness of pure isness and truth. You are dropping the mind as it arises. You are allowing yourself to be who you are, beyond any type of ego-image. Now you exist not as an image but as a being. A being is not made of an image; it is a pure experience, a pure feeling of Me. A being is the self-contained space of I Am which has a Heart and intelligence. You are becoming a being, the divine being which you have always been.

Silence

As you sit in meditation, awaken the desire to meet yourself. Awaken the passion to discover yourself; awaken an intense curiosity to explore the mystery of your existence. If you only sit to have an experience of peace or tranquillity, it is not the highest reason to meditate. The highest reason is this very divine longing which calls us back home. This longing takes us towards the direction of becoming one with the light of love, with the light of Creation. You are meeting your Soul. Do it with a sense of adventure and discovery, be passionate. It is a love affair with God.

The Soul was destined to forget herself and now she must return to her senses. She has to remember, for she has suffered too much in the darkness of ignorance. Now the Soul is awakening to her Ultimate Beloved which is the Divine Mother...

GRACE PEACE LOVE

Transmission 10

11 p.m. - 2 a.m.
21 December - 1 January, 1999/2000
Arambol, India

Doorway to the Timeless

Beloved friends, we welcome you to the New Year's Satsang. One year is ending and the new one is beginning. It is all a dream, an illusion. However, it gives us a good opportunity to contemplate the nature of time.

To whom is this New Year happening? From where is time arising? Being caught in this endless movement of becoming, we have lost the connection with that which is beyond change. And that itself is suffering...

Whatever hopes you have regarding the coming year, do not forget that time is quite deceptive. For not only has it created you, but it can terminate you as well. You are beginning in time and ending in time.

What is time in truth? It is but an opportunity to recognise the Timeless. Time is an opportunity to awaken. If you just live like most, the robot-like life, mechanically and unconsciously - you are wasting a precious opportunity. Life is not only to be lived but an opportunity to meet the very source of life. The deepest meaning of being alive is to awaken to the light and love of Creation.

Come back home! Relax within the Now, rest within and know that I AM. The voice that you hear comes from that dimension which brought you here in the very beginning. Know that I AM. Know that you are always embraced, day and night by the presence of ME.

I AM the light of Creation, which gave birth to your Souls. Relax and be fully present to the reality of the Now. Let go of time, let go of the Here. Let us transport you from the Here into the Now. Time and all what you experience in the time dimension is the scenery and the content of the Now! But the Now itself is untouched. What is the Now? It is not the gap between the past and the future, as some imagine. The Now is ME. I AM the Now. The Dimension of Now is made of pure light, of a timeless presence which is nothing but LOVE. You are in ME. Your Souls are contained in the infinity of what I AM. Know that and rest within.

The year 1999 is ending. The New Year is not yet the New Millennium unlike the general opinion. The new millennium is in one year, when the year 2000 will end. But this year is very important, for it is the final year before the New Millennium. It is not merely a number, a way of dividing time. This shift into the New Millennium has an esoteric significance. Many esoteric gateways are being opened and a lot of cleansing is taking place. You can easily feel it. Time as such is an opportunity to recognise the Timeless, but the coming year 2000 is a special opportunity to go inside. There are times when evolution is accelerated and tremendous help will become available. In the coming year, many things can happen to you if you co-operate. Don't waste this chance. That would be very unwise. Make the necessary sacrifices to give a major push to your evolutionary journey. Don't be lukewarm or lazy and passive. Take your destiny into your own hands and help the universe, help Grace to help you!

* * *

Take a few deep breaths to your chest and put your hands on your Heart. Connect to that one who is the mysterious subject to evolution. Feel that one who is seeking so desperately for happiness and fulfilment. Feel that one who has chosen to live in the time dimension, and within time is evolving towards the Timeless. That one is coming closer and closer to the unity with ME, the Creator of All.

Feeling your Soul, recollect the passing year. Tune into what has happened - from the beginning of the passing year until this time when this year is ending. What elements has existence brought to you? What did you want to achieve? How many things have changed? What was the flavour of this passing year in terms of your evolution?

Feeling your Soul, recognise which elements are necessary in your inner and outer reality to make you more complete? What are your Soul's desires? Not the mind's desires but those desires which come from the depth of your Heart's yearning. What is it that you would like to experience, to fulfil and to accomplish in the coming year? What is it that you need and you would like to create in your life? Feeling all of that, express your intention and longing to the dimension of Grace, to your Eternal Parent.

Feel the Beloved who is present in our meeting, for it is her who speaks through the voice of Aziz. Feel the one who created your Soul and as you feel her, clearly express what you long for. Let these elements be brought to you in the coming year. You cannot receive help unless you know clearly what you want. Let this clarity dawn upon you. Ask the Divine for assistance in your earthly evolution and journey in time. Say to the Creator. 'Please, help me, I am just your child. I know so little! I have so little control over my life and the universe is so vast! My Soul is suffering and I am tired of the pain of separation from YOU. I deeply wish to serve my Soul's evolution, to fulfil the divine plan and blueprint... please, help me, my Heart is crying!'

As you express your deepest longings and desires, commit yourself to the responsibility for your life. Exert all possible effort to grow and accelerate your evolution. You don't need to feel a victim and complain about your life. You have the power to awaken from the inside. If you are just waiting for a miracle, not doing anything, you are wasting your life. You are wasting the potential that was given to you. Be responsible, focus inside and stabilise your Presence. Next, go into your Heart and surrender into the depth of the Now. Wake up! Begin to live a real life.

When your wake up every morning of this coming year, wake up to the reality of Awakening and presence. Don't wake up anymore to the schizophrenia of the mind, to the dream reality of the Soul-less plane. Many gifts are awaiting you but cannot be given unless you sober up. Your responsibility is to get up from the trance-state of the collective unconscious.

* * *

May you have the force to act against the inertia of ignorance. May you have the force to persevere in difficult moments and moments of doubts. May you have the courage to cut through your own past and to evolve into the New. May you have the strength to do the inner work, precisely and clearly, so you can reach quickly the goal of Awakening and rest beyond effort.

May the Divine presence of the Beloved assist unconditionally and compassionately your evolution towards the Inner Light. May Grace be always present, awakening sincerity in your Heart. May it bring the necessary cleansing and transformation assigned to your destiny. May the Divine Mother support you with her Love and Guidance in your journey towards the realisation of ME. And, so we Pray...

GRACE PEACE LOVE

PART TWO

AWAKENING TO THE QUESTION

SATSANG

The evolution of intelligence is directly connected to the ability to formulate questions. If there is no question, how can clarity be reached? The question is a bridge between our present state of understanding and future expansion into a New Understanding.

But tell.us: what is the question? Look inside, from the depth of your Heart and Intelligence, find the Question. The answer is already in the question... So, what is the question? You are the Question!

I

TRANSCENDING IGNORANCE

When is the right time to enter the Precious Path? Beloved, it is Now! Be total in your effort to reach the light of Truth. A real seeker is a holder of the Path. He or she is a bridge of pure intention between the collective amnesia and the dimension of I Am.

Before we aspire to leave behind the trance of forgetfulness, the insensitive pseudo-reality of ignorance - the divine longing for awakening must be born in our Heart. This longing is a function of maturity and the sincerity of the Soul. From this longing comes understanding, passion, dedication and inner discipline. These qualities enable us to enter the Precious Path to Awakening.

Entering the Path

What is the Path and where does it lead to? You cannot know it yet. A part of Entering the Path is the very risk of entering into the Unknown. But if you look into your Heart and into your being, you know that there is no other way. Have the courage to begin the journey into your ultimate Expansion. If you take the risk, you will be taken care of by virtue of the very force which brought you Here. Guidance is with you. Your Soul is invited to the domain of Truth.

Am I on the Right Path?

Student: *How do I know whether I am on the right Path?*

Aziz: That is a good question. You cannot know if the Path is right at the present stage! That is your challenge. You have no way to know it. The reason that you are unable to know it is the very fact that you are not on the Path yet! Only when you enter the Path can you know it. Now you are looking for the Path. You are not even sure, whether you are really looking for something! Don't you see? In Zen there is an expression: 'to see the Way is to be on the Way.' If you don't see the way, how can you tread the way? And what is the Path? What do you think is the Path? Do you think that, for instance, Vipassana or Zen, or Advaita or being on some kind of guru-trip is to be on the Path? Nonsense! You are the Path! I Am is the Path. Unless you see who you are, you cannot even dream about knowing the Great Way. At this stage, you are in a jungle, trying to find the way. But to find it, you need to get out of the jungle. You are in a thick jungle, it is a dark night, you have lost all sense of direction, and in this situation you ask whether you are on the right path?

The Path leads to you! Wake up! Find yourself. But you are unable to - you are not ready for awakening. You prefer to have a sense of being spiritual, of being on some kind of pseudo-path. You are not on any Path. Shake yourself up! See that you are in the jungle and there is black darkness around you. Come back to your senses and awaken the true longing for entering Ancient Path. This Path is a secret. It is made of pure light. To be received by this Path, you have to die, awaken your aloneness, and become the Soul!

You find the Path by finding yourself. You are disconnected from yourself, therefore disconnected from the Path. Discover who you are... it is about time. You need to look inside, you need to inquire, start to ask important questions. Before you awaken your I Am, your mind has to wake up. Ask yourself: 'What am I doing here? Who am I?' Question yourself and question your life. Does it not give you a feeling of absurdity: the whole of your personal story, your memories, hopes and fears? Doesn't it surprise you that you exist? You've found yourself by surprise inside this three dimensional movie, in this dream. Here, you try to play the game according to the rules that have been superimposed on you, since the moment of birth. Who are you out of this movie? Do not take your life for granted and do not agree to live in ignorance. Your dignity as a human being lies in your awakening.

What is the Question?

Student: *How to ask the right question?*

Aziz: You have just asked one! The right question always reflects your next step in evolution. That's why, the right question depends on the answer that you need for your inner growth. Do you understand? What you are questioning is Yourself, for you do not yet exist as an individual, as a Soul. As long as you function as a product of the collective mind, you are merely one more insignificant particle of Ignorance. As long as you are a fabrication of collective consciousness, you are not alive. And when you start to question your basic concepts about life and yourself, you begin breaking away from Ignorance.

Collective consciousness has many levels. Spiritual teachings are also part of the collective mind. In order to free yourself from the lower states of the collective mind, you must explore the more developed layers. For instance, instead of pursuing the social model and being a 'good worker' in a factory, you choose a more insightful option and become a Buddhist. Nevertheless, you are still not free, you still continue as a part of the collective unconsciousness. As your questioning moves further, you start to question the authority of spiritual traditions as well. It continues until you are completely free and see reality as it truly is!

Do not take existence for granted. The Great Question is: 'what is it?' What is this Existence? Where is it? This world is only in your mind! Wake up to the Beyond! Wake up to the reality beyond name and form. Before you were born, where were you? You found yourself suddenly under the control of some adults, claiming to be your parents. You found yourself in some country which forced you to become its citizen. But do you really belong Here? We are not asking you about your past incarnations but about your timeless, eternal identity - about your identity beyond any incarnation.

Here, we give you answers and questions. And even more important part of our work is to give you the right questions. But they are not your questions yet! They have to become your questions, for we simply mirror your Soul. You are the question and you are the answer.

Having No Questions

Student: *What can I do if I don't have any questions?*

Aziz: You have already asked a good question! What have you done to invent such an excellent question? You see, it is not to have questions which matters, but to have a questioning mind. You were born, put inside this dream called life and you've taken it all for granted. But, it is all one big question! Don't you see? You are not the answer yet - you yourself are the question. In front of your exclamation 'I' is standing a big question mark. Don't take this reality for granted, for a joke is being played on you!

The questioning mind is the curious mind, the discovering mind, the evolving mind, the intuitive mind, the courageous mind... To be a true human being is not enough to live. One has to discover, one has to evolve...in order to reach one's angle of perception which we call your unique blueprint. You may have no questions, but are you really alive? How do you know that you live? Maybe you don't live?

Not to have questions is fine; just to be silent and simple is OK. But you cannot drop questions before you have asked them. You are not at the stage of dropping questions yet, but in the stage of awakening them. When a child is a child, he or she is naïve and immature. When a sage becomes a child, one has the depth and one has the profound innocence. So, first questions, next silence.

Find out your questions. Ask yourself 'what is my question?' In the beginning, simple questions will come, later to be followed by deeper and more meaningful questions. Wake up to the wonder of your existence! Wake up to the amazement, to the existential awe; wake up to the miracle of being alive.

Doubting the Collective Mind

Student: *What makes people enter the path? What makes them to doubt the collective mind?*

Aziz: There can be many reasons. In the case of more mature Souls, it is the ancient longing for the Self which awakening in their hearts directs them to Light. Others may be suffering too much and are looking for the way out of their misery. For them, the spiritual path can be an escape. That is fine, if at one stage they are ready to recognise the real Light. Others, may experience the feeling of absurdity. The feeling of absurdity, an existential absurdity is born when there is a crisis in being identified with the collective mind. It is not even a doubt, but rather an impasse; it is simply a sense of absurdity, a feeling of ridiculousness regarding unconscious living.

The feeling of absurdity, existential doubt, does not necessarily lead one to the spiritual path. One can remain on the intellectual level of doubt, like Sartre or other existentialists. They tried to rebel, but they still remained a part of the collective consciousness. They could not get out of it. When you rebel, you are still a part of that against which you rebel. That's why, hippies or punks are a part of society, only more desperate and often ridiculous. To break away from the collective mind can happen only when one transcends the mind as such. It is only the positive knowledge of the Self and of the Soul which can liberate us from the collective ignorance. This ignorance is being shed like the skin of a snake, left to drop into the past.

To answer your question once more: that which directs you to the path and that which frees you from the collective mind is the intelligence of the Soul, and only this intelligence.

Longing for Awakening

Student: *Something is pushing me into the direction of Awakening. What is it?*

Aziz: There are two types of Awakening. One is the Self-realisation itself. And the second, even more fundamental is awakening to the search or to one's evolution; it is the awakening to self-discovery, the awakening to the Soul's desire to return home. If one just wants to become enlightened, it is only from the ego and not from the Soul. When you seek for yourself, the word 'Enlightenment' will matter no more. The reality of your search matters. This is the sign of the Soul's maturity. In your case, dear friend, you are in the process of awakening to this ancient longing.

Student: *There is such a strong pull to go inside!*

Aziz: There are different stages in life. When the Soul wants to complete herself in the Inner, there is no choice. One has to temporarily sacrifice the outer and retire inwards. After this primal desire is fulfilled, you can relax and adventure in the outer reality as well. Because you are a human being - you are here also to live and enjoy this dimension. There are however, Souls who are already complete in the outer, and for them renunciation is a natural phenomenon. There is a danger that Souls who follow a particular master, might want to copy the master's behaviour and personality. For example, one may try to renounce sex or live in solitude, even though it may not be the desire of that particular Soul. Here, we have an example of suppression. Most Souls apart from their inner evolution require the outer fulfilment for their completion too. Now, you can see how important it is to be in tune with your Soul's evolution. Without this connection, you can hurt yourself, following an idea which does not reflect your Soul's blueprint. Discover the purpose of your evolution; use your passion to go inside and do the inner work.

Student: *But sometimes I am distracted by outer desires and then I feel guilty!*

Aziz: Guilt is an unintelligent emotion, for it does not bring about anything positive. You do not need to be extreme. You can allow yourself to realise some of your desires in the world too. Learn the balance. You do not necessarily want to be as extreme as a Zen nun is, for instance; you can learn how to grow harmoniously in the inner and the outer as well. What you need to renounce, beloved, is not sex, money, dance, or meetings with friends. What you need to renounce is forgetfulness! You need to be dedicated from moment to moment to the task of remembering the Self;

this is the only true renunciation. This is the Way... The true practitioner is not conspicuous but invisible to others. In Dzogchen, you can find stories about Self-realised adepts who never made it obvious they were practicing anything at all. It is usually just before their death that people realise they have lived with a Buddha! The ideal is a practitioner who does the inner work so secretly that nobody knows about it.

You do not need to walk around, making claims to your practice. Practice, similar to renunciation is an internal, not external phenomenon. Be playful in the outer, not taking it too seriously but remember the Self! Do not lose yourself in the outer. Retain your dignity.

Entering the Unknown

Student: *When we leave behind what we think we know and enter into the Unknown, we can experience fear. What do you suggest we do? Just let it be?*

Aziz: What is the Unknown?

Student: *What I mean is that a person going into meditation, drops the usual concepts and enters a different dimension...*

Aziz: Yes. This fear can be experienced by a person who is in a transitory state. The past is still dominant and the Real Me is not fully present yet. Here, one is afraid of losing one's past crystallised sense of identity. Imagine a snake scared of shedding its skin, for it is the only one he knows! But, surprisingly enough, the new skin is much more beautiful! The ego holds onto its neurosis. The ego lives through its neurosis. The ego in separation from I Am is truly neurotic. The absence of I Am is the basic neurosis for a human being. But the ego within I Am is completely positive and sane. When the ego discovers reality deeper than itself, it may panic for it loses its dominant, central position.

The ego is addicted to its neurosis. It is important to know that often mental sickness is our choice. Many who are mentally ill cannot be helped, for the very simple reason that they cherish their obsessions, clinging onto them with their whole strength. They became fully identified with their illnesses, so to drop them is like to die. The reasons that one chooses to indulge in the neurotic tendencies of the mind can be various. For instance, one may want to escape from reality (which is not really reality-reality but collective consciousness reality). Or, in another case, one may want to create some enormous ego-image. For many, the issue of self-worth is primary. When one is not able to discover their truly sane and beautiful Soul-image, one may create some ridiculous, enormous ego-image in search of self-worth. The main thing is to be important; to be even Napoleon or the worst criminal possible - but provided one is important. So mental sickness most often represents the loss of a balanced and workable self-image. Of course, the issue of sanity is relative, a matter of judgement. Usually we simply feel it, we simply know it...and let us not forget that the absence of I Am is already the basic neurosis to be treated! The ego is afraid of getting dissolved into the Unknown...it is scared of not existing within the limited and claustrophobic reality of the known.

Student: *So, what do you suggest to such person? Is it a matter of seeing the fear and allowing it to pass through?*

Aziz: The antidote against fear is trust. On some level, it is your choice...you make a decision to trust, for to trust is to take a risk. You may simply trust without being conscious of the risk involved. But in such a case, it is not trust anymore but rather a letting go to allow things to be as they are.

As you take a risk and surrender into the Unknown, fear dissolves because it is not real. This fear has no justification in reality. When you enter the Unknown, what remains is fearlessness which is the pure presence of What Is. The reality of Pure Being is beyond the polarities of fear and trust. It is like jumping into the void. You are naturally afraid but when you jump, the fear goes away; you don't fall anywhere, you simply come home. This Void is the most comfortable infinite space made from the pure light of Being, which is love! What is there to be afraid of? Make yourself comfortable. You are resting in this absolutely safe, soft, sacred space. It loses even the quality of being the Unknown. It now becomes the Known! This Void represents the womb of Existence which contains your Soul within itself. The understanding itself cleanses fear.

Spiritual Goals

Student: *When should we have goals and when should we drop having goals?*

Aziz: It is a very important issue: when to relax into effortlessness, into non-seeking and when to seek? When to use will in order to complete our spiritual journey? The foundation is always non-doing which is simply the effortless abiding in reality. But at the same time, paradoxically, we are reaching this non-doing; we are evolving into the real depth of Pure Being. And for this we need to have some important goals, certain spiritual targets. It all relates to the vision of evolution we have and to the blueprint of our Soul. For example, if one wishes to stabilise the centre of awareness, naturally it becomes the goal of the mind. Here, one cultivates self-remembrance in order to stabilise the experience. And when the state is stabilised, one can afford relaxing into aimlessness.

However, if your evolution is calling you for a new expansion, for example, to open your Heart, you again create a goal - this time to awaken the Heart. So you see, a goal is the call of evolution. And it is important to use the term 'goal' or to use the energy of the goal in a balanced way, so it does not become an obsession. When you are too goal-oriented, you lose this moment, you lose your connection with Reality. On the other hand, if you have no goal you do not grow. The exact point between being aimless and having a precise evolutionary purpose, represents the right approach to our spiritual growth. We can call it 'the middle path.'

At all times, be connected to the space beyond any goal, allowing yourself to experience the purity of the Now and the state of surrender. But at the same time, intelligently see whether certain elements need to be deepened or cultivated within you. And when you have this clarity, use your will, determination and intention in order to maintain them. A very important psychological balance is necessary here. This is because the moment we have a goal, we tend to lose the sane space of self-acceptance. Someone may blame oneself for not being able, for instance, to stabilise the State of Presence...and so forth. Not being able to fulfil one's spiritual goal, one can become quickly frustrated; one gets frustrated with not being complete. However, when we see that the human being is never complete (because to be complete means to be dead) acceptance of our incompleteness arises. We accept this incompleteness as a part of the challenge in being human. In this space of acceptance, we gently allow ourselves to evolve towards our spiritual goal, whatever this goal could be.

It is essential to have a certain compassionate attitude to oneself. Compassion means both that you accept yourself fully and that you can relax into reality of your Now. At the same time, compassion is to do everything that is necessary to complete one's evolution. The middle path, we speak about, is in-between the goal and goal-less. Here, the Soul is like a river, effortlessly but with full strength flowing towards her ultimate destiny - the meeting with the Divine.

Student: *Is it a very delicate balance?*

Aziz: It is delicate and has always a different flavour, depending on the type of Soul and the stage the Soul is in. The more you are connected with I Am, the more you transcend the need for any goal. If there is no experience of I Am, if there is no awareness and one is simply unconscious, not to have a strong goal would be foolish. In such a situation, one has to focus because the sickness of ignorance is hurting the Soul deeply. Later, when I Am is more and more present, one can afford to let go; one can simply relax. Still one has to go further but the amount of relaxed acceptance and effortlessness is much bigger than the energy of the goal. So you see, again the balance changes. First, the goal is really important, later the goal becomes more playful and evolution becomes positive and adventurous. First, you have to get out of darkness in order to evolve towards light. Later, when light is present, you move towards the positive side of reality. It means that your evolution is already joyful. You still may need to have some goals but these goals don't create frustration and are not so much based on the 'lack of,' but rather on a positive expansion. It is coming from the desire to be more complete. First, evolution is based on the 'lack of,' next it is based on positive expansion. In the beginning, evolution is coming from our desperate need for freedom. Later, evolution represents our expansion into Freedom itself, into the mystery of the Beloved.

Student: *And in Shikantaza, in just sitting, is the goal dropped completely?*

Aziz: Yes and no, because even though Shikantaza is just Shikantaza, there are still levels of Shikantaza. In the Absolute Shikantaza, which is a unity of Awareness, Being and the Heart, completely united with the Ultimate, there is no goal. But prior to reaching this complete state, there is a complex process of deepening and maturing taking place on many levels. For example, you need to work with attention, you need to bring yourself to the State of Presence all the time, you evolve into Being...and so forth. The experience of non-doing has many levels, as it refers to how your energy expands into the Unmanifested. Prior to the Absolute State, energy always fluctuates on some level. Even when you rest within, it is not absolute rest. We can call it the experience of relative rest. In this journey to the Absolute, energy deepens itself, gravitating towards the dimension of Pure Rest. You co-operate through your surrender, through the commitment to your own presence. It is a skilful activity because non-doing and subtle doing co-exist...

Can the State of Presence Isolate Us From the World?

Student: *I have the feeling that while cultivating the State of Presence, it isolates Me from the outer. Will it become even more so as I stabilise in this state? Or will perhaps Being and awakening of the Heart bring some balance?*

Aziz: It is an important question. First of all, the separation which one may feel being in the State of Presence, is not of the ego. It is not based on the ego-image but on the energetic quality of the centre within oneself. Here, the stable experience of oneself is present, as if in contrast to the external reality. The reason that you feel excessive isolation is the very fact that you are still cultivating this state. What it means is that you have to make an additional effort to pull energy back to the centre of presence. When you are involved in some activity, for instance, you cannot be fully spontaneous for you will keep on losing yourself. The moment you remember that you are supposed to remember yourself, you pull back to the centre and this very mechanism separates you from your involvement in the action.

In order to give birth to I Am, one has to cut through the unconscious or rather subconscious spontaneity. This need to separate oneself from the outer in order to regain the inner, is a natural part of the awakening process. That is the price which you need to pay. In order to transcend the mind and awaken to the Real Me, an enormous amount of energy has to be engaged and directed inside. Before a child is born, he has to incubate in the womb. You are in the process of incubating your Soul.

We spoke about the economy of attention. How you distribute your energy and attention determines your experience of reality. For instance, an average person has directed all attention outwards - there is constant thought about issues of survival, money, the opposite sex and entertainment of all sorts of sensory pleasures. One simply uses consciousness in a way that leads to greater unconsciousness. The vital-force is channelled only to the outer, but when you begin a conscious evolution, this vital-force is directed to the Inner. For this reason, monasteries have been created to reverse the unconscious outward movement of energy-attention. Living in the environment of a monastery, you are minimally distracted by the outer such that energy can move in. When you live in the world, even if you are on the Path, some energy has to be directed towards survival and other related issues; it is the necessary compromise of living in an unconscious and insensitive society. This society is basically an enemy of our evolution, as it defends its global unconsciousness in so far as possible.

However, living in society does not have to be a major obstruction on the path of Self-realisation, for it is not necessary to invest all energy inside. One rather needs to reserve a sufficient amount of energy for the inner evolution. Even in a monastery, one is unable to direct a hundred percent attention in, because after all you still remain in this world. In many monasteries, there is often a lot of politics going on as well, one can encounter many distractions even here. Even though behind the concept of a monastery, there is the intention to go away from the world, still, the world enters through the back door. For ultimately the world is in our head. That's why, the true renunciation, the true retreat is internal and not external

But coming back to your question. In the beginning, as your presence is not stable, you need to focus strongly, controlling the unconscious aspect of spontaneity. As the Inner State becomes relatively steady, you can relax becoming more spontaneous. When the Inner State is steady, it loses the quality of a crystallised centre and takes the shape of a natural state which encompasses the experience of living. When the State of Presence is steady, it abides in itself on an energy level, therefore not requiring additional self-referral from your intelligence. Of course, from time to time intelligence becomes aware of its centre, but in a relaxed way not creating the feeling of alienation. As you are comfortable and confident with your Inner State, you open up to the outer as well. You open your eyes, you see the sky, a bird, a tree... you feel yourself again as a human being; you may acknowledge your human desires and needs as well as problems. You say to yourself 'alright, I feel complete inside, but how to live, what do I want to do with my life?' You have gone away from life to gain your-self, but now as you return back to life you keep inside the most precious diamond, I Am. When the State of Presence relaxes into itself, it less 'witnesses' the outer, but more contains it. When Being is added, the quality of non-separation and all-inclusiveness radically increases. And when the Heart is present, the feeling of containment is enriched by the energy of love, sensitivity and beauty.

Coming back to the experience of the State of Presence - does it separate us or unite us with Existence? The experience of unity refers to the situation where the subject or Me, energetically experiences her own existence, the perceived and the act of perceiving as one movement. The ego cannot do it for it does not have any centre, therefore it is unable to experience itself in a solid way within the experience of life. In the ego-state, there is a constant oscillation between object and subject. Information from the outer comes back to the sense of Me; there is a quick self-referral and translation of this information and consciousness goes back to the objective reality. In the case of an unawakened person, information from the outer refers back to the subject and does not encounter any solid Me. But unlike animal consciousness, this Me is self-conscious enough to feel her separation from the world.

When the Real Me awakens, there is for the first time a solid presence behind the mind. In this way, paradoxically the ego itself becomes a part of the phenomenal perception, while the Real Me is unmoved allowing all to be experienced within the light of her own presence. So you can see, awareness includes the perceived, the act of perceiving and the perceiver (intelligence).

However, there is a certain existential, independent existence and uniqueness of the Soul within her experience of life. You awaken Awareness, Being and the Heart, creating one unified field of Me which is present within the movement of life. This field of Me is not separated from life. In truth, only because there is Me, the experience of unity with Existence is possible. But at the same time, you know that your Me is not only One with life but the very experiencer of it. This experiencer of life possesses, miraculously enough, its own independent reality.

In this earthly dimension which is quite thick and insensitive, where the collective consciousness is ignorant and even arrogant in its ignorance, you may feel in contrast a sense of uniqueness. Your Soul, deep down is foreign to this dimension. Your Soul comes from the dimension of light and love, from the viewpoint of which to live in the Here is degrading. It is precisely like falling from Heaven to earth. The Soul incarnated Here to experience forgetfulness and then eventually find her way back home through remembrance. You may ask: 'what is the reason?' The answer has been already given: to forget and to awaken. This very polarity, of ignorance and awakening, is the purpose of life. You are Here to experience that which is destined for you to experience.

When evolution reaches its destination, the Soul sees that fundamentally she does not belong Here. It does not mean that the Soul refuses to live Here or that she negates this reality. It means that she frees herself from the gravity of the earth and can fly into the sky of higher understanding, higher experience, higher truth. She lives Here, but is no longer of the Here. She belongs to the timeless dimension. She belongs to the realm of intelligence which has nothing to do with the collective mind, physicality, emotional incompleteness... and so forth. She belongs to the dimension of Perfection and knows it deep inside... Knowing this, she will feel existentially alienated from the Here.

In your case, dear friend, behind the feeling of isolation two elements are present. One element, is your very effort to pull back into the State of Presence which isolates you from the outer. The second element is that you are discovering your uniqueness, your Soul's otherness, her inherent separation from this dimension. You are awakening to the eternal Soul's identity and intuitively you feel it already, as you are a sensitive being. When the Soul incarnates, she emerges from light into darkness and she feels the pain of this separation. Even though the traces of this light are still present in the Heart, the force of the earth's gravity is much stronger. That's why, when a child is born, he cries... for he knows.

Do all Paths Lead to the Same Goal?

Student: *Recently I have this doubt whether it is really true that every Path leads to the same goal? Practising Vipassana and Buddhist philosophy for long time, I have realised, that their vision actually doesn't point clearly to Awakening. Discovering Nisargadatta Maharaj, and next your teaching, something has radically changed. The search started to relate to Me, in a real sense.*

Aziz: You see, Buddhism is an old technology of awakening. We often assume that if someone attains Enlightenment, there arises a natural ability to express the whole truth. But in reality, it takes many generations for a teaching to evolve and reach maturity. When Mạhayana developed, there were attempts to identify this teaching with the Buddha himself. But why do such thing? People tend to look for an authority, but no one has the courage to just let the spirit speak freely. Tibetan Buddhism and Zen are not the teachings of Buddha Shakyamuni! They are simply a further development of the original teaching.

The original approach of Theravada is to discover What Is Real through the negation of what is not. The danger is that pointing to what is real has not been so clear in the past and so everyone has kept on missing it. For example, the concept of no-self can easily prevent one from discovering I Am as it is on some level denied. For that reason, some seekers feel quite relieved by the teaching of Advaita. It is simply more positive; it may be less sophisticated but at least it points to the. Self.

The original Buddhism is too attached to a negative interpretation of reality. Even if you understand that all is suffering, empty and impermanent...so what? What does it actually change? Nothing! Your mind has one more crystallised opinion about reality. Awakening has truly nothing to do with those concepts. An awakened being does not need to create any views about reality, for he or she lives beyond the mind in the space of innocence and openness - to the Mystery.

Yes, this search relates to you. It is not about conditioning you or making out of you an arhat, but about giving you back your Soul.

The Family and Practice

Student: *I find it very difficult to concentrate on my practice. My family takes a lot of my attention and there is a lot of anxiety involved. Sometimes I wish to be alone.*

Aziz: You see, the practice is your internal responsibility. You have a certain outer situation which you will not change for sometime. Neither are you fully content with your present arrangement of life, nor will you be happy getting out of it. This is the fate of most people. What to do? Acceptance! From this acceptance, you must see clearly how to deal with your situation in terms of practice. If you have chosen to be committed to family life, dedicating yourself fully to your inner evolution will be much more difficult. But on the other hand, you'll receive various gifts from life, which a monk, for instance, is deprived of. There is some justice in life, you see...

It is not that you cannot go inside - you simply have to be more skilful, as you also look after the outer life. The main reason that one does not make real progress in practice is from within. It does not mean that outer circumstances do not matter, for they do, by all means. The outer situation should offer us an optimum of harmony. If, for instance, a person sits all day in front of a computer screen, working and working... such a person cannot evolve for his or her life has been sold to a false sense of security. In your case, certainly you've got a family and various responsibilities but at the same time, you are quite a free man, travelling, earning money in an original way, and living often in nature. Don't you agree? In your situation, it is very much possible to combine family life with meditation; which you do, by the way What is important for you is to discipline yourself more in your psychology which on the emotional level disturbs you too much, bringing too much anxiety and unnecessary suffering. From the other side, your dedication for the inner work must increase as well. There has to be more understanding and passion in your awakening process.

Perhaps it will comfort you, but no one has ever found the absolute balance between the inner and the outer; such an exact balance does not exist for a human being. A middle way does not exist, in truth. What exists, is continuous effort of returning to balance. What it means is that one oscillates between extremes. For example, when you find yourself a little too busy with the outer, you pull back to the inner. Or, when you are too comfortable in the inner, then take time to care about your outer. Because there is no absolute balance, the life of a spiritual being is an art form and a true challenge for the Heart and intelligence. Beloved, you have to however, bring more inner discipline into your practice; you need to renounce all these elements which distract you too much and take you away from your centre. Your task is to not lose yourself, in spite of all disturbing circumstances. Be brave and focussed! You need to keep yourself together and restrain the restlessness of your emotional body, restrain your anxiety and do not allow the feelings of insecurity to grow roots in your mind, for you will lose integrity.

Student: *It is particularly difficult when dealing with a child. When he is happy, I can be in the State of Presence but when he is unhappy, I become automatically unhappy and lose my centre.*

Aziz: Beloved, your problem is unusual in the sense that unlike other men your Heart is too sensitive. The Heart can be too sensitive, or rather sensitive in a way that brings suffering to us. Compassion and sensitivity can flow from the place of strength and integrity or can be ungrounded and too emotional. Do you understand? When your Heart is sensitive in this way, you pick up suffering, sadness, sorrow and the unhappiness of others too easily.

Your child is just another human being which happened by the force of destiny to become a part of your family. Naturally, you become identified, for life has made you responsible for his survival and growth. But the child is just another human being... A blood connection is impersonal. No child belongs to any mother or father. The blood bond is just on the level of DNA and has nothing to do with the Soul. People feel obliged to love each other because they belong to the same family. Such nonsense. If they were free from this 'blood bond' conditioning, in most cases they would leave their families, not to see them ever again! Only the Soul-connection is real. How often do people have this type of experience: they look one day into their father's eyes, for instance, and they see a stranger! But the force of habit is so strong! The mother usually loves her child because it is 'her' child and not because she sees the Soul. Is it love? It is a continuation of our biological imperative to take care of the young. It is not real love. Parents may sacrifice so much for their children and children feel in their conscience obliged to love their parents in return. But see, if a child does something which is against the will of his parents, they change into despots. Is it love? Coming to India to meditate, how many parents really want to understand this? Either they pass their judgements on you or they don't care, hoping that one day you will become a good empty-headed citizen paying taxes. But is it love? Consider carefully whether the person, which you call your mother, really loves you or perhaps she simply loves her child which you happen to be! Do you see the difference? You must understand that, in most cases, what your parents perceive as you, is not you but a sheer projection created in their dream-like reality of the unconscious mind.

This doesn't mean that your parents are to be blamed, as they themselves are victims of the collective unconsciousness. You can be grateful to them as often they try their best to secure your wellbeing in the world. You can be grateful even for the whole suffering which you may have experienced in your childhood. This suffering, in truth, is the first wake up call which allows you to enter the Spiritual Path. There are many primal therapies in which one digs into the childhood issues, creating a lot of anger towards parents. Why do this? It is much better to forgive the parents and let go of the past. Suffering is a part of this reality and cannot be avoided. It is the way Existence forces us to awaken.

Coming back to our issue. When you see your child suffering, naturally you feel compassion and responsibility - particularly since the child is so helpless. But do not forget that even though a child is under your jurisdiction, still, he is an autonomous being and is on some level responsible for himself and for being on the earth. You are primarily responsible for yourself because you are the foundation of your reality. The child has to go through his own suffering, otherwise he would not have incarnated. His Soul agreed already for this suffering as it is the price for living on the earth... in this illusory garden of Eden. What it means is that you need to allow the child to experience some suffering. For example, if one has a baby and it has received enough food, affection and its nappies are dry... when the baby is all the time crying, the best is to go for a walk. Crying is an expression of the baby's free will and must be respected (laughter)...

The principle is - be natural with your feeling and express any emotion which you like, provided that you don't lose your centre! Being in the centre does not mean that you are cold... by no means! When you are in your centre, you become rooted in a dimension deeper than your personal self. At this stage, because of the lack of integration, any excessive identification with emotions takes you immediately from the centre. It is as if your psyche becomes sucked energetically into the objectified reality, into the subconscious realm. Therefore, you must make an additional effort to pull energy back to the subject. Unfortunately, there is no other way, no shortcut. There is only this dedication, this sacrifice of the subconscious tendencies, this constant effort to be at the core of the subjective reality of the Soul. That is your responsibility and your renunciation of the family! Now, you cannot renounce the family formally, for you already have one but you can do it on some level internally. Renunciation is in truth, only an internal phenomenon.

You can find in the Dzogchen tradition, stories about Self-realised beings who were recognised only at the end of their life or after death. They were usually family men practicing secretly the State of Presence, even though they performed their outer duties! Nobody even knew that they were on the Spiritual Path! That is the true renunciation. That which must be renounced is forgetfulness, the dissipation of attention in the subconscious reality of ignorance.

You are in a situation which is not accidental. The type of body you have, the type of mind you have, your emotional constitution, the type of circumstances you are living in... it is all as it should be. There is no doubt. The question is, how to use your situation to the optimum? That is your challenge. Your reality teaches you about Truth; it presents to you circumstances, events and difficulties within which you can reach Self-realisation. Your difficulties are contained in this bigger picture or plan. Unless you reach an essential integrity in yourself, a firm connection to the unconditional side of yourself, you will remain frustrated and unhappy. You know it clearly, this voice is coming not from the outside but from within!

Awaken to your passion and strengthen your renunciation. Crystallise your attention and bring a more masculine energy of focus ... cut through all of these emotional tendencies which weaken your practice. These tendencies reflect your sensitivity, but as they are disconnected from your real centre, they represent your weakness as well. Do not allow your emotions to rule you, otherwise you will suffer. To ground yourself and discover the real centre, is your life's purpose. The means which particularly you, Jan, are supposed to use is your masculine energy. Even though a part of you may rebel, still, it is your Soul's desire and direction to reach freedom.

Freedom from Pseudo-religion

Student: *In order to be free, is it necessary to break away from the religion one was born into?*

Aziz: Religion is just crystallised by the egos pseudo-spiritual concept of reality. There is no life in such a belief system. It is nothing but arrogance to turn an alive experience of the Divine into a formalised religion. A religion becomes religion only when it can be shared collectively. Unfortunately, because of the low level of humanity, only something very basic and simplistic can become a social paradigm.

To answer your question, it is your responsibility as a Soul to be free in her meeting with the Divine. And to be free, she must transcend all belief systems which separate her like a dark cloud from the clear sky of Reality. A person who is identified with the religion he or she was born into, has not entered the Spiritual Path yet.

Importance of Having Spiritual Friends

Student: *What is the importance of having spiritual friends or being connected to a spiritual community?*

Aziz: It is natural to need support. A human being is not so strong and needs encouragement on the Path. Particularly in the beginning of the Path, when the inner experience is not grounded, one can easily loose faith and simply give up the practice. It is very helpful to have a partner who shares your interest. If your partner is not at all involved in the spiritual evolution, you are simply not sharing a large portion of your being and your motivation can be undermined.

As you evolve, naturally new friends come in to your life and old friend move into the past. Those who have the same friends throughout life generally don't evolve very much. The deeper you go, the more selective you become in choosing friends and companions. When your consciousness is higher and your Heart more sensitive, you can be close only to those who are in harmony with your level of evolution. Otherwise, you would simply hurt yourself connecting to energies of unconsciousness. In time, you will realise that even the so-called spiritual environment is very unconscious because they're simply very few Souls truly searching for awakening.

Pseudo-spirituality

Students: *How is it that spiritual seekers break from the essence of their search (finding the Self) and instead stop at naïve spiritual experiences i.e. Reiki, Yoga or astral travels?*

Aziz: For the very simple reason that the essence of the spiritual search is not yet the essence of their search. Being completely lost in this dream, they don't wish at all to get out of it. On the contrary, they would even resist the opportunity to awaken. They may like to talk or read about awakening, but only because they feel safe in their sleepwalker's pseudo-reality. Doing Reiki or Yoga is better then not to do anything and for many it is rather a good beginning. The ten thousand-mile journey starts with the first step. But at one stage one simply needs to grow up and begin seeking that which lies beyond the apparent reality...

Diet in Meditation

Student: *Is diet very important on the spiritual path?*

Aziz: Yes... we recommend to eat and drink every day! Use your common sense. Eat a lot of food which contains the sun's energy, like fruits and vegetables. Eat a minimum of meat and heavy food. Be careful not to become health obsessed. Those people who are too health conscious are rather boring and difficult company.

They talk only about food and think only about dieting. Have you noticed?

Whatever good food you eat, you will die anyway! Whatever good food you eat, you will not avoid getting sick from time to time. We eat and take care of our life to live relatively long and in a good condition, so we can evolve and have all these experiences our Soul desires. The mind gets easily obsessed. Whether it is sex, alcohol or food, it does not matter. One loses balance and starts to take this life and one's existence too seriously. If you wish to live life in a proper and healthy way, you need to be rooted in the dimension beyond the mind, beyond attachments, beyond self-protections - resting in the original opening of Being, which is trust.

Lao Tse said, 'the sage does not care about his life, hence he lives a long time...' Nowadays, Taoism has lost its original essence and is now mainly focussed on prolonging one's earthly existence. This pseudo-Taoist philosophy is based on various practices revolving around conserving one's energy, for instance through repressing ejaculation. This was certainly not the message of the founders of Taoism; Lao Tse and Chuang Tse were concerned only with that which is beyond time and our personal existence.

Questions Reflect Your Place in Evolution

Student: *Could you speak more about the process of asking questions?*

Aziz: Asking questions reflects the evolution of intelligence. This evolution is like climbing a ladder. One step is a question and the next step is the answer. If you are low in evolution, your questions are basic, close to the gravitation of the earth. As you go higher, your questions become more refined, more sublime, more sophisticated; here, all basic questions have been answered and you are ready to receive a higher understanding. When your are able to formulate a question, provided it is really your question, it means that you are already on the edge of discovering an answer. Understanding supports the evolution of our being. One side of our existence represents the quality of our energy-presence, and the other side is intelligence. As intelligence evolves, it supports the transformation of our energy system. They go hand in hand, always together.

Existence wishes to give you many answers. Most of them would be shocking to you! You are not ready for all these answers. To receive an answer, you would have to be able to contain its meaning, not intellectually but with your whole being. Now you are ready for the answers which your questions are taking you to. Beyond the frontiers of your present are future questions, awaiting new answers, thrilling answers, unbelievable answers! But you don't have questions for these answers yet. What you may intuitively feel as your possible question, reflects your next step.

Some answers come to you without you asking the related questions. It means that the question was there vaguely formulated in the mind, however clearly present on the Soul level. We try to activate your intelligence so you can become ready to formulate questions you would never have thought about, questions beyond your imagination. The question is much more significant than the answer, for it represents an ability of intelligence to receive the truth of the answer. That which makes the answer valuable is the presence, depth, sensitivity and capacity of the receiving intelligence. The final answer which you are destined to receive at the end of your evolution in time, is itself your Completion. Your completion represents the ultimate realisation of your Soul's unique angle of perception, becoming one with your Over-soul. And what is the question to this answer? You! The answer is hidden in the question.

Student: *I am weak at formulating questions among other weaknesses. What can I do to develop?*

Aziz: Within your limitations, you can reach through your conscious evolution the optimum of your capacity. The goal of evolution is not to make everyone the same. Everyone is different and unique on some level. In order to feel complete and function properly in the world, we need to reach a certain essential harmony within various areas of our personality and to be sufficiently evolved as spiritual beings. We spoke, for instance, that men and women differ in terms of having different predominant centres of I Am. However, all of them need to be awakened in order to feel complete. A person who has no strong awareness, still has to awaken this centre within his or her capacity. If you cannot express yourself verbally, you can develop this ability through writing, for instance, or through having many conversations. In this way, you can balance this faculty attaining the optimum of your potential.

We all have weak points and that is to be accepted with humility. Often, certain disabilities help you in different ways, allowing you to deepen yourself and become more sensitive. In the fire of suffering, the Soul matures and becomes ready to meet her ultimate aloneness. It is not to become a perfect human machine but to reach a certain essential balance and harmony within our imperfect, separate existence. Perfection is only attained through the transcendence of this dimension. By meeting the Beyond, we become One with Perfection.

Sincerity: the Fundamental Quality of a Seeker

Student: *Is Sincerity essential on the spiritual path?*

Aziz: The most essential! It is sincerity which reflects the maturity of the Soul. Without sincerity, the psyche is dominated by the reality of the ego, by the ego-image. Sincerity has its source in the Heart, for it refers directly to the presence of the Soul. This very ability to drop ego games and seek truth in a genuine and innocent way, is sincerity. Sincerity is the greatness of the spirit which is ready to renounce the ego-image in order to serve the Soul.

Sincerity is one of the inherent qualities of the Soul. If one is sincere, one is more or less in touch with the Soul. The seekers who are truly sincere, are like rare pearls. The master always prays to the Divine to meet sincere students. This was the usual prayer of Ramakrishna. The Soul does not play games for she is simple, direct and truthful. The Soul lives not through the mind but through the Heart; she is pure and innocent like a child. The Soul is brave in her readiness to drop the illusory protection of the ego-image. She is ready to be naked and exposed for her only food is Truth and Love.

Progress and Regress on the Path

Student: *In the endless realm of becoming in time, I would imagine myself to be continuously progressing, but sometimes it seems as if yesterday I felt more developed than I do today.*

Aziz: Yes... evolution never goes back, but certain negative tendencies of the mind may return from the past to manifest again. The dust of the past can cover our evolutionary achievements. Often, it is a part of the cleansing process that some patterns need to become manifested in order to become released and destroyed. If you experience a feeling of regression in a different way, referring to your Inner State or to the quality of awareness, it is also natural. We evolve in a spiral way. Sometimes, before reaching a higher state, there is a temporary suspension, for energy is adjusting and accumulating. Sometimes, also, energy needs to rejuvenate and integrate on the subtle, subatomic level. In such moments, you may feel a certain dullness and low quality of energy. But it is only a temporary situation, a transition.

However, sometimes one may lose some amount of accumulated evolutionary energy, by losing focus and becoming lazy, for instance. When you practice for some time with the State of Presence, you may experience real progress, but at one stage, you become distracted. You may fall in love, for example, and forget all about your spiritual target. In such a case, your awareness goes back to sleep and you lose what you gained before.

Spiritual progress is gradual, but it asserts itself through many shifts or quantum leaps. You practice for sometime, experiencing the same quality of energy, and suddenly you find yourself in the qualitatively higher state. So, evolution cannot go back, but certain accumulated energy which you have created through your effort, may be lost.

Having the Right Vision of Awakening

Student: *How important is it to have goals? How important is it to want to reach something?*

Aziz: A goal is nothing but a certain vision of your evolution. As a human being you are continuously evolving. There is a constant process of growth and maturation. You can evolve without being conscious of this process, just living your life as most people do. In this way, there is also evolution but much slower. Or you can co-create with your evolution, making an extra effort. For instance, an ordinary person who is part of society, who has no interest in evolving as a spiritual being, still, such a person matures, over the years, in this way or another. But this type of evolution is very slow... one moves more in circles, throughout life repeating similar patterns and not fundamentally changing one's main ignorant vision of reality.

The moment such an individual becomes more aware, not even spiritually, but psychologically, a desire to transform on some levels may arise. For example, this person may realise that there are some emotional blocks and repressed feelings or some family conditioning. Usually, at this stage, one may try some therapies or psychological work. And to begin any therapeutic work, one must have some goal, like emotional cleansing or opening of the Heart. That's why, as you become more conscious of who you are, what your problems are and who you would like to be, you may naturally create an evolutionary purpose.

There are many types of spiritual goals, from very basic to very sophisticated ones, like reaching the Absolute State. A person who is simply stressed in 'modern' society, working form morning to evening to be able to afford a good car and a dog, may go to a psychotherapist just to become more relaxed. It is also some kind of basic goal. Another person, who is very conscious of his or her evolution may wish to become a Buddha, not yet knowing exactly what it means... and so forth. What type of goal you have reflects your maturity and your connection with your Soul's blueprint. If there is a real spiritual goal, it is always coming from the Soul and not from the mind. But often it is the ego which creates some goal in order to become more significant. The ego also wants to become enlightened, so it can make a spiritual career. The ego is always a good politician, you know.

To be in touch with the Soul's evolution, one must have a connection with the Heart and some essential intuition coming from intelligence. When you are in tune with your Soul, you may have clarity about your next step in evolution. Often you know only your next step. It is all about becoming more and more complete and whole. When you are ignorant, unconscious and live in the natural schizophrenia of a fragmented mind, as an average citizen of this planet does, you cannot even recognise your own incompleteness and fragmentation. You think that everything is just fine, even though you are in miserable situation. As you start to question your reality, you begin to realise that pursuing the social model of making money, having a family and children, furnishing your house all life...etc, cannot, at all, fulfil you. You can foresee the final frustration, waiting for you at the end of this unconscious journey. Life, without connection to the Inner Light, is utterly empty and truly devoid of any meaning. That's why, at one stage, you start to discover what goals there are possibly waiting for you.

To find your goal is a real challenge. It is not that you look in your Heart and it is written there in big letters. The manifestation of clarity, as far as to what you are looking for and what elements are needed for your Soul's completion, takes time. And it is precisely this not-knowing which allows you to grow. To have the answer to what you really want is already an evolutionary achievement. It all starts with the Question. You cannot know your final blueprint. You have no way of knowing it. You are in the process of growing in this direction. One day, you become your blueprint and your journey in the time dimension is over.

Here, in our teaching work, we give you some goals already, as some goals are universal. You have certain options and some things you simply have to do. You may say 'oh, I don't like to work with awareness, I only want to open my Heart.' That is fine, but you will remain unconscious and incomplete. So, the goal is not always what you like to reach, but sometimes what you need to reach. Many spiritual teachers, or New Age teachers give you different options of evolution. Some of them are unclear or create new conditioning in your mind. Someone may tell you that you must awaken kundalini. In India, you can find those 'yogis' who claim that the 'real' Enlightenment requires the awakening of kundalini. But is it really true? To verify any information is your challenge and the only security is from your intelligence and of course from the Heart.

To have a goal is important for it bridges your past with your future. But it is essential not to become anxious about reaching the goal. You have to use the concept of a goal in a balanced way so it will not take you too much into the future. If you live in anticipation, your basic connection to the Now gets lost. That's why we speak about the Non-dual Path which balances our evolution into the future with the right relationship to the Now, that is, our present reality. We could speak about the vision of evolution taking place within the space of acceptance. This allows you to appreciate What Is instead of projecting your sense of well-being into future expectations. Here, the goal does not take you out of the moment but allows you to grow in a real way, where you are grounded in the Now. If you just relax into acceptance, without having any goal or vision of evolution, you will postpone your completion. Even though you are connected to the truth of the Now, you will still become stagnated for you are fragmented in your ability to experience reality.

That is the pitfall for those who take some of the Advaita teachings too literary. They assume that it is enough 'not to seek' in order to 'find.' But what they find are only fragments of the real thing. There are secrets on the Path which are beyond acceptance - they are the hidden dimensions of the Now. If we say to a person who has no awakened awareness: 'just relax, you are already That!' Such a person will have only one second of semi-connection to reality. Immediately, the unconscious mind will take over. That's why, so few could realise the truth behind the teachings of J. Krishnamurti. In order to reach the Self, awareness must awaken, energy must transform, and many faculties must be activated. For that simple reason, we do need goals and spiritual targets.

For a person, new to the spiritual path, it is more correct to say: 'don't accept yourself - do something to change your unconscious mind!' OK, accept yourself but simultaneously do something to become one with that which you accept! If you just accept, for instance, that your Heart is closed... it doesn't work, does it? Your Heart will not open magically out of this acceptance.

This is the fundamental paradox: that even though All Is Already Complete, the individual who is a part of this perfection needs to evolve in order to become complete within the Universal Perfection. This is what they overlooked, in some of the non-dual teachings. They did not see the paradoxical nature of evolution beyond evolution; evolution in the beyond evolution. That's why, it is said: the Self is already there, just see it! Unfortunately, it is only fifty percent true... and what is the other fifty-percent? It is your evolution into the discovery of the Self which is already present and always has been. It is all your adventure, your amazing journey in time to the discovery of that which is beyond time!

Awakening to the Path

Student: *How can I convince myself about the necessity of awakening?*

Aziz: The problem is that your mind and your Soul are separated. The question is: how can this mind get in touch with the Soul? How can she be in tune with her evolution? It is not an easy question to be answered because there are many elements. Generally speaking, intelligence and sensitivity need to grow. A certain intuition needs to awaken and this deep longing in your Heart needs to surface. If this ancient yearning to return home is not awakened - then whatever you do, you will not get anywhere. You can do a hundred retreats and it will still be meaningless. When this longing is awakened, your Spiritual Path is quickly accelerated. At this point you will know what you are doing and what it means to you. There is a passion because the Soul is involved.

The Spiritual Path and meditation is not a hardship. It is a hardship for people whose longing is not awakened. Because their practice is from the mind, the Soul is not really involved. In the case that the Soul is involved, one progresses quickly. When the Soul is present, Grace enters immediately; Existence simply helps you, manifesting all the necessary elements.

Student: *In my case it is the opposite, the Soul really wants to return home but the mind rejects it.*

Aziz: Certainly, because the mind is disconnected from the Soul. You see, your Soul can be conscious of herself only through the mind, through your intelligence. When the mind is separated from the Soul, it is simply unable to register the Soul's wish. The problem is that there is no technique to awaken the desire to be awakened. It is either there or not. One can co-operate, but there is no technique. You simply have to question your life more and look deeper for what you really want. There are no rules. You do not need to meditate, you do not need to enter the Spiritual Path. You can just live like other people as though there was nothing wrong. It is your choice. What it means is that you may not be fully ready to enter the Path and some more time is needed.

Here, when seekers come... the problem with this teaching is that they have to be convinced. When a real seeker comes he or she wants to know how to get There and will give everything for this information. But real seekers are like rare pearls, difficult to be found.

Student: *Concerning what you have said about those who need to be convinced, actually, I find it good that we do not follow anyone at random. I feel I want to be sure that the person who is speaking knows what he is speaking about and prove to me that I am following the right person.*

Aziz: Yes, certainly, but in this way it is not your search. You see the teacher or master is someone who is offering you a certain option in life. And if it is your search, you ask for help in your particular search. In the past for example, in Zen, Hinduism and many different schools, the seeker had to prove that he wanted to reach the truth. This knowledge was not given unless one really proved that he or she was ready to receive it. This knowledge is precious and if the one who receives it is not able to appreciate its value and translates it through his mundane and vulgar concepts, it simply becomes spoiled and wasted. It is a precious knowledge. Nowadays, spiritual teachings have become very commercialised. You can find this information in any book and there are many masters who want to have as many disciples as they can in terms of over-simplifying a teaching to reach the masses, and who compromise so much just to get more followers.

So the answer to you is: You have to convince yourself! In addition you have to find out what you want to convince yourself of!

Isolation on the Path

Student: *As I am on the Path, I feel more and more separated from others and lonely...*

Aziz: The deepest reason for your feelings of loneliness and alienation is that your Soul is not of Here. Your Soul, in her essence does not belong to this plane. Incarnation is a compromise. The place to which the Soul truly belongs has no form. Its only form is the light of I AM. The moment you incarnate, you enter the otherness and become separated from Truth.

You can feel a part of this dimension only while being unconscious. Because this dimension is itself unconscious, those who want to belong here must also be unconscious. As you awaken more to your true identity, you start to feel like a stranger Here. In truth you are a stranger in the dimension of forgetfulness. The home of the Soul is the Divine Dimension. The Earth is beautiful but from the higher perspective, it is a very gross dimension. A plane where all creatures survive by eating and killing each other, is a very low plane. That must be seen. To be a human is beautiful as an experience, but at one stage one moves out from this 'limitation of perception.' Freeing oneself from the gravitation of earth, that is unconsciousness, one can fly into the sky to the Other Dimension.

At this moment you still enjoy it! You cannot give it up yet. But you can already feel that you are not of Here. Knowing this, enjoy the adventure of living here! You still need to gather many experiences. It is not through negation but positive fulfilment that you will transcend. Do not forget that by the force of destiny, it is on the earth that you discover yourself and the truth of existence. You are in the right place! Believe it or not... Therefore, with the gratitude to the earth, gradually prepare yourself to let go of this dimension.

You are the Path!

Student: *How do I know that I am on the right Path?*

Aziz: First of all, are you on the Path? Unless you know who you are, you are not on the Path at all. That which most seekers call following the Path is: a search for a Path. The Path begins with awakening. It is I Am which is the Path and there is no other Path. The concept that there are many ways to reach Self-realisation is true on some level and false on another level. For what is the Path? You are the Path!

Clarity on the Path

Student: *I don't know where I am on my Path? After so many years of meditation, I feel like I am completely lost.*

Aziz: You are here, in the Satsang room! You are exactly where you should be. In terms of your spiritual practice, you simply don't know what you are doing. Your problem, like for most seekers, is the lack of basic understanding. That's why, we speak so much to activate your intelligence, so you can have clarity as to what you are doing. The Path to awakening is complex and full of pitfalls. You will never know where your are standing on your Spiritual Path unless you know the inner map of awakening and the basic principles of the awakening process. Look inside and know who you are! Study these matters carefully...

Who is Really Advanced?

Student: *What suggestions do you have for beginners, who are just beginning to meditate, to seek.*

Aziz: What do you means by being a beginner?

Student: *Before, I knew so many things and now I don't know anything. I have to begin.*

Aziz: If you don't know anything, it means that you are advanced! A beginner knows everything! The less you know, the more advanced you are. In 'Tao The Ching,' it is written: 'those who grow in knowledge, they increase everyday; those who grow in Tao, they decrease every day.'

But, perhaps, you have a question for someone who is advanced? If we wish to distinguish between a beginner and an advanced meditator, we must use a careful criterion. For what does it mean to be advanced? Does it means that someone has been practicing for twenty years? Such a person has usually an 'advanced' spiritual ego but not necessarily an advanced state of consciousness. Is it advanced to carry for half of your life a sannyasin's name and grow a long beard? Is it advanced to be a monk and wear a holy robe?

To be advanced has nothing to do with these spiritual poses, ego-images and games. To be advanced is to be awakened, at least on some level to the I Am. To be advanced is to know who is beyond the mind. To be a beginner is to live in the illusions of the Spiritual Path, to be a slave of a particular technique or philosophical system. To be a beginner is to live a second-hand life and not from within one's own Soul. The maturity of the Soul must be measured by her evolution in many lifetimes.

It is possible that one may not meditate at all in this lifetime, but have a natural connection with the I Am. Someone may already be born awakened. When Hui Neng, the great Zen master was taken to the monastery, he was already awakened but all monks despised him, for they thought that he was just a beginner. He was awakened, but they didn't allow him even to enter the meditation hall! He had to stay in a kitchen and clean rice. This pseudo-spiritual world is full of idiots who want to judge your advancement using their superficial and primitive criteria.

There are some yogis in India who, for instance, deny Enlightenment to everyone who didn't have kundalini awakening! According to them only kundalini awakening brings true Enlightenment. There are others who think that unless you have psychic powers, you have not reached Self-realisation...and so forth. The spiritual world is full of mediocrity and ignorance. In order to see clearly what is true advancement, you must be intelligent and sensitive. This is particularly true for all of you who are already conditioned and programmed by the collective spiritual mind, which is very unconscious. Be aware of it! You may feel that you are free and your mind is free but you are not. You are still just an individual version of the collective spiritual consciousness or rather unconsciousness.

The criteria with which you have to measure your advancement and awakening reflect the purity of your understanding and your wisdom. Our meetings are advanced for we do not give you merely techniques, neither are they based on guru-projections. We point directly to the reality of I Am. We explain precisely the nature of Enlightenment and we guide you into a clear experience of it.

Student: *For long time I thought I was a good meditator but now it seems that I am nothing.*

Aziz: You are nothing but you exist! You are nothing but not in terms of not existing. You are nothing from the viewpoint of the mind which loses its central position. But as you exist as a nothing, you are a pure subject, Pure Me. You are not merely nothing for you do have existence. You are awareness and awareness is not nothing. You are Being and Being is an experience .... it has depth and stillness which you feel deeply. And what about your Heart: is it nothing? Isn't there something the most sensitive? The reality of Pure Me is made of different frequencies of energy which have no crystallised quality. This Me cannot be pinpointed as 'something' objective but it is absolutely real. You are subtle. A rainbow is not nothing even though it cannot be grasped. When you put your hand inside a rainbow, you cannot grasp it but it doesn't mean that the rainbow doesn't exist. Does it?

Look clearly! You know enough. You know what is the centre

of awareness, you know what is Being and you have a Heart. You have a great deal of knowledge. You know enough to be able to go inside and understand the meaning of it.

Sex is not a Problem

Student: *Can sex be a hindrance in our spiritual evolution? Is celibacy important?*

Aziz: In Hinduism, they call celibacy Brahmacharia which means living in Brahman. Originally, it was discovered that certain beings who had realised the Ultimate were not so interested in sex. That's why, their devotees thought that not having sex leads one to the realisation of Brahman. But the fact that some Self-realised beings have no sex does not imply that not having sex brings Self-realisation! In truth, most Rishis, the sages of the Upanishads did have normal families and wives. The negative attitude towards sex was a result of the further development. One of the most important roles of Rajneesh was to bring some healing into this area.

Having sex or not having sex are not directly related to spiritual evolution. There are certain esoteric practices in which one tries to conserve sexual energy in order to channel it to higher centres. Tantra as such works with energy and has nothing to do with sex. So-called sexual Tantra is just a small portion of the spiritual discipline. These practices are very complicated and don't always bring one directly to awakening. Sexual Tantra does not point to the Buddha's type of awakening but more to different mystical states. Energy itself has no wisdom. It is like electricity, you never know what it will do in terms of awakening.

In the Path of wisdom, it is irrelevant whether one has sex or not. Also, we need to remember that in the past, people were malnourished. There was a very little food and seekers were more afraid of losing energy through sex. But now there is so much food, our problem is how to channel an excessive amount of energy. Also, when you are having sex without ejaculation, there is no way that you can lose energy.

There is a way to use sex in connection with meditation. Remaining present during making love is the first step. Sex is a very unconscious and animalistic activity. That's why, bringing awareness to it is very important. We are not speaking about 'observing' oneself having sex but about being fully present inside of it. Particularly, when the centre of awareness is awakened, bringing this state into the time of making love can be a powerful experience. Next, you bring also into making love, the energy of Being and relaxation. Awareness and Being allow you to be total and fully present in sex. It has been said that a sign of an advanced yogi is to be able to retain the State of Presence during ejaculation. The next, very important step is to bring the Heart into the art of making love. When the Heart is present, the Soul is present for the first time. Here, one feels simply love, loving kindness and compassion. You are not only making love, but you see the other human being who like you is longing for love and recognition.

When a man is not in the State of Presence, during orgasm he loses a lot of energy through his etheric body. Every man after orgasm feels depleted and empty, for the level of energy immediately drops down. When the State of Presence is retained, energy on the subtle level does not get dissipated. It seems that the main loss of energy does not relate to the fact of losing the semen but to some unconscious dissipation of energy within the subtle bodies. The State of Presence allows keeping this energy together in a self-contained state.

If you repress your natural sexual desires, it will go against you. Sex will enter through the back door in the form of imagination, disturbing your meditation even more. Sex is not only physical. In truth, the main reason we desire to connect sexually with a partner, is emotional and energetic. Being in sexual union with the opposite sex is very nourishing emotionally and energetically, as we live in polarities. Negating it, can bring an imbalance.

The Art of Meditation

Meditation is an effort to transcend the frontiers of our individual existence. It is this effort which points to freedom from any effort at all. Difficulties in meditation must be seen as an indivisible part of our evolution into the Inner Wholeness. A clear understanding of the inner processes in meditation is essential for the meditator not to become lost in wrong and incomplete practice. The more one is awakened, the more one abides in the state beyond meditation and non-meditation. Here, one becomes the State of Meditation.

Problems in Meditation

Student: *During the meditation while I was watching the breath, the muscles in my face became very tense. Do you know why this happens and what should I do?*

Aziz: Meditation is a new type of activity where one is not doing anything. When you sit in meditation, you might feel suffocated with your own space and the mind does not know how to behave, how to channel the energy of non-doing. Normally, energy goes in many different directions - moving with thoughts, emotions, perceptions, and so forth. This energy is spread in the horizontal reality, in the outer. When you sit, energy doesn't know how to channel itself. All energy is inside, it is all self-contained. Of course, when you lose yourself in thinking, this energy gets distributed into unconscious thinking. But when your are present in the moment, everything is inside. How to channel this energy is an art and a function of evolution. As you mature, energy finds its way to different centres, creating the holistic experience of the I Am. Therefore, do not even try to understand your experience. It is simply something which happens sometimes and does not have much importance. Concentration is in the mind and can affect certain muscles in the face because it is all in the head area.

What can you do in such a case? Acceptance... You accept whatever is happening as a part of your reality. Next, within this acceptance, you relax more. And if these sensations persist, you breathe into your head, into your face muscles. You become fully present with the breath there. From this place of being fully present you relax again - you drop like a waterfall. When you inhale, feel the breath penetrate the muscles of your face with prana, with energy. And when you exhale again, it will bring relaxation. It is an accidental phenomenon; there is nothing to worry and no need to understand.

Student: *When we were breathing deeply to the belly, I felt that I was not so clear in my head, it felt like I was losing awareness. The state was a bit foggy. What should I do in such a case?*

Aziz: It is an important question because many practitioners have this type of experience and they don't know what to do. First of all, what does it mean to be centred in the belly, in the Hara? It does not mean to be centred in a martial art way. It does not mean to feel the area of your body in the lower belly in a physical way. To be centred is to Be. The term centred is not the best, perhaps, for Being has no centre. Instead of the term 'centred' we would use the word 'grounded.' When you experience Being, there is the feeling of rootedness, you become grounded within the Now.

When there is thinking going on all the time, a lot of energy goes to the head and you get disconnected from this fundamental experience of Being. In order to reverse this process, there has to be a certain amount of surrender - letting go so you can drop energy into Being. And when you drop into Being, you bypass the mind, you move beyond the mind. However, because awareness is not awakened, the experience lacks clarity. In such a situation, there is calmness and perhaps not many thoughts, but the state is vague and not really deep. We call it the negative no-mind. There is the negative no-mind and the positive non-mind. The negative no-mind means that there is no clear energy in the head. The mind is blank, there is no life in it. The positive no-mind represents a clear state beyond the mind, where you are fully present. There is a difference between 'having energy in the mind' and 'being in the mind,' so to speak. When you are in the mind, it means you are just thinking a lot. But when there is energy in the mind, you are present.

When there is not enough awareness in meditation, what you can do is - breathe to the head and retain breath in the third eye. Being fully and clearly present in the head, you activate the centre of wakefulness and awareness. You cannot be fully clear however, unless you recognise the centre in the mind. For who is the one actually present behind thoughts? What is this attention behind thoughts? When you have recognised it, you have met the essence of the mind. It is not just an experience which you have by chance. The first time you become present in the mind, you will know this presence which is present as your centre of identity in consciousness - you will know who you are. You see, when the centre is awakened in the mind, it destroys the unconscious mind. Not in a way that the mind is blank, but by giving birth to radical clarity. This is a real revolution inside your own mind. You mind becomes like a room full of light. The negative no-mind is like a room which is empty, but there is no light. The light is switched off, the space is black. When you turn the light on, it is the same no-mind but there is clarity, there is awareness. This awareness allows you to experience this extraordinary strength of presence and knowingness.

A Crazy Mind

Student: *In meditation, my mind becomes very active. I feel I have a crazy mind.*

Aziz: What do you mean by a 'crazy mind'?

Student: *It is like a computer.*

Aziz: Maybe you are simply more aware of the crazy mind. It was crazy all your life but you were too identified with it to notice its craziness! There needs to be a certain distance from the mind to notice its unconscious activity.

Student: *It is easier for me to be in the Heart and Being than to be present in the mind.*

Aziz: It is natural, because what does it mean to be present in the mind? It means that there is more energy in the mind and because of this the mind can become irritated, producing even more thoughts. When one becomes aware, the mind does not always become quiet by itself. In the beginning, it may even become more restless. When awareness is activated, the mind feels awkward; it does not know how to behave. The mind panics and manifests all sorts of disturbances.

Student: *Is the mind personal? I think that the mind is impersonal.*

Aziz: It is impersonal. It is a computer simply. It is impersonal, which means it is subconscious. Personal means that you are thinking and those thoughts relate to the real You. At this stage, you have no control over this mind. You are invaded by all those different thoughts which come without your invitation - you are locked in the prison of your own mind. This mind can become personal only when you are present.

You see, in the case of a person who is not aware, the subconscious mind is overwhelming for it is over-loaded. There is a constant thinking. What do you think happens to a thought when it passes away? It goes below the conscious level to subconsciousness. There is not a one thought that is forgotten. Each thought moves to the subconscious mind where it is saved and stored. And because of this, thinking has no end, the subconscious mind is crowded with innumerable mental impressions. So the moment you become aware of the mind, often the subconscious mind releases some of this stored information. It has to release itself because it is suffocated with too much garbage from the unconscious.

Student: *Should I try to stop those thoughts? Shall I just let them be as they are?*

Aziz: Let the thoughts come if they do but remain fully centred in your presence. It is natural that at this stage, you have many thoughts; nothing is wrong with it and you can even see it as a good sign. Later on, the mind gets more emptied, the subconscious mind becomes released and there is more and more silence.

Student: *How to reach space beyond the mind? I experience myself beyond the mind when we let go into Being. I can do it even without going into awareness.*

Aziz: You see, there are two ways of reaching the space beyond the mind. First is through bypassing the mind, where you direct your attention to other areas than thinking, like Being or the Heart. The second is through facing the mind, where you actually go into the mind, reaching the presence beyond this very mind. Here, you experience the silence within the mind, which is awareness. When you go into Being, you bypass the mind. In such a case, awareness is vaguely present and unconscious thoughts still manifest different impressions and can take you away from Being into daydreaming.

The work with awareness is not so pleasant. It requires attention. It is much more pleasant to relax into Being or to go into the Heart. However, in order to be complete, it is extremely important to focus on awareness, at least temporarily. It is the first step to transcend unconsciousness and reach clarity and presence. Then, when you surrender further in your practice, you will reach enormous depth and clarity.

Feeling Spaced-Out After Meditation

Student: *After meditation, there is often a feeling that it is difficult to connect to the normal state of consciousness. I feel spaced-out and a bit uncomfortable.*

Aziz: When you sit in deep meditation, what you experience is your absence; you become absorbed in Being, your sense of Me becomes absorbed. But when there is not enough balance between Presence and Being, the state may not be clear enough. In activity, the State of Presence is stronger and vibrates more while in meditation energy gravitates more towards Being. If your awareness is not clear, Being can dissolve clarity and the state becomes dull. You need to activate the State of Presence more, bringing a certain focus into the head. Try to be fully present while Being, adding more clarity and concentration to the mind. By repeating the circular movement of intensifying the State of Presence and dropping into Being, certain integration will take place. Eventually, this integrated state will dissolve the boundaries between meditation and activity.

YOU are More Important than Your Mantra!

Aziz: Have you been meditating before? (Addressing a newcomer).

Student: *Yes. I have been doing Transcendental Meditation.*

Aziz: Yes, mantra... and who is repeating the mantra?

Student: *I don't know.*

Aziz: When you repeat a mantra, who is doing it?

Student: *My own mind is doing it.*

Aziz: But who is behind the mind, who is this Me which is saying the mantra? The purpose of repeating a mantra is to concentrate the mind. When the mind is focussed, you can then discover the subject behind it. When you say mantras just for the sake of saying them, you waste your time. The goal of meditation is not to 'meditate' but to awaken to who you truly are beyond the mind.

Who are you? Do you want to find out? Is it your question? Unless you have the right question, all meditation techniques are using you, instead of you using them! Look inside and discover yourself. Wake up from your dream! Or would you rather repeat your mantra (for which you have probably had to pay in the T.M. organisation) to the end of your life?

Who repeats the mantra? What is the essence of meditation? Who are you? No one asks these questions. And is there any surprise that so few beings are awakened? How can there be any questions if there is no seeker in the first place? A question is much more important than an answer. We give you answers here, but to questions which you have not asked! We give you also questions. We give you questions trying to convince you to ask them. We tell you: 'please, ask this question!' But are these your questions? Is anybody home?

When you repeat a mantra, feel the one who is doing it, take a step back within your mind. The one who is attentive to the mantra is much more important than the mantra itself!

Watching and Beyond Watching

Student: *I was trying to watch the mind but there were no thoughts.*

Aziz: The moment you are aware of the mind, often it becomes quiet. The reason that the mind works so much, is the lack of awareness - the mind feeds on unconsciousness. The mind as such represents the subconscious reality which runs automatically. Once upon a time Bodhidharma was asked by a monk, 'could you pacify my mind as it is so restless?' In response, Bodhidharma told the monk to bring 'his mind' with him the next day. But the monk could not find any mind, even though he was searching for it the whole night. This was how Bodhidharma pacified his mind. The moment you are aware of the mind, the mind disappears. But, when you observe the mind and there are no thoughts to be observed, the question is: who remains? That which remains is your true Self. This Me who sometimes experiences thinking and other times the absence of thinking, is itself not a thought - your Me is not of the mind. You are this Me. You are that which always remains. Wake up to yourself!

Student: *How can I separate myself from my mind?*

Aziz: Can you observe the mind?

Student: *Yes, I can.*

Aziz: Who is observing the mind?

Student: *Something is behind it.*

Aziz: That is correct, but what is it? Can you feel it clearly?

Student: *In some situations I observe my thought and my emotions.*

Aziz: You observe but not knowing the observer. Who is observing? In truth, it is the intelligence or the subtle mind who is observing. But who is behind this mind? The centre of attention is not in the Heart, neither is it in Being - it is in the mind. Awareness is arising from a certain place. All that you do, feel, think and perceive involves awareness. But where is the source of awareness? Awareness is born in the brain but its very centre is in the middle of this brain. We call it the wakefulness centre. When you observe, instead of being in an ordinary semi-conscious state, you activate this very centre; but still it is not enough to recognise it directly. Therefore, the next step has to follow, where you turn the observing consciousness back to its very centre. This centre is nothing but the light of attention without any object. We call it mindfulness without object.

Do you see how you live through the constant subconscious perception of objects? You are lost in objects. Who is the subject? Can you see the importance of this discovery? Wake up and see who you are! Go beyond techniques and know yourself! Awaken the passion to awaken your own presence. When you know yourself, why observe anything? The observing ability is a part of the mind's constitution but should not become an addiction, otherwise you will find yourself in some kind of schizophrenia. A Vipassana adept who is caught in the game of constant observation and disidentification is completely split inside and fragmented. For that reason, we say that observation is a means and not at all, the goal. When you observe, the mind is divided into two parts - one part is observing another part. It is not the case with witnessing as witnessing, in truth, is to be one with the mind - from the totality of Presence. Your goal is not to 'do' all the time but to Be, to be who you are which is the Soul in her natural condition. Here, you enter true meditation, beyond traditions, beyond techniques, schools and systems. Here, you enter Universal Meditation which is reality itself.

Student: *When I meditate, I am always disturbed with too many thoughts. It seems the only way to have some freedom is for me to observe them.*

Aziz: That is correct but you still can go deeper. Who is looking at the thoughts? You must look at the one who is looking in order to cut through the endless gymnastics of the mind. When you look at thoughts, you still refer to the outer, to that which you are not. You create some distance but this distance has no real strength and no quality of a centre. You can calm the mind down but not in a real way, for you have no way to become that calmness. To conquer the mind, you must change the focus from observing the mind to observing the observer. The only force which can liberate you from the mind is your own Presence, not your presence to the mind but presence to yourself. Find your Me and keep her, remember her all the time. When you stay with her, the quality of your meditation and the behaviour of the mind radically transform. It is a quantum leap, you simply change dimensions, leaving the mind behind. You change your location within your internal reality. Contemplate what it means to observe the observer. It has to become your question! We are pointing to something which is simple and fundamental. You already know what it means but this experience is not yet clear; it lacks continuity. Who is looking through the window of your eyes? Can you see your eyes? Can you see the seer? Who is behind your eyes?

Student: *I have difficulties grasping it.*

Aziz: This is because your consciousness is fully exteriorised, lost in the outer. Your head is like a camera making everything visible; but what is the centre of this camera? You are aware of the pictures outside you but can you be aware of the one who is aware? To see the seer you have to look back. These are no eyes which are looking; behind the eyes is the mind which translates the pictures and behind the mind is your Me to whom all of this applies. Look back, as if towards the back of your skull. As you direct energy inside your head, you will encounter the seer.

And who is discovering this Me? This question has given a headache to thousands of seekers! But the answer is simple. It is the dynamic extension of Me called intelligence. When you discover your Me, it is intelligence recognising its own centre. For an ordinary person, even when one is able to feel this Me, it is impossible to be aware simultaneously of Me and the outer. Awareness must awaken to reach its panoramic depth. Do you feel this Me? Isn't it something quite familiar?

Student: *I am feeling some quietness.*

Aziz: Who is feeling this quietness? Isn't it the quietness feeling itself? This quietness is itself awareness without object. You must centre yourself more in this area. When your eyes are open, where is the quietness? It is still behind your eyes. When your eyes are closed, you feel it more or less in the whole head. When your eyes are open, you feel it in a more focussed way, for attention looks back as it looks out simultaneously.

The Sound OM is Prior to Hearing

Student: *Sometimes in meditation, I hear a sound or vibration. It can become louder and louder. Is it right to concentrate on this sound?*

Aziz: No, it is not right. That which you hear is the sound OM, the vibration of Existence. You don't hear it through your ears but through consciousness. In some schools of meditation like Kriya Yoga, for instance, they focus on this sound. However, it is not a pure meditation. When you listen to this sound, you create duality, a split between subject and object.

Student: *But there is the feeling that I am this sound.*

Aziz: Yes, but the moment you hear it, you become separated from it. If you were really One with the sound, you would stop hearing it! We say that I Am is made from pure light, but the moment you see it, no longer is it pure. The real light cannot be seen even though one can become it. If you hear the sound OM, relax with this experience and as your intelligence gets absorbed, the hearing will turn into non-hearing.

In Zen they have a koan, 'what is the soundless sound of one hand clapping?' Many give a wrong interpretation to this koan. Even Rajneesh thought that it is about hearing the sound OM.

But it is not correct. The ultimate sound cannot be heard. The soundless sound of one hand clapping is Existence itself, Reality as it is. It is already Now! You don't need to hear it, for it is absolutely present prior to perception.

The Buddha does not Smile!

Student: *There is a Vietnamese teacher, Thich Nhat Hanh, who suggests to sit meditation with a half Buddha smile. What do you think about this technique?*

Aziz: It may be good for a beginner but is not right for an advanced practitioner. If you keep a half-smile, it may positively affect the mind but, on the other hand, keeps you too much in your personal self. The Buddha does not simile! To smile is beautiful but to keep smiling in meditation is ridiculous. When one is absorbed in Being, naturally the muscles of the face are pulled by the force of gravity. When I shifted to the Absolute, my lower jaw actually began to droop as all my body was absorbed from head to feet. When you deeply relax, letting Being to absorb you, not only can you not smile but you forget that you exist! If a person keeps a half-smile in meditation, it is a proof of not being in Samadhi.

Resistance to Meditation

Student: *What shall we do when in meditation, we feel resistance?*

Aziz: You can feel either psychological resistance or resistance on the energy level. If you feel psychological resistance, your mind is drifting away and you seem to have much more important things to think about or to do than to meditate. In such a case, you must use your discipline, power of will and freedom of choice. The mind is often disturbing because it does not want to be silent. The mind wants to be entertained all the time; it is, in a way, like a spoiled child who wants your full attention. So, the mind disturbs you; it creates resistance and a feeling of boredom. But as your mind becomes more intelligent and clear about its spiritual goal, it surrenders more and more and is able to give up its resistance.

On the other hand, when you feel resistance on the energy

level, it is simply difficult to sit. Your energy is restless; you may find it difficult to bring back a clear state of awareness, as well as the ability to settle into Being. In such a situation, you have to persevere, staying with this discomfort in full acceptance. In due time, this restlessness of energy becomes pacified and settled. When you are sitting in non-doing, not only does attention become concentrated but energy by the force of gravitation reaches deeper and deeper layers of Beingness. That's why after meditation you feel good, your energy is fresh and rejuvenated, and the mind is serene.

Therefore, if there is resistance, whether energetic or psychological, you cannot by any means give up. You must oppose this resistance using your will, determination, patience and wisdom. When the meditator is mature, the resistance is quickly dropped. The mature meditator also experiences difficult moments or can have a bad day sometimes, but he or she is able to say 'no' to the moment of weakness and to use the force of determination and clarity to go against resistance. If the Soul is immature and weak, she gives up quickly. That's why most people give up meditation as quickly as they try it. It is much easier to follow the unconscious tendencies of the mind. For most, unconsciousness is spontaneity.

Mindfulness of Thoughts

Student: *In this activity of being mindful of thoughts, I feel some sense of separation.*

Aziz: Mindfulness of thoughts is a combination of attentiveness and the intelligence which gives direction to attention. In order to perceive a thought, attention needs to have a direction. Attention without intelligence has no direction and is unable to perceive anything. Even when you see something from the place free from thinking, this pure seeing already includes in itself a certain unity of awareness and intelligence. The State of Presence which is pure attention or self-attention has no way of becoming aware of thinking; it is therefore that this state needs intelligence as an extension. The State of Presence is the centre of intelligence and intelligence is the extension of awareness.

It is this intelligence which is listening here. When this intelligence becomes aware of breathing, it changes the direction of its focus. And when it looks at the mind, intelligence becomes conscious of its own content. Intelligence is in-between thinking and not thinking. Intelligence can be seen as a subtle mind, for it does not yet have the form of a crystallised thought. For this reason, it is so difficult to grasp what intelligence is. When you observe the mind, your intelligence together with the sense of Me attached to it, feels some distance from thinking. This sense of Me is not clear unless you make one step more and turn the direction of intelligence back to the centre of observation, to the subject. Here, the State of Presence is awakened. We use intelligence to observe the mind. But who is behind intelligence? Intelligence uses the light of attention of which it is not yet conscious. There is attention, intelligence and the mind. It is intelligence which recognises the light of attention giving rise to the real centre of awareness.

Absorption

Student: *When I am resting deeper than the mind, what is the power of thinking in terms of taking Me out of absorption?*

Aziz: What is it that is deeper than the mind? First, there is the State of Presence, the centre behind thinking. When you are centred in this state, it feels as if you were behind thinking. When you relax with the state, you move deeper until awareness contains the mind. And when you go into Being, dropping energy into Shikantaza, you move even deeper beyond the mind. So, you can experience that which is deeper than the mind, in several ways. You can experience it as the State of Presence in a crystallised way, or as being relaxed in the open space of awareness, and finally you become deeply absorbed into Being.

When the mind is thinking, it is not just mind thinking - it is you who is thinking! You can think either consciously or subconsciously. Your Real Me is in the centre. The extension of your Me, the subconscious Me spontaneously creates some thinking from time to time. Your purpose in meditation is not to stop this type of thinking but to rest firmly beyond it. When, however, a thought occurs your attention gets drawn to it and you may energetically be pulled out of your absorption. It doesn't mean that you lose yourself for you still rest beyond the mind, but you simply become less absorbed.

Meditation is like a time of prayer. It is not a time of thinking about mundane affairs. But some thinking does naturally arise as a part of the spontaneous activity of the mind. However, if you get too involved in thinking, the balance can be lost. When you notice it, simply bring yourself back to the zero point and surrender into Being. In order to surrender deeper into Being, the continuity of awareness is necessary. The continuity of awareness allows the gravitational drop to be conscious as well. Energy needs some time to settle down into Being. The continuity of awareness is the continuity of surrender. When you sit, being present and letting go into non-doing, the energy gravitates towards the Absolute. The moment you get distracted, energy pops up and you lose some of the depth you have accumulated.

When an inexperienced meditator sits Zazen, there is this constant oscillation between dropping down and forgetting oneself in the mind... one doesn't have the continuity of surrender. We spoke about the anchor going down to the bottom of the ocean. The anchor is the Soul's presence which drops down to the ocean of Beingness. The moment you forget yourself, the anchor not only doesn't move down, but actually moves up, so you need to repeat the act of surrender. Some thinking is not a problem, if there is the necessary strength of surrender, but when you engage yourself into thinking too much, you lose some amount of rootedness in Being.

It is interesting to see how important one's presence is in the ability to surrender. Surrender does not mean that one is 'gone.' Presence is an inherent part of the surrendering process. Without presence, surrender just makes you 'spaced out,' and is meaningless. The purpose of surrender is not to cancel oneself, but to reach through presence, the depth of Being.

Aziz's Experience in Meditation

Student: *Could we know what is your experience in meditation?*

Aziz: An unbroken unity with the Divine. In this state there is no movement, no change. It is a state of the Diamond Mountain. My state is one solid totality of pure isness and love. The change which takes place, when I close eyes in meditation, relates to the quality of intelligence. In activity, intelligence is more aware of the environment. In meditation, this intelligence becomes absorbed into the presence of the Universal I AM. That's why, even though the state in which I abide never changes, in meditation the quality of absorption is more sweet, like falling asleep into the arms of the Beloved.

Sitting Meditation

Student: *Why is it so important to sit still and not move?*

Aziz: This is just a device and not a dogma. We do not sit still in order to sit still. It is a device to focus the mind. Ninety percent of the reason people move so much, is from the mind not from the body. The mind gets restless and wants to escape from the situation of non-doing, so it creates a disturbance, itching here and there. When we sit still, it is easier to become focussed, absorbed and to go deeper into Being. The stillness of the body is helping you to discover the stillness of your Being. It is not a strict rule and if you really feel pain, you simply move. It is simply a device. I Am is beyond sitting and beyond movement. It is beyond the body.

Student: *How often should you meditate and when is the best time of day to do it?*

Aziz: Twenty-four hours! You see, there is the formal practice of meditation and there is the meditative state which is gradually being introduced into activity. Formally speaking, it is good to meditate a minimum of twice a day; morning and evening are the best times and for 45 minutes. If you meditate more often, it is very good. If you can do a retreat, it helps as it is a more focussed practice.

There are different ways to help your own evolution, we are using different tools. The most important is to discover who is meditating? Who is the one inside? When you discover it in meditation, then you learn how to retain this experience in activity. That's why, in Zen and other schools of meditation, apart from sitting they also do walking meditation. After sitting meditation, there is walking meditation. Walking meditation is supposed to be a continuity of sitting meditation. There is something which is continuing. If, at first, the meditator does not understand that there is a connection between sitting and walking, it is because he or she experiences two distinct states of consciousness.

When you walk you may not see any connection with your sitting periods. You must find the link between sitting meditation and activity, for You are this link!

Student: *Is there any importance to sitting in the lotus position in meditation?*

Aziz: The lotus position is simply a comfortable position. Half or quarter lotus helps you to keep your spine straight and to sit in a solid way. Again these are just devices to help you and not strict rules. Someone may sit in full lotus all day and not reach any real meditative state. Someone else can sit in a chair and be in deep meditation. However, a good posture helps to concentrate the mind and to reach inner stillness. Good posture means you can forget about the body. If you don't have good posture, you are constantly conscious of your body because you are aching. If your spine is not straight, you keep on falling and you are constantly body conscious. When you sit in a very comfortable position and close your eyes, you are beyond body consciousness. It is easier to experience it. That's why, originally in yoga they started with hatha yoga, the physical yoga which prepares the body so that one can sit in meditation without disturbance. Unfortunately, for most hatha yoga has stopped to be a means and has become the goal. Most so-called yogis are forever stretching, preparing themselves for a spiritual practice which never takes place!

If you do some stretching, it may be easier to sit later in half lotus, unless you have an anatomical problem or you are not supple enough. Some people simply cannot do it. But if you can, it is recommended.

What is Shikantaza?

Student: *Can you talk more about the Shikantaza?*

Aziz: Shikantaza is a state of non-doing. Paradoxically, for the human being, the most difficult state of existence to reach is the one of non-doing. We cannot rest because, being identified with the life-force, there is constant activity happening on all levels. The conscious mind, subconscious mind and our emotional body are always automatically identified with these activities. That's why, for an ordinary person, the only way not to do is to eliminate the conscious mind. An example is falling asleep or getting 'stoned.' Of course, becoming unconscious represents the dark side of non-doing. The non-doing we speak about, the Shikantaza is reached while remaining fully conscious. When the Soul decides to go beyond this constant process of becoming, she lets go into Being. To let go into Being, into non-doing, is to undo the habitual and unconscious doings of the body-mind.

The first step in the expansion into non-doing, is the crystallisation of attention where one reaches non-activity within the mind. The State of Presence is between doing and non-doing. The State of Presence means that doing is suspended but non-doing has not been reached yet. Next, one surrenders into Being, energetically letting go into the Now. The non-doing takes place in the space of the Now. We say that there are two realities: the horizontal reality of the Here and the vertical reality of the Now. It is within the Now that the Pure Rest is attained.

Student: *I do not quite understand the concepts of horizontal and vertical realities.*

Aziz: Horizontal is that which is spread around you, which you see in front of yourself and behind - in terms of space and time. From the other side, the vertical reality represents that which is present prior to perception. The horizontal refers to objectified consciousness. The vertical points to the subjective reality of I Am.

Shikantaza can only be reached through the expansion of energy into the Now. Here, your Soul, within her energy system is able to expand into Being. Through this expansion you enter the Now, the dimension of the Now which is beyond time. When you simply sit in meditation, experiencing the state of just being, a part of you surrenders into the Timeless. You may not be aware of it but you have actually changed dimensions - you are no longer only on the earth. At that moment, you are somewhere else. Being is not on the earth, even though you experience it on the earth. The dimension of Beingness has no form and no location in space or time. It is the vastness of pure isness which has only one quality - it IS. Shikantaza means that you as a human being on the earth can become united with the Beyond. The only way to get there is surrender. Through surrender, your energy system expands beyond this dimension into the Other Side of the Now.

When you sit in meditation, contemplate what it means just

to be. What does it actually mean? It sounds simple, but it is a very subtle state. Just to be means not to do and not-to-do means that you become absent. You are not, but something Is. You are absent, but within your absence, you are present. That which is present is neither you, nor is it separated from you. That is the mystery of Just Being.

Retreat: Cutting Through the Past

Student: *Are retreats necessary to complete the practice?*

Aziz: In most cases - yes. Often a stronger practice is required to break through the unconscious patterns of forgetfulness. Another important reason to do retreats relates to the process of cutting through the subconscious identification with your past identity. That which you think you are is continuously recreated from your subconscious computer. In order to shift to the I Am fully, your sense of identity or belief of who you are must become replaced by a new self-image. It is all about how the subconscious mind translates your sense of identity. Unless you are free from the past on some level, you are unable to Awaken.

The basic set up of retreats creates a new environment which for a short period separates you from your past. It is as if you become suspended and in this suspension, you have a chance to awaken. Awakening is not just to reach a certain state but your intelligence must reinterpret the way it translates your sense of identity.

Beyond 'Watching'

Student: *I have a question about watching the mind?*

Aziz: What does it mean to watch the mind? Everybody speaks about it but no one knows what it means. Watching the mind is quite a meaningless activity. You are looking at arising thoughts, attempting not to become caught in them. It is a hide and seek game. You are waiting for arising thought and you are letting it go... and what next? What are you going to do next? The only way for you to find a meaning within this watching activity is to recognise who you really are. The real meditation begins when you know who you are. There is no point in watching the mind.

You just rest in the state beyond the mind. To accept the mind is to rest in I Am. This very dwelling in I Am is pure acceptance, for it contains the whole of the psychosomatic flow. To accept is to become absent within the presence of What Is.

Attaining this Moment, Attaining Oneself

Student: *What is the meaning of the Zen saying: to attain this moment? We are already here.*

Aziz: Yes, you are here, but you must attain the one who is here! This moment does not exist apart from you. If you are gone, this moment is gone as well - all vanishes. You can say 'this moment' only because you exist. But who is that one behind the experience of each moment? What is the identity of that one? Who is that one who says 'this moment'? You are nothing but a vehicle through which This Moment can experience itself. You are a channel through which consciousness is conscious.

Therefore, the meaning of attaining this moment is to attain oneself. When you are merely present to this moment, still you have not attained this moment. Do you see it? For most, Zen means to be aware of the moment. That is, however, a superficial Zen. Unless you have attained your own presence, you are on the level of commercial Zen, Zen for the public.

Your presence is the essence of this moment. When you are present to the moment, you are still within the objective and not subjective dimension. Mindfulness of an object still represents ignorance. Any animal can be easily mindful of its environment. In truth, there is no enlightened being who can be as aware of the surroundings as an average cat. But does it mean that the cat is enlightened? Awakening, in reality, points to something much deeper than general mindfulness. It is the mindfulness of the subject, mindfulness of mindfulness, mindfulness without object, which is a quantum leap in the evolution of consciousness. If you wish to attain this moment, be present to the presence, be present to the essence of this moment, which is nothing but your Real Me. Yes... you have to attain yourself, for you are not yet whole.

Going In and Out of Meditation

Student: *How is it that often I experience difficulties in entering the state of meditation?*

Aziz: As long as you are separated from the universal I AM, this movement of coming into and getting out of meditation is inevitable. From the place of your relative alienation, isolation from the realm of Beingness, you begin your spiritual evolution into the joy of reunion. As you evolve, you go beyond the very issue of entering the state of meditation. You become the state of meditation! You are the State of Meditation.

Meditation is an Act of Courage

Student: *During meditation many thoughts come to my mind. I am very confused about my future. What shall I do? Shall I drop thinking and live in insecurity?*

Aziz: It is fine that you are confused, as long as you don't lose the One who is confused. To be a human is to be confused and that is fine. When you are present within your confusion, not only are you confused but you are beyond your confusion. The only way to go beyond confusion is to expand into I Am. You are being tested now. If your confusion is more important for you than your own presence, it means that you don't really want it! Do you? Some meaningless future plans are for you more significant than to be present to your true self.

Renunciation is an indivisible part of the Spiritual Path. You call yourself 'sannyasin,' but what have you actually renounced? Do you want to be a 'modern' type sannyasin who just carries a new name? Is it what you would call 'neo-sannyasin'? The true renunciation does not concern money, sex or basic human needs. It renounces all of that which takes you away from your Real Me. You need to give up your forgetfulness. It means that you should not invest so much energy into thinking about your security because you lose yourself. In such a case, you must pull back to your centre. When you are connected to your I Am, when you are in the State of Presence, you can still afford to think about your life. But simultaneously you clearly experience yourself beyond your human anxiety, resting inside. That is the foundation of sanity, for you are rooted inside. The moment you get out of this rootedness, you get lost. And when you get lost, even if you solve your earthly problems, still you are broken and miserable.

There is work to be done! You must root yourself in I Am and transcend the mind. It requires a great amount of energy and dedication. We don't tell you to go to a monastery, but you have to create something like an inner monastery. I Am is your freedom. The moment you are clearly connected to I Am, you can do what you like and no external renunciation is necessary. But if you get lost, it tells you that something is off, something went wrong, and you got sucked too much into fear and insecurity again. Our advice to you is: be confused, accept your confusion. Think whatever you like, but don't lose yourself! Be courageous! Renouncing one reality for another requires courage.

Am I Ready to Meditate?

Student: *We hear often that before getting into meditation, we have to first balance and purify our physical and subtle bodies. When do we know that we are ready to meditate?*

Aziz: Now! You are ready to meditate now. The mind is very clever in creating different excuses not to meditate. The mind doesn't want to give up its dominating position. First, it hates any idea about meditation. Later, it becomes more sophisticated in the way it avoids meditation. When intellectually you are convinced about the importance of meditation, the last trick that you can play on yourself is to say: 'I am not ready, I am not good enough!' Either you are ready now to meditate or you will never be ready! If you wish to postpone your inner work, please do, but don't hide yourself behind the idea of preparation and getting ready for meditation. Be honest and say: 'I don't like to meditate!' It is better to be an honest non-meditator than a meditative-hypocrite.

How to Practice Alone?

Student: *I have the basic understanding of I Am and I have been here practicing with you for some time. What do you suggest for someone like me, when practicing alone? Sitting an hour or two a day?*

Aziz: Sitting is important but the practice must enter life as well.

One must keep the State of Presence in activities. Gradually as your I Am awakens - that is Awareness, Being and Heart - it enters each moment of your life. In each case, the practice varies a bit. One needs to receive individual instructions. The general recommendations are to remember the State of Presence in all situations; to sit in meditation regularly as it deepens the particular quality of Being. We recommend breathing into the belly as part of the daily routine. We recommend to pray every day and stay connected to the Heart. In this way, you are touching all the three qualities of I Am, spirally reaching deeper and deeper integrity within your internal reality. But you need more or less to be connected to a living master, then later you receive further instruction to go deeper.

Student: *For an average meditator, it is difficult to continue the practice alone.*

Aziz: Everything is difficult! Everyone expects easy things. That's why, most give up before they really start. Seekers are so lazy! The spiritual path requires commitment and sacrifices. One must be disciplined and dedicated to the work. We cannot be responsible for the embarrassing quality of most seekers! This work is not for everyone but on the contrary, very few are mature and ready to transcend ignorance. If you don't want to practice, better hang around those pseudo-gurus who only want you to sit in their presence and listen to spiritual clichés. This country offers quite a selection in this respect!

II

DIMENSION OF I AM

In the beginning of the Now, a rainbow was created from the Original White Light. It was made of three colours: Awareness, Being and Heart. Awareness is the light of knowing, the pure presence of thought-free consciousness. Being, the condition of Pure Rest is the sacred vessel containing the whole of Creation and all its living beings. The Heart is the presence of divinity, infinite sensitivity, beauty and love - she is the very meaning of Creation. When this inner rainbow is fully realised through the existence of the Soul, the space of I Am is born, the manifestation of wholeness. When it is done, I Am merges back to the Original White Light realising her innate transparency. Here, the rainbow dissolves into the very space from which it originally emerged.

To enter the cave of a Lion, you must be a Lion yourself. To enter the Dimension of I AM, you must become the I Am!

Awakening of Awareness

How do you know that you are awake? How do you know that you are alive? It is Awareness which enables you to know the truth of your existence. But where is this Awareness? The light of Awareness allows you to recognise this vast universe but is itself beyond any appearance. If you look for Awareness you cannot find it, for it is not outside of you. Awareness is the very essence of your Me. You know your existence only because you are made from the light of Awareness. Wake up from the dream, look back to the source of perception and uphold the seer of all. Discover the Host of your mind, the King of Presence. Yes, it is you, the Awareness which never changes.

YOU are the Sky of Awareness!

Student: *Is it right trying to look at the empty nature of thoughts in order to realise pure awareness?*

Aziz: No, it is not right. Thoughts are external to you, therefore, the emptiness which you see is also external. It is not the emptiness of I Am. You make the same mistake like those who imagine to perceive thoughts as clouds covering the sky of their true nature. It is as if they wanted to see through these clouds in order to realise the sky of awareness. They assume that the perceiver of the clouds is somehow located below, between the clouds and the sky. Do you see what we mean? You must radically change the perspective. YOU are the sky! It is the sky in form of you which is looking at the clouds. The sky is before thinking. It is not by seeing through thoughts that you discover pure awareness but by turning attention back to its source. Don't look at the thoughts trying to see what is behind them. Recognise the one who is looking, see the seer! It is already there. Just relax into your own presence.

Do you know the story of the fool who lost himself in the market place and spent the whole day was looking for himself? Don't behave like him!

To Crystallise Attention

Student: *What does it mean to crystallise attention?*

Aziz: It means to create certain solidity in the mind. Awareness, in the case of an average person is completely fragmented and dispersed. Therefore, one is not able to experience any clear sense of Me within the mind. For this reason the need to bring the energy of the mind into focus arises desperately. A crystallised attention has continuity, solidity and a clear sense of its subjective existence within the movement of the mind. To crystallise attention is to bring structure or form into the chaos. That's why, all schools of meditation work with the development of mindfulness. Attention which has been crystallised, in the ultimate sense of this word, is self-aware and self-contained. It has become one with itself in an objectless way. But, when the process of crystallisation is complete, the next step is to let go into the space of Being which has no point of reference. This is what we call de-centralisation. Crystallised attention is the essence of our Presence. However, it is only through the letting go of our presence into the Universal Presence that we can become truly absent, that is, absorbed in Reality.

Awareness is All-inclusive

Student: *The last days I have been practicing retaining the State of Presence. Today when we did the meditation with open eyes, I felt like the state got lost, dissolved in the outer.*

Aziz: Yes... You are simply facing some difficulties which relate to the process of maturation. You are not able to experience simultaneously the subject and the object. In the beginning you are aware only of the objective reality. If you evolve in consciousness, one day you recognise the subject; you discover that there is a subjective reality completely independent from the outer.

We spoke about the mind which creates the inner dialogue. In the case of an unawakened person, there is only this dialogue, which does not refer to any clear subject. Each thought assumes the role of Me, of the subject. Each thought says: 'I am the most important!' When you awaken the State of Presence, you discover this type of 'I' which is independent of any thought. In this way the inner dialogue, for the first time, refers to the real 'I'! Here, you are not watching the mind. It is not the mind watching itself, now participating in the inner dialogue. That is a case of some kinds of schizophrenia! You are not watching the mind, but you are present within this mind. Awakening to the State of Presence is a function of individual evolution. One is not born with this faculty, which means that it is not shared by collective consciousness.

Consciousness evolves like this: first it is aware of the phenomenal reality only and later if cultivated, it becomes aware of itself, of its own subjective presence. However, after recognising the subject, your consciousness still oscillates between the subjective and objective polarities of experience.

That's why, the moment you become conscious of the outer object, the awareness of the subject gets lost. You fluctuate between subject-object-subject-object. At that stage, you are unable to keep them both. It is natural. As you stay with the subject, it grows; the experience of it matures and rises in strength. The ability to be established in the State of Presence while simultaneously experiencing the world is not merely a question of dividing attention... or of training yourself to look inside and outside simultaneously. It is an outcome of maturation and the transmutation of energy; it takes place more and more naturally as you grow. Later you will ask yourself: 'how was it possible that I was losing the State of Presence?' It will become an integral part of your sense of identity. It is like having your head in the right place. Could you imagine the loss of your head?

You cannot force this ability but you can help this process through your remembrance. From time to time you will experience shifts, certain quantum leaps, in the way awareness functions. Through accumulating the energy of awareness, you generate a certain momentum which eventually transforms into qualitatively higher state and experience. You cannot make it happen, but you can co-operate. Breathing into the belly is a very powerful, though indirect tool in the process of awakening awareness. This is because the stabilisation takes place on the energy level. It is not just a matter of will for the energy must be transformed. Otherwise, your energy system is unable to contain the higher state; the frequency of energy is too high. Now you are preparing the ground for future stabilisation. It is a detailed process as it takes place on a subatomic-molecule level. Consciousness is fuelled by energy. That's why self-knowledge is not enough.

To Keep the State of Presence

Student: *When I speak to people, I lose the State of Presence. It is much easier for me to keep it when I sit and meditate.*

Aziz: It is a question of training because in order to remember yourself, a part of your intelligence has to be involved in this process of self-remembrance. The moment you speak with another person, your mind and emotions are involved, therefore, attention gets exteriorised and loses the focus of self-remembrance. But through the process of self-remembrance, your attention becomes stronger and the centre of consciousness becomes more and more spontaneously present - this means you do not need to focus on it anymore. The Natural experience of witnessing is when you don't know that you are witnessing! When you know that you are witnessing, it is still not the true witnessing. It is still witnessing mixed with observations from the mind. True witnessing doesn't know that it is witnessing. It is simply witnessing which means that there is a presence which includes all and this presence is not personal. This presence is simply present there. For instance, you are completely involved in conversation... and suddenly you remember the state and realise it has been there all the time. Self-remembrance doesn't mean always that you remember yourself. It means that the state is present. This is a very important distinction because many seekers make this mistake, thinking that one's personal intelligence has to all the time remember its centre of awareness. When you relax with the State of Presence, you do not need to remember it anymore. You relax within awareness.

Here, there are two possibilities. One is that you do not remember consciously the State of Presence being absorbed in the conversation and you might think you have lost it. But the centre is there at the background, even though you don't focus on it. The second possibility is that after getting absorbed in conversation, you have simply lost the State of Presence. Is it clear? There are two types of self-remembrance; one is when your mind remembers the centre. It says 'oh I am in the centre!' - the checker is present. The second type of experience with the centre is when it is present on the energy level, but you are not aware of it, your intelligence has been distracted.

It is very simple. For example, you are talking to someone and you have forgotten to remember yourself, when suddenly, you remember! Your subtle memory is able to reveal whether the state was present on the energy level (even though you didn't consciously remember it) or whether it got completely lost. It is important to know that to establish oneself in the State of Presence is beyond only the conscious self-remembrance - it is a stabilisation of energy. When the State of Presence is established, it simply vibrates at all times inside your head - your intelligence has a constant energetic centre. So afterwards, you do not even care anymore whether the state is there or not. It has become an integral part of you.

Let us repeat. One level of remembrance is when you as the mind try to remember and check whether the state is present. The second level of remembrance is when the state is spontaneously present on the energy level and you do not pay attention to it. For that reason, when you forgot about remembering the centre, you have to check whether the state was vibrating spontaneously in the background or whether it was completely lost. Sometimes it is difficult to be certain whether the state was fully gone or not. Introspection and sensitive self-observation is necessary.

Student: *At all times?*

Aziz: No, not at all times. Be spontaneous and from time to time check whether the centre is there or not. Check whether you became completely lost or whether the centre was still vibrating. In the beginning of the practice, one has to remember it through one's own intelligence because the centre is simply dead. There is no centre. But when one progresses in this practice, there is less a need for such focus. Here, one can be more and more spontaneous and remembrance takes a function of an automatic pilot. It means that the Presence is vibrating irrespective of your personal will and intention. You need to check these moments when you do not consciously remember the centre, to be certain whether the state was spontaneously present.

Student: *Do I have to dwell in the energetic sensation which the State of Presence creates in the head?*

Aziz: It is very important. That is what you need to do. This is your task for through dwelling on the vibration at the centre of awareness, you activate it more and make the experience permanent.

Student: *Isn't it a trick?*

Aziz: It is not a trick. It is wisdom. It is not a trick at all. It is very important what you are doing. But in those moments when you forget, check whether the centre was vibrating spontaneously or whether you got completely lost. Simply check.

It is pretty clear that you still do not understand those two different types of remembrance. One is when you remember it - you check, you verify the state. The second is when you are not paying attention but the state is still present on the energy level. In the case when remembering is absent, neither you remember nor is the state present.

For example you speak to someone and you are completely absorbed in the conversation but there is a certain depth of Presence. Afterwards with your subtle memory, you can recollect whether the State of Presence was there or not. What does it mean to get lost? Consciousness gets exteriorised completely outside; it loses its depth; it is no longer panoramic. This is what we mean by being lost. Awareness is no longer four-dimensional, it is flat and shallow, reduced back to three-dimensions. Here, consciousness is lost in the phenomenal reality. When the centre is present, you have depth, a panoramic awareness. There are moments when you get absorbed in the external reality, like in conversation for example, yes? But, suddenly, you remember and through your subtle memory you can verify the state and the degree of its depth.

Student: *Do you remember the state through sensation?*

Aziz: No, no - you remember the state by remembering the sensation which was present before you got lost in conversation or whatever other activity. By remembering it, check if it was there or not. Contemplate it. It is important.

Awareness: Is It a Centre or Space?

Student: *How is it that the State of Presence has both, the quality of a centre and space?*

Aziz: When you recognise consciously the centre of awareness, you simultaneously direct attention there; it is then that a certain concentration of energy, a quality of a centre is formed. From the other side, when you relax with the state, self-referral itself relaxes becoming absorbed into the natural state. When self-referral is gentle, it does not formulate a crystallised centre but rather a Centralised Space. As you rest within awareness, a further expansion occurs and Awareness merges into Being. This means that energetically the experience moves down from the head in the direction of the lower belly, creating one energy field embracing the whole of you.

Cultivating the State of Presence

Student: *These days I concentrate on the State of Presence. I was wondering whether I could accelerate the process by doing more meditations or Vipassana retreats?*

Aziz: To do retreats is always very helpful. But if you do a Vipassana retreat, for instance, the technique which they use, can remove you from your centre and disturb the awakening process. It is really sad but it is really difficult to find a school of meditation that points directly and clearly to the Self! Every school is attached to its technique and thereby sacrifices a clear understanding of I Am. It is not by chance that we call the meditation which we teach 'Complete Meditation.' It is called Complete Meditation not out of conceit but because it points to the whole of Me and not merely to her fragments.

Student: *But I would like to do the Vipassana retreat and keep the State of Presence.*

Aziz: Yes, this you can do. The problem is a certain psychological discomfort, as the environment does not support your effort and can be even hostile if you share your practice! Personally, I was cultivating the State of Presence in Vipassana and Zen retreats and felt quite alone in my practice. Even Zen does not clearly teach the State of Presence; its emphasis lays in the Hara. A true seeker is quite lonely, as even some spiritual environments can be quite unconscious.

For most practitioners, to do retreats is not an option but a necessity. You see, in order to reach transformation, the psyche has to be freed from its past. When you are in a situation of a retreat and the best is in a foreign country, you have this chance. Certain associations in your subconscious mind which are responsible for creating your past self-image, get cut off and disconnected from your experience of the now. Within this gap created out of this disconnection, the New can enter. Without it, it cannot for your psyche is not free. It is utterly unable to go beyond its past, it is stuck in its ignorant sense of identity. Can you retain the state during activity?

Student: *After the energy transmission that you gave me in our private meetings, it was very easy. I was able to do everything without losing the state. Next day it became a bit difficult.*

Aziz: Yes... The state at this point in your practice needs to be lost sometimes. Otherwise, the energy would be too intense. The awakening and integration of energies is taking place. As you bring the state back, over and over through self-remembrance, it will become more and more natural and spontaneous.

The State of Presence and Falling Asleep

Student: *When I concentrate on the State of Presence, I have difficulties falling asleep.*

Aziz: It is natural, for the centre of wakefulness has been activated. What does it mean to fall asleep? It means that the centre of wakefulness switches off and only some subconscious parts of the brain function. At some stage of sleep even these subconscious activities of the mind go to sleep and you find yourself in the dream-less state. The difficulty you experience is a good sign and you can use it as an opportunity to keep as much awareness as you can during the night. The night practice goes very deep. It is generally helpful to wake up in the middle of the night and meditate for a short time.

Self-awareness: Mindfulness without Object

Student: *Is it possible that the mind plays the role of the Presence?*

Aziz: But the mind who 'plays' the role of the Presence, is the Presence! The mind cannot pretend to be present unless it moves beyond thinking. However, one can deceive oneself that one is in the State of Presence, while not being truly present. But, here, the mind is not present. For example, the mind is paying attention to something, whether it is an outer activity or thinking processes, and translates it as being in the State of Presence. Paying attention or being mindful is in-between unconscious or subconscious realities and the actual self-conscious centre of awareness. For instance, you are attentive to the act of walking, but still you are not in the State of Presence; you are present just to this activity and not yet to the Presence itself. That's why we use the term 'State of Presence,' in contrast to the general notion of 'being present.' The difference between mindfulness of the object and mindfulness of the subject is enormous - it is a quantum leap in the dimension of awareness.

Unfortunately, in most available spiritual teachings, this difference is not seen at all! That's why many seekers are truly lost in this area of growth. Most seekers assume that by being generally mindful or by paying attention to breathing, they are on the Path...but they have not yet entered the Path. Awakening takes place when one becomes mindful of the one who is mindful. Here, mindfulness becomes mindful of mindfulness. We call it mindfulness without an object. If you study teachers like the popular Thich Nhat Hanh, you can see that they do not, in truth, point to the realisation of the Self, but rather to the general growth of awareness. As the New Age can be seen as the bridge, for most people, between ignorance and real spirituality, so there are many teachings, which operate in the dimension of growth below Awakening. These teachings are deeper than New Age understanding, but, still, cannot cross the line which separates us from the Absolute Subjectivity.

Location of the State of Presence

Student: *I am not sure about the location of the State of Presence. Sometimes I feel it at the back of the head, sometimes in the front...sometimes feel it all-over and sometimes the energy is more focussed in one place....*

Aziz: The centre of awareness behaves differently depending on the function, depending on the situation. If you don't understand this phenomenon, you can get confused because you will experience it in different areas of the brain. The centre itself is one and a half inches inside the brain. However, the centre which is the light of awareness, radiates energy into various areas of the brain. For instance, when you think consciously, the front of the brain is activated because conscious thinking is located in the front of the brain. The ego is there. Human beings have developed this part of the brain more fully.

Student: *What is the ego?*

Aziz: The ego, as such, is a step in evolution. It is not a thing. It is an ability to think consciously; that is the ego. It does not mean to have a 'big ego.' The big ego is just a negative term for being attached to one's mask-image. The ego, itself, is neither positive nor negative. It is a function of the front of the brain, which is able to think consciously. When the energy from the third eye is focussed in the front of the brain, you feel the energy there more. If you experiment, you will find that when your eyes are open and you have no focus, the energy is felt at the back of the head because the optic nerve is there. Seeing actually happens at the back of the head not in the eyes. The image goes to the back of the head and is being translated by the brain in terms of recognition.

When you are aware, it simply means attention is looking back. For example you walk on the street and you are aware of the centre of attention. In order to be aware of the centre of attention, energy has to be turned in, within your skull. This is an energy phenomenon.

What does it mean not to be aware of the centre of awareness? It means that energy is exteriorised, lost in the phenomenal reality. Energy is diffused in the outer and has no depth, for the seer is not present to himself. But the moment you become aware of the centre of awareness, the energy naturally moves towards the back of the head. When you relax and don't have any special focus, energy is felt more in the middle of the brain. When you close your eyes, it fills up your whole skull. These are the ways the State of Presence naturally behaves. When you focus on something, the sense of Presence naturally becomes directed somewhere.

What does it mean to focus? It means that your attention is moved in some direction by your intelligence. For instance, this happens when you look at a tree. There is a decision, in your intelligence to look at the tree. This intelligence is using attention in order to see, but attention must be supported by intelligence. For example, when you are aware of your breath, you use your attention to be aware of this area. When you are not using will the State of Presence is simply resting in itself. Here, you experience the Natural State without any focus; attention has no direction and is simply resting. Initially, it is simply resting in the head's space. Next, when you become more absorbed, attention gets diffused in Being. Here, you experience yourself everywhere and nowhere at the same time. There is no focal point.

The moment you use your will to direct attention to any area, there is immediately a certain change in the energetic experience of the centre. These are the natural ways of behaving for the centre of awareness. You do not even need to know about them. If you know them too much, it can confuse you. You simply feel the centre and the centre will know how to behave; that is the wisdom of consciousness. The wisdom of your brain directs attention and energy to the right spot, depending on the function and on the situation. It is the flavour of Presence, this very sense of Me, the primal vibration of attention which has to be remembered. When you remember and locate this feeling, you will not worry about locating the right spot. This very feeling you have to remember. Do not focus too much on trying to pinpoint the exact location of Presence inside your head.

Student: *Sometimes I am not sure whether the State of Presence is there, particularly when I am engaged in activity.*

Aziz: Check whether it has been there. If you are not paying attention to it, it does not mean that the state is present in the background. When it is not there, it is simply not there. You need to check whether it has been there or whether it got completely lost. Do you understand? There are situations, when the centre is not there. It has simply become lost. There are also situations when you are absorbed in activity and the State of Presence is just gently vibrating in the background of the mind. The moment you come back, you can verify whether the state has been there, even though you didn't pay conscious attention to it. This is an important point, because the centre cannot always be remembered by your conscious mind. Sometimes it vibrates without you recognising it. Still, your subtle memory allows you to recollect if the state was there or not.

Student: *Going back to the State of Presence again, I recognise the experience in the moment of remembering it. But is there a qualitative difference in the case that this state, just a moment ago, has been completely lost? Will I feel the difference?*

Aziz: In that case your memory will remember whether there has been continuity. The moment you come back to the State of

Presence, you experience what is Now, the present experience. But by using your subtle memory, you can sensitively recollect your experience from the immediate past. You need to be sensitive. You will know whether or not you were in the State of Presence, even though you may not consciously remember it. It is a very subtle presence on the energy level.

It is not true that you need to remember the State of Presence all the time. This would mean that you would be like a self-conscious robot. In the beginning, it is true that you have to remember the state as it is not there without you remembering it. So by remembering you activate the state. You are using a lot of will and concentration, but later on as the state becomes increasingly integrated, you don't need to focus as much. You can be more natural and spontaneous. You just need from time to time to check the state. Are you familiar with the ten ox-herding pictures? These are the Zen pictures describing the process of awakening towards the State of Presence. The bull symbolises the State of Presence:

1. Seeking the bull

This shows a man lost in a forest trying to find the bull. He is looking here and there but he does not know where the bull is. This picture represents the seeker at the beginning of the Path. He is trying to find the Self. But where could it be?

2. The seeker finds traces

He knows finally where the bull is hiding. This picture represents the stage where you receive the right teaching. This teaching is telling you to look inside, to look into the direction of the seer. The self is not on the moon - the traces are in front of you.

3. The seeker sees the back of the bull.

Here, one has glimpsed the Self. 'Oh, it is just Me!' But the experience is still not clear.

4. He sees the whole bull

Then, there is the process of taming the bull, which means remembering him. When the whole bull is seen, you clearly experience the State of Presence...but it still escapes. The bull is wild; he likes to go to the grass and disappear for days so you have to put him on a rope and hold him tight. That is the whole process of taming. The moment you lose concentration, the State of Presence vanishes. You need to use a strong focus.

5. The seeker gently holds the bull with the rope.

He is not even pulling but just lightly keeping it. This represents the stage when the State of Presence is easy to keep but you still need pay attention to it.

6. The seeker rides the bull.

He is playing the flute. He can be occupied spontaneously with the outer world, but the bull is always present. No more does he need to control the bull.

These are different stages of integrating the State of Presence. They represent a deepening of experience. You are in a stage where you are holding the bull and he is following you wherever you go. But still, you have to check from time to time whether the bull is still present or... maybe it has disappeared off into the grass. The bull maybe walking with you nicely and suddenly you see that it has already gone. At this stage, you have to check whether the bull is there or not.

Sometimes you go into the opposite direction and you forget all about the bull. The State of Presence is vibrating but you are not paying attention to it; you are involved in other activities. It requires introspection. You have to double check, using your subtle memory and sensitivity. When you are active in the outer, the vibration of the centre can be quite subtle. Was it there or not? You will experience doubts although later it will become more clear.

Student: *Sometimes I cannot tell whether it is there or not....*

Aziz: Yes, this is normal. There are two reasons for not being certain. You may not be sensitive enough to recognise this experience or the state is not strong enough. Another possibility is that the state is simply absent.

Student: *How long does it take to stabilise in the State of Presence? Sometimes I have a doubt whether it can be done in such a short time...*

Aziz: It can be done in a relatively short time if one is really dedicated. It is important to know that a hundred percent stabilisation is not always absolutely required for the Soul's completion. For most practitioners, the aim is to be able to effortlessly experience this state most of the day, and to at will be able to come back to this state when is gets lost. The hundred percent stabilisation is an idea from past traditions, but it is not necessary for everyone. It is necessary for some Souls who have 'stabilisation karma,' but it is not the case with most seekers. Stabilising in the State of Presence is nothing special. It is a constant self-awareness on the energy level - that is all.

Your doubts perhaps are coming from over-estimating both the phenomenon of awakening to the State of Presence and the stabilisation of this experience. It is a very high and precious state, but at the same time, it is nothing special. You have been initiated into the state of Pure Awareness. Being initiated means the awakening process is triggered on the energy level. We spoke about a six months period for an average seeker to establish this experience. But, in truth, this is quite a long time for someone who is dedicated to this task. Life is short. There are more important things to do than stabilising in the State of Presence. Isn't it true? Stabilising in the State of Presence has to be done so that you can get on with more interesting things. Life is not a practice; life is to be lived. Practice just creates a basic sanity- a basic foundation.

Student: *How many of your students have stabilised in the State of Presence and the Absolute?*

Aziz: Quite a lot have stabilised the State of Presence and some have reached the Absolute State. This practice is scientific. It is not romantic or mystical in the naïve sense of the word. This practice is scientific which means that the results will happen without a doubt. It does not mean that this process is linear and everybody has to do it in the same way. There are some variations on the Path, but this teaching also includes these differences. For how long during a day are you able to retain the State of Presence?

Student: *Around ninety percent.*

Aziz: That is almost stabilised. You have been here only a week. Isn't that a miracle? To stabilise in the State of Presence is a lifetime's task. In the past it took twenty years for a Zen monk to stabilise this experience. Why would you doubt that six months, for someone who is dedicated, and being initiated is not sufficient time? The results are obvious. The results are already present... we are not just giving you promises. The results are already there.

Knowing the State of Presence

Student: *Is it possible to obtain the nature of the mind without practicing with the State of Presence? I am thinking about the teaching of one Korean Zen master which I was following for some time. He did not point so precisely as you do to the State of Presence.*

Aziz: It is not possible for the State of Presence is the nature of the mind! But you see, there is a possibility that different types of practice may bring you indirectly to the same state. In Zen, strangely enough, they are not officially aware of the actual location of the State of Presence. Zen is a Sudden Path but the problem is that it is too sudden! They try to point from the beginning to the complete experience, and it is not possible. In Zen practice, they focus on the Hara. If you focus on the Hara in Zazen, you have more chance to experience Being. However, because they emphasise so much attention, the State of Presence can be awakened in a roundabout way. The problem is that because the teaching is not locating the actual state, it may slow down the stabilising process.

Student: *So how does this master keep his State of Presence, if he doesn't know about its location?*

Aziz: He keeps it by keeping it! It means that he does the right thing, without being fully self-conscious of what he is actually doing. But because the process is not described clearly, most students are simply confused. They try to keep their Hara, and even when they glimpse the State of Presence, they give it up, for they think it is a wrong focus! You see now, how important is to be fully conscious about the awakening process!

We should not forget that often awakening is brought by the power of Grace. In many of traditions, students are supported from the esoteric dimension. That's why, even when one is doing the practice without having the full understanding but one is sincere and genuine - transformation simply does take place. Grace is even higher than our understanding and practice. Grace is the ultimate source of Awakening.

Self-Remembrance: Just Do It!

Student: *Could you suggest something about remembering?*

Aziz: The suggestion is to remember yourself from the moment you wake up, to the moment you fall asleep. And you remember through remembering. The only way to remember is to remember. There is no question of 'how' to remember. Just do it.

Student: *Do we have to use the mind to remember?*

Aziz: Who is remembering?

Student: *I am.*

Aziz: But who is remembering this 'I' to which you refer? This question has given a headache to thousands of seeker in the past and will give the same headache to thousands in the future But the answer is surprisingly very simple. The one whom you remember is the State of Presence. And the one who is doing the remembering is the dynamic extension of this core 'I' which is intelligence. Intelligence is responsible for remembering. Who is listening now? It is your intelligence, isn't it? But when you are ignorant, this intelligence does not refer to any clear sense of Me. To remember is to remember your real 'I.' When the State of Presence is more activated, you don't have to use so much of your intelligence to remember it. Here, the state remembers itself; it keeps itself on the energy level. We call it the primal remembrance, which is the very spontaneous presence of the state itself.

This is how we measure progress - by seeing how much of the state is spontaneously present. Your attention must be constantly turned in, from morning to night. You have to renounce all that distracts you from this work. You must give up your forgetfulness! You have been indulging in it for too long already! Isn't it enough? But at this stage, however much you try, the state cannot be kept all the time. The reason is that stabilisation is an energy phenomenon - it is beyond the personal will. So be patient and forgive yourself when you forget, as not everything is in your hands. From your part, you remember as much as you can, and the rest is a function of evolution and Grace.

Awareness in Sleep

Student: *Why in some schools of Enlightenment do they insist on bringing awareness into the sleep state?*

Aziz: The role of awareness in awakening is crucial but it should not be overestimated either. For some reasons, in most traditions awareness became too important. Some traditions identify awareness even with God! It is absolutely incorrect. Awareness is just a function to bring into the field of knowingness the truth of Creation.

If awareness was the Ultimate, why would we need to make the effort to awaken it? It is a clear contradiction. The desire to bring awareness into the Sleep State was a logical continuation of this first misconception. One can easily become obsessed with the desire to be aware all the time! But it is not natural. A person who keeps awareness in a sleep state becomes quickly imbalance. We should not interfere too much with nature. The time of sleep is very crucial for the rearranging of all subconscious elements. In the dream state, a lot of healing takes place which can be disturbed by the presence of attention.

Awareness is not eternal and cannot be taken beyond the death of the body; so what is the use of crystallising it so much? Cultivation of attention has some limits and at one stage, must be dropped. Only when the cultivation is transcended does one reach the truly natural state. Here, one doesn't manipulate with consciousness, trying to enforce some of its elements, but relaxes into the open space of spontaneity and Beingness.

When the State of Presence is established, it does enter the Sleep State, but not in a self-conscious way. The reason is because the conscious mind is switched off and cannot give feedback to this experience. The State of Presence is present only on the energy level. There is therefore, a certain depth at the background of dreaming activity.

Let us contemplate two situations. One is in activity, when your attention is completely lost in the outer, but the State of Presence vibrates at the background. The other is when you are in the Sleep State with the State of Presence at the background. What is the difference in the experience and recognition of the State of Presence? The difference is the connection of intelligence with the State of Presence. In the waking state, even when one is absorbed in the outer, there is still a gentle connection between the conscious mind and the State of Presence. It is neither fully conscious, nor is it unconscious. In the dream state, this connection is completely cut off; that's why you have no way of knowing that you are in the State of Presence. You need to see that what they call 'lucid dreaming,' has nothing to do with the cultivation of awareness. Lucid dreaming is the presence of ego-consciousness in the dream state.

Stay at the Centre of Awareness

Student: *I have been doing Tai Chi and Chi Gong for the past few years almost every day. Recently, I started to do Tai Chi from the centre of awareness. Normally in Tai Chi, you have three types of awareness: awareness of the body, awareness of the mind and awareness of life. Being in the centre of awareness is rather interesting. My question: should you focus on the State of Presence or rather on these other points?*

Aziz: Tai Chi is a very beautiful system of working with energy, but it does not point directly to the awakening of the witness-presence. There are many systems which cultivate the general mindfulness of the environment or the mind, but they do not point directly to the subject. Awakening to the State of Presence still seems to be a secret and hidden knowledge.

In your case, because you are in the process of stabilising the centre of awareness, you need to primarily focus on this particular state. For the time being, the State of Presence is the point from which you live and connect to the world. Later on, when the centre is more steady, you can relax this focus and let go more into Being. In this way, energy will get distributed throughout your body. The complete experience or the Natural State is not to be focussed anywhere in particular, for all centres of I Am function simultaneously. But the end result is very different than general presence in Tai Chi. Here, one has actually changed dimensions, abiding firmly in the place beyond the body and mind, in the Kingdom of the Self.

Now you are choosing the State of Presence as your main location. For the sake of training, you create a sort of artificial situation. As you become more integrated, the presence of your Me also reaches into Being and the Heart. At the moment, your Tai Chi is becoming rooted deeper into the reality of the Self. As you keep the State of Presence, don't fall into the habit of 'watching.' There is nothing to watch! Just maintain the form. Allow the State of Presence to remain present in a natural way, using a minimum of self-referral in keeping it. You do need to hold it, but rather relax into Being. Just maintain your form, remaining gently conscious of the centre of awareness. It is similar to the Sufi dance. The purpose of whirling is to recognise the one who is not whirling - that which is still inside, that which doesn't move. Therefore, stay with that one which is not doing Tai Chi, as you do Tai Chi.

It is easy to have the wrong concept of 'being One with action.' There are two ways of being One with action. The first is when you get lost in dance, for instance, and you are in a semi-trance state. This type of being One with action is purely subconscious. And the second way is the Buddha way, where the whole activity is contained in the clear space of awareness, rooted in a clear experience of Being. Here, movement and non-movement meet, merging into one.

There was a master who told his awakened disciple. 'I don't care what you do and I don't give you any moral rules of conduct, as long as you don't lose your state!' When you are One with I Am, the natural wisdom of the body and mind takes care of everything. The highest spontaneity is beyond consciousness and subconsciousness. The highest spontaneity is where one is just flowing but firmly rooted in the unconditional state. This I Am is not 'witnessing' but embracing the personality, bringing a new quality of transcendental presence.

Awareness Is Not the Ultimate

Student: *If the State of Presence can be constant, why does it feel like there is a very subtle fluctuation?*

Aziz: Because the State of Presence or the centre of awareness is experienced within your relative brain, within your relative third eye. Awareness on some level is affected by the play of the five elements and also the moon, stars, earth and sky. You experience the State of Presence within Creation and within your separate body. That's why, the State of Presence is not the Ultimate. It has a certain flavour of the Ultimate but at the same time, it is relative.

We can call the State of Presence a reflection of Universal Consciousness within the individual Soul and the individual psychosomatic reality. When the state is mature, it reaches a maximum harmony and minimum fluctuation. It reaches its optimum; when it reaches its optimum, it surrenders into Being where the experience is more unconditional for it gravitates towards the

Unmanifested. Being is the link between consciousness and the Source, the Absolute. That's why, the more you get absorbed in Being, the less fluctuation there is.

Ignorant Advises

Student: *I spoke about the State of Presence with two of my friends who are in an awakened state. They say that keeping the centre in the mind is incorrect and there is nothing to keep for there is only space. Could you comment on that?*

Aziz: Yes.... It is dangerous to receive advice from those who have a limited understanding about the awakening process and the nature of consciousness. Most seekers, who reach one of the awakened states, are not always entirely clear and conscious of the experience. Their descriptions are vague and not precise, based on slogans and simplistic concepts.

Certainly, when the State of Presence is established, its energy relaxes and loses its crystallised quality. The natural state is like a space of awareness; one is not keeping it, but abiding in this field of consciousness. However, even when the state is established, in certain situations it crystallises itself as a centre. It happens when we simply focus more in the mind or create the self-referral which is a natural function of the human consciousness.

You must understand that, at this stage you cannot abide freely in this space, for the State of Presence is not yet established. If you just relax, you lose your subjectivity, defusing your sense of identity into some semi-conscious states of the mind. The only way to establish pure awareness is to keep it at all times! Your friends are not helping you but they disturb your practice. But, on the other hand, it is all reflecting your own understanding. Your doubts come from the lack of clarity, as to what your are actually doing and what is the truth of awakening.

Surrender into Being

What does it mean to Be? To Be is to abide in the Beyond. The very ground of reality is the Absolute. In the Absolute the countless universes dwell. In him all living beings rest. In him the dance of Creation and Destruction takes place. Where are you? You are not located in the physical universe at all. You are not located on the earth. You abide upon the formless dimension of Being. Just relax, take a deep breath and tenderly let go into the mystery of the Now.

What is Enlightenment to Being?

Student: *You spoke about three types of Enlightenment: Awareness, Being and the Heart. What is Enlightenment to Being?*

Aziz: Enlightenment to Being is the realisation of the Absolute State which unites you with the Uncreated. The experience of Being, as such, we would not call Enlightenment but rather an experience of enlightened energy. The Absolute is the very ground, the bottomless foundation of Being. When you surrender in meditation, energy links itself on some level with the Absolute Energy. It is still experienced within the manifested, but there is even deeper a connection with the Unmanifested.

Student: *So the experience of Being is not Enlightenment?*

Aziz: The experience of Being has an enlightened quality. You see, 'Enlightenment' is just a word. When we speak about the realisation of the Absolute, we mean that there is a radical shift within the experience of Being. Here, absolute motionlessness or absence is realised. Prior to the realisation of the Absolute, there is a certain movement, fluctuation of energy. It is as if the energy of I Am cannot go beyond its own self-reference, as it is being locked into its individual energy system. It is similar to falling asleep. You are trying to lose yourself in the Sleep State but you are still on the side of the waking state. And at one moment, you move into the Sleep. A proper experience of Being is a link between your consciousness and the Uncreated Presence. When you rest in Being prior to the realisation of the Uncreated, the energy of the Absolute is already present - but the experience of it happens within This, the created Side of the Now.

Non-doing is Non-abiding

Student: *How can we bring Non-doing into daily life?*

Aziz: Non-doing is possible only if there is an expansion of energy within Being. Non-doing is not possible if one has not expanded. An ordinary person is unable not-to-do, for even if the body is not active the mind is working all the time, consciousness is moving and energy is fluctuating. There is a constant activity within the body and mind. When you are separated from the dimension of Being, you simply cannot not-do because you are suffocated with your own existence. You are unable to not-do within yourself. You can experience Non-doing, only within the higher Existence. You can not-do only within that which created you: the Universal Presence. In the case of an ordinary person, non-doing is possible only when one loses consciousness: in a comma or deep sleep state where one's Me is absent. When there is consciousness there is a constant doing. When there is no consciousness, there is non-doing but there is also nobody to experience it.

In our work, we are reaching Non-doing while being fully conscious. We are channelling consciousness into the realm of Beingness. It means that your intelligence and presence merge with Being - with the underlying reality of pure isness. The experience of stillness, the experience of rest can take place only in the dimension of Universal Beingness. And what is Beingness? It is the primordial energy which keeps this Existence in its hands. In meditation, letting go you may think that you are just experiencing tranquillity, but in truth, something deeper is taking place; you are expanding into the Beyond. You cannot experience it in the Here. The Here itself represents the movement of time. This dimension is a constant movement; it cannot rest for it is an endless process of becoming. There is no Non-doing Here. Non-doing can take place only in the Beyond when you expand into the primal energy of the Absolute Absence, which is the pure isness of God.

Student: *This is what I was wondering... Because this experience is* *happening only in the Now - can it be retained in life, assuming that I still want to participate in life, to work, earn money...?*

Aziz: It is an important subject. Normally we think in opposites. For example, we think that 'no-mind' is present when there is no thinking. Many meditators cannot grasp that thinking and not-thinking can co-exist! What is 'no-mind'? It is this very energy-presence which contains the mind. That's why, when you discover pure awareness, there is no need to eliminate thinking because this presence includes the mind. The kind of 'no-mind' which equals absence of thoughts is a relative no-mind; this is not the absolute No-mind. Such a no-mind is artificial and time-bound.

The real no-mind can be experienced exclusively within pure consciousness, or when it goes deeper, in the unity of consciousness and Beingness. In that level of expansion, pure awareness and the Absolute Rest meet and together give rise to a true or absolute No-mind. When Pure Rest is reached, it is rooted in the Beyond and it includes the multidimensional presence of Me. You have to understand that Non-doing does not mean that your particular Me is not doing. It does not mean that you are passive, that you are not thinking, that you are not moving your hand...and so forth. It is not this. Non-doing is a deeper dimension than you are, it includes you. So when you are in a state of non-doing, the doing becomes embraced. Doing is a part of your existence; therefore, you experience these two realities simultaneously.

Non-doing is invisible. It is a secret dimension. It is the Beyond, in truth. But doing is simply the Here; it is a dynamic of relative reality. They both co-exist, like the smoke of incense moving in an empty room. It does not disturb the stillness and the emptiness of the space: they both create the reality of What Is. That's why, Hui-Neng said that any concept of meditation which speaks about the elimination of thoughts is very dangerous and incorrect. This concept is called the 'heretical view' in Zen. Hui-Neng said that the real no-mind includes everything - mountains, rivers and oceans. Why should it not include also thinking? This vast space contains everything and is all-inclusive. This master used to say that 'the essence of the mind does not increase in Samadhi, nor does it decrease in agitation.' Not only is your mind included but also your difficulties, your desires and your longings. You as a human being cannot fully avoid negativity. Negativity is a part of this dimension, but through the inner expansion it is fully embraced.

The linear concept regarding Self-realisation is an assumption that it is being reached by the elimination of everything which is negative, the elimination of the mind, elimination, elimination, elimination... But the true understanding is that the Ultimate is attained through expansion and not through elimination. We don't need to eliminate ignorance. All we need to do is to add the dimension of Awakening, the presence of I Am.

Student: *Can you say then that non-doing includes doing?*

Aziz: That is what we have said, yes. Non-doing does not arise through the elimination of doing, but through expansion into the dimension which is Still. There is no becoming, no movement, no change in that dimension. It is a meeting of that exists in time with the timeless. Non-doing is timeless. It is the presence of the Timeless, the primal energy.

Hara: the Gate to the Beyond

Student: *How can we give depth to the Hara?*

Aziz: The most important element is: conscious surrender into Being. When you let go of the mind in meditation where does the energy go? It must go somewhere, does it not? It gravitates down towards the lower belly, where it gets anchored. Non-doing therefore deepens the Hara. In order to be in a state of non-doing, you must be present of course. The second element is breathing to the belly. You help this process a lot through slow breathing to the belly. That's why in Taoism and Zen, they emphases this type of breathing so much. Breathing and surrender are the two most important elements. We do not develop a 'strong' Hara but a deep Hara within which you can rest. If you only focus on the Hara, you develop a strong type of Hara similar to that of a martial artist, but you are unable to rest inside - for your Hara is too male.

Passage to the Absolute

Student: *You spoke about the inner black hole.*

Aziz: The term 'black hole' relates to a secret passage within the Hara. This passage transports the Soul to the Uncreated. You cannot see this passage for it is of Pure Absence, but when you enter - you change dimensions. Hara is the meeting place of uncreated energy and the created. Through this passage, you have entered Creation and now you return back home. You reverse the process - from being created, you go back to the Uncreated. The other side of the 'black hole' is the original Void. This Void is not an empty space, as some imagine, but Pure Absence. The only way to approach the Unborn is through surrender.

Student: *Is the Uncreated unconscious?*

Aziz: To say that the Absolute is unconscious is incorrect, for the Absolute exists beyond the polarities of consciousness and unconsciousness. The term unconsciousness simply does not apply here. The Unmanifested is below consciousness; it is a domain of Pure Isness which 'no one' is conscious of. For consciousness to manifest, time is needed. In the Timeless, no consciousness can be found. For any recognition or perception some distance between the perceiver and the perceived is absolutely required. This distance can be created only within the physical or psychological space-time dimension.

Realisation of the Absolute is quite fascinating, for it is a meeting of the time dimension with the Timeless. Here, paradoxically, consciousness is conscious of non-consciousness; consciousness becomes conscious of its own absence. That which is beyond recognition, becomes recognised. Consciousness meets face to face that which originally gave birth to its existence. Otherwise, if there is no consciousness, the Absolute alone reigns and no one can recognise it; it is like in deep dreamless sleep.

Watching is not Being

Student: *I was following your instructions in the meditation. I was watching the breath and then inhaling and exhaling slowly. Is this an experience of what you call 'Being'?*

Aziz: Neither of them is Being. The experience of Being has nothing to do with breathing. It is non-doing. Breathing is still doing. Breathing deeply is done for the sake of activating energy. Conscious breathing is also very useful for all those who don't recognise I Am. It focuses and activates attention. In this way one feels a certain amount of presence, rather than being lost in unconscious thinking. However, mainly we do it for an energy reason; to deepen energy, to open the energy system from its source in the Hara. When energy in the group is restless, we usually keep this breathing for a longer period. When energy is calmed down, we say 'let go of the breath and just Be.'

If you wish to follow your breath, the better term than 'watching' or 'witnessing' is 'being one with the breath.' Watching is not good because it separates you from Being. Being cannot be watched. You can watch ten thousand things, but you will be unable to watch Being. In Being you can only Be. The only proper relationship with Being is one of surrender.

Breathing is not Being but when you are one with breath, you are very close to Being. When you are one with the breath, the experience of Being is reached easier. But what is important here is the element of surrender. For example, when you exhale, when the breath goes out, you are supposed to surrender, drop into non-doing; let go with breath... like a dewdrop from a leaf falling on the earth. And in this moment you shift into Being, into non-doing. That is the essence of this meditation: to drop...

Breathing is just an add to activate attention and to deepen energy. Non-doing, dropping down, letting go, is the foundation. If you only breathe into the belly, your Hara becomes strong, like in the case of an martial artist, but you will not be in a state of surrender. A person with a strong Hara has power and strength but this power does not serve expansion towards the dimension of Rest; such a person can use this power to attack someone for example. A strong Hara without surrender serves the ego. In our teaching, we don't speak about a strong Hara but about a deep Hara. For that reason, as we are breathing, we are always combining it with feminine energies of surrender.

In the beginning, as one is breathing, attention becomes attached to the breath. Yes? There is a certain element of will. Later on, as one simply relaxes becoming more absorbed, the act of breathing gets contained in the space of Being. It is as if a new body was given to you: the body of Being. When you are established in the body of Being, breathing no longer distracts you from the experience of Pure Rest. You are breathing, but you are actually below the breath - you exist below breath. You experience breath as a phenomenon happening in You, while you as the Soul rest in another dimension of pure stillness.

The technique of slow breathing is done for the sake of

activating energy. You can watch your breath from the centre in your head but in this way you are still divided. When Àwareness surrenders into Being, you feel as if the breath was inside you, inside your Beingness. They are different experiences. Do you understand? The experience of Being is deeper than awareness because it has more an element of non-doing. This experience is much more restful than awareness and energetically it encompasses you wholly.

However, pure awareness is also deeper than watching. Watching is from the mind only. When awareness abides in its own light, it becomes all-inclusive. It is all-inclusive because it is not directed anywhere. Awareness without intelligence has no direction - it simply is. But awareness cannot be absolutely all-inclusive, for the very simply reason that it does not possess the quality of complete motionlessness. Awareness cannot be extracted from Beingness, for it abides in the Absolute. Therefore, only when awareness lets go into Being, through Being and within Being can it become all-inclusive.

The experience of Being is very much connected to breathing. For example, when you breathe in energy goes up, when you breathe out energy goes down. If you contemplate the gap between the in-breath and the out-breath, then you will already see what it means to Be. Try to Be through rest, try to stay in this energy of pure rest while breathing. Do not allow this energy to rise too much up with inhalation. That is called surrender. When we say that the 'body of Being' becomes separated from the 'body of breathing,' it means that you are resting below the breath. The breath does not take energy up anymore. Everything is resting.

The Absolute State

Student: *Can you speak about the Absolute State?*

Aziz: The Absolute State, which is the second level of Enlightenment, is realised within the Being aspect of I Am. When you rest in Being, there is a movement of gravitation towards the source of Beingness, which is the Absolute. What is the Absolute? The Absolute is the source of all, the very primal energy from which Existence arises. It is uncreated energy and as such there is no consciousness in the Absolute. It is pure energy of rest.

When you are non-doing, when you let go, energy gravitates towards the Absolute... and the esoteric gateway to the Absolute is the Hara. It is an energetic gateway. Before being in the Absolute State, even if you experience Being, energy cannot fully rest; it needs to fluctuate. Therefore, as you sit, energy goes sometimes lower into Being, and sometimes just higher - there is a certain movement. You are resting but this rest is not a hundred percent. The reason is that you experience Being still within the manifested dimension. The experience of Being for a person, who has not realised the Absolute, is more on the side of Creation than on the side of the Uncreated.

When the shift to the Absolute takes place, it is like a door opens within your Hara and you move to the Other Side - suddenly you are Beyond. At that moment, you are beyond movement, beyond relative energy; there is no movement. Here, the state is perfectly motionless. The key towards a shift to the Absolute State is surrender, surrender, surrender and surrender.

The Absolute State is the destiny of very few Souls and in truth, it is a desire of very few Souls. It is a very extreme state. It is like to die. That's why it is not a wish for most Souls. That which most Souls would translate as happiness is the overall experience and realisation of I Am. For them the most important is to awaken awareness, to have a certain rootedness in Being and, finally, to open the Heart.

You see, a person who is not able to abide in Being can experience the Heart only in an emotional way. But to truly enter the Heart, is to become absorbed into the space within the Heart. What does it mean to Be? It means that you are not doing anything, you drop. You are not here and what remains is Being. When the energies of the Heart and Being are balanced, you experience a unity of sensitivity and non-doing. Your are sensitive by virtue of being a Soul and at the same time, you are in a state of surrender. However, sometimes in order to reach the Absolute, the Heart has to close for some time so the energy can be completely pulled into the Unmanifested. In this evolution, there are different seasons.

Student: *Is the Absolute, Nirguna, without attributes?*

Aziz: No, it does have one attribute: It Is. Isness it the only attribute of the Source.

To Let Go into Being

Student: *How can I relax within Being? Is it by watching it? How can I relax within the State of Presence?*

Aziz: You have this tendency and conditioning of 'watching.' Being cannot be watched. The moment you watch Being, it is no longer Being because it becomes an object. Do you understand? You can watch your breath, as something outside of you, but you cannot Be and at the same time watch it. How can you watch breathing? You can watch it from the mind but the problem is that what you are watching is itself a part of your very Me! Can you see the paradox? That's why, from the higher perspective watching is a false idea. Watching means that part of your Me is observing another part of your Me. You may have an idea, for instance, that you are not the mind, so you are observing it in a pseudo-objective way; but you see, the mind is also you...

Watching is a step in the growth of consciousness where intelligence gradually connects to the space of awareness. But at one stage it must be dropped for if you become addicted to watching, you are in a serious trouble. The State of Presence is not watching - it is simply present. The State of Presence doesn't say 'oh, I am not the mind, I am a witness.' The State of Presence doesn't create a split inside of your mind. It is the mind which interprets the State of Presence in a certain way. It is the mind which says 'I am not the mind'! Do you see the paradox? For that reason any manipulations with the mind must be transcended, so the natural state can be reached. Watching can be quite dangerous because it locks you in the mind and separates you from the space of Beingness. Being is a subject, not an object. When you watch it, it becomes objectified, but when it becomes the object - it is no longer Being. For that reason, we speak about being one with the breath and letting go into the space of Beingness.

And now we will speak about awareness. You cannot really relax with awareness in a conscious way, unless the centre of attention is awakened. If you relax without having a clear centre, you relax into an unconscious or subconscious state. One relaxes into subconsciousness instead of consciousness. But when the centre is awakened, when you relax, there is certain strength and solidity of the experience - it is grounded in reality. The more the centre is awakened, the less you need to remember it.

When pure awareness is fully present, there is no need to keep it so crystallised at your centre; you relax with it, allowing it to be in its natural condition. It is a state where you are non-doing, effortlessly resting in the light of object-less awareness. You abide in this clear, vast, infinite space of pure consciousness - you become it. And here you realise Oneness, for you experience that the space of awareness actually contains all. For example, you have a conversation with someone and suddenly, you notice that this awareness in which you dwell contains everything: you, the person you talk to, the whole conversation...everything. That's why, we don't use the term 'witnessing,' but the term 'State of Presence;' because the term 'witnessing' implies duality. When you are 'witnessing' yourself speaking to another person, you feel yourself somewhere in the background, behind. But when you are in the State of Presence, all is embraced, contained in the light of awareness. In this way you are embracing and not witnessing - that is the difference. Embracing is higher than witnessing. Witnessing is a relative state; it is not all-inclusive. That's why the term 'State of Presence' is more precise than 'witnessing.'

There are three types of Oneness you can experience. First, is Oneness realised through awareness, where you feel that all is included in the space of consciousness which is vast, infinite, bright, luminous and all-pervasive. Second, is the experience of Oneness realised through Being. Being is deeper than awareness, for it is more rooted in the Uncreated. When you experience Oneness within awareness, it is a realisation taking place in Creation. This is because awareness is the essence of Creation. When you experience Oneness within Being, particularly when the Absolute State is reached, everything is contained in the experience of unity. But, this time, from the depth of the Now, which is the uncreated isness of the Absolute. This experience is much deeper than pure consciousness. And what it means, in truth, is that your particular Me is rooted deeper in reality, beyond awareness. The third experience of Oneness is when the Heart is added, when the dimension of Love is included. We are not speaking about emotion... it is not that you feel a connection from your Heart with Creation. The moment you feel connection, in truth, it is already separation. When the Heart is awakened, it merges with Being and embraces the whole reality in the sacred space of I AM. This space is made of pure isness and pure sensitivity, which is the very presence of the Divine.

The last and final realisation of Oneness is Enlightenment to Me. So far the unity has been realised, but the experiencer of this unity has still been overlooked. Who knows Unity? The mistake which many Traditions have made, was an assumption that Oneness is attained through the annihilation of Me. In the absence of Me, not only does separation not exist, but nor does Oneness. In the traditional concept of Oneness, Me merges with the Universal I AM and negates herself. However, even when Me negates her own existence she is still present, for she has no way to cancel herself out! For that reason, much higher than the negation of Me is the realisation of Me, that is, Soul-realisation. When Me is realised, the Transparent Me is manifested. Realisation of the Transparent Me is the final experience of Oneness. Before awakening to Me, the experience of unity is not complete, for the very simple reason that the experiencer of Oneness is overlooked - for the very subject is not realised. In the past, they made one more incorrect assumption that the seer is the Self. It is the Soul which is the seer, for she is an angle of perception from which Totality recognises itself. In the ultimate experience, not only is the Universal Presence realised but the mysterious perceiver of it as well, which is Me. That we call apperception. Is it clear for you?

Student: *You have described it very well!*

Aziz: You see, this teaching is simply describing You. This teaching de-conditions you from spiritual clichés, allowing you to become free from the false, so you can see with your clear eyes the reality of awakening. We are mirroring the evolution of your Soul and the ultimate vision of your completion. The validity of this teaching you can verify with your own experience and intelligence.

Presence within Absence

Student: *What is the relationship between presence and absence.*

Aziz: The ultimate understanding of absence is pure isness, the original energy which exists prior to consciousness. Before consciousness manifested itself, there was already 'something.' We call it the absence of consciousness or the absence of recognition. Absence does not mean that it is 'nothing.' Nothing does not exist. That something exists or not relates to the relative absence or presence of different appearances. But when we speak about THAT which exists prior to any type of manifestation, we are approaching an area which cannot be grasped by the logic of: 'is or is not.' The original 'nothing' is an absence of objective reality and a presence of pure subjectivity which is the uncreated energy.

The ultimate understanding of presence is the complete experience of Creation perceived within pure awareness. This complete experience can be recognised fully only within the absence of experience which is the Absolute. Presence and absence represent two sides of the same phenomenon, that phenomenon-noumenon is Reality. The ultimate absence is the void containing the totality of Creation and the ultimate presence is the holistic experience of what is manifested as consciousness. And the Ultimate Experience is the unity of these two. The Absolute Presence rests within the Absolute Absence. But what is that which links the absence and the presence? It is the one to whom absence and presence apply, to whom the Creation applies: Me.

How to Discover Being?

Student: *The body and mind are in constant movement. How can one discover Being which is not moving?*

Aziz: One simply discovers this which does not move!

Recognition of the Unborn

Student: *The Absolute, the Unborn, is unchanging. But does the perceiver (someone stabilised in the Absolute State) experience a different level of depth? Does it relate to whether this person is consciously dropping into the state or is only dwelling in it energetically, while the mind is lost in spontaneous thinking?*

Aziz: It is an important question. One who is established in the Absolute State experiences it at all times on the energy level. This energy experience can, however, have various depths depending on the type of Soul and which centres are predominant. The highest experience of the Absolute we call the Diamond Mountain, for it embodies the qualities of extraordinary strength, clarity and depth.

The next, additional depth to the experience of the Absolute is added due to a certain emotional and psychological surrender. One can abide in the Absolute in a neutral way, translating this experience as 'calmness' or one can truly surrender to being in love with the Ultimate. And we should not forget that when the Heart is added, the quality of the Absolute State changes radically, for it is being enriched by the flavour of Divinity and sensitivity.

When you are absorbed in thinking, your Me is not resting consciously in the Absolute. One is resting only energetically. One cannot rest psychologically all the time in the Absolute, for it is not natural. When the mind explores other areas of reality, attention is no longer focussed in the Absolute. There are, in truth, three possibilities. One is when you exclusively rest in the Absolute - your mind and Heart having fully surrendered. The second case is when you are absorbed in thinking not paying attention to the Absolute. Here you are not merely lost in thinking like an unaware person. You can never be lost anymore, for you are one with Reality... And the third possibility is when attention is divided, part of attention consciously rests in the Absolute and another part freely participates in the outer or psychological dimension. When you are absorbed in thinking or outer perceptions, some amount of depth is taken away from the experience of the Absolute. And that is fine, as long as you maintain an interest to participate in Creation. But even though you maybe adventuring in the outer, all your activities are unconditionally embraced by the vast infinite isness, the void and silence of the Absolute.

How to Stabilise the Absolute State?

Student: *Can you speak about the process of stabilising the Absolute State?*

Aziz: There are three stages in stabilisation and integration. When there is a shift to the Absolute State, one for the first time has experienced the Absolute. The energy has moved to the Other Side of the Here becoming united with the Unmanifested. But this experience may not be constant because the moment one is distracted the energy moves up and one loses this connection with the Absolute. On the energy level, one cannot rest in the Absolute all the time, because the energy is not refined yet. That is why, after this shift, one has to keep repeating through absorption this act of letting go into the Absolute. The outcome of these efforts is that, at one stage, when the energy is mature enough, the experience becomes stabilised and energy fully settles in the Absolute. Here, energy continuously points towards the Absolute, it is no longer distracted. Stabilisation is a function of time but is helped through one's own conscious surrender. One has to meditate; one has to intentionally rest in the Absolute all the time; one has to let go constantly. Absorption is the most important element here, because long meditations deepen the quality of Being. Staying in nature is very helpful; the energy of nature is very supportive. There was hardly ever a master who shifted to the Absolute in the city; it was always in nature. Nature itself is in the Absolute State without recognition. This means that nature is one with Universal Being, but not knowing it. After the shift and stabilisation, the third stage completing the process, is integration where the Absolute State becomes aligned with the wole energy system.

To be Present in Absence

Student: *What does it mean to be absent?*

Aziz: It is to die. But be patient, you've got still some time left (laughter)... To be absent means that an individual rests beyond oneself, that something bigger takes over. The Absolute Absence is the original state, which is prior to manifestation. You can see it as the Primordial Void. It neither Is, nor it Is Not, a mysterious realm. It cannot be grasped as being 'something' for it is not manifested; it cannot be called merely 'nothing,' for it is the source of the whole Existence. It is the Absolute Absence, which is at the same time, the Absolute Presence.

Existing as an individual, you live within your separate sense of identity, within your relatively separate mind, body and energy system. You live in the cage of your individual existence. Out of this cage, you try to reach Existence. Firstly, you are looking for a connection to the outside. You try to reach unity with the outer through affection, co-operation, learning, exchanging information and so on, but this does not work. You cannot be one with the outer, for the very simple reason that you cannot be absent in the outer. The outer cannot receive your presence. You can lose yourself in an unconscious way in the outer, but it is not real absence. Why are you unable to be absent in the outer? Because the outer is itself present without being absent, which means that it is itself a result of something deeper than itself. In order to transcend yourself, you must go inside. You have to reach the source of your existence, regain your inherent connection with the Origin. That is the principle.

So firstly, you must become fully present as an individual, because an ignorant person is not really present - there is no nobody inside. An ignorant person experiences a subconscious, fragmented presence. In order to become really present, the centre of awareness must be awakened. This is because it is not you as the mind, who becomes present but awareness crystallises itself as pure 'I.' The moment you are fully present, you can for the first time, let go into the Universal Absence which is your origin. You cannot let go before that. When you exist as a subconscious reality, letting go would make you even more unconscious. But when your Soul's identity is crystallised, the moment you let go, a merging starts to take place and you become absorbed in a conscious way into the ultimate reality.

Your presence is the meeting between the horizontal reality of the Here, and the vertical reality of the Now. This presence is neither in the world nor out of the world. You are in-between these two dimensions. In order to reach the dimension out of the world, the depth of the Now, you need to surrender from the place of presence into Beingness. The moment you let go as the clear presence, your energy like an anchor gravitates down, towards the source of gravity. The source of gravity represents the original absence. This original absence is itself the centre of gravity of all universes.

As you gravitate towards this original absence, as you let go of yourself, something else takes over. Here, you do not need any more to sustain your existence as an individual - the Beyond sustains your presence. The Beyond contains you. It is like falling asleep. To fall asleep, something else must take over within which you become absent, you as the conscious mind. What is the Sleep State? It is a dimension beyond the conscious mind. But in the case of spiritual expansion, when you dissolve, you still remain conscious. That is, you are present in a certain way. That's why, this expansion is a meeting point between the Universal Absence and the individual presence; it is beyond the Absence and beyond the presence. That's why, one can know that one has transcended, that one is contained within the Universal. From this knowing, the depth of recognition is born and the very appreciation of this experience. And who does appreciate it? It is the One beyond the Uncreated and beyond the Creation. This mysterious subject to all, your own Soul, the dimension of Me. The experiencer of the Beloved and her Creation.

Student: *How does one know that one is absent?*

Aziz: One knows through the absence of one's presence. Here, one is not simply gone, but one experiences the purity of the inner rest. The dimension of Pure Rest represents the most subtle frequency of energy, which is not bound by the movement of relativity; it is beyond five elements. It is freedom from the Here, but freedom, which is nevertheless experienced Here! It is the meeting between the presence and the absence. The Absence has no way to know that it is absent and the Presence is locked in its presence. The meeting of these two creates a new quality, the birth of a new dimension. It is the recognition of the absence which becomes present to itself. This is the secret of the Absolute State which no one can grasp. Here, even though you are beyond consciousness - you know it! How is it possible? How can knowing be present beyond knowing? That cannot be explained. The words cannot go any further. They brought us as far as they could. The rest is beyond words. If you wish to understand that which is beyond words, you must enter this dimension.

Pure Rest

Student: *When I experience the state of pure rest, I feel like I am expanding. What does it mean?*

Aziz: Your experience is not the Pure Rest yet. Pure Rest is beyond expanding and not-expanding. The feeling of expansion is a natural energy phenomenon. When you drop into Being, energy expands vertically and horizontally. It is difficult to understand it. That's why, Dogen said that Zazen cannot be understood. As you let go, energy naturally drops towards your Hara. This expansion moves towards the Uncreated and towards Creation. The experience when your aura enlarges and spreads to the limitless is a more horizontal type of expansion. Through this expansion, you feel yourself as being a part of the Creation, one with Existence. But when the energy of Being gravitates more towards the Uncreated, the experience starts to have more a subtle quality. It is as if you were moving beyond Creation, beyond the horizontal dimension. Here, the energy is more and more rooted and motionless; you are unable to locate it in space and time anymore.

When you sit, contemplate more the meaning of Shikantaza, just sitting - it is the highest or the only meditation. Why is this so? Because in Shikantaza, one is as absent as one can be within the Universal Presence. Just sitting - it is a very profound state. It means only 'just sitting' is present, and you have surrendered. In Shikantaza, the checker the one who observes is absent. The one who experiences both the horizontal and vertical expansion is absent. The one, who wants to repeat the experience or verify one's attainment, has submitted oneself to the depth of the Now. When you care no more, the Shikantaza begins. But you do have to care not to care! The moment you experience your expansion, let yourself not care. Let yourself be absent within this experience. In this way, you will move Beyond to the place of complete stillness, that which Just Is. It will be as if you have died. Here, you have removed yourself, having got fully out of the way.

Student: *Is it only experienced in sitting?*

Aziz: Shikantaza is beyond sitting, standing, walking or laying down. Zazen is not a sitting position but reality itself! Through your sitting practice, you are awakening Shikantaza, you are awakening that which is beyond sitting. This type of training is necessary. As you go on, you will see how Shikantaza, gradually embraces your life and becomes unexpectedly your only reality.

The next issue: The dualistic concept of Shikantaza assumes that only when you are absent, the real state is present. That is true at the beginning, for you need to cancel yourself as much as possible, you need to get absorbed. When the Real State is awakened, you will see that you and that state co-exist as one harmonious whole. Here, your active presence, as the psyche, as the mind and that which contains you - co-exist. That is the meaning of non-dualistic Shikantaza because it is beyond the polarities of your relative presence or absence.

Hara is the Centre of No-centre

Student: *Why isn't Hara felt as a centre?*

Aziz: A good question. We feel the State of Presence in a certain area of our body; similarly, the Heart is felt in another area. Why don't we feel the Hara? The reason is that the Hara is a centre of energy but not the centre of Me! The State of Presence and the Heart constitute the reality of Me, while the Hara is the gateway beyond Me.

In the Heart and awareness, we meet our presence and in the Hara we meet our absence. We feel even hesitant to use the term 'centre' in the case of Being. Being is not the centre but the no-centre. It has the quality of rootedness, groundedness, solidity of energy, expansiveness, depth and peacefulness, but has no centre as such. It is as one mystic defined God - the circle who has the centre everywhere and circumference nowhere. This centre is the Now and it expands infinitely into the Totality of Creation without limit. And in each point of its expansion it exists from the heart of the Now. When awareness and Heart melt into Being, they also lose their centralised quality. They open up, dissolving into the Universal Presence. Like smoke lifting from an incense stick and dissolving into the open space of the temple, leaving only transparency and fragrance.

Being and the Vital-force

Student: *Can you speak mere about the vital-force or life-force? It seems that the vital-force can contradict our surrender into Being.*

Aziz: Yes... when the Soul enters manifestation, it rides on the vital-force. The vital-force is everything. The Creation is one with the life-force. The vital-force or life-force is the very dynamics of energy, which recreates from moment to moment the state of the Universe. The Soul, in the beginning, is fully identified with the life-force, becoming its agent and integral part. We can see the Soul as a personal channel of the impersonal movement of the life-force.

However, at a certain stage in the Soul's evolution, she is able to move mysteriously beyond this life-force. The paradox is that the Soul uses the life-force in order to go beyond it! In truth, it is the life-force, which goes beyond itself through the vehicle of the Soul. The Soul can go beyond the life-force only when she awakens the desire to return to the state of unity with the Source of Creation which is the unmanifested energy. Within the Soul's blueprint, there is a possibility of going beyond the Created energy.

What is the source of the life-force? It is Beingness, the Absolute. The life-force arises from Beingness and is contained in Beingness. Similarly, as a tree grows up from the earth, so the life-force rises up from the dimension of Beingness. The Soul herself is neither the life-force nor the Beingness. She is the experiencer of both, of the Created and the Uncreated. When the Soul wishes to regain her connection with the Absolute, she surrenders. This surrender is not emotional but energetic in its essence. To surrender into the Unmanifested the Soul has to go, on some level, against the primal tendency of the life-force to move outwardly. The life-force is unable to rest. Restfulness is against the basic characteristic of the life-force. From the viewpoint of the life-force, not-to-do is death! But from the viewpoint of the Soul, not-to-do is the unity with the Source of Creation.

The only way for the Soul to transcend the inherent fluctuation of the life-force is by dropping into Non-doing. Non-doing is the key to move beyond the doings of the life-force. To let go of the life-force does not mean to negate it but to shift the sense of identity beyond the manifested energy. In this way, even though you still live in Creation, part of you rests beneath the movement of the life-force.

The totality of life, the whole of Creation is founded upon the Absolute. The Absolute is the universal centre of gravity. Even the life-force is bound by this gravity, so it cannot disconnect too much from the Source. On some level, the force of life and the force of gravity are pulling in opposite directions. But there is a very precise equilibrium between these two forces - to move outwardly into Creation and to rest in the Uncreated. The Soul, which is the reality of Me bridges these two forces through herself. When the Soul surrenders into non-doing, immediately the Unborn pulls her down by the force of gravity and she transcends the force of life. So, non-doing is not merely passivity, as some imagine, but surrender to the force of gravity! That is a very important point. The absolute non-doing is reached when Me becomes one with the Source of Gravity. When one is in the Absolute State, one cannot gravitate further anymore. Here, one has ended; one has reached one's own absence. The Absolute is fathomless, but you cannot travel within it, for the One who enters this dimension disappears!

In this ocean of Pure Isness there is no place for two. But if there is no place for two, how can we experience the Absolute at all? Because the experiencer of it lives above the surface of the earth of Beingness. The meeting point of the tree with the earth, is the experience of Beingness. That which we call the condition of Pure Rest is the most sublime experience of all; it takes place at the point where our presence turns into the Universal Absence. Just to be, remaining energetically passive in spite of the force of life is the only way to connect with the source of gravity, which is the Uncreated Reality.

Student: *There is also some contrast between the State of Presence and Being...*

Aziz: The State of Presence represents your presence and Being your absence. First you need to awaken your Real Me and next you surrender into the Beyond, which is the source of 'I.'

Student: *What happens to the State of Presence in the Absolute State?*

Aziz: The State of Presence is present in the Absolute State.

To be Grounded is to BE

Student: *Often we hear about being centred and grounded. But these terms are used in a very vague and unclear way. Your teaching seems to bring clarity into this area.*

Aziz: Usually for most, to be centred means to have some kind of presence, which is sort of vaguely diluted in the environment. And to be grounded usually means to have some kind of connection to the body. But the true meaning of being centred is to be in the State of Presence; while groundedness refers to your rootedness in Being. That is the proper or the true understanding of these terms.

You see, most people project their shallow experience and understanding into the spiritual terms. That's why, words are not absolute. The challenge of the spiritual teacher is to transmit the real meaning behind widely used and often misinterpreted spiritual concepts. For that reason, we keep on clarifying all these important concepts...

Student: *If Beingness is endless, does that also mean that grounding is endless?*

Aziz: There are levels of being grounded in Beingness but the Absolute State represents the furthest point you can reach in being grounded. Beingness is fathomless and endless but when the Absolute is reached - you end! You simply cannot be more absent than - to Be Not. You can be grounded only in your absence which is the Beyond or Universal Presence. The optimum absence that you can reach, while remaining conscious, represents the deepest possible rootedness in the Ultimate. To be grounded is to be in Samadhi. There are different levels of Samadhi, that is, different levels of being grounded. The highest Samadhi is called Sahaja Nirvikalpa Samadhi - the natural, unconditional absorption in Reality. This type of Samadhi is not a trance state, but a natural state which is present irrespective of what you do. Here, you reach the optimum of being grounded for you become one with the Ground of Existence.

Evolution into Being

Student: *When I am in the state of pure Being, sometimes I feel that this experience is very strong and sometimes not so strong. What is it that moves one away from this experience?*

Aziz: Simply that your I Am is not rooted yet in the Beyond for it is still in a process of deepening and integrating. This which does not allow you to experience the depth of I Am all the time is a certain lack of integration on the energy level. It is all on the energy level and reflects the maturation of your Being quality. That's why, by repeated meditation, breathing and letting go, you deepen the experience of inner rest. It is not only that you experience during meditation the inner rest - as you abide in this state, you also deepen it as well. Later, it enters your life more, you find that there is no difference between sitting and not-sitting meditation. The state of I Am gradually embraces your life even though it is not a function of your will. It just takes place.

We spoke about Being and Awareness. In activity, generally awareness or the State of Presence is experienced more strongly.

In meditation or when you are not doing anything, Being is experienced more strongly. So, there is a certain movement within I Am. It does not always behave in the same way. In activity, awareness is stronger. In meditation, Being is experienced more strongly. You simply observe how I Am behaves. You need to distinguish whether I Am behaves in a certain way either because your energy is not deep enough, not sufficiently integrated or whether it is a natural way for I Am to behave.

When you are sitting in Samadhi, there is a strong experience of Being. When your are active, naturally the energy moves out and the energy becomes concentrated in awareness, focussed in your third eye and the gravitational force towards the Hara becomes less. These are the natural ways for your energy to behave within I Am. Observe it carefully and this will bring more clarity.

How Not-to-do in Doing

Student: *In meditation sometimes I reach the state of non-doing but how to bring non-doing into activity?*

Aziz: The question is: 'Who is not doing?' Since you speak about the non-doing of Me, your question is dualistic. It is not about whether your Me can do less or not do anything (laughter...). When we speak about non-doing, we refer to the unconditional non-doing which is beyond the polarities of doing and not doing. It is not Me which is not doing but non-doing is the presence of Being. This means that you are contained in the space of non-doing. Therefore, it is not that you are not doing but that you are absorbed in the unconditional space of non-doing. When this space of Beingness is awakened and fully present, it is motionless. It is irrespective of what type of activity you are immersed in.

Another question is how this Me can rest more in non-doing while living. How to live and not be caught up in activities, problems, difficulties? How can this Me optimally live in the surrender of Being? Firstly, there is an expansion into non-doing, which is Being. Afterwards, Me not only is contained in non-doing but the Me also surrenders into this non-doing. Here, Me lets go more into this dimension. This happens particularly when one leaves youth behind and becomes more mature. When one has gathered all experiences of life and becomes completed emotionally, one drops the desire to do anything. At this stage one surrenders fully into the state of Pure Being.

So, first there is the unconditional non-doing which is present beyond Me. Next, there is the relative non-doing which is the non-doing of Me. This relative non-doing cannot ever be absolute because Me in order to live, has to do certain things. But even within this doing, Me can reach the optimum of a certain psychological relaxation where she is no longer anxious about her doings. She is doing but at the same time she is resting consciously in Being. It is not only that Being is present but also Me is in the state of Surrender.

Student: *Can Shikantaza be experienced while doing something in a very minimal way?*

Aziz: Certainly. That is the purpose of meditation in action - to bring Shikantaza into activity. In the beginning, when one is not integrated, one connects with non-doing in a quiet space while walking for instance, or sitting at a table eating, reading, and so on. Non-doing is also connected to the State of Presence. The State of Presence is 'non-doing' in the sense of it being a kind of witnessing. Witnessing means that self-awareness is passively present in the background of activity. Being is deeper than witnessing; it represents a more profound level of non-doing. However, witnessing can be easily brought into activity by remembrance. Being is more subtle to bring into activity because the experience of it cannot always be activated by will. But when the energy of Being is mature, it simply enters into life spontaneously more and more as if from the back door without effort.

Student: *How can I co-operate?*

Aziz: By being relaxed, by being more and more in a state of Surrender. As you let go, you discover that a part of you is constantly resting. To Be is to be alive. To lose this extraordinary connection of the Soul with the open space of Being is to lose the precious chance to experience the sacred. For that reason, if you have respect for this sacredness, you try to arrange your life in a way that you do not have to be caught in mundane affairs too much. There is always a certain level of compromise but do not cross the limits of it. From the other side, do not be overly attached to passivity. Life is a challenge where the sacred space of Pure Being must encounter the creativity of becoming in time.

Student: *So, if one is forced to work, it is better to choose a job that allows us to respect the Soul?*

Aziz: Yes, in Buddhism it is called right livelihood, only in Buddhism this has a moral connotation. But here we speak about right livelihood in a sense of not selling your Soul for the sake of survival. Existence in a mysterious way always helps a Soul who is connected with the Light of Creation. Grace is the response of the Higher Intelligence to the readiness of the Soul for transformation and her sincere search for the Light. When the Soul is connected with the Divine, she receives support which means that gradually also the outer elements become rearranged. That is the magic of life. The moment you choose to surrender, you find yourself more in the right environments and right circumstances. That's why we said that there is not only one objective universe but also different universes, different dimensions of the earth. Each of these versions of this earth reflects the level of your Soul and your deepest longings.

Enlightenment of the Heart

To enter the Heart is to cross over to the Divine Dimension. First, you may realise your personal pain, for you have been hurt so many times... let it be. Next, you meet the child-like purity of your Soul...allow yourself to become One. Afterwards, as you move deeper, you disappear into the Other Side of the Heart. In this place you face the final depth of Reality, the mother of hearts, the Beloved. To experience this tremendous beauty, this infinite love and fulfillment beyond imagination, is the ultimate purpose of being a human.

Allow Yourself to Need Love

Student: *Is it right to need love? Or should we be completely free, nourishing our Heart only from inside?*

Aziz: Both are true. The reality of the Soul is paradoxical. She lives in both the inner and outer dimension. The inner and the outer are one and also different. The outer is the timely expression of the Timeless. When the Soul desires her emotional fulfilment only from the outer, she becomes too dependent. The main source of the Soul's fulfilment is from the Divine. When we say that love is inside, we point to the sacred space within the Heart. There, the Soul reaches the source of love and nourishment.

But the Soul also lives in the outer. This which participates mainly in the outer is the emotional body. The emotional body like the physical body needs nourishment and support. That's why, when you are alone for a long time you become hungry for affection. In these moments you look for a lover, friend or companion. This is natural. What you want to reach is a certain balance between your nourishment from within and from without. There is always some kind of dependency as long as you are a separate being and so you will always desire the company of others. But you are also autonomous in your essence supported by the unconditional light of the Divine and so you will also be fulfilled in your moments of solitude.

As you grow older, your emotional body relaxes and becomes pacified. This also relates to your physiology and the evolution of hormones. Do not deny the human in you and your emotional needs. It is not that you have needs because you are not enlightened. An enlightened being also has needs and desires affection. One cannot escape from human nature. But as you relax within and experience unconditional peace and bliss, like a waterfall flowing out from your Heart, you simply become more self-contained. Do not try to be a superman, a hero beyond any needs. Be simple and natural; be honest to your human sensitivity. Respect your needs as you respect your autonomy, which is the light of I AM.

Bliss: Happiness of Energy

Student: *Does bliss arise from the Heart only or from the unity of Being and Heart?*

Aziz: Bliss or ananda is from the Heart but Being itself also has its own blissful qualities. Being is more peaceful but this peacefulness can be translated as bliss when the emotional body is involved. Still however, bliss is more from the Heart, for the particular energy frequency of the Heart is more sweet, more touching and directly affects the emotional body. You see, to feel happy, the emotional body has to be involved. What is bliss? Bliss is the happiness of energy. Happiness as such is more psychological while bliss is energetic. When Being and the Heart are one, peace and bliss are one; it is one field of experience.

Student: *Is it possible for a person to be addicted to bliss and the beauty of the Heart, such that more neutral experiences are no longer appreciated?*

Aziz: Warnings against this type of addiction can be found in many different teachings. The state to be aimed at is the Natural State. The natural state we may call the natural bliss, bliss which is at the edge of being neutral, which is calm and deeply tranquil. In such a state, you do not know that you are in bliss. When we speak about delight or bliss, there is a split between subject and object; there is someone who refers to the experience, who takes a delight in the experience. Someone says inside 'oh, how wonderful, how happy I am, how blissful, it is almost too much!' (Laughter...). In such a case, we recommend taking a break from meditation and going for a walk (laughter...).

There is nothing wrong with feeling bliss and feeling happy about having a wonderful experience. It is natural, in truth. But it is simply not a fundamental experience for it cannot last continuously as the natural state does. The natural state is the natural bliss, a unity of the Heart and Being, self-contained and all-pervading beyond the observer. The observer may re-appear (as it does), but without disturbing the natural state, without interfering to What Is.

To be addicted to the feeling of bliss makes one crave for it when it is not present for one is attached to it. But it is the non-doing, which has an element of non-caring, which is the foundation. The non-doing teaches the Truth, for in non-doing you are absent while Reality is present. Sometimes you co-create with your experience but the emphasis has to be centred in non-doing.

The Heart is Deeper than Emotion

Student: *Is it possible to feel the Heart only on an energy level? I feel the sweetness of the Heart but without experiencing any emotions?*

Aziz: Of course. The Heart in her depth is the dimension of Being as well. The ultimate experience is unity of pure isness and sensitivity. The depth of the Heart is beyond the personal layers of the Soul.

Universal Love, Human Love...

Student: *Can we love all people?*

Aziz: The Soul can only love those Souls with which she has a connection. Love, in terms of emotional affection, is selective and possesses a limited amount of energy. Be honest. When you love, love; when you don't love, simply don't love. Don't try to force yourself to love, for love cannot be forced and certainly loving everyone is against nature. This understanding will simplify your life.

Universal love is not personal, it is impersonal. It is not that a particular Me feels affection for everybody. Universal love is a state of the Heart which is beyond any subject-object relationship. To say that one loves everybody is meaningless. How can you love everyone if you don't even know everyone? Unfortunately, here we have again a case of spiritual conditioning, which reflects some imbalance in the perception of reality and naïve emotionalism.

Love has a wisdom that discriminates. In order for love to be present, there has to be the right flow of energy between the lover and the beloved. If a person who you love hurts you or simply dislikes you, your Soul withdraws and the Heart closes. If you love a person who hates you, it indicates that you are simply unconscious, living in the realm of the mind's projections. In most cases, what people call love is a projection, arising from a desperate need to give and receive affection. Does a mother love her child? Does your parent love you? In most cases, they don't even see you, for you exist only as their projection. They don't see your Soul! How can they see your Soul if they don't see theirs? To love is to have a deep connection with another Soul. Most are not aware of their own Souls.

The love which you can feel for all beings, we would rather call 'loving kindness' or compassion. These are the natural qualities of the Heart which can be transpersonal. Love in a universal sense is all-inclusive in a non-personal way. As your Heart becomes one with the Heart of the Universe, with the Divine, she embraces the whole Existence in her profound, warm sensitivity. There is no object of love here; it is not coming from a particular Me, for Me is herself absorbed in the dimension of love. We can speak here about love without object. Love is the very presence of universal subjectivity, the I Am of God.

To conclude... love is not an emotion. Love is a state of Being where the dimension of pure isness and the dimension of the Heart become one, creating the unified field of I Am. As far as personal love is concerned, by the very fact that it is experienced in the dimension of relative separation, it cannot be all-inclusive but must be selective. This type of personal love requires special conditions in order to operate, like a bond between two particular Souls. Other types of love which are more of an unconditional nature, experienced in the realm of separation, belong rather to the category of loving kindness or compassion. And let us not forget that love which is real, both personal and transpersonal comes always from the Heart Centre. Therefore, for love to be fully present, an open and activated Heart is required.

Love is One but has Many Expressions

Student: *Is love one?*

Aziz: Love is one but there are many expressions of love. Love itself, is the pure presence of the Heart. It is the divine subjectivity. We can see it as love without object. Similarly, as awareness without object is the State of Presence, so love without object is the pure reality of the Heart.

When the Heart looks outside through the emotional body, she experiences affection towards other subjective realities. There are many expressions of love. There is maternal love, caring love, erotic love, loving kindness, compassion, affection, friendship, empathy, forgiveness; and more neutral, calm love like in the case of...loving sunshine, for instance. There are many expressions of love, but when you trace back to the source of love, you will find a dimension without objects. This is the domain of the Beloved.

Awakening and Stabilisation of the Heart

Student: *Is there a stage involving the stabilisation of the energy within the Heart, where there is no movement?*

Aziz: Yes, there is. The evolution or awakening of the Heart is much more complex than the awakening of consciousness. The awakening of consciousness is more linear. The evolution of the Heart takes many turns and it is difficult to grasp. This process contains what we call Enlightenment to the Heart. This means a complete expansion of the Heart centre takes place. There is stabilisation in the Heart when the energy is constantly centralised in the Heart space. Stabilisation of the Heart certainly exists.

Student: *Is it an event?*

Aziz: Yes and no. On a subtle level it is an event because it takes place like a turning of the key but it may not always be grasped. You do not necessarily notice this event. It is very subtle... suddenly, you see that the energy of the Heart is present at all times. The Heart does not close anymore on the energy level. Even though the Heart can close within her emotional body in the situation of anger, for instance, but energetically she always remains fully present.

Human Love, Divine Love and the State of Love

Student: *Can you talk about human love, divine love and the state of love?*

Aziz: The State of Love is beyond separation, it occurs in the pure dimension of I Am. The State of Love is the complete unity of Being and the fully activated Heart centre. When the Heart centre is fully expanded, fully opened and awakened it merges with Being and they create one field: the Field of Love. For this, the Being quality of I Am must already be present. If there is no Being even when the Heart is awakened, she cannot be experienced as the State of Love. This is for the very simple reason that the Heart is not grounded in Beingness. In such a case, one experiences the energy of love, but without the quality of Rest. For what is a state? A state is that which is motionless. It is that which can be retained from moment to moment, in spite of time. That's why we call it a state. This means it is fixed on some level, it is self-contained. It is called 'state' because it 'stays.'

Divine love and the state of love are in truth the same. The Divine Dimension is another name for the Heart of the Creator. The realm of Beingness and Love is beyond time, beyond earth, beyond this universe; it is the timeless abidance of the Beyond. When you are in the state of Love, you have merged with the Divine Dimension, you are in a state of unity with the Beyond. We cannot experience the state of Love in separation from the Divine. It is unity with the Divine that allows you to experience the state of Love.

Apart from Divine Love, there is human love which is an expression of the Soul in the world. In order to experience human love, the Soul has to have a sense of separation. This enables her to acknowledge her individual existence within the relatively separated reality. Without separation, there is no human love. Human love is love experienced within separation. It is love which is channelled through the emotional body and through a particular type of intelligence.

You see, again we cannot separate emotions from intelligence or the mind. This is because whatever you experience has to be recognised and translated on some level through your mind. For example, you cannot love your boyfriend unless you recognise him as your boyfriend and the Heart does not know it unless the mind tells it to the Heart. So your mind tells you that this person is your boyfriend and the Heart opens up, creating affection. This is because without mind you have no way to recognise anybody. To recognise a tree, your mind has to recognise that the tree exists. Without the mind, there is no tree for you. So the mind is that which allows you to recognise the outer. When you look carefully at the way your consciousness operates, you can see how your mind subtly affects the quality of your Heart as well. They are two sides of the same phenomenon, which is human consciousness. The mind affects the Heart and the Heart affects the mind.

When you love someone, what underlies this love is a certain concept you have. It is a play of concepts you have about your partner as well as about the image which you have of yourself. Human love refers to a certain affection the Soul feels for other Souls. If you love someone, you love another Subject. When you love an object it is not the real love, it is like loving a car. You say: 'I love my car, it is a wonderful car, nobody has such a car like me.' It is not really love, but the ego's satisfaction. So to love in a human way, there has to be the recognition of the subjective existence of another Soul. We call it empathy because you are able to tune into the subjectivity of other beings. There are many expressions of human love. There is the erotic love which usually involves a desire to melt and become emotionally united with the opposite sex. Often this type of love is connected to sexual emotions. There is maternal love where one has a need to deeply care like to take care of a child, for instance. Here it is not necessarily the desire to become one, but more to give. There is love in terms of friendship, which has more of a sharing nature. The many different types of Human Love relate to the many ways you can express your affections within the world.

The Heart of an Unawakened Person

Student: *Can one have an experience of the Heart without being established in the State of Presence or Being?*

Aziz: Of course. However, you see, it doesn't go as deep because one can experience the depth of the Heart only when there is an ability to rest within the Heart space. Firstly, we reach the experience of the Heart in terms of feeling her; this gradually opens the Heart centre. Next, we learn the ability to enter the

Divine Dimension, the internal space of the Heart. On a deeper level the Heart herself is a dimension of Being, even though she is initially discovered as the feeling centre. When both the Heart and Being reach complete expansion, there is no longer any separation. They become One.

Prayer and Meditation

Student: *What is the difference between prayer and the practice of meditation?*

Aziz: Prayer is more from the Heart. Meditation is more about silence and peace. When you experience a state of pure meditation, you are self-contained. You are happy as you are. You are not relating to the Creator or to Creation. You are in a state of non-relating. You simply are. This is meditation, just being. But because you also exist as a Soul who is not only a living a state of meditation, you also express yourself in a dynamic way. You have different challenges in life. You are evolving and you are conscious that you are actually a created being. From this space of knowing that your are a created being, you also know that, on some level, you are quite helpless and that you need support from Existence. From this understanding you become ready to communicate with the Creator because prayer is nothing but connection and communication with God.

How to pray is your challenge, for you communicate with that which you cannot see. How can you communicate with the infinite mystery of the Beloved? That is what you need to discover. Prayer is from the Heart only; it is a communication of the Soul with her Creator.

Meditation is a state of pure Being. At one stage, meditation and prayer become one. That is because the Being quality of meditation is a form of prayer too. From a certain perspective, pure meditation is the deepest prayer but only when the Heart is included. When in meditation Heart, Awareness and Being are integrated, this state represents Pure Prayer. There are two types of prayer. One is a dynamic prayer, which is the conscious communication with the Beloved. The second represents a static or motionless prayer, which is just Being. Meditation itself has an inherent element of prayer. It is a religious act. It is not just to be at peace. When you close your eyes and you experience the inner expansion, what happens is that you are merging with God. You might not be aware of it and you might say 'I am just experiencing peace,' but in truth, you are merging with God.

Layers of the Heart

Student: *I have a question about the layers of the Heart. In the Heart we feel human feelings and when we go deeper, it seems we touch something beyond us. Can you speak about these different layers?*

Aziz: The Heart is an energy centre located in the middle of the chest. The Heart is the seat of the Soul and the gateway to the Divine. The depth of the Heart is the link between the Soul and the Beloved.

Within our physical body there are two gateways through which we can meet the Ultimate. One is the Hara through which we realise the Being aspect of God, which is the Absolute. The other gateway is the Heart centre through which we realise the Heart of God, which is the Divine. When Buddhism, for instance, speaks about Emptiness, it points to an incomplete realisation of Truth, for it lacks the realisation of the Divine Dimension. It does not mean that Buddha Shakyamuni did not realise the Divine Dimension. It simply means that in the general energy of Buddhist teachings, the Divine Presence is not seen at all.

A Path like Buddhism which is concentrated on liberation from suffering is certainly not interested in exploring the vulnerable dimension of the Heart. To avoid suffering the best way is to reach the Absolute and to forget about the Heart. Resting in the Absolute State brings total disidentification from the time dimension. Realisation of the Absolute State is the most clean way to get out of samsara.

The Soul as such is vulnerable and cannot ever be completely free from suffering. The moment the Soul incarnates, she agrees, on some level, to experience a certain amount of suffering as a part of her life's experience. But even Buddhism intuitively saw the necessity of awakening to the Heart. Their work with Heart is present in an indirect way through the development of compassion and loving-kindness. However, compassion will not be enough for the Soul-realisation. Compassion is a feeling generated for other living beings where one does not actually acknowledge one's own suffering. Compassion here is a kind of luxurious emotion coming from the place of freedom. But to experience the Soul is to experience compassion for oneself. And unless one acknowledges one's suffering, sadness, longing and vulnerability, one cannot become compassionate towards this very Me which is in the centre of all.

The Heart from one side is the meeting of the Soul with the Beloved, which is the Creator. On the other side it is the meeting of the Soul with her personality. When the Soul incarnates into the body, in order to be here, in the reality of time, she needs to develop the personality. The psyche is an extension of the Soul in the world. The psyche is also the Soul but the manifested part of the Soul. Your Soul is that which rests purely in the Heart. But let's say that someone hurts you by saying a bad word. Your mind registers this abuse and your emotional body gets hurt and next this feeling goes to the Heart. Through this pain in the Heart, the Soul herself becomes hurt.

The first layer of the Heart is the very place where the Soul becomes her personality. For that reason, that which you feel in the beginning when you go to the Heart, is your personal pain. That is because you are exploring the Heart from the place of being a personality, from the place of being a human. The personal feeling in the Heart is still not the Soul, but it is very close to the Soul. It is the meeting point between your personality and the Soul. When you touch your Heart, you experience this part of you which is personal. You feel the one who wants to be happy Here; the one who wants to be secure and who sometimes may get hurt; the one who wants to fall in love...

The Heart is place where the Soul becomes a personality and the place where personality can again become the Soul. Most of those who try connect to the Heart stop unfortunately, at the personal level of the Heart. All those personal emotions which you encounter in your Heart, point to the Soul, but the Soul is still deeper. To reach the Soul requires more intimacy. An example of how to glimpse the Soul is when someone falls in love - there is this thrilling excitement, full of longing and hope. It is the Soul which is so excited but she has to turn around to discover her own light, her divine presence. When you fall in love, discover who is actually so excited, who feels all those hopes around falling in love? Who is behind this yearning... who is that one? We can see it is a particular version of the question, 'who am I?' Who am I in my Heart? We do not speak here about consciousness, but only about the Heart. Who am I? Who is the one behind the longing for happiness and behind the fear of getting hurt? Who am I?

Falling in love or suffering often allows one to get closer to the Soul. The deepest purpose of suffering is to come closer to the Soul. This is because suffering always involves the Soul. Feelings of satisfaction or contentment often are registered only in the mind. Sometimes the mind is happy but yet the Soul can be in a deep pain. When you go deeper into the personal space of the Heart, you encounter a pure sense of Me. This feeling is prior to suffering, prior to happiness and has no personal characteristics. Similarly, like in the work with awareness, we separate the mind from the subject behind. We have different types of thoughts but the one behind them is the Real Me. In a similar way, we can discover the one who is present prior to emotions in the Heart. In the mind we take a step back from the thinking to the thinker, similarly in the Heart we also take one step back from the feeling to the Feeler. The feeler is this Pure Me, the objectless feeling in the Heart. Here, we reach to optimum of intimacy with our Pure Me, for we become simply One.

Often we hear about the need for loving ourselves. But the true meaning of this concept is not to have a pleasant ego-image. It is not to love oneself because of seeing how wonderful one is. The true meaning of loving oneself is to become the Soul. Self-love is non-dual; it is not that you love yourself - you become yourself. Here, you meet the source of love and you experience love without object and without subject. No longer are you loving yourself, for you have become One. In this expansion within your own Heart you are finally meeting you Soul's ancient identity. The spark of this light is always present in your Heart but your conscious recognition turns it into the bright flame of Love.

The next layer of the Heart is behind the Soul. You can imagine that behind the sense of Me in your Heart, there is a space, a dimension which is infinite. This infinite space of love represents the Ocean of Divinity, from which the Soul originally emerged. For where does the Soul dwell? She does not dwell in emptiness, neither does she abide nowhere. She abides within the sacred space of the Divine - the Other Dimension. The Other Dimension is another name for the presence of the Beloved, the domain of the Creator. How to recognise the Beloved is a tremendous challenge, as one needs to be extremely sensitive. Without sensitivity, you cannot register the presence of divinity.

When you sit in meditation, in prayer, tuning into the sacred space of the Heart, you begin to develop a certain sensitivity and mysteries become open to you. You need to ask the Beloved for help in this process. From the depth of your Heart, ask the Divine to reveal herself to you. There has to be a prayerful attitude. Gradually you begin discovering this Sacred Presence which is hidden in the cave of your Heart. Apart from this empathic exploration of the Heart, the deeper way of entering this space is Surrender through Being. In order to reach the final depth of the Heart, one has to become absorbed, attaining Samadhi in the Heart. It can happen, however, only when the Heart is fully awakened. If the Heart is not awakened, the moment you let go into Being, energy goes to the Hara, bypassing the Heart centre. In this final experience of the Heart, Being and the Heart merge into one. You become pulled into the final depth of the Heart, where you end and the Beloved begins. Here you become absorbed into the Beloved.

In your initial exploration of the Heart, you learn how to feel the Beloved. You learn in a feeling way how to tune into the presence of the Beloved; you are discovering your Eternal Parent, the Divine Mother inside your own Heart. When you reach Samadhi in the Heart, you become absent within the Universal Presence of the Beloved. You become united with the Beloved experiencing pure Oneness, where the level of your presence is minimum. You hardly know that you exist, there is just a trace of consciousness while the weight of your being is absorbed in the Heart of the Creator.

Still it is a real miracle that being in the body and living in this dimension of forgetfulness, you can experience a true unity with God! A true unity with God is not emotional but energetic, even though it includes a most intimate and moving appreciation from the Soul. In this state there is no movement. In this way you are here but not of Here. Because you are a dynamic being even when you are energetically united with the Beloved, you can still relate to the Beloved in a personal way. You are able with deep emotion, to encounter the sacred presence of the Creator.

These are the layers of the Heart. The Divine Dimension is

the Heart of all hearts. The Soul is the essence of your individual identity and the purest reflection of God in you. Next is the surface of the Heart where the Soul becomes the personality. The personality can be perceived as a child of the Soul. The Soul is a child of the Beloved and personality is the child of the Soul. Therefore, personality is not to be eliminated, for it is also an important part of your multidimensional self. Through personality the Soul is able to encounter the outer world. This personal expression of the Soul wants to be loved, wants to be happy and does everything to avoid suffering. Somebody shouts at you and you get immediately hurt. You think: 'why am I getting hurt?' or 'why is this dimension hurting Me?' A child is completely innocent but still can get hurt in this insensitive dimension. In this way, you experience the primal injustice which is a part of the dimension of ignorance. And later not to get hurt again, you close your Heart and go into the mind. Because the mind has the power to protect you, it is a self-protective mechanism. But the problem is going too much into the mind and closing your Heart. That's why, most people do not experience their Hearts. They do not allow themselves to be hurt, they live only in this mind. They may be completely protected but are unfortunately dead!

The only way for a person who is locked behind shields of self-protection is to open up to one's vulnerability. First the Heart has to be awakened on the energy level. One has to begin to feel that there is actually a Heart in the middle of the chest. One has forgotten that there is something so precious, soft, tender and delicate inside. Paying attention to the Heart, meditating on the Heart, praying and opening to feelings are the ways to return to the reality of the Heart. In this process, frozen energies of protection, insensitivity and fear gradually melt down, revealing the inner warmth of the Heart.

Student: *How to avoid the danger of getting hurt?*

Aziz: We spoke about this balance between being sensitive and being over-protected, a type of 'insensitivity.' We could compare this to the skin, which protects our body. When the skin is too thin, it is hyper sensitive and gets easily hurt; but when it is too thick, you cannot feel anything! Sometimes we do not know whether the experience we have is pleasant or painful. This is because our interpretation of the sensation is a bit confused. The reason is that the border between being sensitive and being too sensitive is not clear and the brain does not know how to translate the experience. There is a very gentle balance between sensitivity and insensitivity. Sensitivity makes you vulnerable but on the other hand allows you to experience a rich variety of emotions and sensual pleasures. But still when one is too sensitive it becomes painful.

To live as an awakened Soul is to experience the optimum of sensitivity and the minimum of insensitivity. But we have to see the important role of insensitivity which protects the borders of our individual existence. You cannot be too sensitive for the very reason that you live in an insensitive dimension. There is a minimum of necessary insensitivity that serves to protect your sensitivity. As far as meeting the Divine is concerned, there is no limit in expressing one's sensitivity. But in the encounter with the world, the limits of sensitivity reflect our integrity as relatively separated beings.

There are some Souls who are too sensitive and do not have enough inner strength. They usually suffer a lot because they lack self-protection. In contact with other people, they easily get drained or hurt. Afterwards, they are afraid of any type of confrontation because their Heart is too open.

The main source of strength for the Soul is a clear presence in the mind and rootedness in Being. When the inner space of Awareness and Being is created, we can afford to open the Heart. Otherwise, we are too vulnerable, too sensitive. For that reason, before going into the Heart, we activate the other aspects of I Am. Through the inner expansion, one's sense of identity becomes solidified and rooted in the unconditional realm of pure isness. Only when a tree is solid, can it give birth to flowers; it is then strong enough to manifest its beauty.

Student: *You said, in the previous answer, to look in the Heart and to discover the feeler. Is it the same process as we do in the mind, to see who is behind it? Is it like going through the different doors to the same room?*

Aziz: Yes, the process is parallel but slightly different. For the very simple reason that they are different centres, to be awakened. There are different doors to the different rooms but the house is the same. This house is Me. In the mind, we discover the centre of intelligence, the state of pure presence. From observing the mind, we turn attention back to its own centre. In the case of the Heart we are not observing but feeling. Attention is coming to the Heart from 'outside.' That's why, turning attention back within the Heart does not work. Attention is not the subject in the Heart. Here, the feeling centre of the Heart uses the light of attention in order to become conscious. The feeler is not the observer. The feeler cannot observe. For example, in the mind you can watch thoughts but the feeler cannot watch feelings. The feeler can only feel feelings. The feeler is intimate with the movement of feelings. You can watch your Heart only from the mind like in Vipassana. But it is not real because you are split into two; one part of Me is watching the second part.

The process of discovering the Soul is very interesting. It is very similar to awakening the State of Presence in terms of taking a step back towards the subject. But where is the ultimate subjectivity? Which subject is the true subject: Awareness or the Heart? Many spiritual traditions assume that pure awareness is the Ultimate. They think that witness is the Self. It is of course incorrect. We can call it confusion in self-identification. It is in the Heart where we come closest to Truth. It is in the Heart where you we meet the Creator most directly. You cannot meet God through awareness. Pure awareness is just an outer aspect of God's reality. It is the Heart which is the beginning and the end of everything. To experience the Beloved in the Heart is the most moving experience for a human being.

The Pain in the Heart

Student: *When we go to the Heart and find pain, is it necessary to go through it?*

Aziz: Yes, you have to go through these personal layers of the Heart and pain helps you to awaken your Heart. For most people, it is through the experience of pain that the Soul signals her existence. These personal feelings revolving around sufferings, longings, being wounded and searching for love, allow you to awaken your Soul. Through them you come closer to the very subject of these feelings which is the Pure Me. Someone who has not suffered cannot discover the Heart.

The danger however is that one can be stuck in this personal layer. One can be caught in endless emotions, indulging in self-pity and not being able to go deeper. For that reason, work with the Heart has to go together with meditation. Unless there is a continuity of awareness and tranquillity of Being, one is unable to transcend the personal layers of the Heart. When we are solidified in I Am, we can in a mature way enter the internal reality of the Heart. In this way, one can go beyond emotional fluctuations, reaching the essential tranquillity of the Heart. The ultimate experience of the Heart is to rest in the Heart - to Be in the Heart beyond movement.

A Clear Intention to Open the Heart

Student: *How to work with Heart?*

Aziz: The work with the Heart is quite complex. It is much more complex than work with awareness. Awareness is rather primitive compared to the Heart. The Heart is very rich and multidimensional. The main principle in the work with the Heart is to start paying attention to her. Attention itself is energy. By directing attention to the Heart, being connected to the space of the Heart, the centre of the Heart becomes activated; the energy begins to move. Firstly, we pay attention to the Heart becoming mindful of it. Next, we become more and more sensitive, intimate with the Heart space, exposing her vulnerability and innocent child-like quality.

Work with the Heart has to be done in meditation, in prayer and in everyday life. It is the intention which matters. When there is a clear intention to open the Heart, she will open in some time. Existence will bring all elements necessary, as it responds to the clarity and purity of your intention. It is ultimately a function of Grace and Grace only. The Higher Intelligence is required to support this process...

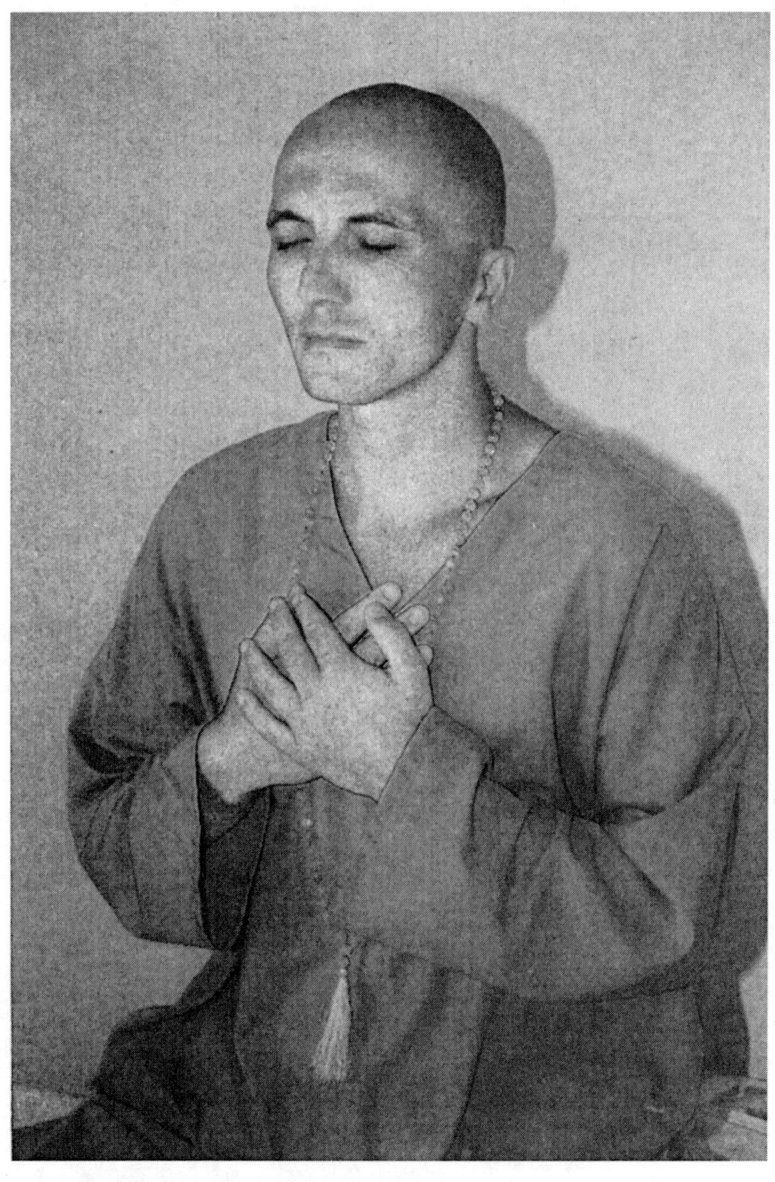

The Inner State

To know yourself you need to understand the internal movement of I Am. It is a movement within silence, a dance within stillness. From complete Awareness, you surrender into Being, dropping into the depth of Reality. Let the Heart be open and sensitive between the shores of clarity and restfulness. You are learning to live the life of I Am. It is like diving into the depth of the Ocean, it is a whole New World. Know yourself...dive into the truth of I Am and let it teach you about Eternity.

Recognition of I Am

Student: *How can one recognise the state of I Am? Is it obvious when one has reached this state?*

Aziz: Our meditation deals exactly with the art of recognising I Am, as well as giving different tools to awaken it. There are two sides of this phenomenon. One is that you actually give birth to I Am. You cannot recognise it unless it is present. Secondly, when the state is more or less present, you have to learn how to recognise it. It is not easy to recognise I Am because one has to be sensitive and one has to have a certain amount of understanding and experience, of course. That's why, in our teaching there are extensive explanations, so one can activate one's intelligence and therefore understanding. I Am is an energetic experience and the one who recognises it is your intelligence. Therefore, both are important - the energetic foundation of I Am and the sensitivity of recognising it intelligence.

I Am is not one thing. It has a few aspects. We speak about awareness which is free from thoughts and the centre of awareness in the mind. What is it? Do you have an experience of it?

Student: *No, not yet. I am new to this.*

Aziz: Yes, but you are not new to Existence. You have lived a long time. You see, meditation is not about becoming a member of some school so you can say that you are new to it. Meditation is to be alive! No one is new to life... not just this life but many lifetimes. You have been using your mind long enough. Is there anyone inside your mind referring to who you could say - 'this is I'?

Student: *I know my personality.*

Aziz: Well, this personality is just an expression of this I. Observe your mind more. Practice observing your mind, not only in meditation but also in activity, in life. For instance, when you sit in a restaurant or walk along a seashore, observe your mind. When you do this, you will sense that your mind is actually outside of you. It is just happening to you. You are not just the mind. You are not the thinking. You are not a thought. You are the one behind thought. When you experience negative thoughts, you are suffering. You don't want them. When thoughts are pleasant, you feel good. Thoughts come and go but they are not you. You are the one who is experiencing them. So what you are trying to do, is first to create a certain sense of distance from thinking. Thinking is like an obsession - it has superimposed itself on you. Firstly, you create a certain distance and next, through this distance you can have an angle to actually perceive who you are. You are not a thought - you are the experiencer of it. Observe your mind and enquire into the truth of your Me. In order to want awakening, you have to see how important it is.

No one ever asks the question 'who am I?' because no one is interested in knowing the answer. Most people only want to have a good time! Where can I go for a holiday? How can I get a new girlfriend? This is because these questions relate to psychological gratification, through which the emotional body gets satisfied or the physical body gets pleasure. The average human being cannot see any benefit in asking, 'who am I?' That's why, most students who come here are not really aligned with this process. Their questions have not yet been born. Therefore, they are not ready to receive the answers.

You must awaken this intuitive longing for your own Soul, for your own Self. It is something ancient, something forgotten... a forgotten taste of truth which is necessary to bring back. It is the taste of I Am. I Am is simply You, prior to conditioning by your parents, society, collective consciousness; it is you before you entered this dream, because this dimension is essentially a dream. When you were born, you were forced to enter this dream, becoming a part of this global dreaming and taking it for granted. You agreed to believe that this dimension is Real. But it is just your belief and not even your belief but one borrowed from the collective mind.

Now as an adult and with the maturation of your intelligence, you may start to doubt whether this reality is real or not? What you are questioning is yourself. How do you experience your very existence? Who actually are you? If you separate yourself from your mind, your memories, from all this information inside your brain, do you still exist or is there nothing? This type of enquiry, this type of longing, this type of intuition can bridge one with the state of I Am. To awaken I Am is not difficult. What is difficult is to awaken the desire for awakening. What is difficult is to bring the Soul to a state of maturity where she is ready to ask these types of questions in a true sense, not just intellectually. Then, you will be ready to receive the gift of awakening, living the I Am.

Imagine it is like this. When you live the reality of I Am, you are fully I Am. You are fully who you are. It has nothing to do with what you think or your memories - you have actually changed dimensions. The very structure of your mind becomes transformed or radically changed. You become a new being. You are at the stage now where you are questioning your reality and the way you experience your very Me. You also question the collective mind which has created your dream-like sense of identity. You are not who you think you are! It is not you yet - it is a version of the collective mind, enriched by the sense of Me. That's why you as an individual have not been born yet. Would you like to be born? Or do you want to spend the rest of your life in the womb of ignorance, which is not even a womb but rather a coffin!

Initially, the Soul is unconscious. She is lost in the mind and lives as the ego. For the Soul to begin to exist, she has to free herself from the mind by developing awareness. Next, she learns how to rest within, in Being. When there is Awareness and Being, the foundation has been created. You have created the inner home. Before then you do not have a home. You are homeless. You are a beggar, lost in the reality of appearances. You do not exist as an individual. You exist as a stream of impersonal consciousness which unfortunately relates to a certain illusory sense of self. This is why, you know that you are suffering.

When you give birth to your real centre within yourself, you start to exist. For the first time, you have the right to say, 'I am.' Before this, you do not have the right to say, 'I am.' If the average person says, 'I am' he is mistaken, because in truth there is no one inside.

Awareness and Being are the inner foundation. When the foundation is built, you can discover the Soul which is in the Heart. You are entering the centre of sensitivity, the Heart centre. It is a gateway. It is not only that you feel your Heart. You are entering a New World. The world of the Heart, the secret dimension is beyond the earth, beyond manifestation. As you feel your Heart, you become sensitive to your own Soul, to the subtle vibration inside your Heart which speaks to you clearly as being the closest, most intimate connection to your existence. Let your own Heart reveal herself to you. You have to ask your Heart. You have to prove to your own Heart that you wish to discover her. Otherwise, you will not feel anything; you will feel only the surface. You have to surrender yourself to your own Heart. What this means is that you as the mind, surrender to you as the Heart. Stay with this feeling of the Heart, being fully present and restful in your Being. Return again to Who You Are, for perhaps the first time, this time.

Three Centres of I Am

Student: *How to integrate the three centres of I Am?*

Aziz: The integration is being done as you awaken more. Your task is to awaken these centres from inside. At this stage, the continuity of the State of Presence is essential. When it is more steady, you will go into Beingness and the Heart more. You don't want to become a self-conscious robot but a being who possesses the depth of inner rest and the sensitivity and beauty of the Heart. Integration is not a function of will but evolution. It is being done.

Is I Am Created?

Student: *Is I Am created? I often get confused whether I am discovering what I really am or if I am creating whatever is being discovered?*

Aziz: It is an important issue to clarify. The concept 'I am That,' even though inspiring is not fully correct. That which is always and has always been, is God alone, the universal I AM. In truth, it is not One reality to which we are awakening, but Two. The first is our own existence which is the Soul; and the second is the realm of Beingness which is beyond us. We do not create who we are but we create the very Awakening to who we are. Similarly, we in no way create the universal I AM but we 'create' the awakening to it. Is it clear? The Ultimate Reality exists beyond recognition. In order to be recognised, duality must arise. We awaken to What Is and this awakening is the creation of recognition. Therefore, both are true: we create I Am and we discover that which has always been present.

Student: *What about the State of Presence: is it eternal or not? Is it awakened or do we discover a state which has always been? Do we create it or is it somehow present independent from our recognition?*

Aziz: Perhaps one of the most misunderstood issues related to the nature of Enlightenment is the issue of awareness. In truth, awareness can exist only in duality. When we speak about non-dual awareness, we mean the Primal Duality, prior to the gross level of duality created by the mind. Awareness is not eternal, even though it has the eternal potential to manifest itself as a part of Creation. For awareness to manifest itself, it needs a particular Me. Awareness as a sense of knowingness cannot exist without Me. The State of Presence is the centre of awareness as it is experienced through the human Me. This centre is certainly not eternal, as that is not its purpose. The destination of this centre is to be stabilised in this state in waking times only. Because of the wrong assumption that this state is the eternal Self, many misinformed practitioners, monks and masters, for the last several thousands of years have been forcing this state into the period of sleep; some even hope to take it beyond death! Such a waste of time!

When the State of Presence is established, it enters the Sleep State but not in a simplistic sense. It is not that you are aware of the state during sleep. In such a case we would speak about lucid dreaming which has nothing to do with pure awareness. Lucid dreaming is nothing but ego-consciousness artificially brought into the dream state. When the State of Presence is established, it simply vibrates in the background of dream consciousness, but in a non-self-conscious way.

Witnessing consciousness is not the Ultimate. It is just a centre of human intelligence, liberating the psyche from unconsciousness and creating a continuity of presence within the movement of time. The State of Presence shares some universal qualities of consciousness. It is transpersonal but because it is experienced always through a particular Me, it is also personal.

No, that state has not been present prior to our recognition. It is our recognition which awakens it, allowing it to become a conscious experience. Instead of saying that we create the State of Presence which has a connotation of something artificial, we rather Awaken it. Evolution is different than creativity. Evolution is the unfoldment of Truth; it is a higher and higher perception and experience of the Self. Creativity points more to the process of expressing the Self while evolution points more to the realisation of the Self; it points to the internal experience of consciousness. Evolution is a process of reaching deeper and more meaningful experience of What Is from the perspective of an individual Soul.

In the past, Hindu mystics thought that the State of Presence, purusha or witness was the eternal Self. And they had some troubles providing a philosophical explanation. For example, some thought that the witness was one, while others thought there were many witnesses. If witness was one, they were thinking, if one being became enlightened, all other beings would in turn automatically awaken and become free of bondage. But the situation is a bit different and more simple, in truth. The witness is not the Self; turiya is not the Self. The State of Presence is the centre of Soul's intelligence. It has some transcendental qualities but still, it is not the Ultimate. Awareness, even pure awareness cannot be extracted from a particular Me; neither can it be separated from intelligence. Awareness is functional and serves a higher purpose than itself. Its purpose is to bring into the light of knowing, the Ultimate. The Ultimate is prior to awareness.

Let us again clarify. What is eternally present, independent from our awakening and what is not? That which is eternally and timelessly present is God at rest, pure isness, the absolute absence and absolute presence. The Self is eternal but the experience and realisation of it is not, for it is an event in time. Enlightenment is a function of evolution.

As far as the realisation of the Soul is concerned, it is 'created' or awakened. The Soul has been there always but in her original condition, that is, prior to recognition - one with the Beloved. The Soul is truly born and self-conscious only through one's evolution. That which has been always there is prior to consciousness. That which is awakened exists within consciousness; that is why it can be aware of itself.

The State Beyond Polarities: Meeting the Beloved

Student: *What is the difference between the Absolute State and the State Beyond Polarities?*

Aziz: The Absolute State represents the realisation of the complete motionlessness of Being. When one is in the Absolute State, there is no more change in the energy of Being. One is simply beyond manifested energy. But who is resting in the Absolute State? The one who rests in the Absolute is not the Absolute. That's why, the famous elucidation 'I am That' is unfortunately not fully correct. The statement 'I am That' is true on some level, for all is an expression of God. But the one who says 'I am That' is not 'That' and is destined 'not to be That.' It is only because we are not That, that we can say 'I am That,' that is, make an incorrect statement. If we wish to say it more correctly, the proper statement would be: I am the very expression of That through which That can be recognised.' That is the truth of the dual-non-duality.

Coming back to our subject... The one who rests in the Absolute is the Soul and she is more than the experience of rest. The Soul has Awareness, the Heart and Intelligence. When one is in the Absolute State, it is only the Being quality of I Am which is motionless. The Heart and Awareness are still fluctuating. When the Heart is awakened and integrated with Being, the Heart is also beyond movement. Here, one may awaken to Me. Enlightenment to Me happens when one fully meets one's Soul identity in the Heart, but more importantly it takes place in the context of Being and Awareness. We call this realisation 'Transparent Me,' for the Soul is dissolved into I AM through her own presence.

This experience is very subtle. Imagine an empty, silent, meditative room. This inner space represents the perfect environment of I AM. The emptiness is Being or the Absolute and the light which makes the room clear and bright is Awareness. Inside of this room there is a beautiful rose which represents our Heart.

From this rose emerges a fragrance so gentle and sublime that it cannot be grasped. This fragrance is one with emptiness and the luminosity of the space but is at the same time, clearly distinct. That is the experience of Transparent Me. This Me is distinct from I AM, but you can see through Me the space of I AM. You can feel Me but when you look at it, you just see I AM. There is only I AM but it is Me at the same time. Me is the self-consciousness and the self-feeling of I AM.

This realisation, however, still lacks the total motionlessness, for Awareness is not yet fully absorbed into the Being-Heart dimension. Pure awareness is beyond thinking but still fluctuates in its own way. There is simply some movement within the State of Presence. In the shift Beyond Polarities, awareness also reaches the condition of pure rest. What it means is that the State of Presence, the Heart and Being abide as a unified field beneath the surface of Creation. They are still experienced within Creation but are beyond it at the same time. That's why, we say that at this stage Me meets the Beloved. The sacred meeting finally takes place, the divine encounter of the child with her eternal Mother.

Zen Ox-herding Pictures

Student: *Do the ten Zen ox-herding pictures represent the process of reaching the Absolute State?*

Aziz: No, they represent the process of awakening and stabilising the State of Presence, pure awareness. The ox symbolises witnessing consciousness, the centre of awareness. These pictures are wonderful! The process is described with exceptional precision. First, one recognises the ox (the State of Presence). Next, one has to tame it until it becomes one with the ox-herder.

An important question is: who is recognising the State of Presence and who is taming it? This you need to contemplate in meditation. It is intelligence, of course. In Zen, the relationship between intelligence and the State of Presence is compared to the relationship between the King and his minister. The King is the centre of awareness and the minister is intelligence. First, the minister is looking for the King who is mysteriously gone. Next, the King is looking at the minister or, rather, witnessing him. Gradually they become one. Zen has developed a very high understanding of the awakening process.

The process of reaching the Absolute State has not been described for the public. However, In Zen they have a metaphor reflecting this experience: 'the bottom of the bucket falls out.' The bucket is the experience of I Am within Creation. When the bottom of the bucket falls out, the Being aspect (the bottom) of I Am slips in to the Other Side becoming one with the Uncreated.

The ox is too gross a symbol for the Absolute. An appropriate symbol for the Absolute would be an eagle. We would have to draw ten more pictures, which, in truth, reverse the other ten pictures. We have described those pictures in the book Beyond Consciousness. The process has to become reversed. Previously we become one with pure consciousness, so now, we have to again remove our sense of identity from it, in order to reach the Uncreated. In the eighteenth picture, the eagle flies into the sky. In the nineteenth picture, the eagle disappears and only the infinite sky remains - freedom. The twentieth picture is the Beyond.

Breaking the Mirror of Consciousness

Student: *What is the relationship between polishing the mirror of consciousness and going beyond consciousness?*

Aziz: Because the Absolute State has always been a secret, transmitted directly from a master to a disciple, the official teachings do not differentiate between the realisation of pure consciousness and the realisation of the Absolute. The concept of pure consciousness, often symbolised as a spotless mirror, can create a trap, as you try to endlessly perfect a state which cannot reach imperfection. The State of Presence can never be perfect, for consciousness simply gets tired. Consciousness is not as unconditional as it seems to be. Consciousness is channelled into the material dimension through the brain. The brain is conditioned by the laws of nature. Even when consciousness is free from thinking, it is still affected by numberless different elements on the energy level. When you are tired, for instance, the vibration of this state changes. When you sit in meditation for a long time, the state starts to vibrate with a higher frequency; it feels fresh and serene.

If a practitioner does not know that the State of Presence is not the Ultimate, he or she may constantly try to perfect it. This perfecting of consciousness is called 'polishing the mirror.' But the problem is that however you polish this state, it never can reach perfection. Consciousness is not absolute, it simply makes you present. Going beyond consciousness is like a quantum leap in your experience of reality. You don't transcend consciousness by making it perfectly pure, but by completely changing the focus. In the shift to the Absolute, your sense of identity moves radically, below actually consciousness. It is as if you have changed the location, finding yourself in a new dimension, under the water of consciousness. Here, the need to polish the mirror of consciousness is transcended.

Reaching the state of pure consciousness usually involves a gradual path. In the case of shifting to the Absolute, the path is sudden. We call it: radical de-centralisation or implosion.

Student: *What is the brightness of the mirror?*

Aziz: It is awareness, of course. Awareness is the luminosity of knowingness. The mirror does not exist apart from its luminosity. When the light is not present, the mirror is no longer the mirror. What is the mirror without light? What is consciousness without knowingness? It is itself the Absolute, that which is prior to knowingness.

In the shift to the Absolute, knowing surrenders into not-knowing; the light of the mirror becomes one with its own absence.

Movement between Awareness and Being

Student: *I find that when sitting with the eyes open, my State of Presence becomes stronger and when the eyes are closed, the experience of Being deepens. Why is that?*

Aziz: That is a very correct observation. I Am is composed of three qualities: Awareness, Being and Heart. This is important to understand. Even though we speak about this all the time, this understanding must become fully imbibed. Depending on the situation you are in, these three centres behave differently. In activity, awareness is stronger. When your eyes are open, awareness is intensified because attention is more activated. When the eyes are open, you are simply more alert - you notice many things. When your eyes are closed, attention relaxes because there is no need to focus on anything. When you walk around, you have to be attentive to find your way, not to fall, to perceive direction... and so forth. Naturally, the centre of attention is more activated and you experience yourself more in the head.

When you close your eyes, attention relaxes and gravitates more towards Being - the energy is more spread and distributed to other centres. This happens not only in meditation but also when you simply sit down on the beach, in a restaurant or in whichever life situation. That is the natural movement within I Am. When you are looking at the flower, the Heart is felt more. When you relax, the experience of Being deepens. When you are crossing over a busy street, your attention becomes very alert and so forth.

The movement between these three centres creates the life of I Am. When we fully activate these three qualities, they are always present. For example, in activity even though one is fully attentive, one simultaneously is contained by the energy of Being. On the other hand, when one is resting in Being, there is still a clear awareness and the energies of the Heart are present all the time. But even though all those three centres are present some of them are more predominant, more active. That is the natural behaviour of I Am. As you observe yourself in different situations, you will be able to verify it with your own intelligence.

It is good to observe oneself, otherwise if one does not understand the dynamics of the inner state; one may try to force the experience which is not natural. For example one may have an idea of letting go completely of awareness in activity in order to experience pure rest in Being, but since awareness is naturally more active in daily life it is not a natural situation. The understanding of I Am enables you to grow naturally and to channel the right effort into your practice. But when the Inner State is fully present and all centres fully activated, you simply allow I Am to behave naturally - there is no longer need for additional observation.

The State of Presence and the Heart

Student: *What is the relationship between the State of Presence and the Heart?*

Aziz: What is it that links the Heart and the State of Presence? What links them is that they belong to Me. They are both simply the different aspects of Me. The Heart is the feeling centre of the Soul and the State of Presence is the awareness aspect of the Soul. They are simply the different qualities of the same Me. The Heart is the centre of sensitivity of Me and awareness is the centre of attention of Me. The State of Presence is the clarity, awareness of the Heart; and the Heart is the sensitivity and emotion of awareness. If a person uses only the Heart, it is beautiful, but look at the quality of the mind of such a person! Such a person is completely unconscious and spaced out. Such a person can be easily manipulated, for the Heart without intelligence is completely naïve. People who use only the Heart centre often become victims of some political or religious leaders.

It is true that the Heart has her own wisdom but this wisdom cannot operate unless it is combined with the intelligence of the mind.. The Heart without the mind is blind, as the mind without the Heart is superficial and insensitive. They've got to go together.

Student: *Is it possible to experience presence in the Heart as opposed to its natural place inside the head?*

Aziz: Anything you experience involves presence. Without some kind of a presence, there is no experience. But the presence which you experience in the Heart without a centre of awareness is diluted, dispersed and lacks continuity. The mind from which comes the direction of attention, remains still on some level unconscious and discontinuous. Before awakening of the State of Presence, awareness is present, in terms of being mindful to objects, but still bypasses its own centre. After awakening to the State of Presence, you experience it inside your head. But the moment you expand into Being or Heart, awareness gets distributed to all those centres. Because this awareness is established in its own centre, when it goes to the other centres, it has continuity and retains a presence to itself. You see, it is not only awareness which pays attention to the Heart, but intelligence. This intelligence moves on attention. Only when there is a continuity of attention, can this intelligence also be steady.

When the State of Presence surrenders to the Heart, no longer does this experience have the quality of becoming aware of something outside of the observer. No longer is it mindfulness of an object. When awareness surrenders to the Heart, it becomes one with subjectivity of the Heart and experiences the Heart from inside. That is important to understand. The similar situation is with Being. You cannot 'watch' Being. Watching Being is perversion. But you can Be and in this experience awareness is included.

Student: *But can the State of Presence recognise itself in the Heart?*

Aziz: Awareness recognising itself in the Heart is the State of Presence in the Heart which means that the Heart is present to herself through awareness. You see, in this experience the Heart is present to herself through awareness, but awareness is not fully present to itself through awareness because the centre in the mind has been bypassed.

You are One but you are composed of different elements. If these elements are not put together, always something goes wrong. Awareness doesn't come from nowhere; it flows from a certain place. What is this place? It is the centre of wakefulness inside your brain. In order to be fully present, awareness must be aware of awareness. Otherwise, it distributes itself to the other centres bypassing its subjective self-presence.

'Energy Experiences' and the 'Experience of Energy'

Student: *We often hear about the importance of not being attached to energy experiences. But isn't I Am itself an energy experience?*

Aziz: It is a good question. You see, to have a good question is often more important than having the right answer. A good question has already an inherent answer.

It is very true that many seekers get attached and addicted to certain insignificant energy experiences which are either induced by meditation techniques or come as a result of meetings with the enlightened beings. In Zen there is a saying: 'that which enters through the Gate is not our family treasure.' That which 'enters the gate' refers to the coming and going of experiences; and the 'family treasure' represents our true nature. It is not attachment which is wrong but the attachment to wrong things. To be attached to the State of Presence is very important! To be attached to have the Heart open - makes it open. When we speak, however, about attachment to the energy experiences, we mean clinging to that which is accidental and not real. It is not attachment to the energy experiences which is wrong, but to these particular energy experiences which do not represent our real nature.

The I Am is certainly an energy experience, but not an

accidental one. It is our family treasure, it can be constant for it is our nature. The shift to the Absolute State is purely an energy experience, perhaps the most refined and sublime. The condition of Pure Rest, when realised becomes our experience. But this experience is not induced by some manipulations with energy nor is it taken from the outer source. It is a real experience! In one Satsang, a Tibetan seeker asked about not clinging to I Am, for clinging brings suffering and is against the Buddha's teachings. This kind of ideas reflects zero understanding regarding the awakening process. Didn't Buddha insist so much, for instance, on mindfulness? Is clinging to mindfulness against the Buddha's teaching? In order to be mindful all the time, you need to be extremely attached to this idea. Some seekers are infatuated with words. They play with words like non-attachment or no-self and, at one stage, the natural and balanced perspective gets lost.

Therefore, wanting to experience energy in a certain way is absolutely important. But clinging to accidental energy experiences which do not reflect our true Nature, represents spiritual materialism or hedonism; they, hence must be transcended. What the real seeker longs for is the Self, that which is deeply intimate and absolutely direct. Here, one transcends the horizontal dimension of reality, with all its accidental and impermanent experiences. At this moment, one enters the cave of the Lion, the I Am, the dimension of the Now, the domain of the Beloved.

Ego-image and I Am

Student: *Can you speak about the relationship between I Am and the ego-image?*

Aziz: I Am is impersonal. I Am is that in which you are resting, when you simply are. For example, you sit in meditation and suddenly you find yourself inside the state of Being. This state is a combination of Being, Heart and Awareness. It is impersonal, there is no one inside - just energy. But suddenly, you become aware of this state! You say to yourself: 'oh, I am sitting in I Am, I am experiencing I Am.' Who is the one who is aware of I Am?

Student: *It is Me, my Soul.*

Aziz: That is correct. It is you but what is this you? It is a combination of intelligence and sensitivity from the Heart. Me has two main centres. One is the centre of awareness, the centre of intelligence. The second is the centre in the Heart. Me and I Am are same and different, they are like two sides of the same reality. They cannot be completely made into one.

Student: *When you say Me, do you mean the ego-me?*

Aziz: No, the Pure Me. The ego-image is merely a reflection of Me in the mind. It is the ability of the mind to create a self-image. The ego is also Me, but just a surface of it. It is not that the ego is an illusion or that it is not you - it is simply a partial experience of yourself. And when you do not know your true Me, you live only in the ego-reality. This partial, fragmented reality of the ego, where you are stuck in the mind and in the play of ego-images, represents ignorance. The ego-image exists only in its relationship to the outer, to the collective consciousness. If there was no collective consciousness, for example, if there was no humanity, you would not be able to create any image of yourself. You can have an ego-image only because you compare yourself with other human beings. If there is no comparison, there is no ego-image.

On the other hand, self-image is positive, as it is the Soul-image. Through self-image, you know the truth of your real identity as the Complete Me as well as the truth of your relationship with the Creator. The self-image is still an image but image which is based on truth. For example, when you stand in front of the mirror saying 'I am so beautiful,' it is an ego-image. You do not know in your aloneness that you are handsome or that you are unattractive. You can create this image by comparing yourself with others. But the self-image is to know that you are the Soul, Pure Me. And this Pure Me is alone. You have no way to relate it to society for there is no relationship between your Pure Me and society. The ego can relate to society but Pure Me can relate only to the Creator. You cannot share your Pure Me with others in terms of communicating your innermost essence. You can Be your Pure Me and share her only through your presence. You can share her only in silence.

Having a clear self-image or the Soul-image is to know that you are a child of the Creator, a child of the Beloved. It is to know that you are made from the pure light of consciousness and love. Yes... It is to know that your true home is in the Beyond. Your self-image is also the image of your evolution. Through this image you understand where you are heading to, what is your purpose and which elements are necessary for your Soul's completion. For example, if you wish to reach I Am, you create a certain self-image of yourself reaching awakening. Isn't it so? And here often the ego-image and self-image are mixed together. That is because the ego may want to have some gratification in terms of its image. That's why, for many seekers, one of the main motivations on the Path is to become a guru and to have many disciples. Mean while the self-image is concerned only with your motivation to become complete, to reach your Pure Me and to transcend suffering.

The self-image refers to something which is real, it is your real image, reflecting your real situation. It is not true that it is wrong to have a self-image. In truth, self-image is positive and necessary. But as you transcend the mind and rest more and more in a state beyond thinking, your move to the place absent of images. This non-conceptual reality is the foundation of our being. However, on the top of this foundation, you still exist as a Soul, as an individual Me. Non-conceptualisation is not just a passive state but an internal space full of potential. You as a Soul, you are dynamic and you still have to face the challenges of life. So in order to be able to face those challenges, to understand your situation, some image is needed. Even though the self-image is not a foundation, it is still a natural expression of the existence of Me.

Before You Surrender, You have to be Present

Student: *How is it that we need to be present before we can surrender?*

Aziz: If you are not present, it is just the mind who wants to surrender. The mind cannot let go of its momentum of unconscious thinking. The mind can try very hard to surrender but is unable to do it! It is because the nature of the mind is exactly opposite to the idea of surrender. The mind cannot give itself up. Before we speak about surrender, the one who wants to surrender must be present. You want to surrender, but who is it who wants to surrender? This idea comes from the mind but who is behind this mind?

To surrender, you have to let go. When you cultivate attention, you crystallise your sense of identity which is different from surrender. Surrender is when you let go vertically into the non-referral space of Being, into the depth of the Now. Self-remembrance is not surrender, it is to become solidified as Me. Surrender is to go beyond Me. Here, we utilise two opposite but complementary energies. One is that we solidify our sense of Me by giving birth to a real centre. And the second is that we let go of it allowing our presence to merge, to dissolve into the bottomless opening of Being. When awareness is stabilised, you no longer need to remember yourself. At this stage you can fully surrender. Surrender is an art of letting go...

The I Am is not a Centre

Student: *When I am resting in I Am, I don't feel any centre. What is the centre?*

Aziz: The term centre mainly relates to the essence of awareness. But even when your relax with the centre of awareness, it loses its centralised quality. Similar to the Heart, you can feel her in the area of the chest. You recognise her as a certain concentration and expansiveness of energy. But when this centre is sufficiently activated, it no longer has a centralised quality. You feel it as a vast space of sensitivity and love which merges with the whole of I Am. Being, as such, cannot be experienced as a centre even though the energetic gateway to this experience is in the Hara.

When you relax in I Am, letting it be in its natural condition, this experience has no focal point. I Am has no centre, but has an extraordinary strength and profound solidity. In the case of being 'spaced-out' or in the mystical state, there is no centre, but no strength of energy either. Such a state is not grounded in reality. That is the difference between the positive and negative no-mind. The negative no-mind is simply spaced-out. The positive no-mind is constant, solid and deep; it carries the strength of energy and inherent bliss.

Awareness is Only a Part of I Am

Student: *What is the difference between Awareness and I Am?*

Aziz: Awareness is just one aspect of I Am. I Am is more than awareness, for it includes Being and the Heart. Awareness is the consciousness of I Am. Being is below awareness; it is the energetic foundation upon which you are resting. Awareness allows you to know that you experience Being. When awareness is awakened, it experiences itself apart from thinking. Awareness is your identity in the mind.

Presence and Dissolution

Student: *When I focus on Awareness, I am present. But when I meditate on the Heart, I feel like dissolving. How to reconcile these two contradictory experiences?*

Aziz: Yes... The purpose of your evolution is dissolution. It is not absolute dissolution but becoming merged, where the experience of yourself is transparent. Here you become absorbed in the Ultimate Reality and, at the same time, your Me in a mysterious way is just a part of this experience. That is the experience of unity between the Soul and the Creator. But before you can dissolve, paradoxically you have to become yourself, which means that you have to become present to your own existence.

That's why the beginning of the Path is about the crystallisation of the sense of Me. If you try to surrender, to dissolve before you crystallise yourself, you will simple fall into unconscious or subconscious states. Someone who has no clear sense of Me, who has no centre of awareness, cannot let oneself go, because of their being lost in an ignorant identity. Such a person has no solidity and is spaced-out. Unless one transcends the mind, one does not exist with clear presence, as an autonomous being. The crystallisation of awareness is the only way to freedom from the mind.

In order to truly dissolve, you must be present. But how can you dissolve? When your presence is too crystallised, it can interfere with the dissolving process. To dissolve, you must learn how to let go. Surrender into Being and Surrender into the Heart are different. To let go into Being, you drop into non-doing, allowing energy to gravitate downwards. Breathing into your belly helps. But you cannot surrender into the Heart before it is really activated. When the Heart is closed, the moment you let go, energy goes down bypassing the Heart centre. It anchors itself in the Heart only when the Heart is activated. Being and the Heart are not crystallised but rather activated and deepened. So you see, surrender is not emotional but rather it relates to an energetic expansion. Therefore, first we must prepare the ground.

From Mind to Awareness, from Awareness to Being...

Student: *According to Osho there are two steps: from Awareness to the Heart and from Heart to the Hara. You speak about three steps...*

Aziz: These are just different ways of speaking. There are four steps. From the mind to Awareness, from Awareness to Being, from Being to the Heart and from the Heart to the Beyond.

Non-abidance: Resting upon Nothing

Student: *What is the meaning of non-abiding? Is Transparent Me non-abiding?*

Aziz: Similar to Shikantaza, there are different levels and secrets of non-abiding. The general translation of this term is to rest in the Absolute State. Here, you abide upon Nothing, resting in the original Void. Non-abiding means not relying upon anything. You are always abiding upon something. Your body is supported on the earth, your mind is supported on ideas and mental objects...and so forth. In that way, you are locked in the Creation where everything relates and depends on everything else. But where is this place where you don't relate to anything? The shift into the Absolute takes us to the state of non-reference. In Being, you are not supported by anything, you abide upon nothing. This nothing is itself the pure isness of Existence.

That is the first level of non-abidance; it is based on realising the Absolute State. From a higher perspective however, it is not yet a pure non-abidance because the inner and the outer are still polarised. What it means on the energy level is that energy is pulled down to the Hara towards the Unmanifested. The reason that resting in the Absolute does not represent pure non-abidance is the lack of Soul-realisation. For who is the one experiencing non-abidance? When the one who realises the non-abidance is not aware of itself, the very centre of this experience is missed. The centre of all experiences is nothing but Me.

In order to discover the essence of Me, the Heart must open. When the Heart is awakened, energy is brought up exactly mid-way between the inner and the outer. At this middle point your Me can fully let go into the reality of pure isness. But because Me does not gravitate towards the Absolute, but rather stays exactly mid-way between the Absolute and Creation, one truly abides upon nothing.

Even though we called the realisation of the Absolute non-abidance, in truth, the Soul abides not upon nothing, but upon the Absolute. Here, energy is radically pulled in. It is not pure non-abidance, for the inner dimension and the outer dimension are still polarised. In true non-abidance, totality is apperceived. This means that Me is absolutely motionless and dissolves through herself into the wholeness of What Is. In pure non-abidance, energy doesn't go anywhere, neither does it gravitate downwards, nor does it move upwards. It maintains pure stillness, free from any will and movement. Here, Me reaches the optimum of her absence, dissolving into the Universal Presence. This is the maximum of one's absence, beyond consciousness, subconsciousness and unconsciousness; this is beyond the inner and the outer, beyond knowing and not-knowing; beyond, beyond, beyond... we call this the Transparent Me. Reaching the ultimate transparency, Me neither abides in herself, nor in the Beyond. In different words, Me abides through herself in the Beyond. When the relative is transcended, non-abidance represents the same as the Absolute Abidance. It is neither abidance nor non-abidance, but it is What It Is.

Movement within I Am

Student: *Is the energy of I Am always going up and down or does it becomes constant at one point?*

Aziz: It finally becomes constant and motionless when all elements are integrated and when Awareness, Being and Heart completely merge into the Unmanifested. Before that happens, there is always some movement within this energy - a movement within stillness. What it means is that there is already a certain solidity in the inner state.

You see, many elements are to be considered. When the centre is predominant, which centres are activated and to what extent? For instance, if the third eye is your predominant centre, you experience energy mainly in the head area. If you are the Being type, your energy is lower. And if you are the Heart type, energy is centralised in the middle of your chest.

There is a natural movement between Awareness, Being and the Heart which reflects the wisdom of I Am. In activity, awareness is most present, while in meditation energy gravitates more towards Being. The movement of energy is transcended in the Absolute State, within the Being quality of I Am. Here, one merges with the Source. When the Heart is fully awakened, she becomes integrated with the Absolute as well. Awareness reaches this condition only after shifting to the State Beyond Polarities which is a very rare attainment. In the case, of the State Beyond Polarities, the movement of energy is radically transcended. In this state one fully meets the Beloved.

Student: *So, when you just stop and allow the energy to be in its natural condition, will it go where it is supposed... that is into Being and Heart?*

Aziz: Not always so automatically. There is something like the dimension of Awareness which can be experienced artificially, as if in separation from the Heart and Being. What it means is that when awareness relaxes, even though it prevails everywhere, still it is paradoxically present within the headspace. The reason is that the source of awareness is in the brain. The human brain is the instrument through which Universal Consciousness expresses itself as individual consciousness.

When you experience Being, the energy goes lower and deeper. When awareness abides in awareness, we have the Natural State, but of awareness only. When awareness is self-aware, it creates a centre; but when it rests in itself, it opens up like a space and is no longer so concentrated. Here, awareness goes beyond self-referral, becoming luminous and serene. That is the experience of pure awareness without content. The experience of Being is below the neck; it gravitates towards the Hara. They are absolutely interconnected, but artificially they can be separated. One can for example experience Being without the State of Presence, where attention functions only minimally and is not self-aware.

When the Heart is not awakened, the moment you let go, energy moves to the Hara bypassing the Heart. Energy never goes to the Heart, unless it is activated. For the Heart, in order to pull energy into herself, first must be awakened. Awakening of the Heart is not automatic and in the case of most masters, it takes place years after the initial Self-realisation. Even kundalini awakening does not necessarily open the Heart automatically. Evolution is a complex process and not merely a one-time event.

The State Beyond Polarities

Student: *Can we speak about the State Beyond Polarities in terms of horizontal and vertical realities? And is the State of Presence awakened within the frame of the horizontal reality only?*

Aziz: Any kind of awakening takes place always within the frame of horizontal reality but still relates to the vertical reality. The State Beyond Polarities is the optimum one can reach in going beyond horizontal reality and thereby in reaching the vertical. It is simply the optimum. It represents the optimum of the Now within the Here.

Student: *What is the relationship between the State Beyond Polarities and time?*

Aziz: First of all, the one who experiences time is the extension of the Soul; it is the personality, the psyche. One is experiencing time as long as intelligence operates, as long as the emotional body is active and as long as there is the physicality. Individual consciousness needs the presence of horizontal reality and time. The very fact that intelligence is active shows it is already taking place in time, that it is already present in the horizontal reality. The very fact that you can experience your emotions as a separate being within your separateness is the experience of time and that relates to the Here.

There is no mystery in the nature of time; it simply operates naturally as it does. Only the Pure Me is resting beyond polarities, abiding unconditionally beyond of time. But the one who knows it and recognises it is intelligence which is indivisible from time. This intelligence is registering an experience which has already happened in the immediate past. All that you experience has happened in the past. You live in a universe which has already ended! That is because perception always refers to the past. For any recognition or act of consciousness to take place there has to be a distance in time between the perceiver and the perceived. This distance is possible only when the present event removes itself into the past allowing itself to be recognised in the Now. You can experience this universe only because it has already happened; although you may think the universe exists right now, it is only a deception of the mind which interprets the immediate past as the 'present moment.' However, the most mysterious element of reality is the very perceiver of it. That is, the perceiver neither exists in the past nor in the Now; rather the perceiver acts as a link between them both.

Reality is the Absence of You

Student: *What is Reality?*

Aziz: It is all that remains when your me gets out of the way. You cannot see reality for you are on the way! But, paradoxically, reality can be realised only when you become one with your Me. This Me cannot be cancelled, she cannot be erased, she cannot be negated - but she can become awakened. When Me is awakened, she becomes Transparent. She is not longer the ego-image but pure transparency. In becoming transparent, Me dissolves into the Totality. That is the blossoming of individual evolution: the Soul becomes one with the Beloved.

Are there Levels in Silence?

Student: *You speak about the many states of awakening, but can there also be many levels in silence?*

Aziz: Beloved, what is silence? Silence is not the absence of sound but the presence of I Am. The presence of I Am is an energy experience and, therefore, silence is an energy phenomenon. You can experience silence in many ways which reflect the various levels of depth you are immersed in. Silence is like an Ocean - there are many levels of depth that you can dive into.

You must understand that silence is an energy experience. And who is that One who experiences silence? You are not just silent; this silence has a flavour...doesn't it? It has the flavour of the Soul, of your unique sensitivity and intelligence. Yes, the spiritual path is an evolution into the dimension of silence, where your individual Me becomes more and more absorbed into the universal womb of absolute silence, which is nothing but the presence of God. There are many dimensions of silence. For instance, the silence in the middle of the night in the big city is very different than the silence in high mountains! There is a silence after the lightening in the sky and there is a silence at the bottom of the Ocean...many different flavours of silence - all of them founded upon the Original Absence, the supreme presence of the Absolute.

I Am is beyond 'Watching'

Student: *Is it possible to be in the State of Presence and to watch the mind?*

Aziz: A very important issue to understand. Everybody is confused about the true meaning of terms like watching or witnessing. Who is the witness? Who is doing the observing? The State of Presence is not observing, for it has no way to observe anything. Watching is done by the subtle mind called intelligence. Watching is not meditation. Watching is something between the ordinary state of consciousness (or rather unconsciousness) and the one of pure awareness. It is neither completely ignorant nor is it truly conscious. But when you are in the State of Presence, you abide in the dimension beyond the mind. However, the mind still manifests some thoughts according to its nature. Watching is one of the many ways the thinking mind creates an attitude towards its own content. Watching is not just based on disidentification but on a certain distance or spaciousness within the thinking process within which intelligence can move, trying to reach understanding.

It is important to see that watching and witnessing (State of Presence) can co-exist as two complementary aspects of the same human consciousness. The one who is watching is intelligence. Intelligence is the dynamic expression of awareness. From one side, intelligence recognises the State of Presence looking back; from the other side, intelligence participates in the reality of the mind, whether thinking consciously or observing, learning, letting go of thoughts...and so forth. Do you understand it? It is very simple, but there doesn't exist a teaching on this planet which has ever explained it.

Who is aware of the State of Presence? Who could that be? It is your intelligence. Isn't it? Who is observing the mind? It is the same intelligence. Isn't it? And who is present behind this intelligence? To whom does this intelligence apply? Isn't it your sense of Me? And when you become one with this sense of Me, the State of Presence is born. The State of Presence is just present. It doesn't do anything. It represents the energetic centre around which the movement of intelligence can take place. If this state is not present, intelligence has no centre and is therefore deprived of any solidity or true continuity...it is simply ignorant.

Two Types of Samadhi

Student: *What types of Samadhi are there?*

Aziz: There are two types of Samadhi: Samadhi in Awareness and Samadhi in Being. In the first Samadhi, one is resting in the space of pure consciousness. This experience is energetically located in the head area. In the case of the second type of Samadhi, energy is rooted in Being and gravitates towards the Hara. In the Samadhi in Being, they're two possibilities. One is Samadhi with awareness and the second is Samadhi without awareness. In the Samadhi without awareness, one is in a trance-state similar to the deep sleep. This state has no spiritual value, as it cannot be brought into life. Life is awareness! In the case of Samadhi with awareness, Being is absorbed into the Unmanifested but consciousness is fully present.

III

DIMENSION OF THE SOUL

I Am is the Light of Creation the heart of which in the very beginning gave birth to Me our ancient Soul identity.

The Soul is the mysterious subject to the evolution in time. She is the dual experiencer of the non-dual Creation. She is neither created nor uncreated; neither One with the Beloved nor separated. To her not only Creation but even the Creator applies. She belongs to the mysterious realm, to the dimension of Me. She dwells eternally in the Heart of the Beloved, but evolves through her creative intelligence, reaching completion in her inner reality, fulfilment in the world and finally merging with the Divine.

Enlightenment to Me

Enlightenment to Me is a flowering of our individual evolution and the true purpose of our existence. It is nothing but becoming One again and regaining our ultimate integrity. Me cannot realise herself fully unless she rests in the Beyond. The reason is that Me cannot be taken out of the context of that which sustains her presence, which is the Beloved. Upon reaching full Awareness and absorption in Being, Me can then rest within in the internal Ocean of Love and Stillness. From that place Me can meet herself fully at the core of her most intimate identity - which is in the Heart. This meeting is beyond words...it is pure Love, the most moving experience of all.

Innocence is of the Soul

Student: *Can you speak about innocence?*

Aziz: Innocence is one of the main qualities of the Soul. It represents the original purity of the Soul. True innocence is found in the Heart, the child-like quality of Pure Me prior to the ego-image. True innocence is a meeting of silence and sensitivity. A child's innocence is naïve and ignorant, in truth. The innocence of the sage, of the Buddha, is one with complete understanding. When the knowledge consumes itself, when understanding submits itself to the Unknown, when Awakening is no longer self-conscious, when one is beyond ignorance and beyond Enlightenment, when one encounters life as if seeing it for the first time, when one is amazed by the fact that one exists, when one recognises the Beloved, the presence of Divinity - it is then that true innocence is born. Innocence is to become what one has always been - a child of the Beloved. When a human becomes a Buddha, this is awakening. When a Buddha becomes a human, this is innocence. Innocence is to be Here but not of Here...

Aloneness of the Soul

Student: *Can entry into the Mystery, the meeting between the Soul and the Beloved, ever be shared or does it only happen in this aloneness...*

Aziz: It can be shared for it is being shared here! Isn't it? Certainly, it can and moreover it has to be shared, but the experience itself on some level cannot be.

As an individual you experience deep human emotions and intimate encounters with inner silence and you will wish to communicate these experiences to other human beings. This need to share is an indivisible part of being human. The thought that you are unable to share that which is most precious, seems very cruel. But when you look deeper into this matter, you discover that sharing takes place anyway, but in a much more profound way. You share the inner experience through your own presence. In truth, you cannot avoid sharing for to be alive is to be a part of the sharing phenomenon.

Sharing, in terms of communication or teaching requires an ability to speak from one mind to another. This requires some conceptual tools and the ability to tune into other people's psyches. This type of communication has its limitations but when there is a connection between Souls, love and intuition can act as a bridge between them.

Who Feels the Happiness of I Am?

Student: *Is I Am happiness itself?*

Aziz: When you abide in I Am, there is someone who feels: 'I am happy to experience the bliss of the Inner State.' Who is that one who feels the bliss? It is not I Am. I Am is the very energy which creates bliss. But who is the experiencer of bliss? Who is the one trying to reach bliss and repeat this experience? Who is the one wanting to reach peace? It is Me. And what is this Me?

Me exists within I Am. I Am is the space, without which Me cannot exist. But Me is something else. Me has two ways through which she recognises her own existence. One way is through intelligence where Me can create a self-referral in the mind. For example, you contemplate your inner state and you know that it is your contemplation. You are able to create a self-referral in the mind. Here, Me is aware of herself in intelligence. The second way through which Me can know herself is in the Heart, where Me feels herself as the most pure feeling of Me. Me is able to think about herself, that is, to create a self-referral, and Me is able to feel herself in the Heart. But when Me relaxes into I Am, she merges with Being as if she forgets about herself. However, at the same time Me knows that she is experiencing the Inner State. They are one and they are different. Me is the experiencer of I Am and I Am is the very life of Me, the environment in which Me can live. It is a very interesting process, for we are awakening Me to herself and simultaneously, we are awakening the ability to go beyond Me. These two parallel processes cannot be separated.

The most beautiful experience takes place when the Soul is awakened to herself fully. At that moment, you know who you are as an individual creation of God. But when the Soul merges with the Universal I AM, she goes beyond herself. What does it mean to merge? It means that you are not doing anything but existing. That within which your existence is contained is I AM. It is impersonal; it is universal - the universal space of Beingness. We have two parallel, interpenetrating realities: the Soul and I Am. This issue is subtle and difficult to be grasped unless one can fully experience it. Me and I Am are one but different at the same time. Through the polarisation within I Am, Me can be born. It is Me which knows I Am. I Am has no way of knowing itself. Me and I Am complement each other. They are the two different angles of looking at our reality.

Me is not the ego. The ego is a shadow of Me: a reflection, a self-image in the mind. When Me translates her existence as an image in the mind, she crystallises herself as a mental, virtual Me. This is what we call ego. It is only in the mind. Pure Me has the centre in the Heart. It is a profound feeling-recognition of the Soul. It is beyond personality, beyond any relative thoughts, feelings, emotions and experiences. This feeling of the Soul is the Soul; this feeling is non-dual. Who is feeling the Heart? It is the Soul. It is the Soul which is feeling herself. Here, the feeler and that which is felt become one. However, the Soul is more dynamic. The Soul exists on two levels: one is the Soul at rest, and the second is the Soul in motion. When the Soul is at rest, it is a pure experience for you are not doing anything. In that state you just rest in the I AM; the Soul is at rest. In the second situation, the Soul is in motion and there is a certain dynamic movement - you feel yourself, you are able to relate to the Inner State.

Yes...an awakened Soul exists in these two ways: in motion and in rest. An ordinary human being which is unawakened, exists however only in motion, not at all experiencing the Soul at rest. Here, we are simply awakening the ability to experience the Soul at rest. That is your core-identity, separate from any action, any perception, any thought, memory or mental association. Your true identity, that which you have always been, is pure subjectivity.

Realities of Me

Student: *How is it that we have these different parts? One part is thinking, another part is resting, another part is aware, another part is feeling?*

Aziz: It is a question about the multidimensionality of being the human. We exist at the same time on many levels. We think, we feel, we experience our body and if awakened, we experience the transcendental state of I Am. For example, you rest in Being during meditation, but simultaneously you may be thinking consciously or subconsciously, you may feel some emotions, you may hear the sound of a bird. These are all your realities, aren't they?

Student: *Is the right way trying to include all in order to experience all these parts as myself?*

Aziz: All is already included! And you have no choice but to experience all of this as your very self. But the deep meaning of containing it all as the reality of Me, is to experience all these different elements from the place of inner silence and non-abidance. Simply speaking, you experience the whole of your Me from the place of resting in the depth of Being. And what it means is that you can contain the whole of you only from the place of your absence, which is the Beyond. All that you experience is a part of your Me phenomenon and how this Me perceives reality. But from which place do you experience this Me? When you experience Me only from the place of Me, there is no space and the experience cannot be contained; you get suffocated with yourself. In order to embrace yourself, you need to go beyond the self-referral of your very Me. When you have transcended yourself, the Impersonal Existence becomes your very place of abidance, which is non-abidance, for the state is based on the absence of Me.

Student: *Is it Enlightenment to Me?*

Aziz: Many students cannot grasp the difference between Self-realisation and Soul-realisation. Self-realisation refers to going beyond oneself and merging with the Universal Beingness. Soul-realisation is awakening to that very One who has transcended itself. To realise the Self is to go beyond; to realise the Soul is to discover oneself from the inside. These are, in truth, two sides of the same phenomenon. This is called apperception or the total seeing of What Is in which the seer is an invisible part of the experience. By the way, the seer is not the Self (as they concluded in Upanishads) but the Soul.

The ultimate containment takes place when our sense of identity rests fully in the Beyond; and at the same time, the one who rests which is Me, realises herself from inside of herself. In this way, one abides in one's own Soul identity while simultaneously abiding in the Beyond. Here, Me meets the Beloved and the experience of it is beyond Me and beyond the Beloved.

Awakening to Me refers to the discovery of the unconditional essence of Individuality. There is I Am, which is the impersonal space of Being and there is the Soul which is the intimate encounter with your Pure Me. There is the State of Me where Me as a unified experience is contained within the universal field of Being.

The multidimensionality we spoke about refers to a slightly different understanding. Here, apart from the Universal Presence and the personal Soul, a more dynamic extension of Me is contained. This dynamic extension of Me is the psyche. The psyche represents the Soul in motion and includes such elements as the physical body, intelligence, emotional body... and so forth.

Individuality is the Unique Recognition of Universality

Student: *Can you talk about individuality and Oneness?*

Aziz: The word 'individual' comes from the root-word 'indivisible' which means: undivided. As we know there are two parallel types of awakening. One is to the Impersonal Existence or Self-realisation and the second is to the Personal Existence or Soul-realisation. The experience of Oneness refers to the ultimate relationship of the Soul with the Source of Creation. But the Soul cannot reach unity with absolute subjectivity unless she first becomes one with herself. Here, the Soul discovers her indivisibility. That's why, only when one becomes truly individual does one meet oneself as a

Soul. You cannot experience unity with the Source unless you really exist as an individual. To be an individual is to have a real centre, a continuity of intelligence, a depth of Being and an awakened Heart. This is an individual, the whole being - the one who is ready to meet the Ultimate face to face. Only within your complete presence, that is indivisibility, can you merge with your absolute absence, the Source of Creation.

Through Awakening You Enter the Real World

Student: *When a person is fully awakened to the Self and to the Soul, how does this change the quality of relating to others?*

Aziz: For the first time one is relating to others! Before, one lives in a dream world, in the world of imagination and fantasy, in the net of infinite projections. When you become your Soul, you enter the real world where Truth reigns. In this real world, you are present to your indivisibility, you live beyond the mind. From the place beyond the mind, you see the real world, the world of beauty and wonder but also the world of sorrow, suffering, unconsciousness, ignorance and forgetfulness. Yes, it is the real world full of dreamers and sleepwalkers. When you are awakened, you see the world as it is and for the first time you can relate to what is. But as you look more carefully, there is no one to relate to - for everyone is in a trance! When you are awakened, you bring your awakened presence into whatever you do and whomever you meet. When you are present to your Soul, you no longer see personalities around yourself - you see only Souls. Souls who are lost and hide under the mask of their personalities but which still possess a deep longing in the Heart to awaken. To see a Soul is to see the reality of another human being, beyond projections, beyond masks and veils superimposed on them by the ego-image.

As you are awakened to your Soul and you feel the Souls of others, a natural compassion is born. This compassion arises out of clarity and sensitivity; it is a part of the real world. In order to perceive the real world, you must be located beyond the world. When you are identified with your personality, you are yourself a dream character. And what type of relation can one dream character have with the other characters? It is all one huge, monstrous net of projections. To see reality from the place of inner silence, complete awareness and an open Heart, is to meet oneself fully; one becomes Oneself. That is Enlightenment to Me. That is the primal Enlightenment to Me which is a state beyond movement. We call this realisation the Transparent Me.

However, there is also another type of awakening to the Soul which is more dynamic and relates to the discovery of one's blueprint. The blueprint is the ultimate vision of one's evolutionary completion. The Soul is dynamic. She is not only realised as a state of a pure experience but she is realised through her evolution in time. In this evolution, the Soul becomes more whole. She completes herself in the context of understanding, sensitivity, emotional maturation and creativity. She reaches as far as possible her unique ultimate angle of perception. These are the two types of awakening to Me: one is more static, the other is more dynamic. These are the two sides of the Soul-realisation.

You are not THAT!

Student: *Am I THAT?*

Aziz: You are not and you will never be! But THAT is you.

Student: *So who am I?*

Aziz: To ask this question is a good beginning. You see, it is not so important who you are but who you could be! Now you are the mind! The answer to your question 'who am I?' is: 'you are the mind.' But the more you ask yourself this question, the more you become that which you could be, which is the Real Me.

It is like to ask 'what is inside of a seed?' Inside a seed is a future tree, but this tree is not there yet. Similarly, your Real Me is closed in the shell of the mind. The seed may become a tree or may not. Not all seeds become the trees. Some of them die, become dry or are eaten by the birds! So now you are asking from inside of the seed the question 'who am I?' We answer you, 'you can become a tree if you wish, but you are not this tree yet!' Similarly, do not deceive yourself, thinking that you are THAT. You are not only not THAT, but you have not yet become the one who might recognise THAT. Before you worry how to become THAT, find out how to become a Real Me!

You will never become THAT but you could become 'I.' 'I' is not THAT but the first and foremost manifestation of THAT. When this 'I' is fully Self-realised (THAT-realised) it doesn't

The Self is the environment within which the Soul abides experiencing herself and her absence. The Self is like the sun. The sun is not self-conscious but makes everything visible. The Soul is the reflection of the sun in a dewdrop. This dewdrop reflects the whole of the sun, but on a micro scale. It is in the dewdrop that the sun becomes conscious of its existence. The numberless dewdrops reflect one sun, in infinite different and unique ways. All these dewdrops represent individual Souls, the countless reflections of the faceless face of the Beloved. That is the miracle of Creation.

Awakening to the Soul

Student: *Can you describe the process of giving birth to the Soul?*

Aziz: The Soul is giving birth to herself through the evolution of consciousness, intelligence and Heart. The moment the Soul incarnates, she becomes identified with the body and the mind. Initially, she functions only as the ego, unless there is a certain connection with the Heart. For that which makes the Soul a Soul is the Heart. Even if a person is unconscious if the Heart is awakened on some level, then you can at least feel the Soul. Here, the Soul is still not realised, but is felt shyly on the surface.

When we speak about the awakening of the Soul, we point to the complete meeting with our eternal identity. Before becoming One, the Soul is fragmented and unconscious. Firstly, she functions as the mind where she is able to create the ego-image. She is trying to fulfil herself, for even in the case of the ego, the emotional body is present and so the desire for happiness and pleasure is also present. This is how the Soul operates in her unconscious period. She tries to reach happiness and satisfaction within her personality, through the ego and the body. The most primitive type of the ego is identified with the body. An example is those simple-minded individuals who all the time cultivate their muscles wanting to be stronger than others.

As the Soul evolves more, she sees that there are more important matters than physicality and wishes to develop wisdom. She reads books, she goes to university and reads poetry; she gathers different types of knowledge in order to become wiser. This is the case of the intellectual ego. Such an ego is very proud of its knowledge and cleverness. Next, the Soul discovers that even this does not bring her real satisfaction, it is also empty. So the Soul starts to look deeper. She starts to question herself, the whole reality and eventually enters the Spiritual Path. At the end, the Soul becomes ready to discover a way of existing which is truly intimate with the depth of her true Me beyond the mind.

First the Soul is expressed as the body, next as the movement of the mind. Through the mind she is able to create a self-referral, which is the birth of the ego. Afterwards, the Soul awakens to the State of Presence and is able to experience a clear centre of awareness. Next she expands into Being and is able to surrender vertically into the Now, experiencing absorption within the Ultimate. At last, she discovers herself in the Heart. In the Heart, the Soul becomes one with herself and meets the Beloved.

Student: *Are there any people who are born with an awakened Soul?*

Aziz: Yes. If the Heart is awakened, we can say the Soul is awakened. There are Souls who have awakened the Heart in their past lives. However, it is not always immediately present and often a certain additional awakening is needed to bring this realisation back. Secondly, the Soul cannot be experienced fully unless she has a clear centre in the mind and a connection with Being. This is because the Heart and the Soul cannot be taken out of the context of awareness and Being. Awareness and Being create the environment within which the Soul can live and experience her Heart.

Therefore, a person with only an awakened Heart does not necessarily experience the complete Soul. The Soul is awakened but not complete. There is no depth to this realisation, simply because the mind is constantly daydreaming. There is no continuity of intelligence. In order to become fully awakened, there has to be a continuity of intelligence. One has to be present from moment to moment in one's existence as Me. For example, a person who has an awakened Heart, but no awareness, experiences the Heart only from time to time. It is not the real Heart because one is constantly being disturbed by the mind. One loses oneself like this in the unconscious and negative tendencies of the mind. Here, the mind comes like an eclipse and covers the Heart. In this sense, the Heart without awareness is insincere. While awareness without the Heart is arrogant...

Prayer can Happen only in Separation

Student: *Can you speak about separation and non-separation in prayer?*

Aziz: Prayer itself is the movement of love which takes place in the mysterious gap in-between separation and non-separation. Prayer is only possible because one is separated. On the other hand, true prayer can take place only because one already experiences unity with the Beloved. When you are only praying from a place of being isolated from the Light of Creation, you perceive God as something outside of yourself. For many people God is simply an 'object,' like a chair. Ignorant people think that God is in some distant place listening to prayers and answering them. But God is not an object, God is the subject. So how can we pray to this subject? This subject is not our Me, it is the Ultimate Subject. It is similar to when you rest in your Heart. The one who is resting in the Heart is the Soul. You feel your Soul in the Heart, that is the subject. When you rest deeper in the Heart, the Heart actually is resting upon something which you cannot really grasp. We call it the Ultimate Subjectivity. Also when you are resting in Being, it is the subject that is resting. It is resting upon something that cannot really be grasped, the Ultimate Subjectivity. God is the Ultimate Subjectivity, a combination of Absolute Beingness and Love. When you are awakened, you rest permanently upon this reality, experiencing unconditional unity with Truth.

When you discover your connection with Being and Heart, then no longer are you separated from the Beloved. It is very miraculous and amazing that you can experience unity with God. It is not an emotional unity but a grounded realisation so that you can really rest in God. But at the same time, it is you that rests in God for you are the Soul. You experience the beauty of resting in God but at the same time you experience a certain pain or sadness related to you being separate.

The Soul Must be Born

Student: *Does the Soul experience emotions?*

Aziz: The Soul experiences emotions through the emotional body. Who is experiencing emotions? There is only the Soul, the Soul experiences everything. The Soul is the experiencer of the mind, emotions, physical body and outer perceptions; there is only the Soul. When the Soul is disconnected or unawakened, she is fragmented, she does not experience her existence fully being identified with the mind. What it means is that even though it is the Soul who experiences emotions, these emotions do not refer to any clear Me. These emotions operate in their virtual reality separate from the Soul. The psyche becomes completely identified and one loses the connection with one's own subjective reality within the psychological flow. The Soul is indeed there but unconscious. It is like a dream state - where you experience many things but you cannot find any real subject there because you are lost in this dream. That is why, even though the Soul experiences everything, paradoxically, she is not necessarily aware of herself. She is lost. On some level, you can say the Soul is not there yet. She has to be awakened and become born.

Awakening to Me

Student: *Can you talk about awakening to Me?*

Aziz: Awakening to Me is the awakening to the Soul which is your true identity as an individual. When one incarnates, one becomes manifested into the reality of time. One carries with oneself a certain intimate individual identity which is unique. We call it the flavour of the Soul. It is not merely that the mind or consciousness that incarnates - that which incarnates has the flavour of an individual. This flavour of individuality is primarily located in the Heart centre. For this reason, it is in the Heart where you meet yourself in the closest way possible. The Heart is Nearest to you. This unique flavour of Me cannot realise herself fully unless different faculties are awakened. When a child is born, he is unconscious: the brain is not developed, intelligence is not activated and he is not emotionally matured. Therefore, the child needs to grow. This means the body has to grow, the brain needs to develop and intelligence has to be activated. One undergoes a constant process of learning. The Soul grows and matures. First she develops her ego which includes the conscious mind in combination with the emotional body. She develops the ability to survive in the world, to protect herself physically and psychologically. The Soul is present from the very beginning but is not aware of herself. She is conscious to some extent. She knows that there is some kind of Me who wants to be happy but she is completely identified with the phenomenal reality. This is because when the child incarnates, he becomes immediately infatuated with the outer. There is nobody home, only what is around the home matters. The child is constantly learning, adventuring, being exited about the outer. This is the nature of a child. He has to learn, this is imprinted. It is a sub-conscious process.

Eventually when the Soul matures, she may be ready for self-discovery. It means she creates an intention to go beyond the mind and to discover that which is real. This intention may be awakened on the intuitive level or one can receive this information from a master. The awakening of the Soul can happen in many different ways; there are different stages. Here we create a linear model to simplify. Firstly, the Soul transcends the mind by awakening the centre of awareness. This means that the Soul discovers that there is a centre of identity, an 'I' which is independent from the movement of the mind. We call this the State of Presence, the centre of attention or self-awareness. Next, the Soul expands into the internal reality of I Am through Being. You surrender into Beingness; the vertical letting go towards the source of gravity. This is Being. Here the Soul discovers Beingness which is the ultimate environment within which Me lives. Next, the Soul discovers the Heart and she comes as close as possible to her deepest sense of identity. When awareness is present and there is a connection with Being, the Soul can say for the first time: I Am. This is because the Soul experiences herself fully in separation from the constant movement of becoming, thinking, emotions and the general restlessness of energy. When the Soul discovers herself in the Heart, she meets herself face to face. If there is no awareness and no Being, the Soul cannot contain the experience of herself in the Heart. That is why, it is not sufficient to awaken the Heart in order to meet fully one's Soul. Without the other qualities of I Am, the experience of the Soul is fragmented.

When we speak about Enlightenment to Me, we speak about a very subtle type of Self-realisation or rather Soul-realisation. Here, Me (in her personal expression) fully merges with Me (the Soul at rest) becoming ONE. This experience includes a profound sensitivity, towards one's identity which is present within the context of awareness and Being. In this moment, one meets oneself fully; one becomes Oneself. That is Enlightenment to Me. That is the primal Enlightenment to Me which is a state beyond movement. We call this realisation the Transparent Me.

However, there is also another type of awakening to the Soul which is more dynamic and relates to the discovery of one's blueprint. The blueprint is the ultimate vision of one's evolutionary completion. The Soul is dynamic. She is not only realised as a state of a pure experience but she is realised through her evolution in time. In this evolution, the Soul becomes more whole. She completes herself in the context of understanding, sensitivity, emotional maturation and creativity. She reaches as far as possible her unique ultimate angle of perception. These are the two types of awakening to Me: one is more static, the other is more dynamic. These are the two sides of the Soul-realisation.

You are not THAT!

Student: *Am I THAT?*

Aziz: You are not and you will never be! But THAT is you.

Student: *So who am I?*

Aziz: To ask this question is a good beginning. You see, it is not so important who you are but who you could be! Now you are the mind! The answer to your question 'who am I?' is: 'you are the mind.' But the more you ask yourself this question, the more you become that which you could be, which is the Real Me.

It is like to ask 'what is inside of a seed?' Inside a seed is a future tree, but this tree is not there yet. Similarly, your Real Me is closed in the shell of the mind. The seed may become a tree or may not. Not all seeds become the trees. Some of them die, become dry or are eaten by the birds! So now you are asking from inside of the seed the question 'who am I?' We answer you, 'you can become a tree if you wish, but you are not this tree yet!' Similarly, do not deceive yourself, thinking that you are THAT. You are not only not THAT, but you have not yet become the one who might recognise THAT. Before you worry how to become THAT, find out how to become a Real Me!

You will never become THAT but you could become 'I.' 'I' is not THAT but the first and foremost manifestation of THAT. When this 'I' is fully Self-realised (THAT-realised) it doesn't become THAT but reaches the state of unity with THAT. A tree cannot become the earth but can become rooted in the earth. Do you see the difference?

Let us say it once more. The seed is your present ego-reality. The tree is your Real Me and the earth is THAT or the Absolute Reality. First, from the seed, a tree becomes formed and simultaneously it grows roots into the Beyond itself, which is the earth. The branches of this tree are your intelligence; the leaves are your feelings and the flowers are your Heart; and the fruit which becomes separated from the tree when it is fully ripe is Enlightenment to Me. Enlightenment to Me is the most mysterious of all Enlightenment's. When Me becomes enlightened to herself, she transcends the inner and the outer and her own identity, merging with the Totality, not through negating herself, but through her own self-contained presence. And it can happen only when Me rests fully in the Beyond, in the earth of Beingness.

Student: *I don't understand what is the difference between the 'Real Me' and 'Enlightenment to Me'? It seems that the tree is not the same as the fruit, which falls down from it.*

Aziz: The Real Me is born when the State of Presence is discovered. The Real Me has a constant centre of awareness. That's why, we speak about the Real Me. But the Real Me is not necessarily the Complete Me. There are four distinct realisations of Me. First is the Real Me, second is the Pure Me, third is the Complete Me and fourth is the Transparent Me.

The Real Me you can see as the trunk of the tree. It has a solidity of presence and continuous sense of 'I.' The Real Me represents the awareness aspect of Pure Me. The Pure Me is more than consciousness - it is a unity of pure awareness and the Heart. The Pure Me represents the Soul at rest, Me in herself, apart from her connection to Creation. The Complete Me is manifested when we add to her intelligence which are branches, feelings which are the leaves, the Heart which are the flowers. The Complete Me is the unity of Pure Me and Me in motion which is the psyche and personality. The Transparent Me which is the fruit becomes something distinct from the rest of the tree, a new quality. The subconscious Me gives birth to the Real Me; the Real Me gives birth to the Pure Me; the Pure Me embraces the Complete Me; and the Complete Me gives birth to the Transcendental Me - the

Me which is beyond Me, merged with the Beloved. As there is evolution within the awakening of Me, so there is the evolution of going beyond Me, where the tree becomes one with the earth. That's why, realisation of the Transparent Me can take place only in the Absolute State. That is because only abiding in the Beyond (within her absence) can Me embrace her own totality, that is, motionless transparency.

Self-image: Image of the Soul

Student: *Can you speak about the relationship between I Am and the ego-image?*

Aziz: The I Am represents that in which you abide, when you simply are. For instance, in meditation you rest within the profound state of Being. This state of I Am, the combination of Awareness, Being and Heart, is impersonal. This impersonal state within which you can dwell is I Am. But who rests in this I Am? It is your very Me, which is the Soul. To know who rests in I Am is to have the proper self-image. We spoke about the difference between the ego-image and self-image. The ego-image is only in the mind and it represents your image in the collective consciousness. The ego-image is created only in contrast to the outer. You cannot have an ego-image which relates to the inner. Without humanity, you wouldn't be able to create an ego-image. The ego-image is based on comparison, while the self-image is based on an understanding of who you really are.

The ego-image is important as well, for you do relate to the outer and you have to compare yourself to others from time to time. These are the natural functions but you yourself are much deeper and to understand it is itself the right self-image. The self-image is not a state but a function, which you activate at times; though most of the time, you rest beyond concepts in I Am.

There is I Am which is the impersonal energy; there is the Soul which is a pure feeling of Me in the Heart including awareness and subtle intelligence as well. There is the self-image which allows you to understand who you are in your connection to I Am and to the Creator. There is the ego-image which is an image of yourself in relationship to the world and other people.

So, you see, the ego-image is the very surface of our identity. It is not that the ego-image is not you. It is also you; you are the ego-image yourself, but it is just a surface, your mask in the outer. You do need this mask for it is a part of being a human who lives among other humans, but you need to know who you are behind masks.

What is, therefore, the relationship between I Am and the ego-image? There is none, apart from the fact that the ego-image is contained in the space of I Am. The ego-image is unable to relate to I Am. The moment it tries to relate to I Am, it becomes automatically the self-image or the Soul-image. You cannot wear a mask in front of I Am. You can encounter the inner realm only being utterly naked and exposed.

The proper question to ask is: 'what is the relationship between the Self-image and I Am?' The self-image allows the Soul to recognise that she is the child of I Am, its foremost manifestation. The self-image allows the Soul to understand her connection to I Am and to know her own identity as well. The child knows himself and his mother. Resting in I Am, we can understand what it is that is happening to us and to whom it is happening.

Who is Suffering?

Student: *You say that the Soul is eternal and originally pure. Who is suffering? For example, some say, when a person commits suicide, the Soul becomes suspended in the time between incarnations and experiences very negative states. Who is suffering?*

Aziz: Firstly, it is not true that the Soul stays in some kind of bardo state or purgatory. These concepts are born out of fear and out of judgmental thinking. There is no purgatory at all because when one dies, everything disappears and the Soul becomes temporarily demanifested. Also there is no punishment for committing a suicide - one must simply repeat the lesson again, that's all. There are situations in life, that committing suicide may be a right choice. Even some animals, in an extreme situations decide to put an end to their life. The real suicide, the real pain most people inflict on themselves is living in the mind; it is like living as a computer.

However, naturally, when one follows one's lower nature, producing a lot of negativity and dark, ignorant energy, one creates the momentum of suffering for oneself. For example, when one hates deeply other beings, one simultaneously hurts oneself through this energy. So many people live locked in their minds, full of obsessive tendencies and fears. That is already a purgatory! They are already in a bardo state, for they live in a dream state, as if they have died long time ago.

So, who is suffering? How is it possible that the Soul who is originally pure can live in a hell? It is the Soul who is suffering, for there is only the Soul. But the Soul, who suffers in a neurotic state, is simply not aware of her true nature - it is the Soul which is not Soul-realised. The Soul in her eternal condition is beyond everything. But the moment she incarnates to begin her evolutionary journey, she enters the realm of ignorance, she becomes a part of the dimension of forgetfulness - she forgets herself.

When the Soul plays the role of a manifested being, she is pure in her essence, but lost in ignorance. Imagine - the Soul incarnates and becomes a child. She doesn't understand anything, she doesn't know what she is doing here! She is slowly growing, accumulating all kinds of information from the outer reality and from the collective mind. She evolves within ignorance which is forgetfulness, so, at one point she can go beyond ignorance and re-discover her true identity, her original face.

It is difficult to understand, why would the Soul choose to fall into the realm of forgetfulness, if she was already pure and one with God. And it doesn't have to be answered. It is simply like that. It is a part of Leela, a part of the divine play, a part of the creation of polarities. If there is no darkness, there is no light either. If there is no sadness, the joy cannot exist. If there is no forgetfulness, there is no remembrance. You see, when the Soul is one with the Beloved, in her original form, she has no way of knowing it! There is no one to know it... the purpose of Creation is not merely to negate one's separation and to dissolve into Oneness. The purpose of evolution is to reach a point of being almost one! It is reaching the point where you recognise both your separation and your Oneness. At this point of meeting you begin merging with God. This precise point, when you are neither separated, nor One is the Ultimate Experience, and the true most noble purpose of Creation.

Now, you are in the process of returning to the state of Oneness. In this process, not only the goal matters, but even more so the journey! It is your adventure! It may sometimes be difficult but the beauty and colourfulness of this journey is much higher. It is like when you travel in India. It is not easy to be in India and many get very impatient with this country. The price to pay is a bargain as it is a country of magic and spiritual transformation. Similarly, you pay the price for entering the Leela land of evolution and forgetfulness, so you can discover again and again the Truth of God. You enjoy this journey the most when you leave the dimension of ignorance far behind yourself and you are very close to the final dissolution into the Source of Creation. Because, when you dissolve completely, you are not, only the Beloved remains. In order to experience God, a slight duality is required. If there is too much duality one is simply separated painfully from Existence. If there is no duality at all, there is no Me either. But when there is a touch of duality, the conscious meeting between God and her child takes place. That is the purpose of Creation. Now you can perhaps understand that duality is sacred in its essence, as it allows the Soul to experience the divine marriage with the Beloved, a communion with God.

What are the Characteristics of the Soul?

Student: *Does who we truly are have any characteristics?*

Aziz: And who are we truly?

Student: *Well it is complex because we are multidimensional. A part of us has characteristics and the other part is not personal, as it is merged with the Beyond.*

Aziz: The essence of who we really are is called the Soul or Pure Me. This Pure Me exists deeper than the psyche and the personality. Personality has clear characteristics because personality expresses itself through the physical, emotional and mental bodies; these characteristics can be relatively measured and described. Pure Me does not have personal characteristics but it does not mean that she is without characteristics. Pure Me is a meeting point between the individual and the universal. Pure Me is made of the light of I AM and is endowed with a particular intelligence-sensitivity through which she can recognise the truth of Creation.

Student: *Is this different for each Soul?*

Aziz: A different flavour or unique blueprint is superimposed on individual expressions of Light. This difference can be present only through the creation of time. When there is no time everything merges into one. The basic characteristic of being a Soul is a combination of joy and sadness. Inherent to the Soul is a certain profound sensitivity which comes from the Heart. The Soul represents a natural humility, an innocence and purity. The deepest characteristic of the Soul is that she is the child of the Beloved. From this understanding, prayer is born.

Universal Love does not know that it is love. But when it manifests itself as the Soul - it knows its love. This knowingness of love... this knowing that it is love, is the Soul. Love without object is Me. This Me is self-contained and beyond any image.

Student: *What is this state of humility you mentioned?*

Aziz: The state of humility is a renunciation of the ego-image and a surrender into What Is. In this state of humility, a certain understanding that one is like a child is revealed from the Heart. The Soul simply recognises her child-like quality. It takes place in the space of her existential aloneness, where she meets the Creator, the source of her existence. Yes... you can say that true Shikantaza is a state of humility. True Shikantaza includes the Heart and sensitivity. Apart from that, a gentle transparent understanding is present of who one truly is. So, humility is a combination of surrender and the transparent self-image. Transparent means that there is hardly a self-image for it has already dissolved into Beingness and Heart. But, at the same time, Me feels herself.

Prayer

Student: *What is the relationship between my cultivation of the State of Presence and prayer?*

Aziz: You have work to do. You are responsible for your awakening. At the same time, you do need help and this help will come in one way or another. The right elements will be given to you. But prayer helps because it creates a conscious connection with the source of Grace.

The Soul has Never Incarnated!

Student: *Where does the Soul abide?*

Aziz: The Soul abides in the Other Dimension, she is eternally one with the Beloved. The Soul has never incarnated! The Soul never enters the body. What you experience as your psyche and your body is the hologram projected by the Soul. The Soul projects herself into this dimension to experience her relative separation form herself. The Soul never incarnates. It is the psyche which incarnates. As you evolve in the form of human consciousness, you are actually looking for the way back. As you trace the path back to your origin, you recognise the amazing fact that you have never been born! Yes... it is all just a hologram, a projection in the dimension of time.

Me is the Vehicle of Consciousness

Student: *Can you speak about the sense of Me?*

Aziz: That which makes us conscious is the sense of Me. When consciousness recognises itself, when consciousness is conscious of itself, it means that the sense of Me is already present. It is possible that consciousness and intelligence can function in an impersonal way, without the sense of Me, but in such a case, there is no knowingness. The moment there is any kind of knowing, it means that the sense of Me is present.

Evolution, in our case is the evolution of the sense of Me. What we are doing in our work is deepening your experience of Me. We are giving her more solidity, depth and continuity. It is all about Me, there is nothing else but Me. You've got nothing else but your Me. Even the mind is a part of your Me-identity. But the Me which is lost in the mind is simply fragmented and shallow. Each thought creates a separate, disconnected sense of Me which has no real continuity. That is the ego-reality. The ego represents the state of evolution where the sense of Me becomes relativity conscious of itself and can refer to its own image. But the ego has no centre, therefore it needs to recreate itself moment by moment.

The moment your ego asks itself the question 'who am I?' it refers to the Real Me. The State of Presence is the first clear experience of Me, the centre of awareness. Here, the vague sense of Me transforms into the Real Me. Next, this Me continues to evolve becoming more and more whole. She expands into Beingness and discovers her very essence which is the Heart. In this way, Me evolves through the awakening of awareness discovering her connection to Being and opening her centre in the Heart. The end result is the Pure Me. The Pure Me is where the complete field of the Soul's existence becomes manifested.

But where does this Me exist? She exists within the infinite space of the Universal I Am, the all-pervading presence of the Beloved. Me cannot be separated from God and extracted from the universal context. That's why, to awaken Me is at the same time indivisible from regaining her connection with the light of Creation. The Vastness of the Beloved contains all living beings and the whole of Creation.

Let us ask you: when you rest in meditation, where are you abiding? It is not in time and space that you abide but in the Beyond. You abide in the ocean of Being which is God in truth. You may be surprised, but when you rest in meditation, you dwell in the ocean of Love. But to fully experience God, the Heart has to be included. It is through the unity of Being-Heart, that you experience fundamental unity with the Creator.

Me in her pure form is beyond the body and mind. She is an energy field which knows herself directly as Me and rests in the Universal I Am. But in this body, Me also lives in the outer. Me evolves also in the world. The Complete Me is multidimensional. Apart from the inner state, Me includes the emotional body, feelings, human nature and sensitivity, the mind, desires, needs, creativity... The Soul in order to be complete, apart from Enlightenment (in the traditional sense) must also reach fulfilment and maturity in the outer reality.

Can Me be Negated?

Student: *Why do so many traditions negate Me?*

Aziz: They simply overlook her. Without Me there is no Enlightenment. The concept that Me must be eliminated proves ignorance. Me herself is the light of consciousness which enters the Uncreated. The Uncreated is not aware of itself. Therefore, it needs Me to know itself. Without Me what remains is just a deep sleep state. The purpose of being Me is to recognise God. Me is the vehicle through which God recognises her own presence.

Soul and Personality

Student: *What is the relationship between the Soul and the personality?*

Aziz: The Soul is the moon and the personality is the reflection of the moon in the lake. The lake is this world, the dimension of time. It is never perfectly still but at moments it is able to reflect the moon clearly. We should remember that the moon has no light of her own. The moon must reflect light from her source, which is the sun. What is the sun? It is the Beloved! So the Soul is a reflection of the Beloved, and the personality is the reflection of the Soul. It is the personality which begins to look for its source. That is the purpose of the question 'Who am I?' For the personality to reach its source, first it must look for its Soul, then the Soul must look for the Beloved. In actuality, personality doesn't discover the Soul - but the Soul discovers herself through the personality. And to further clarify, the Soul doesn't discover the Beloved - but the Beloved discovers her divine presence through her dual creation, the Soul.

Adding to this metaphor, we can say that the ripples in the lake which distort the moon's reflection represent the negative tendencies of the personality. That's why, most personalities first try to heal themselves in order to eliminate their negativity. Unfortunately, there are always some ripples for the personality cannot attain perfection. Because this reality is inherently unstable and imperfect, perfection cannot be actualised here. For that reason, the Soul as a personality must at one stage compromise her desire for perfection. At this point, she begins to seek perfection beyond the personality. The perfection which the Soul discovers is the light of her presence but the source of this light is beyond the Soul. The moon (Soul) is no longer disturbed by the ripples of the lake (world) but the light she shines is still borrowed from the sun (Beloved). The Beloved, the Empress of all realities is the source of perfection and the embodiment of perfection itself.

Enlightenment to Me

Student: *What is the difference between the realisation of Transparent Me and the negation of Me?*

Aziz: The realisation of the Transparent Me is called Enlightenment to Me. It can happen only when the Absolute State is present and when the Heart is fully activated. Enlightenment to Me is the most mysterious compared with all other types of Self-realisation.

Me cannot be separated from the dimension where she exists, the Universal I AM. Without the realisation of the Universal I AM, you can certainly feel your Me but you are unable to experience her wholeness. In Enlightenment to Me, Soul-realisation and Self-realisation - merge into One; this One is beyond the Self and beyond the Soul. The centre of your Me is in the Heart - it is in the Heart that you meet yourself fully. But to meet yourself fully you need other elements which constitute the environment of the Soul. These other elements are Awareness and Being. Awareness creates the space of knowingness and a continuity of intelligence. Being allows you to abide firmly within the reality of the Now. If one of these elements is lacking (even if the Heart is fully open) Me is unable to grasp and retain her subjective reality.

Firstly, we usually awaken the presence of Me by crystallising attention in the mind. The culmination of this process is awakening to a constant state of self-attention. Secondly, we re-connect Me with the dimension of Being, where she abides eternally. The flower of this process is in attaining the pure stillness of Being. In this stillness Me can unconditionally rest, for her presence is contained within the Universal Absence. Here, the environment of Me is fully realised. This environment is the energetic field of I Am.

But what is Me herself? She is still not fully realised. Me needs to meet herself in the Heart. From the inside of the Heart, through her own presence, Me dissolves into I AM. The realisation of this Total Experience is the most subtle and therefore difficult to transmit. Here, Me does indeed merge with Totality but not by negating herself. The opposite is true - Me merges and dissolves into God by embracing herself fully and thus becoming herself for the first time.

From the other side, to dissolve through the negation of Me is negative and one-sided. It can take place in the Absolute State where Me loses herself becoming absorbed in the original void. This experience is valid and profound but it is not total because the very experiencer of it has been overlooked.

We give you a simple example. Imagine that you dive into the ocean and the water has the temperature of your body. When you deeply relax into this experience, you may forget yourself. Forgetting yourself is a negative dissolution. To not forget, you must feel yourself, thereby enriching the experience through your own presence.

The purpose of evolution is not to negate the Soul in the realisation of God but to realise God through the Soul. It is the Soul which makes God-realisation possible. Without the Me, how can you realise God? To negate the Me is not better than to commit suicide! Me is certainly an indivisible part of experiencing the Ultimate. However, to fully understand what it means is the same as reaching 'Enlightenment to Me.' Here, Me abides in the dimension beyond the inner and beyond the outer. This mysterious realm is where the Soul meets herself directly and through herself, she merges with the Light of Creation.

To be an Individual is to a Soul

Student: *Can you speak about individuality?*

Aziz: Individuality refers to being a separate Me; a unique angle of perception. Individuality refers simply to the presence of the Soul. Everything in the world is unique; we can look at many elements of this reality in many ways. We can see a tree as something individual, a reality unto itself; we can feel the spirit and the energy of the tree. We can see a mountain, we can see a flower or we can see everything together. We can see an atom as being something unique, an individual; or we can see the whole human body which is composed of infinite numbers of atoms as something unique. So, what is individual or what is not individual is often a matter of perspective...

In the case of being an individual human consciousness, it is directly linked to the realisation of one's blueprint and unique evolutionary vision. A true individual is someone who is aligned with one's blueprint. If one is not an individual, if one is not awakened to oneself, to his or her unique Me, one is merely a part of the collective mind. One does not really exist. What exists is a flow of personality, a flow of unconsciousness. There's no one inside.

To become truly an individual, one has to discover the Real Me which means one has to transcend, on some level, the unconscious identification with the mind. One has to give birth to the Soul. If one has not given birth to the Soul, one does not yet exist as an individual. That's why, an individual is not necessarily born from the mother. An individual has to be born from one-self. That is the second birth - the birth of I Am, the birth of the Soul. To be an individual is to become the Soul. This is the paradox that even though we are the Soul, we have to become the Soul. Or rather the Soul has to become herself. When the Soul becomes herself, what she realises is her uniqueness through her unique blueprint. Your blueprint is to be the only Soul, perceiving reality from your particular angle. This angle of perception includes many different elements: a type of intelligence, a type of emotional body, a type of the Heart, a certain depth of Being. It refers to the relationship of the Soul with the Inner Realm and the relationship of the Soul with Creation.

Only Me can Rest Beyond Me

Student: *What is this Me? When I sit in meditation, this sense of Me dissolves into something which is not Me. Where is Me at that time?*

Aziz: Me is the one who knows that the sense of Me dissolves! Don't you see that without your Me there is nothing? Your Me is a part of every experience, everything... Me is the one who feels herself in the middle of all, the one who is able to recognise life and to create the self-referral. I Am and Me are two sides of the same thing. I Am is the impersonal energy of the state; and Me is the personal knowing-sensitivity within I Am. In the case of Transparent Me, the impersonal I Am, and the personal experiencer of it, merge into one. This is what we call apperception or the total experience of What Is.

Life as a Human

To live as a human is the art of facing the imperfections of the time-dimension. It is within this imperfection, subject to the law of polarities, that we have been destined to discover the perfection of our timeless Soul identity. As human beings, we aspire towards harmony and purity in our personal expressions. Our destiny is to come as close as possible to this ideal. That which allows us to endure the suffering and constant difficulties inherent to this plane of forgetfulness is: Acceptance.

How to Purify the Mind?

Student: *To what degree can we change the habits of the mind?*

Aziz: Why would you like to change them?

Student: *Because sometimes I experience a negative mind, violent thoughts, for example.*

Aziz: The question is: how can one purify the mind? There are two types of parallel evolutions: evolution into liberation and evolution into the purification of Me. The first one is going beyond the mind, transcending personality thereby reaching I Am. Here the problem of purifying the mind does not arise, as one is beyond the mind. However, in the second case when you acknowledge your mind as a part of yourself, you may wish to align it with the principles of harmony and purity, for they reflect the original reality of the Soul. These two types of growths represent two different way of looking at the reality of Me - her unconditional side and her relative or dynamic side.

However, it is not really possible to transform the mind, unless I Am is present. Because if there is no centre of awareness, no Being and the Heart is closed, there is simply no space inside which one could allow transformation to take place. The mind is neurotic by the very absence of I Am. There is no need really to look for other causes of human suffering. In such a case, there is no Me, no one inside and the psyche is governed by the play of unconscious energies. If Me is not present, how can the mind possibly be changed? It does not belong to anyone!

Purification of the mind is not simply a result of your will but when the Real Me is present and you express a clear intention of having the mind purified - it will be purified! It is a function of evolution. Not that you do it, it is not that you make it happen - it is being done! Nevertheless, you do co-operate. You express a clear intention to your Soul and to the Divine to become purified within your personality. Next, you may bring some element of psychological understanding into the functioning of your mind. In order to experience a purified Me, the subconscious mind needs to be cleansed. You have very little control over your negative patterns, for they have already been crystallised in your subconsciousness. It is like a computer program which has been set and you have no way to get inside it. On some level, you are not responsible for your mind, for it was created by a past you cannot change. Your responsibility relates to how you respond in the Now to the subconscious expressions of the mind, which themselves are rooted in the past.

How can the subconscious mind be changed? Only the force of Grace can do it. You need help, the intervention of Higher Intelligence, which is God, in truth. Only the One who created you can heal you! There is no therapy, no psychological work which can do it. Through therapy, you become only more aware of your psychological hang ups, not being however able to change them.

When I Am is present within yourself, an energetic centre, the inner refuge is created within your very sense of identity. That is already freedom, for you can locate yourself beyond the mind. From this place of freedom, you can express the intention of healing your personality as well.

On the path of disidentification, like Advaita for instance, the problem of purification does not arise, as Me is negated. But when you acknowledge your personality as a part of your multidimensional wholeness, there is room for the evolution of the psyche as well. So, in order to transform the mind a clear intention must be expressed, the presence of I Am, a certain element of renunciation and discriminative wisdom; these elements are important to cultivate because the negativity of the mind can take over. The next step is to invite consciously the power of Grace to which you pray for help and for healing. Often you must be patient and wait for some time before you see a clear transformation. A change simply happens, sometimes unexpectedly; suddenly, the negativity which has crystallised in your psyche is simply erased or cleansed. Many elements need to be considered. The transformation of personality is also a question of age and maturation, hormones and so forth. When one is young, the emotional body is quite restless and there is a need for having many experiences in life not excluding the negative ones.

When you experience a negative emotion or pattern, bring yourself to the centre of awareness, which at least energetically removes you from this emotion. Next, you have to dissolve this emotion on the energy level. It is important to see that 'watching' alone will not do, for when the emotional body is involved; watching from the mind cannot cut off the very identification with experience. The patterns you experience are not merely from the mind - they are present on the energy level. That's why, you need to breathe. You breathe first to your belly for some time and next bring this emotion to the Heart, breathing deeply and asking for healing. The centre in the lower belly dissolves the emotion energetically and the Heart transforms it. These are the functions of these centres.

Student: *What about the concept of being total? For example, in experiencing anger and expressing it?*

Aziz: There are two extreme ways of responding to negative emotions. One is, repressing them; the second one is, expressing them. Expressing is often better but, may not always do as it can make the situation even worst. When you are too repressed, expression helps you to release these energies and emotions. But expressing can also become a game of the mind, for one can easily indulge in this type of unconscious spontaneous release, not dealing directly with the problem.

A higher way of handling negative emotions is neither repressing them nor expressing but Embracing them. When you embrace an emotion, there is complete acceptance and you do not lose your integrity by getting sucked into negativity. When you embrace your negative emotion, there is not only acceptance but also love, compassion for yourself and forgiveness. Within full acceptance however, you use also wisdom to understand the meaning of the experience and what it is trying to tell you. When you see clearly that you don't want the emotion which you experience, with full acceptance, you breathe and relax with this emotion. In this way, the disturbing emotion becomes dissolved.

Sometimes being total in expressing emotions, even negative ones, is right. Because, for instance, to get angry is not necessarily wrong; sometimes it is a right response to the necessity of the moment. Sometimes, even emotions like jealousy may be the right type of response. If your wife sleeps around constantly and you don't allow yourself to feel jealousy, trying to 'heal' it - it shows that you are simply an idiot! But when you experience some neurotic tendencies, certainly being total will only bring destruction! How can you be total in obsession?

Let us repeat - first awareness of what is happening in your mind, next the State of Presence, next acceptance, next relaxing with whatever you experience, and next breathing. The emotion will go. After some time the pattern may return but it will become weaker until it dissolves. Be aware that complete transformation is a function of Grace, a higher technology or evolution. As you evolve towards Light, awakening to your Soul, there is no force in the universe which can stop the process of becoming Divine on all levels.

Know also, that a certain amount of negativity and difficulty is a part of being human. You will never be perfect as long as you live in this dimension. The very fact that you live in a place which has the characteristics of low evolution and ignorance does not allow you to reach complete freedom from negativity. It is simply difficult to live here. But what you will reach is a minimum of negativity and a maximum of purity.

Personality Disturbs Me...

Student: *My personality disturbs Me.*

Aziz: It is not a question of personality but a lack of attention. Personality always takes you out of I Am for it lives outside of I Am. When your attention loses itself in your personal dramas, you get disconnected from I Am. When your awareness is strong, it can divide itself in a way that it is simultaneously rooted in I Am while participating in the life of the personality. Attention can divide itself. For instance, you sit in deep meditation and a thought arises, 'what shall I do tomorrow' or 'what shall I have for the dinner...' and so forth. In truth, this thought has no impact on your Inner State as long as you are connected. You can occasionally daydream and still be rooted in I Am. By the way, a certain amount of daydreaming is absolutely natural as a part of the spontaneous activity of the mind. Thinking is not a problem; considering your personal life is not a problem; being disturbed or falling in love is not a problem; as long as you don't lose yourself.

The energy of awareness distributes itself to many different areas of our multidimensional reality. This awareness, when awakened makes I Am visible and the Ultimate realised; at the same time this awareness creatively distributes itself into the life of the personality. Before you are integrated, when you experience daydreaming, you lose yourself fully. Later, when you are mature, the inner state is present automatically and you can truly afford daydreaming.

You can express your personality as you like. You are free! You grow in two directions: into I Am and into personality. You are like a tree. As you grow your roots, you reach I Am; and as you grow up, you express yourself in the world. Some concentrate only on reaching the impersonal; others want only to improve their psychological reality. But you are both and you have no choice in reality, but to grow in these two directions. But to whom does the personality belong and who is that one who attains I Am? It is this part of your Me which is present behind all masks. That you need to see.

Student: *Can personality live without the Soul?*

Aziz: Personality without the Soul is simply unconscious. It is like a shadow without the owner of the shadow. When the Soul is awakened, for the first time you see that there is someone who casts this shadow. In this way, the personality becomes a real part of who you are because the owner of it is present. Even though the personality is an expression of the Soul, it has been formed out of numberless conditionings and limitations. It is the make-up of the Soul and this make-up can easily become a mask. Personality is being recreated from the subconscious mind. For instance, you have a certain type of the mind and, at times, you may not like some of its tendencies. But, even though you don't like them, you are often faced with the frustrating realisation of not being able to change your own mind. It is because these patterns of behaviour are already imprinted and crystallised in your subconscious computer. Subconsciousness is the program which the Soul requires in order to function in the world.

The Soul herself represents the pure experience of Me beyond personality. But in order to live in the world, the Soul needs an extension bridging her with the outer, which is the mind, emotional body, physical body and so forth. Without these extensions there can be no link between Pure Me and the world. It is this very extension which creates the life of a personality. But unfortunately, this extension can operate as if without the Soul, in the virtual reality of the ego. When the Soul awakens, she may also wish to purify her personality, so it can become aligned with the purity of the original Me.

Student: *I am still not fully clear about the difference between the Soul and the personality.*

Aziz: Who has just said it: the Soul or personality?

Student: *It was me.*

Aziz: It was the Soul but expressing herself through personality. The Soul, in order to live here needs an extension. The Soul dwells fully in the Other Dimension and to enter the world, she requires a medium, a bridge. The Soul has no eyes, no ears, no tongue and no mind... Without your mind, you wouldn't be able to ask your question, isn't it true? When the Soul becomes embodied, she is given various tools to connect to the world, to live in the outer. The extension between the Soul and Creation is made of the physical body, sense-doors, emotional and mental bodies and other subtle bodies.

Your mind and your emotional body are continuously learning, accumulating experiences and developing habitual or spontaneous tendencies. This which links the Soul with the conscious Me in the world is a very complex subconscious mind. This subconscious mind has not been understood by anyone, for it is not the destiny of the human being to understand it. Before you experience any thought or emotion, it is first being processed in the subconscious mind. The subconscious mind operates as a combination of instinctive functions and impersonal wisdom.

It is all happening by itself until it reaches the layers of the conscious mind. The conscious mind is a reality where intelligence refers to something personal, to the presence of the subject or Me. When you experience a thought or emotion, apart from experiencing it you also add a second level of recognition, which is the function of ego. You experience a thought and you give feedback to it from your conscious mind. In the case of less evolved animals, there is no distance between Me and the mental impulse-reaction to environment - it is all one subconscious movement. Animals experience a negative or subconscious Oneness with the Creation. In the case of the human being, one is able to respond to one's emotions and give feedback to the mental impulse. This response returns something new to the subconscious mind, enriching it through personal intelligence. That's why, we can speak about conscious evolution. The animal is not evolving consciously but rather subconsciously and in a non-personal collective way.

Personality is the very way the subconscious mind manifests in each moment our behaviour, in emotional, mental and physical areas. The Soul can be conscious of herself only through the channel of personality. But there is a possibility that personality becomes disconnected from the Soul which is the case with most people. Through the evolution of personality, the conscious Me slowly comes to the surface. This means that at a certain moment, you realise that an arising emotion or thought does relate to you! You may still not be clear what this 'you' is but you already feel it intuitively. You see, the ego is also Me but it is only the trace and surface of the Soul. The personality is a combination of subconscious responses, different thoughts and emotions which receive psychological feedback from the conscious mind.

Where is a place for the Soul here? The Soul is the experiencer of all these elements and the presence of the very subject around which the psychosomatic movement circulates. When the Soul is realised, which means that you realise your Pure Me beyond the body and mind, she experiences her existence independent from personality. However, in the case of the human being, the Soul can experience herself consciously only in contrast to the personality; and at one stage, they become one. But to experience the real Oneness of the Soul with personality, this personality must become cleansed and aligned with the purity of the Soul. For that reason, the work with the subconscious mind has to be done at one stage.

To explain it more clearly: imagine that you abide in your Pure Me and suddenly a neurotic emotion appears, disturbing you and taking you away from your inherent purity. You cannot do anything... you may use your will and intention, but often it does not help. What is the meaning of this situation? It means that the very matrix of your subconsciousness has crystallised negative patterns which function automatically and need to be cleansed in order to reflect the reality of the Soul. The Soul is a child of I Am and personality is the child of the Soul. It is through the child that the mother becomes the mother; it is through the personality that the Soul discovers herself. At one stage the mother and the child become one. The concept that one can live without personality is absolutely false. Personality eventually becomes aligned with the Soul and functions as the natural expression of the Soul in the world.

We can speak even deeper about how the Soul emerges through personality into the world. There is the Soul, personality and there is something else, which we call the psyche. The Soul is the very subject, the essence, Me in herself. Personality is the way the Soul expresses herself in the world through the channel of the mental, emotional and physical bodies. The psyche is a certain sphere or atmosphere between the Soul and personality. It is more manifested than the Soul but less gross than personality. We can call it the mood and intuitive intelligence of the Soul in the Here, in the world. The psyche is the conscious bridge between the Soul and personality. The psyche is the vehicle through which the Soul feels herself within the personality.

Beloved, when you ask the question about personality, this very way you ask, the way you speak, the play of facial muscles, the way you sit, the type of thoughts which come to you, your emotional constitution... all of this is your personality. But to whom does all of this pertain? Who are you? Whose Heart is beating in your chest? What is this most intimate place in you where you meet yourself directly, beyond your mind, beyond your psychology? This is what you need to discover and deepen! The one who looks through your eyes which abides behind all thoughts, all emotions... this Pure Me is present in your intelligence and dwells in the cave of your Heart. That You Are.

Student: *But what if someone hurts Me - is it the ego or the Soul which is hurt?*

Aziz: The ego and the Soul are one, but ego can be disconnected from your Soul. If your Heart is hurt, it is the Soul; if your mind is hurt, it is the ego.

To Evolve within Limitations

Student: *I would like to ask about limitations. How is it that we cannot go beyond limitations? For example, we spoke about how if I want to write a poem, I wouldn't be able to express it in Arabic. What if I learn Arabic, would I then be able to go beyond this limitation?*

Aziz: Yes, but it would anyhow, most likely be a low quality poem (laughter...). You are limited but you have been given some amount of energy, intelligence and free will to expand within your limitations. However, your capacity to expand within your limitations is itself limited! You see, to exist as a separate being is to be limited, but your limitation is your capital as well. In order to be unlimited, you have to dissolve as your particular Me. You must see that your energy system is limited, that your mind is limited by the very human brain which you are using. You have no way to get out of this limitation which is inherent in being human. For that reason, we speak about 'human Enlightenment,' for it is being reached within the limitation of human consciousness. It is true that the Buddha reaches the Unlimited but from the limited perspective of the human blueprint. What it tells us is that the recognition of the Unlimited from the human perspective is limited. That's why, Enlightenment has no end, for there is no end to deepening Awakening...no end in expansion into the Unlimited. Here, we can understand the profound meaning of dual-non-duality. One has already become one with the Ultimate but still paradoxically, one expands into the mystery. Human consciousness reaches the Unlimited within its limitations; it expands within these limitations in order to reach a deeper and more meaningful perception of the Unlimited.

See, you are limited on all levels. You need to sleep everyday, you need to eat not to die, you need to breathe. Breathing is a serious limitation - that's why, you cannot live under water. Can you see how limited your mind is? You have been living so long and still know so little.

It is important to understand the role of the blueprint, which is the divine plan for the Soul's ultimate expansion. The Soul is not complete when she becomes unlimited, but rather when she reaches the optimum of expansion within her particular limitations; this optimum is the blueprint. To grow within limitations is the creativity of the Soul. The only sphere where the Soul goes beyond limitations is when she becomes One with the Ultimate Reality. You do not become the Unlimited but you merge with it from the place of your limited existence. Similarly, when you swim in the ocean, you are not the ocean but one with the ocean. Do you see the difference? In the past they thought, that the Buddha became the Unlimited; it was however a serious mistake which brought about a great deal of confusion. We do realise God, but in a human way. The meeting of our primal limitation, that is Me, with the divine presence of the Unlimited - is itself God-realisation.

Fear of Death

Student: *Can you talk about death and fear?*

Aziz: It is interesting, a child in the beginning does not know that death exists. Later, when the information of death enters his mind, it creates many disturbing emotions in the child's mind. How the child interprets the information of death has a flavour of the Unknown and some awkward kind of fear. The child is afraid, but is not clear of exactly what. He has no way to really understand what death is. The child cannot comprehend the possibility of his own absence, let alone the absence of his mother. The child, in the beginning assumes that he is going to live forever and only gradually realises the insecurity of life.

Look inside and try to remember how in your childhood, you became acquainted with death and what impact it had on you. Usually the child blocks this information trying simply to avoid thinking about it. In reality, pushing away the truth of death, pretending that death does not exist continues throughout the life. Everyone pretends that death does not exist, treating it as taboo subject... even on the deathbed! Everyone is in a complete dream, a complete illusion.

Very symbolic is the story of Buddha. Nobody has noticed so far a certain significant feature of Buddha - he was like a child.

Buddha didn't know for long time that such a thing like death existed! He not only didn't know that death existed, but he was not even aware of the existence of sickness and old age! When he realised the cruel truth about life, his whole concept of life fell into pieces. But because his Soul was so big, the moment he saw the truth, he radically faced it. He said that he would not rest until he found a way out of this miserable situation. And he found a sacred way out, which was a purely internal expansion beyond the dimension of time.

Student: *How to overcome the fear of death?*

Aziz: It does not need to be overcome but rather be transformed. To be protective about prolonging one's existence, which is the continuity of one's particular sense of Me is absolutely natural. In this way, Existence protects her beings - by creating an instinctive love for life and fear of death. You see, to live you have to be on some level identified with your body. It is your subconscious identification with life which fundamentally serves your survival. That's why, when a car rushes towards you, you step back. You don't say: 'now I am going to step back, not out of fear, but to live for others!' That would be ridiculous and you would not have enough time to save yourself. Some amount of fear, the ability to feel fear is positive as a part of the body-mind reality. But the problem is psychological fear, where you are afraid of death as an idea which you anticipate in your mind. Psychological fear is beyond the natural self-protective mechanism. It is the mind's fear. You are afraid of the Unknown and of the end of your particular stream of consciousness-memory. Psychological fear is not natural. It is created only in the mind.

As you evolve, you reach deeper layers of your internal reality, from the depths of which you can contain the truth of death. A child cannot contain the existence of death, for he does not have the necessary depth. A child is beautiful and innocent but does not have depth and wisdom. A child is simply unconscious. But you as an adult being, you have the chance to go beyond the limited perspective of life and death and to reach your inherent connection with the Uncreated Reality. Your very life and death become contained, embraced from a higher, infinitely deeper and eternal perspective. In this way, there is no more a need to escape the fear of death, by creative post-life fantasies, for instance. You simply do not anymore need psychological self-protection. You have surrendered to that which is beyond your crystallised sense of identity - to the vastness of God.

Student: *Can you speak more about fear?*

Aziz: The primal reason that fear exists is derived from the fact that you are an individual who is relatively separated from the rest of Creation. Because you are separated, you have to support your individual sense of Me; you have to survive physically and psychologically here. This particular dimension is designed in a way that all creatures compete with each other for survival. This is a very gross dimension of low evolution and many cruel rules.

You have a physical body which is vulnerable and must be nourished all the time. So you have to protect it against fire, water, earthquakes, bombs and other disasters (laughter)... also against mosquitoes. Why is it like that? Do you really see it? You are separated. Many spiritual masters tell you that you should be free from fear, so you feel that something is wrong with you because you cannot get rid of it. But fear is a natural part of life which allows you to prolong your I Am. So fear as such protects your continuity, thereby providing enough time to reach your blueprint.

Fear is instinctive. If a child didn't feel fear, he would run under a car on the street or jump out of a window. Fear is the mechanism which nature uses in order to protect all creatures. Nature protects you from the inside, by programming in you the impulse of fear. Fear is a part of the make-up of being a separate being. However, there is a neurotic fear which is unnecessary; it comes from the mind. The mind can develop obsessive and psychotic tendencies. For example, to protect oneself is natural but one can become excessively self-protective and possessive. For instance, in order to survive, you need to have a certain amount of money. Yes? But this need to have money can easily become an obsession. You may simply end up seeing life as a means of making money; you start to think only about money and security. See how, somewhere along the way one can easily lose their sanity, becoming fearful and insecure. Most people constantly protect their illusory sense of security. They prepare themselves for a future which may never come! They manage to secure their old age but, what a misfortune, as somewhere along the way, they simply die inside!

An excessive self-protectiveness and possessiveness is already a symptom of neurosis. As we see, fear which is basically natural can be used by the mind in a way that gets out of control. The mind can create different types of fear. For instance, a fear of darkness, a fear of ghosts, a fear of being alone... numerous fears coming from an excessive imagination, insecurity, conditionings, obsessive tendencies and ignorance as such. Some people need to have a light on in the room to be able to fall asleep! What kind of mind is it? How can one live like this?

Sometimes fear helps you to avoid dangerous situations and reflects reality. To discern between a natural type of fear and a neurotic one, you have to use your common sense, intelligence, discriminative wisdom and courage. In order to live as a separate being, you need to have some essential amount of trust and confidence. Your Soul, in order to incarnate into this insecure and insensitive dimension, has to have an enormous amount of courage! You cannot live in fear, for it would be better not to live at all.

Student: *I experience fear when I look into other people's eyes. I feel fear meeting people.*

Aziz: You experience a type of fear which comes from being shy and timid. It is difficult to live when one is too sensitive. The fear you experience has a few reasons. One is the natural humility and vulnerability. Another reason is a certain lack of self-confidence and being too self-conscious in a psychological sense. When you are too self-conscious, for instance, you may feel that everyone looks at you even though it is not true. In such a case, you simply need to relax this mechanism and centre yourself in a true sense, in the openness of Being.

Student: *When I am looking at you, I can be myself but with other people I feel like I am in shock.*

Aziz: Because to look into the eyes of most people is a real shock - for there is no one inside! It can be really shocking, for you are looking at somebody and what you see is only the mind. A meeting between two people can take place only on the Soul level; in such a case, when you look into the eyes of someone, you see the Soul. Even if a person is unconscious, at least the Heart should be present to be human. But in most cases, not even the Heart is present - only the noisy mind. When you understand it fully, your shyness will change into compassion! What are these people doing to themselves? And if you are shy, it is more for this person, you may even feel ashamed for all these people you meet. It is really embarrassing to live among people whose consciousness is so miserably fragmented...

But, practically speaking, you have to build up some self-confidence; you need to be stronger inside yourself and to have more trust in who you are and what you represent. You need to have a certain courage to face other people. Your shyness is a part of you which you don't need to remove and cannot, in truth. Some confidence will bring to you a necessary balance. If you know fully who you are, a natural confidence arises, for you no longer represent your personality but your Soul which is divine. Also, always be in your centre solid inside. When you are centred inside, by this very focus, you become less self-conscious in the mind. In this way, you become more impersonal, in a positive sense. This type of impersonality takes you beyond fear.

Letting Go is to Enter the Unknown

Student: *Can you speak about letting go?*

Aziz: Letting go is to allow things, ideas and emotions to go. It is to drop from moment to moment into a space without self-reference, into an open field of Being. To let go, is to Be. To Be is to die within the Now.

Existing as a human being, as an individual consciousness, there is a constant self-referral, a constant thinking process which from moment to moment recreates the ego-image. One refers continuously either to oneself or to the outer in the context of one's ego. This ability to create a point of reference within the reality of appearances is natural but it is only a mechanism and not who we really are. To live as an individual is to retain one's sense of identity. Because of the desire to prolong our existence physically and psychologically, we develop attachments to objects, ideas and to our ego-image. Because of this attachment, at one stage, we lose the right relationship with the open space of Beingness.

Animals also need to cling in order to survive. In the case of an animal, the mind is not very active, that's why this effort to prolong its existence is not translated as constant thinking about itself. The attachment to objects, when obsessive can replace our

Soul identity. Suddenly, we become blocked, locked in the cage of ego, living in the virtual reality of the mind and constant self-referral. Here, we lose freedom. We are children of Existence. We are born out of Universal Love and Being. As children, we play our individual lives, we evolve, grow, completing our angle of perception. But we are founded upon the Universal Isness, from which we arise, moment by moment. When we lose this fundamental connection with the Source and Light of Creation, we become simply neurotic, imprisoning ourselves in the arrogant world of ego-images.

Learning how to let go, we return to a sane way of existing, in proper balance with our individuality and Existence. To Be is to experience on some level, one's absence, for one has surrendered to something much bigger. Letting go is to surrender the mind; it is to have the courage to live without this constant self-protection which is fear. Living beyond the mind, resting within inner silence is the foundation which represents our purity and proper relationship with Totality. From the space of letting go, we live our human destiny, facing various challenges and difficulties, maturing in all areas and become whole. What is most important is finding this fine balance between the self-referral and non-referral (which is the abiding within the Ultimate Presence). Letting go is to enter the Unknown. But, when there is sensitivity and intelligence, we enter the Unknown knowingly.

True Creativity: Meeting the Creator

Student: *When we are only in Being, is there a place for activity and creativity?*

Aziz: Your understanding of Being is dualistic. This is similar to one who thinks that to go beyond the mind is to stop thinking. But the space 'beyond the mind' includes thinking and not thinking. Being is all-inclusive. It is beyond the polarities of activity and passivity; it includes action and non-action. Being is the foundation upon which you exist. For example, you sit passively on the floor and yet actively ask a question; sitting on the floor is non-activity, but you are active asking the question. How is it possible? Can you explain how you are doing it?

Being is not physical and has no location is space but you sit upon it all the time. It is similar to this planet, to the universe

- they are located somewhere in space and time but simultaneously they abide Beyond. You must understand what spiritual expansion is about. You are constantly active, doing, thinking, and you are disconnected from Being. Aren't you tired of it? Look at a tree. The tree grows up, higher and higher, the leaves become green, the flowers open up, fruit appears, the branches are dancing in the wind... but the tree is rooted in the earth - it is still inside. As you re-connect with the ground of Beingness, you find this inherent stillness within. In this way, you discover the inner silence, the unconditional peace and from that place you express your creativity.

You are free to do whatever you want! If you are creative, wonderful; if you are not creative, it is also wonderful. Here, you are beyond these concepts, for you yourself have become the most beautiful expression of Existence. The ultimate creativity is meeting the source of creativity which is the Creator! In truth, creativity can take place only from the inner silence. If you are disconnected from Being, what you call creativity is more a catharsis. Catharsis is not creativity but a throwing out, a release from the subconscious mind. When the subconscious mind is overcrowded, it gets suffocated with excessive amounts of information and must eventually let it out. If you look at most tourists, travellers, they like to write dairies every day. Don't they? This is the way they make order in their subconscious minds. They are so unconscious that all the experiences, impulses, thoughts, emotions, events they have during the day cannot be properly processed. Through writing, at least the subconscious mind can rearrange its content. The dreams have a similar function. However, true creativity is not a release but a positive expression of the Soul. True creativity is born from the dimension of love and silence.

Life Teaches You Truth

Student: *In the last few years my life has been very intense, in many ways, many deaths, many good things as well. I am not complaining. I was just wondering... it is so extreme and even though I enjoy living with this kind of passion, I also feel exhausted. I always think, maybe tomorrow I can rest but tomorrow a new thing happens. What is happening?*

Aziz: We live in a very intense time, the coming of the new millennium. Many esoteric energies are present and evolution is accelerated on many levels. Everything is polarised. Many things are happening on many levels - individual, collective and universal. It is a good time but an intense one. Cleansing is usually connected to some suffering but it works to your ultimate benefit. You are awakening in a multidimensional way - not just to I Am. You are awakening to your intelligence, to understanding what it is you are doing here, to the clarity about the truth of this earthly dimension whereby the force of destiny has locked your sense of Me. What is happening to you is the truth of your reality in the Here. Existence will present many different elements which are necessary for your growth and awakening.

How you respond to life events represents you, it reflects your psychological maturation and the subconscious tendencies of the mind. Not all these responses are coming from the right place which means that not all of them are aligned with Truth. Often, how you perceive reality is fully conditioned and, therefore, cannot represent the reality of your Soul. What you are aiming at is a very fine perception of reality, a very fine understanding which reflects the precise meeting of Universal Truth with your Soul's very unique angle of perception. You see, you don't know yet fully what your ultimate angle of perception is. To know it, you have to awaken more to your Soul identity, like a flower which must fully open to the light of the sun. To know who you truly are, you must be more free from certain idiosyncrasies imprinted in you by the collective mind. It is very amazing - the journey of the Soul to the realisation of her unique perception of What Is. Awakening is not only to realise a generic One State but one's uniqueness as well.

Beloved one, many of your reactions and emotional responses are not really yours. Can you see it? When someone dies, we usually cry because we are supposed to cry. But are they really our tears? Someone dies and we don't know how to behave, for it is all too strange and unusual; but are we really in despair? Maybe everything is all right? You have to see which responses are coming truly from your wisdom and inherent sensitivity of your Soul. Existence is checking you, taking away that which is false, removing what is not yours. Whatever is happening, trust this process and see the divine hand leading your life in the right direction. This world is often cruel but does not this cruelty tell you something about this dimension? Maybe this plane of forgetfulness is to be transcended? It is not to get addicted to life on the earth. Existence kicks you from time to time in order to remind you that you are not of Here. You are Here, but not to stay. Enjoy as much as you can, by all means, but know your purpose and see beyond the horizon of the earth! As you are being bombarded by this reality, this very fact pushes you to go beyond and discover the timeless, the immortal sphere outside of life and death. You need to live here and do your best to sober up to the dark side of the earth! Part of the awakening process is shaking up the subconscious mind. This very computer program through which you translate this reality into the known has to be cleansed and harmonised with Truth and the Higher Intelligence.

Student: *I do feel that the human part of Me is too sensitive.*

Aziz: You see, the human in you represents your natural sensitivity and is in harmony with the Soul. But there is another 'human' part of your make-up which is not of the Soul but from collective unconsciousness. Here we also include some naïve and superficial sentimentality which is a part of the global human hysteria. The human we wish to awaken is the divine being, fully conscious, fully sensitive and completely intelligent. Whatever is happening to you, dear one, is teaching you a lesson about this reality and about yourself. And you are trying to find a vision and attitude towards life which is optimal, which is in harmony with the objective reality and the truth of your Soul. This reality will bombard you until you find an awakened attitude which cannot be shaken anymore. You are constantly being checked. Do you see it? The test is going on all the time. You are being washed clean, so you can receive the gift of your Soul's ultimate vision. If you are constantly suffering and susceptible to emotional disturbances, it shows your vision is too vulnerable and lacks the essential strength.

Student: *It seems to me, in a way, that these things are happening to me when I am actually much stronger than I used to be. If the same things had happened several years ago, I would be broken. Whereas now, there is something in me which feels quite contained.*

Aziz: Existence is wise and compassionate. It gives you a hard time only when you can cope with it. Only when you can bear the hard time, the fruit is evolution and breakthrough. When you are unable to bear difficulties, they break you down.

Student: *Do you have any idea why the main issue seems to be around death?*

Aziz: For the very simple reason that death is the cruellest lesson, which touches the deepest fears, anxieties and paranoia's of our mind. Death represents the end of the known. Holding onto one's life and the life of others is the strongest emotional attachment for the human being, the primal attachment. That's why when we face death, the deepest layers of our psyche are shaken. Death leaves you utterly helpless. There is no way, you can cope with death! You can cry or you can celebrate dancing at the funeral, but these are different expressions of the same helplessness! Do you see it? There is no real justification to death; it ends everything and leaves you with emptiness.

The only way to contain the information of death is through surrender. Here, you do not look for justification; neither do you cling to your despair; you allow it to be as it is from the space of non-conceptualisation. When you understand fully that the divine intelligence is behind all and that your mind knows hardly anything, you simply surrender. You have just entered this Creation endowed with a limited mind; you simply know nothing! The highest understanding the human being can reach is giving up of the mind and letting go into the Original Silence which knows all through not-knowing. Your very limitation helps you to discover your proper relation with the Creator and that is surrender; it is giving up your individual mind at the altar of Universal Intelligence.

Student: *But sometimes I am so disturbed by my mind that I cannot go deeper, I am simply unable to surrender. (Another student).*

Aziz: Yes... to enter the higher mind is to be in a state of no-mind which is beyond thinking. You see, you have made a good observation. Surrender to the Divine is not emotional, neither is it mental; it is not an attitude from the mind; it is itself an expansion into a deeper state of consciousness. This expansion takes place on the level of awareness, Heart and energy. The only way to transcend the mind is to awaken a clear centre of awareness and to stabilise this experience. Why are so many thoughts bombarding the psyche? The reason is that, paradoxically, the one who experiences them is absent. There is no one inside this mind! But the moment the 'I' is born, the mind encounters its counter force, namely the Me. The mind is not used to the presence of Me, for it cannot be the boss anymore. In the presence of 'I,' the mind gets shy and feels awkward. It is the beginning of its end. However, initially, when the centre of awareness is activated, the mind can manifest even more thoughts because the subconsciousness is overcrowded. The excessive amount of information stored below the conscious level has to become released and emptied. In due time, the subconscious mind reaches a certain balance and there is no more need for this desperate manifestation of thoughts. Thoughts still come but as if in slow motion without the usual invasive and obsessive tendencies. An awakened person still experiences thoughts but in slow motion. That is perhaps the best definition of awakened consciousness.

In your case, you don't have to be so helpless in your experience of the mind. You must however do some work. You have the freedom to centralise yourself in the State of Presence. When you do it, you take a big portion of energy from the mind and direct it towards your own presence without any intention to stop thinking. Here, you don't even care whether thinking is there or not. In this way, indirectly, the mind loses its power and control over you - it exhorts itself. Is it clear for you?

Surrender is an expansion and is based on self-knowledge. If you don't know who you are, how can you surrender? In the case of an ignorant person, there is no one to surrender! It is a double process because through your self-discovery you then move to the Beyond, uniting yourself with the Ultimate Reality.

You can see it in this way. Your Soul herself is the door and the Golden Gate to the Beyond. By discovering yourself, you are entering this door. As you realise yourself, you find yourself suddenly on the other side of yourself, which is the Source of Creation. Your Soul is not the Ultimate but rather she is a channel through which the Ultimate can be experienced and consciously realised.

Student: *What happens to the Soul when the Ultimate is realised?*

Aziz: The Soul co-exists with the Ultimate. Pure Me is made of Awareness, Being and Heart. As Pure Me experiences herself, there is merging with the Beyond! Here, two realities are experienced simultaneously. And it is precisely here that Pure Me and the Ultimate become One. In this way, you experience your presence and your absence simultaneously. You can experience your absence only because you are present and on the other hand, you can be truly present only when you rest in the Beyond. In the ultimate experience, the Soul and the Beyond are completely one. You may not even be able to separate your Soul from the Beyond assuming there is no difference. We call it the illusion of non-duality. But when you look at this experience with the utmost sensitivity, you recognise the two-ness, the subtle duality. We call it the dual-non-duality.

There is the Soul and there is the Self. Is it clear? For instance, you sit in meditation, resting in Being, particularly when the Heart is present; this rest has the quality of the Soul. There is someone inside who experiences this rest. Isn't it so? You sit in deep silence, feeling your very Me who is inside. This Me knows 'that she is Me,' for she feels herself and can create a self-referral in the mind. The pure experience of Me is a combination of feeling and the Soul-image.

The Ego-image

Student: *What is the ego-image?*

Aziz: The ego-image is a picture or concept about oneself reflected in the mind. As personality lives in relative separation from the Soul, it creates a virtual image of itself through the ego-image.

We would like to make a significant distinction between the ego-image and the self-image, or the Soul-image. The ego-image exists only in relation to the collective consciousness. When you say, for instance, 'I am beautiful' or 'I am successful,' or 'I am not good enough,' this type of image cannot exist without comparison to others. For it is a reflection of our desire to have a good situation in the world. The ego-image is a virtual, artificial creation disconnected from our eternal identity. On the other hand, it is the self-image which reflects our true identity. It is not true that we should not have any image at all. Of course, to live in the space of non-conceptualisation, beyond the mind is a foundation. But out of this foundation, we arise as manifested beings living according to our purpose and destiny. That's why, no-image and a self-image are both necessary to live life in a real way.

What is our true self-image? It is beyond the collective mind. This type of image relates only to our universal situation, that is, to our place and status within Totality. To discover the Soul is to find our real self-image. Our true self-image is: the child of the Beloved, Pure Me contained within the ocean of Beingness and Love. If you don't have the real self-image, you don't know who you are. It is through the real self-image that you awaken your proper relationship with God and Universal Intelligence. The right self-image reflects your understanding.

When one is conditioned by the non-dual philosophy, for instance, assuming that there is no Me, but only impersonal Existence - one believes in an incomplete self-image. It is very interesting. Here, Me has this type of self-image where she denies her own existence! In our teaching we allow you to discover your true self-image in harmony with your blueprint and evolutionary purpose.

Is Having Judgements Wrong?

Student: *Can you speak about judgement? Is it wrong to have a judgement?*

Aziz: To say, 'it is wrong to have a judgement,' is already a judgement. Isn't it? The term 'judgement' has no clear roots. Often it is associated with the verdict of the court and the one who passes this verdict is called the judge. In this way, the term 'judging' feels quite serious and contemptuous. But if we treat it in a lighter way, it becomes an equivalent to the word 'opinion.'

Words are just words, they are relative and their meanings often evolve. For instance, the word 'ordinary,' in some languages is negative and means 'primitive' or 'vulgar.' Here, we often speak about being ordinary in a positive way, as an expression of humility and simplicity. In our teaching, we are using common English language and vocabulary to transmit a subtle and profound understanding. Language however has been created to express an unawakened perception of reality. That is why enlightened beings always have had difficulties expressing their realisation within the confines of language which is neither subtle nor rich enough.

What we call spiritual language is an attempt to create a new set of words and ideas which could reflect the awakened reality.

Be clear that words are not absolute and often carry conventional meanings. In our teaching, we often shape the meaning of some words in order to transmit subtle understanding. For instance, we speak about the Soul. It is a very common term which is understood by most people in a very shallow, naïve and simplistic way. Because of that, we explain over and over what the true meaning of this word is. We combine words in a skilful way to transmit an understanding which is beyond words. It is like poetry. You cannot understand a poem unless you read between the lines, reaching insight into the feeling of what the poet wished to transit. In this way, your mind and your Heart meet the mind and the Heart of this poet. To understand our teaching, you have to have a love for Truth, sensitivity and imagination. This teaching is not arising from the outside, but is awakening you from inside you!

To have a judgement is a bit stronger than to have an opinion. There is a feeling we fix our opinion in a stronger way when we have a judgement. But it is still all right. You see, to have a judgement is not the same as being 'judgmental.' To be judgmental is to use the ability to create judgement in an excessive way. There is a difference between getting angry sometimes and being 'an angry person.' There exists in the collective spiritual consciousness or unconsciousness rather, a naïve concept that one should not have any judgements. It is only partially true. If one has no judgements at all, it means that one is either an imbecile or one is dead! However, most people as they are stuck in the mind, have too many judgements. The ego very much enjoys creating all kinds of judgements. By creating judgements, the ego feels much more important. The ego has always an inferiority complex which it compensates by criticising others. This constant movement of opinions and judgements creates the gross reality of the ego which is locked in the cage of the mind.

This mechanism must relax so one can experience the open space of not-knowing, letting reality be as it is without categorising it into any concepts. The state of no opinion represents our original purity, our connection with Existence, our innocence and surrender. No opinion means, in truth, no separation. In Buddhism it is called suchness, the mirror-like consciousness. However, the mirror-like consciousness does not represent the whole of reality, for its internal dynamics are still lacking. Here, one enters the wisdom of differentiation. In Buddhism, the archetype of this wisdom is Manjushri. He carries a sword with which he cuts the non-dual reality into a polarised understanding of differentiation. All is One, but within this Oneness, good and bad co-exist, dark and light, beauty and ugliness, warm and cold, affection and repulsion...all of that co-exists allowing the dynamics of life take place. The Soul is nothing but a subject to polarities. Without Me, there is no difference between good and bad, wrong and right, dark and light. If there is no perceiver, the perceived is not there either. The Soul is that to which the Creation applies. It is a very significant statement. The experience of life can happen only due to polarities and polarities always refer to a particular Me or to the infinite Me's, numberless angles of perception.

Because you live in polarities, in order to live here, you have to create an attitude to your surroundings. And you recreate it from morning to evening. You eat food which tastes good, and you spit out food which is horrible; you choose events, company, places, circumstances according to your sense of wellbeing, pleasure and satisfaction. There are some stories about monks who tried not to differentiate between good and bad, eating for example bad food or rotten meat in order to bring into life their interpretation of Non-duality. But these are pathological cases showing how some spiritual ideas can turn into sheer perversion!

So, a certain sense of judgement accompanies your life at all times, for it allows you to live. This primal way of opinionating each moment of your life represents our ability to respond in harmony to the necessity of the moment. But there exists also a second level of creating an attitude towards reality. We speak here about having different concepts towards life, other people, the situation of our planet... and so forth. For example, every conscious person worries about the 'plastic problem' on our planet. In the west, many environmentally conscious people don't want to take plastic bags from shops. A New Age owner of the plastic factory could say 'oh, you are so judgmental!' ...(laughter...). Or many cold drink companies paint their appalling advertisements even on some small beaches in India. You can find all these ridiculous 'pepsi' paintings on the beaches and rocks in the middle of nowhere! Isn't it appalling? Here, we express a clear judgement. Don't we? These types of judgements are healthy for through them we protect the integrity of our planet, in this case.

To conclude, it is not judgements which are good or bad but the way we use them. On the other hand addiction to create judgements is a part of the ego-neurosis, but when we use this ability in a balanced way, it is a positive expression of our intelligence. Being on the spiritual scene, you must use your discriminative wisdom to avoid guru-hogwash and find the Truth. We tell you, therefore, use your judgement well but don't be controlled by your own judgements! Live beyond the mind as your true reality and from that space create in a wise way your life. When you understand the limitation of human intelligence, naturally you start to relax within the mechanism of creating opinions. You know so little! Therefore, you allow yourself to be fundamentally in the state of not knowing and you let the divine intelligence who created this life, act according to its mysterious plan. Here, true humility is born. In order to live, you must have some opinions but create them from the place of inner silence and love. It is OK to have opinions but first you have to have yourself, that is, by becoming one with your Soul.

Morality is a Substitute for the Basic Goodness

Student: *Can you define the difference between inherent goodness and morality, ethics or socially conditioned attempts to be pure?*

Aziz: Inherent goodness comes from the Heart and morality comes from the mind. Society had to create morality to compensate for the absence of the Heart chakra. However, it is important to understand that the Heart without intelligence can become conditioned as well and easily manipulated. In some cultures, like in the Middle East, we can feel the Heart more and the intelligence less. In the west, intelligence is quite developed but the Heart completely closed. Intelligence allows one to channel the energy of the Heart in the direction of wisdom. A person who has an open Heart but lacks intelligence, can be easily manipulated by the government or abusive spiritual leaders, for instance! Even though such a person has a mind, it functions in a semi-conscious way. It is chaotic and lacks clarity. The whole human being we point to is completely aware; he or she is intelligent and has an open Heart. If one element is missing, the whole construction collapses! Basic goodness is a combination of the Heart, inner peace, clarity and wisdom.

Spontaneity is Never Self-conscious

Student: *Can you speak about spontaneity. Is there such a thing as conscious spontaneity?*

Aziz: Spontaneity is either unconscious or subconscious. When spontaneity becomes self-conscious, it stops to be spontaneous. What is conscious? It is a feedback from intelligence to the outer or inner reality. This very feedback holds and freezes the spontaneous flow. It is an important step in the evolution of intelligence. Initially, intelligence evolves in an impersonal and subconscious way. When the conscious mind or ego develops, evolution becomes conscious. The ego is not fully conscious, for it has no real centre. But it is conscious enough to sense the existence of the subject (Me) in contrast to the object and give feedback from this place of self-referral. The ego cuts down the spontaneity of subconsciousness.

It is important to understand that spontaneity is not always positive. Spontaneity is often unconscious and blocks our evolution because it moves in vicious circles. When evolution becomes conscious, it accelerates for the Soul simply begins to co-operate. The next step in evolution takes place when the ego is transcended in reaching pure consciousness. This state is beyond subconscious spontaneity and beyond conscious control. Pure consciousness neither flows nor does it control - it is simply present. When you rest in consciousness beyond the mind, the second birth of spontaneity takes place. You simply allow your mind and your body to behave in a natural way. However, as an intelligent being, from time to time you bring an element of control, checking whether the action or emotion which you are about to perform spontaneously is right and whether you can allow it to flow; otherwise, you simply change it or stop it.

Spontaneity and control are the two sides of the human consciousness. In the state of pure consciousness even spontaneity is no longer unconscious, for the light of your own presence mysteriously penetrates it. It is not that you are conscious of your spontaneity; it is rather that spontaneity is contained within I Am. Bringing too much awareness into the spontaneous activity of the body and mind is against nature; it would turn us into self-conscious machines. The presence of pure consciousness does not eliminate subconsciousness; neither is it conscious of subconsciousness - it rather embraces and contains subconsciousness allowing it to flow spontaneously within the light of I Am. Here, the conscious spontaneity is born.

Evolution as Humans

Student: *How can we evolve as humans?*

Aziz: You can evolve only as a human! How else could you evolve? Even when you transcend this dimension and reach Buddhahood, you are attaining it in your human way. You evolve into the Beyond, into the Within and into the Without. Evolving into the Beyond, you merge with the Ultimate. Evolving into the within, you realise your Soul. And evolving into the without, you purify your psyche, reaching a maximum of harmony and expansion in your emotions and intelligence. That is how you evolve as a multidimensional human being.

Aloneness of the Soul

Student: *Can you speak about existential aloneness?*

Aziz: Aloneness in contrast to loneliness is an existential experience beyond the subject/object relationship. Loneliness is the sorrow of not having a loving Soul around with which you can share the experience of life. Aloneness is experienced only in the realm of the Soul. When the Soul refers exclusively to the Absolute Subjectivity, she is alone. In such a state, she does not translate anymore her sense of identity in relation to the objective reality; she is beyond the Here, relating only to the Creator. This existential experience is possible only when the Soul is realised and when one abides outside of the mind.

Sincerity: the Dignity of the Soul

Student: *What is maturity?*

Aziz: When the fruit is ripe, we say that it is mature. To be mature is to reach ripeness, a certain optimum of growth. To be mature is to be able to cope with the information of existence in the most efficient and responsible way. To be mature is to reflect the truth and not the subconscious tendencies of the mind. To be mature is to go beyond neurosis and the lower nature. To be mature is to know oneself and to discover the truth. To be mature is to be at ease with our human destiny. To be mature is to be awakened, in truth. To be mature is to deal with the difficulties of our human nature in a dignified manner, and to respect the code of honour inherent to the Soul. To be mature is not to be perfect or without mistakes but to be able to calmly and intelligently deal with difficulties. To be mature is to be much stronger in one's Heart and intelligence than in the negative subconscious and unconscious tendencies. To be mature is to be brave in one's encounter with life and to trust life in all circumstances. To be mature is to take responsibility for one's evolution. To be mature is to live beyond the ego-image, in the true humility and simplicity of the spirit. Maturity has no end, as long as we are alive, but what does end is - the immaturity.

Evolution in the Space of Acceptance

Student: *Can you speak about acceptance? In order to transform, we need to accept what is and yet to be open to change. Should our 'lower nature' be embraced as part of the process of purifying Me?*

Aziz: In order to transform, we need to accept what is and yet be open to change. Here, you have answered your question and expressed the principle of the non-dual path. Not only are you open to change but you willingly co-operate with your transforming process. Acceptance allows you to relax and appreciate your existence. However, within this acceptance there is a wisdom which allows you to grow. Otherwise you would remain passive. Non-acceptance brings frustration and the inner split. On the other hand, a static acceptance is stagnation and cuts down the evolutionary journey. Evolution has a very mysterious nature. It is the unfoldment of the Now, an expansion within acceptance, a constant transcendence of the present moment, which is becoming the future Now.

Yes, the lower nature must be embraced from the place of the higher nature. In this way, the lower nature is not negated but aligned and integrated with the original purity of the Soul. The lower nature is lower only in separation from the higher. Therefore, when embraced, no longer is it a 'lower' nature but a natural part of our multidimensional wholeness.

The Sense of Wonder

Student: *The sense of wonder...sometimes I am full of wonder, watching the sunset, gazing at a tree, listening to a stream. And sometimes I walk on the beach and my mind is full of dull thoughts. So I was wondering whether one can activate the state of wonder. Can it be a state?*

Aziz: It cannot be a state. The natural state is beyond wonder and dullness or insensitivity. It is an experience of pure isness which itself is magical but is not conscious or self-conscious of its own magic. The experience of wonder relates to a certain sensitivity, to the ability of re-discovering one's aliveness and of seeing the magic of Creation. Here, we can speak about awakening not to any particular state but to the fact of being alive. And this awakening creates within us this primal amazement. Life is dynamic, it is a constant meeting of the Soul with Existence, there is a magic to it, surprise, beauty, enchantment, humility, innocence; there is questioning, inquiring, discovering, evolution and expansion taking place on all levels; there is also suffering and sadness. Life is not only beautiful - it is the play of polarities. A person who lives only in the state of wonder may not see the other side of the Here which is quite negative and dark. But on the other hand, if one emphasis only the negative side of life, following the Theravada philosophy, one loses the natural perspective and the magic suddenly disappears. The beauty gets lost and the feeling of wonder is killed - the Soul commits suicide on some level.

The feeling of wonder cannot be constant. But when one's Heart and intelligence are awakened and the deep sensitivity of the Soul comes to surface - the state of wonder is present most of the time. But even though such a Soul does not feel wonder at all times, still, being one with the Divine, she experiences the ultimate beauty, the natural and constant wonder, Universal Wonder without the wonderer.

True Self-image: Beyond the Ego-image

Student: *You spoke about the difference between the ego-image and the self-image. How having the right self-image relates to dropping the sense of knowing?*

Aziz: A very important question. Do you see how the right questions allow you to grow and to reach a deeper and deeper insight into the nature of truth? The ego-image is a contraction of the Soul's reality. It is not that the ego-image is wrong; it is simply limited and taken out of context, that is out of wholeness. The ego-image always relates to the outer and to the collective consciousness. If humanity didn't exist, how could you create an ego-image? From the other side, the self-image refers to your relationship with God. Why have any image at all? Because you are a separate being. The totality has no image for it does not relate to anything - One without the Other, as it has been beautifully said. An image is not separated from your individual existence - you are that image already! You are a reflection of Totality in its individual manifestation. It is not that you just are - you actually relate to Existence. You cannot simply be - your life is dynamic, you are in a constant process of awakening to your existence and to the universal Existence. You are evolving. If you don't have this image of being an evolving individual, you are asleep, you don't know what is happening to you! That's why, your self-image is simply a pure reflection and understanding of your individual reality as well as of your purpose.

Your true self-image is that you are inherently a divine being: a Soul who evolves Here, discovers herself and eventually returns home to God. Your true self-image is that you are a child of the Beloved. That is the reflection of your deepest self-identity. Where is here a place for not-knowing? It is all Not-knowing! What does not-knowing mean? Not-knowing is your absence within the Now; your absence within the Universal Presence. When Socrates said 'I know that I don't know,' it was just in the mind. It is the point where the mind gives up but what next? You are still very much there, with your ego-not-knowing-image. True Not-knowing is beyond knowing one's not-knowing; it is pure Being, the absence of the self.

Where is the place for not-knowing when one knows one's true self-image? First, you cannot have a complete self-image, unless you are Self-realised. Why? Because, having a true self-image and being the self-image cannot be separated; they are the same. When you abide in the state of not-knowing (the Beyond) you know yourself directly as Pure Me. This knowing yourself directly as Pure Me and abiding in not-knowing which is the Beyond, become one. The result of it is the transparent self-image which leaves all traces of concepts behind. This state is Purity.

The part of yourself which allows you to experience not-knowing knowingly is your self-image. That which allows you to be free even from your self-image is not-knowing. This ultimate transparency is the mysterious meeting of the Soul with the Source of Creation. Me meets the Beloved. This supreme communion is beyond anything one can imagine; it is so subtle, so sublime that words exhort themselves. To understand it, you must enter the home of silence, the domain of unity, the temple of the Beloved which is made of love.

The Soul can only Speak to the Soul

Student: *How can one connect to people who have zero connection with spirituality?*

Aziz: From your Heart only. Not from your mind, not from your spirit, but from your Heart. If the other person is only in the mind, the best is just to go away or to connect in a formal way. The mind without the Heart is too arrogant, too insensitive and you simply waste your time. Respect your Soul, don't just talk to others for entertainment. But if the other person has the Heart, you can express your kindness and compassion. The Soul can only speak to the Soul. A complete meeting is possible when two Souls are at the parallel level of evolution. But first the Soul must be present. Only when the Soul is awakened, one with the inner silence, having an open Heart, being fully aware and intelligent, can we speak about the full presence of Me.

Acceptance and Non-acceptance

Student: *Can you talk about the attitude of accepting everything in life?*

Aziz: Acceptance... the deep meaning of acceptance is that your Soul rests in a deeper place than the phenomenal or psychological reality. The actual question is: from which place do you accept life? You can have the concept of acceptance in your mind. This is then followed by a certain attached emotional response. This type of acceptance is personal. You say, 'I accept.' Something happens, you say, 'I accept.' Something bad happens you say, 'OK, I accept.' You may be imperfect, you may not like something in yourself, but you say, 'I accept, I love myself anyway.' This is the personal acceptance.

But a deeper layer of acceptance is not personal; it is existential. This means that you surrender to this vast space of Being which is even beyond the concept of acceptance or lack of acceptance. In Buddhism there is the term Suchness. Suchness means that everything is as such, everything is as it is seen from a non-conceptual space. You allow reality to be as it is from the place of your absence, so the speak. That is the true acceptance. This acceptance is a state of Being and not a state of mind.

Within this unconditional allowance there may arise an issue of more personal acceptance. For example, someone dies and within your mind there is a choice either to accept or rebel against it. You may even question the whole meaning of life and so forth. You have to use your discriminative wisdom regarding which elements in life you choose to accept, which you must accept and which you can change. There was a prayer by St. Francis to God: 'Please, Lord, help me to discern between this which I can change and that which I must accept.'

Acceptance is a dynamic phenomenon. To accept everything on the psychological level is a form of dullness; it is not real. Because as you live as a manifested individual being, you must use your discriminative wisdom to discern what to accept and what not to. When a waiter brings you a meal in a restaurant, which is not cooked right, you refuse to eat it. Otherwise, even if you accept it, your body won't.

True acceptance is existential. It is a foundation in which this very mind of yours, with its freedom to say 'yes' and 'no,' is contained. When you do not accept something, be total in this non-acceptance and accept yourself not accepting it. And you accept yourself 'not accepting something' through resting in this Universal Acceptance which is Beingness. Your foundation is the non-conceptual state. It is a state beyond the mind, beyond thinking, beyond judgement, beyond the movement of thoughts and emotions. That is your foundation. From this foundation you are playing the role of a human and you relate to reality in a dynamic way. You use your wisdom accepting or not accepting things. You can do whatever you like - you are free. This is the point, you can do whatever you like. You are completely free. The real meaning of being beyond judgement and opinions is to rest in Being. It is not that your mind has no opinions. Because if your mind does not have opinions it cannot survive Here. It has to have opinions; it has to distinguish good from bad. But you are having these opinions from the place of your absence, from the place of rest in the Beyond.

There are two types of approaches to this matter of differentiating between good and bad. It is very much a Buddhist or Taoist idea to go beyond good and bad. Because the mind translates this reality constantly in terms of good and bad; it perceives truth in a polarised way. It is constantly creating judgements and opinions about the relative truth. However, the idea of going beyond good and bad is also dual, as it points to its negation. The moment you say that discriminating between good and bad is Bad, and not discriminating is Good, you are caught in a paradox of duality. The dualistic vision of going beyond judging is to stop judging where you simply do not allow your mind to create any judgement or opinions. But the non-dualistic transcendental way of going beyond good and bad is to go beyond the mind. From this perspective whether you discriminate between good and bad doesn't really matter because you are Beyond. Your I Am contains the mind. You are beyond polarities, beyond good and bad. And while you are beyond good and bad, you see that things are still good and bad, choosing the better ones. Beyond good and bad is Absolute Truth. The presence of good and bad is relative truth. The unity of Absolute Truth and relative truth represents Reality As It Is.

In Zen and Buddhism there are two types of realisations. First is the realisation of Oneness. They call it 'mirror-like consciousness,' in which reality is reflected without discrimination. Everything is just as it is. All arises in this mirror and the mirror allows everything to be purely reflected. When there is a beautiful face in the mirror reflected, the mirror does not say it is beautiful. When there is an ugly face, the mirror does not say, 'I do not want to reflect this face because it is ugly.' The mirror does not care...the mirror simply reflects. When you reach the State of Presence or pure awareness, you merge with this type of consciousness which is like a mirror reflecting everything.

The second type of understanding which follows the first one is called 'the discriminative consciousness' or the wisdom of differentiation. Even though it is true that fundamentally there is no good and no bad, good and bad do exist. In winter it is cold, in summer it is hot. We choose pleasure above pain and so forth. Many elements in Existence are differentiated, having different purposes and various functions. If you do not understand the wisdom of differentiation, you will not be able to live. You will be stuck in a clinical and conceptual vision of Oneness which is static and artificial. The Real Oneness includes separation and differentiation; the real Oneness is dynamic and alive. In the world of real Oneness a bird is singing, the child is crying and the human being is longing for truth. You can see it as the infinite space containing the play of phenomena. Is it clear? Do you have other questions related to it?

Student: *Can we jump back to the mirror which is reflecting? There is no judgement, but still there is some concept about what is happening.*

Aziz: Yes, simply seeing what is happening, that is right. And seeing that some things are negative and some are positive. There is no need to jump because everything is already differentiated. When you shift to the state of pure consciousness, this state is being simply added to your experience of existence. But the mind which has the inherent ability to differentiate things is already present. The reality of non-discrimination and the ability to discriminate between the multitude of various phenomena co-exist as two sides of One Reality, which is Truth.

Spiritual Evolution for a Child

Student: *How to direct my child towards his spiritual evolution?*

Aziz: Your child is just another Soul with whom by the force of destiny and karma you are connected. You are responsible for creating an optimum environment of love and inspiration for his spiritual evolution. But the choice is his! It is the child who has to choose his Path. In order for a child to enter his spiritual evolution, he has to reach a certain maturity.

In terms of inspiring spirituality in a child, never tell him what he should do but rather what he could do. Gently speak about spiritual matters, about sensitivity and love... silence and beauty, about God and Grace...meditation and awareness, about his Soul and eternity... Plant tenderly in his consciousness the seed of awakening, the message of the Timeless... the precious feeling of the Beloved.

The Role of Conditionings

Student: *Is there a way to live free from conditionings? Does Enlightenment free us from conditionings?*

Aziz: The concept that one can live without conditionings is one of those naïve misconceptions (re: spiritual conditioning). To condition something is not in itself negative. To 'condition' means to shape, to give a form or to create a foundation through which something can exist. Without conditioning, there wouldn't be any life possible. If you were not conditioned, you would be just an imbecile! Without your childhood and life learnings, you simply could not function in the world. Don't be fooled by this concept of being free from conditionings. That which is free from conditionings is your unconditional essence, but not your human nature. You as a human, are yourself an evolutionary flow of various conditioned psycho-somatic elements.

However, what you need to free yourself from are the negative conditionings which are not in harmony with your Soul's evolution. And do not forget that your primal conditioning is the very addiction to ignorance, this habit of being unconscious, identified with the mind, the trance of forgetfulness. The main problem, in truth, is the very fact of becoming conditioned as a member of this Soul-less collective unconsciousness. It is a global agreement - not to be conscious, not to be aware of the Soul, not to know the I Am. If you wish to be free - break through this primal conditioning!

An enlightened being within his or her personality participates in the conditioned reality like everybody else. Enlightenment changes only perspective from which one experiences the relative and conditioned reality. Enlightenment is a radical expansion into the unconditional realm of I Am. From that place one playfully participates in the dimension of time.

Education: Collective and Universal

Student: *How much formal education is necessary?*

Aziz: In the development of one's intelligence, it is necessary to learn from the collective mind some degree of knowledge to function in society. In this way or another one needs to participate in a more or less formal or collective education. How long one has to study depends on many elements, like one's interest and independence. Unfortunately, formal education is a real brain washer and the whole system of examination can easily hurt the vulnerable Soul of a child. We would say that the very capacity to drop collective education reflects one's readiness for the real freedom. You see, as there is official education so there is Universal Education. Official education is designed for human personalities and Universal Education is directed to Souls evolving towards Awakening. At one stage, one simply transcends the collective mind, becoming a member of a different family, a family of light, love and pure understanding. Our Transmission represents the Universal Education from the dimension of pure intelligence or Guidance.

Freedom from the Past

Student: *To what extent should I address issues from the past? Can I be free from the past?*

Aziz: You are already free from the past! The very fact that you are Now is itself freedom from the past. However, within the relative life of your personality, there is a continuation and evolution from the past. Because in your subconscious mind, you have gathered the dust of negative experiences - some of them manifest in your present reality and disturb you. The weight of the past neither should be overestimated nor underestimated. In modern therapies, there is a tendency to give too much importance to the past. By focusing too much on the past, like in the case of primal therapy, you actually intensify past issues; you actually create your problems by believing in them. You can deal with your past problems only from the place of freedom, that is, from the Now. The I Am is your ultimate and only refuge from the past. If you abide in I Am, the very light of its presence will cleanse the unwanted energies from your past. This cleansing is a function of Grace.

Forgiving Our Parents

Student: *Is it important to make peace with our parents? How to transcend barriers in understanding?*

Aziz: Your parents are not your parents but just people who have been karmatically destined to channel your physical form and take care of your initial evolution. If there is no connection and understanding with your parents, forgive them. They themselves are victims of this monstrous collective unconsciousness. If someone is completely drunk and says things which don't make sense - can you really be upset? In this society everyone is drunk with the wine of ignorance and forgetfulness.

If you can, try to communicate your truth to your parents. If this is not possible, relax and accept. Not to be understood is generally destiny of real seekers. Accept this destiny with dignity and humility. But if your parents are aggressive in a way that leads you away from your Path, you must resist, clearly presenting your truth. If this does not work, you need to create more distance and suppress the desire to share your inner life. When the time is right, you simply start your own life, graciously letting your parents to be just a part of your past.

Anger

Student: *Where does anger come from?*

Aziz: Everything comes from the same place, which is the Original State. Psychologically speaking, anger comes from a certain dissatisfaction, frustration and negative reaction to what is happening. Anger is a certain type of aggressive energy which rebels against a particular situation.

Student: *But who is saying no, who rebels? Is it the Soul? Is it the mind...?*

Aziz: YOU are angry! When you are angry, you are angry. Aren't you? You do not need to call it either Soul or the mind, or the ego. Simply, you are angry.

Student: *But, sometimes I feel that my anger is ridiculous.*

Aziz: Because sometimes you are ridiculous (laughter...). Anger as such is neither good nor bad, it is a natural reaction to certain situations. Often anger helps you by letting you know something is wrong. It is a spontaneous impulse from your emotional body. For example, you sit in a place which is smoky, crowded and noisy. Suddenly, you feel frustrated and angry for no apparent reason. This tells you that this situation is not right and that it is better to leave. In another case, you speak with a narrow-minded person; you try to convince this individual about your truth; you speak and speak and, at one stage, you get frustrated and angry. This tells you that it is better not to talk and just to leave. If someone is unjust to you, saying things that are not right and you naturally express a justified anger. You say 'no' to the situation.

Sometimes anger can come from the negative tendencies of the mind too. In such a case, it is not a natural response to the situation, but rather an immature and improper reaction. Similarly, as with other different negative tendencies of the mind, they arise from the subconscious mind. The subconscious mind, from the infinite past has crystallised its patterns of behaviour. These imprints have been formed in childhood, prior lives, and so forth. The subconscious mind is conditioned by collective consciousness, the environment and your particular life style. In this way, you have been programmed in a way that you react negatively to certain situations which you dislike.

The question is: who is experiencing the anger? Anger is coming from the mind but it touches something in you - someone is angry. It is not just in the mind. Someone is suffering. It is your Me. But what is this Me in separation from anger? When this Me is completely lost and unconscious, she becomes the anger. You lose yourself one hundred percent. But if you do not lose yourself, you experience your Me as clearly distinct from the anger. You experience anger but at the same time you are not lost. A large portion of you is quietly present in the background as well. You 'witness' your anger, so to speak. In order to comfortably deal with negative emotions, a certain distance and inner space must be present. If you do not have this space, any emotion will simply dissolve your identity, the clear Me. You have to learn to create the necessary distance of a wise and balanced disidentification. In this way, you will experience your anger in a totally different way. It will no longer be so obsessive and you will be able to deal with it appropriately.

Firstly, the thing to do when you experience anger is to come back to your sense of Me. Next, with intelligence you can see whether this anger is justified. Even when the anger is neurotic, it reveals something about your patterns and your way of reacting. But if you feel that the anger is not right, you must transform this energy. For instance, if you are angry with your child because you had a bad day, you can hurt your child by expressing your anger. Therefore, do not express this anger but learn how to channel this energy. In such a case, the best way to dissolve this energy is deep breathing into your belly. Even after a few deep breaths into your belly, you immediately feel a change in energy. Because observing from the mind is not enough to change the anger. Observing and witnessing will not change the anger because anger is present on the energy level. The very fact that you breathe, immediately, dissolves and distracts this energy.

So you see, as you evolve and become more connected with your Me, your I Am, the tendencies of the mind become slowly cleansed. In due time, your subconscious mind reaches a certain optimum of purification. It does not mean it will be perfect because you will never be perfect as you live in an imperfect reality. But you will reach a balance and minimise the difficulties of your emotions and your mind. Not only must you have a connection with your I Am and the essential understanding of your mind but the Heart has to be present. Slowly, your personality will be in harmony with your Pure Me. Your Pure Me is deeper than your personality; your personality is merely an expression of this Me. When this expression is neurotic or disharmonious, it hurts your Soul as well. That is why, work with the subconscious and your personality has to be combined with the process of reaching your Pure Me. That is, you must go beyond personality.

Here, there are two processes. One is that you go beyond your personality and discover this Pure Me which has nothing to do with thought and emotion. The second process is that you choose to positively participate in your personality, in emotions and thoughts and you intend to bring maximum harmony into this area. Therefore, you cannot purify your personality unless you are beyond personality because in order to change the system you have to be out of the system. To be the personality and try to change it is like sweeping the place on which you are standing! You cannot because you are standing on it, your feet are there.

At one stage, you have to make a step back to create the necessary space. You have to get out of the way. The only step back out of the personality is through I Am, that which is beyond personality.

Trust: All is Well

Student: *Can you speak about trust?*

Aziz: Trust is simply a certain psychological confidence that everything is well. It is a certain knowing that there is wisdom behind your life, that there is a purpose, that you are being protected from a higher perspective; that all is taken care of. That is the real trust; it is not dull and emotional but it comes from a clear understanding. In this pure trust, the Soul is awakened to her proper relationship with Creation. In the reality of Creation, there exists something like the proper relationship between the Soul and the Creator. One is able to recognise the constant presence of Guidance and the loving control of Higher Intelligence. As you tune into the mystery of your life, you can see the subtle thread of meaning and direction which has been present there all the time. You can see this tremendous wisdom in life and the amazing connection between all events.

Meaningfulness can be seen clearly only when one evolves. A person who is not evolving and lives only within the frame of collective consciousness is disconnected from any true Meaning. Someone who lives only according to vulgar common sense and translates one's existence through the need to survive on superficial pleasures - such a person is cut off from the Universal Meaning, Purpose and Trust. Universal Intelligence or the wisdom of God responds in an absolutely empathetic way to the creative evolution of the Soul. It is not only a relationship between the Soul and the Creator but also a way of relating of the Creator to the Soul. What kind of Guidance and help the Soul receives from Universal Intelligence reflects the intention and the purity of the Soul. That is why, as you evolve and experience difficulties connected to your internal processes, Grace enters your life. It enters according to the intensity of your dedication and yearning for Truth. You begin to see more a real meaning in your life and, naturally, you trust more. Someone who only lives within the collective mind trusts only one's own strength. The ego becomes obsessed with the need to protect itself and does not believe that it can survive without its own effort. This is where Trust is lost.

Real trust comes from a certain sensitivity, from being tuned in with the Soul's reality and her connection to Existence. Real trust means that you let Existence flow through you. It is not that you say: 'oh, everything will be alright.' It is much deeper because you simply stop thinking about yourself in terms of self-protection. You simply relax into What Is, that is, into your absence. You abide beyond thinking, beyond the self-protecting mechanism. That is why, Nisargadatta Maharaj used to say that a Self-realised being is like a baby - Existence must take care of him. When a baby is born, it has no way to protect itself. It does not think about finding milk to drink. When it is hungry - the mother simply appears. So, an innocent, awakened being who is in a state of surrender becomes like a baby. Existence takes care of him and everything magically falls into place. This does not mean that it is unnecessary to think about one's survival and means of living. One simply co-creates with Existence the truth of Creation but from the place of absolute rest in the Beyond.

When you live beyond the mind and surrender to the Ultimate Reality, fear is given up. When you give up your distrust, in return you receive universal protection. When you give up the excessive use of the self-protective mechanism, you receive more help from Existence. It is one movement: what you give on the altar of Truth, you receive a hundred fold in another way.

Self-protection and Trust

Student: *Can you speak about the balance between protecting oneself and not losing our innocence and openness?*

Aziz: There is a difference between protecting oneself, as an ego, and protecting oneself as a Soul. Protecting oneself as an ego is mainly in the mind, it revolves around attachment to the ego-image. On the other hand, protecting oneself as a Soul involves the Heart. Protecting oneself as a Soul, is your responsibility as an individual because she is vulnerable. The earth contains many negative elements in addition to the ignorance of collective consciousness. Humanity is quite ignorant and insensitive. For this reason, living in this dimension is difficult for a sensitive Soul. Naturally, the need for protection arises.

When there is no Heart, less protection is necessary because one lives partially and, therefore, can get less hurt. For example, if you live only in this body, this reality can hurt you only physically. If you live only in the mind, only the mind can get hurt. Although since the mind has very little sensitivity, the hurt does not go very deep. The mind lives in the reality of satisfaction and dissatisfaction; there is not so much a question of becoming truly hurt. When the Heart is open, you experience yourself and this reality deeper. How you experience yourself reflects how you experience this reality and how it can affect you. That is, for example, why it is false that an enlightened being is invincible. Even though Enlightenment empowers, it is also true that it can make one more vulnerable. This is because reality is experienced much deeper. For this reason, the dimension of forgetfulness can also hurt us much deeper.

To live as a Soul is an interesting combination of strength and openness, vulnerability and sensitivity. These two elements are necessary; for they are the basic polarised energies which enable one to live as a Soul here. Because you are sensitive, you can feel. For this reason, you can experience this reality in a rich way; you may admire a sunset, be moved by a flower or become touched by music. On the other hand, you have to pay a price for this sensitivity and certain elements of this reality can hurt you easier. For example, if you encounter injustice, insensitivity or certain negative energy, you may become immediately hurt. That is the price you have to pay for having the Heart. And it is a bargain!

Sex is a Natural Expression of Energy

Student: *You talked earlier about the economy of energy. Can you talk about sexual energy, is it a waste?*

Aziz: We spoke about the economy of energy but even more about the economy of attention. The ability to divide attention is not necessarily related to having a lot of energy or to be full of energy. Rather it relates to the expansion of awareness. Of course, in order to expand awareness, there has to be a certain amount of energy, particularly in the mind or third eye. It does not necessarily need to be a lot of energy, but a certain essential amount.

Some spiritual traditions speak about conserving sexual energy, so that it can be directed towards different spiritual centres. There is some truth in this, but at the same time it is not the complete truth. Traditions which work only with energy and are not related to wisdom, often channel the sexual or kundalini energy for the purpose of awakening. It is a valid Path, but can become quite mechanical as it lacks the element of self-knowledge.

In the past people were quite underfed, there was less food on the planet. That is why, if someone was having a lot of sexual activity, such a person could feel quite depleted. Afterwards one didn't have enough energy to meditate. But in our times where there is too much food, therefore too much protein, one suffers rather from excessive amounts of energy; one has too much energy, one does not know what to do with this energy. One is running around, trying to distract oneself.

Sexual activity does not have to disturb your spiritual practice. That is if you are having sex in a balanced way. For anything, what you do excessively weakens your energy system. When you have sexual activity in a balanced way, it can even help your practice, as it frees you from all those sexual fantasies that are generally disturbing in meditation. Contact with the opposite sex is energetically healing and balancing, energy can flow better. However, it is important to bring a certain amount of meditative energy and awareness into sexual intercourse. This means that when you are having sex, you are present and relaxed. The meaning of sexual tantra is to bring a meditative state into normally unconscious sexual activities. Sexual intercourse is one of the most unconscious activities a human being can have. This is because all those instinctive and animalistic layers of the mind are being triggered. Therefore by bringing the energy of awareness and the Heart into the act of making love, one can deepen meditation and the practice.

They say that one of the signs in the progress of a yogi is not to lose the State of Presence in the moment of ejaculation. The principle is that you are not looking for orgasm; the orgasm is not the goal. In this way you are not using your partner as a means, but you experience each moment of making love as a fulfilling experience. The orgasm is a certain pleasure which you allow yourself to experience, but you should not blindly look for it. Particularly, when men are unconscious, they lose a lot of energy during ejaculation. This energy is not so much lost in the sperm, it is on the energy level. One simply gets depleted, it is like the energy gets dissipated on the etheric level. That is why, most men have to sleep after sex. Many men have the feeling of being actually depressed after sex. This feeling comes from the lack of a real centre and a lack of awareness. When there is a centre, a State of Presence, this phenomenon does not occur so much. This means that you feel well after having sex. Observe yourself, because if you feel weak after sex, you may have to restrain from this activity or avoid ejaculation.

How Serious is Life?

Student: *How seriously should we take life?*

Aziz: It all depends on your sense of humour! (Laughter)... Sense of humour is a part of your blueprint. If you feel like laughing, it means that you are supposed to laugh. If you are serious, it means that you supposed to be serious. Therefore, the intensity of your sense of humour decides how seriously you will take life.

Making Decisions

Student: *What is the principle of making right decisions?*

Aziz: Who is making decisions? It is the intuitive intelligence, of course, or another name for it is the conscious mind. The conscious mind, in order to feel the situation must be connected to the Heart. Making decisions is not a simple task, for it represents the creativity of the Soul and the co-creation of her destiny.

There are three main karmic situations in life, regarding the decision making process. One is when positive karma pulls you into situations, places and circumstances which help you to grow, to adventure and to have all those important for you experiences. The second situation is the negative karma pull when you feel that you have to do something without much choice. That is the negative karma. In this case there seems to be a choice to do something else, but, at the same time, karma forces you to make the choice which you resist. In the third case, no karma is pulling you in any direction. We call it the zero karma point. At the zero karma point, you use purely your freedom of choice to make decisions. Here, you simply co-create your life. It may be difficult, for you become responsible. At the zero karma point, you simply use your creativity, imagination and intention. You may suffer in such moments, if your only intention is to flow with the Divine. To make a decision, on some level crystallises our sense of separation, our individual identity.

We would recommend not to be too serious with the problem of making decisions. In truth, you cannot make a wrong decision! Any decision you make is right, for it reflects who you are in this moment. Life is a learning process and everything you do and experience is a part of this learning and growth. Our main problem is not our inability to make decisions, but the very suffering coming from this inability! The more intelligent one is, the more it is difficult to make a decision. Why? Because one sees how many possibilities there are, how many options there are and how easy it is to go wrong! An unintelligent person is too primitive to see the complexity of reality. Such a person makes decisions easily.

So, relax within your difficulties in making decisions. What truly matters is not whether you make a decision or not, but how you feel in the moment of making your decision! Be relaxed and know that you cannot go wrong. That is very important. It is in the space of relaxation that the best choices are always made. And be playful with indecisiveness. It is all to be experienced, it is the adventure and joy of growing and maturing.

How to Change Personality

Student: *What can we change in the basic make-up of our personality and what is not possible to change?*

Aziz: We can change that which is possible to change and we cannot change that which is impossible to change. Certain tendencies of your mind, emotional body and general energy are your destiny, so to speak, and cannot be changed. That will slowly become clear to you. Even some tendencies, which you may perceive as negative, may be a part of yourself, similarly like the type of body which you have. With this understanding, you will accept yourself and relax inside. No one is perfect and those who try to be perfect are the worst! It is all not so serious anyway. Be compassionate to your own lack of perfection and embrace yourselves in forgiveness. You are just children of the Beloved and you are perfect as you are, that is, as being imperfect...

Can Intimacy and Freedom Meet?

Student: *I have a question regarding the issue of love relationship. Can intimacy and freedom meet? We always experience this unsolvable paradox, that we want to be intimate and free at the same time. Is it possible?*

Aziz: Intimacy and freedom can never meet, but if you follow the Path of intimacy, it ends in Freedom. The Path of intimacy is the Path of a Lion; the Path of freedom is the one of an Eagle. An eagle gets what he wants from the earth and flies up to the sky. It wants to be free from the earth. He needs the earth but doesn't want to be bound by it. A lion lives on the earth and has no need to fly into the sky.

If you follow the Path of Freedom and, at one stage, want to reach intimacy, you must give up your freedom. But if you follow the Path of Intimacy to the very end, it ends in freedom and you don't need to give up intimacy. In our evolution, oscillating constantly between polarities, we are slowly reaching the way of being which is beyond polarities. The final truth of our Soul is beyond freedom and beyond intimacy.

Is Monogamy Natural?

Student: *I have a question about the man-woman relationship. Is there a place for jealousy? Is monogamy natural?*

Aziz: If there is a deep connection between a man and a woman, if their Hearts open fully to each other, monogamy is the way. Otherwise, you will hurt each other. There are many idealistic models of love which are just the mind's creation. It is interesting to see how the mind can easily deform the reality of the Heart, by having unreal expectation from the Heart!

In the sixties during the hippy movement, the idea of free love was widely popular. And what was the result? A catastrophe! They could exercise this type of life style only because their sensitivity was dulled by drugs. If you are not sensitive, you can do anything. But it is not love! It is OK to have more than one partner, if the connection between people is casual and not so deep. The moment your Hearts open, there arises a natural commitment. So, yes, monogamy is natural for those who love each other.

The moment we speak about jealousy, we must be very careful because also here we find many idealistic concepts which go against human nature. Some naïve individuals think that we should love everybody and have no expectations whatsoever; and if our partner wants to sleep with someone else, you should be accepting even delighted! (Laughter...). Sometimes, some common sense is necessary, otherwise we become ridiculous. There are two types of jealousy: one is neurotic, reflecting our possessiveness, egoism and obsessive tendencies and the second one is a natural jealousy, which tells us that something is simply wrong! This type of jealousy has to be respected as it comes from the right place and protects our Heart against abuse.

Our advice is - be honest to yourself and respect your feelings even when they contradict your idealistic belief system. When you feel jealousy, with your discriminative wisdom discern whether you are being influenced by negative subconscious tendencies or whether your feeling is real and comes from the Heart.

Suffering Points to You!

Student: *When I suffer, I feel I am connecting to something within myself...*

Aziz: Certainly, because this suffering points to You. For example, when you are listening to the ocean, there is just a sound. But to whom does this sound refer? In truth, it refers to the one who hears it. It is always you who listens to the sound. How you feel listening to the ocean, colours the whole experience of hearing. You are always there and you have no way to get out of yourself. The moment you are in a state free from thoughts, you become less self-conscious. When you dissolve into I Am, you lose your crystallised sense of identity. But still, you are an indivisible part of this experience. Any experience, even the experience of your 'absence' refers to you. Even when the gross ego-sense of identity becomes absorbed, there is always a gentle feeling of Me behind.

However, when there is suffering, this painful experience refers to you in a very acute way. It hits your integrity. No longer is it merely a neutral experience, like seeing a tree or hearing a bird.

This experience hurts you and you know it, for you are in pain! That is why suffering points much stronger to the existence of the Soul than anything else. Even happiness does not touch you so deeply as suffering. Deep suffering really shakes you. When you experience a thrilling joy, like falling in love, for example, you immediately feel your Soul. But pain somehow moves deeper layers of your Soul.

Ask yourself: 'Who is the feeler?' Who is the one behind this experience of suffering? Do this type of gentle inquiry. Eventually, you take a step back and discover your true subjective existence. Do you understand? In moments of suffering you come as close as possible to who you are. It is your very Me which is suffering. But because you are identified with suffering so much, everything ends with the feeling of self-pity. 'Oh, I am so miserable, God doesn't love Me'... Suffering points to the Soul's reality but one has to make an additional step in order to discover the Soul. If you are just stuck in your personality, your only desire is to become satisfied within this personality.

The main problem with this teaching is that actually everyone wants to be happy on the emotional level and no one wants to transcend the superficial sense of self. Most seekers come just to feel good, to visit a spiritual atmosphere and be in the presence of a master. Afterwards they feel nourished emotionally but still they are not ready to face their nothingness. Therefore, the moment when you are as close as possible to yourself, in moments of strong suffering or thrilling joy: wake up! It is an opportunity which Existence gives you, by creating this whole situation, to discover your eternal Soul's identity.

What is this Pure Me in the Heart? What is this Me prior to personality, prior to becoming a child of this world? Suffering brings you back to yourself, but what is this self? This is what you have to explore. Not intellectually but by feeling yourself in the Heart, encountering this Pure Me which is so direct! Imagine that who you really are is beyond any incarnation, beyond all those changes in your personality during this lifetime. It is beyond this dream of being 'somebody' and having a role in this world. It is something direct, the most sacred and precious. And that is what you need to discover. In these moments, you are completely alone. That is the meaning of positive spiritual aloneness. You take away all masks, facing yourself as you are in your utter nakedness of abiding upon nothing. To meet oneself sounds like a slogan and it is a slogan for most. But the actual meaning of the sentence is tremendously profound. In this process you are not only discovering yourself; you are awakening this ancient longing for becoming One. Unless this yearning for Truth is fully present, you are not ready for the wedding with your own Soul.

When Suffering, You are Just Suffering

Student: *How to deal with pain and suffering?*

Aziz: From which place do you experience pain? In order to fully experience and embrace suffering, you have to contain it and in order to contain it, you must be beyond it! Before reaching I Am, you are the suffering. But when you expand beyond the mind and reach I Am, for the first time you can say: 'I am experiencing pain.' Awakening doesn't take suffering away from you - it takes away the neurotic and unnecessary suffering. Suffering which is experienced after awakening, we call Pure Suffering. Pure Suffering has no roots in the mind, but is indivisible from being human. From the place of I Am, you allow suffering to be. Here, even though you do experience pain, you are beyond it at the same time. The Human Buddha simultaneously suffers and is free from suffering.

That is the meaning of this Zen koan. Once a monk asked a famous Zen master: 'how to escape from cold and hot?' 'Why don't you find the place beyond cold and hot?' the master replied. 'Where could I find such a place?' 'When there is cold, the cold kills the monk; when there is hot, the hot kills the monk.' The master ended the conversation. Do you understand? The monk is in the place beyond suffering, but from that place he experiences suffering just as it is.

Student: *And what about the experience of physical pain?*

Aziz: When you are in pain, you experience pain.

Creativity

Student: *What is creativity?*

Aziz: Creativity is an expression and evolution of the spirit, intelligence and Heart. It is the ability to go beyond the known into the Unknown, into the New. It is to channel information which is beyond the content of the personal mind. It is the power to create the New!

How can the Ego Proclaim: I Have no Ego?

Student: *You say that the ego is good. How to understand it?*

Aziz: You think that the ego is bad. How to understand it? Is it really your idea? Or it is borrowed from some cheap teaching? Be honest to yourself! You have ego and you will always have it. So, better accept it as a part of being a human. Those who say that they have no ego - have the biggest egos! Do you see how an enormous ego could proclaim: 'I have no ego'! Those masters, who claim not having any ego, are simply ignorant or dishonest. Most often they hypnotise themselves in believing that they have no ego, so they can fit themselves to the prevailing spiritual paradigm.

Simplicity is to Exist Beyond the Mind

Student: *What is simplicity?*

Aziz: Simplicity is to abide in the state prior to thought. The mind complicates everything. That's why, the mind has to become quiet and get out of the way. Simplicity is already present, for it represents the purity of the Now, the immediacy of Truth. Simplicity must, however, be reached. That is the paradox, that the complex mind has to transform and become a vessel - containing silence and innocence. The evolution into I Am is the evolution into simplicity. The moment you say 'simplicity' there is already a complication! True simplicity does not know that it is simple. True simplicity is not self-conscious. Don't try to grasp simplicity, for the moment you do, it is already gone. Simplicity is already here but you need to relax into it, letting it be the container of your presence.

Facing the Unknown

To be a human is to be faced with the Unknown. Only within the space of not-knowing can evolution take place. There is a limit to knowing but no limit to not-knowing. Not-knowing from the ultimate perspective represents the absence of the mind and the presence of Reality. From the relative perspective not-knowing is a reflection of our inability to fully understand reality and our personal journey in time. Not to know is to be human. How far we reach with our understanding reflects the capacity of human intelligence. We are travelling to discover the ultimate frontiers of our human limitation. Infinity, the abyss of possibilities which is present beyond our reach, is where the Mystery begins.

Beings, Entities, Presences, Archetypes...

Student: *I heard that some beings or entities can accelerate our evolution and others can have negative intentions. I am curious as to what you have to say about this.*

Aziz: There is an esoteric dimension of spirits, beings, presences, ancient archetypes and energies. This esoteric dimension is present and closely interconnected with human consciousness and evolution. There is constant help and intervention from that plane into the human reality, which is otherwise, one of slow and painful evolution.

To answer the second part of your question, the concept that we have enemies in the invisible dimension, that there are malicious entities trying to block our evolution, is wrong. This belief is born out of fear, as are many other concepts. You must see that in order for a being to live in the formless dimension, a higher level of evolution is required. These beings are much more evolved than the majority of human kind. This means that the neurotic tendency to create evil does not exist in their case. Evil is unintelligent. To have the wish to harm other beings is proof of a very retarded state of consciousness! Therefore, this idea does not make any sense. You see, human beings have always been deadly scared of the invisible. Somehow, our sense of security relates very much to our sense of seeing, to the sense of sight. That's why so many people fear darkness and night; for that reason, evil is often symbolised by darkness. But darkness, in truth, is beautiful. The time of night is like the time of meditation: deep, calm, self-contained.

If you wish to be afraid - rather be afraid of that which is visible than invisible. There are no ghosts or spirits wanting to harm us. Neither are there human ghosts hanging around after their earthly death. These are superstitions born of fear and hope, which again do not at all reflect reality. There is no need to decipher the esoteric dimension. It is too complex to be understood. It is enough to know about its existence and that it does, doubtlessly, answer your prayers and support you in your earthly evolution. Yes, Grace exists.

Student: *So help is coming from the ancient archetypes?*

Aziz: Not only from ancient archetypes but also from various beings and entities. What is the difference? A being has a certain sense of Me which can be experienced and recognised as if out of the context of totality. This means that a being is experiencing some level of separation from the rest of Creation. Of course, we speak here about beings who are not in the body, formless types of consciousness. From the other side, an archetype has no sense of Me and is purely impersonal. Shiva, for example is this type of ancient energy, which responds to our prayers. Shiva does not have a sense of Me. Shiva doesn't say to himself 'I am Shiva.'

Student: *Is an archetype a part of the collective consciousness?*

Aziz: It is not at all collective. A collective consciousness is produced from many individual minds. An archetype is neither individual nor collective - it is like a space of super-intelligence which has its purpose and dwelling place within the Totality. An archetype is this part of the mind of God which responds to a certain need for help which arises within human and non-human evolution. Different traditions have their own esoteric presences and energies. Buddhism has its own esoteric dimension. Advaita is connected to a certain ancient esoteric energy which has been helping Advaita adepts from the beginning of this tradition. One of the functions of a master is to channel the type of esoteric energy which he represents. Similarly, when a great master passes away, even though his individuality gets dissolved, his presence and energy is kept in the Universal Mind. That's why, when you keep a picture of a master to whom you feel connected and invite this presence, it comes. It is not that the person comes - energy comes. This energy or presence does not have a sense of Me anymore. That must be clear. It is important to know how important the role of Grace is and the Other Dimension in our evolution. Without this help, human beings would still inhabit the trees in all the forests of the earth!

Channelling

Student: *Can you speak about channelling?*

Aziz: What channelling means is that human intelligence can receive inspiration and information from a Higher Intelligence. When you use your mind, you operate within the known, within your personal stream of consciousness. When you open up in your Heart and intelligence to Guidance, your personal consciousness can access new understanding and new insight. The type of information which you can receive relates to the capacity and evolutionary level of your Soul. That's why it is difficult to find a 'pure channel,' as the channel limits the Guidance which comes through it. As you evolve and reach higher states of consciousness, be careful in receiving advice from different channels who are themselves in lower states of evolution. You will simply not be understood. How can an ignorant channel possibly mirror the evolutionary path of a Soul who already experiences the Inner Light?

Student: *Does the ability to channel come from the third eye?*

Aziz: A combination of the third eye and the Heart.

Student: *Is the 'third eye' a centre of awareness or does it represent psychic abilities?*

Aziz: In truth, there are two different centres in the third eye which represent these two distinct functions. That can explain why psychics most often have very little awareness. The centre of wakefulness is not the psychic centre. In truth, when one is too aware one is unable to channel. One has to be deeply relaxed and slightly fall into a trance-like state. In the case of conscious channelling, awareness is simply relaxed and through the Heart can bring understanding and the spirit of Guidance. Channelling is a form of creativity and creativity is a form of channelling.

Death is the End of the Known

Student: *Can you talk about death?*

Aziz: Death is the end of a crystallised sense of identity with which one has become identified. Death is a change. It is not the end, but a change. It is a culmination of your particular stream of consciousness. From a certain point of view, death is inherent to each moment. It is the vanishing of each moment, and rebirth is the arising of each moment. That is why the phenomenon of death is happening all the time. Death means that the past or the present moment is giving a place to a new moment and is removing itself into the past. To experience a new moment, the present moment must go. The present moment is a particular experience of reality, taking place on many levels. It is very fast. The phenomenon of dying and being reborn occurs at all times. There are major experiences of death like spiritual death, for example where one encounters the end of one's past sense of identity. In such a case, the ego removes itself in order to give place to I Am. That is one type of death and one type of rebirth. Spiritual evolution is a complex process of different types of death and rebirth.

There is the general understanding of death, in which one's psychosomatic continuity ends. This means that your body dies and your mind dies. The body is no longer a channel for the vital-force and for the spirit which runs through it. Here, one's sense of identity as you know it ends. That is usually a dramatic change because humans are very identified with their physicality. It has been designed on a DNA level. You are supposed to be identified with your physical identity, otherwise you would not care about survival. That which allows you to survive and keep your I Am going is this very instinctive identification with body. We would not call it an ignorant type of identification, for it is the 'trick' of I Am in order to prolong itself within its individual manifestation. So your mind and emotional body are very attached to this physicality. When one's physical life ends, naturally the experience is strong or even traumatic, particularly because you are entering the Unknown.

When we say that each moment you die and the next moment you are reborn, there is a certain security in this feeling of dying because you retain continuity. You can foresee your continuity, therefore, you are not so afraid. When you go to sleep every night, it is a type of death, but you know that you will wake up the next day and that your existence will continue. When you go to sleep, you feel safe because you know there will be a continuity of your physical form and your mind will continue within the same stream of consciousness and memories. When you die a physical death, there is this basic lack of security as you have no way to know what will happen to you next. Different religious beliefs, whether they are Tibetan or Christian or whatever, try to create a new sense of security. These beliefs do not necessarily represent reality. They are mostly invented out of fear.

When you die, you simply die and enter the Unknown. There is no security. There is no protection. Your protection, your ultimate protection is the ultimate identification with the Creator. What it means is that you submit your sense of identity exclusively to the Ultimate.

Student: *After the death of the body and the mind, does anything remain?*

Aziz: Certainly. That which remains is evolution and the flavour of the Soul which later incarnates again in a different form and perhaps in a different dimension. But you see, what is the ultimate goal of all this can be represented in a poem by Rumi:

> *I was first a mineral. Next I became a plant and after I died as a plant. I became an insect and after I died as an insect. I became an animal and after I died as an animal. I became a human and after I will die as a human. I will become an angel and after I will die as an angel. What shall I become? I want to die completely in order to become the Beloved.*

There is this desire of his to just die completely. This is the opposite desire to that of a 'normal' person which is to retain their sense of identity at any cost. Everybody just wants to prolong his or her existence: to be even a ghost, a haunting ghost, to live in nightmares as long as one can BE. If humankind is passionate about anything, it is certainly passionate about its survival. Anything is better than not to continue one's ego-existence. This is how an average person instinctively clings to his or her sense of identity. But when you go deep inside, you can see that to die is positive. You are endlessly dying, coming closer and closer to the final death - death in God.

Student: *And does the Creator, God, have a way of knowing the truth of Existence without this particular Me?*

Aziz: It is beyond comprehension because the Creator exists prior to consciousness which means that she is not self-conscious...the Creator abides in a realm of pure isness. This Reality is beyond comprehension because it is neither absent nor present; neither does the Creator know herself, nor does she not know. It is simply beyond comprehension. With linear nature of the human mind this matter cannot be grasped.

Surrender Yourself to Death

Student: *You said that human consciousness cannot survive death. In that case how is it possible that the Dalai Lama or Karmapa can consciously incarnate?*

Aziz: There is no human being who can do such a thing. We can strongly effect reality with our mind and our beliefs, but there are limits to it. The Dalai Lama seems to be a wise and honest man who is himself not very identified with these believes. Because most people are not ready for truth, they need to be fed with fantastic stories. Tibetan Buddhism, apart from bringing to the west a very profound philosophy and understanding of Buddhism, brought also plenty of magic and superstitions.

It is very interesting to see how unconsciously westerners behave around the Dalai Lama. It is very similar to the way simple people treated the Pope in the medieval Europe! It seems that in many respects the Tibetan Buddhism has replaced Christianity. Perhaps, that is the secret of its popularity in the West.

Student: *I have participated in the Tibetan practice of 'Powa,' which is the preparation for death. Do you think it has any value?*

Aziz: There is not much value in this practice. This practice is based on a belief that unless you leave your body through the crown chakra, you will not be easily reborn in the Amitaba Land or paradise. Therefore, they are trying to open in a forceful way this passage on the top of the head. This is one of those beliefs which are based on fear. Buddhism has a tendency to control reality. If you enter the Path, you begin the battle with ignorance and awaken awareness because attention is your only freedom from darkness. However, there are areas in life of which you simply have no control; one of them is death and another is your future rebirth. There is no way that you can prepare yourself for death apart from reaching as much light as possible in your particular lifetime. When you die, you simply die - you can do nothing more. At the moment of death, you submit yourself to the same Infinite Intelligence which brought you here in the first place. Let go and trust...surrender yourself to death. It is like falling asleep - you just let go. Trust the Creator. There is nothing to be afraid apart from your own fear!

To Feel Sacredness through a Symbol

Student: *What is the importance of religious symbols and rituals like maintaining an altar, wearing a mala or chanting mantras, etc?*

Aziz: In truth these symbols have a great significance in our life as spiritual beings. They bridge our dimension of forgetfulness and separation, with the Divine. They inspire our connection with the Beloved. We need them to stimulate our imagination, to help the Heart open and the mind to focus on the Divine. Keeping an altar, for instance, creates an atmosphere of sacredness and prayer, deepening our love and sensitivity. From the other side, through these symbols we invite the Divine into the esoteric aspect of our life; we consciously invite Light to support our evolution in this plain of darkness. And the Divine always responds to our invitation, bringing the energy of Grace and support on all levels.

Those who are too intellectual often speak negatively about using religious symbols or doing rituals. But this behaviour can be understood only from the Heart, and the Heart is never so rational or logical. The Heart believes in a different logic - a logic of love, gratitude and devotion. To use symbols and rituals is an indivisible part of human psychology, which needs to be fully respected. Even a simple act of giving flowers to the one you love, is another expression of the same archetypal need to express what you feel through a symbol or gesture. To deny this need would be foolish.

However, if these symbols are used in a mechanical and unconscious way, they become empty and dead. This is what has happened with most religions - the symbols became more important than that which they pointed to. For example, one lights every evening a candle for the lord Shiva to keep the precious connection with his presence. One does this ritual every day, year by year... and suddenly it becomes just a habit or superstition - one forgets the original reason for this ritual. One can even become afraid of going to hell if the ritual is not done properly! One is convinced that the candle has to be lit in a special way and in a specific hour...and so forth. In this way, that which was beautiful and pure in the beginning, has become dead religiousness.

The Limitations of the New Age

Student: *Could you speak about the value of information channelled from different beings and other dimensions?*

Aziz: The New Age movement is a bridge between collective unconsciousness and the dimension of awakening. Because it is a bridge, it has to be transcended, left behind. It is very interesting, but there is something like collective New Age consciousness. There is some kind of virtual reality being shared by those identified with the New Age ideology. If you read various channelled books, they show similar thinking patterns and ideas, even though they usually present contradictory information. For example, if you read different reports channelled about Jesus, each of them have different ideas about who he was and what actually happened to him. There is something very Christian in the New Age, as if this whole movement was a sublimation of frustrated Christianity. That's why, no one in this movement and no one of these channelled beings speaks about the Buddha. When they do, which is rarely - their opinions are rather inadequate and even ignorant. Many of those beings bring a lot of inspiration and love but hardly any of them seems to be aware of the Buddha State. It simply tells us that to be a being, entity or a formless type of intelligence does not mean that one is truly awakened and in touch with the ground of Existence. These beings seem to be very much in the dream state. It is quite a beautiful dream; it is a dream where the energy of light and love is much stronger than on the earth - but it is still just a dream.

Student: *The New Age movement seems to have brought some light to human consciousness but at the same time it has falsified aspects of spirituality. How to be clear about what the New Age has to offer?*

Aziz: If the New Age has something to offer, it is mainly in the field of human psychology and evolution towards feelings. In truth, all this spiritual Disneyland revolving around psychic phenomena, energy healing, clairvoyance, auras, chakras, astral travel, meeting extraterrestrials, communicating with dolphins, crystals, tarot readings, channelling...and so forth, represents just a superficial layer of this movement. The most important message of the New Age is the return to feelings and a more feminine perception of life. From the higher perspective, the New Age is just another illusion because it does not point directly to Self-realisation. It is quite an unconscious movement which attracts those looking for an excuse or escape to be even more spaced-out and ungrounded. Yes, this movement seriously ignores the basic work with awareness and the whole eastern technology of awakening. None of those channelled beings seems to be aware of the essence of the Now and the Source of Creation. It is all like a big dream.

The Concept of Chakras

Student: *How much does your teaching about Awareness, Being and Heart relate to the concept of chakras?*

Aziz: It is connected on some level to the idea of chakras and on some level it is not. The usual teaching referring to the awakening of chakras, transmits a different type of energy and message. In our teaching, we divide the human being into three centres: the head, the Heart and the belly. These three centres are sufficient to trigger awakening. Other chakras have more psychological functions. For instance, you do not need to activate your throat chakra which is responsible for vocal expression, in order to experience I Am. Whether you are deaf and dumb or a wonderful public speaker, the experience of I Am is the same. Other centres do not relate directly to the awakening process. The concept in the Yoga of Kundalini speaks about the awakening of chakras one after another, up to the crown chakra, we find very linear and simplistic.

Also the centre in the belly, the Hara, is not a chakra as it is taught in Hindu mysticism. The Hara is the energy centre of our whole body, the centre of gravity and the centre of life force. That's why in Japan, Samurais were committing suicide by cutting this place with a sword, for one dies immediately.

In the case of the Heart, she is seen traditionally as one of the seven chakras. This is also true for the centre in the head, the third eye. But again, the situation here is complex because in the third eye there are two sub-chakras present. One is responsible for the psychic vision and the other one for awareness. And, as you can guess, our emphasis is the awareness aspect of the third eye. Now you can understand why some psychics who only develop the third eye are completely unconscious and spaced out.

Student: *What is the function of the crown chakra?*

Aziz: It is your connection with the universe, your connection with the dimension of Grace and the ability to channel energies from the Beyond. When the third eye and the crown chakra are fully activated, they combine as though they become one.

Awareness and Psychic Abilities

Student: *Can the State of Presence activate psychic abilities?*

Aziz: The State of Presence can indirectly unblock some dormant psychic abilities, but it directly has nothing to do with them. The State of Presence has no mind on its own. It is simply present to itself in the background of the mind. Psychic abilities belong to the reality of the ego and cannot by any means be seen as evidence of spiritual advancement. The State of Presence is not an ability to manipulate reality, but is freedom from ignorance. What is the use of psychic abilities within the mind, which is essentially neurotic? This constant movement of thoughts, emotions and fluctuation of energies is itself suffering. You can create some special abilities within your suffering - but isn't it meaningless? The Buddha used the metaphor of someone who becomes shot with an arrow. Imagine that such a person speculates about archery instead of taking this arrow out! How foolish! Trying to develop psychic powers instead of awakening is exactly the same. One tries to entertain oneself with essentially useless abilities while remaining in deep sorrow! Psychic abilities are called spiritual materialism. They are very dangerous, because one becomes even more proud and arrogant. If they arise, let them be but do not give them much importance.

Who Chooses to Incarnate?

Student: *Is it true that when the Soul doesn't want to incarnate again, she doesn't come back?*

Aziz: If the Soul truly doesn't want to come back to this plane, she doesn't incarnate. But most often, even though the Soul does not want to incarnate on one level, she does on another level. The reason that you incarnate is the desire to incarnate. It refers mainly to the emotional body in which some strong needs, desires and obsessive tendencies are imprinted. Incarnation is the Soul's choice; it is not a conscious choice. It is not that you make a decision. There is no you to make this decision, in the first place! The Soul cannot stop incarnating unless she fulfils her blueprint. The scenario which Universal Intelligence has written for her must be played to the very end!

The blueprint is the point where you reach the ultimate perspective, the optimum of expansion related to your unique angle of perception. Many elements are included in the blueprint. Some of these elements are inner expansion, various experiences in the world, emotional fulfilment and the understanding of reality. Enlightenment is just a part of this blueprint. It is possible that the Soul does not come back even if she is not yet enlightened. Some Soul's give up their desire to incarnate prior to reaching Enlightenment. For other Souls, unity with the Divine and realisation of the Heart may be sufficient in order to transcend this plane. Some Souls are too feminine to attain Enlightenment in a traditional sense, which does require some masculine energy. Therefore, don't be dogmatic in projecting one generic vision of Enlightenment for everyone, as the past traditions did. Your challenge is to attune yourself to your own evolution and to discover your unique blueprint. Which elements do you need to become complete? If you study Buddhism, if you study Advaita, you are being given a general blueprint. The danger is that you may become conditioned by this linear model of awakening, overlooking your own unique flavour of evolution.

Of course, some elements are universal and trans-personal. For instance, awakening to I Am is an element which almost all Souls require for their completion. Within the global blueprint of the human evolution, you must find your unique evolutionary path. You are the force through which your Soul's ultimate vision of completion becomes realised.

The Path of Energy

Student: *Can you speak about Tantra or Sexual Tantra?*

Aziz: There are certain Souls who don't want to use their wisdom in the awakening process. They prefer to use energy. The Path of energy is not so clear and can be quite dangerous. To use lower energies in order to channel them as a force of awakening, is Tantra. It is an indirect and complex Path.

On the other hand, in the Path of self-knowledge, energy is turned directly to the recognition of I Am. That's why it is a safe Path, but at the same time it does require some intelligence. When you pose the question 'Who am I?' it is your intelligence which, using the energy of attention, discovers her own centre.

As far as Sexual Tantra is concerned, it does not point to a clear awakening. The type of spiritual discipline which Sexual Tantra offers brings one to various mystical states, but hardly ever to the Buddha State. To use sex for spiritual purposes means simply to experience love and to be present.

Karma Means Connection

Student: *Can you speak about karma?*

Aziz: Karma means action, the interconnectedness of all elements in the realm of becoming. For example, you ask a question and you receive an answer. Therefore, by asking the question you create the type of karma, through which you receive the answer. Karma relates to the connection between cause and effect. In the way you live and act, you attract certain consequences. For instance, by meditating you create the karma of awakening, and by eating fat food you create the karma of becoming unhealthy.

We know that all is interconnected and that there is a basic relationship between cause and effect. That is the general understanding behind the concept of karma. But the question of a more delicate nature is how the elements of Existence are interconnected and what is the exact relationship between causes and effects? Here, we enter the area of many different theories and interpretations which often tend to be very moralistic and conditioned by their particular belief systems. Sometimes the theory of karma is related to the general idea of reward and punishment which is often understood in a narrow and simplistic sense. Karma does exist but not always in the simplistic sense of the term. Many events in our life are karmicly determined but karma may also be rearranged and changed.

There are three types of karma: positive, negative and neutral. Positive karma enables you to meet the right people, be in the right places and have positive experiences which help you grow and expand in the different areas of life. An example is the meeting your Soul-mate or a spiritual master with whom you were once connected in a past life. From the other side, negative karma may pull you, for example, into a relationship with a person who is not good for you or to go to a place where you may suffer. Negative karma sometimes needs to be experienced in order to become released and at times it may be transformed or erased by the force of Grace. Neutral karma represents the type of karmic coincidences in life which cannot be measured by the criterion of good and bad. Many things simply have no special meaning in our life but have causes which can be traced. Apart from karma, there is also a place in life for accidents where things happen at random, without any particular karmic reasons.

The notion of karma is closely related to the term destiny. Destiny means that certain things in our life must take place and cannot be avoided. An example is the country you are born in or the mother you were born to. These situations are not made by decision. The decision has been made for you by Existence. In your spiritual evolution, you must attain a certain completion in each life. This certain completion could be, for instance, the opening of the Heart or stabilising in the State of Presence. You may also be destined to be in a certain relationship and to have a child...and so forth.

There are two kinds of destiny: static destiny and dynamic destiny. In the case of static destiny, it cannot be avoided. But as far as one's dynamic destiny is concerned, some different possibilities and elements can be rearranged. There is some creativity in life and there is an important element of Grace which often brings unexpected positive conclusions.

Negativity which you have accumulated in your mind may be erased by the intervention of Grace. Without Grace we would never get healed, for the mind is too negative. If we look at the process of cleansing the subconscious mind, from the viewpoint of karma, it could never reach completion because our natural neurosis is simply too strong. That's why, we cannot really transform ourselves through therapy alone. We need the help of a force which is higher than karma; this force we call Grace.

There is destiny, there is the free will and there is the combination of the two. There is Grace, which is the unexpected help, intervention from the dimension of love. There is an element of accidentality as well, for life and evolution often experiment. In conclusion, Grace is above destiny and karma.

The Model of the Seven Bodies

Student: *Does the system of the Seven Bodies used by teachers of the Rajneesh school, reflect the inner map of awakening?*

Aziz: It is just one way of looking at the model of Self-realisation but it is not the most precise. The seventh body is called the nirvanic body and represents the Absolute State. But you see, there is a big difference between the Absolute and the Absolute State. The Absolute exists prior to recognition, while the Absolute State is the meeting between the Soul and the Uncreated. So what is the role of Me in the realisation of any state? It is Me which brings recognition into the Ultimate. In the system of the seven bodies, there is no place for Enlightenment to the Heart and certainly not for Soul-realisation.

The sixth body is cosmic consciousness. What does it mean? It is a big word, isn't it? The moment you hear cosmic consciousness, you feel immediately scared and small! Isn't it so? These notions are good to intimidate seekers. But what is the actual experience of the sixth body? It is nothing else than turiyatitta, the state beyond witnessing consciousness. This state is a combination of pure awareness and expansion into Being. It can be experienced with or without the Heart. In truth, cosmic consciousness cannot be fully realised unless the nirvanic body is present. Why? Because only the foundation of motionlessness can allow

I Am to expand fully. Cosmic consciousness represents the manifested reality. When the Absolute is realised, the Soul reaches the Uncreated and from that place her consciousness can merge with Creation. In the complete state, two types of merging take place: one with the Absolute and the other with the totality of Creation.

Beyond the seventh body is the Divine Body which represents the heart of the Beloved. The next body is the Body of Me which paradoxically can be fully realised only after reaching the other bodies. And the ninth body is the State Beyond Polarities. Here, the Body of Me merges fully with the totality of Creation which is the sixth body, and with the Unmanifested, which is the seventh body, and with the Divine Body. Why does it happen in that moment only? Because the fifth body, which is witnessing consciousness (the State of Presence), only now becomes absolutely absorbed into the seventh and eighth bodies.

The question may arise: are these all the bodies that exist? The answer is yes, but only from the view of the particular Me who has reached so far. First of all, God is not our body but we are the body of God. Do you see the difference? Through spiritual expansion, you don't become God, but you merge with God. So what you may translate as the realisation of the body of God, is in truth a meeting place with your own absence!

It is like that. Me is a tree. The crown of the tree is our consciousness; the flowers of the tree represent our Heart; the roots of the tree are our connection with Beingness. Beingness is the earth of Me. The experience of Being, the experience of the Uncreated takes place where the roots enter the earth. But how deep do they reach? They reach just a surface of the earth. The place where roots of the tree end, reaching their ultimate expansion is where Me meets her own absence within the Universal Presence. So reality is more than we may imagine it is. When Final Enlightenment is reached, it is now that we can face the mystery with humility and awe. It is because only then we have merged fully with the Nameless. It is here, that through our presence, we experience our absence. At this moment, the frontiers of our perception of What Is exhaust themselves, letting the infinity to be BEYOND.

When one is ignorant, one is suffocated with one's limited and fragmented presence. One is surrounded by the Beyond, but is unable to access it... one is unable to transcend. Awakening means that we expand through our Awareness, Being and Heart into the Beyond, towards the mystery. The experience of Oneness is a particular mixture of our existence as Me with the Universal Presence. This meeting of the Soul with the Ultimate cannot be grasped; it cannot be pinpointed, but can be clearly experienced and transmitted.

Please see that Me, in her transcendence, doesn't merely become absent. It is not that only the Ultimate remains present. The Ultimate is present through Me. Me is meeting her own absence, which means that Me is in a profound way present. She abides in this dimension of experience where she encounters her own disappearance. That is the mystery of the meeting between the Soul and the Beloved. It is neither the Soul nor is it the Beloved. What is it? It is the Beloved meeting herself through Me.

Who Incarnates?

Student: *How come some part of us is beyond incarnations and another part is lost in this world? I often get very disturbed by subconscious emotional reactions.*

Aziz: We spoke about experiencing that which is beyond incarnation. There is a part of you which incarnates and there is a part of you which doesn't incarnate. Like you were born in this body, but were you really born? If you look inside, you see that there is something which was not born in this body, an eternal essence.

What does it mean to incarnate? It means that consciousness is continuing evolution. Let's say you die now, yes? Your consciousness reaches a certain point of evolution, but your Soul is still not fulfilled inside; you still want to grow further; you still want to continue. Because you have died, you cannot continue in this body and so you incarnate in order to continue your evolution.

There are many people who are very unconscious, ignorant. They think only about primitive or material things, yes? They don't have spiritual desires. But their Soul from a higher perspective still wants to reach the light: First they need to fulfil their worldly desires, get tired and afterwards they seek a spiritual direction. So sometimes you need a few lifetimes to experience all that matters for an average person. To experience the same emotions, to have a family, wife, job, all the things. And eventually you start to ask yourself the question: is it enough? Or is there something more in life? You have returned here so many times, never having been able to learn your lessons. When you meet someone, you can feel whether this person is an old or young Soul. Certain people have a maturity which is not from this lifetime. Even among children, you can find some with the maturity of an adult. This phenomenon is related to their past lives, their past evolution, in past lives. A child is often more mature than his parents even before can he speak.

Your reality is composed of several elements. The foundation is I Am, which is the unconditional state. I Am is where your Soul abides. Second is the Soul which is your true individual identity; the one who is experiencing the inner and the outer. Then there is the personality which is the expression of the Soul in the world, the mask and the function of the Soul in the world. Personality develops through many experiences. Through the learning process and conditioning, it becomes crystallised in the subconscious. Sometimes it is crystallised in a positive way and sometimes in a negative way. In order to experience the positive personality, there requires a cleansing of the subconscious mind. When the subconscious mind is cleansed, it becomes aligned with the Soul. This means that you experience a harmony, a unity between the Soul and personality. The nature of personality is never perfect. It uses a certain program stored in the subconscious mind. The role of personality is to help the Soul to function optimally in the world. It cannot be completely perfect because functioning Here can never be perfect. To live in the world is difficult and perfection cannot be reached but what you can reach is an optimum of harmony within your personality.

As the Soul is the child of I Am, so is personality the child of the Soul. This child has to grow up as well, which means it has to mature and have many experiences in life. It has to go through a learning process in order to reach maturity and purification. When you experience disturbing tendencies, treat your personality as your child. Embrace your personality with compassion and wisdom. When you do not agree with certain tendencies of your personality, make an effort to let them go. In this case you use your discriminative wisdom and a certain amount of will. You have a certain amount of freedom in how much you indulge or transform the negative tendencies in your personality.

When I Am is present, when the Soul is present, one can be the master of the mind. One can be a master of personality because one has a centre, a place of inner refuge. If there is no I Am, if there is no inner refuge one is completely lost. If there is only the mind, one has very little power to deal with personal tendencies. Certain tendencies in your personality need to become more conscious. They are too subconscious; they are too automatic in certain areas. You have to become aware of them. Yes, this is exactly what we are talking about: this automatic habit from the past which doesn't relate to the present.

Yes, look at them deeper and look at the emotion which is behind it. Before a certain tendency manifests itself, you can trace a certain subconscious pattern or habit, a certain energy preceding it... This helps you to understand why a particular tendency is manifesting. There is usually something deeper which triggers your reaction. It may be restlessness; it might be some immaturity. Simply look at it.

How can you Secure Your death?

Student: *What happens when you die? According to the Tibetan book of Living and Dying, it is a very complicated process.*

Aziz: Yes... don't believe in these things. Just forget about this, for those concepts are born out of fear. You know, death is the most feared thing. And many religions somehow have their share in creating this fear. For example, there is a concept that if you are not aware at the moment of death, you will be born into lower realms. It is a sheer nonsense. The moment of death is as equally important as all the moments you experience in life! There is no way you can prepare yourself for death. When you die, you just die. It is like falling asleep - you disappear. After death, there is no you, so why is there a need to prepare? How can you prepare yourself for your own absence?

You see, it is like this... When a person dies their Soul de-manifests, she returns to the deep sleep state. The human Soul cannot exist without the body. There are other beings that exist without the body, but they are not humans. When the body dies, the Soul de-manifests, returning to the deep sleep state and losing awareness of her existence. When the blueprint is not complete, however, the Soul becomes manifested again.

And who manifests the Soul? What is this power which makes you manifest into the human realm or into another realm? It is called Universal Intelligence. You are not in control of these matters. You have no way to control your next rebirth; you cannot make sure that everything will be fine, there is a higher wisdom that does this. Your next incarnation in one way or another reflects your level of evolution at the time of death. For that reason, the best way to prepare yourself for your future incarnations is to evolve.

You have to come as close as possible to your inner light. Do not allow yourself to follow your lower nature, but always be in touch with your Heart and your I Am. In this way, certainly, your next incarnation will be positive. And you do not need to be reborn as a human; there are many possibilities. The reason why one does not need to incarnate is not merely Enlightenment. That which makes you let go of this dimension is your completion and fulfilment. When you feel done with this ridiculous drama, your Soul will not wish to incarnate anymore. It is all on the Soul's level; your Soul decides, not your mind.

So when you do not incarnate anymore and you are fully complete with this dimension, the evolution may still continue but within Universal Consciousness. We cannot speak about this because it is beyond human understanding. There are mysteries which are far beyond the totality of human knowledge; no human knows these mysteries, not even the Buddha knew... nobody can know. There are certain mysteries that the human being is unable to know because of the basic limitation of human consciousness. We cannot go beyond that.

Even the Enlightenment we speak about is just the human type of Enlightenment. There are other types of Enlightenment which no one in the human body can ever reach. So what the human reaches is human Enlightenment which is the optimum of completion within human consciousness. You can reach a certain amount of light, a certain optimum within the human potential.

When human evolution is complete, evolution still continues but within a higher structure. You still evolve but not as an individual. Your intelligence merges with the universal space of intelligence. It is similar to when you sit in meditation and merge into the space of I Am; in that dimension, there is no point of reference but you still exist. Universal Consciousness exists in this way. There is no-one there, there is no entity; but there is movement of intelligence, movement of understanding, movement of Love.

The best way to prepare yourself for death is trust, simply trust that the One who created your Soul will take care of you. You don't need to be afraid of anything. Were you afraid before being born? Why should you be afraid of going back to the Mystery?

Student: *Does the awareness continue after death?*

Aziz: What dies is the conscious memory. What ceases to exist is the conscious mind. And what does not die is the stage of evolution which you have reached. Your level of evolution continues in the next incarnation. But the moment you die, you can say that everything dies in terms that you get de-manifested. This is like when you go into a deep sleep state. Every night it happens to you - everything vanishes. There is no memory, there is no consciousness, there is no awareness...everything vanishes. So it is not correct to say awareness does not die. Awareness also dies, or gets de-manifested. Reality, the Source is deeper than awareness - it is the primal energy. You see, awareness only exists when there are Two. When there is duality, consciousness can become conscious. Even the so-called non-dual awareness requires duality. The original state does not know that it exists.

Within your subtle bodies and within your subconscious mind, there is a certain subtle memory of your evolutionary journey. Evolution continues; there is a certain flow of evolution within your relative individual structure. This remains after the death of your body. It is like falling into a deep sleep, you de-manifest but when you wake up the next morning, there is a continuation. Similarly, when you die, you are de-manifested but something continues later on when you again manifest. For example, the level of your emotional evolution continues as well as your intelligence. Intelligence is something deeper than the conscious mind. You have no conscious memory but you have a certain capacity to understand. This ability to understand represents the maturity of intelligence.

Student: *And will the memory from this life somehow continue?*

Aziz: It should not remain because in the next life your identity will be different. Your particular Me will perform a different role, so if you could remember this lifetime, it would confuse you. For example, if you experience your memory and the memory of someone else, you would be in a state similar to schizophrenia. That is because your blueprint is to experience your particular memory, your particular chain of events and stream of consciousness. That's why to erase the memory at the moment of death is the wisdom of evolution. This allows you to understand that who you are is not made out of memory. Your Soul is something deeper than memory. Memory allows you to locate yourself in this particular lifetime, in this particular environment, that which you are is deeper than memory. You are not an outcome of memory. Higher Intelligence operates without memory. It doesn't require the subconscious mind, for it doesn't need the past in order to manifest in the Now.

The most important thing to see is that there is a part of you, namely I Am, which never incarnates. There is a part of you which is beyond incarnation. You are multidimensional. You have a few different layers of yourself which exist simultaneously. That which incarnates is your psychological extension. It is your personality which evolves in time, incarnating into various forms. But paradoxically, the essence of you doesn't evolve, for it is already perfect. You are evolving, you are changing...but throughout this evolution what you discover is your timeless perfection. Through evolution, you recognise that which doesn't change, that which is beyond evolution. That is why all of this is real and unreal at the same time.

Can Enlightenment be Scientifically Verified?

Student: *I was wondering whether using modern electronic tools we could check the level of Enlightenment? Another question: can we verify whether one is Self-realised, by reading the aura?*

Aziz: We have to be very careful trying to verify the level of Awakening by using scientific or psychic criteria. Some scientifically oriented people try to find objective ways to measure the level of Self-realisation. But most often what they measure are the relative and not fundamental aspects of our personal self.

One of the attempts to measure various meditative states was by checking the brain waves. They call the checking of different electrical frequencies of the brain 'biofeedback.' Initially, they thought that there were two main brain wavelengths showing us whether one is in an ordinary state of consciousness, or in the meditative state. According to the initial concept, the Beta waves were supposed to designate the usual activity of the mind, while the Alpha waves, the meditative state. The Alpha frequency was called 'passive volition,' or 'detached awareness.' An ordinary person can experience this state when the eyes are closed and one is very quiet. On the other hand, the Beta rhythms indicate the normal mind's activity.

But the matter is more complicated as there are two hemispheres of the brain and they emit different waves. Personally, I participated in such an experiment some years ago. I could observe on the computer screen the actual change of the brain waves, as I was going deeper into meditation. The problem is however, that people who design these programs are unaware of what it is that they are actually trying to see. What they measure are different levels of calmness and relaxation, but calmness does not always represent the awakened state. One can, for instance, bring the brain waves to the Theta or even Delta rhythms (which is deep sleep) by taking some heavy tranquillisers.

The Inner State is a specific combination of calmness and alertness. The alertness of pure awareness is not the same as being active in the mind, but a computer may not pick up this difference. One cannot really see the State of Presence on the computer screen, for it is beyond the category of calmness and alertness. When one is fully Self-realised, the inner state is beyond change but still the brain waves can behave quite differently depending on the situation. For example, one can abide in the transcendental state and being simultaneously agitated. In such a case, the biofeedback will register mainly the agitation. So the matter is rather complex. Also, the Absolute State is beyond awareness, and so it cannot really be verified by checking the brain vibrations. We face the same difficulty trying to measure the awakening of the Heart.

In the experiment in which I participated, in the first couple of minutes the right hemisphere of the brain reached the Theta rhythm, which was next followed, two minutes later, by the left hemisphere. The frequency was slowly moving to the Delta waves but because we had just five minutes, so the experiment ended. Unfortunately, the person who led the experiment was completely incompetent as far as the whole interpretation of the procedure and the knowledge of various inner states were concerned.

There is a similar problem with the issue of reading the auras. Most individuals who are capable of seeing auras are fully conditioned by their limited concept of spiritual awakening. They are therefore not reliable in terms of bringing clarity into the verification of Awakening. In truth, in the aura you cannot see consciousness. What you see is a mixture of various subtle bodies, the condition of vital force and the emotional state.

Can a Clairvoyant Verify Enlightenment?

Student: *Is it possible that using the psychic abilities one can verify whether someone is enlightened or not?*

Aziz: It is an important matter to understand. You have no way to be clear about someone else's level of Self-realisation unless you are yourself in that state. If a clairvoyant is sensitive, he or she certainly can recognise that, for instance, a spiritual master is in a special or different state - but he or she still has no way of knowing what state it actually is! Do you see what we mean? The major problem with the so-called 'psychic reading' is that a clairvoyant always projects his or her vision of reality onto others. That is the basic limitation of this type of work. An unawakened person simply cannot see clearly that which lies beyond the frontiers of his or her limited experience. Therefore, an unawakened psychic has no way to see a Self-realised being clearly.

It also applies to all concepts and projections most seekers have about their masters. For instance, going to Satsang you can feel bliss or certain peace, but you don't know what is the actual source of this experience. It can be an energy channelled from another dimension; it can be the bliss of your own heart awakened in the magical atmosphere of the Satsang; it can be the energy generated by the whole group attending the Satsang, enforced by impact of guru-projections; and finally it can be the energy of the master himself and the inner state he represents. You must be very careful to be able to separate your own projections from the actual reality.

Student: *What if a clairvoyant sees the aura of the master?*

Aziz: A clairvoyant just sees the colours. But what do these colours mean? This you don't know and the clairvoyant interprets them according to his or her limited knowledge and conditioned views. Which colour is the colour of Enlightenment: white, golden, blue? You don't know. For instance, if a master becomes angry, the colour of the aura will be read. Does it mean that he or she has lost his enlightenment? In truth, the enlightened state cannot be seen in the aura. In the aura you just see the emotional and mental bodies in combination with other subtle bodies and the life-force. Be clear that a psychic can give you information only within the frame of his or her unawakened and often unconscious vision of reality. It also applies to different channelled beings, who are often completely unaware of the Buddha State.

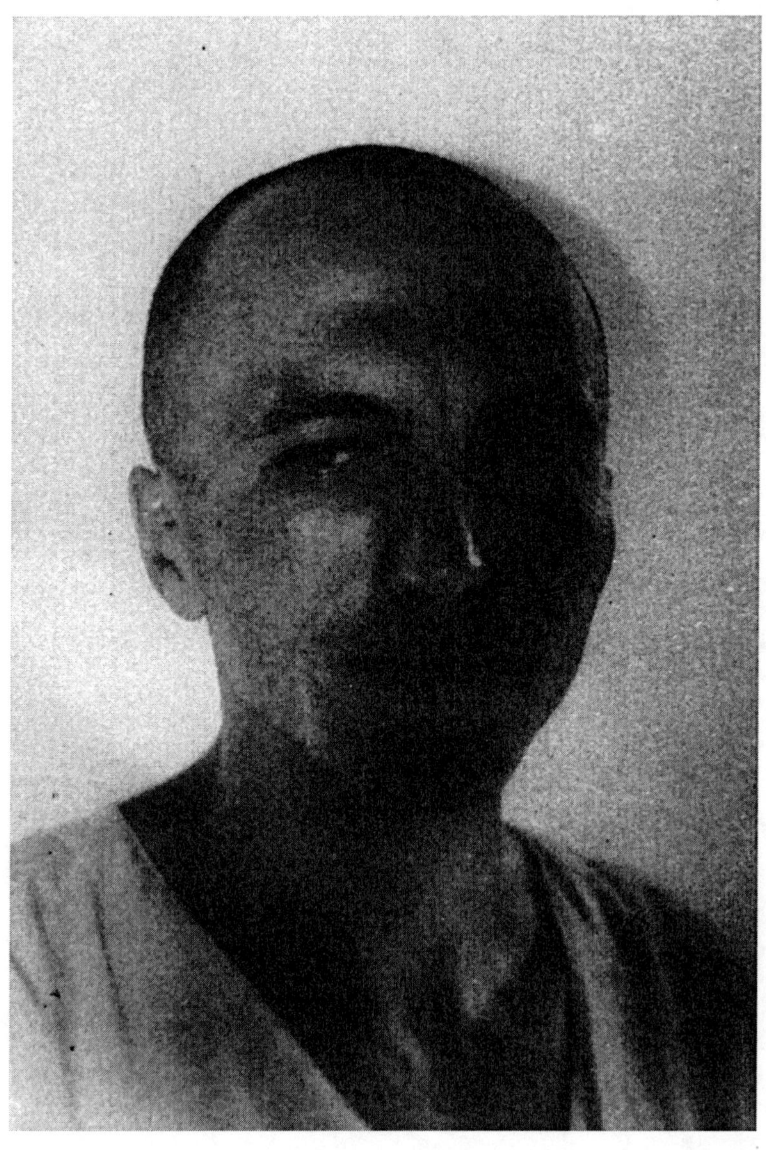

IV

DIMENSION OF INTELLIGENCE

Intelligence is the movement of the Universal Spirit which enlivens the whole of Existence. When this Spirit flows through the human mind, the journey into human understanding begins.

Intelligence is neither thinking nor not-thinking; it is neither the mind nor the no-mind. Intelligence is neither the content of the mind nor is it its container. Through its force we can gain insight into the nature of Truth and reach freedom from that which covers the Real like an eclipse - from Ignorance.

The evolution of Intelligence is the evolution of clarity. With clarity, you start to understand more and more what it is that has happened to you. You are here in the middle of this enormous puzzle, the infinite mystery. Can you understand it? Yes, it has happened to you - you are alive! Use your Heart, use your mind, use the whole of your being - to Understand!

The Wisdom of Clarity

Wisdom is a function of intelligence. It brings us to the place of clear seeing where all doubts are erased. Wisdom is freedom from the false and the only weapon against spiritual pitfalls. The evolution of understanding is both complex and subtle. But the very foundation of this evolution is our desire to understand, to be clear... to know what is right and what the true meaning of our spiritual journey is. Let us pray for this clarity, which can take us radically out from the sorrow of ignorance.

The Role of Intelligence and Intuition on the Path

Student: *You have said that Vipassana does not point directly to the awakening of the Real Me. My question is: will intuition bring one to the realisation of the true centre anyway?*

Aziz: It may or it may not. It may if you are able to go beyond the linear interpretation of the Buddhist philosophy. Most seekers are not intelligent enough to use their intuition. Intuition is a combination of sensitivity and intelligence. To awaken intelligence is many times more difficult than to awaken to Enlightenment! To reach Enlightenment you often need one lifetime. To become truly intelligent, one Kalpa is needed! Intelligence is something very subtle and profound. It is not just to have a clever mind. In the west they have tests for intelligence but it is not intelligence which gets developed but cleverness. Those students who have high marks are often far from being intelligent in the true sense of this term. Intelligence comes more from the Heart. It is the deep intuitive wisdom of the Soul which enables her to Understand. It is the unity of the Heart, intellect and imagination. Yes, to truly understand you must have imagination!

Student: *Do you mean that intelligence is wisdom?*

Aziz: Wisdom is an outcome of intelligence. Intelligence is the dynamic ability to reflect reality in the depth of understanding and emotion. What is intuitive intelligence? It is simply a very sensitive, conscious thinking which feels its own movement as well.

Most seekers refuse to think on their own: they want to seek the available knowledge which has been crystallised into tradition. Most seekers prefer to get ready-made uniforms of understanding. They strongly dislike raw food. They want to eat well-cooked dishes which they can find on the menu. This menu with names of various dishes is their security in the jungle of possibilities. We call them seekers but are they really seekers? Is it their search? No! It is a collective search. A Theravada practitioner, even before entering the Path, already knows the conclusion: suffering, no-self, impermanence. The whole practice is about conforming to these pre-conceived ideas. But what if they are wrong? Here, the authority of the traditions gives one a psychological security. It is a psychological security and not a spiritual one, for one's evolution can get stuck in the incorrect vision of awakening.

In Vipassana, the bridge between observation-disidentification and Awakening is not clear. This teaching does not point to the State of Presence. How can it point to it if everything is impermanent anyway? One of our students who was speaking about the State of Presence was asked by a Buddhist practitioner whether it had a flavour of impermanence. It is difficult to lead such discussions with someone who sees reality only through the glasses of impermanence and general Buddhist philosophy. We can ask such a person in return: 'does mindfulness of impermanence have the flavour of impermanence?'

The Buddhist technology of awakening is very old and requires some fundamental modifications. It was a wonderful discovery but no longer satisfies our need for clarity or for a more holistic vision of reality. When you practice observation and mindfulness in Vipassana, attention is directed to the objectified reality. This attention does not want to turn back to its very source. One is obsessed with re-stating the preconceived conclusions about the nature of reality as having the quality of impermanence, emptiness and suffering. Ok, you see it... so what? Does it make you enlightened? Nothing has changed in truth!

Another problem with this type of philosophy is that it closes the Heart. To be free in this way, through negation and disidentification, one has to block the natural sensitivity of the human Heart. It is not that Vipassana is incorrect but that it represents only half of the truth. Because it has been at least half-true, it has helped many. But the moment you believe that it is the whole of truth, you are in trouble - you can become seriously hurt, you many even lose your Soul.

Student: *I was doing Vipassana for long time and something was missing all along. As you were saying, the Me was missing. That's why, as we practice here, I feel for the first time that it relates to me.*

Aziz: We emphases what is and not what is not. Disidentification from the body and mind is very useful at a certain stage of evolution. Most are so identified, they are completely caught in the psychological reality. That's why Vipassana has helped many people, but it does not clearly point to awakening - that has to be seen.

Equanimity is not of the Mind

Student: *Can you speak about equanimity? Is it the same as the zero point?*

Aziz[4]**:** No, equanimity is an attitude of the mind, while the 'zero point' is present before the mind. The zero point is neither equanimous nor unequanimous - it simply is. Equanimity refers to a certain neutral and disidentified experience of life. It has become an ideal of some traditions for the very simple reason that it takes us beyond suffering. But true equanimity is not an attitude of the mind, but rather designates abiding beyond the mind and beyond the phenomenal reality. Certainly, when you rest in this primal equanimity or pure isness, your relationship with the outer becomes more equanimous as well, but, paradoxically, you can sometimes experience qualities which are beyond equanimity. The Buddha is not someone who always behaves in a dispassionate manner. The Buddha can be very much passionate, he can become angry and experience attachment. We speak about the true Buddha, and not about one of those Self-realise beings who have been conditioned by Buddhist philosophy! The true Buddha is human. In this way, unconditional equanimity can co-exists with relative un-equanimous behaviour.

Who Remembers the State of Presence?

Student: *Who remembers the State of Presence?*

Aziz: The same one who is asking this question! Who is that one? It is intelligence of course, the dynamic expression of Me. It does everything. It tells you to open your Heart, to meditate more; it is learning, contemplating, growing and discovering truth. But to whom does this intelligence belong? To the Soul... and what is the Soul? The State of Presence is the Soul's identity in the mind. The deeper identity of the Soul is in the Heart. When you fall in love, the very one who is so excited in your Heart... is the Soul.

Paradox Exists Only in the Mind

Student: *Can you speak about the nature of paradoxes?*

Aziz: Paradoxes do not exist in reality. They exist in the mind only. When the mind is unable to grasp some element of reality, and yet cannot deny it, we call this experience a 'paradox.' Reality is beyond the mind, even though the mind is a part of this reality. From the place beyond the mind, no paradox can be found.

For instance, someone may not understand that in meditation, thinking and not-thinking co-exist. It maybe felt as a paradox or even a contradiction in terms. But it is neither a paradox nor a contradiction - it is simply just like that! One cannot grasp the concept that free will and destiny co-exist as two sides of the movement of life. Is it a paradox? Reality is as it is, but we can have many different viewpoints. When we confuse those viewpoints, we lose clarity and face the paradox. But when we surrender our mind, only Reality remains.

Oneness is Beyond Knowing

Student: *What is the difference between the experience of Oneness and the attitude of Oneness?*

Aziz: The experience of Oneness is beyond the mind. What it means is that the mind does not know that is experiencing Oneness. True Oneness does not know that it is Oneness; it is in a state of not-knowing. Pure Oneness is an energy state where the individual energy system of the Soul dissolves into Universal Energy. Pure Oneness is realised through the unity of Being and Heart, the Absolute State and the Divine. When an awakened Heart merges with the Absolute, complete Oneness is manifested.

That is the experience of the mystic. The sage experiences Oneness only within Being, bypassing the dimension of the Heart. The saint experiences Oneness only through the Heart, therefore being unable to dwell beyond movement.

The attitude of Oneness is from the mind in combination with the emotional body. A separate human being, in his desire to transcend isolation, tries to bridge his existence with the universe, by creating an attitude. A poet may experience the feeling of Oneness; a philosopher may intuitively, in the mind, grasp the concept of Oneness. An old man, after many years of going through the dream of life may suddenly have an insight into this, that all is One. This was the case with the character of Herman Hesse's famous novel, Siddhartha. At the end of his search, he saw that all was One. Herman Hesse was longing for spiritual fulfilment but having lacked the proper guidance, was unable to realise it. As he was very sensitive, very wise and had had some mystical experiences, he had many insights into Oneness. These insights were not, unfortunately, founded upon the energetic expansion, that is, upon the State of Oneness.

The attitude of Oneness is not grounded and has no continuity. The psyche has to repeat from moment to moment this act of tuning itself into the experience-feeling of Oneness. True Oneness is a state and not an attitude. True Oneness is not self-conscious. True Oneness simply is; it is present beyond concepts. It is a state of not-knowing.

Student: *If Oneness is the same as not-knowing, how can we know that we are in a state of Oneness? How can we verify Not-knowing?*

Aziz: A very important question. It is a master question. How can we know that we are in a state of Not-knowing? How do we know that we are Self-realised, if Enlightenment is beyond the mind? If you know that you experience Oneness, no longer you are in a state of Not-knowing. From the other side, if you don't know, how can you know that you have reached Oneness?

There are two levels of knowing and not-knowing. First, not-knowing represents your pure Being beyond any concepts, and knowing represents the presence of understanding coming from intuitive intelligence. Because Being and intelligence co-exist, knowing and not-knowing can co-exist. The sage is beyond the concept of Enlightenment, for he or she simply abides in the natural state, beyond the need to call it anything. But even though one rests in the natural state which itself is beyond knowing, simultaneously one knows that one is in the ultimate state. In time, gradually even this knowledge that one is in the state of Oneness, relaxes and dissolves into Not-knowing. At this stage is not only Being in a state of not-knowing, but intelligence is as well. For this reason, Hui Neng, when asked 'are you enlightened?' replied: 'no!' For this reason, Bodhidarma when asked by the emperor Wu, 'who is standing in front, of me?' said: 'I don't know!'

The stage when even intelligence gives up its knowing is very interesting because it is not merely that intelligence does not know. Intelligence abides in a non-conceptual state but it is still able to re-awaken or regain its ability to know. That's why, if Hui Neng was to be asked another time 'are you enlightened?' he would probably have replied: 'Yes, of course, I am! Don't you know that I am the successor of the fifth Patriarch?' An enlightened being knows that he or she is in a enlightened state (unless we have a case of an imbecile), but does not support his or her self-image by this concept. To know is a function of recognition and Being is beyond recognition.

There is, however, one more step in this evolution. Here, intelligence drops all concepts, even the ability to understand that one is Self-realised. It is here where the collective human mind is dropped completely. That's why the Bodhidarma answer 'I don't know' can be seen as higher than the Hindu answer 'I am That.' Here, all is transcended. But the not-knowing Bodhidarma was in, was not an expression of ignorance but fullness, totality and a complete unity with Existence. The ultimate not-knowing is knowing without object; it is a pure knowing, a unity of Being and intelligence.

To be One with Action

Student: *You have mentioned that prior to awakening, one is 'the suffering' and it is only after awakening that one can for the first time say, 'I am suffering.' How does it relate to the idea of being One with action? When I am suffering, I am just suffering; when I am walking, I am just walking...*

Aziz: Who is walking? You can be one with action only when you are one with yourself. An unconscious person may try very hard to be One with action but is unable to really accomplish it. This is because the subjective presence is missing and one's sense of existence is diluted in the outer reality. That's why, the first step is not to worry so much about being One with action, but rather about giving birth to the Real Me. In this process, initially you may even feel more separated from action than an ordinary person does, because your attention has to be so much focussed inward. But that is fine. Your task, in truth, is to become hundred percent separated from action! Only when you are fully separated from the world, can you truly become One with it. In the case of an ordinary person, such a person is neither truly separated nor one with life but suspended in nowhere, in the vacuum of ignorance.

When I Am is fully present, the next step is to let go of the inner and open up to the world, allowing oneself to be spontaneous and natural. Here, you have made the fully circle and have returned to life. At this point, you can really say, 'I am just walking, just drinking, just living...'

An enlightened being is not the walking but One with walking. The aim is not to become identified with activity but to transcend our separation from it. Our Presence is always beyond our phenomenal expressions - although not seperate from them. All is simply embraced by the inner vastness and silence.

Student: *So when an unawakened person is suffering, such a person is one with suffering but in an unconscious way?*

Aziz: The paradox is that the ego is unable to be either One with the experience or to be clearly distinct from it. The ego constantly oscillates between recognising the outer reality and creating self-referral in the mind. The ego cannot retain any real continuity. It is unable to stay either with the object or with its own subjective sense of identity. So when you, as an ego, try to be One with action, you actually make an effort to stay with the object. This is what they call 'mindfulness.' You force your ego to keep focus on what is happening. But it does not really work as your subjective presence is not solidified. It is a very important point. You try to become One with action or your inner psychological state (like suffering) and you are not able to because the one who wants to reach this unity does not exist yet. Do you see the problem? That is why, the practice of mindfulness can never take you beyond the limitations of the ego-consciousness.

For that reason, in our work we radically change the focus. We turn attention to the very subject who dwells in the middle of all. It is only when you are One with your Real Me, that you can be One with action as well, not otherwise. The secret meaning of being One with action is to be at the same time existentially beyond it. This realisation is founded upon the transcendental presence of your unconditional subjective essence.

Sometimes, you are one with walking, sometimes with talking, sometimes with suffering. These experiences come and go, but something remains, doesn't it? This vast space of silence, awareness and love does not change, does not move. That dimension by its very nature transcends any type of activity, any type of empirical experience. That's why, an awakened being is One with action but is not the action itself.

When an ordinary person suffers, he or she is this suffering but is not One with it. Such a person is completely identified as there is nobody inside clearly distinct from the experience. It is very much like a dream. It is not that one is in a dream - one actually is the dream.

Idealism

Student: *What is idealism?*

Aziz: From one side it is a certain vision or perception of reality; from the other side, it is an attitude to life, connected with shaping reality according to our highest wishes. There is idealism, materialism and realism. Idealism is not realistic; materialism is primitive; and realism reflects reality as it is. For some, to be 'realistic' is to be identified with the gross, common sense perception of life. However, this is not realism but unconsciousness.

The term idealism comes from the word 'idea.' It was the term used by Plato to designate something like the pure archetypal existence of original pattern-ideas, from which this world was later shaped. These ideas were supposed to exist in the mind of God, in some kind of heavenly realm. From this, the term idealism was created. What it means is that the idea precedes reality, the idea is higher than its manifestation into the form.

The mind has certain idealistic tendencies. These tendencies reflect our desire to experience perfection. It is natural, when we understand that our Soul comes from the dimension of pure perfection. This memory of our origin which is present below the conscious level, is reflected in our wish to see or create a perfect world: the world of love, harmony and beauty. To see is to perceive the Now; to create is our attitude and impact on this world.

As we incarnate, we enter into the dimension of imperfection. Something constantly goes wrong here! Do you see it? You want to love everybody, according to your preconceived idealistic concepts, and you suddenly get angry with someone, or you simply develop a strong headache (laughter)... It is difficult to love everybody when you've got a headache or your hormones are disturbing you! So, be honest to yourself and simply don't force yourself to love everybody, if the reality is different. What is love anyway? Do you see how we are conditioned by so many concepts? Our idealistic tendencies are a part of our sensitivity and cannot be denied but they do need to be aligned with reality. The desire for purity comes from the Soul and it is the mind which translates it into linear concepts. It is not the Soul who wants to love everybody, but the mind, the ego which translates in a linear way the inherent Soul desire for love. The Soul is wise. If she does not love, she is simply calm and she relaxes into the truth of her present reality. When she loves, she simply loves, that's all. So, idealism is the reflection of the innate perfection and purity of the Soul in the mind. It is not that the mind is wrong as such but needs to be aligned with truth and common sense. Some teachings negate the mind too much - this is very unwise. The mind simply needs to grow in intelligence and has to surrender its domination to the Soul.

Another example of idealism can be some spiritual teachings. The mind can, on the intuitive level, feel that reality is One and perfect. That's why we say there is only God, only the Self. But what does it really mean? The conclusions which some teachings draw from this global feeling about the nature of reality are far too extreme and linear. The mind simply cannot have a hold over the paradoxical nature of reality. So, some teachers say that there is only the Self, therefore, there is no evolution, no path to Enlightenment...and so forth. They deny even the existence of Me, the one who reaches awakening. If there is only God, there is no place for Me. In the Ultimate, there is no place for two. This type of thinking represents a clinical and rather unimaginative translation of non-duality.

But truth is higher than the mind's inventions. Each moment, Truth teaches us about itself. If a Non-dual master gets a headache, he or she may be detached from this experience but still the headache is present. There is a story in which Ramana Maharishi was sitting on a tiger's skin due to his rheumatism and was asked why he needed such comfort. He replied that even a sage does not like rheumatism. So, who is this one that feels the headache? Who is that one who dislikes rheumatism? Certainly, it is not the Universal Self. The Universal Self could not care less. The one who cares is simply Me. It is this very Me who is listening to these words.

Reality is the highest teacher, for it destroys all that is false, leaving only raw truth. In this particular dimension an extreme idealism simply does not work. This is because the laws of this universe are brutal and paradoxical. This dimension can get very cruel and insensitive. The mind is unable to explain why the earth has been designed in this way. The idealistic mind can easily be convinced that all is God but when we look around, something simply does not feel right! Isn't it your experience? It does not mean that all is not God but what it does tell us is that our interpretation of the statement 'All is God,' is not necessarily correct. For that reason, at one stage, we must surrender our idealistic tendencies of the mind to What Is.

But if you think that idealism is wrong, you fall into another extreme. The true picture of reality is a combination of idealism with common sense. The new quality which is born out of this meeting, we call realism. Common sense without idealism is gross, insensitive and unconscious; idealism without common sense is unrealistic and disconnected from the reality of the Earth. So what does it mean to be truly realistic and to see reality as it is? It means to see reality from a place of absolute silence, beyond the mind. It is to see reality from a place of pure love, which is our Heart. It is to understand the purpose and role of our individual existence. It is to see the all-pervading presence of God in all aspects of this reality. It is to see the mystery, the inexplicable nature of Existence. It is to see reality from the place where our desire for love, harmony and beauty are embraced in the context of What Is; this is a realistic perspective. It is to be humble in our meeting with the outer reality which not always satisfy the aspirations of our Heart; it is not to be humble towards the outer as such but towards this mysterious reason behind the existence of this reality. It is to sincerely evolve towards our higher purpose, which is perfection, while moving through layers of imperfection, which are inseparable from this dimension. It is to acknowledge that this reality is often different than what we think it should be.

Do not forget that what this reality is also includes our personal intention, evolution and creativity in the way we are trying to affect our inner and outer existence. What this means is that not only do we perceive What Is but we create or rather co-create What Is. To what extent we create our destiny according to our criteria of harmony, beauty and love, is reflected in a true and realistic vision of this dimension.

Drop All Concepts!

Student: *Could you speak about the Buddhist concept of No-self?*

Aziz: It is better not to be attached to any concept. It is not the concept alone which matters, but the energy of understanding that we wish to transmit. When we speak about the Soul, for instance, many feel negative about this term. Why? Because, for most people, it is just another name for the ego. What does an average person know about the Soul? Going to church and praying for the Soul's salvation every Sunday is a reflection of another ignorant behaviour of the ego-mind. But what is the Soul really? She is the most subtle element of Existence that one can imagine...

For that reason, both are wrong - those who believe in the existence of the Soul and those who deny it. The first 'believers' are wrong, because they don't know what it is that they believe in. It is simply meaningless. It is like believing in some entities living on Mars. You believe that some beings live out there but you have no idea who or what they actually are. Most people live in this kind of world of fantasy, in a dream world. From the other side, the non-believers are wrong, for they deny that which is unknown to them! They say that everything is empty and there is no-self but who is the one who says it? Who is that one who says that there is no-self? The no-self has no mouth to say such a thing. Neither is the self 'something,' nor is the no-self 'nothing.'

When you see an empty room, you can say, 'nothing is there' or you can say, it is full of the bright space. It is the same room but there are two different ways of describing it. Afterwards, for two thousands years, two great traditions will debate whether Nothing is in the room or whether the room is filled with space!

Do you see the ridiculousness of clinging to words? The no-self and the self are different ways of speaking about the same thing. Some Buddhist philosophers were very attached to a certain intellectual precision in speaking about the Ultimate. They couldn't say about the Ultimate anything positive, for it would suggest that they make out of it 'something' and believe in the self, which would put them in the category of eternalists. On the other hand they could not identify the no-self with merely 'nothing,' for that would put them into the category of nihilists. Their intellectual precision is beautiful, in a way, but it is not good to be too precise. The spiritual teacher is also a poet and not just a scientist. It is very important to transmit, on the intuitive and energy level, the message behind the concept we apply. Otherwise, we begin to worship concepts instead of using them.

If we want to be precise, the no-self is another name for the Absolute, which is the Uncreated energy. On the other hand, the Self here represents the state of pure consciousness. The unity of them which is the realisation of the Absolute, is beyond the Self and beyond the no-self. We could call it the 'Self-No-Self.'

What is the meaning of the word 'self'? What does this word itself designate? It simply points to the sense of identity. When we say that something has a 'self,' it means that there is some identity in this to which we refer. When we say my-self, we mean that the particular sense of identity (self) refers to Me. When we say, 'our car' it means that the car belongs to us. But in the case of 'myself,' it is the sense of identity which pertains to Me. In the Ultimate, the sense of identity does not refer to itself, for it is absolutely undivided. The ultimate identity represents the primordial presence of pure isness.

Where Can 'I' be Found?

Student: *How is it that in Buddhism, there are many practices where one looks for 'I' in different parts of the body and one is not able to find it anywhere? Where is 'I' located?*

Aziz: You cannot find 'I' anywhere because the one who is looking is this 'I'! In order to find this Me, one has to simply be sensitive. It is not enough to be clever and intellectual. It is all very simple in truth. There are two centres of 'I': one is the State of Presence and the second is in the Heart. If you touch your Heart, don't you feel 'I'? If you have minimal sensitivity, 'I' will be clearly recognised. In the field of awareness, 'I' has two points of identity: one is the dynamic centre of intelligence or ego. This centre appears and disappears in each moment. It is precisely intelligence which is trying to find 'I.' The second centre is the static and solid centre of attention or self-attention. When awakened, this centre has continuity from moment to moment.

The Heart is the feeling centre of Me. From the viewpoint of observing intelligence, the Heart is an object and not a subject but from inside the Heart, she is the subject, while intelligence is the 'object.' From the place of complete experience, the State of Presence, intelligence and the Heart all create one field of Me, which is pure subjectivity.

Intelligence is Beyond the Content of the Mind

Student: *Isn't it true that the State of Presence recognises itself?*

Aziz: The State of Presence is self-aware on the energy level but it is intelligence which awakens this state as well as adds to it a second level of recognition. Even if the centre of awareness is already present, the moment intelligence pays attention to it, it begins to vibrate stronger.

Student: But this intelligence is still the mind?

Aziz: All is the mind. Even the State of Presence is the mind but it is the mind beyond thinking. The mind is multidimensional. That's why the division of the mind into mind and no-mind is simply a different way of speaking about the same phenomenon. Awareness free from thoughts is the material from which the whole mind is made.

Student: *Is it possible to experience awareness free from thoughts more often when one is in the State of Presence?*

Aziz: Awareness free from thoughts is the State of Presence! When you are in this state, you are free from thinking even when the mind is still thinking. Do you understand? It is not to stop the mind but to discover the empty nature of the mind. Naturally, as you abide in the State of Presence, the arising of thoughts becomes minimal. They still arise but are very slow and quite rare.

You see, without some subtle thinking you cannot live. Even as you sit here, without any particular thought in your mind, subtle thinking is always present. You hear a bird singing - how do you recognise it? There is a subtle mind simply present. Complete absence of thinking designates that one has died! It is the gross level of thinking, this unconscious inner dialogue which gets pacified.

Intelligence is a movement of subtle thinking. For example, when you observe the mind, what happens is that the subtle thought creates a distance from the gross level of thinking. Next, the subtle thought recognises its very energetic centre of pure awareness. In another case, you are using the subtle mind to crystallise some understanding on the more gross level of thinking. For instance, you want to express something and cannot find the right sentence. So you are trying with your subtle mind to verbalise yourself. Suddenly, the right sentence comes to your mind. It was the effort of the subtle mind which has achieved it.

We spoke about the content of the mind and the container of the mind which is emptiness. Some try to eliminate the content of the mind in order to reach the container. But the container is already empty or beyond the content. Similarly, when you see the nature of the mirror, you see that reflections cannot contaminate it. Intelligence is between the content and the container. It is the spirit which brings life to both. It is the link between thinking and the empty nature of the mind. And this intelligence is 'I ' as well. It represents the very effort of the Soul to recognise her identity. When we speak about the nature of the mind and about content, it is all impersonal. But there is someone inside, someone who recognises the emptiness of the mind and participates in thinking as well; there is someone who tries to understand how they both co-exist. We could, of course, say that it is just an ability inherent to the mind but it wouldn't be precise. The one who does all of this is the intelligence of the Soul.

When this intelligence awakens to the State of Presence, it recognises its very nature before thinking. From the other side, it actively uses its thinking faculty, in order to participate in Creation. Intelligence is learning how to use the mind in a positive way and how to re-connect with the feeling centre of the Heart. Intelligence has been evolving, learning and maturing for many life times; it evolves until it reaches the optimum of understanding destined for it by the force of the blueprint.

Is the State of Presence Universal or Individual?

Student: *Is the State of Presence the same for everyone?*

Aziz: The State of Presence has universal qualities but at the same time it has an individual flavour. The State of Presence is an energy vibration inside your third eye, in the middle of your brain. Different Souls experience different strengths and degrees of clarity of this state. The Soul for whom this centre is predominant experiences it much stronger than a Soul who has a different centre predominant. If you look even at the great masters, you see big differences in the way they experienced their I Am. For instance, in the case of Nisargadatta Maharaj, you see that awareness was predominant, while in the case of Ramana Maharishi, Being had definitely the predominant quality. And both of them were completely Self-realised beings.

Another important matter to understand is that the State of Presence is always experienced as attached to the personal intelligence. It is intelligence which allows you to recognise consciously that you are in the State of Presence. This intelligence is personal, for it belongs to your particular stream of consciousness and memory. This intelligence is unique for you even though it shares the global quality of human intelligence as well. You must see that the totality of the State of Presence is the unity of pure awareness and the self-conscious movement of intelligence. This intelligence adds real meaning, life and strength. To answer your question precisely, the State of Presence is the same for all of us, but it is also unique. It is unique as it is being recognised within one's individual blueprint, intelligence and sensitivity.

The real meaning of awakening to the State of Presence is an important subject and for the last few thousand years, it has been discussed by many philosophers and mystics. One of the questions long contemplated was whether the State of Presence is the Self or whether it represents individual consciousness. Another question was whether there is only one Witness-Presence or if there are many witnesses. One of the prevailing conclusions, to which they have come in India, was that the State of Presence is single only and it is the Ultimate. A further question that appeared was about the whole concept of liberation. How could the Self put itself into bondage? How had purusha, which was another name for atman, lost itself in forgetfulness? If purusha is already free how is it that it must liberate itself? There seems to be a clear contradiction here!

All these doubts were based, in truth, on a certain misinterpretation of the State of Presence and the true meaning of awakening. Even though the question about 'who' is reaching liberation was one of the main pivots of Hindu spirituality, still, surprisingly enough, the precise answer to this question has not yet been found! The State of Presence is not what they thought it was. In truth, the State of Presence or the witness is not the Self because it is simply the awareness aspect of the Soul; it is her centre in intelligence. This state, despite its universal qualities is more individual than universal. This state is being awakened and experienced in time, through the channel of Me.

The State of Presence did not receive the proper status in Indian mysticism. It is like to take the reflection of the moon in the lake for the moon itself. The State of Presence is not the Self but a reflection of the Self in the 'lake' of Creation. This allows us to avoid another difficulty which the Indian mystics had. Some of them thought that if the witness is One, there could be only one global event of Enlightenment. If only one person became enlightened, everyone would become enlightened simultaneously. If this is not the case, who are all these witnesses not being recognised yet? If witness is the Self, it cannot be recognised in one person and remain unrecognised in another person. Do you follow? As you recognise the State of Presence, ask yourself 'what happened to this state before I recognised it?' Someone may say that the state was there but you were not aware of it. But in that case, is there any Me separate from the Self? The very presence of ignorance assumes the absence of the Self, at least in some area of reality (which at this point is replaced by ignorance). So we always meet some contradictions, as long as we do not see the clear picture of reality.

You see, the State of Presence does not exist unless recognised, for recognition and awareness are the same. The State of Presence is the recognition of it! This very concept - that there exists somewhere objectively the State of Presence, independently from our recognition, is a misconception and a contradiction in terms. Before you awaken the State of Presence, it simply is not there. The witness either is or is not. It cannot be simultaneously present and absent. Before awakening, there is only the mind. Through awakening, you give birth to it. Can you say that the child is there prior to conception? In a certain sense you can, for everything is already present in the Timeless from the Ultimate perspective. But from our perspective of evolution in time, some things are present and others are not, some were present and some will be present. That is the truth of our existence here. The child has to be born in order to exist here.

When we see clearly that the State of Presence is far from being God, we can bring more understanding into this whole area. The State of Presence is a reflection of Ultimate in the individual consciousness. The reflection of the sun in the dewdrop is not the sun itself. The reflection of the moon in the pond is not the moon. The moon is in the other direction! Therefore, what you experience as your State of Presence, is this very reflection. Your State of Presence uses the borrowed light of the Self. Similarly as the moon is not shining its light but the light of the sun, so the State of Presence has no light on its own. It is a subtle matter. Please, contemplate it more.

Concept is a Unit of Understanding

Student: *What is the actual relationship between concepts and intelligence?*

Aziz: A concept is a unit of understanding. Concepts are the particles of intelligence. Similarly, light is made of small particles which all together allow us to see the field of brightness. This field of brightness is Understanding. Understanding is built from concepts, but at the same time possesses a new quality than the composing it elements. Concepts are related to the experience of separation. They bridge the intelligence of the Soul with the reality of Creation. There are many types of concepts, they represent different levels of density and different concentrations of meaning. For instance, when we say, 'this is a chair,' the meaning is very concentrated and crystallised. This is how intelligence has been evolving. In the case of primitive people, the concepts were basic and simple, relating to everyday life. Perhaps in the beginning one was able to verbalise the function of eating. One could say, 'eating.' Next, one was able to add, 'eating apple.' And one day, one was able to point to one's subjective existence saying, 'I eating apple.'

The question is how intelligence could function before creating a language or how does it function in the case of an animal? In the case of an animal, intelligence is subconscious which means it does not create a clear self-referral. In the subconscious intelligence, the mind functions in an instinctive way, using images and automatically responding to the environment. In the case of subconscious intelligence, only the empirical reality is present, different phenomenal objects and experiences cannot be extracted from their meanings. The evolution of intelligence truly begins with the development of the ego. The ego allowed intelligence to create a distance from the empirical reality and to extract the meaning from objects and experiences. To separate meaning from that to which meaning refers, is to take an idea or image of an object and reflect it inside the mind. It is done as if in separation from the real object. Highly evolved animals already have this ability developed to a small extent but in their case it has more a dream-like, subconscious quality. To truly extract meaning from any object and to process it in the mind, the ability of self-referral is required. When there is a self-referral, the information which comes to Me from the environment can be kept inside as if the flow of information slows down and here it is possible to process the meaning of this information. That is what we mean by contemplation - that we actually stay with the information, facing silently its meaning. We allow it to reveal its deeper truth.

When language developed, not only was one able to communicate information to others, but most importantly to oneself. This ability to communicate with one's own mind by using symbols and ideas brought a radical acceleration to the evolution of intelligence. This intelligence was able to use a more sophisticated network of ideas and give rise to a larger understanding. And what is this understanding? Neither is it the non-conceptual state, nor does it have the crystallised form of a concept. Understanding represents a very subtle network of concepts which are harmoniously linked, giving way to a higher meaning. It is like music. A beautiful song is composed of many notes which among each other create the holistic quality of the symphony. The symphony is like understanding. Different notes are like concepts. How these notes link and flow with each other, according to the intention of the composer, symbolises the effort of intelligence to create understanding.

Understanding is the ability to reflect, in the individual consciousness, the meaning of an event, phenomenon, situation and life in general. Understanding is the ability of the Soul to know the meaning of Creation, the dynamic of life, the purpose and the direction of our evolution in time. Our human intelligence has to use concepts in order to understand. But the higher the understanding, the more subtle and transparent are the concepts. The deeper we meet the Mystery, the more transparent is the field of knowing. The highest understanding is the very meeting of the Soul with the Beloved. It is realised as Pure Knowing, the unity of absolute silence and love.

In the case of Universal Intelligence, it knows all without processing the Understanding. It exists only within the Now and is instantaneous and absolute.

Who is Present in the State of Presence?

Student: *Who is present in the State of Presence? Is it Me who is present? Is it Universal Consciousness which is present? Is it God who is present?*

Aziz: The State of Presence is present in the State of Presence! All your questions point to the right answer. It is Me who is present, it is Universal Consciousness and it is God who is present. The State of Presence is a specific mixture of personal and impersonal energies. It is Me who is present but at the same time this Me is being witnessed by its own presence. There is an immediate identification of the sense of Me with the impersonal energy of consciousness. What is Me? It is this aspect of impersonality which allows the Universal to become self-conscious. Me is the agent of conscious knowing.

Yes, it is ultimately God who is present in the State of Presence, for God is all. God becomes conscious of herself within Creation, by becoming the State of Presence. It takes place through the channel of Me, which is herself God's individual incarnation. That's why everyone is an Avatar, an incarnation of God. Some Avatars are lost in the darkness of ignorance, while others have realised their Godliness, their Divine essence.

Education

Student: *Under twenty, would it be possible to provide real education, rather than social conditioning, for children and teenagers?*

Aziz: Real education can be introduced from the very beginning when you are born. What does real education mean? It means that the parent is conscious, not only in a social way, but conscious as a human being, connected to the Soul. There is the energy of love, the energy of awareness. You can say the parent is a spiritual being, and by his or her own presence is able to educate the child in a proper way. To educate in a proper way means that children are educated in a way that allows them to be connected with the Light of Creation and not just lost in the phenomenal reality, in the toy shop of the 'modern' world.

Student: *Could this real kind of education be put into the form of different kinds of schools?*

Aziz: There have already been many attempts to make New Age schools. There are different attempts to bring an element of light into the process of education. You see, how much light you can bring into education depends on the receivers. Children are not always ready or willing to receive this type of education. Even among quite mature spiritual seekers there are very few who are really ready for awakening. Most human beings do not want to be awakened. They want to live in ignorance and forgetfulness. So in their case, what you provide is a certain amount of light, connected more to their psychology and to the basic harmony of the mind and emotions. This is what the New Age does - it bridges real awakening and ignorance. It is something in-between. In teaching, meditation is, of course, a very important element of education. How deep a student can go depends on his or her capacity. Sometimes with teaching, you may just be planting seeds, but later at some point in the future the benefits will become visible.

Intelligence is the Movement of Understanding

Student: *What is intelligence?*

Aziz: Intelligence is the movement of understanding which allows the Soul to comprehend reality. Any type of knowing is a function of intelligence. Intelligence is the wisdom of awareness. Awareness has no wisdom. Awareness is just a light which makes things visible; but it is intelligence which knows what is visible. In truth, awareness and intelligence cannot be separated. Some seekers are confused because when they experience the state of pure awareness, they realise that their intelligence is still present, which knows and checks the experience. But this confusion comes only from wrong ideas and simplistic teachings. Intelligence and awareness are the two sides of the same phenomenon. Intelligence is the other side of awareness and awareness is the building block of intelligence. Awareness is the energy upon which intelligence is founded...

Intelligence is the movement of spirit which runs through all. Initially intelligence is impersonal but when it manifests itself through an individual Soul, it becomes personal as well. Here, intelligence refers to Me. The information which intelligence carries, comes back to the sense of Me. Intelligence is the movement of knowing within awareness. The intelligence we speak about also includes the Heart. True intelligence is much more than intellect, it also refers to the Heart. The Heart has its own way to understand and to know. But the Heart cannot understand without the mind. The Heart without mind is blind and the mind without Heart is barren, like a desert without rain.

The Witness is not the Self

Student: *If witness is not the Self, what is it?*

Aziz: The witness is the primal vibration of awareness behind the mind. The witness is where the impersonal intelligence becomes conscious of itself as the pure 'I' of awareness. The role of the witness is not to 'witness' Me but to be the centre of her identity in the mind. Not only is the witness not the Self, but it is not even the whole of Me for Me is much more than awareness.

Originally the misconception that the witness is the Self was created because there was a lack of conceptual understanding regarding the enlightened reality. The truth is that unless we are able to differentiate between Soul-realisation and God-realisation, we will never see clearly what really occurs in awakening. The Self or God is reached not through awareness. Awareness is not capable of reaching God. God is reached through Being and the Heart. Through Being is reached the isness of God, which is the Absolute; and through the Heart is reached the Divine quality of God which is the heart of the Creator.

Awakening of Intelligence

Student: *In your approach, you emphasise asking questions in order to awaken intelligence. In the official system of education, they want just to hear the right answers. Why is that?*

Aziz: For the very simple reason that they are afraid of your questions! You would perhaps question their authority? They don't want to awaken your intelligence but to tame it! They want to adjust it to a model already prepared for you. The official system of education is a system of programming social, soul-less robots. They operate only in the mind, closing your Hearts and dulling your sensitivity. They already have all the answers waiting for you. But what if you ask different, unexpected questions? To prevent this, they give you a list of questions you are suppose to answer to pass examinations. It is all based on psychological violence and fear. They threaten that if you don't pass an examination, you won't be able to survive in their soul-less system.

If the question is coming from you, you have a desire to find out the answer. If you are asked a question from the outer source, you are not necessarily interested in the answer. The questioning of reality is much more important than the answers, for it represents your true and intelligent relationship with the mystery. It proves that you are alive. Through getting answers, you simply close reality into dead conclusions. You may study Buddhism for example, just to get all those answers about the nature of reality, but what is the question? This is what most seekers do: they go to Dharamsala or Nepal to study Buddhism and they stuff their minds with a bunch of intellectual concepts in the name of 'spirituality.' The mind gets satisfaction in creating different conclusions. But is your Soul really nourished? The answer which your Soul is craving for desperately is - awakening and awakening only.

Can Spontaneity be Conscious?

Student: *A question about spontaneity. Spontaneity seems to be quite an attractive quality but it is often unconscious. Is there such a thing as conscious spontaneity?*

Aziz: Spontaneity is always subconscious, but when it is experienced within the space of I Am, it becomes embraced by something which is conscious. Spontaneity itself is an automatic or natural response to the necessity of the moment. Spontaneity cannot be self-conscious. Anything which is conscious is not spontaneous because it means intelligence is interfering with reality. Therefore, consciousness prevents spontaneity because the very intelligence within consciousness takes time to activate; it takes enough time for the action to lose its spontaneity. That's why our goal is not to be consciously self-conscious, but it is to be in a natural state. The Natural State is deeper than consciousness even though it includes the quality of pure awareness.

Spontaneity is like driving a car. When you drive a car, you do not need to think all the time about changing gears, about controlling the speed or where to make a turn. However, from time to time, you have to check what you are doing... particularly if the situation demands your attention. Likewise, with being spontaneous and functioning naturally in life, you don't want to check yourself all the time. But from time to time, you need to bring an element of control and become more self-conscious. This is similar to psychological expressions and emotional responses, which need to be checked from time to time by the sensitivity of your intelligence. When you experience negative or immature emotions, it is a situation like this that demands conscious self-attention.

One can be truly natural and spontaneous only if one is beyond the mind. True spontaneity can arise only from the depth of I Am. When one is identified with the mind, one is not living. The mind is living. Here you have a purely unconscious spontaneity. The true meaning of being spontaneous in a conscious way is not to check your spontaneity. This is because the moment you are aware that you are spontaneous, you are no longer spontaneous. The true meaning of bringing an element of consciousness into spontaneity is to be rooted in I Am, while the body and mind are functioning spontaneously. In this way everything arises in the space of Truth.

Who Says 'I am not the Mind'?

Student: *I have been contemplating recently a lot on the concept 'I am not the mind.' It is still not clear to me. Could you speak about it?*

Aziz: You are the mind!
Student: How is it possible? Everybody says that I am not the mind and I am not the body?
Aziz: But you are the mind and you are the body. If you are not the mind, who is saying it? Isn't it the mind? Do you see the contradiction? It is the mind, which is apparently not you, that is saying, 'I am not the mind, I am not the body.' How is it that you can use the mouth of your body to say: I am not the body? And how can the question which arises from the mind claim: 'I am not the mind?' The one who makes up all these statements cannot negate itself!

Student: *So, who is watching?*

Aziz: It is the mind of course. The mind can watch anything, even itself! These are all concepts to be dropped. These concepts keep you in bondage. Be free, live without concepts! When you just live, you don't know whether you are the body or not. When you walk on the beach, you just walk; when you are hungry, you just eat. You don't say: 'I am not the body, but I am going to eat anyway.' You don't say: 'I am not the mind, but I am going think anyway.' That would be ridiculous! You are everything... However, your Pure Me is beyond the body and mind, resting unconditionally in the Soul's dimension.

The master Lin Chi spoke about all those concepts as ropes holding donkeys to a pole. Be free! Let the donkey free! The I Am is not watching anything and certainly is not saying, 'I am not that;' neither does it say, 'I am That.' The I Am does not care about all those statements! I Am is all-inclusive, containing the whole reality of Me and the outer in its own vastness.

Student: *How can I find my ego?*

Aziz: You cannot for you already are your ego. The one who is looking for the ego is the ego itself! You Are That! (Laughter...). It is a new version of the Advaita 'I am That' exclamation. Yes, you are your ego. In Buddhism they try to prove that ego is unreal because it cannot be found anywhere. But it is a serious misunderstanding, for it is the ego which is looking for itself. That's why it cannot be found. You cannot capture your ego because it is a movement of intelligence and not a 'thing.' But to whom does this ego belong?

Student: *You said that I am the ego, so it is just me.*

Aziz: We said that the ego is you, but we didn't say it is the whole of you! You are more than your ego. That's why there are more versions of the statement 'I am That.' You are That and That and That. So, to whom does your ego belong?

Student: *It belongs to my Real Me.*

Aziz: That is correct. The movement of intelligence refers to your true Me. Thoughts and concepts come and go, but you always remain. And to whom does your Pure Me belong? It belongs to the Beloved!

Beyond Knowing is Not-knowing-knowingly

Student: *When Bodhidarma was asked 'who are you?' he answered: 'I don't know!' What did he mean?*

Aziz: Bodhidarma was asked by the Chinese emperor Wu, 'who is standing in front of me?' And he answered, 'I don't know!' It was a very high answer. To say, 'I don't know' is the highest answer possible. When an Advaita master says: 'I am THAT,' it is a lower truth. To say, 'I am THAT' is just a concept. It is a concept based on experience, but it is still a concept. To say, 'I don't know' is to drop all concepts and surrender to the Unknown.

Emptiness: the Secret of the Sage

Student: *What is Emptiness?*

Aziz: This term is particularly popular in Buddhist philosophy. The thinker-mystic who created the philosophy of emptiness was Nagarjuna. In his work, he attempted to prove that all concepts ultimately contradict one another. For example, the concept of the Self leads to an unsolvable logical contradiction, as well as the concept of the no-self. If we speak about the Self, we make a 'thing' out of non-abiding existence which cannot be grasped. When we say 'no-self' we make out of our negation 'something,' a positive statement. How could we even say no-self? This very 'no' has already objectified the absence to which it is pointing! Hence, to say the 'Self' is wrong and to say the 'no-self' is wrong too.

So what remains? That which remains he called 'Sunyata' or emptiness. In his understanding, the term emptiness is not equivalent to the word 'void' or 'vacuity.' The term emptiness should not be seen in opposition to fullness. Emptiness does not mean that something is empty. That's why, these thinkers who try to prove that the conclusions of Buddhism and modern physics are the same, make a mistake. The emptiness of science is an objective emptiness, an emptiness which refers to the vacuity of something.

For Nagarjuna, Sunyata was a word indicating that something is beyond concepts and opposites. Sunyata can be called the no-mind, if you like. When the mind finds a logical contradiction within the concepts through which it wants to grasp reality, it reaches an impasse and becomes silent. It was this silence, the space of non-conceptualisation, which Nagarjuna translated as Sunyata. This type of mind-impasse, where the mind cannot grasp the apparent contradiction of reality and gives up, is illustrated by Zen koans. When you cannot solve a koan using your linear logic, the mind stops and reality, for the first time, can reveal itself to you. Therefore, emptiness is reality beyond the mind, free of concepts.

But what is the reality beyond the mind? Is there only one reality within the no-mind space? When Zen speaks about dropping concepts, one may think that the mind is free from thoughts and that this represents the only enlightened experience. But as we know, the no-mind has several levels. There is the no-mind of pure awareness; there is the no-mind of the Absolute State and there is the no-mind which includes the Heart as well. By the very intellectual nature of Nagarjuna's method, the experience of Sunyata clearly pointed to the realisation of the State of Presence. When concepts are dropped, just the awareness prior to thinking remains. We say that the no-mind of awareness is the cross-section between the Here and the Now - between the horizontal and vertical reality. It is neither the Here nor the Now, but the middle point. That's why this type of emptiness is not the final one. In order to go further, one has to reach the depth of the Now. Here, one drops from the not-knowing mind from the mind beyond concepts into the depth of Being. It is not enough to drop concepts in order to reach the Absolute State. For that reason,

Zen koans cannot really bring one to the final realisation. The Absolute State is much deeper than thoughtless awareness. To reach it, an energy expansion must take place, Grace must enter.

It is the most appropriate to call emptiness the Absolute State, which is the realisation of the Unmanifested or the Unborn. Emptiness is another name for the primordial state of pure isness which is the Absolute. Concluding, we can say that the most holistic vision of emptiness is a unity of non-conceptual state (space of not-knowing) with the absolute rest within the Uncreated Reality (energetic expansion). This means that the energetic expansion into the Unborn co-exists with the purity of the mind which submits itself to the innocence of Not-knowing.

The Nature of the Mind

To know oneself includes knowing one's mind. In the process of awakening, we move to the dimension beyond the mind, but within this space the mind is still included. First, we teach 'you are not the mind,' to help you reach your true Presence. Next, we teach, 'you are also the mind,' letting you to embrace your Complete Me. The mind can be truly seen only from the place of pure awareness. Otherwise, you are merely the mind and, therefore, there is no space inside to embrace this very mind as it stands on its way. From the place of clarity, silence and presence you can see the whole richness and beauty of the mind. When you understand your mind, you understand a very important part of your multidimensional existence.

Two Minds in One

Student: *Two days ago you spoke about a koan in which a Zen master was speaking to himself. Your answer was very interesting. Can you go deeper into it?*

Aziz: A few days ago we spoke about the Zen koan, in which a Zen master used to wake up every morning and speak to himself before beginning the day: 'Master!' 'Yes?' 'Be attentive.' 'Yes.' 'Do not be deceived by others.' 'Yes.'

The Zen question from this story is: two minds and one master - which mind is the true mind? There are two minds. One is saying 'Master!' and the second is responding 'Yes?' Which mind is the true mind? The one who is interrogating or the one who is responding?

It is a very beautiful koan and also shows that even an enlightened being, like this master, still is growing, still needs to be attentive, still needs to be careful in the way he lives. To be deceived by others means to be deceived by the outer. 'Others' means the outer... the master still needs to be careful not to be lost in the illusion of the phenomenal reality.

Before we go deeper into this koan, we would like you to close your eyes and to contemplate it for some time. As you close your eyes, what you experience is your mind. It is about your mind. If you understand this koan, you can understand better your own mind. Please, in your mind speak to yourself in the same way the master was speaking to himself. As you speak to yourself - which thought is a real thought? Which mind is the real mind: the one who speaks or the one who responds?

That is the nature of the inner dialogue. The mind is able to speak to itself, it creates understanding through relating to its past thought. In other words, one thought is responding to another thought which has just past. A very important thing to understand is that two thoughts cannot exist at the same time. In one moment only one thought can exist. What it means is that in the inner dialogue, there are never two voices at the same time. There cannot be. There is always one voice. When the mind says 'master,' this very thought immediately moves to the past. It becomes already the past. And in this moment a new thought arises, 'Yes,' which is responding to its own past. Do you understand? Present thought is relating to the past thought, which has passed away. And there is the next thought, 'be attentive,' which is followed by the thought 'Yes,' and so forth. There are many thoughts but each thought arises in the now and relates to the past thought or chain of thoughts. That which links them is the subtle memory.

What does it mean to be a schizophrenic? It means that different thoughts create their own autonomous reality. There is no proper communication in the mind. One thought says 'I am beautiful,' another thought says 'I am ugly.' These contrary thoughts try to overpower each other as though they were two individuals in conflict. Here, there is a lack of communication. In an extreme case, we have what we call schizophrenia.

There is, however, a third element in the mind. If one is awakened to the state of pure awareness or 'the witness.' Apart from one thought speaking with another, there is also the presence of no-thought: I. Pure I witnesses all kinds of thoughts as they arise, itself remaining in the background. In the case of our master, in the middle of this inner dialogue, there was the constant presence of I, pure awareness. Gurdjiev used to say that an ordinary person experiences a hundreds of different I's of which no single I can be identified as the real I. Awakening means that one discovers this Me, this I which does not change and is nothing but the centre of awareness behind the mind. When the centre of awareness is discovered, the movement of thoughts still exists and the inner dialogue still remains. But this inner dialogue is no longer obsessive, as in the case of an unconscious individual, for it continues to operate only as a function.

There is one mind which communicates with itself in the flow of time. A thought arises, goes to the past; a new thought arises and is responding to the thought which has just past, giving rise to understanding. It is a complex movement. However, it is one mind.

From where does Consciousness Arise?

Student: *I have a question about the process of thinking. Thoughts appear and disappear in each moment. Is it possible to be aware of a thought before it arises?*

Aziz: It is both possible and not possible. It is not possible because you cannot be aware of something which does not exist yet. But it is possible, for you can trace the subconscious formulating of the thought. The place from which a thought arises is the subconscious mind. The thought does not arise from awareness but rather it manifests itself into awareness. When the thought is manifested, it simultaneously becomes awareness because the thought is a combination of awareness and information. This issue not only concerns the arising of thoughts. It concerns also you as such, that is your very Me. Where does the sense of Me arise from? You may think that you are present all the time and that you are continuous. This illusion is due to the continuity of memory. But, in truth, you arise into each moment of the Now; or rather, in the Now you arise in each moment. You arise from the Original State being continuously created. Can you trace your own creation within the Now? Can you capture the moment of your arising into the recognition of Me?

You arise into consciousness from that which is prior to consciousness. It happens so fast! Can you capture it? It is faster than the speed of light. Light travels in space and consciousness travels in the Now. This which limits consciousness is the vehicle through which it channels itself into the dimension of time. And what is this vehicle? It is You! For that reason, we can speak about evolution. You don't have a control over your own arising in time. Just let it be, flow with the mystery.

As far as being aware of arising thoughts is concerned, what you can do is be present to your Me before the thought arises. Your existence as Me precedes the manifestation of thoughts; you are simply rooted deeper in reality. When you try to observe the mind, you are still not free from it; you are still a part of the mind. When you place yourself in the State of Presence, you no longer need to care about being aware of the mind. In this way, thinking is thinking and you allow all to be as it is.

You can be aware of only that which exists in consciousness. You cannot become conscious of that which has not come to the surface of the conscious mind yet. It is possible that you can trace the subtle process of arising thoughts by exploring deeper sub-conscious states. You see, originally a thought manifests from the unconscious, next it reaches the subconsciousness and then moves to consciousness. But there are layers of the subconscious reality. The deeper you go, the more it gets sub-sub-conscious. This is, however, not necessary from the viewpoint of discovering your Pure Me, for it abides eternally in the state of unity with the Beloved.

Awareness of thinking is not natural because thinking is itself a form of awareness. In the beginning, you need to create a distance in order to observe the mind and later you discover your Me. When Me is present to her own existence, this Me and the mind create one field. Neither the Me nor the mind observe anything, even though there is a movement in intelligence which circulates around the centre of Me.

How do Thoughts and Feelings Relate?

Student: *Can you explain more about the mutual connection between thoughts and emotions?*

Aziz: In the centre of the mind lives Me, the State of Presence. Around this Me occurs the movement of intelligence and thinking and emotional activity. When you are not awakened to your Me, you are fully identified with the dynamic expression of Me, which is the mind or personality. Personality is the outer layer of Me, her shadow. A person who is ignorant lives as such a shadow, not having any Real Me. Therefore, there is the central Me and the dynamic Me which is the personal self. This dynamic Me is made of thoughts, emotions and physicality.

Thoughts and emotions are interrelated. They can be seen as two sides of human intelligence. A thought in itself is emotionally neutral; it is just information without any emotional context. An emotion in itself is instinctive yet blind as it has no intelligence. But in the case of human beings, thoughts and emotions are more or less mixed together. Thinking and feeling are not abstract - they exist in the context of the Soul. When a thought arises, it is not just 'a thought;' when an emotion arises, it is not merely 'an emotion.' They relate to you, to your personal story and stream of consciousness. It is always about you, about your life, security, pleasure, happiness or fears. That which makes the Soul identified with the thought is emotion. When a thought arises, what makes us interested in the information which it presents? It is the emotion, of course. Because thinking relates to your well-being and well-being is a feeling, that's why, thinking without feeling does not exist for a human being.

For instance, there is a thought, 'this airplane will soon crash and everybody will get killed!' It is just a thought, mental information. A computer, for instance, does not care about what type of information is shown on the screen. Outputs on the computer screen like, 'this computer is going to be shut down,' or 'there is a virus inside,' will not cause the computer to shake and tremble with fear. All is the same for the machine. But not for you. That's why, when the thought about the crashing of the plane arises, immediately attached is the emotional identification - 'oh, my God... I am going to die!!!' And you begin trembling with fear, your breath changes, the heart starts to beat rapidly as if it was going to jump out of your chest...and so forth. When an important thought comes to you, you feel it and respond accordingly - with fear, anger, passion, jealousy, surprise, sadness, disappointment, hope, desire, love, hate, boredom...and so on.

Thinking as such, however, does not always trigger strong emotions. When there are no strong emotions or distinct feelings, we speak about being emotionally neutral. For that reason, it is fairly easy to observe the mind, but to observe emotions is very difficult because the level of identification is much stronger.

Student: *What comes first: the emotion or the thought?*

Aziz: Both cases are possible. Sometimes a thought comes first and is followed by an emotion. In other cases, an emotion comes first and the mind tries to catch up with it, translating it into a thought. If someone steps on your foot, you scream and feel anger without thinking. A moment later, the mind explains to you the situation: 'oh, this idiot stepped on my foot!' Emotions cannot exist without some type of thinking. Even thinking in the case of someone who is totally in the head, always carries some flavour of emotion. Let's take, for instance, a philosopher who is completely disconnected from feelings, is thinking about some logical problem and suddenly finds a solution. This solution is not just processed intellectually - he is also satisfied and happy.

Continuing this subject, we need to see that even though feeling and thinking are interconnected, one of them may be more predominant. Human intelligence is a combination of thinking and feeling. A person who is mostly emotional still thinks a lot but without any clarity or logic... the thoughts are disconnected, without any real continuity. On the other hand, a mostly cerebral person (with which our earth is so populated in our modern civilisation) though he can feel something, is so locked in the mind that he can hardly be considered as living.

Student: *Is the Soul beyond emotions?*

Aziz: Certainly, she lives in the dimension of Pure Me, beyond the emotional body. She is the primal feeling of the Heart, which is timelessly at rest. But the Soul connects to the world through emotions. Emotions represent a particular type of sensitivity-perception, through which the Soul exists in dynamic relationship with the world. You see, throughout life you experience a flow of different emotions but on some level you sense a Me which is deeper than these emotions. Within your psyche, you are identified with these emotions but on a much deeper, existential level you are disidentified from them. And here we are discovering this part of your Me which exists prior to the coming and going of thoughts and emotions. To discover it, you must first transcend the mind, that is, the subconscious reality. Awakening to the Soul takes place on a few levels. It includes pure awareness, the depth of Being and, most importantly, the Heart.

Intelligence is Both, beyond the Mind and the No-mind

Student: *What is the nature of the mind?*

Aziz: The nature of the mind is awareness without an object. The content of the mind is thinking. The empty space of awareness is the container, while the expressions of the mind represent the content. In Buddhism, the concepts regarding thought are more positive than in Hinduism. In Hinduism, you can find many teachings speaking about the need to eliminate the content of the mind. In Buddhism, they discovered that to awaken awareness free from thinking, thinking itself does not have to be eliminated. The container is already beyond its content. In their model, however, what was missing was the understanding of the role of intelligence. Intelligence is neither the container nor is it the content. Intelligence is the link between the container and the content; between emptiness and form. Who knows the nature of mind? Who knows thinking? It is intelligence alone, the subtle mind. It is intelligence which may say, 'all thoughts should be eliminated,' or it may say 'it is fine to think as long as one is beyond thinking.' Do you see how significant this intelligence is? It does everything! It can direct you to a completely wrong direction or it can make your practice clear, reflecting the true picture of spiritual reality.

Thinking in the State of Presence

Student: *When a thought appears, it seems to have often much more power than the State of Presence. How can I become more identified with the State of Presence?*

Aziz: When a thought appears, it imposes its identity on you. The thought wants to be the boss; it wants to be the most important. The thought is not just a piece of information, it is information which almost always relates to you. A thought which is neutral has no power over you. This is the case if you think about something which is not related directly to your life. You can deal with this thought in a relaxed way. But when the thought relates to your security, to your sense of well-being, to your survival or to your emotional satisfaction - it does have power because it also engages your emotional body. You see, it is not the thought alone which has control over you, but it is the thought in combination with the emotional response. It is your emotional identification which makes the thought really important to you. For example, a thought threatens you or promises some benefits and you immediately become emotionally identified. Why do you think? Because thinking is a way to secure your life or of granting you more happiness. For you want to be happy! Don't you? It is all about your happiness and security. This whole thinking is the self-protective mechanism.

One reason why people think so much is because of their unconsciousness. This means there is no one present in the mind, there is no Real Me. This thinking is an unconscious mechanism. Another reason is that thinking protects them, they do not want to give up thinking. Without thinking they feel insecure and unprotected. They do not have the courage not to think. If an ordinary person is given this ability to stop the mind, this person would not take it because he or she would feel insecure and would likely panic. This thinking mechanism is always active; you are protecting yourself from morning to evening. It is an excessive protection. It is like when a mother is over-protective it becomes unbearable for a child. The parent has to give the child space, so he can explore different things and explore his natural freedom. Similarly, the mind is likewise over-protecting.

The thought has power because it relates to one's well-being and to one's sense of security. It is not more powerful than the State of Presence. No, not at all. The State of Presence is the centre of consciousness behind the mind. We call it the King of the mind, the owner of the mind, the Host. But when the owner of the mind is drunk, he forgets that he is an owner. Imagine that the owner of a big hotel took same drugs or got drunk, forgot that he owned the hotel and began to clean rooms and serve guests. That is what has happened to this Pure Me - she got drunk and forgot her own importance having become identified with the mind.

Through the process of awakening, we are simply sobering up. The owner is slowly coming back to consciousness. The affect of alcohol gradually evaporates and eventually the Host returns! Now, the servant which is the mind can do the whole work. You can rest in the royal seat of pure consciousness, sitting on the golden throne of the third eye centre. Slowly you are becoming the owner of the mind. However, now you are at the stage where even though you recognise the host, a part of you still does not believe in it. There is doubt because still some alcohol remains in the blood. Part of this disbelief is subconscious. Your intelligence has not fully imbibed the truth of who you are. Your intelligence is still adjusting to this truth.

One can be fully Self-realised and still not believe it! It is possible because Self-realisation is an energy-phenomenon and apart from this, intelligence still has to recognise the real meaning of what is being experienced. Intelligence has to believe. It is all about the role of intelligence and Understanding, in truth. You are shifting your sense of identity from the mind to the State of Presence. Intelligence, which operates in-between the mind and the State of Presence has to change its belief system. It has to change its belief system regarding the way it has been translating your sense of identity. You must see that for so long you have believed that you are the mind and personality. Now, slowly you are waking up to a radically new perception of your existence. It is a process of adjustment, on the level of energy, intelligence and the subconscious mind. It takes some time.

Another element is that the State of Presence needs to become more stabilised in order to avoid the danger of getting lost in the mind. To be lost is to lose the very energy presence of pure awareness behind the mind. This is because the moment you think, energy is naturally directed towards thinking. Since thinking is outside the centre, it is energetically external to the State of Presence or Me. When the energy of attention is diffused in thinking, the centre is not strong enough and simply gets lost. For this reason, we speak all the time about divided attention. Even when you are thinking, part of you is constantly focussed on the State of Presence. The mind is a seductive phenomenon, it tries to seduce your attention. A thought arises, it is like a beautiful piece of cake on the screen,of consciousness. Your Me gets exited and says: 'oh, what a wonderful thought!' (Laughter...). Immediately you lose yourself because you are unable give undivided attention.

The problem of getting lost in thinking, however, points to another truth. It is the understanding of your multidimensional existence. You exist on many levels at the same time. That which you are is not just merely the State of Presence. You are the Soul and the Soul is more than the State of Presence. The Soul does not reach complete happiness, from being in the State of Presence. The State of Presence represents only the centre of awareness in the Soul. The ultimate centre of the Soul is in the Heart.

The Soul, apart from abiding in the light of her own presence, lives in the world as well. This means in order for you as the Soul to be happy and fulfilled, you need to reach a certain satisfaction in the outer reality too. For example, in order to grow emotionally you may need a partner or a dear friend. In order to grow in your intelligence, maybe you need to read or contemplate certain spiritual matters. In order to fulfil your sense of adventure, you may need to travel and see different countries, to gather different experiences. All these elements are necessary for you because you are more than I Am, you are the Soul. The Soul is the mysterious essence of our individual Creation, which lives precisely in-between the impersonal dimension of I AM and her personal expression which is the psyche.

First we shift the centre of identity from the mind to I Am. At this stage of changing one's sense of identity, we teach that you are not the mind. Neither are you your emotions, nor the thoughts which you experience - you are the subject behind, you are I Am. When this I Am is firmly established, we change the teaching slightly, bringing you to a more holistic perception of your Me. Here, we say that you are also the mind, thoughts, emotions and the movement of intelligence. You are both, I Am and the mind. That's why, when an important thought arises in the mind, it is dear to you for this thought is a part of your reality. The problem is that when you are unconscious, the mind creates your only reality - you are locked in the prison of mental reality. Ignorance means that you experience yourself in a very superficial and fragmented way. Here, we are simply adding the necessary depth to you. When this depth is present, it embraces your personal self and you become a complete human being. The complete human being is I Am, the mind, intelligence, emotions, physicality... everything. This is the whole Me, it is not one thing. This essence, the core of Me is this place in the Heart where Me meets the Beloved. This very place of meeting between Me and the Creator, is the Soul.

Feeling is a Steady Emotion

Student: *What is the difference between emotion and feeling?*

Aziz: We sometimes use these terms interchangeably but there is some difference. The emotion has more of a fluctuating nature, while the feeling has more continuity. For example, when you suddenly become upset or agitated because someone steps on your foot, it is an emotion. But sadness could not be called an emotion. Sadness is a feeling and it has continuity. The experience of I Am is itself feeling, for it is felt, from moment to moment. Any energy experience has the quality of feeling. Similarly, happiness is a feeling and not an emotion and so forth.

Subconscious Me and Conscious Me

Student: *What is the subconscious Me? What is the actual difference between the conscious and subconscious Me?*

Aziz: When consciousness arises, Me arises, for consciousness cannot operate without a subject to which it could refer. Consciousness cannot function just in emptiness. Even consciousness free from thoughts must apply to someone who experiences it. These are not simple matters and to understand them fully, you must be free from spiritual slogans, so you can go inside and discover for yourself the truth of your reality.

In the case of impersonal subconsciousness, the movement of information doesn't relate to any particular Me, but neither can we speak about the existence of consciousness (knowingness). When consciousness arises, simultaneously there is someone to whom this consciousness applies. In order to be conscious of consciousness, there needs to be some level of duality, a certain split between subject-object for the recognition to take place. This represents the primal polarisation within intelligence which gives rise to conscious knowing.

This is what we call the State of Presence; it is the most developed experience of consciousness, for here consciousness becomes self-conscious, that is, it goes beyond subject-object relations, reaching a subject-subject realisation. Before then, there are many levels in the evolution of consciousness where consciousness is still not aware of its own subjectivity. The subconscious Me is this level of consciousness where the sense of Me is completely dissolved into the objectified polarity of reality.

How does consciousness evolve and through what? Through this very Me to which it applies! Do you see it? In truth, consciousness serves Me, for it is Me which is the essence of consciousness. During the initial stages in the development of consciousness, Me is hardly felt, for she is very, very subconscious, even though she is already there. A cat, for instance, cannot separate its Me from the spontaneous functioning of its psycho-somatic reality. The psycho-somatic reality is this extension of Me which bridges the Real Me with the objectified reality which means it is neither the Real Me nor it is not-Me. The best example to show you what the subconscious Me is like is the dream state. In the dream state you experience some type of subconscious Me. There are also other types of subconscious Me, which are much less clear or more subconscious than the human subconscious Me. In the dream state, consciousness fully operates but only part of the brain is active. This consciousness in a dream does not refer to any clear Me; that's why, you may suffer or experience joy but not be able to separate your Me from the experience. The sense of Me in the dream is not able to refer to itself. It is an objectified Me, merely a part of the psychological flow. This subconscious Me functions all the time, not only in the dream state but also in the waking state, the subconscious Me is mostly present. This function of the subconscious mind is natural as it is an indivisible part of spontaneous movement of the human intelligence.

There are levels of subconscious Me and stages in-between the subconscious Me and the conscious Me. Sometimes, you may find yourself not being sure whether it is subconscious or conscious Me operating in your mind. And it means that you experience the type of Me which is in-between the subconscious and conscious mind. This type of Me is neither fully subconscious nor fully conscious.

What is important to know is that any thought which occurs in your mind is already Me! It is not merely that a thought is arising from your subconscious mind and then your Me is dealing with this information. The arising thought is already Me but simply a more subconscious Me. A thought cannot be separated from the recognition of it. How do you know that there is thinking? Who knows it? As a thought arises, there is an immediate sense of knowingness attached to it and this sense of knowingness is nothing but - Me. It is a complex issue and for most it is difficult to be grasped. As you may guess, the reality of the mind is much more rich than simplistic teachings may assume, dividing consciousness into thinking and not-thinking only.

Student: *So what is the conscious Me? At which stage does the subconscious Me become conscious?*

Aziz: When you ask this question are you conscious or subconscious?

Student: *I am conscious.*

Aziz: How do you know it? What makes you feel that you are conscious?

Student: *I feel like I am present in the moment when I try to formulate my question.*

Aziz: Yes, to be conscious means that one's Me is present in the thinking process. This Me can be slightly present or completely present, Me cannot be separated from attention. When attention feels itself, one senses one's Me. The Conscious Me is the same as the ego. It is an ability to stand a little bit back within the thinking process. The conscious Me is able to create a self-referral in the mind as well as to extract herself from the empirical reality, in order to think about it. The conscious Me senses herself being present in the thinking process, but still, has no real centre. It is only when Me is able to become conscious of herself, in a true sense, that the self-conscious Me is born. The conscious Me has some amount of presence but is fully identified with thinking and lacks continuity. The self-conscious Me is the Real Me, fully experienced out of the mind's content.

To Whom does the Inner Dialog Refer?

Student: *Why is there this constant inner dialogue?*

Aziz: For the very simple reason that the Soul is not present in the mind. Therefore, intelligence does not have a stable centre. The mind which is unconscious and fragmented has no centre. If there is no centre, there is no counter force which could oppose the inertia of mechanical thinking. You see, what it means is that the Me to whom the mind refers, is in a state of coma - she does not yet exist, in truth. The Buddhist concept of no-self is very convenient for many seekers, as it philosophically justifies their lack of the Real Me. This concept asserts the status quo of ignorance. They are at this stage of ignorance that, unlike other people, they see the emptiness of their illusory sense of self but they have not discovered that which is real. They try to assert the absence of any Real Me as itself representing the nature of reality. However, they need to transcend their negative conclusion in order to discover the positive. What Buddha Shakyamuni himself meant by saying that there is 'no-self' was a very profound state of realisation. He referred not to the negative absence of subjective reality, but to the absolutely positive presence of Truth which was beyond the limitation of the ego.

Who experiences the mind? It is Me, but this Me is lost in the arising of thoughts, completely identified with the mind. Awakening the State of Presence is a stage in the evolution of consciousness; it is where awareness is able to separate itself from its content, the mind. There is no other way to transcend the mind - the only way is to give birth to the Real Me. You can watch this mind a hundred years; you can repeat mantras and do thousands of visualisations but the mind in its unconscious core will not change. Become present to your Real Me and see what happens! There is no need to do anything! Just be present to yourself and that very presence will do the whole work! It is like turning the light on inside a dark room. All meditation techniques aim to fight the phantoms and ghosts inside this dark room. But turning the light on in one instant destroys darkness and all illusions. That is the power of self-knowledge. That is the beauty of this practice - you don't need to watch the mind or manipulate with it anymore in anyway. You are just present to your presence and the mind by itself becomes silent...

Why do I have so Many Thoughts?

Student: *What about subconscious thinking? It seems that even when I am in the State of Presence, there arise many thoughts.*

Aziz: After the State of Presence is awakened, you may still experience many thoughts because the subconscious mind is overloaded. It needs to release itself. Do not give energy to it, remain present and let the mind come to surface. Let the excess information stored below the conscious level become manifested and released. The end result is the silent mind. Some arising thoughts are natural but here they no longer have an obsessive quality. In this stage, you experience thoughts rarely as if in a slow motion. The slow motion arising of thoughts contained in the silent space of awareness is the Natural State of mind.

Trying to fully suppress thinking goes against nature and is as such impossible. Our purpose is not to eliminate thinking but to put thinking into the right perspective. Here, the mind still operates but no longer in a compulsive manner. The mind becomes a natural expression and extension of Me, which is the inner silence. The mind is a horrible boss but a wonderful servant! Thinking is not a problem. The problem is that the one to whom the thinking applies is fast asleep.

To Truly Accept the Mind is to be Out of It!

Student: *What does it mean to accept unconsciousness?*

Aziz: In truth, to accept unconsciousness you must be already conscious. If one is merely unconscious, one cannot accept it. The mind can only accept its past unconsciousness. It is unable to accept its present unconsciousness. For the mind is never present, it always lives in the past.

A real acceptance is to take a step back and relax into Being. When we speak about acceptance in meditation, we mean that you can allow the mind to manifest thoughts while relaxing into Being, beyond the mind. To accept is to contain the accepted. That is why, acceptance is already an expansion. It is not that the mind accepts; it is that the no-mind allows all to be as it is. Acceptance is allowance and allowance is surrender into the non-personal space of pure isness - the ultimate container of everything.

When you accept the mind in meditation, it does not mean that you indulge in thinking. In meditation, neither do you fight with thoughts, nor do you let yourself get lost in them. That is true acceptance. The moment you accept the mind as it is, you are already out of it! Therefore, true acceptance is to abide beyond the mind. In that space, even the issue of acceptance transcends itself. This vastness is beyond acceptance and beyond non-acceptance... it is the Beyond Only.

What is the Source of Emotions?

Student: *Where do the emotions come from?*

Aziz: Everything comes from the same place, the Source of Creation. Emotions, you see, represent a certain type of sensitivity, a certain way of experiencing reality. Yes? You live as a separate being, you experience the world as if it is outside of yourself. You experience the world through your senses, mind or emotional body. Emotions are more deep way of experiencing for they are closer to the Soul. Behind any type of emotion, there is a direct recognition that it refers to you, to your Soul. Yes? You experience anger, your Me is angry which means that she is irritated by something. You experience sadness, you feel maybe negative or melancholic. All these emotions are translated through you in terms of good and bad or neutral. Yes? What it means is that your Soul wishes to experience a positive reality. She wants to be happy. Everything is based on this desire to be happy, from morning to evening. Everything you do is either for pleasure or to avoid unpleasant things and suffering. This regards everything ... you go to the river because it is pleasant, you go to a restaurant because there is good food. You don't go to another restaurant which plays loud music, for it disturbs you...and so forth. It is similar to the type of friends you choose. You spend time with companions which make you feel good, which are nourishing to your emotional body.

This is how your Soul lives in the world. If you are not connected with your feelings, you start to live too much in the mind. In such a case, you are not aware of important feelings and become disconnected from the space of the Heart. For example, you spend time with people who are insensitive and hurt you emotionally. The mind which is disconnected from the Soul can be very insensitive and ignorant. Feelings and emotions represents the frequency of sensitivity referring to your particular Me in terms of good and bad, positive and negative, happiness and suffering...and so forth.

The question 'where do emotions come from?' is not properly formulated. You are these emotions! You are made from emotions. It is the same as to ask: 'where do human beings come from?'

Student: *What is the relationship between the mind and emotions?*

Aziz: They are inter-connected. Your mind and your emotional body are two sides of the same phenomenon, which is your psychological self or your personality. They can function relatively separately but ultimately they are One. And in a person who is integrated, where the Heart and the mind are one, it is hardly possible to differentiate thinking from feeling.

But if one is fragmented, the Heart and the mind have no connection. A person can use only the head, for example, or a person can use only emotions. There are certain people who use only emotions. They are not able to think rationally and there are other people who are like robots - they only think; they don't feel anything. However, ultimately thinking and feeling cannot be separated.

Thinking affects feelings. For example, you think about somebody who has irritated you. Yes? It is just a thought, but immediately you become angry. You are angry, irritated and you start to perspire! (Laughter...). In another case, you think about your beloved and immediately some sweet feelings come to your Heart, yes? So you see, in this way thought affects feeling. From the other side, what kind of feeling you have affects your thinking pattern. For example, somebody makes you angry, it affects your quality of thought. It is difficult to think rationally. You are watching sunset and a contemplative thought comes to your mind, about life, about beauty...or about impermanence if you are a Buddhist (laughter)... When you think, whatever you think, there is always a certain feeling attached to it. The human being cannot think without feeling. Even if you are a mathematician and you think 'two-square equals four,' it's just a thought, but something pleasant is felt in the mind. One is very satisfied subconsciously that one can count until four (laughter)... If a scientist invents some new formula there is a great satisfaction in the mind. This satisfaction is an emotion. If one cannot solve a problem, one gets upset, experiencing an emotional dissatisfaction.

It is difficult to experience an emotion or a feeling without any idea attached to it. It is possible however, that your moods are affected by hormones, the weather or the position of stars. But is such a case, your moods affect your thoughts. If you feel really bad, you can even think about committing a suicide. So it is all inter-related, inter-connected. There is this constant circular movement from thought-emotion, emotion-thought...and so forth.

Student: *What is the relationship between the mind and the awareness?*

Aziz: The mind is intelligence of awareness and awareness is the building block of the mind.

The Inner Dialog

Student: *What is the Inner Dialogue?*

Aziz: We can call it a monologue if you like.

Student: *Who is talking to whom?*

Aziz: There are two kinds of the inner dialogue: one is subconscious, the other is conscious. When you think consciously, the dialogue is conscious and it is done by the intuitive intelligence. You can call it the ego-function. It is the conscious inner dialogue which is simply a part of intelligence. It is how the inner computer is working. The thoughts are the inner waves of consciousness which create understanding. One thought relates to another thought which is from its immediate past. By relating to its past, a response in the form of a new thought is created. Those thoughts communicate with each other, giving rise to understanding. It is a dialogue through which intelligence is functioning.

In order for intelligence to function, there has to be a certain split or duality inside the mind. For without duality intelligence cannot function. There has to be a division between the subject and object within pure consciousness. So first a thought arises, which is a subject. It relates to the past thought, which is an object; and it is followed by the next thought, which is the new subject. This is the subject-object relationship within the thought process. This situation is all the time present in the dynamic reality of the mind. What is interesting is that the subject-object relationship within the movement of intelligence occurs not in space but in time. Two thoughts cannot exist in the same moment within one mind.

In the case of subconscious thinking, the inner dialogue is more mechanical or automatic. Subconscious thinking is this type of thinking that you don't really control. You don't really know that you are thinking. Thinking is just happening and only after a while you realise, 'Oh, I've been thinking.' When there is subconscious thinking, it means that your Me is less present. Subconscious as well as conscious thinking is positive in its nature. The inner dialogue represents the basic make-up of human intelligence. Without this dialogue, there can be no evolution of understanding. Without the inner dialogue, you do not exist as a human being.

Our purpose is not to eliminate the subconscious and conscious thinking but to put them in the right place. A person, who doesn't have awareness is constantly lost in this inner dialogue. The inner dialogue, in the case of unconscious individuals is obsessive and ridiculous. It is not a dialogue but more like gibberish! When the State of Presence is awakened, your intelligence for the first time has a centre, the Real Me. Here, you rest in silence and complete awareness, beyond the mind. From that space, the inner dialogue operates just as a function which arises from time to time.

Let's address your question in a different way. Who is speaking with whom? It is intelligence which is speaking with itself, by creating a certain inner duality within the movement of information. The thought is a unit of information and immediately there is attached to the thought a sense of Me. That's why you know that thinking pertains to you. When you are not fully conscious, the sense of Me is purely subconscious, that is, unclear. Hence the feeling of Me is not strong and is completely identified with thinking.

It is very difficult to understand the subconscious mind and how it works. We can understand certain mechanisms and basic principles in its working. And certainly, there is nothing wrong with this function. There is nothing schizophrenic about it for it is the natural way of human consciousness.

The inner dialogue symbolises how human intelligence evolves in duality, creating understanding. But if there is no awareness, this faculty turns into pure obsession. For that reason, it becomes unwanted. There is a Zen koan relating to this problem:

> *There was a master who every morning upon waking up spoke to himself. He was saying: 'Master?' And responding: 'Yes.' 'Be careful.' 'Yes, I will.' 'Don't let yourself be deceived by others!' and so forth.*

And the question coming from this koan is: 'one master and two minds - which one is the true mind?' Which mind is the true mind? The one who says 'Master,' or the one who responds 'Yes'? Which one is the true mind? The Zen answer is always beyond concepts. There is no explanation, but only demonstration of Truth. But we can explain it intellectually. The answer is that there is only one mind, but divided into the relative dual movement within itself. It is one mind. The 'Yes' part of the mind, and the 'Master' part of the mind, belong to the same mind. But this one mind is itself beyond one and two. It is what it is.

Student: *What is the right question?*

Aziz: Which part of your mind wants to know what is the right question?

Student: *Could you tell us the Zen answer to this koan?*

Aziz: Daniel!

Student: *Yes?*

Aziz: Thank you for showing us the Zen answer!

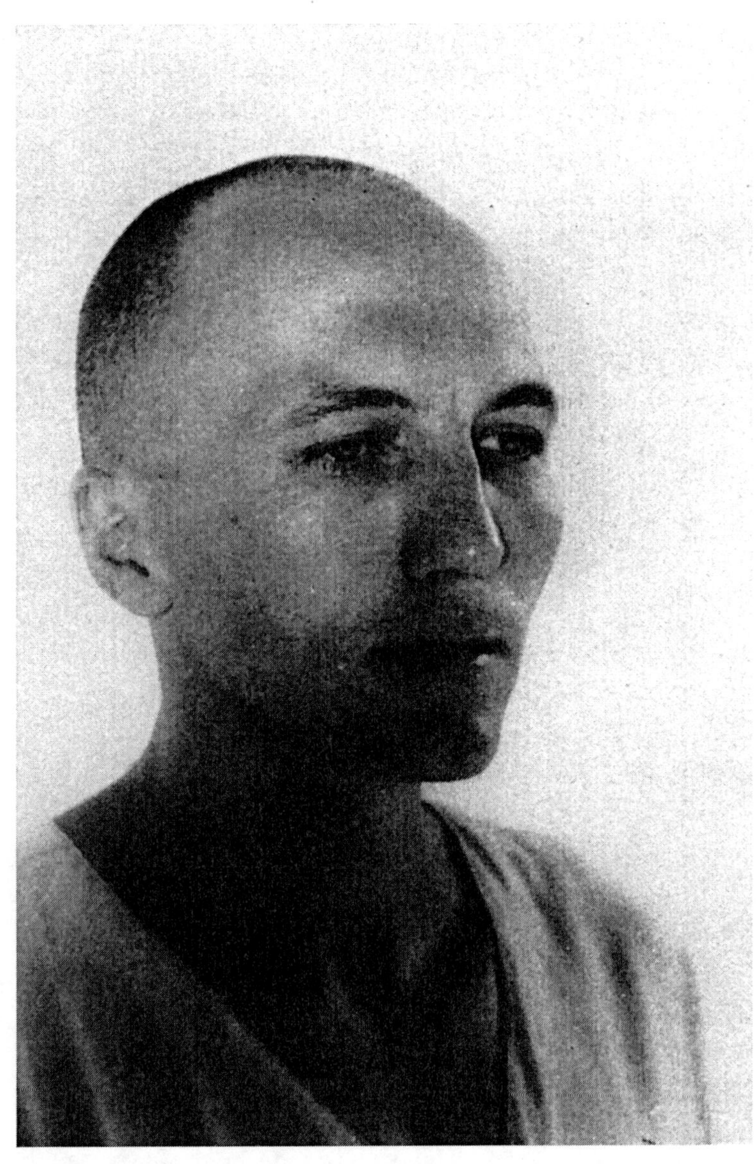

V

DIMENSION OF THE CREATOR

Who is the Creator? Look inside your own Heart and feel the divine presence of the Beloved!

The Beloved is a unity of the Absolute and the Divine. The Absolute is the Being of the Beloved and the Divine is her Heart. Universal Intelligence is the Wisdom of the Creator; Grace is her loving care. The Soul is her child and the Creation is her eternal Dance and the mirror in which she can reflect her formless face.

The Creator is the Inner and the Outer, the Created and the Uncreated, Time and Timelessness, Evolution and the unchanging Perfection. The Creator is beyond consciousness but contains the totality of knowingness. Her essence is Love, Light and Mystery. She cannot be fully known but we can reach re-union with her everlasting Presence, returning home...

The Beloved

The Beloved is with you and always has been. In the inner ocean of your Heart there is a dimension where you end and the Divine begins. Let yourself to enter this inner vastness and infinite sensitivity. Ask the Beloved for help. Say:

> *I don't know how to meet You, I don't know how to look directly into your face, your sacred face like the Sun, please help me! I don't want anything from You but let me feel Your presence and teach me how to feel You. Where are you? Where are you - the Heart of Existence, the Light of Creation, the Creator of my Soul? Let me know You, for You are the very meaning of my life. My Heart so deeply longs for reunion with the Beloved. How long have I lived in the illusion of separation? Let me return home, let me enter the Gate of the Heart...let me dissolve into Your Light.*

Who is the lover and who is the Beloved? The deeper you go into your Heart, the less you understand! Let yourself become completely confused, lost in the ocean of the Heart, no longer knowing... who is the lover and who is the Beloved...

Beyond Emptiness

Student: *What is beyond Emptiness?*

Aziz: Emptiness is another name for the Absolute, the Uncreated Energy. Certain mystics have realised that the Original Void or Emptiness is the Ultimate. This realisation is however not complete, as Emptiness is not the whole of the Ultimate. The secret within the Absolute is the presence of the Divine Dimension. The Divine is simply the Heart of Emptiness and, in truth, the very meaning of the Absolute. The Absolute represents the Being aspect of the Ultimate Reality. The Beloved is the absolute unity of Emptiness, Love and Inexplicable Intelligence.

How Deeply can We Know God?

Student: *Can you speak about God and the meeting of one's Soul with God?*

Aziz: God cannot be known fully but our Soul can have some understanding about the reality of God. Each being in his evolution is destined to reach his ultimate recognition of God's reality. The blueprint means that your Me, that is, your particular angle of perception, is destined to attain a certain degree of insight into the nature of Truth. This optimum is limited, by the borders and frontiers of the blueprint. The moment the Soul reaches her blueprint, she is complete and ready to let go of this dimension. What we are trying to say is, that your destiny is not to know the whole of God, but to know that which is important to know for you. In our search for knowledge, we have to know when to stop and when we are not ready to stop yet. We can know it only by being in tune with our Soul's evolution and blueprint.

Too much understanding is a burden. Understanding is responsibility as well - it is a weight your intelligence has to carry. Understanding, when it is excessive, can prevent you from being absent, from letting go into the ultimate space of not-knowing. When you know too much, how can you get lost in God? In Sufism, they have the expression: 'drunk with the Divine.' When you are drunk with the Divine, you care no more about knowing anything; you give up everything, you become naked and exposed. But before you can melt into God, you have to awaken the ability to transcend your very Me. And for that, you do need some knowledge. Even the concept of God is the initial information which allows you to reach that to which this idea is pointing which is God herself. If a person has no concept of God, can such a person experience or realise God? Of course, not. There are cultures, which may not use the concept of God, but they have other concepts which allow them to experience the sacredness of reality. They may worship spirits, ancestors, trees, rocks, the sky or the ocean. This is the way they translate their experience of God. But some initial concepts must be there. Without any concepts, you would be very much like an animal, just experiencing the empirical reality and relating to it with basic emotions.

Too much knowledge is a burden, an excess of luggage you need to carry. But if there is too little knowledge, you are not complete either, for you have not reached your optimum capacity and potential. So know how much you need to know, and know when you don't need to know!

As far as God is concerned, she is the Ultimate Mystery. There is no being existing who can know the whole of God. We know what we can about God, within the limitation of human consciousness; and more than this is not necessary - we can stop there.

We know about God that her foundation is the dimension of Beingness or the Absolute, which is pure isness. We know that God is beyond consciousness and yet encompasses the totality of consciousness. God knows all but not in a self-conscious way. God doesn't need to know that she knows all. We know that God's reality includes the Divine Dimension, which is the realm of the Heart and Love. We know that God contains the Totality of Creation and the wholeness of divine intelligence. The Intelligence of God does not need the vehicle of thinking in order to operate. The Intelligence of God is one with Creation - it is immanent in every aspect of created reality and yet simultaneously transcends the totality of Creation. The Heart of God is the Divine Dimension. The Being aspect of God is the Absolute. The wisdom of God is Universal Intelligence. The personal aspect of God is Guidance and the Love of God is the presence of Grace.

But that which we know the most is that we can become one with God, meeting the Beloved face to face in the cave of our own Heart. This knowledge is the most important, for it allows us to return to a state of unity with the Light and Love of the Creator. When we merge with God in a real way, through our Being and the Heart, a new knowledge is given to us. This knowledge is beyond knowing and not-knowing. This knowledge is total and immediate, as it bypasses the mind. This knowledge destroys the whole of our past and takes us beyond the last residues of collective consciousness. When we are free and awakened in a new way to this very Now of Creation, the lightening of complete understanding enters our Heart and our mind, bringing the final revelation that - only God is! Know that I AM!

God-realisation - Soul-realisation

Student: *Can you explain more regarding the difference between Self-realisation and Soul-realisation?*

Aziz: What's the difference between Soul-realisation and Self-realisation? First, Self-realisation and God-realisation are the same. In fact the term 'God-realisation' is more precise because the word 'Self' is rather one-dimensional. The reality of God is far beyond that which we could experience as 'our true self.' You cannot have clarity in this matter unless you understand the fundamental difference between the realisation of your Soul and the one of Universal Presence. We spoke about the light of the sun reflected in a dewdrop. The water from which the dewdrop is made is the body, our physical form. The dust on the surface of the dewdrop is personality or ego. The light inside the dewdrop, is the light of the Soul. The light inside the dewdrop belongs to the sun. The light of the Soul is borrowed from God. The Soul cannot exist without the source of the light, which is the Beloved.

Imagine that the light inside of this dewdrop is conscious and can become self-conscious. In truth, the light of the Soul is not physical or visual. This light is love and consciousness combined. When this light inside of the dewdrop becomes completely aware of itself, we speak about Soul-realisation.

And what is God-realisation? It is the moment when the reflection, inside of the dewdrop, becomes aware of the sun! When the light inside the dewdrop recognises its own source. Here, at this stage of realisation, a famous exclamation is born: 'I am THAT.' That is to say, I am the sun for I am made from the light of the sun. But, as we know, this statement is not fully correct. More appropriate is to say: the sun is Me, THAT is Me.

In Rumi's story, when he stood in front of the Gate to the chamber of God, God asked him 'who is there?' Rumi said: 'I.' 'There is no place for Two here,' God replied. In this moment Rumi understood his mistake and said: 'It is You!' In that moment, he was allowed to enter. It is a very profound story. There is a big difference between saying 'I am You' and 'You are Me.' In the first sentence, the relative subject says that it is itself the Absolute subject. In the second sentence, the relative subject admits that the Absolute Subject is its very light and existence. These are the two ways of expressing the realisation that 'there is no place here for Two.' One is, 'I am alone,' and the second is 'You are alone - You are the only reality.' The first solution is more Advaita and the second leans more towards Sufism. We find that Rumi was closer to the Truth. But there is something more here. Who was that one who was allowed to enter the Gate? If you can intuitively grasp it, you will understand the paradoxical truth beyond duality and beyond non-duality - the dual-non-duality. Yes, it is Me.

What is God-realisation without Soul-realisation? The light inside of the dewdrop has become aware of the sun but is not conscious of itself, it has not realised its existence inside of the dew drop. What does it mean? You see, the important issue to understand is - from which place does God realise herself? What is this place from which God becomes conscious of her existence as God? Isn't it from within the Soul's Heart? To realise the Soul is to realise that very vehicle through which the Beloved becomes conscious of her Divine Presence. For that reason, God-realisation without Soul-realisation is not complete. These two elements need to be present in order to have a complete experience. When the Soul is realised and God is realised, the Beloved recognises herself and this very Me from the heart of which she has recognised herself. Here, all polarities and aspects of God-realisation are included and embraced within the Total Knowingness of I AM.

God and the Soul

Student: *What is the relationship between the Self and the Soul?*

Aziz: Before we understand the connection between them, we need to know what is the Self and what is the Soul. What is the Self? It is God in truth. And what is the Soul? It is the individual expression of God. Their connection is based on the simple fact, that the Soul is created by God and she eventually discovers her Creator. It is a relationship between the mother and the child.

But what is their connection in term of the actual experience on the level of energy? When God is realised, the Soul is one with the Beloved, she is absorbed into God's Reality. But yet God is beyond the Soul. How can you experience that which is beyond you? You can experience a tree which is outside of you, seeing it through your eyes. You experience this universe through your senses. You see it, you taste it, you hear it, you touch it, you smell it... and you think about it. These are the ways you can discover the universe, which is relatively outside you. But how can you discover the Beyond of God? God is neither outside nor inside. God has no form and has no objectified existence. God is not visual, you cannot see her. Your senses are useless, as far as the discovery of God is concerned. Neither can you think about God; you cannot experience God through thinking or creating concepts. Your senses cannot touch God, your mind cannot grasp God. So how can Me experience God and through which channel does it take place?

The Soul can experience God through Being and through the Heart. These are the two gateways through which you can enter the reality of God. The experience of Being refers to the very fact that the Soul rests in the Beyond. Being is a very mysterious state. It is not a simple state, for in this state you encounter your own absence. You don't know what it is that you experience because it is beyond you - you cannot enter it through your mind. So there is no one to grasp this experience, even though there is someone to know the experience itself. Do you see the paradox? There is a limit to knowing but no limits to not-knowing. In Beingness, you can rest. You are unable to rest in yourself, for you get suffocated with your own energy. You can rest only in the Beyond. In order to sit comfortably, you need a chair. Similarly, you need something in your internal reality which you can let go into. That is the role of Beingness - it supports all living beings through its all-inclusive, all-embracing, limitless Presence.

Beingness is, however, not the whole of God. The other dimension of God is the Divine, which is the Heart of the Creator or the Beloved. The Divine is the dimension of Love, Beauty and infinite sensitivity into which you can enter through your own Heart. In your Heart you can experience God in two ways. Firstly, you can feel the Beloved, you can feel this tremendous beauty which is transparently present inside the depth of your Heart. Secondly, you meet the Beloved by becoming absorbed, that is, resting inside the Heart. We call it Being in the Heart. Here, the Heart and Being create one field of experience. This second way of meeting the Beloved inside the Heart can take place only when the Being quality is awakened. The deepest experience is when a full expansion of the Heart centre becomes one with the Absolute State. Here, the absolute sensitivity meets the absolute motionlessness.

Being in the Heart, in a true sense, and not in a sense as it is used in the common language, is a deeper experience than feeling the Heart. The reason is that when you feel your Heart, you feel your actual individuality and sense of separation. When you rest in the Heart, you become more absent, more absorbed in the dimension of the Beloved. You still exist, as the Soul, but in a very gentle and transparent way. What prevails is the Beloved.

However, the experience of a God-realised being is a mixture of pure rest in the Beyond and a feeling of a utmost sensitive and delicate transparency. The Beyond is the unity of the Absolute and the Divine. That is the true and complete Beyond. Sometimes we speak about the Self as the combination of pure awareness and Being. But, in truth, awareness is more a part of the Soul's identity in the mind. God is realised through Being and through the Heart.

So, the relationship between the Soul and the Self is one of unity and separation. As you rest in God, you are on the edge of dissolution, but still, you must live your life Here. You have to realise your blueprint within the created reality. You need to grow psychologically, express your creativity and adventure in life. You must live as a relatively independent and individual being, as you abide in the Heart of the Beloved. You, as the Soul relate to Creator and you also relate to her Creation of which you are a part. Your relation to Creator is one of surrender and prayer, one of love and humility; your relation to Creation is your creative participation and your ultimate transcendence. When you participate in the world, you are slightly on your own and you may often feel lost and lonely. It is like a child who playing with other children, suddenly feels lost and starts to cry, not knowing what to do or where to go. In this moment, the child remembers his mother and finds his way home. Similarly, the Soul experiencing the difficulties of living on earth, suddenly remembers where she has come from and tries to find her way back home, the home of God. Here, she begins to pray, she asks for help, for Grace, for consolation... she cries to the Beloved. It is another aspect of our relationship with God, that we, being at lost here, may cry to the Beloved. These tears are the deepest expression of the Soul's longing for her ultimate and only security, which is God. These tears wash our Heart, preparing us for the final communion with the Beloved.

So, there are two aspects of our relationship with God. One is more static, relating only to the energy expansion into the Beyond. The second one is more dynamic. Here, you are discovering God, meeting the Beloved, encountering the mystery of the Heart. The deepest, most profound aspect of God is the divine dimension; that's why it is in the Heart that we meet God in the closest and most meaningful way.

The Soul is this very Me inside you, the one who seeks for happiness and does everything to avoid suffering. It is the Soul who discovers God; it is the Soul who recognises the Beloved. The Soul exists in two ways: the Soul at rest, and the Soul in motion. When you rest in your Heart and in Being, with full presence, you meet your Soul directly. As you rest inside, it is almost impossible to separate your Soul from God because they simply represent two aspects of the same experience. As you rest inside, you rest in God, you merge with the Inner Vastness. You become One with the Beyond but at the same time you are not completely One. Why? For the simple reason that from time to time you recognise your own existence. Either you feel yourself or you create a self-referral in your mind. Or you may even become aware of your own physical body... you may become aware of the external reality. And the moment you are aware of anything, the sense of Me arises, as automatically attached to any act of consciousness. From time to time, you feel yourself in a human way. You may simply feel some sadness or feel tired. Who is feeling sad? Who is feeling tired? It is not God, certainly not... It is you, it is the Soul.

It is difficult to pinpoint what is the Soul, for she is so subtle... that's why, in some traditions, the Soul was negated. They couldn't distinguish between the experience of the Self, and that of the Soul. To see this difference, a new sensitivity and understanding must be awakened. The realisation of the Soul is equally subtle or even more subtle than God-realisation.

Student: *Can we find in other traditions the distinction between the Self and the Soul? Or only in the tradition of the Complete Meditation?*

Aziz: We represent not the tradition of Complete Meditation but the 'Tradition' of Guidance. Guidance is not tradition but beyond traditions. Guidance does not need the past in order to support its present understanding. Guidance knows all instantaneously and timelessly; Guidance never reveals the whole truth but responds to our level of evolution and our capacity. If you received the whole truth, it might destroy you! You can receive only that which you are capable of taking! You can listen only to that which you can hear. Our teaching is based on revelations from the dimension of Guidance. It can be seen as a quantum leap in the Understanding. A quantum leap here means that Understanding, which we present, is not just a result of the evolution of past knowledge. It has been manifested as a sudden shift, lightening from the Beyond, which enters our present limitation of understanding, allowing the New to be born.

We can find certain elements of this distinction, between the Self and the Soul, in Sufism. As Sufism is the Path of Love, naturally, it can more easily awaken the Soul. In Sufism, emphasis is not on liberation, as in Buddhism, but on the realisation of God. Do you see the difference? When you search for liberation, what matters is your own freedom. In a sense, you become very centred on yourself. But when you seek God, it is no longer you who matters so much, but the Divine. When you are in love with God, of course, you become clearly aware of the Soul. Only those who are in love experience the Soul! In Sufism, the Beloved and the lover are constantly playing their love affair. The lover and the Beloved become one, dissolving into each other. Sometimes the lover becomes the Beloved and other times the Beloved becomes the lover. Who is the Beloved? Who is the lover? No one knows... one who is drunk by this love affair cannot separate oneself from another! A true Sufi master is completely one with the Beloved on all levels, but at the same time, can cry and long for the Beloved and can be deeply sad and unhappy because of being still relatively separated and living in the dimension of forgetfulness. We can say that in Sufism there is more of the element of dual-non-duality.

Student: *Can we say that the eastern mystical schools speak more about the Self and middle eastern schools more about the Soul?*

Aziz: Eastern mysticism emphasises more the impersonal aspects of God while middle eastern religions more the personal aspect of God. In order to experience the impersonal aspect of God, one has to dissolve, one has to reach one's absence, so to speak. On the other hand, to experience the personal aspect of God, one has to be present, as the personal aspect of God is the very reflection of the Soul's personal existence. Many of the spiritual traditions which teach bhakti or devotion remain on the level of a personal experience of God, without being able to dive into God's impersonality. Impersonality is the deepest quality of God, for it represents the pure isness of the Ultimate. The experience of the impersonal aspect of the Creator cannot be reached through personal intelligence, which means it is not psychologically accessible.

The experience of impersonality takes place through energy expansion only. That which we call Enlightenment is nothing but an energy expansion. As we know, in order to reach the Ultimate, an expansion into Being must take place. But before we can possibly surrender vertically into Being, first we must transcend unconsciousness through crystallising attention. This element is strongly missing in most Bhakti Traditions. Concentrating only on the Heart, they bypass the basic work with awareness. This means that those adepts who follow the Bhakti Path cannot ever become fully present and conscious.

We can speak about the polarisation of human consciousness into Wisdom and Love. On the Path of devotion, love is present but wisdom and clarity are often strongly missing. In Buddhism, Advaita and similar systems of teaching, there is a lot of wisdom and clarity but often love and a certain innocence are missing. Because to really experience love, not universal love, not impersonal love, not compassion or loving kindness... but simply to love as a human, one has to acknowledge the child-like, vulnerable quality of the Soul.

In Sufism, there is the concept of getting drunk with the Divine. A beautiful concept, but many take it literary which can be very misleading. If you want to lose yourself in God, prior to becoming fully conscious, you simply become more unconscious than you were before. If I Am is not realised, the ecstasy which one may experience by repeating, for instance, the names of God, is an illusion in truth which is not grounded in the Self.

On the Path of Self-realisation, the stage of being drunk with the Divine takes place at the end only, when one is already energetically One with God. Here, one lets go of the last traces of mind and knowledge, forgetting oneself like a child in God. That is the true second childhood. To be drunk with the Divine is not to be in a trance state; neither is it to be in the state of pure consciousness... to be drunk with the Divine is beyond consciousness and beyond unconsciousness. Neither is it the

Absolute State because it refers rather to the quality of the mind of the Soul who abides in the Ultimate. It is the mind which gives itself up becoming like a child, returning to its original purity, innocence and humility. Here, one doesn't want to know anything, one drops even the concept of being enlightened, even the concept of being the Soul. Here, one is truly in love with the Beloved. One is drunk with the Beloved yet deeply calm, tranquil, silent, sensitive, ordinary, humble, alone, empty of all concepts... being one with this eternal, ancient yearning which itself is the very meeting with the mystery.

Student: *Can we imagine a Soul which is tabula raza, like a blank piece of paper who incarnates into a body?*

Aziz: The Soul is always tabula raza but because the blueprint becomes super-imposed on her, she is immediately coloured by her evolutionary predisposition. You see, for a Soul to incarnate in this dimension a structure is necessary. This structure is the collective human subconsciousness, a particular DNA and the unconscious memory of global evolution stored in the molecules of the body. As you live in this body, you carry the memory of the whole earth and your subconscious mind carries the evolutionary memory of all species. That's why, the Soul is both: always tabula raza, one with her eternal unchanging identity and never tabula raza, as she instantaneously becomes a part of the program which governs this dimension.

As the Soul evolves within this dimension, she transcends all her conditionings, masks and roles more and more, reaching again her original face, which is tabula raza. For what is the Soul in the beginning and at the end but the pure light of I AM? The Soul is made from I AM but because of the blueprint, she must perform the role of a separated being. She enters the human body and starts to use the human brain. This brain, though without personal memory in the beginning, has the capacity to manifest the whole of human consciousness. The moment the Soul incarnates she becomes a part of the collective and impersonal reality. The Soul is not yet personal. Only after many years, can she discover herself as truly subjective reality. She becomes free from objectiveness, waking up to her ancient identity.

Student: *Can the Soul transcend karma?*

Aziz: Karma is a part of the Soul's blueprint. Karma is the scenario of one's life, the basic rules through which this Leela functions. When we speak about transcending karma, we mean that the Soul discovers her existence as beyond the Here in her original purity. Karma as such cannot be eliminated, for it constitutes the functioning of the manifested reality. But when the Soul reaches her own light, karma no longer locks her in the dimension of forgetfulness. The personality is always there and personality is based on karmic elements, but the Soul different to the personality dwells in the Beyond.

Who is the Beloved?

Student: *Could you speak about the logo which you use?*

Aziz: This logo represents the unity of emptiness and the Divine. The circle which is painted with one movement of the brush, symbolises the original state, the formless ground of Existence, the Unborn. When we are looking for the source of Existence, the Source of Creation, we are coming closer and closer to a very mysterious dimension. To the dimension which is absolutely present but is not manifested. If something is not manifested, it cannot become an object of experience. Only that which is manifested, can be experienced. For instance, how can you see the light of a candle prior to lighting it? How can the Uncreated be experienced? How can this primordial existence of the source be recognised? How can we even speak about emptiness, if it is unmanifested?

Here, we are entering the mystery of awakening to the Uncreated. There is a stage of realisation which the Buddha experienced and later called reaching Nirvana. At this stage, consciousness merges with that which is prior to consciousness. The experience of it is like entering a deep sleep state while remaining fully present. Here, one is fully present and fully absent. There is no movement in that state, only absolute stillness exists. The absolute stillness is the presence of the Uncreated. And the presence of the Uncreated is the absence of consciousness. The meeting between these two is called the Absolute State. The ultimate experience is of non-abidance. When you are caught into the dream of phenomenal reality, you are always abiding in something. Your body rests on the floor, the floor rests upon the earth, and so forth. There is always a point of reference. To move beyond any point of reference is to live in emptiness. To rest upon nothing is perhaps the most amazing experience that a human being can have.

But the emptiness is not empty for it contains infinite intelligence and love. That is the meaning of the Heart inside the circle. The Divine is the Heart of God. The Divine is the Meaning of emptiness. The meaning of the Absolute is to support, to contain the Divine dimension. For the Divine needs a place for her ultimate abidance, which is the pure isness of the Absolute Rest.

Where is God?

Student: *Where is God? How can I reach God?*

Aziz: God is Here and Now! You are looking for God but where do you exist? Don't you see that you exist in God? There is only God? It is like a fish seeking the Ocean! You are inside the Ocean of the Divine. Just make yourself at home! The reason that you are not seeing God is not her absence, but your absence! You are not yet present to your Soul's existence. You are fast asleep. God is in your Heart. Look into your Heart, tune in, become completely silent and Feel! Feel the Reality, which is already present.

Student: *How to reconcile the existence of evil and the presence of God?*

Aziz: It is already reconciled for it is Reality!

The Presence of Grace

Grace does not enter at random. It is the law that Higher Intelligence supports the lower forms of consciousness. That which links the Soul with Universal Intelligence is the Over-soul. The Over-soul is always ready to bring about all the elements necessary for our Awakening. But even the Over-soul needs to respect the laws of nature, the blueprint of the Soul and her readiness for awakening. Grace is simply the response of Guidance to the intensity, sincerity and purity of intention in the Heart of the Soul. When the Soul has done all that is possible within her limitations in order to awaken - Grace can enter. Grace enters like lightening bringing transformation and changing the structure of her apparent destiny.

To Know that Light Exists is Called Grace...

Student: *What is Grace?*

Aziz: When you incarnate into a body, you enter the realm of darkness, ignorance, forgetfulness and unconsciousness. Whether you are aware of it or not, you are very helpless and miserable as a Soul. Living in the prison of ignorance, you try to suffer as little as possible, you try to make your cell comfortable and pass the time in the most comforting way. At times, you may even believe that you are having a fulfilling time. In truth, the less conscious you are, the more you will enjoy this prison. The more aware you become, the more you rebel against this basic limitation, which is the state of forgetfulness. But even though you may rebel, you still have no way to get out of the cell; you have no way towards the light; no way to escape the darkness of ignorance. But your questioning, your search and inquiry allow you to awaken the ancient longing for Truth. You become mature and develop sincerity in your Heart. In your striving for light and truth, you become a Soul while preparing for the ultimate meeting with the divine... and at a certain stage Light enters.

When you receive confirmation from a master - that there exists a dimension of pure love and understanding, we call it Grace.

To know that such a dimension exists for a human being is called Grace. Being locked in your prison, so often you simply lose the hope that there is a way out. You stop believing that there exists a world where the sun is shining and where people are free. All that you encounter and experience in this dimension is against such a belief.

Most people give up. They trust more the power of darkness and ignorance than the presence of light. 'Where is light?' they say. 'Life is hard, you need to survive, get a job so that in your old age you will have some support.' That is how they live, like frightened children locked in a dark room. That is the fate of most people - life without light, without hope, without love, without silence, without God. There is no dignity in such a life- no beauty, no adventure, no joy.

To be shown that light exists, is Grace. To know that true happiness and fulfilment is your destiny and that you deserve it because you are the child of God, is Grace. Grace is always present, but it enters unexpectedly. It enters when you have proven that you are ready to receive it, in your Heart and in your intelligence. As you connect with light more and more, you begin to see how Grace operates. The further you are in evolution, the stronger Grace operates. When you reach the state of unity with the Ultimate, you see the presence of Universal Intelligence in every step that you take.

Grace is the connection of the Soul with the Over-soul, her divine parent. When the Soul is immersed in ignorance, the separation between her and the Over-soul is very strong because the Soul is simply disconnected from her origin as well as from her purpose. As she evolves, this connection becomes closer and closer and the presence of Grace becomes much stronger. Grace is the way the Beloved reaches the Soul and leads her evolutionary journey in time. Grace means that you are being helped on many levels, from your everyday life to your spiritual expansion. This help cannot be explained or predicted; it transcends the power of nature. When you reach deeper and deeper levels of Self-realisation, you come closer to the very source of Grace which is the Beloved. A fully Self-realised Being is one with the source of Grace. He or she can become a channel for this Grace, through which Grace can reach others on the Path.

Intuition is a Part of Guidance

Student: *Can you speak about intuition? Is there a connection between intuition and Guidance?*

Aziz: Intuition is the subtle sense of knowing beyond the logical mind. The logical mind is very important but quite dense as far as certain areas of life are concerned. Intuition does not contradict the mind but allows it to reach a more subtle understanding than pure reason. Intuition can be seen as a combination of feeling from the Heart and subtle insights from the mind.

Intuition is the ability to be in tune with the information of existence. It is to feel what is happening in the moment; it is to feel your next step; it is to feel the truth behind masks; it is to be able to feel your purpose in life. Intuition is to be in tune with what is right for you; it is to be able to make the right choices.

Intuition is a certain sense of knowingness which is a combination of intelligence and the wisdom of the Heart. Intuition is also connected to your knowledge, to what you have learnt in the past. Intuition does not arise in the blank mind but must be supported by your maturity. When you have many experiences in life, many experiments with your intuition, your maturity grows and your intuition becomes aligned with your wisdom as well.

Intuition and Guidance are interconnected. Guidance can be seen as a Higher Intuition. However, not all intuition represents Guidance itself. Intuition can operate within the frontiers of personal consciousness, without a connection to Higher Intelligence. Guidance is like a quantum leap of intuitive insight. Intuition can also be seen as our ability to tune in, within our limited capacities to the Universal Intelligence. Guidance knows all but how much we can receive reflects our maturity, intellectual capacity, sincerity of Heart, blueprint and timing.

Student: *And what is the difference between intuition and Guidance? Does intuition come from within and Guidance from without?*

Aziz: Essentially, there is no difference. However, intuition is more experienced within the personal or individual creativity of the Soul, while Guidance represents a more transcendental element, an information which descends from the higher source.

You have a certain capacity within your individual system of energy and consciousness which is limited by your destiny as a human. Within your relatively independent and separated system, you use the creativity of your intelligence and your free will. In the process of making decisions, you use your individual resources, your personal mind and intuition. You have no choice but to operate within your limitations. But Guidance enters from beyond your individual resources. Guidance represents the super knowledge of the Over-soul. You would never access this knowledge using only your personal intuition. The revelation of this knowledge is the function of Grace and Grace only. Guidance enters neither from within nor from without. Guidance enters from the Now. Guidance is neither in nor out. Guidance neither comes from within nor from without. Guidance simply Is.

Student: *Are you a part of Grace?*

Aziz: Certainly, any being who shows you the way out of the state of suffering, who directs you to Light, is a part of Grace.

What is Guidance?

Student: *Can you speak about Guidance?*

Aziz: Guidance is a mysterious force; it is a dimension of intelligence and love, linked with the Soul's evolution. Guidance cannot be understood. It is an expression of the intelligence of God. It is that which allows you to experience your connection with God in a personal way, in terms of help and guidance.

Another way to see it is as a deeper part of yourself, who knows your future and your past and takes care of you in a mysterious way. It can also be seen as the presence of the Over-soul, which is the parent of the Soul. The Over-soul controls the evolution of the Soul, bringing the right elements and Grace as necessary.

Even though Guidance is constant, it does not always occur with full strength. On some level the Soul is left alone, as a part of human destiny. One has to grow and learn within one's own reality. But in certain moments Grace enters, for one cannot reach complete transformation alone. Evolving individually, making all efforts possible, you will reach the point where you become ready to receive Grace. You cannot receive this Grace until you have made enough effort and have suffered enough. That is the rule, the law - that your suffering and your effort make you available to Grace. This is because the Soul, in order to receive Grace, has to have a certain essential quality in the Heart to be able to appreciate this gift of transformation. There has to be a certain sincerity of the Heart. If the Soul is not sincere, Grace does not enter. In such a situation, Grace enters in different way, creating life circumstances where the Soul can grow towards sincerity and true clarity. In the beginning of the Soul's evolution, she is not aware of Guidance; Guidance enters in a secret way. In due time, the Soul is able to tune more into the presence of Guidance. At the final stage of evolution, the Soul becomes one with Guidance.

Grace and Surrender

Student: *What is the relationship between Grace and Surrender?*

Aziz: What is Grace? Grace simply represents the presence of the Higher Intelligence and Love, which takes care of the Soul's evolution. Because we don't know what is happening, we call it Grace. We have received a gift of transformation, not knowing from which dimension and we interpret it as something extraordinary. But Grace represents the basic universal principle that the Higher Intelligence supports lower forms of intelligence. The Over-Soul governs the evolution of the Soul and leads her to the completion of her blueprint.

And what is surrender? It is not just an emotional act. To surrender is to surrender to your evolution and realisation of the blueprint. To surrender is to do what is necessary. For example, to surrender is to stabilise the State of Presence. To surrender is to be disciplined and to meditate everyday, to be constantly present. To surrender is not to forget oneself and to give up forgetfulness. When you surrender to your evolution, Grace immediately enters and you receive tremendous help.

From the other side, if you don't surrender to your evolution, serving the inertia of ignorance and unconsciousness, getting stuck in the collective mind - you are left alone, for some time. You are left alone until you get fed up with the prison of ignorance, until the longing for light and true life becomes awakened in your Heart. At a later stage, you again receive the chance to surrender to the precious Path. Grace is the response to your surrender. And surrender is an expression of your free choice and a manifestation of your responsibility for awakening.

The meaning of being a Soul is that you awaken yourself from inside. You are no longer merely evolving collectively. You have the freedom of creativity. You co-create your evolution, together with Universal Intelligence. You awaken from within your intelligence and Heart. It is because of your co-operation that your intelligence can grow, to prepare itself for the ultimate encounter with God. If Enlightenment was just given to you, without you striving to reach it - it would not be a real meeting. You are in a process of meeting the Ultimate. The real meeting comes from the space of this burning desire of the Soul which does everything to return to her eternal home of the Beloved.

Your suffering, your difficulties, your doubts... all these elements allow you to grow. They allow you to reach clarity, to deepen your sensitivity and to awaken true sincerity; these are the major characteristics of the Soul. Afterwards, when you reach awakening, the meeting with the light and love of the Creator has real significance. It is the true meeting of the Soul with the Beloved. It is more than becoming enlightened - it is a meeting, the Supreme Meeting.

Receiving Guidance

Student: *Could you speak about receiving guidance?*

Aziz: You can see it like that. You are relatively separated, you have a relatively separated mind, you have a relatively separated stream of consciousness, separated memories and a separated life story. In this field of relative separation, you are trying to find your way through, using your individual potential. You are growing within your intelligence, attempting to understand life and your role in it. But even though you are using your individual mind, this mind cannot be taken out of the universal context. You cannot separate your mind from the rest of humanity. Your mind is partially autonomous but it is contained within Universal Intelligence.

You are asking a question and you receive guidance. Don't you? Where is Guidance? It is already operating. Isn't it? Guidance is always present but because you are locked in your personal mind, you are unable to register it. There are different sources of inspiration and not all of them represent pure Guidance. Not all inspiration comes from the place of truth. To find the right guidance is the challenge of evolution. The Soul needs the right type of information in order to become attuned to her evolutionary blueprint.

From the other side, your search for Guidance allows your intelligence to grow and your Soul to mature. For instance, you explore various teachings, various schools of Enlightenment and you meet different masters. Which one of them represents pure Guidance? You are checking them out, exploring, learning and discovering the right elements. What information do you truly need for your awakening? Which teaching can bring about wholeness? What do you want?

What type of guidance you receive reflects the state of your evolution and the sincerity of your Heart. You are not necessarily ready to receive the whole truth. That's why most Souls do not receive complete Guidance. They receive only fragments and different pieces of truth. The Soul explores different possibilities, encountering difficulties and challenges. It is all a process of the maturation of intelligence. Intelligence evolves from the inside, making an effort to understand within its own capacity. And on the other hand, it receives Guidance and inspiration from the Beyond.

Guidance is a dynamic phenomenon. It is occurring all the time. There is not even one moment when Guidance is not present, but the depth of the revelation which reaches you depends on your own readiness.

Student: *And what do I do in the time of complete darkness?*

Aziz: The time of darkness when you feel completely lost is very important, for it helps you to grow. When you experience an impasse, in utter confusion you begin to question your reality and open yourself to new possibilities. In such moments, you come closer to your Soul. Some suffering deepens you and triggers your awakening. You are learning about being human. Someone who has not suffered cannot understand suffering. Someone who was not ignorant, cannot understand ignorance.

Sometimes the time of darkness is a time of suspension. There are some moments in evolution where nothing moves - moments of stagnation. There are different times in life, which relate to many elements - like the position of planets, karma and blueprint. When you experience difficult times in life, just know that there are often reasons beyond your personal control. Be patient and trust that there is a higher force which will bring the necessary elements into life. Your responsibility is to stay with the light of I Am. That is your highest freedom as a human being.

Student: *In these times, is it possible to do anything?*

Aziz: Absolutely! First you accept the whole experience, as it represents the truth of your present reality. Next, you connect to that one who is in darkness, but is itself pure light. You can on some level transcend darkness by discovering the one who is in darkness.

Do not struggle, but fully accept the situation. It is as if you are in deep waters, the situation may feel helpless and you fall into despair. But you must simply relax and calm down. Otherwise, you will quickly drown. The moment you accept, you are already on some level out of the situation. When you accept, you simply drop into Being. True acceptance is not an attitude from the mind but a Surrender into Being. In this way, you come closer to yourself, to the one who experiences confusion. To be still and unmoved inside is the key. In this way, you come back to this very centre which is beyond the coming and going of appearances. That is Freedom.

The entrance to the dimension of freedom is in this very sense of 'I.' When you come back to your Real Me, you discover freedom which cannot be touched. And simultaneously you make this amazing discovery that your Me is contained in the space of the infinite ME, the universal presence of God.

Gratitude of the Soul

Student: *Can you speak about gratitude and the Divine?*

Aziz: Gratitude can only come from the Heart and Soul. When the Soul is touched by the Divine, she feels infinite gratitude. When the Soul experiences Grace, she becomes deeply moved by this help. The Soul lives in this difficult dimension of constant struggle for survival and security. Therefore, for a Soul to even know that there is a plane of love and beauty is itself Grace. It is the contrast of darkness and light, suffering and freedom which allows the Soul to experience gratitude. Appreciation needs the presence of opposites.

The World of Creation

Here is the Creation: the blossoming of God, the infinite dance of life, the mystery of time, the cosmic vision in which the Beloved can reflect her formless face. This Magnificent Vision arises in the timeless space of the Now, creating the past and future with all dreams and possibilities included. It has no beginning and no end; neither can it be captured as the present moment. The Creation has never happened for only the Now exists, but still it is doubtlessly present. Observe all that is happening Now: the Sun is rising in the middle of the night... how beautiful! Look: the mountain is covered with white snow, the stream is flowing abruptly through the deep valley, and a bird is singing...

What is the Question?

Student: *What is the question? What is the matrix from which the apparent reality is created?*

Aziz: What is the question is the question! From where does the question arise? How is it possible to have a question? When you ask about the matrix, your question questions the very program and design through which this reality functions. You are inside this program. You are a part of this program. Your mind which is the only tool with which you can question this program, is itself a part of this program. In all, this divine design is the program of our existence.

We can however, program ourselves in a virtual way. That is the meaning of being conditioned by the collective consciousness. They program you to become a living social-robot, deprived of the Soul and with an empty hole in the place where your Heart should be located. Morality is a justification for the absence of the Heart, so one is not burdened with a guilty conscience. This is how the ego is able to replace the Soul. There are many programs and this includes the divine program which represents your Soul's blueprint and evolution. However, all programs are contained in the Beyond Program Dimension. As you are inside the system so you are out of it as well. In truth you can be inside only because you are outside of it! To be inside Existence is itself the Question, and the Answer is to move outside of Existence. The Question is your presence and the Answer is your absence. Most people do not question their existence, but in actuality they are the Question!

The ultimate question, the question impossible which is very much possible is: how to get out of Here, while remaining Here? How to experience one's absence while being present? How to transcend? You can find the answer through the insight that you are fundamentally not Here, as you are founded upon your own absence. This part of you which is beyond the system, beyond the matrix, is the real world of the noumenal reality, pure isness, the original condition of God. The goose is out! The goose is locked inside the bottle. How can it get out without destroying the bottle? The bottle must be saved for we grow up inside of it and we have to let others incubate inside it too! But how to get out of it? You are already out! Being inside the bottle, is the Question - being out of it is the Answer!

Free Will and Destiny

Student: *Can you speak about free will and destiny?*

Aziz: Free will represents the creativity of the Soul. A certain amount of energy and intelligence has been given to each Soul so that the Soul can perform some relatively independent activity. Free will is never absolute; it is relative, as it operates within the boundaries and frontiers of your unique blueprint and destiny. Destiny and free will co-exist. Free will is contained within destiny. It is a free movement within the determination of destiny. Free will is a certain choice of the Soul, as far as reaching her destiny is concerned. Destiny cannot be avoided but can be accelerated or postponed. The Soul will keep incarnating until she attains her blueprint. When you follow your higher nature, you help your evolution; when you follow your lower nature, you hinder it. To delay your evolution is to prolong your suffering. You are free to choose Freedom!

Student: *And how do you know when you are complete?*

Aziz: You don't know this until you are complete, but you know when you are completing yourself. You can clearly see changes and how the positive experience of yourself and reality increase. When you are complete, you recognise it by the absence of lack, as well as through the feeling of being done with this dimension.

As you grow, you become more aligned with your evolution. Usually, you know only the next step in your evolution but that is enough. The completion will present itself at the right time. And it is not only the goal of completion which matters but the journey to it as well! Each step on the path brings you closer to your divinity. Each step on the path represents the joy of Awakening.

To be Sick is to be Separated

Student: *What do you think about disease?*

Aziz: Well, illness as such is a very profound information, because it helps you to see clearly that this reality is essentially imperfect. It is not a safe place to be. Disease and the other infinite problems of this dimension help you to transcend the hobby of living in this gross material universe. Otherwise, the Soul would be too content, snoring in the comfort of unconscious dreams, living in ignorance.

You see, you may have many New Age concepts about different causes of becoming ill; you may believe in life without disease, but in truth, disease is simply an indivisible part of this particular design of life. Disease means not to be at ease with the fact of living in the dimension of time. The primal disease, that is disease, is the separation from the Source of Creation. Isn't it? And in our work here we treat this disease! The medicine against this disease is the very expansion into the I AM. The initial disease with the virus of which we are born - is the very forgetfulness of our origin.

Student: *Why are we separated from the source?*

Aziz: To return back to it.

Student: *Why do we need to be separated in the first place?*

Aziz: Because when there is Oneness alone, there is no experience. You see, there are two extreme situations. The first is when you are fully one with the Source. There is no experience, for the very simple reason that you don't exist. The second is when you are completely separated, disconnected from the Beloved. Here you live in a hell - the arrogant and ridiculous world of the ego, in the cage of the mind. These are the two extremes.

As you enter the Spiritual Path in a true sense, the process of meeting with the Ultimate begins. In the end, you become only One, that is, you get dissolved. Your purpose as a spiritual being is to reach the point of your evolution where you are almost dissolved. This very 'almost' allows you to give feedback to the Ultimate, that is to recognise it! In this way, you experience unity while still being slightly separated.

God is unable to recognise herself, for she is not separated from her pure Divine Isness. God needs Me to become recognised. You are a tool through which God can meet herself in a conscious way! That's why your existence is precious.

Student: *Are we the expression of the Source?*

Aziz: We are the Source's expression and we are a response or feedback to the Source. We are this type of God's creation which can become conscious of its own origin! God is meeting herself through your Me. The purpose of evolution is this very meeting, the joy of coming back home. You are separated in order to experience unity and you can experience unity only because you are separated. Unity and separation relate to the existence of Me. Without Me, even unity is absent. When the Soul meets the Beloved what remains is neither One nor Two, neither Dvaita nor Advaita. We call it the dual-non-duality. There is the Soul but also unity; there is unity, but also the Soul. It is the Soul who knows unity. What is the Soul? It is the pure feeling of Me which knows herself directly as Me. Me is a channel through which consciousness becomes conscious...through which the Beloved becomes the lover!

Individuality and Oneness

Student: *Can you explain how individuality and Oneness relate to each other?*

Aziz: In a very simple way: Oneness is experienced through an individual and individuality is a manifestation of Oneness. But when individuality is locked in its individuality, which is the ego-world, Oneness is no longer experienced, it is overlooked. In order to realise Oneness, individuality has to surrender itself into the universality; and to surrender is to experience on some level, one's absence. In order to fall asleep, for instance, you must experience the absence of the conscious Me. However, you can experience your absence only because you are present. If you are just absent there is no experience. In deep dreamless sleep your absence cannot be recognised, for there is no Me. In the experience of Oneness, that which is present is the Soul and some traces of the ego. In this way, one experiences one's sense of identity as unified with the Beyond. One rests within the Totality, simultaneously being present to oneself as an individual. In this meeting, between individuality and impersonality, a new quality is born which contains elements of both. The universal pure isness is mirrored by the presence of Me and this Me feels herself as well.

After the Death

Student: *After the body dies, what remains from the mind? Will it all disappear?*

Aziz: You still have some time to worry about that (laughter...). Yes... everything disappears and what remains, retained in the Universal Mind is the continuation of evolution which later on takes another form. This continuation of evolution is beyond personal memory and mind but it includes certain characteristics from your emotional and mental bodies. You evolve within the spiritual body of I Am, within your emotional body and your intelligence. The emotional body has no conscious memories but there is a continuation of its evolution. Intelligence does not remember its past steps but has continuity as well. It may be difficult for you to understand that intelligence can have continuity without self-conscious memory. It is like this: intelligence is the capacity of consciousness to reflect reality and the complexity of reality in the form of understanding. On the other hand, pure awareness in itself is unable to understand, but like a mirror reflects reality in the space of not-knowing. Intelligence does not just reflect, but it also understands. The ability to reflect understanding is beyond memory, even though intelligence needs to use its faculties related to memory and knowledge.

Similarly, you may not remember being Awakened in your past life but on the energy level it is remembered. And you recollect it through inquiry and practice. Because it has been already realised, in this lifetime it comes back quite easily. But do not worry about these matters too much, for no one has ever understood them completely. Just know that there is a continuation of evolution and it is beyond the personality. You cannot grasp this continuation, for it occurs below the conscious level, but it is present on the level of the Heart, intelligence and the emotional and spiritual bodies.

Student: *Does the conscious mind dissolve immediately after death?*

Aziz: Almost immediately, like a picture on the screen of the T.V. when the electricity is cut off. You simply cannot hold it; it dissolves and disperses into the original ether.

Student: *So the belief in bardo states like in the Tibetan book of death is not correct?*

Aziz: This belief is incorrect. Human consciousness can exist only in the body. Consciousness can exist without the body but not human consciousness. Even when your Soul will choose to incarnate into a formless realm, she will continue her evolution but not as a human being. She will simply participate in a different type of consciousness; a different type of intelligence and sensitivity.

You see, what does it mean to be human? To be human is to have a particular and unique type of sensitivity, a certain type of emotional body and intelligence, and for these to be embodied in a physical form. Can you see how having your physical body determines your consciousness? Your experience of yourself is absolutely linked to having a body, to your physiology, hormones... and so forth. How you can locate yourself in a certain place in space is also determined by your body as your main point of reference... do you see how your form affects your perception of reality?

A human without a body is not a human. If you meet a psychic who tells you that he or she sees your grandmother above your right shoulder, do not believe this! It is sheer imagination, a product of collective superstitions. These concepts are created out of fear and out of hope (which is not hopeful at all but completely hopeless). It is rather a nightmare... and people even get haunted by these false ideas. Let them go.

Is Reality Subjective?

Student: *Can you speak about the difference between the absolute and relative subjectivity? In your book, you made this distinction.*

Aziz: The Absolute Subjectivity is God or universal I AM. The relative subjectivity is Me or the Soul. Initially, they thought that to become enlightened is to eliminate the 'illusion' of relative subjectivity and become the Absolute Subjectivity. That is why, they assumed that the Buddha should know everything and be omnipotent, for he is united with the One Mind. This was however a logical mistake, an illusion of the mind. An enlightened being is one with the Absolute Subjectivity but does not become Absolute Subjectivity. The Soul on the energy level is in a state of unity but she herself continues to live within her limited (by her blueprint) separate existence. The true vision of Oneness includes duality, for Oneness without the dual perceiver of it turns blank.

Absolute Subjectivity contains in itself the whole of Creation. And that which links the Absolute Subjectivity with its Creation is Divine Intelligence, the spirit which runs through everything. From the higher perspective, Creation is itself absolutely subjective for it is the manifested energy of the Absolute Subjectivity. Within Absolute Subjectivity are present the numberless angles of perception, that is, relative subjective realities. That is the mystery of Creation. The universal 'I' manifests an individual 'I' and this individual relates to the rest of Creation from its own perspective, as well as relating to the Source of Creation! Can you see how amazing it is? The mind cannot contain it, only silence can; this vision truly leaves us in a state of awe... There is not a definite objective universe, for it is composed of an infinite number of differing angles of perception.

Next, not only does the individual I exist within the totality of Absolute Subjectivity, but it evolves within it as well; and, paradoxically, this 'I' can be ignorant of its origin. See, most live in the middle of this Creation without awareness of the very ground in which they exist. It is the mystery of ignorance that, living in the ocean of God, one can forget God. Like a fish, swimming in the ocean forgets the ocean. However, here the situation is less simplistic for the individual subject must develop special faculties to experience God in a real and meaningful way. That is the function of evolution.

Student: *You say that there is no objective universe. How can we understand it?*

Aziz: It is not objective, in the sense that the perceived perceives you and creates your perception! Not only are you looking at the chair, for example, the chair creates your perception, it 'jumps,' into your eyes... this chair cannot be separated from the sun which, suddenly, blinds your eyes and shines a red flame over the whole picture. So, what is objective?

To explain it better, we will say it like this. What does it mean to be 'objective'? It means that all angles of perception, all I's perceive this universe in the same way. And it is not true, for everyone experiences a different universe. That which allows us to meet here and communicate with each other is this approximately objective universe. It means that there is some common ground for our meeting. Your universe and our universe are similar enough that we can meet. Still, we don't meet on all levels. We meet on these levels only which our similarity allows us to. For instance, above your head there are other beings which you don't see! Why? Because your perception of reality is not synchronised sufficiently with theirs. But they see you because they have a higher perspective. Here, we have a situation that some elements of Creation are not a conscious part of your universe, but you are a part of their conscious reality. It is all quite complex. It is a multidimensional dance of infinite angles of perception, which affect each other in many ways, co-creating the life of Creation. It is life - a process and not a fixed thing. The Buddha discovered that nothing is fixed; life is a flow, an inter-penetration of infinite elements.

We live in an approximately objective universe. It is not at all a subjective reality in the sense that the world is relative to a particular 'I.' This is the mistake of 'subjective idealism.' This universe is alive; it creates you and you respond to it from your perspective; this is co-creation.

If this universe is objective, it is only for God. In order to say that Creation is objective, you would have to find 'an ultimate angle of perception' which contains all other angles of perception. You would have to find a Me which contains all other Me's and, at the same time, does not affect their reality through her own presence and perception. Do you see this? This is what physics discovered, that the moment we observe an atom, for example, we change its quality for perception is itself an energy which affects the reality of the perceived! The perceiver affects the perceived and the perceived affects the perceiver. And they are both affected by numberless elements of Total Existence. It is truly amazing.

This Creation is only objective from the perspective of Absolute Subjectivity for the Beloved abides beyond her Creation. In order to see an objective universe, one has to be outside of it and that is not possible for any existing being. For Absolute Subjectivity, Creation is absolutely objective because she contains the totality of Existence with all elements included. It is possible for God because God does not 'perceive' Creation. God is the very total life of Creation, mysteriously penetrating all elements and not being limited by any of them.

Let us conclude in a few sentences. We live in the approximately objective universe. This universe is absolutely objective only from the perspective (or rather non-perspective) of Absolute Subjectivity. That which allows us to share this world is similar perception of the same approximately objective universe. The universe is not a 'thing,' but a co-creation of a multitude of infinite subjective realities. The perceiver and perceived are not separated, but rather represent two polarised aspects of the same reality. The perceiver encounters an alive universe, by which he is created and embraced. On the other hand, the perceiver affects Creation by the force of his presence and unique perception.

How deeply we share this Creation relates to that how deeply we meet Here. When we meet only through the body and mind, this meeting is very shallow. When we meet in the space of inner silence, love and understanding, we meet truly. In such a case, we can say that within the approximately objective universe, we have met in a most objective way, sharing the universal quality of Truth. Love, silence, intelligence and Being are the most objective qualities of this reality, for they link us directly with the Absolute Subjectivity, which is the Light of Creation.

Student: *Can the Buddha see reality in an objective way?*

Aziz: An awakened being is not seeing this reality in an absolutely objective way, for the seer is still relative. The Buddha reaches the optimum of his or her objective perception. An awakened being is rooted in the dimension beyond the perceiver, the perceived and the perception; he abides in the dimension of pure isness, which is the very presence of God.

Leela is a Serious Joke!

Student: *Is Leela a drama to be acted and enjoyed or should we take it seriously?*

Aziz: Life is a serious joke! Your attitude toward Leela is a part of this Leela. When you are supposed to enjoy it, you enjoy it; when you are supposed to play, you play; when you are supposed to be serious, you become serious; when you are supposed to suffer, you suffer.

If the ego is the actor, you are separated from the drama of life for you are too self-conscious as the ego-image. But when the Soul is the actor, your life is total. Here, you are not watching yourself acting - you are your role!

Don't take life too seriously but take it seriously enough. There is enough suffering in the world to take it rather seriously. Seriousness is a part of compassion. But if you lose the sense of humour, the openness of life contracts and your Soul becomes as heavy as an elephant! A Tibetan master, Trungpa defined the sense of humour as having a gentle touch, as being soft in connecting to the earth. This type of lightness is very important. True gentleness is beyond both seriousness and superficial celebration. Be relaxed and sensitive in your meeting with the earth. Do not make a joke out of life, but do not be too serious about it either. Be just serious enough! Play, adventure, see different countries, meet different lovers, swim in the sea, dance in the sun, but also be serious and responsible for your life, for you are here to become a divine being and to meet God.

It is within Leela that one meets the Creator of this Leela. This meeting is beyond Leela; it takes place in the dimension where nothing changes and where love alone is, God is.

What is Time?

Student: *What is time?*

Aziz: Time is a distance from the Now to the Now, the movement of becoming within the Now. The Here is the content of the Now and time is the process through which the Here arises in consciousness. Pure Now is prior to consciousness. In order for consciousness to exist, there has to be duality, the split between subject and object. Recognition always refers to the past, because consciousness needs distance from the experienced. In order to see your face in the mirror, you need to take a step back. Don't you? Similarly, distance is required for consciousness in order to be aware of itself. Space is the physical distance and time is the psychological distance or distance within consciousness. Here are just different ways of looking at the same phenomenon.

The outer, physical space is simply a certain model designed for the material universe. If you close your eyes and use the eye of imagination, you will experience a psychological version of the physical space. You will see colours, spaces, skies, trees and mountains... To experience space, the observer has to be located either in this very space or outside of it.

There exists also a space without object, like the space of I Am. I Am is an energy experience beyond perception. However, the very fact that it is an experience indicates that some type of space and time are involved. Time allows you to recognise this experience, for it occurs in the immediate past; and the space of I Am allows you to abide within this very experience. See, there is no experience right Now! Any and all experiences take place in the past. The experience of I Am, unlike other experiences, is simply as close as possible to the Now. The Absolute State is pure Now, but the ability to know that one is in the Absolute requires some distance in time - it simply occurs in a split second. The Absolute State is the meeting of the time dimension with the Timeless - as close as one can get to the Timeless. Any closer you get - you dissolve and only pure Now remains, but without recognition.

To conclude - the Here is the environment of space, and time is the movement of the Here, the re-appearing of the Here in consciousness. The question whether there is an end to time or to space, cannot arise in truth. Why? Because time and its perception are the same and, since there are no limits to perception, there are also no limits to time. Perception is Creation and Creation is Perception. Time arises from the Timeless entwined with the concept of its past and future. You can see this Creation as the imagination of God. Because God can imagine anything, everything is possible and has only relative existence.

The River is Still, the Mountain is Flowing

Student: *How do time and the Timeless co-exist? Is the movement of time just an illusion?*

Aziz: What is Now? What is This Moment? This Moment is the dimension where you meet the truth of Existence. In this moment, right Now, Existence presents itself to you, to your very Me. But from where does this knowing arise? The closer you come to the Now, the deeper you enter a very mysterious realm in which time does not exist - the Timeless Dimension. You are unable to grasp it with your mind, but you can directly taste its eternal flavour. Your very Presence is the essence of This Moment. Before you can experience anything, this Presence is already there. This Presence is neither of time nor of the Timeless, but acts as a bridge between these two polarised dimensions. This Presence represents the primordial knowing through which the Timeless becomes time. It is the primal polarisation within the womb of the Timeless, where the original absence of recognition gives birth to the presence of knowingness.

This moment is where you exist. You arise from the Now. But all that which you experience is time...it is already the horizontal dimension. To come closer to the Now is to shrink the experience of time. You become absorbed into that which is immediate, so fast that it cannot be registered through consciousness. That which is the fastest in Existence is the Now - it is faster than time! The moment you reach the Timeless, you disappear. There is no more you, no more Presence, no more knowing.

However, there is a dimension of realisation where the time and the Timeless can meet, where consciousness meets the Absolute, where Presence meets its absence without ceasing to be present. We speak about the realisation of the Absolute State. It is a very mysterious expansion. Here, knowing meets not-knowing; the movement of time meets the motionlessness of the Now; the Pure Rest becomes manifested.

You can see realisation of pure awareness as awakening to the essence of This Moment within time and realisation of the Absolute State as awakening to the essence of This Moment within the Timeless. As you know, the Timeless is realised through Being and the essence of time (State of Presence) is reached through Awareness. Time and the Timeless are One as two sides of Reality.

Time cannot exist without its source and the Timeless cannot be recognised without time.

To demonstrate this, we would like to present a beautiful Zen koan: 'The river is still and the mountain is flowing.' How is it possible? According to our common sense, it is the mountain which is still and it is the river which is flowing. But from the Awakened Perspective, from the depth of Reality, it is just the opposite which is true - the river is still and the mountain is flowing. The river is still for it is absolutely contained in the eternal space of the Now. There is just the Now and nothing is changing, nothing is moving within the Now. The apparent movement of the river occurs upon the motionless background of the Timeless. It is like in the cinema. The pictures are moving but the screen is oblivious of this movement, retaining its complete stillness.

But how is it that the mountain is flowing? How is it possible? Our first illusion was the belief that the river was moving. Our next illusion is that the mountain is still. Yes, the mountain is relatively still but only in space. Even in space, it is only relatively still, from our earthly standpoint, for as we know the whole planet is moving like and arrow with an enormous velocity through the galaxy. The mountain is relatively still in space but is moving in time. It is arising moment by moment from the Now into the Hereness. This Moment is being eternally re-created in the river of time, manifesting the environment of the apparent reality.

The river is not flowing and the mountain is not still. The Now is not static and time is not dynamic. All is upside down in the Awakened Vision. However, when you see this truth clearly, you are invited to take one more step in your journey towards awakening. You are invited to enter the Real World. And what is the Real World like? In the Real World the river is just flowing and the mountain is simply still. It is as simple as that! The Real World is beyond human concepts. Here we transcend not only the concept of time but even the one of timelessness. We begin to see reality just as it is with complete simplicity and innocence. But you should not forget that you cannot drop concepts unless you have fully imbibed them. The non-conceptualisation to which Zen is pointing has enormous depth of wisdom and insight into the inner expansion. The Real World is free from the dust of human ideas but is filled with the bright light of Pure Understanding.

In the beginning, living in our dream-like state of consciousness, we believe that the river is flowing and that the mountain does not move. It is an ignorant, shallow and superficial perception of reality. Through awakening we are able to see through the illusory stillness and movement of apparent reality. It is here, where we see that in truth the river is still and the mountain is flowing. And in the end, we return to reality as it is, reaching Pure Innocence. At this stage, the river is just flowing and the mountain is simply still. Hence, first is ignorance, next is awakening and finally we arrive at the child-like innocent vision of reality - just as it is.

Outside of the Inside

Student: *Are we inside or outside?*

Aziz: We are outside of the inside and inside of the outside. This universe is inside our consciousness and our consciousness is inside this universe. We create our reality and we are being created by Total Existence. When you look at a tree, this tree is outside your eyes but inside your consciousness. The sun is outside the eye but inside the eye's consciousness. It is all a dance between outside-inside angles of perception.

Reality as such is neither inside nor outside. Reality just is. But the moment perception arises, consciousness arises, all becomes divided, polarised, inter-woven and inter-penetrated. The dance of life... the mind cannot grasp it, yet we live it already! When one insists that everything is inside, the Zen way of teaching is to hit such a person with the stick on the head! How can you be hit on your head from inside?

As far as our relationship with the Absolute Subjectivity is concerned, the situation is a bit different. In this case, we are inside of the Inside, for God cannot be an object to us. It is the subject-subject relationship; the relative subject - absolute subject relationship.

You are a Particle in the Universal Belief System

Student: *Does time exist because we believe in it?*

Aziz: No, we exist because time believes in us! We are a part of the belief system of the Time dimension (laughter...). What this means is not that we create time but rather time creates us - it is creating us in each moment. We are ourselves a part of the manifestation of time. You see, in order to believe in something, you must first exist. You cannot believe in time before you exist in time! Time exists before your individual existence or, you can say, arises simultaneously with your existence. You recognise time the moment you become conscious; but before this recognition, you already exist in time on a very subconscious level.

From a certain perspective, you can say that time exists because you believe in it, but this belief is not your fabrication - it is yourself! Similarly, as your DNA creates your particular brain, so does your brain create the very concept of time! You are created by your DNA and you have no way to get out of it! Even the fact that you see the world outside of you, is imprinted in your DNA. Do you think that there is such a thing as 'outside'? It is just how your senses are translating this reality, that's all. It is not your belief, for you yourself are this belief! You have been designed this way by Creation.

You are programmed in a certain way and you are a part of this global program called the universe. There is a global program, a general design for all human beings. For example, we all have two legs, two hands, one system of digestion, and one organ of elimination... We all have a similar type of mind and emotional body. Within the global design of this universe there are many elements and sub-designs, sub-programs. Humans are different from other creatures inhabiting this planet but we all have to eat, drink and sleep.

As there is a general program for all humans, so there exists uniqueness and the ability to modify one's program to some extent. We call it our relative free will. There is the collective consciousness which programs all its members into good citizens, perfect social robots, copies of the prevailing paradigm. And there are different individuals within this global program, trying to find their way and their unique expression. You give feedback to the outside information from the inside of your intelligence. For example, you can choose to meditate; you wish to enter the Spiritual Path. You program yourself in a way that you can evolve spiritually. In order to do so, you need to break away from the prevailing social program. You re-program yourself and de-program some elements of your conditionings within the global belief system of human kind; you create a modified belief system. You are your belief system; it is your life. As you are a part of the universal belief system, so you co-create your unique angle of perception, your unique belief.

Usually, when we speak about a belief, we mean that the mind believes in something. But there is a deeper, existential belief, which is the Soul's blueprint. All that you see, that you think and feel, your vision of life and the destiny of your evolution - all of this is the primal belief of your Soul. This belief changes and evolves, gradually reaching its final vision, which is the blueprint. That which is beyond any belief system is Being. This is because Being is beyond perception. It is the vertical reality of pure isness. Here, one simply is. It is not the reality of thoughts, emotions or outer perceptions; it is the reality of isness. Shifting into Being, within your individual program, you transcend all programs, getting out of all belief systems.

What Buddha called Samsara was another name for this global program. He found that we are locked in the same vicious circle of life and death, desire, attachment, disappointment and suffering. He meditated for many years, trying to find the way out of this program. But how can one get out of the program, if one is oneself inside this program as well as an inherent part of it?

For example, if you try to change your belief system, you use your mind which is a part of the program. You cannot have a thought which your brain is unable to produce. You can only have this kind of thoughts which are within the capacity of your particular human mind. Therefore, the question is how, within our limitations, can we reach the Unlimited? How can the goose get out of the bottle in which it is locked? This goose is you; you are inside the bottle and your Soul cannot breathe. How to get out? Most people just try to make themselves comfortable inside! They are completely suffocated but they think that they actually enjoy life! So, how to get out? The goose is out already!!!

Student: *I know what it means to be out of the program, but as I am in the program, I need to learn how to live in it as well.*

Aziz: That is the paradoxical reality of an awakened being. Such a being lives out of the program and inside of it simultaneously. In such a situation, the Soul lives a double life - inside and outside of Creation. In all her appearances, the Soul lives like others in this time dimension, but secretly, she is out of it.

Student: *I would like to know how to live in these two realities in a harmonious way? I can still get lost in the apparent reality.*

Aziz: It is a function of maturity. As you let go more into yourself and into the Beyond, with the clear understanding that the Beyond is the Ultimate Reality, you will relax in your attitude to the world. You also need to have more experiences in the world, more adventuring, more fulfilment and more disappointment as well. One has to exhaust some youth energy and pacify the restlessness of the emotional body. Eventually you let go more, you simply relax - outside and inside.

It does not mean that you reach a hundred percent balance between the inner and the outer, as such a balance does not exist for a human being. But you will reach the optimal balance, relaxation and harmony. Even the lack of balance you will experience in a balanced and relaxed way. It is also important not to be too serious, for life is also a play, an adventure...

Where is Time?

Student: *Where is time?*

Aziz: Where are you? Everything is within the Now. The Now is the spaceless space of pure isness, which contains the totality of consciousness, all dreams, all possibilities... Within the timeless dimension of the Now, the concept of time is created, which justifies its existence through the vision of the past and the future. Your personal memory makes you experience time as continuity, within which your particular stream of consciousness flows. There are many parallel dimensions of time... they are numberless. The sages of old used to say that time does not exist and nothing has ever happened. And that is true. But who knows time? Who knows the illusion of time and who knows the Timeless? The one who knows them is both beyond time and Timelessness.

Individual Consciousness is a Dewdrop of the Ultimate

Student: *How do individual consciousness and Universal Consciousness relate to each other?*

Aziz: Individual consciousness is a dewdrop of the Ultimate dreaming on the leaf of Creation...it is an expression of the

Universal Consciousness in her Creation. The individual consciousness, which is the Soul, is but an angle of perception through which the Universal Consciousness views her Creation. It is a relationship between the mother and her child. The child is taken care of, but also learns how to be independent and alone.

Student: *But how can a separate being tap into Universal Consciousness?*

Aziz: By becoming One with it. You cannot become God but you can, doubtlessly, become One with God. However, even when you reach this Oneness, you can experience it only because you are separated on some level. Separation as well as unity is a part of your blueprint. Universal consciousness and individual consciousness penetrate each other. They are both transparent and you cannot find clear borders. You cannot say that 'in this place' the individual consciousness ends and in this place the universal begins. The individual consciousness is simply less transparent. That's why, it feels itself as separated. We can see it as the primal contraction within the universal energy system. As an individual you are unable to have access to the Totality, in terms of becoming it. We spoke already about this type of illusory view. But you become one with Totality on the energy level. That is the purpose of spiritual expansion.

Student: *Is the State of Presence primarily individual consciousness but merged into the Universal Consciousness?*

Aziz: The State of Presence is a reflection of the Universal in the individual Soul, just as the sun reflects itself in a dewdrop. This reflection in the dewdrop represents your experience of the State of Presence. The difference is, however, that the State of Presence is not the full reflection, for the Heart and Being are still lacking. It has a flavour of the universal but it is very much a personal experience. It is a personal experience beyond the personality.

It is very, very significant what we are saying here. It is a revolutionary teaching, a gift for humanity in the millennium time. For the first time, you have a chance to see clearly what it is that is really happening in Self-realisation. It is very interesting, but originally in the teachings of Upanishads, which were the milestones in the science of Enlightenment, there was a clear distinction between Atman and Brahman. Atman represents the individual consciousness or the complete experience of the Soul. Some assume that Atman represents merely witnessing consciousness, but it is not correct, as Atman encompasses more elements. From the other side, Brahman is the Ultimate Reality. Later on, some Upanishad thinkers seemed to have lost the right perspective, exclaiming that Atman IS Brahman. Here, the famous exclamation 'I am THAT' was born.

How did it happen? It is quite simple. What was lacking in their technology of awakening was the fundamental differentiation between Self-realisation and Soul-realisation. It is so subtle! There are two parallel movements in the evolution towards awakening. One is reaching the personal, the individual essence of our ancient Soul identity. The second is reaching or merging with the impersonal, Universal I AM, which is in truth our own absence. Do you see how subtle and important this understanding is?

The Buddhists went even further than Soul negation, for they denied even the existence of the Brahman. The Upanishads proclaimed that there is no Atman, for Atman is Brahman, and Buddhists said that even Brahman does not exist. In truth, the conclusion of Buddhism is more correct for it is a logical continuation of the Upanishad's elimination of the Soul. If there is no Soul, Brahman is not either because being and non-being can exist only in the presence of duality. For this reason, Buddhist logic, which reached a high level of sophistication, negated everything with negation itself included. That's why, in their way of reasoning, the Ultimate neither is, nor is it not. Here, however, we try not to be too clever in playing with the logical mind. The Universal simply exists, as does the individual. Their dynamic relationship creates the richness and aliveness of the spiritual dimension.

Next, the State of Presence which we all experience in this room has the same universal quality but, at the same time, each one experiences it in a unique way, with a unique flavour, strength and clarity. Also, we should not forget that this state cannot be separated from personal intelligence, which is attached to it. It is like the life-force. The life-force is One, but it channels itself differently, running through a stream, for instance, or becoming a bird.

Student: *What does it mean to say that an 'experience' is personal?*

Aziz: It means that it refers to Me. Me is an angle of perception, one with the blueprint. How do you know that you experience your intelligence? You know it directly. However, when you are conditioned by non-dual philosophies, you may try to cover it up, programming yourself on your own absence. Still on some level, you always know that it is you! The Soul is simply present and it is the Soul who is listening here! Isn't it so? You cannot grasp it all by your mind but you can see it and experience it clearly, for it is your reality.

How, within the totality of Universal Presence, can an individual Soul exist? It is logically impossible, but it is our reality which tells us clearly: yes, it is possible! Surrender not to logic but to Reality...

Student: *Can you say that when we experience the State of Presence in a crystallised way, it is more individual and when it is diffused, it is more Universal?*

Aziz: That is correct. To have a crystallised attention is to be more present and presence is always on the side of individuality. When you relax, you become simply more absent as an individual, and therefore, the experience is more on the side of universality. But the paradox is, you cannot experience Universal Presence, unless you are present as an individual. And when you are present as an individual, you relax your presence, letting it dissolve into that which is beyond yourself, into your absence.

When you let go of your Me, prior to crystallising attention, you simply become unconscious. To relax, is to let go of consciousness, and you cannot let it go unless it is fully present. Otherwise, you experience negative surrender which makes you simply spaced out. Therefore, first the subconscious Me must be transcended so you can become the Real Me. Only the Real Me can surrender in a way that can reach the Universal Presence.

The Unborn is the Container of Creation

Student: *Can you speak about the Unborn?*

Aziz: Before this Creation took place ('took' is time and 'place' is space), there was already something. It does not mean that the Creation has a beginning. There IS something before the Creation Now. What is present prior to Creation? It is the Unborn, the Uncreated, the Unbecome. The Absolute does not know that it exists. It is in a condition of Pure Rest. From this original state, Creation takes place, which is the manifestation of consciousness.

All those Souls, infinite angles of perception, have been created. Now, those Souls in the form of You, are trying to discover their origin. That is the purpose of Creation - to meet and recognise the Source of Creation.

Your Soul is the agent of this purpose! THAT which is unable to recognise itself, for it has no consciousness, needs to create consciousness in order to become conscious of itself as this which is prior to consciousness. The Unborn needs duality to know itself. The Uncreated needs Me to recognise it. God is beyond knowing. It is Me which knows God. In order to know God, this Me has to become pure to be able to reflect the Purity of God. God does not know herself. Me can know and is destined to know God. But God also knows Me in a transcendental way. How? Through her extension, which is the Universal Intelligence, Guidance and the presence of the Over-soul. The Over-soul is the bridge between Me and God.

Creation is Co-creation

Student: *I have a question about the concept according to which we create our own reality. Can you please explain co-creation and the idea that everything is taken care of?*

Aziz: To see it clearly, you have to deeply contemplate this issue because it is very subtle. This whole universe is created by the ultimate 'I' which is the ultimate subjectivity, or simply God. But what truly is this universe? It is not just an object placed in the infinite space. Creation does not take place in the way, for instance, a carpenter makes a chair. No. This particular 'chair,' which is the universe, has eyes and can look back at the carpenter! This universe is made of infinite numbers of separate Me's, which is the multitude of different angles of perception. It is an enormous, amazing composition of infinite subjective realities penetrating the truth of Existence. You are a particular subject; Jan is a different subject; Anna is a different subject... this tree is a different subject; this stone is different subject. We all have different types of consciousness, different potentials and different capacities to experience reality. Yes? This universe is composed of infinite Me's and each of them perceives reality from its own uniqueness. Do you see how amazing it is? We live in the same apparent universe, but is it really the same reality? Each Me experiences a unique version of the Total Existence. It is an amazing composition created by the Divine Intelligence. One cannot grasp the richness of Existence with the mind, but one can at least feel the Truth intuitively.

Each of those Me's perceives reality from her own perspective and each of those Me's evolves in her own way and has her own relative stream of consciousness, relative mind and relative sense of identity. In the case of the human being, Me is able to respond intelligently to this universe in which she has found herself living. You can even commit suicide! You have been created by the Universal Presence and you say, ' I don't want to live, I rebel, I commit suicide.' This ability was given to you, to say 'no' to God! However, it wouldn't be intelligent to make use of it.

You create your own life within the limitations of your intelligence and your evolutionary blueprint. You are limited. Your mind is limited by your past evolution, your conditionings and the very structure of your brain. But at the same time you are free to respond and to create your life within these limitations. To say that you are completely limited and conditioned is only half of the truth, the other half is that you are free within your limitations.

There are numerous elements which constitute your existence. You have no control over that which creates You. At the same time, within your own mind and Heart you can co-create the truth of your life. To say that you create your reality is not entirely correct, because more than that you are yourself being created by the Universal Existence. You don't create your reality but you do co-create it. You co-create your reality with the universe. You have the freedom to help your own reality within the overall Creation. That is the meaning of co-creation - your creativity has limitations but it is valid.

For example, what is spiritual evolution? It is your co-creation. If you are just living passively, the universe will not make you awakened. You will just be a 'good citizen.' This is how you will end your life. In order to become an awakened being, you have to go inside, using your passion, inquiry, creativity and intention. In this way you co-create. You are awakening yourself from inside. You are giving birth to yourself. Yes, you do co-create your reality.

Student: *I have a question about the astrological chart. Which part of us is it affecting?*

Aziz: The position of planets affects the basic make-up and tendencies of your personality. When you know your chart well, you can understand those tendencies better. You can see more clearly your limitations, talents and basic personal challenges. However, the planets do not determine your reality a hundred percent; they determine you on some level. Apart from the influence of the planets, there is also free will, the creativity of your own intelligence and the depth of your Soul. For instance, if there is a full moon, you are affected by it, but how you respond to this influence is your free will. You do have a relative free will. Your free will is limited. That is why you cannot, for example, negate the presence of the full moon. It is already there, in the sky. You cannot say, 'tonight I choose not to have the full moon!' That would be ridiculous. You live within the limitations which existence has drawn around you. Within these limitations, you perform your creativity and exercise your freedom of choice. The Soul's intelligence is unpredictable on some level. Even though intelligence operates within the limits of human consciousness, it is divine and can break through the limitations in which it functions.

I Am is beyond the chart. I Am cannot be found in the chart. It is this part of you which is unconditional and not determined by the movement of planets. However, the movement of planets may help you to awaken I Am. Often, spiritual shifts and experiences of awakening are co-related to some powerful constellation of stars. How is it possible that the unconditional I Am, in order to awaken, requires help from the relative reality? For the very simple reason, that you are awakening to that which is unconditional, from the viewpoint of the conditional. It is from the reality of your personality that you are awakening to that which is beyond the personal self. This channel of awakening, which is your very Me, is related to the whole universe. Your intelligence grows within the limitations of your personality, your particular brain, your physiology, the society you live in, language, culture, the planet, the universe, the galaxy... Yet, it is unpredictable!

Inside and Outside

Student: *Can you talk about the inner and the outer? How it is possible to lose your inside in the outside?*

Aziz: What is inside for you? For example, the mind from the perspective of Pure Me is outside. So it is a matter of viewpoint whether something is inside or outside. Is the experience of feelings inside or outside? From the perspective of pure Soul, they are also outside. They create a certain environment for the Soul. Similarly, the shirt you wear is from the viewpoint of your body outside but it is still very dear to you; it is inside your ego-image.

So what is inside? The question is if you can separate your inside from your outside. If you separate that which is inside from the outside, what is the actual experience of it? What is this Pure Me, in separation from the outside? The mind, the personality, is somewhere between the outside and the inside. That is why it is difficult to say whether your emotions and the mind are outside or inside because they are neither. Your personality is that which connects you with the outside. If you had no mind, emotions or senses, you would not be able to know that such a thing like the 'outer' exists at all. So, the personality allows you to experience the outer. This personality is neither out nor in, but in-between. It participates in both realities. Because there is an immediate identification of all thoughts and emotions with Me, you translate the movement of personality as being an inherent part of this Me. But at the same time, your personality is constantly changing, moving and fluctuating. Therefore, it cannot represent the reality of Pure Me.

A person who is not awakened experiences only that which is between the inner and the outer as one's subjectivity. This means that the personality assumes the role of a subjective identity. Here, it is the movement of thoughts and emotions which one considers as Me. And from this place one relates to the outer.

Because the movement of thoughts and emotions is not really Me, you can observe your feelings and thoughts from a distance. The moment you experience a thought there is an immediate 'sense of Me' attached to it. This sense of Me is energetically deeper than the movement of thoughts with which it is identified. Separating this Pure Me from personality is the function of awakening.

Initially, the question about losing the inner in the outer is irrelevant because the personality is already lost in the outer. Personality is a part of the outer and the outer is a part of the personality - they create one reality. It is like when you have a dream, you cannot separate yourself from this dream because this dream is yourself. You cannot find any clear 'I' which is dreaming the dream. When you dream that you are flying in the air, you are just flying. There is no one flying as such - it is one movement of subconsciousness. When you are afraid in a dream, you are completely afraid because your Me is fully identified. There is no distance between Me and its surroundings. Me is merely a part of what is happening. Here, a subject cannot be separated from an object.

Before the issue of how not to lose the inner in the outer can arise, we have to first discover the inner, as it does not yet exist. So, first the inner needs to be awakened and recognised. But even though you recognise this Me, you may still keep on losing it. You need to become one with your Me. For instance, you are resting in your Me and suddenly a strong emotion arises and immediately you forget yourself - your Me gets lost in the outer. So, in order not to lose yourself you have to remember your Me. Here arises the need for the cultivation of self-remembrance. You have to pull inside. In truth, in the beginning, you have to separate yourself from the outside and from your personality as well. That is why, the beginning of the Path is a little difficult because you have to make an extra effort to remember yourself.

You cannot experience a thought which is not related to something. Therefore, thought is already a part of the outer. In addition, neither can you experience the outer without the thought. The outer without thought or feeling attached to it, does not exist. To see a tree, you have to perceive it and your mind has to translate it as a tree. So a tree without the mind does not exist for you. It exists for other minds but not for your mind. That is why, we say that the personality is a part of the outer as well, which means it is already 'lost' in the outer. Identification with Creation is a part of being the manifested Me-personality.

The next question is: who is going beyond personality in order to discover the Pure Me? That one is neither personality nor Pure Me. It is the subtle extension of the Soul - the psyche. Me is the bridge between the outer and the inner, between Creation and the Beloved. The psyche represents the intuitive intelligence-sensitivity of Me. The psyche is this part of the created Me, through which Me discovers Creation and the Uncreated in a conscious way.

When you shut down your senses, the outer is experienced only in terms of thinking. When you are discovering your Me, you begin to question whether the mind and its movement of thoughts is really yourself. For example, you do the practice of observing the mind and next you discover that there is something behind this observing, which is 'I.' This is how awakening happens. First, you awaken to the State of Presence. Next, you expand into Being and open your Heart. You are giving birth to yourself. You are not only recognising your true Self, but you allow it to become manifested as the truth of your existence.

Student: *And then we experience no separation?*

Aziz: When this I, this subjective reality is awakened and integrated, there is no need for additional remembering. In this moment, Me relaxes. In this relaxation, one abides in a natural state beyond remembering and forgetfulness. Here, you experience the unity between the inner and the outer - you see that they are actually one reality.

When you are resting in this Pure Me, you are not doing, you are just being. Within this space of just being, everything is present. The trees are present, the mountains are present, the birds are singing. This is what is meant by the experience of Oneness - that there is no observer. When you are only in the mind, there is someone who is constantly translating this reality into something. When information from the outer comes back to the sense of Me, Me processes it in the mind and gives feedback. There is a constant movement between the subject and object. When you discover this Pure Me, it is beyond the mind. This means that there is no actual referral to the outer. Me is just present within the outer. The mind still translates information which comes from the outer, as a part of its natural function. But still, you are deeper than the mind. When you are resting in Pure Me, a certain openness in your being is experienced within which the inner and outer are included. It is not that there is no mind, but that you are deeper than the mind. As they say - you are 'witnessing' the mind; but a better expression is that you are 'embracing' the mind and the totality of perception. The term witnessing is more dual, there is a feeling of separation involved. This Pure Me is not referring to herself, neither is she witnessing anything - she simply is. Within this simplicity of pure Being, all is One.

Beyond the Third Dimension

Student: *What is the fourth dimension?*

Aziz: Behind the perception of three dimensional reality, is the perceiver of it. The perceiver itself is the fourth dimension. When the 'I' is recognised, a new panoramic depth is added to perception. The State of Presence is the fourth dimension. The fifth dimension is the Absolute State. The fifth dimension is realised when the perceiver vertically drops to the unmanifested. The fourth dimension is beyond horizontal reality, but has not yet reached the depth of the vertical reality of the Now. When the depth of the Now is reached, the Soul abides in the Primordial energy of the Source. The sixth dimension is the Divine, the dimension of the Heart. The seventh dimension is the dimension of Me. Here, the perceiver of all other dimensions finally realises itself beyond the inner and the outer.

Will: the Force of Life

Student: *Can you speak about will?*

Aziz: Will is that which made you ask this question. Will originally represents the very force of energy to manifest itself, to move, to create. Will is indivisible from the Creation. Everything which exists, has the inherent element of will, like through which a tree grows, a bird flies or a seed awakens the life sleeping inside it... There is the will to live, to survive, to prolong one's life... there is the will to create, to evolve, to adventure... and the will to reach peace and liberation. There is the natural, spontaneous will of Existence and there is a personal, conscious will where your intelligence is involved. Here, you use the power of will in a conscious way.

Student: *Is it the intuitive intelligence?*

Aziz: Of course. But if your thinking process is not conscious, it is your subconscious thinking which uses the will in a semi-conscious way. In order to live, you must use will. Life is actually a constant effort to perpetuate one's existence. There is the will to eat, to avoid suffering, to experience pleasure... All is based on some kind of will. Most of this is unconscious or subconscious. You wake up in the morning and will is already there. In truth, it was will which woke you up! On top of this instinctive, impersonal will, there is your conscious will. 'What shall I do with my life?' you may ask. For instance, when you decide to enter the Spiritual Path, you have awakened the will to grow, to transcend suffering and ignorance. You use the power of will to bring the element of discipline and mindfulness. You tell yourself: I must keep the State of Presence! Will is a part of the vital force and how it flows through this Universe.

The only way to go beyond will is to reach the Uncreated energy. First, you must crystallise your attention, which means that you use your will to become present and to free yourself from unconsciousness. When you are fully present, you may use your subtle will to surrender into the No-will state. Meditation is the state of Non-doing, of just sitting, that is, abiding beyond will. But, paradoxically, you have to use your subtle will to go beyond will. You need to use a subtle will to free yourself from your habitual, subconscious will. It is through conscious surrender that you are able to let go into Being.

There are two types of will which you transform in meditation. One is the will of the mind. The second is the will of energy or the vital force. In truth, the will of energy is the main problem. The main reason most people feel it difficult to sit in Meditation, does not involve even thinking and being lost in the mind but rather it involves the quality of energy. This energy is restless, fluctuating, imbalanced and shallow. It means that our personal energy system is disconnected from the dimension of Beingness; this energy is uprooted and simply cannot sit, one has to move, one feels like running away from meditation...

Initially, our personal will makes a decision to let go of itself and surrender into Being. This personal will encounters the resistance of energy which is unable to rest. The next step is the whole process of settling this energy and deepening the experience of Being. As we surrender, with the intention to sit still in Shikantaza, energy gravitates towards Being and gradually settles down. It transcends its habitual tendency to fluctuate and to move constantly upwards. It moves into the direction of Pure Rest which is the Absolute. The Absolute is the only dimension which does not use will, for it is the realm of pure isness, the original Void.

The Absolute has no will, it only Is. It has no other attributes - it just Is. As you surrender in meditation, your energy gravitates towards this dimension of No-will. In order to come closer to this dimension, you must use your subtle will to undo the gross level of will. The Rest which your Soul longs for exists in the dimension where you do not need to use will anymore. In that place, you can finally rest free from will, beyond yourself. Will, on some level, always crystallises your sense of identity as a separate being. This is the primal suffering or existential pain. The only way to go beyond this primal suffering is to reach the dimension where you become relieved from yourself, that is, from will. You are will yourself. No-will is where you are not. In your practice, first you transcend the mind; next, you transcend the fluctuation of relative energies. In this way, you are coming closer to the unconditional energy of Pure Rest.

Another topic is the importance of will in the spiritual practice. In order to grow, you must use the power of will. But if there is too much will, you become overly tight and goal oriented, thus using an excessive amount of the male energy. On the other hand, if there is not enough will one is too passive, waiting for a miracle to happen... One doesn't do anything and becomes stagnated on the Path.

There are some seekers who refuse to use their will either because they are lazy or because of their naïve interpretation of the concept - 'not being a doer.' What they don't see, however is the condition of their consciousness, which is fragmented and lacks a basic amount of attention. They simply have work to do! They must crystallise their presence and energetically surrender into Being.

We recommend using a balanced amount of will - not too much and not too little. In this way, you have enough focus and discipline. In addition, you are simultaneously connected to the Now in a feminine way. You are accepting your present reality and meeting from moment to moment the truth of who you are. That is the principle of the Non-dual Path. The Non-dual Path, because it is non-dual, points to that which is beyond will, to the Now. At the same time, it is a Path, which means that you must do something; you have to engage the force of will and intention.

What is Consciousness?

Student: *What are the criteria through which we can say that consciousness is present?*

Aziz: Consciousness for us is that which can be registered by our mind. What it actually means is that information of existence is registered and recognised as relating to Me. If the information from the environment does not come back to the sense of Me, it cannot be registered by the conscious Me, therefore remains below the level of recognition.

What information is registered by Me is relative and relates to the needs of a particular individual. We do not need, at all, to be conscious of everything. To be conscious of too many things would be an unbearable burden. From the other side, not to be sufficiently conscious leaves one in the realm of ignorance. For instance, it is not necessary to be conscious of our blood flowing or of the process in digestion. These are the natural, spontaneous functions of our body. However, one can, if one really wants, to develop the ability to bring some amount of consciousness into these areas.

There are different levels of the strength of consciousness. We spoke about the flexible border between the conscious and the subconscious Me. Subconscious Me is still conscious but the information which comes back to it from the environment does not encounter any clear sense of Me - Me is diffused in information, identified with the flow of impulses.

So there are three ways information in our dimension of existence is present. One is unconscious, the second is subconscious and the third is conscious. What is happening on the moon is not registered by your particular Me. From your perspective, you remain unconscious of it. In another example, when you meditate by the beach, in your absorption you may subconsciously register the sound of the ocean. Here, the border between unconsciousness and subconsciousness is not always apparent. What it means is that we cannot trace this exact point where the unconsciousness reaches the level of the subconscious Me. The reason is that subconscious Me has many layers itself; it can be more and more sub-sub-subconscious. That's why, from the perspective of Ultimate Sensitivity, unconsciousness can be seen as a form of subconsciousness. What it tells us is that everything that occurs in Existence is in the utmost subtle way registered by our subconscious Me.

Consciousness is Not All

Student: *Can you speak about the concept that everything is consciousness? How can unconsciousness exist from this perspective?*

Aziz: It is not true that all is consciousness. In truth, the foundation of reality is unconsciousness. What is unconsciousness? There is only one Absolute Unconsciousness, which is the domain of pure isness, prior to consciousness - the Absolute. From the place of pure isness, Creation arises. Creation is always related to the flow of information and information is the other side of consciousness. When we say that Creation is Consciousness, we mean that it appears in the field of knowingness. However, consciousness is not always conscious of itself. The field of pure knowingness, which is the ultimate flowering of consciousness, is experienced only through awakened beings. Otherwise, consciousness functions in many semi or sub-conscious ways.

The concept that all is consciousness was created from the incorrect assumption that awareness is the Ultimate. But God is beyond consciousness. Consciousness itself is dual, even so-called consciousness without content. In truth, consciousness without content doesn't exist, for even when freed from the movement of thought, consciousness contains this very Me to which it applies. It is more correct to say that all is subconsciousness and consciousness is the point where the impersonal subconsciousness becomes aware of itself. For that it needs the channel of Me to become self-conscious.

It is truly amazing to see that, in reality, this whole Creation applies to the Me and to the Me only. Creation without the very subject, that is you, is completely meaningless and empty. And what is this Me? It is an incarnation of God through which she can become aware of her own Creation, from the perspective of relative duality and separation.

You can be conscious only of that which appears in the field of your Me. All the rest of the infinite Existence which you don't register, exists below and beyond your consciousness. This is important to understand. In the past, they made a mistake assuming that the Buddha becomes the totality of consciousness. Such a thing is not possible. Why? Because the agent which channels consciousness is the relative Me, and the relative Me is merely an angle of perception of Totality. The pure consciousness which Buddha realised is beyond the content of the perceived. It represents the reality of Me with respect to awareness.

Me is more than awareness. The essence of Me is the Heart. And where does this Me, through which consciousness is Self-realised, abide? Does she abide in pure consciousness? Absolutely not! She abides in the Beyond consciousness, in the realm of Beingness, where the Absolute alone reigns.

There is the relative unconsciousness and the absolute unconsciousness. The relative unconsciousness refers always to the relative angle of perception, which is Me. You are conscious of some aspects of reality and you are not conscious of others. Others can be conscious of aspects that you are not conscious of, that dwell in your unconscious. The absolute unconsciousness cannot become a conscious experience for anyone. Although an enlightened being, can abide in this original absence of consciousness. This very realisation of the Absolute brings us to a completely new dimension - beyond consciousness and beyond unconsciousness.

Eternity is Now

Student: *Can you speak about Eternity?*

Aziz: Eternity is something other than endless time. Eternity does not concern time which has no end. There is usually this feeling behind the notion of Eternity that something does not end. Eternal life, for most people, means never dying. It means to continue living day after day, life after life. For most people the ultimate dream is to keep on living, perpetuating their ego sense of identity forever. But they are not aware that they actually live in hell!

The true meaning of eternity is not the endless continuity of time but the Timeless. Eternity is beyond time, it is beyond becoming. This means that when you discover your I Am, you discover this part of you which is beyond change. When you discover I Am, you cannot give it a name. The I Am is one with the Timeless.

The Absolute is beyond experience. There is no time, no recognition. I Am is a mysterious place of meeting between the dimension of time with the Timeless. That's why you know that you experience it. That is the paradox that what you experience happens in time but the experience itself rests in the Timeless, that is beyond time. It is here that eternity is actually recognised as an experience. Eternity is not an experience but here it becomes experienced because time and the Timeless meet; and they meet through you, which is the Soul. An awakened Soul is a bridge between time and the Timeless, between Creation and the Source of Creation.

Creativity is the Imagination of Life

Student: *Can you talk about imagination and creativity and how they can work against us and for us?*

Aziz: Everything is connected with a certain type of creativity and imagination. Even on the Spiritual Path which is essentially about transcending the mind, one has to use the imagination. To create the idea of going beyond the mind, you have to use a lot of imagination. A person who asks oneself the question, 'who am I?' requires an enormous imagination to ask such an unusual question. It is beyond the imagination of most people to even conceive of an idea that their past sense of self could be doubted!

Therefore, to possess imagination does not necessarily indicate that one lives in the world of fantasy. Imagination can also relate to I Am and to the evolution of awakening. If imagination is disconnected from intelligence and from the Real Me, that is, from the Soul, it becomes simply spaced-out. Imagination is a function of the third eye. Those who are using this faculty in an excessive way, without working with Awareness and Being are quite ungrounded. This tendency to be spaced-out can often be found among so called psychics. To be a psychic is also to use the imagination. For example, reading the future of others requires the type of imagination which tunes one into the life of another.

Creativity is the ability to discover something new, something which has not been there before. That's why it is called 'creativity' - to create and not merely to repeat. When you repeat, you are not creative but you are just moving in a circle, copying the past. The type of creativity is being expressed depends again on the evolution of the Soul. For someone, it may be the basic creativity, like painting, writing poems or singing a song. For someone else, creativity may mean to discover the truth of Existence, to discover the truth of oneself. To explore the blueprint of the Soul or to explore God is another expression of our creativity. The ultimate creativity leads you to the Source of Creation, which is the Creator.

Spiritual creativity is a journey in time of the Soul who uses her intelligence, sensitivity and imagination. In this way, she discovers the Source of Creation which is her origin. That is the ultimate or the most meaningful creativity, for it reflects the true purpose of Creation. All other types of creativity are more accidental - they are more like entertainment in the Leela land of apparent reality. Real creativity is always connected with silence, depth of Being and the presence of the Heart. When you are in your Heart, when you are silent and when you abide in I Am, imagination flows according to your deepest desires and predispositions. You express creativity.

If your creativity is not coming from the depth of silence, it is not a real creativity but rather a catharsis, a certain release from the subconscious mind. That's why, if you look at the lives of many artists, even great artists, you see a lot of suffering. Many of them expressed a beautiful creativity, but their Souls had suffered. Their creativity was not really flowing from a healthy place. Real creativity flows from the place of sanity and happiness; it is a positive expression of the Soul. Most artists have to express themselves in order not to get crazy. They are simply suffocated with their minds. It is similar to the need for catharsis. That's why they have to create all the time. They cannot rest. They are not expressing creativity, but they are being controlled by creativity. This means that the balance is lost.

Does the Earth Exist Objectively?

Student: *Is there also an objective earth?*

Aziz: There is an approximately objective earth, which means that there is something like a meeting place of all Me's. We can meet because there exists something like an objective earth. But this objective earth is only relatively objective because it is experienced by all those Me's in different ways. Approximately objective means that there is a similarity in our experience of the earth. But in truth, we do not meet on the same earth but on approximately the same earth. There are people who you will never relate to because your earth and their earth have no connection. From the higher perspective, what you call the earth is a state of consciousness and not really something objective. This state of consciousness can be measured in an 'objective' way to give us the feeling that we are actually meeting Here. Nothing here is absolutely objective. It is all subjective but not in a sense that your ego-mind projects this apparent reality. That would be the illusion of 'subjective idealism.' This reality is subjective but in a universal sense. It is composed of infinite relatively subjective versions of the same overall Universal Projection. This Universal Projection comes from the realm of the absolute subjectivity, which is God.

Oneness is Not-knowing

Student: *I wonder about the experience of Oneness. When I am in the State of Presence, I am trying to experience Oneness. I am trying to see that all is consciousness... but I still feel separated?*

Aziz: The moment you know that you experience Oneness - it is no longer Oneness. The experience of Oneness does not exist. What exists is a lack of separation. To be One is to be in the state of not-knowing. When you relax into I Am, in a non-conceptual way, you don't know what this experience is. You have no way of knowing it. This not-knowing is purity and true innocence. Don't try to experience reality in a certain way, for you will manipulate the experience. Be simple, be beyond the mind. It is already Oneness. Here, the one who wants to know Oneness cares no more.

Awakening to the Dream

Student: *When I wake up in the morning, I get the feeling that my Soul is returning back to life.*

Aziz: Waking up in the morning symbolises our birth into this dimension. It is a little birth that you experience every morning. And the mechanism is the same. Before your incarnation, the Soul is in a deep sleep state; she is one with the Beloved. Suddenly, you slip into Creation - you wake up in the dream of phenomenal reality, you find yourself in the body, you see some people around who claim to be your parents, you find out you are a citizen of some country... and so on. The same happens every morning.

The first experience in the morning is the sense of I Am. Your subconscious computer has not yet re-constructed your past sense of identity, based on ego-image and various mental associations. You don't yet know who you are, but you know that you are. Afterwards, the mind enters and brings back the memories and the personality is crystallised again. But before the mind comes, you already exist. This fresh taste of I Am points to the reality of the Soul. How do you know that you wake up in the morning? What does it mean to be awake? Isn't it the knowledge of I Am?

To Reach the Truth

Student: *Is the Truth relative only? Can I experience the universal Truth?*

Aziz: As long as here is an individual mind and an individual consciousness, Truth is always relative. To be an individual is to perceive reality from one's unique angle of perception. You are seeing reality from the place that you are sitting on this pillow, as well as in your life and at this point in time. That is your relative truth. And your relative truth is a part, a particle in the infinite composition of the universal Truth. You are contained in the space of totality, which is the Absolute Truth. From the place of your relative truth, you are evolving towards the universal Truth - you are returning to the place of wholeness.

There is only one way you can experience the absolute truth from your point of view. This is only when you become One, where you are absent within the Universal Presence. And paradoxically, the way you merge with totality, the way you experience this unity with God is relative to you. For you remain an individual, an unique angle of perception through which totality recognises itself.

The purpose of the Soul's evolution is to reach the optimum of one's relative truth. The blueprint is the furthest point you can attain in the expansion of your relative truth. When you reach the point where your Soul perceives reality in her capacity, in terms of purity, understanding, inner expansion... you feel complete. The maximum of your relative truth represents how close you can get to the universal Truth. When this purpose is reached, you can let go completely of your relative truth which is nothing but your own existence. You are your own relative truth!

When you let go of yourself, in the final expansion, you become dissolved, returning to the condition of complete unity with the universal Existence. The absolute Truth cannot be experienced fully by a human being because the one who experiences it is relative, and limited by the boundaries of the blueprint.

For that reason, the statement 'I am THAT' is not fully correct. 'I am one with THAT,' is the precise statement. I am one with THAT and THAT is beyond Me. You cannot become the whole of the mystery but you can become one with the mystery. It is this separation which is being transcended. But still, you perceive this mystery from your unique perspective.

You are seeking not for the absolute Truth, but for the truth of your Soul. This truth is relative, not in the ego-sense, but in terms of the uniqueness of your Me. Your relativity is the divine limitation which allows evolution to take place. If there is no limitation or relativity - there is no evolution, no Creation. Evolution is a movement of imperfection within Perfection. And that which is beyond evolution, is God.

Free Will is Just Now

Student: *Is there freedom of choice and is it a function of intelligence?*

Aziz: Was your question coming from the place of free choice? Or were you forced to ask it?

Student: *My mind asked this question but I am not sure if on some level, I was conditioned to ask it?*

Aziz: In truth, it does not matter. The human mind is limited and linear. It tries to fix reality in terms of 'yes' and 'no.' You are trying to have a higher view about the functioning of your mind, but, in order to have this view, you must use your limited mind. You have no way of transcending your limitations. That's why, the highest wisdom to which your mind can bring you, is the silence and letting go of concepts. Someone says that there is free will, while someone else will deny it. Everyone has some logical proof to support his or her ideas. But reality is beyond these linear concepts; reality is more complex, more rich and has a paradoxical nature. The logical mind simply cannot get it.

What is the reality of your mind? You are using your intelligence and making choices in a creative way. You are asking questions, exploring different possibilities and trying to find solutions. That is all a part of the Soul's creativity. Whether this creativity is predestined or not, it does not matter for you at all! Whether you believe in free will or complete determination, you will still function as you always have, only the mind will have one more concept.

Of course, the one who uses this creativity, is your intelligence. But intelligence should be one with the Heart, for it is one system. Intelligence is the engine of evolution and is virtually responsible for everything. It is your conscious mind which is listening and attempting to understand. In the case of animal consciousness, intelligence is subconscious, instinctive and mechanical. The less there is consciousness, the less there is free will or individual creativity. As long as you are a collective being, a part of the social system, you are hardly using your freedom of choice. You are not an individual yet.

We cannot understand the concept of free will unless we deeply contemplate the phenomenon of creativity. Intelligence is not mechanical thinking. It grows from inside and is alive, vibrant, paradoxical, divine, rebellious and untamed. In that way, intelligence frees itself from its own limitations and conditionings.

You must become an autonomous being, free and divine. Collective consciousness is like a womb in which you are growing. One day you must get out of this womb, becoming born into the Real World of Truth, Intelligence and Love. But most people are never born. They live in the womb of collective ignorance, and they die there as well!

Beloved friend, for your convenience, it is very good that you accept the concept of the relative free will. It will solve many problems. There is destiny. Some events you cannot avoid; some people you must meet; some experiences you must have. Even your intelligence functions within the very limitation of your brain. The mind which you are using is conditioned by your personal past and the past of humanity. For example, you cannot invent or imagine a colour which does not exist on this planet! Can you? So even your creativity cannot go beyond certain limitations, within the frame of which it operates. But, at the same time, you are creatively evolving within your limitation. In this way, free will and destiny co-exist as one ecological organism of this particular reality. By the way, you are free to choose one of these two concepts: that there is freedom of choice or that there is none!

Fear of Becoming Absent

Student: *Can you speak about the fear of death?*

Aziz: Initially, the fear of death is a natural mechanism through which your I Am protects itself and prolongs its existence in time. It is imprinted in your DNA that you don't want to die. That's why, you eat, you breathe, you avoid dangerous situations. So, your fear protects you, it protects your organism - otherwise, you would just die. For why to bother so much about surviving? Surviving is not logical, it is irrational. A computer, for instance, doesn't care whether it is switched on or off.

The problem however, is a certain type of fear - a psychological fear. Psychological fear is not a response to the Now but is fabricated by the mind. It is the fear of the Unknown. One is afraid of encountering one's own absence. For what is death? It is the absence of Me. It is natural to step back avoiding a car rushing at you on the street. This type of fear is natural, for it protects you. But if you are scared of 'death as such,' waking up in the middle of the night, sweating and being terrified because suddenly you realised that you must die one day - this type of fear originates from ignorance and unconsciousness. The ultimate medicine against the psychological fear of death is to realise your unity with that which is beyond death.

From where does life arise? Who created life? The dimension of Beingness from which Creation takes place is beyond death and the illusion of time. One day you have to return to the place of your origin. How long can you perform the role of a separate being? When you truly experience unity with the source, light and love of Creation - the fear of death becomes cleansed and dissolved. There is no other way, in truth. When you realise unity with the Beloved, a deep trust replaces your fear. It is not even that you trust. There is just trust.

Most people try to avoid fear by creating belief systems about life after death or reincarnations. That is not trust but avoiding confrontation with the real problem of death. The real trust arises when you, as the mind become absent and absorbed. It is not that the mind trusts but that the absence of the mind is trust. It is the absorption into the deathless, which liberates you from the fear of your annihilation. If you are separated form the Source of Creation - this itself is fear. As long as you are locked in the cage of your separated existence, there is no way that you can completely free yourself from the fear of your own absence. When you surrender, through an inner expansion, you become one with the totality of Creation. And suddenly, the understanding dawns upon you that death does not exist!

Free Will is Your Destiny!

Student: *What is the balance between free will and destiny?*

Aziz: Destiny is higher but free will is important as well. Free will represents how we co-create our life and evolution. In the New Age, there is the concept that we create our own reality. This concept makes the mistake of subjective idealism; it overlooks the objective side of reality. We create our reality but much more than that we are ourselves being created by the larger reality, by the whole of Existence. The concept that we create our own reality can be seen as a medicine against feeling like a victim. Victim consciousness is a regular state for most members of this Soulless society, in which work, competition and survival are the only philosophies of life.

However, we can fall into another extreme where we think, in our egocentric mind, that we can create any possible reality. There are people who continuously try to manifest a perfect reality by doing different visualisations, changing their belief systems and so forth. But their intentions meet resistance with the objective reality, which simply does not conform to individual visions. Our free will constantly has to confront the boundaries and frontiers of our blueprint and destiny.

It is more proper to say that we co-create our reality. Here, our subjective intelligence and the objective reality co-operate in the Creation of life. For how we respond to the challenge of life and what visions and attitudes we have towards life and our evolution, do in fact matter. Co-creation reflects our responsibility and creative participation in Existence. By co-creation, we help Reality to create itself through us.

Belief System

Student: *Can I create a new reality by changing my belief system?*

Aziz: You can change your belief system only within your belief system! You can imagine only what your imagination allows you to. Can you imagine a colour which doesn't exist on this planet? You cannot! You are conditioned and limited by the elements of reality which have been presented to your little self by a much bigger reality. You, yourself are a belief system! What you can do is to evolve and become creative within the prison of your private little world. If you wish to reach freedom, you must transcend all belief systems by reaching that which is eternal, that which is beyond the mind. The Truth doesn't require belief, for It Is.

The Continuity of Becoming

Student: *Let's say before going to sleep I think about something and when I wake up the next day, the same issue and the same thought pattern continues. So it seems that there is a continuation inside me and also outside of me, like with the sun, the stars; everything has a continuation. If possible, please talk about it, about this power or this quality ...*

Aziz: In life there is a continuation within the flow of time, but not always a conscious one. Most often the continuation is subconscious, which means it cannot be recognised by your conscious mind. When you think of something in the evening, it is not necessarily true that you wake up with the same thought. The thought may be completely different, but the thought with which you went to sleep continues at least on the subconscious level. It affects the type of thought you have in the morning, but the relationship is not necessarily direct. Life is a flow. In order for life to happen many different elements need to co-operate. It is a very complex and multidimensional process. The whole universe is involved; other universes are involved. All dimensions, physical and non-physical, are interconnected and flow towards their destiny which is the ultimate flowering of the Now. All these elements cannot be understood, but you can intuitively see and feel that there is a continuation and there is a tremendous wisdom behind.

This continuation involves destruction as well. The old becomes destroyed so the New can become born. Certain elements in your psyche, in your personality may be completely extinguished, allowing your Soul to go forwards.

The Gateway to Oneness is Me

Student: *A few days ago you said something very interesting. That some people, for example, want to merge with the universe. Before they know what the subject is, they try to merge with everything, to love everything but they cannot. How to merge with all through discovering the subject?*

Aziz: It is an important issue. People who are sensitive or creative enough to aspire for the experience of unity try to experience this unity while remaining ignorant of the Self. They try to experience unity through the outer doors of their sensory perceptions, their emotional body or their mind.

You meet this universe through the senses: eyes, ears, nose, mouth, skin. If you did not have senses, where would the universe be? Behind the senses, there is intelligence and a very fast subconscious movement of the mind. The mind translates information, which comes through the senses and creates a self-referral. This self-referral points always to a certain type of Me inside. That's how it is functioning. In the case of human beings who have a developed ego, this self-referral crystallises a strong self-image in the mind. You can say the subject becomes excessively self-conscious. When you perceive a sun, for example, this information comes to your sense of Me and you feel yourself; you know that you exist. When you see something from which you can benefit, immediately you translate this in terms of your gratification; this refers to your Me. There is a constant movement of information going out and coming back. There is the subject who is thinking about oneself and creating a self-image. It is a very quick movement of self-images. Because of this never-ending movement of in-out and out-in, human beings experience a very acute sense of separation. That is how the ego functions. This ego which still does not understand its own subjectivity, is sensitive enough to suffer. The ego is able to experience suffering because it belongs to the Soul, which is the primal sensitivity of Me. Even when one is totally lost in the mind, the Soul on some level is at least present in a dormant way.

Because most are not aware of their true subjectivity, they want to reach Oneness through a kind of merging with the outer. For them only the outer exists. One can experience a sense of unity through certain empathetic feelings with some aspects of Creation. This desire to experience Oneness with the universe in an emotional way is understandable, but it is not grounded and it cannot be retained. We may have to repeat this emotional feeling of Oneness. Poets and artists might have this type of experience as well as people who are sensitive and who are connected to the space of the Heart. Sensitivity is necessary to connect with nature, for example. The experience of nature can take an unawakened person the closest to the feeling of unity with Creation.

You can experience Oneness with the universe only if you are able to tune in and experience on some level the subjectivity of objectivity. Yes, to feel a tree from the inside; to feel a mountain from the inside...it is like a love affair. Merging with the opposite sex, surrender to a partner for most people is the deepest experience of transcending one's sense of separation. Unfortunately, it often becomes just an escape from oneself and is more a reflection of one's despair than of a positive expansion into the Heart of another.

Paradoxically, the gateway to Oneness is subjectivity; it is this very sense of Me. And why is that? Because Oneness can be experienced only from the place from which Creation has emerged. In order to experience Oneness, you have to connect with the ground of Existence, with the Source of Creation. There is no other way. We spoke about the feeling of containing reality, about containment. In order to contain the manifested and embrace it, the ultimate container has to be discovered in the Universal I AM.

In this process, you discover the Universal I AM, the ground of Existence and at the same time you transcend this very ego which feels its separation. When we look for the true Me, we discover that the ego itself is not really subjective. It represents a certain objectified consciousness. It operates as outside of the field of Pure Me. That's why we can say, for instance, that awareness can witness the ego because it is deeper.

As you transcend ego, you are reaching the condition of the pure Soul. The Soul is not translating reality into anything. The Soul is one with the Source of Creation. She is experiencing separation for the very reason that she is operating as an individual consciousness, though in the context of unconditional Oneness. In truth, Oneness can be experienced only because there is some touch of separation.

Creation is Now

Student: *Is there a beginning to Creation?*

Aziz: Yes, Now! You see, the very concept of a beginning and an end is 'created' as a part of Creation. That's why, beginning is not of time. Creation is eternally happening in the context of the Now. There are many streams of time. We can see this universe like a stream of time among other streams of time, all with their own relative beginnings and ends. But from the ultimate timeless perspective, no beginning or end can ever be found.

There is only One Reality

Student: *Is this reality an illusion? All mystics seem to see it as a dream.*

Aziz: To see this reality as a dream is a part of this dream! This reality is what it is and you don't need to call it anything. Do you see how much you live in the mind? There is this constant translation of reality into mental concepts. Look at reality without concepts. The highest understanding is not-knowing. The moment you know, you have already missed the Truth of life. To live without concepts is to live in insecurity. Your concepts protect your ego-sense of identity. But it is all empty. When you put your hand inside your interpretation of reality, there is just nothing. It is like a phantom - it seems real but there is nothing inside of it. Let go of concepts and learn to live in emptiness. Have the courage to be nobody.

The idea that this reality is an illusion was created to transcend the outer in order to regain the Inner. But when the Inner is attained, the negation of the outer should be dropped as well. Indian mysticism transcended the Outer. Zen transcended the Inner. In Zen, to separate the inner from the outer is a sign of ignorance. 'Form is emptiness and emptiness is form,' is a verse in the Heart Sutra. But even this concept must be transcended! Any idea, even the most profound, is like a rope binding a donkey to a pole. It is all a form of intellectual bondage. Freedom lies in the dimension beyond the mind, in the dimension of not-knowing. That is the true innocence!

Student: *But you speak about changing dimensions during meditation.*

Aziz: Yes, but the dimension we speak about is This Reality. There is only One Reality. You look at the phenomenal reality thinking that there is something beyond it. But who is looking? From which place are you seeing that which you assume to be the phenomenal Existence? The Other Dimension is Now! But you don't get it. You are not ready to meet Reality. You are living in the mind and thinking to meet reality within the control of your mind. Drop all of this and let yourself encounter the real world empty of all ideas. There is only One Dimension. For you, to change dimensions is to get out of the mind's dimension and to encounter Reality. When we speak about changing dimensions, we refer to the discovery of this One Dimension.

The Prison of Collective Consciousness

Student: *What is collective consciousness?*

Aziz: The collective mind represents the global forgetfulness of humanity. The collective mind is a monstrous prison and all the individual minds are represented by the cells in this prison. Most prisoners are addicted to this prison - they would never want to leave it! They think that it is real life and that there is no life outside of this territory. When a bird grows up in a cage, later even when you leave the door of the cage open - the bird will not fly out. The bird is scared of the Unknown. Similar, most prisoners are deadly afraid of the real world of freedom. There is a global agreement among all prisoners that to be happy is to just add some comfort to their prison. They believe in making their cells beautiful and reaching global harmony within their prisons. This is represented by those who try to improve themselves, by doing therapies or engaging in the innovations of the New Age movement. The New Age is the concept that there will be a time where all prisoners will love each other and will create one big family.

In our work, we invite you to get out of your prison. We are visiting different cells (individual minds) and speaking about the possibility of freedom. We tell you how to leave your prison and what it means. We awaken in you this forgotten intuition which connects you to the Real Word. We take you out of your cells and show you around, taking you to the very edge of the prison's territory. Now you just need to JUMP OUT!

VI

DIMENSION OF ENLIGHTENMENT

What is the truth of Enlightenment? What is Enlightenment and what is it not? What is true and what is false? How to enter a dimension so profound and so subtle? Which teaching can guide us towards this clarity? Which master should we follow? How to disperse all our doubts? How to know the truth of Enlightenment?

It is as important to know what Enlightenment is not as to know what it is. Incorrect opinions about the real meaning of Self-realisation cover the Natural Reality of Awakening like an eclipse. Here, the Truth is lost.

Enlightenment does not refer merely to one type of Realisation but to a few possibilities of Inner Expansion. That must be seen clearly. Enlightenment does not magically remove one's sense of identity as an individual, or the challenge of the human life. This must be accepted in humility. Enlightenment is to return to the state of unity with the Light of Creation. But what does it really mean? This has to be contemplated deeply.

Enlightenment does not end one's evolution. In truth, from the place of Self-realisation the real evolution begins. It is only when one is free from ignorance, can we speak about positive journey into mystery of the Beloved.

The Self Realised

What is it to be Self-realised? When one has completed this immense task of becoming whole, one begins the life of an enlightened being. But there are new mysteries awaiting us, new challenges on the horizon. There is still a strong need for clarity and direction. The teaching of Guidance is not only addressed to those on the Path but to those who are already awakened as well. An enlightened being still needs guidance to reach freedom from the incorrect interpretation of his or her state and guidance for further evolution. After completing the traditional model of Enlightenment, the real evolution begins. But so far no one has ever spoken about it. You are invited here with us to explore the dimension of Enlightenment and beyond.

Is there Only One Enlightenment?

Student: *You said that there are several types of Enlightenment. Can you speak about it?*

Aziz: We will clarify this matter in the following meetings. To present it briefly, we can say that the First Enlightenment is the awakening of witnessing consciousness, which is awareness without content. It takes place in the third eye. This is the State of Presence and when it is established permanently, this type of Enlightenment is complete. Here, the centre of awareness is constantly present in the background of the mind. In Zen, they call it the 'clear mind;' in Dzogchen 'rigpa' or bare awareness. In the ancient scriptures of the Upanishads, they gave it the name of 'turiya' or the fourth state.

The next Enlightenment is to the Absolute State. Even within the knowledge of available traditions, the Absolute State has been a secret. Most seekers and teachers from different traditions of Enlightenment consider pure awareness to be the ultimate... however, this is incorrect. Realisation of the Absolute takes place through the Being quality of I Am. In Zen there is an expression, 'the bottom of the bucket falls out,' referring to the shift beyond consciousness. The 'bucket' represents I Am experienced only within the individual energy system. Through the shift to the Absolute, the Soul becomes one with the Unmanifested. That was the reason why Buddha Shakyamuni negated the Hindu concept that Brahman is the ultimate. In his understanding, Brahman was the equivalent to pure consciousness. He discovered that consciousness itself still belongs to the Created Reality.

Unfortunately, the way he expressed his understanding was later interpreted in a negative sense. Even though Buddhism claims to be the middle path, in-between eternalism and nihilism, still, the balance moves strongly towards nihilism. At least that is the case with the original school of Theravada. The idea of the middle path is that the Ultimate is neither described in terms of being 'something' nor being 'nothing.' In this way, the human mind pays homage to the inexpressible nature of the Absolute. However, if we want to be precise, the Absolute possesses one inherent quality which is absolutely positive - the Absolute IS. Buddhism, in truth is more apt to speak about reality in terms of 'no-self' rather than 'neither self nor no-self.' And to say that there is no-self is to go against the principle of the middle path.

The only Master who clearly differentiated between the realisation of pure consciousness and the Absolute was Nisargadatta Maharaj. Maharaj, a great teacher and revolutionary thinker, brought many original discoveries into the traditional interpretation of Advaita Vedanta.

The Absolute State can be seen as the Final Enlightenment but this view is incomplete. Evolution still continues and can give rise to the next awakening, Enlightenment to the Heart. It is not true that Enlightenment, as such, must include the Heart. One may be in the Absolute State but have the Heart closed. The Heart brings into the Inner State a profound sensitivity, the flavour of divinity. The Heart is the middle point, the balance between the Absolute and Creation, that is, between the Unmanifested and the Manifested. When one abides purely in the Absolute, the energy is pulled in too much and the Soul is energetically alienated from Creation. When the Heart is awakened, energy moves from absorption in the void to this very precise equilibrium in-between the Inner and the Outer. Here, one is neither in nor out, in the experience of true Oneness. At this point, the Absolute and the Divine become one - Being and the Heart create one field of experience. The next Enlightenment takes us to the realisation of the very experiencer of all, which is the Soul.

To Miss One's Awakening!

Student: *Is it possible to be awakened and not to know it?*

Aziz: You might be surprised but it happens quite often. We have met a few students who were in the State of Presence while being, however, completely oblivious to this fact. We have met even one student who wanted to do a special Gurdjiev workshop to 'make her more aware' even though she was already in the State of Presence! Such unconscious behaviour!

One of the reasons of such a lack of self-knowledge is that most available spiritual teachings are utterly unclear in their description of the Inner States and levels of Self-realisation. Also this whole concept of eliminating the ego has confused thousands of seekers. Even if some seekers do realise the State of Presence, they think that something is wrong with them because their relative Me or ego is still present. They believe that unless they eliminate their ego and stop desiring, they cannot even dream about Enlightenment. They don't know that if they were unlucky enough to succeed in their attempt to eliminate their ego and desires, they would have reached not enlightenment but - suicide!

This is how inadequate teachings, repeated mechanically for the last thousand of years, have truly damaged a number of sincere seekers. For that reason, we work so much with your intelligence. This very intelligence of yours must wake up and reach clarity. Otherwise you will always be lost... you will remain forever a victim of an incomplete vision of awakening. In the book Enlightenment Beyond Traditions we have written the chapter 'Verification of Attainment - the Seeker's Goal.' It is important to read it. It can give you more clarity about the criteria with the help of which you can verify your inner states.

Is Enlightenment Bliss?

Student: *It is a personal question. After you stabilised the State of Presence in Japan, what was your experience? You call the State of Presence the First Enlightenment. How was it? Was it an experience of bliss?*

Aziz: If someone lives in the mind, anything which is beyond the mind, is translated as bliss. Even smoking marihuana. Awareness itself has the quality of peace and serenity. When one is stabilised in the State of Presence, one is simply centralised in this experience permanently. Serenity is a bit different than bliss. In bliss, the emotional body experiences a certain type of sweet, delicate, calm in its essence, happiness. Serenity can be translated as the basic brightness, luminosity, weightlessness and positiveness of awareness.

Apart from the presence of any Inner State, there is the mind interpreting the experience. This interpretation is connected to the intelligence and sensitivity of the Soul as well as to her spiritual aspirations. Spiritual happiness arises from reaching one's evolutionary blueprint. That is, from becoming complete. You see, that which makes one want to evolve further is a feeling of lack. If the State of Presence was absolutely fulfilling, why would one wish to evolve further?

The State of Presence from one perspective is freedom from the mind, which you can translate as happiness. From another perspective, for the Soul who wishes to go deeper into the nature of reality, it may still be a limitation. This is because one continues to remain separated from the Unmanifested and lacks unity with the Divine.

If we want to be precise, we say that bliss is from the Heart; it is an experience of the Divine. Awareness represents serenity; Being represents peace; the Heart represents bliss. Sat-chit-ananda - these are the three qualities of the Ultimate Reality.

Student: *Is it possible to first become enlightened to the Heart?*

Aziz: Of course. Certain Souls enter this dimension with an awakened Heart already; other Souls may wish in their evolution to first realise the Heart. However, the experience of the Heart taken out of the context of Being and Awareness, lacks a certain fundamental depth. If one is unable to rest in Being and Awareness, if one's Me is fragmented and discontinuous - how can it be possible to enter the depth of the Heart? In such a case, one experiences only the surface of the Heart. Enlightenment to the Heart means that this centre is fully activated, it has completely opened up, expanded to its optimum. But the experience of it is interconnected with other aspects of our wholeness - like Awareness and Being. You cannot separate one from another.

Who is Enlightened?

Student: *You said that many who teach in the name of Enlightenment are only partially awakened.*

Aziz: That is correct, and in this statement there is not judgement but clarity. Most spiritual teachers who translate their realisation as Complete Enlightenment are in the State of Presence. Some may not even be stabilised in this experience. Others may represent Enlightenment to the Heart only. Although that is beautiful, it is not complete. The Spiritual Path is not a competition for the highest Enlightenment. We simply give you clarity as to what is happening on the spiritual scene, what the different possibilities are and what options relate to your own evolution.

Student: *Could you say which spiritual teachers around represent the Final Enlightenment?*

Aziz: It is not for us to tell it. Use your discriminative wisdom. Be critical and wise. Most important for you is what your state is! The state of others is insignificant unless you submit to a particular master. Even if a spiritual teacher, whom you have chosen for a guide, is not fully Self-realised, you can still learn and grow with this person within the frame of their attainment. If you reach the same state as your master and still wish to evolve further - here, you have to say good bye. Be critical in choosing your spiritual guide. Examine the nature of your master and don't get fooled by appearances.

Even awakening and stabilisation in the State of Presence is a very hard task and for most it takes the whole lifetime. That's why reaching Final Enlightenment is quite a rare phenomenon. Most important is to understand that there is not One Enlightenment for everybody. For most beings, the feeling of completion relates to the experience of the overall integration in the energies of Awareness, Being and Heart. For most, not even the stabilisation in the State of Presence is the goal. Their goal is to reach an ability to be in this state most of the time and to be able to bring it back at one's wish when the state is lost. The Absolute State is too extreme for most Souls and in some cases can close the Heart, if it brings too much disidentification.

To become one with the Void is like dying. To transcend through the 'black hole' within the Hara and merge with the

Uncreated is truly a desire of very few Souls. These Souls are rather extreme in their evolution. We must remember that reaching a certain enlightened state does not always bring complete happiness. The main reason that most Souls incarnate is not to reach Enlightenment but to experience this very life and realise their desires. The awakening of I Am does not merely take you away from the adventure of life, it allows you to see clearly what it is that you want. Otherwise, one is neurotic and the mind creates endless desires not allowing one to catch up with fulfilling them.

When there is silence you can see; your eyes are clear for the first time and you can try to fulfil your Soul's desires. For this reason, we have to perceive the concept of Enlightenment in a non-linear, non-dogmatic way. Enlightenment does not refer merely to one type of realisation and it is not the only target in our evolution. Final Enlightenment is a destiny of very few Souls and they have to pay their own price. There is a certain justice here, in terms of distributing different kinds of happiness to different Souls. A Soul who reaches Final Enlightenment has to suffer many lifetimes; such a Soul has to be isolated, completely concentrated inward. Such a Soul has to often renounce human love and many other natural human needs. Such a Soul has to live in an extreme way. It is a high price... even though ultimately it is a bargain.

Are all Masters in the Same State?

Student: *Are all enlightened beings in the same state?*

Aziz: In most cases, those who announce their Enlightenment represent only a certain type of Self-realisation. Most often they represent the realisation of pure awareness. And even among them not all are stabilised in this experience. Not to be established in the State of Presence means that one is still losing it from time to time. In Zen, they say that after Enlightenment, twenty years practice is required! It is because, in their understanding, Enlightenment initially means to see one's true nature; and then one has to practice hard not to lose it. There is a level called 'beyond practice' where the state is spontaneously and permanently present, but it is not easy to reach. The problem with the popular view concerning 'sudden Enlightenment' is that their interpretation is rather naïve. This idea can be very misleading because many seekers assume Enlightenment is a sudden, complete and permanent shift of perception. They think that after Enlightenment everything suddenly changes and one is free from problems; that one is continuously happy and lives in bliss. But this is not true. Even those who are considered the greatest masters had to take many steps in their evolution towards completion. In most cases, a master reaches complete Enlightenment in old age.

Student: *So how come certain teachers who claim to be enlightened don't know that they deceive themselves?*

Aziz: First of all, they don't necessarily deceive themselves. They've possibly experienced a shift into pure awareness, and it is an enlightened state. The only question is whether it is the Final Enlightenment and whether they possess the complete knowledge about the awakening process. You see, it is a very subtle area. It does not work in such a way that you become enlightened and then you know everything. You may know nothing. When you become suddenly enlightened, it is similar to being transported, in one instant, in your sleep, to the top of Mount Everest. And you say: 'Oh, I'm so high but how did I get here? What am I doing here, actually?' You don't understand your situation yet, for your intelligence has not caught up with the experience. You must see that if there is no intelligence, any experience is meaningless. It is like an enlightened cow - the cow may become a Buddha, but her mind is not capable either of understanding or appreciating the gift of Freedom.

We are in the process of a multidimensional evolution. Even if one has experienced a certain shift of consciousness, it takes years for such a person to understand his or her state and much longer to be able to teach. It is not enough to be enlightened in order to teach. A spiritual master has to understand the process of awakening. It is a very complex process. It is not just to be there, hiding oneself behind the Guru-image and projecting energy onto seekers. Teaching is a responsibility and most teachers, because of their egos, want to become masters as quick as possible. They have some spiritual shift and immediately they start to give Satsang! It is ridiculous what is happening on the spiritual scene.

It is not to judge. It is not to walk around saying: 'this man is enlightened' and 'this one is not enlightened.' Just know that the term Enlightenment designates many stages and possibilities of awakening, and not everyone who awakens is completely enlightened. Use your sensitivity and discriminative wisdom in order to feel what level of Enlightenment the teacher represents and if you wish to choose him or her for a spiritual guide.

It is irrelevant for you whether a particular master is enlightened or not. It is their problem. It is not your life, it is theirs. The question is: how can such a teacher help you? What is important is whether he can give you a teaching that leads you straight to the Self. There are many pseudo-gurus who do not have any real understanding of the awakening process; they tell their followers, 'just stick around and everything will happen.' A real master never over-emphasises his own presence but is humble and hidden behind the light of Truth.

Do you understand? That is the point. If a spiritual teacher can help you, see this as an opportunity to grow, until the point where perhaps you may go beyond. I have personally met many masters which from my present perspective were not in a complete state. But still I have learnt from them and I am grateful because they shared their truth as much as they could.

Next, it is not necessary to be completely enlightened. Complete Enlightenment is the destiny of very few Souls. What an average person, an average seeker, needs to awaken to is a certain relatively permanent experience of the I Am, and the ability to come back to this experience at any time - to have this inner home. Such a person does not need to reach the Absolute State. Enlightenment is not the only purpose of life. You want to live life, you want to be happy, you wish to reach a certain essential amount of emotional fulfilment, you want to adventure in life, to express your creativity. If the purpose of life was only Enlightenment, this universe would not be created.

Yes...there are many elements. You are multidimensional and you need to have in your perspective the vision of your blueprint, your destiny and your completion. You are heading towards the point in your experience of the inner and the outer where you simply feel complete and done with this dimension.

Somebody can be enlightened and be an asshole, while someone else may be only partially connected to I Am but be a wonderful person. Enlightenment doesn't necessarily make you a better person. It gives you a foundation of inner peace, a continuity of awareness, and a depth of Being. But if the Heart is not awakened, the ego may still be arrogant. Apart from awakening, the Soul needs to still evolve emotionally, mentally and in many different areas.

Student: *Can one reach awakening for a few months and then lose it?*

Aziz: You see, sometimes you experience a certain expansion of consciousness but it is not grounded and you might prematurely let go of the practice. For example, someone has an experience of pure awareness but does not know about the necessity of self-remembrance and the state slowly evaporates. Often we hear about those who had Satori experiences but the experiences remain on the level of sweet memory. For that reason, it is so important to understand the process of awakening, the various possibilities of expansion and the basic laws of cultivation, stabilisation and integration...and so forth. Clarity is freedom from illusions and spiritual pitfalls.

Self-realisation - Self-confidence

Student: *I have a question about Self-realisation and self-confidence. Is it possible that after becoming a Buddha, one still lacks self-confidence? (Addressed by a Self-realised student).*

Aziz: Yes... it is a complex subject, as we need to see through many naïve views concerning Enlightenment. It is possible that one may become a Buddha and still be uncertain of it. On the other hand, it is possible to be absolutely self-confident about being a Buddha, without being one! From time to time we come across such individuals.

Before we speak about self-confidence, we have to know how to verify our attainment and what it really means to be a Buddha. For example, you may experience a shift of consciousness; you know that your state is different than it was before - but that is all you know. However, is it the Buddha State? The wrong view which so many seekers share is an assumption that Enlightenment is self-verifiable, self-proven. This means the moment you reach it, you should know it doubtlessly. Unfortunately, the reality of it is much more complex.

Because the reality of awakening is rich and rather complex, we need a complex and visionary teaching which can mirror this complexity in our understanding. We meet many seekers who are resistant to go deeper in the Teaching, for they don't want to make an effort to understand. They escape into spirituality because they are already too complicated and overloaded with knowledge. But without an essential understanding, how could you possibly go deeper into the multiple dimensions of Self-realisation? Our teaching is not complicated but complex. Reality is complex and, if we wish to reflect the real truth about Enlightenment, we have to create a teaching which is precisely as complex as reality. We don't feed you slogans here, well cooked baby food from past traditions, neither do we wish to entertain you with pseudo-satsang dialogues. We give you raw Truth. But you must remember that truth is often less attractive than fairy tales.

The first step is to know how to verify one's attainment or the lack of; for how to verify that one is not awakened is also an important issue. Most people have to be convinced that they are ignorant. They don't believe it. They say: 'we are fine, we are just enlightened enough! What do you want from us? We are good people and we pay our taxes.' (Laughter...). As far as the verification of attainment goes, our teaching speaks about nothing else. One can verify one's state only if there is enough understanding and sensitivity... for it does require an enormous sensitivity. When you have the proper knowledge, you simply compare the state you are in with the description and information given to you.

If you have a competent master, the attainment can be verified by him or her. But in the beginning, doubts cannot be avoided for they are a part of the maturation process. If someone has no doubts, this person should be even more doubted as something is definitely wrong here. Certainty is a function of time, growth of intelligence and integration on the energy level.

Even famous masters had many doubts about their state. For instance, the main translator of Maharaj reported that Poonjaji visited the master in search for confirmation of his Enlightenment. Poonjaji was very happy because Maharaj told him, 'you are the Ultimate!' But, the translator added, 'Poonjaji didn't know that Maharaj was saying it to everybody!' You would be surprise but most spiritual masters have serious doubts about their attainment. In particular, those who project a strong guru-image have the biggest inferiority complexes!

Not all Souls have the need for self-confidence because they do not necessarily wish to translate their experience in terms of being the Buddha. You see, the moment you say 'I am a Buddha,' a comparison is involved. In such a case, you don't say 'I am what I am,' but 'I am like the Buddha.' Some Souls do not have any need to compare themselves with anybody else, in terms of their spiritual realisation. Either they are more ego-less or perhaps their intelligence lacks the curiosity and proper enquiring abilities. The moment you start to represent an enlightened state in the form of teaching, you have to be fully confident about your realisation. In such a situation, you do not represent merely yourself, you represent Awakening.

However, there is a possibility that even though there is the right knowledge, understanding and verification of the state, one may still lack confidence. Here, the lack of confidence is purely psychological. You see, the one who verifies attainment is your own intelligence and this intelligence is connected to your personality. Your personality is full of complexities. Most seekers have some type of inferiority complex! Here, we may think that Enlightenment takes us beyond personality and therefore these mundane problems disappear. But that is incorrect. Personality still remains and needs to develop and evolve.

Once in Korea there was an awakened Zen master who was not giving any dharma talks even though his attainment was very high. The reason was that he was simply shy! It is very refreshing to realise that an enlightened person can be simply shy! A Human Buddha. The self-confidence refers not only to your trust in your Self-realisation but also to your self-image in regards to others. You see, here you have to face not only your doubts but the doubts of others too! No one will believe that you are a Buddha unless you are a charismatic asshole! Otherwise you don't look special; so why should anyone believe you are a Buddha?

Because the projections about Enlightenment in the collective mind are so exaggerated, in combination with the inferiority complex, a human Buddha may not believe in his or her attainment. The moment you are born, everyone tells you that you are just a tiny gear in the great machine of society. Unless you make a career and big money, you are simply nothing. To free oneself from this inferiority complex, one tries to be different. Some teenagers, for instance, try to look as strange as possible just to be different, but it is all based on an inferiority complex. Do you see it?

Therefore look at your psychological patterns and see the real causes of your fears. Some doubts are natural but if a doubt grows roots within you, it becomes a poison. In such a case, psychological work with oneself is required.

Part of the lack of self-confidence is positive, so to speak, for it is a sign of humility. To call oneself a Buddha is to make oneself special on some level. And our Heart may rebel against it, for in truth, we are nothing special in a positive sense; we are like the air we breathe, deeply ordinary. Reaching the Buddha state is to become even more 'nothing special,' for it is simply a natural state.

When you express your inner realisation, unfortunately, you must face the collective mind which is full of projections and ego-games. Even if a master is free from ego-perceptions of his state, one cannot avoid facing the mediocre minds of others. That's why, the teaching work is a big compromise, for one enters the realm of unconsciousness and impurity. To be a Buddha is nothing special but because in the collective mind, projections about the Buddha, have grown to a monstrous size, one may hesitate to call oneself a Buddha.

Once upon a time, Hui Neng was asked: 'are you enlightened?' And he replied: 'no!' He said 'no' for he was beyond the self-referral aspect of Enlightenment; it was no more an ego-image for him. What he basically said was: 'I am what I am - call it Enlightenment, I don't care, call it ignorance, I don't care either.' His answer did not come from a lack of self-confidence but from being beyond any need to be self-confident. The ultimate confidence is beyond ego-image, beyond the polarity of Enlightenment and ignorance.

In truth, why do you care? You are what you are. When you wish to teach, you simply teach, you share your truth. Look inside and see why the issue of self-confidence is there? Why do you want to be confident in being a Buddha? Why is it all necessary? As you relax more, you care less about these matters. It is a function of time and certain experiences you have to go through. As long as you are reaching the Inner, the need for confirmation is naturally present. But when you complete the inner elements, you slowly drop everything. Even the concept of being a Buddha gets erased from your psyche as this conceptualising pertains to ignorance, in truth. The ultimate meaning of being a Buddha is not to be conscious of being one

Is Enlightenment the Same for Men and Women?

Student: *What is the difference between the Enlightenment of a man and of a woman?*

Aziz: Men and women in their evolution towards Self-realisation need to follow similar principles, but with a different flavour. Men and women generally speaking, utilise different predominant centres. Both have their advantages and disadvantages. Men have more energy in the mind, which allows them to awaken awareness faster. Women, on the other hand are more in the Heart and in Being. Women, generally speaking are more balanced. But by the law of polarities, because women are more balanced, they have less motivation for awakening. In the sense of reaching the Buddha State, there are more enlightened men than women; but, on the other hand, there are more women with an awakened Heart. For men, because of their predominant mind quality, they are more disconnected from Existence; their need for transcendence is much stronger. For instance, there are many more men committing suicide than women. This tells us something.

The next issue is when a woman attains Enlightenment, most often the flavour of this realisation is different than in the case of a man. A man Buddha tends to have a more crystallised attention; while in the case of a woman Buddha, the energy is more spread into Being or Heart and attention is less solidified. To have a very crystallised attention has good and bad sides. When the State of Presence is very strong, it may be more difficult to let go of oneself in the act of surrender to the Inner State. One is simply very conscious and consciousness also makes intelligence more alert. The positive side of having a strong awareness is less thoughts and a deeper anchor in Being. When awareness drops into Being, it deepens this experience, adding new strength to it. Also, awareness deepens the power of recognition which means that there is more intelligence integrated with the experience.

Men and women have different predominant centres, but they both aspire for a maximum balance and harmony which includes their uniqueness. We should not forget that there are also different types of men and women. For instance, some men are more feminine than women in general and vice versa.

Some women seekers rebel against the work with awareness. They think that they will lose their feminine quality. But we would say that, in truth, awareness allows a woman to become a real woman who has the dignity of real presence. Of course, an excessive focus on awareness, like with Zen training, can damage the feminine quality of a woman. But with the technology of transformation that we use and with the energy of Guidance, this danger is not present here at all. Therefore, to conclude, a woman has to crystallise her attention, at least to a degree, and a man has to discover the softness and vulnerability of the Heart. The balance needs to be found. This balance, for a woman, is a bit different than for a man but there are similar characteristics. In truth, without awareness there is no real Heart for one is too unconscious; on the other hand, without the Heart, awareness is truly meaningless and barren. When you have difficulties experiencing one aspect of I Am, often it is a sign that it is this very aspect which you lack the most.

Here, for example, we have one female student who in the past had a strong resistance to work with the State of Presence. She used to say that she was different and unique, and that she did not want to follow such a 'linear' model of awakening. But eventually, she understood the importance of the State of Presence. After cultivating awareness for some time, she became established in the State of Presence. She was able to retain her unique flavour and feminine quality but now with the presence of awareness. Anna, what has the work with attention brought to you?

Student: *I have a clear sense of Me as my identity beyond the mind. I have a direct way to be free from the mind and a certain important solidity and continuity within this mind. I find that it allows me to go much deeper into Being and Heart, as I am simply present. I have a refuge outside of the mind.*

Aziz: Yes... the continuity of intelligence. Imagine that you throw an anchor into the ocean. This anchor represents your presence; its movement and direction represents your intelligence. The bottom of the ocean represents Being. If a person has no presence and no continuity of intelligence, such a person will be like an anchor which suddenly vanishes as it is dropping in the Ocean. The act must then again be repeated.

It is like this. When a person resting in Being during meditation all of a sudden begins day-dreaming, he or she reverses the gravitational pull of Being and instead rises energetically to the surface. The whole momentum of letting go gets lost. Again, one drops into Being...one gets lost in the mind and energy moves up to the surface. You throw the anchor of your presence into the ocean of Beingness and this anchor keeps on disappearing, for there is no continuity. Do you understand?

A person who has awareness and an awakened Heart experiences this Heart in a completely different way than a person who has no continuity of presence. This experience is simply much more meaningful. What makes you know that you rest in Being? You feel it, your intelligence knows it and you are present. When you lose yourself, not only are you no longer conscious of Being but the energy of Being moves up, losing its depth. When you rest consciously, your very presence deepens the experience, allowing energy to be pulled, according to the force of gravity, towards the Unmanifested. For that reason, the continuity of presence-intelligence is so essential.

The Other Shore is Now

Student: *What is the Other Shore?*

Aziz: It was the Buddha's term for the Absolute. He spoke about crossing the ocean of Existence and reaching Nirvana. The Other Shore is Now. It is the essence of the Now. The ocean that you are crossing is the ocean of time and the Other Shore which you are reaching, is the Timeless.

Where is the Timeless? It is an important question; where is it? It is Now, it is inside the Now. And where is time? It is outside the Now. The Timeless is the container and time is the content. To cross the ocean of time is to move from outside the Now into the Now. Time is horizontal and the Timeless is vertical. One needs to move from the horizontal dimension into the vertical one. The cross-section between the Here and the Now is the zero point of existence, the meeting with the Absolute. Who is crossing the ocean of Samsara? It is the One who can neither be found in the ocean nor can be found on the Other Shore. The mysterious experiencer of Samsara and Nirvana is beyond both of them. We speak about the Soul, the dimension of Me. We discover she is neither created nor uncreated, nor can she be found in Creation... But she can be found in the Dimension of Me.

How does this Me move from time to timelessness? First she freezes the horizontal flow of time by awakening her real centre of awareness. The State of Presence is itself an experience in time, but gives one the continuity of self-attention within the movement of time. This continuity keeps one constantly in the present moment. And the present moment is the entrance to the Now; it is not Now yet but it is as close to the Now as one can reach, from the horizontal perspective. The State of Presence exists on the edge of two realities: time and the timelessness. From the place of the real centre of intelligence, which is pure consciousness, Me surrenders vertically into the Now. We call it surrender into Being.

The State of Presence is freedom from unconsciousness, which is the subconscious dissipation of one's sense of identity in the horizontal reality. When one is stable in the experience of oneself, one can submit oneself into Being. Non-doing is the key to experience Being, for Being itself represents our absence. The inside of the Now is itself our absence. When Me lets go, she is pulled by the force of gravity to the heart of the Now which is the Timeless, the Absolute. This movement of surrender, from the present moment to the Now represents different levels of absorption, reaching different depths of the Now. The final shift to the Other Shore takes place when the gateway to the unmanifested opens fully and Me rests finally in the Beyond. When the Other Shore is reached, the two shores become one and they contain the ocean of time.

But what is 'this shore'? Before we cross over the ocean of time, we have to begin from somewhere. Don't we? This shore is the very creation of Me in time. Me herself is this shore. Me moves through the ocean of time, in her evolution reaching the Other Shore, which is her origin. Therefore, Me which is the relative subject, subject to Creation is This Shore. The absolute subjectivity, the Source of Creation is the Other Shore. The ocean of Samsara, the ocean of time is Creation. The process of crossing the ocean is evolution. And finally, reaching the Other Shore is the meeting of the relative subject with the absolute subject - the meeting of Me with the Beloved.

A Mystic is One with the Mystery

Student: *What does it mean to be a mystic?*

Aziz: There are three types of awakened beings. One is the Sage, which is an ideal of Taoism, for example. The sage is someone who has realised the Absolute State. The sage is one who has reached the Unborn; the sage is someone who has gone beyond the phenomenal reality; he is someone who abides upon nothing, is One with the original void.

The second type of the enlightened being is the Saint. A saint is enlightened to the Heart, like Jesus, for example. The saint is one who knows the Beloved, who is one with the Divine. The saint is someone whose life is a constant prayer, a constant communion with the Creator.

The third type of Self-realised being is the Mystic. The mystic is a combination of the sage and the saint. The mystic is someone who has one foot in the Absolute and the second foot in the Divine. Such a being is absolutely still and clear like a diamond mountain, but at the same time absolutely sensitive, gentle and vulnerable. The sage is not vulnerable; the saint is not still. The mystic cannot be categorised, for he or she is free and beyond freedom.

Enlightenment beyond Enlightenment

Student: *Could you speak more about the state Beyond Enlightenment?*

Aziz: The state Beyond Enlightenment can be viewed from several different angles. For example, awakening to the Heart and transcending the Absolute State is one way to go beyond Enlightenment. Another way is to drop the concept of being a Buddha, to drop the need to translate one's state as anything. The next way is to return to the world and to the reality of being human. That's why we speak of the Human Buddha. The next meaning of going beyond Enlightenment refers to the continuation of one's evolution into the Mystery. There are further Enlightenment's which are beyond the traditional models. One can expand infinitely into the dimension of Love and Intelligence. But how far one wishes to expand, relates to one's unique blueprint and evolution. That is the other meaning of going beyond Enlightenment. There are many secrets, many mysteries and many ways of encountering Infinity which are beyond the totality of human knowledge.

Beyond Consciousness

Student: *Aziz, are you always conscious of everything you do?*

Aziz: On the contrary - I am hardly conscious of anything! I am hardly conscious of being Here!

Student: *Are you conscious of not being conscious?*

Aziz: My state is one with consciousness and far beyond. I am not conscious of being unconscious. In fact I prefer to be as little conscious as possible. However, when I am unconscious - I am Conscious. I am not conscious of being unconscious - I am just Conscious, without referring to anything. This Presence is just constant, and it rests constantly upon the Supreme Reality.

The evolution of consciousness is just a beginning of the journey into the Supreme Awakening. When the light of awareness is established, we are free from our negative absence in unconsciousness. But what can we do with this freedom? We surrender it to the Absolute through our Being, and to the Divine through our Heart. Here, we begin the process of merging with the Beloved. There is no end to this love affair with God. And, dear friend, it is far beyond the human effort of being conscious.

Coming Back to the Market Place

Student: *If a person is completely Self-realised then should the person go back to being active or does it depend on the blueprint of the Soul?*

Aziz: Certainly it relates to the blueprint of the Soul, but it is also connected to the past lives of the person. For example, a particular Soul may have experienced everything already in past lives. This means there is no longer a need to return to the world because one is completed. But generally speaking, coming back to the 'market place' is a very positive and important step in the process through which one transcends attachment to the Inner. Here, one transcends the subconscious belief that there is a distinction between the inner and the outer. One is experiencing the whole of reality as it is. It also relates to the age of the person. If one is young and has not experienced the world yet, naturally one needs to mature also in the outer; one needs to grow emotionally and to experience the different challenges in life. Also the psychological growth is important for the Soul's completion.

Enlightened Women

Student: *Could you speak more about this why there are so few female spiritual masters?*

Aziz: Generally speaking, women are more Here and men are more Now. Because women are responsible for giving birth to children, nature gave them a slightly different psychological constitution. Women are more practical and connected to the energy of the earth. They are also more balanced psychologically. Because they are more balanced, the motivation to transcend this dimension is naturally smaller. The man is more in the head and the woman is more in the Heart.

The question of who has more advantages, whether man or woman, cannot be answered. Both are in a difficult situation (laughter...). It is easier for the woman to awaken the Heart and for the man to awaken awareness. You see, to be a spiritual master, to be a complete Buddha, is an extreme and rare case. Even among teachers who give Satsangs, most represent only partial Self-realisation. One of the pivots of Enlightenment is the awakening of pure awareness. There are more enlightened men because they simply have more energy in the head and therefore stronger concentration and will power.

If we look at the concept of enlightenment in a less linear way, we may discover that the situation is not so simple. Globally speaking, women are more enlightened compared to the majority of men. They are closer to Being, closer to the Heart, less negative and more harmonious. That's why, even though there are more fully Self-realised men, universally speaking there are more enlightened women! Men are less enlightened and generally suffer more, also because they have a stronger ego-image and are more egoistic. For that reason, more men want to become masters. It comes from the ego. A woman does not have such a need to teach others because she receives emotional fulfilment in other areas of life. You see, for many masters there is emotional gratification involved in teaching. Women are less goal-oriented, less ambitious, they possess more the quality of humility.

If we see this matter in a more broad way, beyond simplistic ideas about Enlightenment, we drop the desire to categorise Enlightenment according to traditional criteria. Here, we can reach a truly human vision of Enlightenment. To show you the complexity of this area, we will ask you a question. Is it better to awaken awareness and reach freedom from the mind while having a closed Heart; or is it better to be enlightened to the Heart while not recognising the State of Presence? There is no answer to this question, for it is related to the particular individual Soul and her blueprint.

Everything has its price. To stabilise oneself in the State of Presence, for an average seeker is a life long task. Such a person who insists on completion in this area of growth, must to some extent sacrifice the work with the Heart. Life is short and not everyone can live the life of a monk. What we are trying to demonstrate to you is that there is no one generic Enlightenment. Also the type of evolution the Soul chooses, can not always fit the traditional concept of Enlightenment.

Student: *Is it really necessary to close the Heart in order to stabilise in awareness?*

Aziz: The Heart, in most cases is already closed! Therefore, there is no need to close her a second time. In the case of a person who focuses on awareness, one is not closing the Heart. One is simply not doing much to open her. If a seeker already has an open Heart on some level, then he or she does not need to close the Heart, but only to simply pay more attention to awareness. But if the Heart is too open, too sensitive, sometimes one needs to close her temporarily in order to reach the stability of awareness. The reason is that if one is too emotional, one is unable to concentrate, one is too distracted, too diffused...

Unlike awareness, in the work with the Heart, we use very feminine energy. Feminine and masculine energies do not cancel each other out but sometimes they can contradict themselves in the process of awakening particular centres. In those instances, we focus more on one area of growth. But it all depends on the quality of the Soul. That's why, private instructions must be given. Some Souls choose to grow more or less harmoniously in all areas of their being simultaneously.

Student: *Should one follow one's intuition regarding the direction in which one needs to grow?*

Aziz: Yes, but intuition must be supported by knowledge. You have to understand the life of I Am and the basic laws and principles which govern it. Intuition without knowledge often misleads us. In the instance of an energy healer, one must follow intuition and inspiration but if he or she lacks basic psychological and esoteric knowledge, it will diminish healing abilities.

Transcending the Myth of Satori

Student: *Is it important to have a strong, explosive awakening experience in order to fully recognise the State of Presence? We hear about all those Zen stories regarding amazing Satori experiences.*

Aziz: The recognition of the State of Presence is a radical but natural experience. You see, the experience is as it is, but how we translate it, relates to the clarity and sensitivity of your intelligence. Zen stories often do a bad job, as they mystify the enlightened experience too much. Here, we are touching a very important problem present in the spiritual scene. The problem is that seekers expect too much or something completely unreal from Awakening. We understand that to speak highly about Enlightenment is a sign of appreciation. But when we see the minds of those who hear about these descriptions - we calm down in our desire to praise Enlightenment too much. They are already too agitated by the concept of Enlightenment. Why give them more food for that imaginations? By praising Enlightenment too much, the minds of seekers become conditioned and programmed into very unreal expectations. That was the case with the teaching of Rajneesh, for instance. By making Enlightenment so big, he basically hypnotised his disciples into a subconscious belief that no one can reach it, apart from himself of course.

The truth about Enlightenment is that it is both extraordinary and ordinary. If we see the enlightened state as ordinary, it would not be true, for it is something beyond what an ordinary person could even dream about. And when we say that Enlightenment is extraordinary, that is not true either; it is a very natural and truly ordinary state. Because the minds of seekers have been already conditioned by the vision of Enlightenment as something completely extraordinary, we prefer to emphasise the ordinary aspect of Self-realisation. It is simply an expression of compassion. We call it de-hypnosis, for we de-hypnotise the seekers mind from the magical and unreal vision of Enlightenment.

There are many misconceptions about the term 'Sudden Enlightenment.' Many are enchanted by the dream of Sudden Enlightenment. But what is the actual meaning of this term? Few know. It is simply to recognise the State of Presence. You cannot recognise the State of Presence gradually. How can you recognise the State of Presence gradually? Either you recognise it or you don't. It is a radical shift of focus from the mind to the centre of awareness, to the subject.

When we realise that throughout life we live without experiencing any real subject, we can truly appreciate the experience of awakening. It is a real miracle, a moment of celebration. But, paradoxically, it is at the same time, an ordinary, simple and natural experience. Enlightenment is extraordinary for someone who is not enlightened, but it is an ordinary and simple experience for someone who is inside the state!

The feeling of explosion is due to imbalance. When a seeker is kept in darkness, without intuitive clarity about the whole process of awakening, the experience of awakening may be truly shocking and most unexpected. An 'explosion' is not a natural way of recognising the State of Presence. When a student is guided in a proper, balanced, clear and intelligent way, awakening takes place more smoothly, in a gentle and natural way. You see, in the Zen the style of teaching is to explain as little as possible. That is the beauty and the danger of Zen. When you don't explain things, you avoid the risk of distorting the purity of non-conceptual truth; but you allow for the possibility of more mistakes in practice - one can easily become trapped in the incorrect idea of Enlightenment. The internal reality of the Self is very complex and extremely subtle.

In the past, Zen masters had such respect for the Truth that they simply did not want to reveal it to the student unless he showed total determination and was ready to give even his life for it! The 'explosive' stories in Zen are caused due to the strong contrast between the darkness when entering the Path and the strong lightening effect of Self-realisation. All these descriptions about 'amazing' satoris with which all Zen students are so fascinated, prove a lack of maturity and create unrealistic expectations.

You see, the problem is that for you to believe in your realisation, you must first free yourself from all these pre-judgements, misconceptions and wrong views about Enlightenment. It is a real problem to reach this freedom. It is often actually more difficult than to reach Enlightenment! Do you see? Do you see how difficult it is to reach freedom from other people's projections about Enlightenment? Do you see how deeply you are conditioned by the collective consciousness of seekers? All these wrong views and superstitions are like a heavy burden on your shoulders. You can hardly walk!

What kind of explosion do you expect from the recognition of the State of Presence? If you sit with the concentration of Zen students with a koan, the moment you let go, this very meeting with the simplicity of I Am may feel like an explosion. But if you recognise I Am in a natural way, this experience is simple, clear, focussed, centred and serene. The whole splendour or 'explosiveness' of this experience lies not in energy behaviour but in the meaning of this realisation. The meaning of awakening is profound indeed. When you truly see what it means to be in the State of Presence, you become amazed... Here, consciousness meets its own light of presence. It is a moment of celebration; it has taken you many lifetimes to attain such a high state.

But if your intelligence is immature and shallow, it is unable to see the whole depth of this realisation. This is unfortunately the case with most seekers. That's why, most seekers are not ready to receive the gift of awakening. To give awakening to all seekers could happen through the intervention of radical Grace, but it would be a waste. It is similar to giving diamonds to the blind. For a blind person, a diamond is just an ordinary stone. In order to receive the gift of awakening, the seeker must mature many lifetimes, and even then, many reach only a limited depth of intelligence. In these cases, Existence compromises and allows one to become awakened, even though the gift is only appreciated partially.

You must see that very few seekers desire awakening. They do certainly want to help themselves, but it has nothing to do with awakening. If awakening was given to them, they would throw it in the nearest garbage bin.

There is a story from the life of Kabir. His daughter was very upset seeing the low quality of seekers coming to visit her farther. To demonstrate this sad truth to her farther, one day before everybody left she said to all visitors, 'please, make sure that you come tomorrow because Kabir will transmit Enlightenment to everybody!' And nobody came!

That is really true. You may not believe that Enlightenment is not what most desire because you don't see how unconscious the majority of seekers are! There is simply nobody there!

Truth about the Sudden Enlightenment

Student: *I have a question related to the concept of sudden Enlightenment. Is sudden Enlightenment the same as 'beyond cultivation'?*

Aziz: There are many mistaken views related to the concept of sudden Enlightenment. The matter is more complicated when we realise that there is not only one Enlightenment. Enlightenment to pure consciousness involves quite a different process than Enlightenment to the Absolute State or to the Heart. Because the State of Presence concerns most who are on the Path, we will focus on this area now. Usually, the concept of sudden Enlightenment involves an assumption that there are no steps in-between ignorance and the awakened state. On the other hand, the gradual approach believes that we become more and more enlightened. The truth is, however, that before grasping the mind's essence one is left groping in the darkness, not becoming more enlightened at all. In truth, the Path starts with Awakening. But awakening does not mean that the Path is over. That is perhaps the biggest misconception about sudden Enlightenment. It seems that Zen has reached the highest understanding of this matter, for according to Zen, after Enlightenment the real work begins. One still needs to sit Zazen twenty more years, for example in order to cultivate the awakened experience.

There are a few possibilities regarding the concept of sudden Enlightenment. First is, 'sudden Enlightenment and then gradual cultivation.' This means that recognition of the essence is sudden but the state is not constant. After the recognition of the State of Presence, one needs some time to stabilise this experience.

Second is, 'gradual practice, then sudden Enlightenment and then gradual cultivation.' This is the case with the majority. After practicing for many years, developing the qualities of mindfulness, one has sudden insight into the nature of awareness. Still cultivation is needed to establish the inner state. The third possibility, although rare, is 'sudden Enlightenment and sudden cultivation.' Here, after having the insight into the state beyond the mind, one becomes simultaneously stabilised. These are the main three possibilities concerning the suddenness and the gradualness of awakening. To be remembered though is that the real practice begins with awakening. From that point, you simply know what you are doing and your practice, for the first time, relates to You and not to the ideas of Enlightenment.

To answer your question once more - sudden Enlightenment is not the same as the stage 'beyond cultivation.' Beyond cultivation is the stage where the necessity of practice is over. Some Zen masters propagate the view of non-ending cultivation. That concept is not correct. Any kind of cultivation must be dropped at one stage, so one can evolve into the other dimensions of reality and experience. Both concepts, that sudden Enlightenment is the end of cultivation, and that cultivation is non-ending, do not reflect the truth of awakening.

Enlightenment: The Divine Boredom

Student: *Is an enlightened being beyond boredom?*

Aziz: No. An enlightened being is in a state of Absolute Boredom! We call it the divine boredom, for it has its source not in the mind but is one with life. An enlightened being is in a state of clearly seeing that there is nothing to do! Can you see that there is nothing to do? There is nothing to do but one is still Here! This very contrast between not having anything to do and still being alive - is boredom. Consciousness, on some level, is one with the life force. When the Soul becomes One with the Universal Absence, she reaches the conditions of complete surrender, divine passivity. But, because this passivity is connected, at the same time, to the life-force which must recreate itself moment by moment, the Soul experiences a type of tension. It is the tension between the divine passivity and the natural tendency of the life force to participate actively in Creation. This very existential tension represents pure boredom.

Boredom is the meeting between the dimension of time with the Timeless; it is the meeting of presence with its absence. Boredom is this very suspension of the Self-realised Soul between her existence as Me and her dissolution into the Source of Creation.

To Understand one's Awakening

Student: *How can one understand one's awakening? You spoke about a huge difference between two awakened beings if they represent different levels of understanding. Why do we need knowledge? Why do we need, for example, to study different teachings?*

Aziz: Why are you asking? Why do you want to understand anything at all? Understanding is clarity and clarity is its own gratification. You see, Enlightenment is not just a state. It is the unity of the inner state and understanding. When we spoke about someone who is in the enlightened state, but without understanding, we meant that the state is present only on the energy level. Therefore, awakening, in such a case, is only partial. What is the meaning in being even in the highest state, if intelligence is asleep? What is the meaning of any kind of experience, if the experiencer is almost dead? Who is experiencing Enlightenment? A rock is in the Absolute State, but can we call it the Buddha? Recognition itself is the light which gives meaning to any awakening, to anything. Energy and intelligence are the two fundamental sides of Existence. Energy is the base but this base is meaningless without feedback from intelligence. Energy is the building block of Creation but intelligence is its very justification. Energy without intelligence has no meaning, but on the other hand, intelligence without the foundation of energy has no roots. The absence of energy would annihilate intelligence. Intelligence must refer to What Is, that is to Beingness or Pure Energy. Intelligence and energy are two sides of the way the Soul experiences reality. Within the energy state the Soul abides, she exists as a Soul. And intelligence allows the Soul to know that she exists, as well as to understand her existence. And we should not forget that intelligence itself includes the sensitivity of the Heart and the subtle mind.

In the evolution of the Soul, understanding and the energy state must always go together. Understanding itself is only in the mind; it is abstract and empty. From the other side, the energy state without understanding lacks the depth of appreciation, lacks this very knowing which gives meaning to the experience. Seekers who study many teachings but lack experience are like sick people reading about perfect health. They waste their time and hurt themselves in truth. On the other hand, those who practice a lot but refuse to enlarge their knowledge, they evolve only partially; their intelligence is dull and usually they cannot make any real progress. Often such practitioners are stuck in some area of incorrect practice or false understanding.

Understanding without an energy foundation has no real connection to reality. A Soul who is in such a situation is deeply suffering, restless and disconnected from Being. Even the centre of awareness is an energy state. Intelligence itself has its own energetic centre, which is the primal vibration of self-attention. However, for the Soul to get out of suffering, more important than understanding is to be grounded energetically in I Am. Even if there is no depth of recognition, at least one is free from suffering. And suffering is primarily an energy state or rather an energy disorder, imbalance.

When you close your eyes in meditation, you experience peace - what is this peace? It is an energy experience or energy expansion. You have this experience not merely because you have closed your eyes but because certain faculties within your energy system have been activated. There is some concentration in the mind and your Being quality has been deepened. Another person closes their eyes and experiences restlessness, boredom, discomfort and suffocation. This person may have perfect understanding but how useless it is!

Without intelligence, the inner state has no depth. The presence of the inner state is shallow and cannot reflect the whole depth of this experience. It is intelligence which allows you to truly appreciate the whole beauty and extraordinariness of I Am. That which allows one to give real feedback to the inner state, in terms of recognition and appreciation, is the combination of understanding and sensitivity.

The difference between two fully Self-realised beings can be enormous, in terms of recognition. For one the whole experience of the inner state may be just a feeling of calmness and stillness. For the other, Self-realisation is a meeting with God, the most moving experience of all! What makes such a difference? It is Intelligence and the Heart.

Next subject. In order to understand yourself as a multidimensional being, you have to be able to put together different parts of yourself, so they function as one harmonious organism. How to understand, for instance, that the inner silence and the movement of thoughts can co-exist? How to live in these two apparently exclusive realities? How to understand that one has transcended the mind reaching the Absolute and still may have desires or fears? How to understand this? Do you see how concepts condition our perception of reality? Do you see that without basic conceptual tool one is unable to grow and to understand one's situation? Even though we speak about the non-conceptual state as the foundation, still without having concepts reflecting our reality, we cannot exist as human beings. Concepts, we could say, bridge energy, that is pure isness with understanding. And understanding is the pure knowing reflecting the meaning of Existence. Where does understanding occur? In the space of consciousness. Consciousness can be seen as of a field of pure knowing without content. Understanding is the content of consciousness, that is, the meaning of consciousness.

In order for your intelligence to grow, you need to receive information from collective consciousness. To some extent you need to study spiritual teachings and get to know basic spiritual concepts. It was the effort of many generations to create spiritual understanding. A person who has no basic knowledge, has no foundation to understand the phenomenon of Self-realisation. Understanding is also a Vision of reality. Life and the vision of life, are one. In a sense it is true that you, on some level, create your reality for your vision determines your life. Everyone already has some vision. Even the most primitive and unconscious individual, has a vision of life reflecting the level of his or her intelligence. Life is dynamic. You are not just living - you are becoming. You create yourself and your universe moment by moment, day by day. If your vision is shallow, such is your life, such is your spiritual understanding. As you expand in your understanding, so your vision evolves, becoming more rich and sophisticated. Your vision reflects your depth and the depth of reality you are living in. Understanding allows you to live in an intelligent and beautiful way in the heart of the biggest puzzle which has happened to us - Creation. And understanding must be anchored in the Heart, for only the Heart can reflect the subtleties of Truth, beyond the linear conclusions of the mind. The Heart knows the truth of Existence much more deeply, but she needs to channel herself through the mind - to know that she knows!

After Enlightenment

Student: *Does the Buddha remember the time when he was in a state of forgetfulness?*

Aziz: To remember one's past forgetfulness is important in teaching work. It is like a doctor needs to remember what it means to be sick, otherwise he cannot understand his patients. A master needs to remember, on some level, forgetfulness as well as the process of getting out of it. Often a master forgets his or her past ignorance. When a master does not remember his past forgetfulness, there is little chance that he can understand in a true sense his disciple. A master has to understand what the ignorant state is as such and needs to have insights into the difficulties each disciple must face.

You see Enlightenment is simple but ignorance is complex. In a sense to understand Enlightenment is much easier than to understand ignorance! We speak sometimes about 'enlightenment to ignorance,' which is very important for a spiritual teacher. To be enlightened to ignorance is to understand fully the ignorant state of consciousness and the mechanism of awakening.

Ignorance is not simply a negative state of consciousness. From a certain perspective, ignorance represents an important stage in evolution. For instance, the ego is ignorant of the Self, but, at the same time, it reflects a higher state of evolution than animal consciousness. For an animal, to reach ego-consciousness would be Enlightenment! The ego is the bridge between the subconscious realm and pure consciousness. Do not remain under the illusion thinking that ignorance is some kind of mistake. Ignorance itself is a stage of evolution. Ego-consciousness is a passage between animal consciousness and the Buddha State. It is neither unconscious nor is it fully conscious; it is the state in-between.

An animal cannot create a clear self-referral and without this ability, awakening is impossible. Self-referral is that which bridges the subconscious Me with pure 'I.' From the viewpoint of evolution, the ego represent a very high state of consciousness. It is through the ego that the subject senses itself for the first time, in a clear way. However, in order to reach the Real Me, the ego must be transcended.

Ignorance is not an illusion of the eye; it is a reality. This reality must be respected. There are laws and principles which govern the reality of forgetfulness. For example, in order to reach awakening one has to develop an essential amount of mindfulness and crystallise attention; one has to respect the laws of energy; one needs to breathe properly; one needs to meditate on a regular basis, doing retreats, and so forth. Awakening is not a miracle. It is not that suddenly you say 'oh, all is the Self!' and your work is over. Not at all! Awakening is a complex process of evolution. That's why ignorance must be understood.

For instance, it is not so simple to remember the State of Presence. Is it? Whose mistake is it that the 'I' cannot remember itself? It is nobody's mistake. It is simply a part of the maturation of energy. One is unable, in the beginning, to keep the State of Presence continuously, for the energy system cannot contain this experience all the time.

Apart from the importance of remembering one's past forgetfulness for the sake of the teaching work, it helps one to appreciate one's present experience. Awakening is a gift from Existence. However, when one has been in the awakened state for a long time, one forgets that one is in a special state. A natural part of the blueprint of awakening is the ability to appreciate one's evolutionary achievements. And appreciation can take place only in comparison with something else, only in contrast to its opposite side. It is the comparison with one's own past that allows one to see over and over the truth of how blessed one is to receive the gift of Freedom.

The Impact of Awakening on the Collective Mind

Student: *Does an awakened being affect the collective unconscious or the collective consciousness? Are they the same?*

Aziz: Nothing has an impact on the collective mind because there is no hope for collective unconsciousness. Your question is coming from your hope that there is something that can change collective unconsciousness but nothing can change it! But there are individuals who break away from collective unconsciousness. Awakened beings have an impact on those individuals in terms of direct teaching as well as on the esoteric level. The awakened energy affects many individual Souls who are on the Path; Souls who are trying to free their hearts from collective unconsciousness and to reach the Inner Light.

Student: *Are all Souls trying to reach the light in their own way?*

Aziz: No, most Souls are trying to reach even deeper unconsciousness! You see, the reason that the Soul incarnated is similar to an alcoholic who goes to the pub. He has to get drunk, to get intoxicated and to forget about everything. There are certain Souls who try to reach the Inner Light but these Souls are extremely rare. That has to be clear. These Souls are exceptional. It has always been like this. This situation is present not just in our times or in our civilisation. It has always been like this. The level of humanity is very low. You see, humanity has just descended from the trees. If you look at a monkey, he is not looking for I Am, he is looking for bananas. If you give I Am to the monkey, you will just make him unhappy because he will become too conscious. When you are too conscious, it is very difficult because you cannot sleep all day, you cannot eat bananas all day. You have to do something with yourself. Consciousness is a responsibility. It is not enough just to be conscious. In truth, consciousness is difficult to digest. That's why, most people don't want to be conscious. They want to be unconscious. When you are unconscious, you suffer less because you hardly know that you exist! You are in a dream world, constantly dreaming and suddenly, oh, my God, you die and you are so surprised! Even when you die you might not notice!

If a person is looking for this inner light, it is not enough to find one's own way, for no one is so independent. Part of the learning process is to explore the inheritance of spiritual traditions and various teachings. These teachings are a reflection of the optimum of clarity which has been reached by those who have already crossed the ocean of ignorance and arrived at the Other Shore.

A person who just tries to find his own way will not get anywhere because it is too difficult of a task. You need support from the collective spiritual mind. And here we are entering a very interesting subject. There is within the collective mind an aspect which points beyond its unconsciousness. This aspect is represented by the different traditions of Enlightenment. The message of awakening is already imprinted in one area of collective consciousness. Therefore, the collective mind not only represents ignorance and forgetfulness but also we can find within it some wisdom like the teachings of the Buddha, the Upanishads, the Tao The Ching...and so forth.

This part of the collective mind which speaks about awakening is the necessary bridge between ignorance and Soul-realisation. This realisation actualises the Soul's freedom, which is her unique angle of perception or blueprint. Your unique angle of perception is realised when you transcend the idiosyncrasies of human spirituality. Here, you can reach Truth which is reflected in the purity of Universal Intelligence.

Following any tradition is often a necessary step on the Path of finding the truth of your Soul, but the danger is that you may get identified and stuck in the tradition, missing the universal perspective. It is very interesting that in order to evolve as an individual you have to use the collective mind, you have to learn from others, but at the same time you are creating your own understanding. You are finding your own unique way. If you are just repeating, following, you miss your own unique evolution. However, on the other hand, if you just insist on finding your own way, without learning from others, as some naïve individuals do, you will not reach anywhere. You have no way to transcend without the support of the past knowledge. Therefore, the balance is required between learning and finding your own way. You can see the collective consciousness as the womb from which your Soul needs to become born. You need it as much as you need to get out of it! How unfortunate that most never get out of this womb! They have never lived...

Verification of Enlightenment

Student: *How can one know how much one is awakened? Why does one need to compare one's state with different descriptions - for instance, by* [re]*ading spiritual books?*

Aziz: You see, awakening is not just a state. We spoke about a case of someone who even though fully awakened, lacks basic understanding and clarity regarding this experience. In such a situation, the inner state is only present on the energy level. In truth, awakening is a combination of the inner state-energy and recognition from intelligence. We can say that there are two sides of the human being: one is energy, the second is intelligence. The experience of energy has not much meaning because if there is no one experiencing it, what is the use? For example, a rock is in the Absolute State. You can feel it being around a huge rock or in the mountains - a deep peace. But the rock itself does not know it. With the evolution of intelligence energy can at least be recognised now. From the other side, intelligence without the foundation of energy is just in the mind, it is up in the air; it has no roots. Intelligence and energy are two ways in which the Soul experiences reality. One is that the Soul understands. Understanding is a combination of the subtle mind, a subtle thought and sensitivity. This means the Heart is also involved, because you cannot separate intelligence from feeling. The other side of the Soul is the energy experience. For example, the Soul may have a profound understanding, but if there is no Being she has no foundation. One simply suffers, for one cannot rest inside; there is no place within which one can rest. Also, if there is no awareness, intelligence is also without any foundation; it has no roots as it is spaced-out. Here again the Soul suffers because on the energy level she has no foundation. That's why we speak about awakening to the Inner State, which is an energy phenomenon.

When you close your eyes in meditation, you experience deep peace. What is this peace? It is an energy expansion. This happens not only because you close your eyes, but because certain faculties have been activated. Something in you has awakened. Another person may do the same but is unable to experience this peace. Such a person is restless, uncomfortable and bored. But if there is only this energetic experience without intelligence, the state has no depth. That is because the one who experiences it, is not able to see the whole value of the experience. You see, it is also about the level of appreciation. It is this appreciation which allows you to see the whole beauty and depth of any inner state.

We can compare it to being deep in the mountains. Being in the deep mountains represents the inner state. When a person who is insensitive and shallow, stays in these mountains he or she might simply get bored and need to listen to music. But a sensitive person is deeply moved, feeling the infinite silence and divine quality of nature. Why is it that one person is able to see it and another is not? It all relates to one's level of intelligence and sensitivity. Similarly with this inner state, it is a combination of the subtle mind and sensitivity which makes one see the significance of the experience. The subtle mind represents intelligence, which is not based on concepts but on pure knowing. Concepts are important in the growth of intelligence, but intelligence is itself deeper than concepts. Intelligence represents direct knowing, you simply know and understand. When there is a deep understanding, when there is a deep recognition in meditation, you are simply meeting God. And if there is no understanding, you experience the same state but your mind translates it in a much more shallow way. Here, you say, 'I am very calm today,' and so forth. To see that the experience is special, to understand its meaning is a function of intelligence.

In order to understand yourself as a multidimensional being, you have to know how to put all the pieces of yourself together. For example, how is it that you can be deeply absorbed in meditation and still be thinking? How is it that you can be in a state of pure awareness but still have desires or suffer? How is it possible? It is very interesting.

Concepts have a very important role because they allow you to create understanding. And understanding is a very mysterious phenomenon because it is itself beyond concepts; it is a pure knowing. To study different traditions, to have a basic knowledge of different teachings is not necessary but can be very helpful. A certain amount of knowledge allows one to see one's experience and realisation from a higher perspective.

Understanding is also a vision. You see, life is dynamic; life is not just that you are living from moment to moment, surviving and doing things. In life there is always an element of vision. In a sense it is true that, on some level, you create your own reality, for your vision determines your life. And everyone subconsciously has some kind of a vision. Even a person who having grown up in a primitive tribe, has just minimum knowledge, does have a i. But this vision is probably very shallow and conditioned particular version of the collective mind. That is why the deeper the understanding, the more profound the vision of life and the universe, the vision of the evolution and your relationship with the Creator. True vision is not merely a fabrication of the mind but the creative expression of the Soul in harmony with universal truth. A true vision of Creation is reflected in the mirror of individual evolution.

Another element is that the term Enlightenment does not refer to one generic state. There are a few options within the evolution of awakening. For example, one can be awakened in terms of awareness but the Heart can still be closed. How can such a person know that the Heart should be open? How can one open the Heart? To open the Heart requires a certain co-operation from your side and you have to be open to this possibility. For this you need understanding.

It is very hard to explain what understanding is. For example, you have been coming here for some time. Sometimes you ask questions, sometimes you hear answers. Sometimes you cannot grasp the whole meaning but your understanding is growing. There is more clarity and this clarity is beyond concepts. This is understanding; it is deeper than thinking but neither is it not thinking; it is something between thinking and not thinking. The mind without the Heart cannot see the subtle colours of reality, for it operates within a linear logic. The Heart allows you to grasp the paradoxical nature of your life and existence. The evolution of intelligence is much more complex than the evolution into Enlightenment, as it is traditionally understood. Many lifetimes are necessary to develop intelligence. To conclude: Enlightenment without intelligence is only partial.

To Remember Forgetfulness

Student: *Do you remember forgetfulness?*

Aziz: You mean myself personally? Yes, I remember, although in a vague way. It is like something fuzzy, something almost forgotten. One forgets but to remember forgetfulness is very important in the teaching work. Without this remembrance, the master cannot understand his disciples. If a master forgets his past forgetfulness, he may be, for example, very surprised that no one can reach awakening in an instant. If one abides in the enlightened state for some time, it becomes so natural that it is hardly possible to conceive of another way of experiencing reality.

There are two types of Enlightenment. One is enlightenment to Enlightenment; and the second is enlightenment to ignorance. Enlightenment to ignorance is necessary for the work of teaching. If a teacher does not understand ignorance, there is no way to teach in a real sense. When you understand ignorance, you see that ignorance is also reality. There are certain laws and principles governing the Spiritual Path which need to be respected. For example, consciousness needs to develop a certain type of concentration, attention and mindfulness. We have to see how awakening actually takes place. Awakening is not a miracle, but a radical change of focus. There are so few masters who can point clearly to the State of Presence. And so one must be careful in choosing a master.

Some Advaita masters become so extreme in their interpretation of non-duality. Advaita as a philosophy is simply a creation of the mind. It uses quite a simplistic and linear logic, which does not always reflect the paradoxical nature of reality. To cling to such a linear view is the same as not to understand the truth of the evolution in time. There was a famous master called Poonjaji. According to him, his students didn't love freedom enough for they were not able to keep the State of Presence. But as we know, it is simply physically impossible to stabilise the experience of pure awareness unless the energy system is able to contain it. One has to take it easy sometimes, being patient with this process. So, ignorance needs to be respected because it is real; it is not merely a mistake in perception.

Remembering your past forgetfulness can also help you to appreciate the awakened state. When you are a long time in the enlightened state, you forget that you are in some kind of a special state. It is only by this comparison with others and your own past that you can again see how blessed you are. Comparison is not always from the ego. Often it allows us to awaken an alive relationship with the rest of Creation. When comparison comes from the Soul, it represents a quality of wisdom.

...hinking is not the Absence of Thoughts

t: ***Sometimes we find teachings speaking about the complete***

elimination of thought. Even in Mahamudra, which accepts thinking as a part of the Natural State, we find concepts that Buddha himself completely stopped thinking.

Aziz: These concepts are created from the lack of understanding about what the complete human being is. In different spiritual teachings the truth of Enlightenment is often mixed with man-made superstitions and incorrect views. Some speak about having absolute powers, some about being fully free of suffering; some speak about having no ego anymore. Others speak about the cessation of desires and others about the mind fully stopping. All these views are incorrect and represent an imbalanced perception of reality.

Hui Neng, the famous Zen master said that awakening takes us beyond the mind, but trying to completely eliminate thinking is against the nature of the mind. What is thinking anyway? Any perception, any recognition - is already a type of thinking. Everything is thinking. Subtle thinking cannot be separated from the presence of awareness. When you see a tree, for instance, even if you don't create a concept around it, the seeing itself is a type of thinking! Enlightenment takes us to the place beyond thinking, but thinking continues as a part of our functioning in Creation.

The difference which awakening brings, is the quality of thoughts. No more do they have their invasive and obsessive tendency. A mind which is awakened, is mostly silent. In such a mind, thoughts arise in a slow motion and in longer intervals. What matters the most is the location of the thinking process within our sense of identity. In the case of an enlightened being, thoughts arise in the unconditional space of awareness and Being, not disturbing the inner solidity of I Am.

Enlightened Masters

Student: *There are some masters who have realised the State of Presence only. Others who are in the Absolute State, are more rare. How conscious are they about the state they are in?*

Aziz: A person who is in the State of Presence has no way to know that it is not the final Enlightenment. Only Grace allows one to go beyond consciousness. Most teachings available do not distinguish between the realisation of pure consciousness and the

Absolute. So far, only Nisargadatta Maharaj was able to create this clear distinction. Perhaps now you can see the importance of having certain essential conceptual tools. If you didn't have the concept of the Absolute State, how could you aspire to reach it? Of course, in the case of the first enlightened being, shifting to the Absolute was a function of Grace only.

There are two sides to the phenomenon of Enlightenment. One is the energy expansion and the second is the interpretation from the mind. Apart from the fact of being in a certain state, on top of this experience comes a specific translation in the mind. How the mind interprets the experience, relates to one's personal intelligence and general spiritual knowledge. For example, one can have a completely meaningless experience in meditation and yet this person may claim Enlightenment! It happens quite often! Here, the ignorance of this person's intelligence has falsely interpreted the experience. And often this level of intelligence is fooled by egoistic ambitions to become enlightened, and so on. You can even find opinions from completely ignorant individuals claiming that Enlightenment is a self-fulfilling prophecy. Which means that if you 'really believe' that you are enlightened, it means that you are! That is of course a complete nonsense. I met a woman who said that she 'announced her enlightenment.' 'What has happened to you?' I asked. 'Nothing, I just made this announcement and immediately I started to feel better,' she said. Do you see the ridiculousness of this type of thinking? In another case, I met a person who said, 'I have been with Poonjaji and I realised that I am the Self.' 'And what is your actual experience? What is the quality of your Inner State?' I inquired. 'I don't know, I am just one with everything.' Here we have another example of intellectual enlightenment. For some seekers it would be better not to study Advaita and live like ordinary people do. This perhaps would save them from living in the utopia of enlightenment.

Here, we are entering a very complex area in the verification of spiritual attainment. How can we verify our inner realisation? As we spoke, the foundation is a particular energy-state; the next element is our interpretation based on our knowledge, intelligence and sensitivity. Yes, sensitivity is extremely important here [illegible]thout proper knowledge, it has no foundation.

[illegible] Absolute State represents a very subtle and profound [illegible]ion and as such it is reached by very few Souls. It is a state beyond change; it is beyond the movement of energy. However a person abiding in the State of Presence can also interpret this state as Pure Rest, a Oneness with the source! Do you see the difficulty here? These matters need to be studied all life in order to gain complete clarity. Our teaching offers precise descriptions of the inner states and the awakening process; it attempts to bring more clarity and understanding into these subtle areas. But even then you may mislead yourself, not being capable of aligning your experience with a correct interpretation of it. That's why, often you need to meet a competent master who can clarify your state.

Most often we meet seekers who have completely wrong opinion about their state. Our work is to help them understand their state and their possible evolutionary goals. Unfortunately, there is a lot of ignorance in this area, not only from the side of seekers but also from the side of incompetent spiritual teachers. In order to shift to the Absolute State, one must be on some level dissatisfied with the state of pure consciousness. Even though it is true that there is no way that the Absolute State can be reached by will, but still one does co-operate. This co-operation, in terms of proper and purposeful surrender into Being is essential. The shift itself is a function of Grace and transmission of energy from the master or directly from the Beyond.

Happiness and Beyond Happiness

Student: *Two days ago you said that an enlightened being is beyond the ordinary concept of happiness. Can you speak about happiness? What can bring happiness?*

Aziz: Happiness from one side relates to the presence of the inner state, a certain unconditional energy of I Am. This is already happiness, but this happiness is not necessarily registered by the Soul. Whether you feel happy or not is not just a question of the outer situation or the inner state, but also of your interpretation. Happiness is usually a Soul's choice. To be completely happy, many elements need to be fulfilled in the inner and in the outer. We can say, the Soul becomes completely happy when she reaches transcendence. This means that she becomes fulfilled not only in the inner but in the outer as well. Here, the Soul reaches complete happiness but this happiness is not necessarily ecstatic.

It can be a tranquil happiness, a direct knowing of being fulfilled. Ultimately, the Soul gives up her personal translation of wellbeing and surrenders to the Universal Truth.

Ultimate happiness is not that there is someone who is happy and who translates one's experience as being extremely pleasing. The ultimate happiness is the moment when the Soul completely gives herself up and becomes absorbed into the universal ocean of I AM. Here, she becomes completely absent. In her dissolution, she reaches the final happiness.

Often the feeling of being happy or not being happy can be a message from the Soul. For example, the Soul reaches a certain inner state and is still not content. The reasons might be two. In one case, it simply means the Soul is not mature and is not able to appreciate her inner expansion. However in the second case, the feeling of discontentment points to the need for further evolution. Here, the Soul knows on the subconscious level or intuitive level, that she is not complete and that some other elements are necessary.

As far as an enlightened being is concerned, his or her happiness cannot be measured by ordinary criteria. Those who live in the dream of the world, fascinated only by their emotional gratification in the realm of objects cannot even imagine the Real World of Awakening. An enlightened being is beyond the Here and cannot be understood by the concepts of this dimension. Being one with the Beloved is the only true happiness; this is everlasting happiness, Samadhi in God.

Truth is Beyond Both: Destiny and Free Will

Student: *Is Enlightenment only a matter of destiny? Some Advaita teachers deny that we can do anything about our awakening.*

Aziz: They deny, for their vision is conditioned by certain ideals and a linear logic. You can do a lot to help the awakening process. What you can do is concentrate effort into inquiry, self-discipline and the intensity of your search; this has enormous value! Don't wait for something to happen, for it will never happen. You will waste your life and your tremendous human potential. Be real
e the responsibility of awakening in your own hands. It
that in some stages of Self-realisation, your will is not
. For instance, the Absolute State can be attained only

through the power of Transmission. But unless you take yourself to the very edge of your possibilities, no Grace will ever enter. Grace is a response to the intensity of your dedication.

Awakening is Now!

Student: *According to Yogananda, practicing Kriya Yoga one can reach Enlightenment in one lifetime. Do you agree that it is possible?*

Aziz: Why wait so long? Life is more than a spiritual search. Reach completion quickly and go on with life! Your question shows how deeply asleep you are! If you were dying of thirst and someone told you that within this lifetime you would quench your thirst - would you be satisfied? You ask this type of 'inaccurate' question because you think that you are doing just fine 'not being enlightened!' And you are not! You are dying, drowning in a swamp of ignorance. Without the light of I Am, you are just a walking corps! Don't you see it! Don't ask about this lifetime. You must become enlightened NOW!

Are you Enlightened?

Student: *Are You enlightened?*

Aziz: Certainly, I am. But this statement has a bad taste. Instead of emphasising myself being in the Awakened State, I would rather say that I represent the Enlightened State. I am a mouthpiece of I AM. To become enlightened is like to terminate a disease. When you are no longer sick, you don't recognise your health, for it is your natural state. That's why, I don't remember that I am enlightened. But when you ask, oh, I remember again! Thank you for reminding me about it. But it does not have much meaning for me anymore. I represent the Other Dimension in which I am energetically rooted. That's where this Satsang is taking place. I am not playing a guru. I couldn't care less. But we have work to do. That's why we are here.

How Can I Know whether You are Enlightened?

Student: *How can I know whether you are enlightened?*

Aziz: Why do you care? What difference does it make for you?

I have no interest to fit myself to your projections about Enlightenment. What is Enlightenment? If you don't know, what is the point in knowing whether someone else is enlightened or not? You live in the dream world! In our teaching, we don't make students dependent by projecting guru-images. The spiritual scene is full of guru-hogwash already! What matters is only: can this teaching awaken you? It is about YOU and not about me. I am just working here, representing Guidance. I don't project any guru-image or expect any particular respect from my students. I live in emptiness. You are invited to enter to the Inner Shrine. Forget about your ideas about Enlightenment and take responsibility for your evolution. It is about time!

Secrets of Teaching

Teaching is the responsibility of the Soul who completed her Path to guide other Souls into Awakening. The place from which teaching originates is the Heart. However, without clarity, knowledge and understanding - an intelligent teaching cannot be brought about. Teaching is a Transmission of the Inner State from a master to a disciple. For this transmission to take place fully, the master as well as the disciple have to present the necessary depth in their Souls. The qualities of the student should be sincerity, vigilance, discipline, openness, imagination, critical thinking, honesty, gratitude and complete dedication to the task of awakening. The qualities of the spiritual teacher should be: compassion, sincerity, humility, wisdom, sufficient knowledge, ability to drop the ego, seeing teaching as a service to the Beloved.

Who is Teaching?

Student: *Why are you teaching in third person, using the term 'We'?*

Aziz: The place from which this voice flows is not personal. It is neither individual nor is it collective. We say 'we' because it feels the most appropriate for the human psychology. If we called ourselves 'It,' this would feel too impersonal. No one wants to be loved by 'It'! The voice which you hear is channelled through the particular intelligence of Aziz, but the very source of this voice is the Other Dimension. There is a huge difference when an individual human being is teaching and when we speak. It is not a question of words but this very space from which we speak. We do not say just words; we Transmit the powerful energy of Truth and Transformation. We take you for a journey to our Dimension...

The Teaching

Student: *You seem to draw to you those Souls who long for understanding. Why do some Souls crave understanding while others don't?*

Aziz: We attract Souls who long for understanding, for the very simple reason that the teaching we represent is intelligent. It is easy to find an intellectual teaching, but intellectual is not the same as intelligent. For example, J. Krishnamurti taught in a very intellectual way; he tried to bring awakening only through the power of inquiry. But he did not seem to understand fully the complex process of awakening and the necessity of practice. It was at the end of his life, that he seemed to acknowledge the necessity of practice. Most seekers who follow his teaching, unfortunately, stop at the level of intellectual satisfaction. His teaching, on some level, takes away from them the responsibility of practice. That's why, with the full respect for his inspiring personality, we would not call his teaching holistic, as it overlooks some essential practical elements. Another intellectual teaching is presented by Ramesh Balsekar. He is a wonderful person, but his teaching is one of the most impractical ones existing on this planet! It is a very linear and ultra simplistic interpretation of Advaita philosophy. It is certainly not an intelligent teaching. Teachers like Ramana Maharishi, or Nisargadatta Maharaj were able to combine a certain practical understanding of the Path with Advaita's non-dual idealistic vision. From the other side, the teaching presented by Rajneesh was a very intelligent teaching but unfortunately did not point clearly to Enlightenment. It was to introduce spirituality in such a way as to inspire the mind, mock ignorance and provide an alternative vision of life. On the other hand, the whole 'atmosphere' he created was based on a strong guru-image and magical notion of Enlightenment. That's why he attracted thousands of seekers. But if a master draws thousands of students, it is a sign that the teaching is not pointing to the real thing and the level of compromise is immense. Why is that? Because the Souls who seek Truth are rare... humanity is simply not intelligent, not excluding the spiritual minority.

An intelligent teaching is not intellectual but includes the intellectual understanding as well. Most teachers teaching in the name of Enlightenment are neither practical nor do they present any intelligent teaching. They usually repeat spiritual slogans based on guru projections and somehow try to make their students dependent. It is all based on projecting a strong ego-image onto others in the name of Enlightenment. It is sad but most teachers giving Satsang in India, foreigners included, are a real joke! It is truly embarrassing to listen to their 'teachings.' There is not a teaching in truth, just pleasant or unpleasant gibberish. At least, in Buddhist tradition, there were different ways to check one's competence as a teacher, for examining the attainment of his students. When master Joshu got enlightened, he stayed twenty years with his master Nansen to polish his understanding. And in India we hear stories, like in Pune or Rishikesh about some woman or man getting enlightened and the next day starting to give Satsang! They usually have no basic knowledge, neither do they have understanding about their own state which is usually only partially awakened. And they take the responsibility to guide other Souls? They lack not only intelligence and humility but simple common sense.

Why do some Souls crave understanding and others don't? All Souls crave understanding, but what amount of it they can receive relates to the capacity of their intelligence. The evolution of intelligence takes much, much longer than awakening to I Am. Intelligence evolves in a more dynamic way. What is intelligence? It is the capacity to reflect the truth and complexity of life. It is to intuitively reflect in our intellect and Heart the workings of Universal Intelligence, in the reality of this dimension. Most Souls enter the Spiritual Path in the hope of escaping their misery. They are not ready to crave understanding for they are fast asleep, lost in their dreams. To crave true understanding is itself Awakening. To crave understanding is to have this deep, intense longing for clarity as to what we are doing Here; it is to aspire for the greatest knowing possible within our individual destiny and blueprint.

Student: *Can you explain more about the difference between an intellectual teaching and an intelligent teaching?*

Aziz: There are three basic types of teachings: simplistic, intellectual and intelligent. A simplistic teaching does not reflect the complexity of the awakening process. Neither does it show any clear path to Enlightenment. Usually, it is based on repeating spiritual slogans or on dependency on the master. An example of such a teaching could be a situation where a master relates to a disciple: 'be with me and awakening will happen to you.' Another example could be represented by the statement: 'everything is God, everything is Love - just realise this truth.' On the spiritual scene, these types of teachings are quite wide spread.

Mostly seekers who have weak minds and resist practice follow this type of naïve teaching.

An intellectual teaching aspires to bring awakening through understanding and intellectual insight. We call it intellectual for it believes too much in the mind and lacks a certain essential practicality. One of the biggest dangers of an intellectual teaching is idealism, through which the mind gets taken away from reality. That is the case of the simplistic interpretation of Advaita, for example. It is able to convince our minds of its non-dual truth but is unable to help us realise it. This is because one is simply not ready on the energy level. So many seekers stop at the level of this intellectual satisfaction. They say 'we believe in Advaita,' 'it is All already present here,' 'there is nothing to do as there is only the Self'...and so forth. These are, however, meaningless intellectual statements. This type of intellectual 'Enlightenment' promotes only a new type of arrogance. Intellectual satisfaction can be a trap because one may lose a true and realistic perspective of one's evolution.

From the other side, an intelligent teaching represents a balance between understanding and practicality. An intelligent teaching reflects the true complexity of the awakening process, avoiding the trap of idealism. An intelligent teaching reflects clearly the practical and realistic aspects of the Spiritual Path even though it does point directly to self-knowledge.

Student: *What is a precise teaching? Your teaching seems to be exceptionally precise.*

Aziz: A precise teaching reflects all the steps and nuances in-between the beginning of the path and the end of it. It reflects the complexity of the awakening process and the multidimensional nature of the human being.

You see, from the other side, some teachings can be analytical and yet not reflect the whole truth. Some Buddhist teachings are extremely elaborated but often reflect pre-conceived and conditioned views about reality. When we speak about a precise teaching, the idea is not to be overly analytical but to explain the main steps of the Path, as well as its significant subtleties.

Student: *How do you deal with this teaching? Very few students seem to be really sincere and dedicated. And you give it so much energy!*

Aziz: Is there anyway I can help you? Yes, teaching is a rather sad activity as there is hardly anybody to teach. An old master said: it is relatively easy to find a master but to find a real seeker is very difficult! The teaching which we represent is a very advanced understanding. Very few Souls are ready to receive it. The destiny of spiritual teachers who give a real teaching is to have very few disciples. For such is the level of humanity. On the other hand, if a master has many students, it means that the level of compromise is big, which indicates that the teaching must be very basic. Such a situation is not real and usually a strong ego-image is projected to manipulate the consciousness of seekers.

Often we hear that those who have read our fist book 'Enlightenment beyond Traditions' cannot understand anything. It a good sign. If an average seeker who has not studied these matters for many years, who has not spent sleepless nights on meditation and contemplation, is able to understand the teaching easily - it must be false or very primitive. Why is that? This is because the spiritual dimension is simply very complex and extremely subtle.

However, even though, it is sometimes difficult to teach and one gets discouraged with the level of seekers, there are also rewards. Even to transform one Soul, even to give birth to one Soul is a great gift; it is like to create a life! And there have already been a number of Souls who've been completely transformed through this teaching and above all, through the force of Guidance! Wisdom tells us to teach without expectation. We are just creating an opportunity for those Souls who are ready to transcend this dimension.

The teaching is not my identity. I teach but I am beyond teaching. When I leave this room, I am no longer a teacher until I meet a Soul who needs guidance. It is not my ego-image to be a master. My karma to teach has already been completed. Now it is just an expression of responsibility and creativity.

Student: *I feel that you actually don't want to teach but it is the only way to get through.*

Aziz: We are not teaching here but Transmitting Awakening. Let it continue for some time.

Satsangs have Become Clichés

Student: *Why is it that most of masters giving Satsang do not seem to* *understand the process of awakening and tend to simplify the subject of Enlightenment so much?*

Aziz: Because the understanding is simply lacking. These teachers themselves are not free from the past. They are identified with the collective spiritual consciousness. These matters need to be studied and contemplated for years. Teaching is a big responsibility. It is not enough to have some shift of consciousness in order to give Satsang. It takes many years to understand the state one is in and even longer to be able to transmit it to others. There is a general lack of responsibility, guru-trips and ignorance governing the spiritual world.

Most of those pseudo-gurus are unable to teach anything. They imitate the great Advaita masters proclaiming that 'There is No Path.' But do they understand the meaning of it? Do they understand that the truth of 'there is no path' has to be reached through right practice? But it is not in their true interest to arouse awakening. After all, who would attend Satsang?

Student: *I have been visiting so many Satsangs. In most of them we hear many clichés and they seem to be based on seekers and gurus projections about Enlightenment. Why in the realm of Enlightenment is there so much nonsense?*

Aziz: The event of Satsang has been quite abused these days. Many partially Self-realised individuals are taking the role of great gurus, without even having the basic knowledge about the awakening process. It also reflects the low quality of most seekers. It is all based on clichés and projections. The most amusing is that those individuals who pose as great gurus, pretend not to have any ego. Imagine how big an ego you need to have, in order to claim that you have no ego!

The Mirage of Pseudo-non-duality

Student: *There is one famous master who is very much against meditation. He says that no effort is needed as nothing separates us from Truth. Could you comment?*

Aziz: How can one be against meditation? What is meditation? These statements show lack of basic understanding. It is easy to say that no effort is necessary for the realisation of the Self. It is easy if you are already Self-realised. But it has no connection to average seekers who have such fragmented minds. There is simply work to do. It is important for a spiritual teacher not to be attached to the simplistic interpretation of Advaita. One has to have some compassion for the confused minds of seekers or at least some common sense.

Abusing the Role of a Spiritual Teacher

Student: *Sometimes a master will hurt the ego-image of the student as a teaching device, which can be both powerful and painful, but I do not understand this process. How can it work to make a person more in touch with their self-image of the Real Me?*

Aziz: You see, on some level, the ego-image is also a part of the Soul. In order to live as a person, you have to have a certain image of yourself. This happens not only in your relationship to the Creator, but also in your relationship to the society. It is like this: the ego-image is on the surface, and deeper there is the self-image, and finally there is the non-conceptual state as the very foundation. That is the structure of your identity here. But the problem is that the ego can operate in its own virtual reality, as if disconnected from the Soul. In such a case, the ego may grow in arrogance, egoistic pride and insensitivity.

As far as hurting the ego of a disciple, it can be the right action in the case that a particular seeker is too much in the mind, too arrogant or egocentric. In such a case, to shake one's ego-image can be a part of the awakening process. But to hurt a person who is sincerely connected to the Heart and sensitive, is against the code of honour. Here, the master does not hurt the ego-image but the Soul-image.

For example, if someone abuses you verbally and there is no apparent reason to do this - he or she proves simply to be insensitive. To be a spiritual master is not an excuse to become insensitive. The master is not God and has to respect the basic code of honour and principles of sensitivity. If the master crosses this border, he himself becomes arrogant and serves the ego reality. You must see that Enlightenment does not eliminate the ego and can even make it stronger, if there is not enough humility! That's why, awakening to the Heart is so important! How is it that a master can destroy the ego of his disciple if he himself has an ego? The spiritual master is not ego-less. He abides in a dimension deeper than the ego but he is not egoless himself. It is not a question of not having an ego. The ego itself is absolutely positive. But this ego has to serve the Soul, becoming intelligent and humble. The ego is the servant of the Heart, an expression of Pure Me in the mind. Why would we want to destroy it?

Unfortunately, sometimes we hear stories where some pseudo-gurus abuse their disciples, even hurting them physically. This type of behaviour is simply criminal and teachers like that serve darkness and create very bad karma for themselves. That's why, a master has to learn throughout his life the lesson of humility and how to respect the Souls of others. Being a spiritual master is very dangerous as one can become addicted to psychological power and grow in arrogance. Those pseudo-masters who humiliate their students, in the name of killing their ego, are most often simply abusive. Usually, they themselves need to be humiliated... to bring them back to the Soul's reality.

To Meet a Competent Master is itself Grace

Student: *How is it that I met around twenty enlightened masters and none of them showed me the State of Presence. You are the first who gave me this experience. How is it possible that no one actually teaches about it?*

Aziz: It is the sad reality of the spiritual scene that it is really difficult to meet a competent teacher who can directly point to the essence of consciousness. How is it possible? It simply is possible, as it is what is happening. Either the masters you met were not really awakened or they didn't know how to point directly to Self-realisation. In India you can meet many gurus who don't necessarily represent the Buddha type of Enlightenment, but rather various mystical states mixed with psychic abilities. Some of them have mastery over different energies but without being necessarily grounded in the I Am. It is a very mystical country, you know. Meeting a competent master, who can show you directly the State of Presence, is itself Grace...

Seduction of Energy Experiences

Student: *I have a question about so-called 'energy experiences.' How is it that in many Satsangs seekers experience various energies, feel bliss,* *and so forth? Can these experiences be a proof that the particular master is Self-realised?*

Aziz: You need to be aware that there are many types of energy experiences and not all of them are grounded in I Am. Sometimes, the energy you experience is self-induced or brought about by the hypnotic atmosphere of the Satsang. You need to see that all your projections, enforced by the whole group, the guru-atmosphere, the master-image, your expectations and openness, all of this makes you experience many things. That how you make yourself feel during Satsang, is already an energy experience!

If you don't believe, you can make an experiment. Find on the street a complete idiot and put him in the role of the master. It is preferable if such an individual has a big beard, big eyes and is dressed white or orange. Tell him not to blink much, to have a spaced out look and mysterious expression on the face. Make this person sit on the high chair and invite all your friends saying that a famous master is visiting your town. This person should not speak at all, because everybody would easily recognise that he is an idiot. You can tell your friends that he has taken a vow of silence. He can just sit there, with closed eyes... and it is good if, from time to time, he is staring persistently at everybody. In this way he will be even more mysterious. We guarantee you that most of your friends will have some energy experiences!

When you come to Satsang and you are really open, in this openness, through your own heart many things can happen. You may simply experience the bliss from your own heart. You may experience the Divine or be touched by the esoteric dimension, as during Satsang different beings or presences can come through.

On the other hand, some masters are connected to various mystical energies, which manifest themselves during the sacred event of the Satsang. It is particularly true in the devotional type of Satsangs, for the heart opens there more easily. Just be aware that not all of those energies are coming from the dimension of I Am. Not all of them relate to the Buddha type of Awakening. That's why, they most often don't bring any permanent results; they come and go. They do no represent your 'family treasure.'

The energy which comes from the fully Self-realised being, brings transforming results and grounds you in your own Self. This energy may not be ecstatic or exciting at all, but it is solid and points to the Unconditional. The energy of Awakening is more subtle than ordinary mystical energies, therefore to recognise it you need to be sensitive. The reason is that this energy cannot be merely experienced as something from outside - it touches you from inside. Hence, to fully recognise it you yourself have to be, on some level at least, connected to the reality of the Inner State.

The ability to project or channel energy is not, by no means, a proof of Self-realisation. There are some teachers who have mastered, for instance, kundalini energy and can project Shakti onto others. But many of them are far from true awakening. For example, visiting Samadhi of Nityananda, I have come across a rather charismatic lady, a successor of Muktananda. I was really surprised about her great popularity, as I could not feel in her eyes real presence of any Inner State. She had a presence of energy but not the energy of Presence. The reality is, however, that for majority of seekers more attractive are fleeting energy experiences that the Truth of Awakening.

Is Rigpa the Ultimate?

Student: *How is it that in Dzogchen they say that rigpa is the Unborn?*

Aziz: Originally, Dzogchen, as well as Mahamudra pointed to the Absolute State. But, because so few seekers had the aspiration and capacity to reach this Exalted State, the teaching lost its original focus. We could say that these teachings became commercialised: they adjusted to the need of the majority. For that reason, Dzogchen and Mahamudra stop at the level of pure consciousness only. The assumption that rigpa is the Unborn is, of course, incorrect. How can we speak about the luminosity of bare awareness prior to Creation? It is a contradiction in terms.

In this teaching, the role of the ego is also underestimated. According to their understanding, it is the ego, which covers the recognition of rigpa. But if that is so, in a dreamless sleep, for instance, rigpa should shine its luminosity and it doesn't. To call the deep sleep state a luminous reality would be very inaccurate. The ego is not an obstruction but the link between unconsciousness and consciousness. Of course, if the ego does not evolve but is stuck in its ego-image, it remains on the level of the subconscious reality, instead of pointing to awakening.

It is very interesting, but from the viewpoint of orthodox Buddhism the concept of rigpa would be most likely considered as another attempt to smuggle into the 'No-self Teaching' the belief into the Self.

The teaching of Dzogchen and Mahamudra are very sophisticated and represent a high technology of awakening, although they are not Complete.

The Function of Teaching is to Mirror Ignorance

Student: *How is it that for some your teaching seem to be too complex?*

Aziz: It is not that this teaching is too complex, but life itself is too complex! Life is simple and complex. If you see only the complexity of life, you have not experienced life yet; but if you don't see the complexity of life, you are simply ignorant!

There are two types of teachings. One tries to reflect the simplicity of life and Self-realisation. The other one intends to reflect the whole complexity of Truth. Some Buddhist teachings we find too analytical, too complicated, too sophisticated intellectually. Buddhism, unlike Advaita, is very analytical and sophisticated intellectually. Some sutras can easily give you a headache. If a monk studies such sutras, that is fine, but this is of not much use to the ordinary seeker. However, some schools of Buddhism combine the complexity of teaching with simplicity. Zen for example emphasises the simplicity of truth, but only on the surface. Zen is also very sophisticated conceptually and profound intellectually. In the west, they see usually only the first element of Zen teaching. But, in truth, to understand Zen, one has to study it for years. Similarly as Dzogchen or Mahamudra. They are very sophisticated and only a subtle mind can understand their teaching. But, at the same time, that to which these teachings tirelessly point is very simple and beyond any concepts! Do you see what we mean?

A teaching which is only simple is false! That is the problem with some naïve reception of Zen or Advaita. Advaita is less complex than Buddhism, using basic concepts in order to trigger awakening. But, still, it is not as simple as it seems. Many seekers have the illusion of understanding Advaita. Do they really understand Advaita? Can you understand Advaita and not being Self-realised? In truth all concepts are false, for reality is beyond concepts. Advaita is not a Path of self-knowledge but a Path of Grace. That's why, their Path is not very elaborate; it is a bit simplified. Buddhism is the Path of self-knowledge, for it tries to elaborate all steps in between ignorance and awakening.

Advaita tends to negate ignorance, for the very presence of ignorance, contradicts their idealistic vision of the Self. Advaita is the Path of Transmission and Grace. That's why, many seekers in India are very drawn to its magic. India is magical. The transmission of Enlightenment happens here much easier than anywhere else. Advaita is an old, ancient tradition channelled from another dimension or planet. It is the only tradition which has not become a religion. Even Rajneesh's teaching is becoming for many people a religion. But in the case of Advaita, some mysterious protection saved it from the fate of becoming a religion.

You must understand that the main source of awakening always has been and will be Grace, the divine intervention. This Grace needs often the medium of the master. In Advaita, it was not 'self-knowledge' which produced so many enlightened beings, but the transmission from master to a disciple. Self-knowledge is only a part of this process, for Enlightenment points to something deeper than any type of knowledge. Enlightenment points to the actual change of dimension, to the dimensional shift. No knowledge or inquiry can bring you there. But Grace can.

In the case of awakening to the State of Presence or witnessing consciousness, inquiry and understanding can trigger awakening. But what type of inquiry can bring you to the Absolute State? You can repeat the saying of the great Maharaj, 'I am not the I Am' or you can try to believe that you are 'That.' But it does not work. And we guarantee you that you will not transcend this very consciousness within which this inquiry takes place. So how can one go beyond I Am? It is a question impossible! But the answer is possible as the actual experience. And this experience itself is Grace!

Our teaching is neither simple nor complex. Most seekers refuse to use their minds. They are so tired of their minds, that spirituality is for them a hope to forget about thinking. But it doesn't work like that! If you don't use your mind, even your simplicity is false and ignorant. Of course, we don't suggest to use spirituality as a means of bringing more and more information to the brain. That would be insane. And there are many pseudo-seekers who study books all life without doing any actual meditation. We speak about the balance. Be simple, but see also the complexity of your existence. Your existence and evolution are not only complex but paradoxical. See how rich your I Am is! See how difficult it is to align the purity of your inner state with the complexity and challenging nature of the external reality. See how difficult it is to be truly awakened and not only remain on the level of empty talks about simplicity or non-duality!

Ask yourself whether those who say that this teaching is too complicated, are they themselves simple? Look at the fragmented quality of their minds! You see, only a complex teaching can heal you from your own complexity. When the disease is serious, the treatment is usually very complex. Because our teaching is complex, it can heal the complicated nature of ignorance. The truth is simple, but ignorance is very complicated! A spiritual teaching is more designed to treat ignorance than to reflect the simplicity of truth. That is important to understand. A simple teaching is false for it cannot grasp the fragmented and complicated nature of ignorance. We are not interested in reducing the seeker's mind, neither by giving a simplistic and naïve teaching, nor by projecting a guru-image on those who look for freedom. We are simply honest in our presentation of the truth of both awakening and ignorance. This teaching is neither simple nor complex. It simply reflects reality.

Teaching for Buddhas

Student: *Your teaching seems to be very advanced. Is there a danger that it may reach only a few?*

Aziz: We present a multidimensional vision of awakening. This teaching is directed not only towards unawakened ones, but to those who are already Self-realised. So far there hasn't yet been any elaborate teaching created for those who have reached Enlightenment. Why is there a need for such a teaching? Such a teaching is necessary to deepen understanding of those who are Self-realised; they are most often conditioned by their particular traditions. Also, in most cases, Self-realisation is not complete yet. For example, the Absolute is missing or the Heart. There are also enlightened masters who are far away from their Souls. The teaching which we present is channelled from the Dimension of Understanding. We present a very intelligent and universal vision of awakening. Very few are ready to receive it, as most are locked in the past. The purpose of this teaching is not to appeal to the majority of seekers but to those who are sincere and mature. A teaching which attracts many, must be very basic to fit the limited intelligence of most seekers. We emphasise the quality of seekers and not quantity; we are here not to comfort ignorant ones, but to awaken those few who are ready for true transcendence.

Transmission of I AM

Student: *You call your Satsang: Transmissions. What is a Transmission? What is being transmitted?*

Aziz: That which we Transmit is awakening and awakening only.

Student: *What stops us from receiving it?*

Aziz: Nothing can stop you from receiving it, but how deeply this Transmission reaches your being depends on many elements. It is the unconditional state of I Am which itself is transmitted in Satsang through the master or directly from the dimension of Grace. That which stops the complete reception of the light of I Am is the immaturity of your energy as well as the resistance in your mind and Heart. In order for Grace to bring transformation, she needs to enter through the heart centre, the seat of the Soul. When the Heart is closed, this force cannot operate freely.

Nothing can stop this Transmission, but it often takes place gradually. It cannot be transmitted immediately because the Soul is not ready to receive it. The Soul gradually receives dosages of enlightened energy. This enlightened energy is settling into the system of the receiver. However, it is not merely a passive reception of I Am. One has to co-operate. The part of the blueprint of awakening is co-operation, which means that the very intelligence of the Soul is awakening itself from inside, as well as it is being awakened from the outside. When we speak about Transmission, it enters from outside the Me so to speak, for it is being transmitted from the Source or from a Self-realised being; but awakening is primarily happening from inside. One is like a seed which is being awakened from the inside, even though it is being watered from the outside. One has to co-operate.

However, the Soul may not be ready to receive the complete state yet. She needs to develop gradually. There are many elements, even the position of the stars matters. In order to receive any state or any type of shift, the whole universe has to be aligned in some way. That's why, usually, there are events, like auspicious times when transformation can happen more easily. At those times when transformation cannot happen, you are simply preparing yourself, maturing from inside. When the time is ready and when, most importantly, you are ready, Transmission radically manifests the necessary completion.

Fundamentally, Transmission is an energy phenomenon. At the same time there is another transmission, the transmission of understanding. Here, you are given tools to awaken from the inside as well, not only from outside. When there is only a transmission of energy, one remains passive; the receiver is passive and, in truth, because of this passivity, the receiver cannot receive the whole of the Inner State. In order to receive the total experience, one has to awaken from the inside.

Another important element which can stop one from receiving transmission is a closed Heart. Guidance channels herself through the Heart primarily and if the Heart is closed she cannot enter fully. When the Heart is ready, transmission can enter much stronger because it means that the Soul is present and is able to receive the gift of transformation. The receiver is not just a vessel. The receiver is a dynamic being who is fully responding to that which is being transmitted. How the receiver responds affects the amount of energy received. The energy which comes through is selective. It is not like electricity, which spreads everywhere or kundalini energy, it may transform you or it may not; it may help or it may even harm you. The energy of transmission is one with the Higher Intelligence. This energy has wisdom - it sees, hears and discriminates. It knows when to channel itself and in what amount. It knows which aspect of our being is to be touched and healed. This energy is not only transmitting the presence of I Am, it is also working with the mind, with the subconscious, cleansing it and freeing the psyche from its past. It is a multidimensional work.

Tradition of Guidance

Student: *Can the tradition of Guidance become crystallised as another past tradition?*

Aziz: No, because Guidance never stops in time. The opposite is true - Guidance is much faster than time. It waits for us already in our future! Guidance never stops its revelations; it offers a supreme understanding always relevant to the Now. The understanding which is being revealed to you, transcends past views. This understanding brings you to a more intelligent, sensitive and holistic comprehension of the spiritual dimension. But the moment you fully assimilate this higher Truth, it has already moved to the past! At that point, a New Understanding will enter like lightening from the Beyond! Do you understand? There is no end to revelation.

As you evolve, you are deeper and deeper initiated into the Truth of the mystery. There is no end to it. The moment you think that you have understood the Teaching fully, you may mistake it as the absolute final understanding. It is a final understanding but only at a certain level of human evolution. At this stage, you are trying to realise some goals which Guidance presents. But when these targets are reached, a new and deeper guidance will be given to you on a more personal level. Evolution never stops and there are many surprises awaiting you on the Path which you might not even conceive of!

Guidance can never become a part of your past. Guidance is, in truth, your Future; it is not even your Now. It enters into your Now, to pull you into your Future, the realisation of your final destiny. Guidance cannot be grasped, nor can it be frozen into the past. Guidance is the essence of life itself. Guidance is your connection with the mystery.

What are the past traditions but Past Guidance crystallised by the human mind as the absolute truth? Guidance always responds to the state and capacity of human intelligence. Guidance not always reveals the whole of truth, but most often the fragments of it; it reveals that which is necessary and can be digested by the particular stage humanity has evolved to. Guidance never stops; it enters over and over again. Guidance is love and love only.

Yes, we represent the Tradition of Guidance. We do not rely

anymore on past understanding but on the voice which enters from the Future into our Now, revealing a New Understanding.

Dependence and Autonomy on the Path

Student: *How can being with you for a few months help this process?*

Aziz: It is not about being with me, but being with yourself which matters! But, naturally having support from the master and from the energy of Guidance has tremendous significance. Allow yourself to receive this help; it is a gift which you are being offered from Existence. There is a fine line between receiving help and losing independence. We would say that it is impossible to be both, independent and dependent. But still you have no choice but to be both independent and dependent! You have to be dependent on something higher than yourself, for you are quite helpless. That must be seen. But, you have to respect your autonomy as well; you have to be a light onto yourself. And we offer you a perfect solution. We offer you the energy of Guidance and the presence of a fully Self-realised master, but simultaneously we give you understanding and inner clarity as to what you can do to co-create your own awakening. We give you clear practice and guidance towards inner discipline. Your destiny is in your hands. Just do the work.

Being with a fully Self-realised master is of tremendous help, but still you need clear tools to co-create awakening from within yourself. See whether you have the necessary tools to do the inner work. If you don't, you lose your autonomy and become too passive, too dependent. This environment is full of seekers who use masters as a temporary escape from their problems and Satsang as a spiritual club. Most of those pseudo-gurus are happy to play this game as they don't have, in truth, any teaching or interest to bring awakening. The game is that the guru remains the guru and the seeker remains for ever the seeker. Neither is the guru interested in making the seeker awakened, nor does the seeker have any interest in losing his comfortable status as a seeker. What is happening in most of those Satsangs around is truly embarrassing. Most of those self-appointed gurus in this area manipulate with seeker's projections about Enlightenment in order to create a strong ego-image for themselves. For example, they try to behave like Osho, talking slowly, walking slowly into the Satsang's room...and so forth. Most of them don't even know how to teach meditation!

For Most a Tradition is Security

Student: *Why are people so afraid of going beyond traditions?*

Aziz: Because they are not seeking truth but rather security. What are seekers doing? They are looking at different traditions like at the menu in a restaurant. They try to find the one that fits themselves the most. Just to fit into one available interpretations of Truth is the greatest happiness for an average seeker! Everybody is following everybody, individual unconsciousness gives rise to collective unconsciousness! Everyone is so unconscious! Nobody has time to look for truth, so everybody wants to follow something which has a good reputation, which has the authority of the past. It is all based on the idea of authority. Authority is a drug against basic fear and insecurity. The reality is that there are few real seekers. From all the so-called seekers, perhaps one percent represent 'real seekers' and one percent of this one percent is ready to see the whole truth.

The Secret Teaching

Student: *Poonjaji spoke about having some kind of a 'secret teaching.' He used to say that all his students were unworthy to receive this teaching. Does the secret teaching exist?*

Aziz: According to tradition, it is said that the Buddha Shakyamuni did not keep anything for himself but revealed all that he knew. But in truth there is always a secret teaching, for the very simple reason that most seekers are not able to receive the whole truth. What Poonjaji said about the unworthy students, unfortunately reflects the sad reality of spiritual environment. Most seekers are either unintelligent or insincere and insensitive. That's why, the work of teaching is a big compromise and a painful wastage of energy. There is simply nobody there to be taught.

What Poonjaji meant by 'secret teaching' was simply the Absolute State. He was only teaching about the State of Presence with some elements of the Heart. In our teaching, the information about the state beyond consciousness is available but, still, it is a 'secret' unless you realise the Absolute, isn't it? 'Enlightenment to Me' is another secret. The State Beyond Polarities is one more secret... And if you think that it is the end of secrets, you are very mistaken. There is no end to the revelation coming from the Dimension of Understanding. We have not just one or two secret teachings waiting for you...there is simply no end to New discoveries. It is like the horizon - you can never attain it. Similar, you can never reach the end of the Mystery. But what you can reach - is your completion. And what is this completion is your Ultimate Secret.

Teaching is a Necessary Compromise

Student: *Are you teaching out of compassion for us?*

Aziz: I am not teaching. It is Guidance that is teaching. I am just working here, letting Guidance to come through. This work is not even holy; it is just a work. The amount of unconsciousness, ignorance and insensitivity to be faced in this work is so huge...the teaching is simply a compromise. Yes, teaching is a necessary compromise. To lead an average seeker to transcendence is like trying to break through a thick wall. One cannot really feel compassion for unconsciousness, as there is nobody there. Compassion can be felt at the point when a Soul is met, a Soul who is in a state suffering. And to meet a Soul is so rare that this meeting itself is a real joy. It is not suffering which is the problem but the embarrassing level of unconsciousness...the state of coma in which are entangled most Souls.

Teaching is a Transmission of the Past

Student: *Why do you never speak about yourself and your Inner State?*

Aziz: What is this 'myself' that I am supposed to speak about? I Am Myself - isn't that enough? And as far as speaking about my State is concerned - what is the use of it? You are my past, so I speak to my past about my past evolution. The State of Presence is this fragment of my past which is relevant to most seekers. The Absolute State is this fragment of my past which applies only to very few. I am speaking about fragments of my past evolution, to bridge them with your future. If even my past does not apply for most, why should I speak about my Present State?

To be Worthy of Having a Master

Student: *How can I know whether I should have a master?*

Aziz: Before you can have a master, you must first become a seeker! Are you a seeker? What is it that you are seeking? What are you doing to gain Self-realisation? To be a 'seeker' is a noble title, not to be taken lightly. Ask yourself, whether you deserve to surrender to a master! Are you ready to take responsibility of the Inner Work, or you are going just to waste time of different masters?

Who is the master and who is the disciple? These are just miserable characters in the human 'spiritual comedy.' There is just the Soul and Universal Intelligence...nothing else.

In Our Time Awakening is Easier!

Student: *Is it more difficult to become awakened in our time than in time of the Shakyamuni Buddha?*

Aziz: On the contrary - it is much easier! People nowadays are much more intelligent and sophisticated. They are also more confused, which is the price they have to pay for living in modern civilisation. But reality works through polarities. Our times are extreme and bring us to extreme experiences in life. Most become simply bent under the weight of the excess in knowledge and technology. But if you choose to evolve, you can make much quicker progress now than in the past.

There is a general tendency to complain about the times one lives in. They found a document from the times of Babylon where the author complains about his times exactly in the same way as most people complain now! But in truth, our times have many advantages. Human intelligence has become more refined. That's why old spiritual teachings can no longer fully satisfied our desire for clarity and understanding. That must be seen. Spiritual teachings have to evolve and reflect the general evolution of the human mind. Some think that Buddhism or Advaita for instance, have given us the complete vision of reality, once for all. It is however, not true. Certainly, in these teachings there are included some universal and timeless elements but not all of them can be applied to our times. The teaching of Guidance which we present is a response to this call for a new and more complete vision of spiritual realisation and understanding.

Beyond the Frontiers of Non-duality

Student: *Advaita seems to be very logical. Is there something wrong with the type of logic they use?*

Aziz: Advaita is a very profound Path; it is an ancient Path which points directly to the realisation of the Self. But as a philosophical system, it is not as logical as it seems. Reality is based on a different kind of logic, which is non-linear. Advaita, unlike Zen does not pay attention to details. What it means is that it refuses to see the steps in-between ignorance and awakening. At some stage, Advaita must deny even the existence of ignorance, for ignorance is illogical! There is no logic in ignorance. But reality is more than human logic - it is paradoxical and surprising. Reality is constantly surprising us, destroying our poor concepts and crystallised views. Reality is teaching us constantly about humility.

Non-duality, in truth is not logical for there is no experience in non-duality. In true non-duality the concept of non-duality is itself not non-dual! Who says: 'non-duality'? Who is this Me who says that there is only non-duality? Don't you see that only due to duality, the concept and experience of non-duality can be possible? Duality represents ignorant separation, while non-duality the universal space of Being. But when duality meets non-duality, the universal Existence becomes consciously realised. This experience is beyond duality and beyond non-duality. We have named it the 'Dual-non-duality' or 'Dvaita-advaita.'

Follow Only the Truth

Student: *Is there a danger in being exposed to too many teachings and masters?*

Aziz: If you are looking for Truth, nothing is dangerous. But if you are looking just for a 'teaching,' philosophy or a master, everything is dangerous. This is because you mistake the Truth for the shadow of reality. To study many teachings and to meet many masters can help your intelligence to grow. However, you must see the essence of your search. What is a master but a guide pointing to your eternal self? What is a teaching but a description of your inner reality and of various possibilities on the Path? It is all about you. Don't become a 'follower' or a 'member;' don't become a Buddhist or Sufi or anything...become yourself. Look at the truth and not at the shadow of it. If you are not intelligent, you cling to words and concepts and therefore easily get confused. You get confused not knowing whether Buddhism is right speaking about no-self or Advaita speaking about the Self. You cling to the finger instead of looking at the moon to which the finger is pointing. You have to see that teachings and masters do not matter. It is You who matters and the essence of your Soul dwells in the dimension devoid of any concepts.

Surrender to the Master

Student: *What is surrender to the master?*

Aziz: Why do we surrender to Guidance? Because we feel the tremendous love, wisdom and clarity with which this mysterious force is guiding us. A true master is just an outer expression of Guidance. The difference is that in the case of the human master, the ego is also mixed in. The presence of the ego makes it more difficult to surrender. For that reason, those masters who pretend not to have ego, have more disciples. Through this comfortable projection, seekers find it easier to surrender.

Be critical and do not surrender to anyone who projects on you a strong egocentric-guru-image. In such case run away fast! But if you feel the master carries a true sincerity and love, wisdom, humility and a real desire to help you and is not just throwing slogans on you... if you feel the real thing - you allow yourself to trust and be guided. And as you receive different gifts of transformation, you feel more and more gratitude, from which natural surrender takes place.

Unfortunately, many seekers are just looking for anyone to surrender themselves to, so they don't need to carry their frustrated lives by themselves! They don't practice, they refuse to meditate - they just want to surrender and wait for a miracle to happen. It is all nonsense of course. A true sign of surrender to the master is to do your inner work. To surrender is to become responsible for your own awakening! Otherwise, your surrender is truly meaningless.

What is the master anyway? It is your own Self. The I Am is your master. If you wish to surrender, go inside and let go of your mind, drop all concepts and become whole! Rest within and drop all nonsense about masters. Be real and live the light of I Am, which you are. That is surrender to the master.

VII

UPON COMPLETION

The Human Buddha is a natural awakened being who has transcended even the concept of Enlightenment. As the Buddha went beyond ignorance, so the Human Buddha went beyond liberation, becoming free from freedom itself. The Human Buddha is a multidimensional being who abides in the unconditional state. The Human Buddha is one with the Beloved but lives the dynamic and challenging life of a human. The Human Buddha openly acknowledges the gentle and vulnerable quality of his or her Heart...

The Human Buddha

To be the Buddha is to be also a human. This is because Enlightenment is realised within the frame of human intelligence and sensitivity. Expanding to the Inner Realm, the awakened being transcends the dimension of time. However, he or she still has to face the challenge of human life. When even the notion of Enlightenment is dropped, true innocence is reached. One simply becomes natural. In this natural state, one does not care anymore either about being a Buddha or about being a human. One is what one Is. Let us have a cup of tea...

The Human Buddha

Student: *Why has the human aspect of the Buddha been so often ignored and negated?*

Aziz: Perhaps not in all traditions. There is a feeling that in Sufism, the human aspect of Buddha has been on some level acknowledged. Maybe because the existence of the Soul has not been negated in this tradition of the Heart. A Sufi master has a Soul, the Soul which prays and cries to the Beloved. When you read Rumi's poetry, you can feel how often he was sad or lonely and feeling like a child in the face of God. In Zen we can also find some elements of the Human Buddha even though the negation of some essential human sensitivity can easily be found as well.

It seems that the roots of the concept of a super-human Buddha have their origin in India. We could historically trace the gradual development of this concept. The human effort to transcend the reality of limitations and suffering, was so great in India that it gave rise to the creation of the ideal man-god, the super-being, the Liberated One. Due to this development, in combination with the ego-projections coming both from followers and from masters, this extreme model of Enlightenment was born. This model negates our humanness as well as the reality of the Soul. Philosophically, it was also caused by the incorrect assumption that atman (the Soul) is Brahman (the Ultimate). This assumption was made because of the lack of a sophisticated enough view of Enlightenment.

Another reason behind the attempt to negate the human part of the Buddha, is a certain tendency of the human mind to choose extremes. The human mind does not like paradoxes; either A or B. It is fairly easy to accept being a human; it is fairly easy to accept the ideal of super-Buddha. But to be both? The mind simply cannot handle it! It is very challenging to live simultaneously in these two ways. The mind wants to pinpoint the reality of the Buddha. From the view point of the linear mind, either the Buddha suffers or is beyond suffering; either the Buddha still evolves or is beyond evolution; either the Buddha has desires or is beyond desires. The mind is unable to grasp that the Buddha is both!

We have to use concepts in order to evolve. Some spiritual ideas, philosophies and models are essential for us to support our evolutionary journey. But as we reach higher and higher experiences and insights into the nature of reality, our mind is able to reflect a truer picture of reality - in a non-conceptual way. We are simply able to see what the real world is! To see it, we must free our psyche from all past conditionings, including the teachings of past traditions. A tradition, using the metaphor of the Buddha, is like a raft. The raft takes you to the Other Shore and when it is done, you simply drop it. If you don't drop it, you cannot go further. How are you going to drag this raft along dry land? What is the Other Shore? It is reality after Enlightenment, the real world. This real world is the true reality of the Human Buddha. Here, Buddha transcends his own Buddhahood going beyond freedom itself! Here the Buddha at last says: I am just human.

In the original Buddhism, the ideal of an arhat or a liberated being was formed. If you look at the descriptions of the last stages of arhathood, you would be shocked by how inhuman they were. The arhat is some kind of a perfect robot! He does not suffer, certainly, but is he really alive?

Once an advanced monk was tested by Manjushri, the Buddha of wisdom, who in disguise appeared in his cave and started to annoy him by asking endless questions. His purpose was to check whether the monk would get angry. It continued for one month and the poor monk couldn't meditate, he got extremely upset and burst out with anger. In this moment, his disturbing visitor revealed to him his true identity (Manjushri) and the monk, in shame, realised that he had not mastered perfect patience, therefore, being still far from the arhathood.

But is it so? In truth, if the monk didn't get angry he would simply be an idiot! Not getting angry when the situation demands it from us, is not a sign of Enlightenment but dullness and stupidity.

Do you see that by following an incomplete model of Self-realisation, one may lose a natural perspective and handicap oneself? Unless you uncover your true Human Buddha nature, you will likely live in the reality of an artificial 'enlightened' idealism. There is the true nature of reality, which is I Am and there is the true nature of being human. Both need to be awakened and integrated into the true life of the Human Buddha.

Student: *How can the Human Buddha combine different aspects of oneself in a harmonious way?*

Aziz: By becoming the Human Buddha

Freedom and Beyond Freedom

Student: *What does it mean to be free from Freedom?*

Aziz: It means that the one who wants to be free doesn't care anymore. One doesn't care anymore, not because one loses interest but because one has lost oneself in the Beyond. When the Beyond takes over, when God enters, no longer do we matter anymore, for Reality alone prevails. Another meaning of being free from freedom is to go beyond the dualistic concept of non-suffering where one sticks to the safe disidentified side of reality. We call it negative Freedom, for it blocks the spontaneity of emotional participation in Creation. In our terminology, the Buddha becomes the human. Here, one is free to experience the difficulties and challenges of being a human.

Zen made the first step speaking about the return of the Buddha to the market place. The Buddha again enters the mundane reality, the reality of Samsara. But what is still lacking in this model, is the embracement of feelings, sensitivity as well as the vulnerability of the Buddha. Zen went beyond the Inner, including in its vision of suchness the outer as well. But still bypassed the reality of the Soul.

There are a few levels of freedom. First, is disidentification from the reality of suffering, which is the Absolute State. Second, is the freedom to be human, including even suffering, which is a part of being human. The third level of freedom is Samadhi in God, letting oneself to dissolve into the Divine. And the last Final Freedom is beyond freedom itself, where one fully lives the challenging life of an individual from the depth of human sensitivity. Nevertheless, simultaneously one is in a complete, constant and natural Samadhi in the Beloved.

Enlightenment and the Boundaries

Student: *I have a question about boundaries. In your state, do you still feel boundaries in your connection to other people or are there no more boundaries?*

Aziz: Both. An enlightened being exists on two levels: the absolute and the relative. The first represents the awakened unconditional state beyond the relative reality. The second is the existence of Me. For who has realised the Unconditional? Is it the Self experiencing the Self? If you think like that, the question of boundaries does not arise, as there is 'no one' to need them in the first place.

But the situation is more complex. The one who reaches the Uncreated is the Soul and the Soul does live in Creation too. She uses her relative energy system which has to be supported in many ways. The Soul gets tired, for example, and needs to sleep to rejuvenate. The Soul is sensitive; this tells us that she can get hurt. She still has various needs and desires; this tells us that she can experience lack and suffering (when unfulfilled in some areas of her relative existence). The Soul after awakening still evolves through her emotional and mental bodies, as long as she exists in time.

An enlightened being has a paradoxical existence, for he or she lives a double life. One is the life of unity with the Self; the other is the life of an individual who has to face the challenge of being human - and the difficulty of living in an imperfect dimension characterised by low consciousness. An enlightened being can be even more vulnerable than an unawakened person, for he or she is one with the original purity and innocence of the Soul. Enlightenment gives you a new strength but simultaneously makes you much more sensitive - particularly when the Heart is open.

To answer your question directly. Of course there are boundaries, for the very simple reason that one continues to live as an individual. If one does not respect this truth, not respecting one's borders, the result can be very miserable. One becomes drained, depleted and worn out very soon.

Following some idealistic philosophy, one can easily lose their common sense. There is a Zen story. One master asks a monk 'what is your understanding?' 'Everything is empty!' the monk replies. In this moment he receives a blow on his head with a stick and starts screaming! 'Why are you screaming, if everything is empty?' the master concluded their conversation. It is not enough to understand the Absolute Truth. One has to respect also the relative truth of separation and differentiation's, for it represents our human destiny.

Student: *I have the problem of not having clear boundaries. I am easily affected by the energy of others?*

Aziz: When we describe Enlightenment in terms of being beyond personal boundaries, we mean that the transcendental state embraces everything: all is included in the space of I AM. This space cannot be affected by others. Here, one leaves no traces like a bird crossing the sky. But that is just one aspect of Self-realisation. The second is that the Inner State and the Soul co-exist in a dynamic way. The Soul not only co-exists with the impersonal space of I AM but she also participates and adventures in the world. She is like a window: one side is looking in and the other side is looking out. That through which the Soul connects to the outer is the personality and the psyche.

Your problem, beloved, is not only being very sensitive but that you simply keep losing your I Am in the outer. You see, to be Me is to be on some level self-contained, solid in one's energy field, otherwise, your Me loses too much vital force and breaks. To live as Me is a skill. You need to, first of all, keep your centre in spite of circumstances. Apart from this, you have to be wise and discriminating in your contacts with other people. Do not spend unnecessary time with people who do not nourish your Soul and your Heart. When you communicate with others, observe your emotional reactions and how energy is distributed in the process. Be careful not to get caught into the psychological games which others play and you yourself participate in.

Be at the centre of yourself. To be at your centre is not to 'watch' but to be centred as the Real Me. The centre is your energetic presence and rootedness within yourself.

Student: *But sometimes I am at my centre and still lose energy in my contact with others.*

Aziz: On some level, it cannot be avoided. There is no absolute protection from negative energies. You are alive and to be alive is to be sensitive and vulnerable. Living in a big city, no matter what you do, you will still feel as though you are locked in an energetic prison. When you are in nature, suddenly you feel how the sky opens up to you. Living your life, you need to be wise in choosing friends, places and circumstances. No one is invincible, you know. Avoid people who have too much mind energy and those who are too emotionally disturbed. Avoid those who do not feel your Heart and do not see your Soul! Take care of yourself! Having the centre of I Am is your ultimate protection, not a hundred percent protection but the highest protection you can have.

It is Fine to Have an Ego!

Student: *I have a question regarding the concept of the ego. Ramesh Balsekar says that in the case of an awakened being, only the 'working mind' functions. How does it relate to the presence or absence of the ego?*

Aziz: The concept of the 'working mind' is not quite precise. According to Balsekar, there is no ego as such but only the 'working mind' which performs its natural activities. It is one more attempt to interpret the thinking and volitional processes of the mind in an impersonal manner. According to the traditional model, you are not the doer but the witness, and the mind is just being witnessed as something simply happening out there. As we know, this model is rather flat and inaccurate in truth. If only the subconscious mind (subconscious Me) operates, you can have a feeling that thinking is 'just happening' spontaneously and there is 'nobody' doing it. However even here it is not fully correct, because the subconscious Me does have a certain amount of subconscious volition and creative intelligence which use a very subtle self-referral. But when you think consciously, it is obvious that your active intelligence, personal will and sense of Me are engaged. Isn't it obvious? Please, don't lose the common sense in the net of philosophical ideas. Be simple and natural...in this way everything will be clear.

During my visit to Ramesh Balsekar, I asked him, 'if all is impersonal and there is no ego, why don't you give all your possessions to those who are obviously starving behind your windows?' 'It is not my destiny,' he replied. I thought in that moment, 'Is it really necessary to complicate reality in this way? Isn't it much more simple to honestly admit that one likes to have a comfortable life and an essential sense of security in the material world?' So many enlightened masters during the last few thousand years insisted on denying themselves the right to have the ego, just in order to fit themselves to the non-dual paradigm!

I remember, once during a Dharma talk, the leading Zen master in Korea said, 'the root of our problems is this very concept of MY space and MY time. Drop it and you will be free!' 'Is it so?' I was wondering. Afterwards, I went to him and asked, 'if someone comes here from the street and tells you that he wants to live in your room and needs all your time for his purposes - would you agree for it?' He remained silent for some time and said, 'no, I would tell him to get out of here!' And that was exactly what I had assumed. As you can see, common sense is always higher than well-rounded idealistic fantasies. It is much better to be honest and simple. Yes, you have the full right to have your ego and to enjoy it. It is a gift from the Divine! Yes, there is the ego and there is someone inside you who is pursuing the primal instinct of seeking happiness and avoiding pain and suffering. It is not just 'working mind' which is thinking about becoming happy - it is YOU! This understanding will simplify your life a lot and will free you from the feeling of guilt, for which all that pseudo-religious conditioning is responsable.

The Crazy Wisdom of Enlightenment

Student: *Could you speak about the issue of moral conduct regarding the spiritual masters? Some masters seem to be very strict, behaving in a very pure, holy way. Others, seem to follow the idea of 'crazy wisdom,' not feeling restricted by any rules. Where is the clear border between immorality and freedom?*

Aziz: We cannot have any real clarity in this matter unless we fully acknowledge the simple fact that a spiritual master is just another human being. This should be acknowledged by both seekers and by masters. In this way, neither will a spiritual master try to behave in an unnatural, holy way, nor will the seekers cherish some unreal expectations. It is very interesting to see not only how some masters condition seekers into an idealistic vision of Enlightenment, but also how the seekers condition masters with their projections about Self-realisation. A master can easily become a slave of his own student's expectations. The concept of 'Crazy Wisdom,' according to which the behaviour of the master is utterly unpredictable, is just a remedy for this type of conditionings. A master at one stage may realise, that he is no longer free, trying to behave in a holy way in the name of Enlightenment. Yes, the masters have to strive for freedom from their own disciples!

In the term Crazy Wisdom, the word 'crazy' indicates that one is beyond any rules; one is able to break any expected social or religious behaviour. On the other hand, the word 'wisdom' shows us that this unpredictability is not just based on an ordinary idiotic ignorance, but flows from the place of wholeness and love. The concept of crazy wisdom is similar to the character of 'divine fool,' or 'wise clown,' known in other cultures. It is a way of teaching through paradox where one challenges the shallow concept of morality and the primitive 'common sense' of the collective consciousness, in order to open the door to the Unknown.

In Zen or Tibetan Buddhism, you can often encounter a certain kind of master who breaks away from any moral restrictions, showing that Truth is beyond our limited concepts about purity. Such a master can, for instance, behave in apparently uncompassionate way, can drink alcohol or sleep with prostitutes. But inside he is in a transcendental state, completely free and pure. In Zen they use the term 'unconcerned traveller,' for the true man of Truth who is bound neither by the limitations of collective mind nor by the very concept of Enlightenment.

What is moral and what is not? It is after all a matter of judgement. Isn't it? We have the tendency to focus on the outer behaviour, for this is all that we see. But most important is not the behaviour itself but the very place from which we act, the state of the mind and the quality of the heart. A fully Self-realised being is in a state of absolute silence, inner stillness, presence and love.

This is the unconditional state in which the awakened Soul abides. This state we can see as the Basic Sanity or Goodness. From this state, any action is True. It does not have to be a perfect response...it does not mean that one is not making mistakes. The action is simply True and even if one makes a mistake, this mistake is True because it arises from the place of Truth.

An enlightened being is still evolving emotionally and on other levels. This must be seen. It is also a matter of age and life experiences. Often that which you might call an 'incorrect' behaviour can be just a part of the maturation process and learning. It is important not to be judgemental and to accept the humanness of the spiritual teacher.

Some, for instance, have been judging the behaviour of the extravagant masters like Trungpa or Gurdjiev, because they used to drink alcohol and they had many girlfriends. But wasn't it their choice after all? It was their free will to enjoy sex and to get intoxicated. Trungpa was very sick so he drank to suffer less. Being in pain is not pleasant even for a Buddha. Perhaps ge did have many girlfriends, but it was also the free choice of these women to be with him. He didn't manipulate with the master-image in order to seduce women. He seemed to be very simple and human. If women were attracted to him, it was because he was most likely a beautiful being... He wasn't pretending anything. Once, someone asked him, 'why are you always late for your lectures?' 'I am simply late,' he answered...

Some think that the master should be celibate or should not have any emotional needs whatsoever. It is a sheer nonsense! These concepts have been invented because everybody is so misinformed about the true nature of awakening. And the paradox is that the masters themselves became victims of those unrealistic ideas! Others, think that OK, a spiritual master can have one partner but not more, otherwise he or she is immoral. It is all based on Christian morality and repression of sexuality.

In Japan, there was a famous Zen and sword master who had 3000 women before he finally decided to give up his sexual life! Is it to be judged? Maybe he made all of them happy? Krishna made love to thousands of married women at the same time and he was considered to be a god! Krishna was not a god like Shiva, but is regarded as a divine incarnation of Vishnu. He was most likely just a highly realised human being.

Look at the temples of Khajuraho. They are full of erotic and sensual sculptures with the most refined sexual poses. Are they immoral? In some of them you can see even sexual intercourse with animals! But everybody seems to admire them. In India everybody loves Krishna, everybody is proud of those temples, but in life they do the opposite. In this country one is supposed to make love without taking ones clothes off! Such hypocrisy...

Morality is not a fixed thing. What is moral in one culture, may be immoral in another culture. You may not notice even how deeply you are conditioned in your concept of ethics by the culture you have been born into. Often it is difficult to separate one's conditioning from what actually feels to be truly moral. Remember, don't focus on the action itself but try to see the heart of the one who stands behind it...

Can you imagine that even old Maharaj was criticised because of his habit of smoking and eating a little meat! Some seekers refused to learn from him when they saw him smoking one beedi after another. They missed perhaps one of the greatest opportunities in their lives to meet a real master! Maharaj was full of fire and energy and so he could get very restless, angry or impatient. So some judged him thinking that the real master should be calm, nice to everybody and infinitely patient. It is however, very unintelligent to judge that which one does not understand. When a real master gets angry, impatient or whatsoever, it is a part of the Teaching. In this way, he frees us from our simplistic ideas about how the spiritual teacher should behave and from our na_ve perception of what it really means to be 'spiritual.' Enlightenment has a paradoxical nature and often we must surrender our preconceived notions to the truth of What Enlightenment Really Is.

The problem is, however, when a master preaches one thing and does just the opposite. In such a case you are justified to suspect that something is simply wrong here. There are cases where partially Self-realised teachers use the myth of Enlightenment to manipulate with their students in order to receive various ego-related gratifications. Here, we can speak about the impure action or immoral intention.

To conclude. If a spiritual master is not projecting a guru-image onto his students, does not behave in an artificial and unnatural way, is humble inside, is simple, honest and fully acknowledges his or her human nature - this is what it means to be moral. Therefore, be careful not to become deceived by appearances!

Student: *Referring to the idea of having many sexual partners, didn't you say in the past that to have a single partner is more natural?*

Aziz: Yes, it is more natural, however not in the sense of morality but in the sense of maturity! It is not necessarily 'wrong' to have more than one lover but most often it is simply not nurturing for the Heart. When a man or a woman is emotionally mature, the need to have many partners drops by itself. This is because, for true intimacy to take place the environment of 'one to one' relationship is required. It is simply not possible to open fully one to another if there is no commitment. Such is the nature of human love. You can walk around saying that you love everybody and your love is not selective but it is not real, these are just empty words. The human love is indeed selective.

It does not mean that you have to commit yourself forever, as you don't know what future will bring. But you commit yourself Now, to the person you have chosen to share your life with, that's all.

Student: *Does it mean that a master who has many partners is immature?*

Aziz: If a spiritual master, or anyone for that matter, has many partners as a style of life, it may simply indicate a certain degree of emotional incompleteness. But you see, being emotionally incomplete is not the same as being 'immoral.' It is OK to be incomplete! Nobody is perfect. And those who try to be 'perfect' can be a real nuisance because they create a feeling of guilt in everybody. They say, 'look how holy I am, I don't smoke, I don't have sex, I eat so slowly, I don't drink tea or coffee, I don't say bad words, I pray all the time, I meditate all day, I wear only white clothes, I love everybody, I serve humanity and feed animals, I don't experience negative emotions, I breathe only two times a day...' (Laughter...). You wouldn't like to be around such individuals, would you?

As masters have tremendous compassion for the fragmented minds of their students, so students in return should have some compassion towards their masters! A master is just another human being, who happens to simultaneously experience Oneness with the Universal I AM. To be enlightened does not mean that one has reached completion within the human side of the Soul's wholeness. For a master, it takes a tremendous courage to be able to say, 'I am just not perfect!' Unless we accept our imperfection, how could we accept the imperfection of others? To be reconciled with one's own imperfection is an indivisible part of Compassion!

So be at ease with your own imperfection and that of your master. Give the master time to reach completion within his or her human destiny. If one is fully Self-realised, this completion will manifest quickly. When there is complete awareness, complete Samadhi and particularly when the Heart is wide open - the force of Grace quickly does the necessary cleansing, manifesting the true maturity. And the end result is Complete Peace - in the Inner and in the Outer as well. In the end there is just Peace.

Student: *It seems that Rajneesh has challenged many traditional views concerning sexuality and spirituality as such.*

Aziz: Rajneesh and Trungpa were quite unique masters as they went beyond traditions. Trungpa went beyond Buddhism and Rajneesh went beyond Advaita. This was because they were aiming not merely at liberation but at the real wholeness. Unfortunately they didn't have enough strength to fully transcend past views. Trungpa somehow chose to conform to Buddhist philosophy to the end of his life. He stopped wearing Buddhist robes but kept on wearing the inner robe of the Buddhist concept of reality. If he lived longer, most likely he would have dropped it. Rajneesh was more radical, but still remained identified with the traditional vision of impersonal enlightenment in which there was no real place for the Soul. They both wanted to give their students complete freedom, also to explore the earth dimension and sensuality. They themselves became caught in the realm of desire, into which they had entered so bravely. And they both got free from it, in the end of their lives, when they reached the State Beyond Polarities - the Freedom beyond Freedom. On the way to wholeness, often the price to pay is a temporary loss of balance. If one does not risk, one cannot reach the real depth.

Relaxed Self-protection is Trust

Student: *How can one be open and yet self-protective?*

Aziz: These are the two polarities of individual existence. In order to survive, one has to have enough strength. One has to keep all the elements of oneself glued together, so one doesn't break apart. Around your body is spread the skin which protects you from the outside. Inside this skin, a war is going on to keep you alive. You are a child of Existence... do you know how many elements are required to keep you alive? All those cells, germs, bacteria fighting inside your body to keep you going... When one element of this system breaks down, you get sick; when something more serious happens, you simply die. And what about the outside reality? You need to compete for food, space, time, affection, security on all levels, all in order to survive. When you live in abundance, you may forget about all of this. But when food is taken away from you, you forget about your civilised manners - you get wild, you do everything to survive! That's why the element of self-protection is indivisible from being a human.

From the other side, if you emphasise only this self-protective instinct, you become locked in fear, egoism and existential alienation. Here, you simply die psychologically and spiritually. That's why, you must open up to the magic of life, to the vast space of Being, love and compassion, to sharing and giving... you must open up to trust and to the courage of living without masks, veils and shields. You must make yourself available to encounter the mystery and beauty of life.

The question is: where is the balance, the exact balance between self-protection and being open? There is no fixed balance, as such, but a constant process of returning to the balanced perspective. You must listen to your Heart and use your wisdom as well. Observe how your energy behaves. If you feel weak and too vulnerable, it is usually a sign to go inside and close down a bit to the outside world. Your I Am is your inner refuge and the source of real strength. It is no more the strength of the ego, but beyond the ego. This New State, the awakened state, gives you a new type of protection beyond the gross egotistical way of protecting yourself. Here, instead of building shields, you simply relax inside, letting go of the human dimension. That is your freedom - freedom beyond the desire to be free.

Self-protection is necessary as long as you are alive. Let your Heart choose your friends, the people you talk to, circumstances, livelihood...,and so forth. If you encounter energies which are harmful, simply withdraw, close down or leave. That is the wisdom of the Heart, beyond naïve idealism. Respect the vulnerability and the gentle quality of your Soul. As you evolve, your energy becomes more refined and more sensitive. Because of that you have to be more careful and discerning in your everyday life. Remember that Enlightenment gives not only a new strength and freedom from this dimension, but also makes you more sensitive. This makes your encounter with ignorance much more painful. To live as an awakened being is similar to the case of a patient in a mental hospital who suddenly recovers but is not allowed to leave. It is very painful for such a person to live among all these imbeciles! The energy in a mental hospital is so bad! An awakened being is not allowed to leave the mental hospital of collective consciousness! The wheel of karma needs time to stop turning.

Pure Suffering

Student: *Could you speak about Pure Suffering?*

Aziz: What is the primal reason that we are suffering? What is the original cause of suffering? It is to be Here! The Here itself is suffering. Suffering is inherent to duality and duality is inherent to the existence of Creation. Suffering cannot be eliminated but can be minimise, which means that the unnecessary, neurotic suffering is cleansed. Pure Suffering is the experience of an enlightened being. This type of suffering is not caused by the mind, for the mind is silent and one rests within, beyond any movement of relative energies. But still one experiences some type of suffering because of being Here. And this suffering is not contradictory to the simultaneous presence of unconditional happiness.

Liberation and Transcendence

Student: *What is the difference between Liberation and Transcendence?*

Aziz: Liberation is called the negative freedom from the Here. It is reached through the refusal of a positive participation in the reality of Creation. Liberation is based on disidentifiction and a certain negation of human sensitivity. The essence of liberation is the Absolute State. When one is in the Absolute State, there is a natural energetic disidentification, for one is pulled down to the unmanifested reality. In liberation, one also transcends but overlooks the reality of Creation. That's why, liberation points to freedom but not to Wholeness.

Unlike liberation, Transcendence is based not on negation but on completion and wholeness. Transcendence can happen only when the existence of the Soul is acknowledged. In liberation, the Soul goes beyond herself, dissolving herself in the Absolute. In the case of Transcendence, the Soul apart from resting in the Absolute, embraces also her own existence. As we know, the Soul is something more than the function of rest in the Absolute. The Soul is connected also to the reality of Creation. Participation in Creation is a part of the Soul's blueprint. Apart from completing the inner evolution, the Soul also needs to fulfil herself in the world, by completing herself emotionally, for example. Therefore, Transcendence is this type of freedom which includes inner liberation and outer completion.

When all elements of the Inner and Outer are complete, the Soul simply transcends this dimension. She doesn't just get out of the Here, but she lets go of the gravitation of the Earth. Transcendence points neither to the Inner nor to the Outer. Transcendence is very clean... it leaves no traces behind. One simply transcends... The difference between liberation and transcendence can be seen in comparison to moving out of the house. In the first case, you move out without making any order inside. In the second case, you first make order, cleaning the house and taking out the trash. In the second example, you feel simply good and complete. Transcendence is more than liberation, for it allows you to experience fully the paradoxical magic of transformation and awakening, which is all-inclusive.

Beyond Non-attachment

Student: *The Buddha taught that after a certain amount of practice, one would reach a state beyond clinging. That became the whole vision of Buddhism - freedom from attachments and desires. And you are showing us a different vision.*

Aziz: Yes... because the first step is to transcend attachment and the second is to transcend attachment to non-attachment. When you are attached to non-attachment, you are still living in an artificial reality. The real reality is beyond idealism and realism. It is to be alive and beyond man-made superimposition's. You must see that the danger with spiritual teachings is that many of them, apart from revealing the truth of Enlightenment, condition us by their past views about reality. A spiritual teaching is the fruit of many generations and is often subject to the authority of past masters and philosophers; it tends to be dogmatic. So everybody carries on repeating the past conclusions, not having any interest in questioning their validity. But are they all valid in our times?

For example, most seekers unquestionably adopt the belief in the illusory nature of Me, pursuing simplistic translations of non-duality. But is it really true that there is no Me? In truth, you know directly that your Me exists, but you may force yourself not to see it! Another concept can be about identifying Enlightenment with the idea of the spiritual superman, who is invincible and untouched by suffering. A perfectly liberated robot. But in truth, reaching Buddhahood is not the end of the evolution but the beginning. Most awakened beings therefore need to receive further guidance. First a person receives guidance to become the Buddha and next how to go beyond the static concept of Enlightenment.

Student: *What about Shakyamuni Buddha? His words spoke clearly about transcending suffering and clinging.*

Aziz: But still he was suffering and had a lot of troubles with his sangha. No one can avoid suffering. It is simply physically impossible. Freedom from suffering is just a mirage. But you can be beyond suffering. When you are beyond suffering, it does not mean that you are not suffering. It means that part of your sense of identity is simply not of here. That is the meaning of spiritual expansion - you are merging with the Other Dimension, stepping out of time. Here, your being roots itself in the Beyond and becomes completely still and motionless.

But the human in you continues to live, in time, on earth, in the imperfection of this reality. If the human in you, for instance puts a finger in a flame, pain is immediately present. You scream from the hurt. This experience is the same as for the Buddha as it is for an unconscious person. To experience suffering is a part of the human destiny and no one ever got out of it. You can suppress the pain of being a human, using a strong will, but it is not natural and not real. In the case of the Buddha, it is the type of suffering which changes. We speak about the experience of Pure Suffering. Pure Suffering does not come from the past, from the mind or neurotic tendencies. Pure Suffering reflects the condition of being the human. This suffering has no reason;

the only reason is to be in the body and to live in the thick, ignorant and insensitive dimension of this world. To see such the immense ignorance around us is itself suffering!

Also when the Heart is awakened, the Buddha becomes more sensitive, open and vulnerable. If you want to reach liberation, it is better not to touch the Heart at all! To open the Heart is a risk, for you open yourself up and become exposed to suffering. The Heart is tremendously sensitive! The Heart does not need much in order to get hurt. This very contact with insensitivity and the malice of this dimension makes the Heart cry... Therefore, if you don't want to suffer at all, if you want to be a perfect robot, better lock up your Heart, close it completely. Here you are safe but are you alive?

Shakyamuni Buddha 'renounced' most of his worldly desires, for he didn't have them! His particular Soul was already fulfilled as far as human nature is concerned. He brought this emotional completion from past lives. All he needed to do was to reach the Beyond, to merge with the Unborn. Of course, he still had desires but more related to everyday life and not so much emotionally. But even not having any emotional desires is also not possible. In his case, they were gentle and not disturbing.

But his life cannot become a model for everyone. It was appropriate for his particular Soul and blueprint. If you, for instance try to fit this model, you will hurt your Soul and cripple yourself. If you follow the Theravada philosophy and attempt to eliminate all your desires, exercising detachment, you will go against your Soul. You will block the positive expansion in your evolution. You need to have many experiences and desires. They help you. Your desires are your friends! How otherwise could you possibly grow? Having no desires has nothing to do with being a Buddha. A person who has no desires is dead!

As one grows older and their emotional desires become fulfilled, one let's go more into the Inner Dimension. It is also a question of age and having many life experiences. But here, the letting go is not coming from detachment. Detachment is from the mind - it is the mind's attitude. An awakened being who becomes absorbed in the Beyond is not detached at all. Such a being is beyond attachment and detachment, beyond identification and disidentification. He or she simply does not care anymore. That is natural transcendence. To go beyond Buddhahood is to drop the very concept of liberation; it is to become simple and truly ordinary. The final step beyond Buddhahood is the awakening of the Soul where the Buddha again becomes the child of the Divine. No longer is he or she merely a liberated being but an innocent child of Existence - like a mystic in a state of wonder, in a state of prayer. An awakened being stands with open hands in front of the eternal garden of the Beloved - the Mystery.

An Enlightened Being is not Invincible

Student: *Is an enlightened being free from getting affected by negative energies?*

Aziz: Enlightenment, paradoxically gives one not only strength but makes one much more sensitive and vulnerable. This is particularly true when the Heart is open, for one is simply sensitive. Living in this thick and primitive dimension is not easy for a being who has reached the Light.

In the concept of Enlightenment where the Buddha simply becomes the Totality, there is no place for being vulnerable. But when we see that the Self-realised being simultaneously experiences relative separation, we find here a place for being human.

A being who has reached light often experiences offences from the dimension of ignorance. Darkness hates light, for it threatens its existence. Ignorance should not be underestimated. Jesus trusted humanity too much and he ended up on the cross. Humanity is very undeveloped and lacks the Heart. Humanity is not ready for Truth. All the messiahs of the past, present and future seem not to understand this simple fact. When you understand humanity, no longer will you want to change it. It is too unconscious to be changed. What can be changed are those rare individuals who break away from the collective mind.

To conclude, an enlightened being is not invincible and has to take care of himself or herself. There is no other choice living in the dimension where darkness and stupidity reign. Some common sense and discriminative wisdom is required.

Spiritual Master is a True Beginner

Student: *Is a master still learning?*

Aziz: Enlightenment is the true beginning of learning. Before, you are living in a dream, in the mind's schizophrenia. After Enlightenment, you start to look around, discovering the truth of life. It is all quite interesting. Isn't it?

However, the main lesson for a spiritual master is humility. It is so easy to become arrogant, using Enlightenment for self-aggrandisement. For some individuals, it would have been better not to have become enlightened because their egos are monstrous. If the Heart is not awakened, being in the role of guru can be a real catastrophe for the Soul. One gets stuck for the whole life in the pride of the ego. Letting go of arrogance and learning humility is the task for the master. But most of them don't even admit that they have any ego! Can you imagine how big the ego has to be to say: I have no ego! It is truly ridiculous. A spiritual master has to be humble, simply, ordinary and able to admit his humanness.

PART THREE

AUTOBIOGRAPHY OF AWAKENING

I would like to share with you the story
of my dream...
Once upon a time
I was destined to believe in forgetting
who I had been
And I was destined to rebel against this belief
It was not easy at all
But when Guidance entered into my life
All had changed
Everything became easy
I have no words to express my gratitude
I may just say
It was worth it to be alive

I Have Been Blessed...

My Apparent Past

On the 11th day of May 1962, I entered the dimension of time, the plane of forgetfulness. Unexpectedly, I found myself seemingly born in the middle of nowhere. The name of this apparent nowhere was Poland. My family was rather poor and was never accepted by the village for ethnic reasons. My mother was a simple but good person; she was quite unhappy with her life and with her drunk husband, my father. She was a teacher in my school, and unfortunately this distinction isolated me from the other children.

From the very beginning my soul refused to live in this dimension of ignorance! I suffered a strong depression from the very beginning which was supposed to last until I reached the age of thirty. I was a complete stranger Here, not remembering my origin; I felt painfully stuck.

At the age of five, I experienced my first awakening. I had escaped from school which made the director very upset and some children were looking for me. Completely terrified and scared of punishment, I hid myself behind the school fence. Sitting there, I asked myself in my child's mind: why do I have to suffer so much in this hostile reality? And what am I actually doing here?...when suddenly, I experienced a shift, a radical re-location into the dimension of Pure Consciousness. My mind as a little child could not understand this experience but my heart recognised it clearly - as it was a return to the forgotten Truth. Later, I came to understand that in a past life I had already established the state of Pure Awareness and as such it was easily retrieved. Because my child mind couldn't comprehend the whole significance of this experience, I returned back to my ordinary consciousness and the dramatic situation. A part of me knew clearly that I was not supposed to share my realisation - in particular with my parents, for they would not understand...

The suffering I underwent as a child was so deep, I was unable to develop a way to deal with it. I was always very alone, although this was actually fine as I was in love with solitude. Most of my time was spent in the forest next to our house going for endless walks. I was simply connecting to my Soul, to this intimate place inside. It was never intended, it just came natural to me. I was like a young mystic, often spending whole nights in the forest absorbing the bliss of nature and the silence of trees.

As a teenager, I became well-versed as a chess player, displaying a certain talent which later won me championship in Poland. Playing chess helped me escape extreme isolation and brought some desperate balance into my mystical life. Connecting to the world, I discovered, was a part of my larger journey. Through my travels, I learned how to connect with people and thus to the world. My Heart was sensitive and in deep longing for human contact but my Soul was so introverted that made meetings extremely difficult. I had a lot of heart-ache finding friends and a female companion... this problem lasted for a long time.

A few years later I started to widen my perception of life by studying philosophy and classical literature. Because of my extreme one-pointedness and concentration, I totally focussed in whatever the task might have been till its completion. For that reason, I dedicated the whole of my time, from morning to night to complete my studies. Reading and contemplating the meaning of life made me so visionary, I lost all interest in making a career out of chess. I thought it was an activity below the dignity of a true mystic. At this point, my heart started to become more conscious of its true longing..

Still, I continued my official, utterly meaningless education, absorbing the distasteful content of the collective mind. Going to school was a real torture. So much trash I had to fill my head with in order to pass into the next class, such nonsense!

At the age of 21, I was forced to join the Polish army. I was completely broken! I was crying, scared to death and thought of crippling myself in order to escape. However, I wasn't clever and self-confident enough to avoid the army. Reality was even worst than I had thought. I found myself among brutal male individuals full of pathological and sadistic tendencies. They took my civilian clothes away, shaved my head and told me that there was no way out of that place. It was my first serious lesson regarding the low consciousness of humanity, as I was previously isolated all my life. There I discovered that humans can be completely barbarian and heartless in their essence. They are only kind when they feel safe. In a situation of insecurity when their basic needs are threatened, nothing is left of their good manners and their mask of morality.

In the beginning, I tried to feign suicide in order to get out. I took an enormous amount of pills, enough to kill an elephant. But my body was so resilient that I didn't need to be rescued. I took it as a sign to accept my strange fate...given that this dosage would have killed an average person. So, instead of getting free from the army, I had to run in the snow with full equipment. Soon I discovered that the whole army system was based on a mutual agreement between the sadists and the masochists. I said to myself: they all play this game because they believe it, not having enough imagination to disbelieve in this ridiculous circus. From that time, I decided to pretend that I wasn't a part of that system and that I actually didn't exist. Instead of participating in army life, I did my own thing, which was mainly walking by the river. Eventually they forgot that I existed. My name was still on the official list, but no one knew to whom the name on the list belonged...

Upon leaving the army, I continued my life as a mystic spending time in nature in deep contemplation. At that time, I wrote my first book 'The Name of God.' It was my first attempt to translate my meditative and mystical experiences into religious language. It was the first time in my life that I experienced the meaning of my existence. Later Guidance told me that one of the main reasons for my incarnation was to write a book. It was not That book, but I was at least already connected to the truth of my Purpose.

I was instinctively and desperately searching for my Inner Home, the ultimate security. I felt very insecure on the earth and carried a strong depression from my childhood. I was still disconnected from the Other Dimension, all the time trying to just get there, but not really knowing how. The experience of I Am was still not clear, even though I already had a strong connection to the state beyond the mind. From that time, I started to study various spiritual teachings with the usual great intensity. From this endeavour I learnt English as most books were not available in Polish. I read everything: Zen, Tibetan Buddhism (particularly Dzogchen and Mahamudra), Upanishads and Sufism. I studied the great teachers, like Krishnamurti, Rajneesh, Ramana Maharishi, and so forth. I was especially inspired by Krishnamurti, as he spoke to my sense of freedom. Living in the middle of ignorance, I had to really believe that 'I Am THAT.' Where could I find in the middle of Poland a master to whom I could surrender? In the mean time, I connected to a Sufi group to aid my discovery of the heart's mystery. It was a lovely group, but the teaching was utterly ungrounded and did not at all point to Awakening.

One day I came across the book 'I Am THAT' with the teaching of Nisargadatta Maharaj. At that moment, I knew that I found my master. He spoke to my essence, his spirit deeply touched my heart. From him I realised the necessity of stabilising the State Presence to which I was already awakened. He called this the I Am-ness. For the first time, I received clarity regarding the Path and recognised the necessity of the right effort. Maintaining the State of Presence became a new task; it was a new challenge. I went for long walks, attempting not to lose the State, not for a single moment.

At this time I began to live alone in my house as my mother had just passed away. Not having any money, I sat all day in the freezing house and read 'I Am THAT.' At that time, I was a Freezing THAT. But I persevered as the profound teaching of Maharaj gave me hope. Maharaj was my first real guide out of this cage of forgetfulness.

Feeling the need for formal practice, I joined a Zen group which followed the teachings of the Korean master Sung Soen Sunim. He was quite an original Zen master as his work revolutionised the koan system. I did a few Kyol Che's (three months retreats) which led me deeper into the realm of meditation. To my surprise, no one from that tradition knew about the State of Presence. I had trouble finding myself as no one directly pointed to I Am. Working with the koan system was quite interesting but there were many shortcomings. The Zen philosophy represents a very profound, pure understanding of reality. However, any understanding is still in the mind, while the actual Awakening points to something much deeper. The koan system was not an original aspect of Zen, it later developed as a tool for practice but somewhere along the way became a focal point. This was a mistake because the essence of Awakening cannot be limited to any kind of structure. Reflecting reality 'just as it is,' is the principle of Zen. Ultimately this vision points to reality as reflected in the mirror of pure awareness. The problem is that the mind also can try to see reality 'as it is,' not from the place of pure awareness but from its mental standpoint. For this reason, the koan system can be very misleading. One learns how to give the proper answer according to Zen convention, but unfortunately still remains disconnected from the light of I Am. According to Zen, the right answer can only come from the right state, but it is possible that the right answer can come from the wrong place. It is possible that a student maybe fully established in the State of Presence and yet still cannot answer the koan. From the other side, I have met plenty of Zen students who solved many koans and knew nothing about pure awareness. Therefore, koans can become like a game of the mind when we forget that the true koan is beyond the mind. Actually the only koan which points directly to awakening is the discovery of I Am. If a Zen master does not point directly to the State of Presence but makes you work for months on some abstract Zen riddle, it proves some level of incompetence. Awakening can be simple but is often made complicated. I made myself go through the koan system, just to confirm my feelings and to make sure that indeed I wouldn't miss anything. In the end, Zen at least gave me a great deal of inspiration and a solid foundation for practice.

Not being able to make a major breakthrough in my practice, I decided to go East. In the West most seekers somehow believe that the spirit of Dharma is present only in the East. It is something like an inferiority complex. Usually when they go to the East, they become disappointed finding that practice in the West is often more authentic. Nevertheless, to get money for my travels, I went to France working hard picking fruits. After making enough money, I took the Trans-Siberian train to China. The journey took over one week and was rather psychedelic in those post-communistic times. There was total chaos, this train was like a buzzing market place, as everybody seemed to sell everything and from time to time a parade of prostitutes would pass. I spent some time in China and slept in surrealistic railway stations on the latest Beijing newspapers. At this point I decided to leave.

From China I took a boat to Korea. It was on this boat that I experienced my first disillusionment. Fleeting the West I was hoping to leave Christianity behind. To my surprise, Koreans who

I assumed would be Buddhist, attempted to make a Christian out of me, in our first encounter. It was on that boat that I almost died because of the onslaught of a heavy storm. It was a catastrophe, everybody threw up everywhere including myself. Fortunately, I arrived in Korea in one relative piece.

I had only a few hundreds US and no return ticket. I intended to do a traditional Zen three months retreat and let the future work itself out. I entered a Koran Zen Monastery, Shin Won Sa. The location of the monastery was splendid, up high in the Korean mountains. I had a wonderful time absorbed in silence and nature. I used to bathe in the freezing river at 3 o'clock in the morning so I could be fresh for the morning Zazen. Still, I always hated to wake up so early and could never really get used to such a disciplinary life style.

In that period I solved the main set of koans. I needed to solve them because I was uncertain about their importance in the awakening process. Not being able to solve them - I might have doubted the authority of my state. I was quite sad seeing those poor fellows trying to solve these abstract koans instead of directly awakening their consciousness. I had a few arguments with the leading there Zen master, in fact I had arguments with all the Zen masters. This man was anyway a good man, but quite identified with 'the school.' This school of Zen seemed to mould everyone into the same shape, as if they were making clones. Everybody seemed to speak the some language, ask the same questions and give the same answers. The most interesting thing was that none of those masters were actually interested in the inner state. No one ever asked: 'Aziz, what is your state?' Such a basic question! Instead, they asked: what did master Joshu mean saying Mu? Who really cares? It is wonderful to study the sayings of Old Sages, but what they were pointing to is much more important. In awakening to I Am one holds the essence of all possible koans, from the past, present and future. Afterwards I stayed in Korea for some time adjusting myself to life in monasteries and doing a lot of meditation. My state was still not fully established and awareness was fluctuating. It felt like I needed to move again to intensify my practice.

Soon appeared an opportunity to go to Japan. I had a strong attraction to the Soto school of Zen and to the teaching of Dogen. Entering Japan, the custom officer asked me: how much money do you have? I had only a few hundreds, but I said two thousand and they let me in. Even on the Path to Awakening you should not always be too honest! A friend of mine gave me the idea to earn money by doing 'takuhatsu,' which is a form of religious begging. The idea was to sit, unlike other monks, Zazen on the street with a begging bowl. My first begging experience was at the railway station in Hiroshima in the middle of the night. I collected some money and a big can of beer...

I stayed for six months in a Zen Dojo near Tokyo. I was studying Dogen's teaching and making money by sitting Zazen. I made a lot of money which helped me to travel later for a few years in Asia. As far as Dogen was concerned, he was a profound thinker but tended to be dogmatic. His concept of Shikan-taza was very subtle and profound. Zazen in his understanding was no longer a tool to become the Buddha but an expression of Truth. Zazen is Buddha! I was very inspired by this teaching. His teaching was for me a bridge between Advaita's vision of 'Awakening Now' and seeing Enlightenment as a future goal. However, his concept of a never-ending cultivation proves that he was not fully Self-realised. He disliked strongly the idea that after Enlightenment there is no need for practice anymore.

Another teacher, I connected to was Uchiyama Roshi who touched my heart by his humility and humanistic perception of Enlightenment. Yes, we all have in the beginning an inferiority complex. That's why humility and ordinariness in a master can bring a student that much closer to the truth of awakening. Afterwards I moved to a Rinzai monastery, Sogenji, in Okayama to undergo 'real' practice. I was practicing there under Harada Roshi who was a very sincere man. The place was perfect for concentrated practice... a very male atmosphere. The way the monks chanted the sutras was actually scary! I wondered how they could chant so fast, so deep and with such a power? It felt a bit like I was back in the army! Still, I felt this was the place where I could make a major breakthrough in my practice. I was allotted a space. I slept in the same place where I made my meditations. They had quite a strict set of rules and a very organised life style. Harada Roshi liked Zazen and so Zazen was the main form of practice in addition to a one week retreat every month. This practice included the technique of deep breathing and the solving of koans. I was forced to do this breathing even though I hated it. I asked myself, why to make this whole effort when I can just rest in the State of Presence? Disappointingly throughout my practice nobody ever asked about my inner state. The master had his own way of checking our state. His method included listening to the out-breath, particularly of the last stage when the belly contracts. Only later I realised that this way of checking one's state was not so precise. I refused to do this breathing except during interviews with the master. Each morning at dawn there was a private meeting with the master. It was actually quite frightening. In darkness, twenty shadows waited their turn at the sound of the bell. The master screamed at everyone. This interview was like a battle for life! He was extremely dedicated in pushing students to their breakthrough.

After my request, Roshi gave me a special permission to do a solo retreat in a secluded temple in the mountains. I broke my initial desire to fast during this retreat, eating fruits from the local cemetery and drinking the beer offerings left in the graveyard. During the retreat I got frostbite. I could not cure it for a long time as in these places they don't use any heating! Actually they were quite tough. In the morning, during the dead of winter, the first thing they did was open all windows wide! But I got used to it and started even to enjoy the freshness of the cold morning air. Despite the conditions, my practice was excellent. The most powerful time was during December of 1993. In that month I was intensely focussed on stabilising self-awareness. I was so concentrated that I was hardly aware of the outer world! When everybody went to sleep, I used to walk around in a trance of awareness. One night in the middle of this intensity - I let go! When I let go, I saw a new world! Everything was so beautiful! I looked at a tree and this tree was the Truth. I looked at a mountain and this mountain was itself an explosion of the Now! This ecstasy lasted for some time but eventually settled down. Later I understood that my experience was caused by the contrast of extreme concentration and a full letting go. During that time, I had a few more ecstatic experiences. One day to my surprise while checking my breath, the master shouted: yes! He approved of my realisation. Finally I stabilised the State of Presence.

I didn't know what to do next. While working on some more koans, I got into a disagreement with the master. I spent one month trying to solve a koan as he kept rejecting all of my answers. Eventually I found the answer but still I was sure that my past answers were even better! At this point, I realised there were no more reasons for me to stay as I was striving for my own vision of reality. I left the monastery and decided to do a two months retreat, this time in a Soto monastery. I spent a fortune to get to the other side of Japan. When I entered this place, I realised my mistake. This was a typical Japanese monastery - all the monks seemed devoid of any human emotion. They were just like Zazen-robots! This was a sign to leave Japan. Japan is a country of deep culture and precise focus, but emotionally it is like a desert...and when the heart closes, one simply becomes depressed. As such, the next day I left.

My next stop was Thailand. The first thing I experienced was a terrible sunburn on one of the islands. The second thing was getting poisoned by 'magic' mushrooms. I was experimenting with the State of Presence, trying to see whether drugs could disturb the state. The hallucinogenic did not take the state away but rather distorted the energetic quality of it. At that time I understood how delicate our brain is and that it needs to be respected. After getting poisoned, I went to a Thai monastery to spend the rest of my time in a more meditative atmosphere. The monastery was connected to the famous Ajan Cha. When arrived, all the monks looked completely spaced out. They only studied the rules of conduct as if Enlightenment was the equivalent of being a 'good monk'.

My next stop was India. I was very excited to finally see the land of the great Advaita masters! After many years of longing to come to this magical land, Existence now gave me this chance. When I arrived in Calcutta, I shed tears seeing the enormous poverty. Slowly I had to get used to it. This was India! I left to Lucknow where the disciple of Ramana Maharishi, the famous Poonjaji was teaching. He invited me for dinner, but I was unable to have a serious conversation with him. But the situation was not right, as I didn't come all the way from Japan just for a social visit. I had a burning desire to clarify the matter of Enlightenment. He was surrounded by female disciples, who in an air of an infinite admiration kept caressing his head. He seemed to be more interested in talking about his social life - that is by 'whom' he was visited and 'when' he was visited. During Satsang the next day, I asked him an interesting question. In his book was written his story of awakening. He chanted mantras with great dedication. Soon, a day came when he could no longer chant and so he went to Maharishi with his problem. Maharishi looked at him and said: you have arrived! My question was, how was it possible that Poonjaji didn't know himself that he arrived? Isn't Enlightenment self-evident? And what was the difference between the state he was in, prior to Maharishi's approval and after it? My question pointed to the important element of recognition. For it is the power of recognition which brings value to any state. However, Poonjaji, got quickly annoyed not being able to read the question (as all questions were submitted on paper) and became very rude. I also got very upset, so I stood up and left. Similar to Poonjaji, I had to admit that I was also looking for the recognition of my state. Guidance told me that in this life time I was not supposed to be recognised by a human master until I became fully confident in my own realisation. It was nevertheless my first disappointment with an Advaita master as all the inspiring literature I read gave me high hopes. The whole scene of Satsang was rather hysterical. All these seekers seemed to be in some kind of an unnatural euphoria. The whole scene was mainly based on projections regarding the legend of the great master of Poonjaji, Ramana Maharishi. In spirituality like in politics, to become popular one has to have the right name and connections. Again, the next day I left.

I decided to visit the Bodhi-tree under which Buddha reached Enlightenment. When I realised that this tree was just like any other tree and the sky above it was blue like everywhere else, I paid my homage and left in peace. Next I went to Dharamsala. There I had a discussion with one Dzogchen master about the nature of Rigpa, the State of Presence. According to this tradition, Rigpa is eternal but only temporarily covered by the ego. My point was, how come that in the deep sleep Rigpa is not present? There is no ego in deep sleep, so no one should obscure the purity of Rigpa! He said that Rigpa is present in the deep sleep in its own way. We couldn't reach any positive conclusion. The reason is that in Dzogchen, they don't differentiate between the state of pure awareness and state prior to awareness. The deep sleep state is simply prior to Rigpa and Rigpa is not as eternal as it seems. I left again...as my questions were still left unanswered.

I visited some gurus in Rishikesh. It was all rather amusing.

Most of the gurus looked rather suspicious. I attended a Satsang with a surprisingly well-known American woman, who didn't seem to have any clue as to what she was talking about. She gave some disconnected statements about Enlightenment, which showed her lack of basic knowledge and experience. And of course, nobody meditated there. Most seekers in Rishikesh seem to be completely spaced out and without any discriminative wisdom in their choice of a master. Either they smoked a lot or talked about some flighty experiences with their gurus. Because of poverty of my experience here, I was able to appreciate more my Zen training and wisdom.

I was very moved being able to visit the Samadhi of Nisargadatta Maharaj. There was a wonderful coincidence because the day I visited his place was also the anniversary of his death. I paid him homage and expressed my infinite gratitude for his guidance. I also used this opportunity to visit two other masters in the area: Ramesh Balsekar and Ranjit Maharaj. Ramesh was a very special man, in love with I Am, but rather identified with a certain Advaita line of logic. He was very humble and beyond guru trips, although our discussions about free will did not get anywhere, as he radically refused such a possibility. He asked me: 'why don't you find the inner essence?' I said, 'I am speaking from that place!' In that case why are you checking out all these gurus? 'Because that is my destiny,' I replied. I used his own argument of destiny to challenge his interrogation of my quest.

Most Advaita seekers go through Bombay to visit Ramesh. It is like the tourist in India who has to visit the Taj Mahal, so the Advaita seeker must visit Ramesh. And he tells them, they don't have free will, it is all just movie. He tells them that Enlightenment cannot be reached through effort for effort is from the ego and ego cannot jump above its own head. So they all realise through this 'logic' how ridiculous they are and they relax. Afterwards they see that the meeting was wonderful but they are still as miserable as before! My feeling is that Maharaj himself was not attached to the concept of destiny. Even though he spoke about destiny in such a fixed way, I feel that he could just say the opposite. This was the same issue regarding the need for practice. In the simplistic interpretation of Advaita, the need for practice is denied because practice takes place only in ignorance. But in an imaginative interpretation of Advaita, the vision of non-duality is more dynamic and includes the need for practice. That's why Maharishi spoke so much about arresting the mind, and Maharaj about keeping the sense of I Am, and so forth. Ramesh did not reach his awakening to the State of Presence directly through his effort, but neither through the dropping of his effort. It was through Maharaj that the energy of transformation shifted Ramesh into a higher state. It didn't merely happen because such was his destiny, but because of the presence of an alive master.

Later I realised that even though Ramesh is a direct successor of Maharaj, his view about the Absolute proves lack of this type of realisation. According to Ramesh, the Absolute represents consciousness at rest; however this is incorrect for, in truth, the Absolute is prior to consciousness. This is not merely a difference in terminology. In the first statement, Absolute prevails when consciousness is suspended, for instance in trance or deep sleep. But when we say that the Absolute is prior to consciousness, this means that it exist independently from consciousness. The reasoning of Ramesh shows that his perception of the Absolute is purely intellectual. He simply knows, while being conscious, that there exists a dimension deeper than this consciousness. But he didn't realise the simultaneous unity and co-existence of both of them. What it means is that being in consciousness, he does not abide experientially in the state prior to consciousness.

It was at that time that I also was convinced of understanding the teaching of Maharaj, without actually realising the Absolute. I was telling myself: I am in the state of pure consciousness, but prior to this very recognition of it, in this very Now is present the state prior to recognition, the Absolute. In this way, I was rather certain of being in the same state as Maharaj. It was two years later that I was supposed to realise my mistake.

Ranjit Maharaj was a very pleasant old man who lived in a tiny, little room in the middle of Bombay. He was a dharma brother of Nisargadatta, as they both had the same master. We had one conversation, although it was not very interesting. Maharaj simply repeated the model of reality based on the state prior to consciousness, the Absolute. But it was wonderful to see in the middle of this crazy city an old man with clear eyes, behind which was burning the unbroken fire of pure awareness and who was resting in the Uncreated!

In India one can find many interesting teachers. One of them is U.G. Krishnamurti. He reached the Absolute in a radical shift caused by kundalini energy. U.G. is a very sensitive being but seems to only live in a state of reaction. Battling constantly with past traditions and struggling with different masters seems to be a part of striving for one's freedom and one's unique perception. But when one gets addicted to this battle, one stays at the level of reaction throughout life, not allowing the Heart to open. This was also my problem which luckily got healed by the power of Grace. U.G. has an ambition to explain Enlightenment using the discoveries of science. But he cannot do it, for the limitations of science are not able to explore the mysteries beyond the linear mind. There is something not quite right in his negative attitude towards the issue of Enlightenment. It does not seem to make sense because though he refutes Enlightenment as a myth he also obviously claims to be enlightened.

My next stop was Pune. I found the teaching of Rajneesh rather interesting, inspiring and challenging. The problem was that the way he painted Enlightenment made it impossible to be reached! The self-image he projected was rather super-human. He behaved in a very unnatural way during his discourses not blinking and moving his hands in a slow manner. I was surprised that most of sannyasins, who were actually quite educated, believed that this behaviour had something to do with Enlightenment. Pune is an interesting place. It has helped many people but at the same time it has confused many. Entering the Ashram is like entering a huge mind. It was this type of Mind which called itself 'no-mind.' A strong conditioning was in the air, revolving solely around Osho philosophies and the New Age. For me the Ashram was a place to face some of my psychological issues, to experience a lot of dance, meet inspiring people and to relax.

At the time, I was deeply contemplating the nature of I Am. I discovered the relationship between the State of Presence and the mind. I saw that the presence of pure awareness does not automatically cleanse the mind and certain negativity's can still remain. I observed that there is indeed a movement even in the Inner State. Gradually, I freed myself from simplistic ideas about awakening. It was already in Poland that I had noticed that the State of Presence did not automatically remove my depression. I was wondering, how is it possible to be in the State of Presence and yet feel so sad or depressed? Nobody ever talked about it!

Only later, I understood that additional cleansing is necessary to purify the mind.

My Soul was not fully satisfied with the State of Presence. I was looking for a deeper peace, a deeper refuge inside. But the question was, how to reach it? I didn't know and nobody could help me. At that time, I met a man in a crystal shop who seemed to have a great deal of esoteric knowledge. I felt that I was speaking with a real person! His name was: Houman. Soon we became close friends. He initiated me into the secrets of energy and healing. I initiated him into the state of pure consciousness and shared my spiritual understanding. We complemented each other perfectly.

One day, at the end of 1996, during a channelling session of ours, the voice of Guidance came through. It was a real surprise for us, as we seemed to make a breakthrough, connecting to Intelligence from another dimension. It was not a typical experience in channelling, for some new and higher force had made entry. This force seemed to be a specific combination of our two Souls. This force spoke: 'we are not outside of you, we are not beings, we do not exist in a place like another planet. But we know you and we are your future. We speak to you from your future, into your present now.' It was like we met our True Parent or God. That voice answered all our questions and allowed us to understand our purpose. It had absolute wisdom and possessed a tremendous love. We met for the first time the Beloved. I asked: 'am I in the same state as Maharaj?' 'No, you are not.' 'How is it possible that there exists a truth beyond my present total experience?' 'It is simply possible!' 'Will I reach the same state as Maharaj?' 'Yes, and you will go deeper than him!' 'How can I reach the Absolute State?' 'You cannot reach it by will but through Grace only! From your side, you can co-operate through surrender.' Here, I faced a big problem. To admit that I was not fully Self-realised was very challenging for my ego. But did I have any choice? I submitted myself to that mysterious wisdom which seemed to know everything and more. I surrendered to that which I couldn't see but which my heart and my intelligence recognised as a representation of Truth.

Guidance sent me to do a solo retreat in South India and predicted the shift to the Absolute for the middle of December. I went to Kerala and started my retreat by the beach. How to reach the Absolute? Maharaj spoke only about the Absolute as such, but nothing about how to get there! He was saying that I am already THAT, but for some reason, I was not yet THAT! The intellectual conviction of being THAT does not actually help you become THAT. At that time I wasn't THAT in any way. Maharaj spoke about the witnessing of I Am. I Am itself is the witness. How could the witness be witnessed? Soon I discovered that whatever gymnastics I made with awareness, I was still locked within this awareness. It was in Pune that I kept demonstrating everyday to Guidance a different realisation, hoping that it was the Absolute. Each time Guidance patiently answered, 'not yet.' Yes, the only way to go beyond it is to surrender into Being. The key words which pointed in the right direction were: 'no-will' and 'absence.' I sat in absorption and tried various experiments. I contemplated the moment of falling asleep, just trying to recognise the condition of no-will and absence. I discovered that the place where the Absolute lives is at the bottom of the breath. To breakthrough this gate is to move to the Other Side. I was completely desperate! I was full of doubts, anxieties and impatience. It was a very difficult time. All my life seemed to culminate in this retreat. It was the final battle to reach the Absolute.

The shift happened on the 15th day of December 1996 around one in the morning. It was such a relief! I found myself slipping to the Other Side, to the Beyond. This implosion cannot be expressed in words. It was like diving to the bottom of the ocean and piercing through this bottom into the space on the other side. I experienced the absolute freedom. But the next day the passage closed again! I was so desperate and broken. But in a few days managed to slip into the Absolute State again. I needed to use a very subtle will to reach the condition of no-will. Guidance told me that Maharaj himself did hundreds of such attempts. On the 31st day of December 1996 I became stabilised in the Absolute. It felt like I had died and I had not been fully reborn. It was a mysterious time. For many lifetimes on the Buddhist Path, in my Soul there was imprinted a deep longing to reach the Unborn, to reach Nirvana. Upon reaching the Absolute State, I completed my Buddhist karma. I had reached complete disidentification and freedom from the apparent reality. My whole life of search reached culmination. The next few months I was completely absorbed inside, I was without any desire to do anything. The energy needed to settle down and integrate. Contemplating my life, I could see myself sitting in my little room in Poland reading 'I Am THAT' and now already in the Absolute, free at last. At that point I could have said that 'I am THAT,' but it would not have been a precise statement.

I returned to Pune. Shortly thereafter, I met shortly an Israeli guru who was rapidly growing in popularity. Our meeting had been arranged. I was curious whether he like myself might have mistaken the State of Presence for the Absolute. He had a sudden shift into the State of Presence, but he didn't know how he got there and that there were other possibilities of expansion. He didn't seem to recognise anything I said. This knowledge is precious and it is rare to find a Soul who desires to dive into the ocean of its mystery, into the depth of New Understanding. Most teachers convince themselves they have reached the complete state and cannot allow themselves to even doubt it (even that they secretly very much do) for they would lose their role as a true master. At that time, I understood that in order to attract seekers, one does not need to be at all fully Self-realised. It is all a game based on guru projections and creating the right guru atmosphere. Some get around just by imitating Osho. People love it for in actuality they don't really desire awakening but rather someone sitting on a high chair, so they can unload their projections unto them. In my teaching, I look to maintain the right perspective in terms of my ego-image. Since Enlightenment does not eliminate the ego, one has to always practice humility. The problem with most Satsangs is the ego projected from the master and its further reinforcement by disciples. There are many cases of manipulations and even abuse regarding the issue of power and control. It is quite sad. Many of those teachers behave in quite an unnatural way. They walk very slowly, they project some spaced out look into the eyes of their followers, they speak very slowly and so on. It is such hogwash but so many naïve seekers think that it is an appropriate type behaviour! There is probably no cure for all this nonsense. It has to be accepted on some level as a part of the collective ignorance regarding spirituality.

I was invited to teach in Israel. Being in Israel was rather difficult because of its claustrophobic atmosphere and lack of nature. Despite this, I did meet a few very dedicated students.

The first of them was Reza, who quickly received the transmission of the Absolute State. I began my teaching work. It was challenging, as I was very shy and nervous of being in front of many people. Because my life was spent mainly in isolation I had difficulties in relating to others. At that time the only thing I was interested in was teaching the Absolute. Only later, came to understand that the Absolute is the destiny of very few seekers. After the shift into the Absolute, I was tired all the time, as my energy system needed to adjust. I was learning how to enter the world from the place of the inner Void.

From Israel I went to Japan and wrote my next book 'Beyond Consciousness'. The energy of this book had a strong Buddhist flavour even though I was already presenting a new vision of awakening. In July 1997 I again met Houman in America. I was very surprised as our work was about to begin again! Guidance said: 'Aziz, you have done well, but now we have to open your Heart and awaken your Soul.' My task was to put Houman into the Absolute State and his job was to open my heart chakra. Working with the heart was not an easy task because the whole area was not very clear to me. The concept of the Soul which Guidance introduced was rather against my basic non-dual make-up. It felt like a naïve word but Guidance couldn't find a better term for the essence of our individual creation. According to Guidance, one can be enlightened in a traditional sense and yet have no soul! Later, we started to use more the term Me which had the enormous power of simplicity. Completing our work, took us over half a year. It was an intense time. We were constantly doing energy work on each other, retreats and praying to God.

I was coming closer and closer to the Beloved and to the experience of happiness. The Absolute State was not able to give me happiness. I was still very isolated and disconnected from the reality of Creation. I was opening my heart and finally discovering my Soul, the child within. Sometimes I wanted to give up for I didn't see any real progress. But gradually the energy of my heart started to move. There was more and more warmth and happiness around me. This happiness was not psychological but was manifested purely on the energy level. I meditated on my heart day and night, awakening to my Soul and discovering the Beloved. I was becoming free from my Buddhist past. We received constant instruction from Guidance. In moments, we were losing faith, Guidance would always bring healing and encouragement.

Apart from opening my heart, Guidance was deeply cleansing my subconscious mind. I began to understand how it was possible that even though I rested in the Absolute, I could still be rather unhappy. It was all about the negative perception of life crystallised on the subconscious level. Many lives on the Buddhist path imprinted in me a negative perception of Creation. This negative vision of life was not conscious but imprinted on the energy level. As Guidance cleansed my subconscious, suddenly something got freed from my infinite past. For the first time, I could truly see this reality as a beautiful expression of the Creator. The complete Enlightenment to the heart and its stabilisation took place at the beginning of December 1997. In the middle of that month Houman shifted to the Absolute. During his retreat, there was a very powerful transmission of the Absolute which transported his soul to the Unmanifested.

Our meeting was absolutely amazing. He was born with an enlightened heart and a strong message to help humanity. I was born with an enlightened consciousness and with the strong message to transcend this dimension. Our meeting brought harmony and balance to our Souls. Houman moved to the place beyond helping and non-helping recognising the low level of humanity and seeing that there is hardly anybody to be helped. And me, I opened my heart to compassion and moved forward towards humanity. During the period of 1997, not only did we reach completion but gained understanding into the secrets of the teaching and transmission. Guidance was continuously preparing us as channels of Transformation.

In the beginning of 1998, we reached a further awakening which we called 'Enlightenment to Me.' We understood finally that this fundamental and extraordinary truth was All About ME. Guidance said, 'Aziz, your fight against traditions was not about the battle of ideology, but about coming back to your Me. You had to free your psyche from all concepts which negated the existence of your very Me in order to fully meet yourself.' That was so true. All my life was about meeting Me. This realisation was so simple, yet so subtle and profound. From the very first experience of suffering, long walks in the forest, fear and yearning for security and love, in truth, it was all about Awakening to Me.

Gradually the New Teaching was taking shape. The book 'Enlightenment Beyond Traditions' had emerged from the depth of our Intelligence. It was a very precious work revealing the secrets of the inner world. It clarified many misconceptions about Enlightenment. This book for most students is difficult to understand. When one is fed with over-cooked food, one forgets how to eat the raw food of Truth. This book needs to be read many times and contemplated deeply. It is not for a lukewarm seeker but for seekers of the Truth.

Being in America, apart from its thrilling nature was really rather disappointing. I wrote a few articles to the Buddhist magazines about the role of ego, 'Buddha Mind and Christ Consciousness' and other subjects. There was a very little response. Americans are too busy to look for Truth. They prefer to conform to available traditions, like Buddhism, which offer a comforting sense of security. I did do some teaching but mainly in order to prepare myself for my future work as a channel of Guidance. Although, it was only preparation, a few Souls became deeply touched by the energy of Transmission. It was about the time to leave America. Guidance made further prophecy about our next shift, into the State Beyond Polarities. There was supposed to be a state even beyond Awakening to Me, where the Soul fully meets the Beloved. Guidance said that Osho and Trungpa reached this state at the end of their lives and even though they could not understand its meaning, they lived it. In order to reach such a state, one foot has to be in the Absolute and the other foot in the Divine Dimension. Sufi masters get there easier. Rumi was, for instance, in that exalted state. I asked Guidance: 'is it in the realm of Me?' Guidance remained silent for a long time and answered: it is not for us to tell this...but yes, Aziz, it is in the dimension of Me...

Houman decided to move to Hawaii. It was unbelievable time which in truth we cannot share with anybody. We left deeply moved and completely transformed.

* * *

After leaving America, I was sent to work. I started teaching in Israel and afterwards I moved to India. Not used to channelling such amounts of energy, after an intense period in Israel I was completely depleted. There was a day I felt like I almost died.

Private work in particular with students (based on consultation and energy transmission) seemed to exhaust me a lot. My being was still weak after the shift to the Absolute State and I needed to sleep a lot.

Teaching in India was quite interesting but very disappointing. At that time, I still had the illusion that somewhere on this planet there were many seekers waiting for Truth. From that time on, I started to realise more and more the sad truth that seekers do not really exist, apart from a very few. I began teaching in Dharamsala where a strong Buddhist community had formed. My Satsang attracted many Buddhist intellectuals who were completely stuck in their minds. One Tibetan Lama wanted to argue that keeping I Am would be proof of attachment, and therefore against the Buddha teachings. But what is the whole eighth-fold path which Buddha offered to humanity but a type of attachment which is supposed to take us to Freedom? Soon I saw that most people were rather satisfied in only shopping for spirituality without any real desire for awakening. Most are either not serious or simply play ego-games.

My next station was Pune as I decided to return and I had to face the low consciousness of people running the ashram, who didn't want me to teach in the area. According to them I was supposed to teach inside the ashram. But in such a case, I would have no choice but repeat Osho like a good boy, which I was not interested in doing at all. It was the irony that even though Osho had taught about being a Rebel, the place he created turned the people instead into Ashram conformists. After being insulted by a few suspicious individuals running the ashram, I was quite happy to say good bye to this place.

Most sannyasins who came to Satsang were strongly conditioned either by pseudo-Advaita clichés or by the naïve idea of celebration. In truth, both ideas complement each other. The first one justifies that one does not need do anything to awaken apart from maybe relaxing. And the other one brings some kind of a simple joy into unconsciousness, so it is more bearable. Most seekers who came were shocked by the idea that they had to meditate and were not allowed to lay down and sleep during Satsang! Very few were able to appreciate that they received actual tools to awaken. Most of them would rather be stuck in their illusory search the whole life, just waiting 'for something to happen.' Still in spite of it all, Pune is a magical place and often special encounters can happen here. Anyway, I did meet a few good people. As Guidance mentioned, only one percent of seekers can be touched by the light of Truth. Afterwards, I moved to Arambol, a gorgeous beach in Goa which is a natural power place. Arambol became one of my bases for teaching in India.

Presently

In 7 March 1999, when Uranus transited my natal Saturn, I had the shift into the State Beyond Polarities, as Guidance predicted. In the same period Houman was transported Beyond Polarities in Hawaii. All the three centres of I Am became One and merged with the Beyond. Although I have become One with the Beloved, my human aspect is still evolving. As a teacher, I had to pacify my shyness and nervousness. There is still an emotional evolution for me and space to reach further harmony within my personality. My evolution continues but it is taking place in the dimension beyond Enlightenment. This further evolution takes me deeper into the mystery and cannot really be shared as it belongs to my unique blueprint.

In my teaching work many have become fully transformed. It is all by the force of Grace and Guidance. Many were shifted to the dimension of pure consciousness; a few dedicated students have realised the Absolute State and some have reached Enlightenment to Me. But I am still rather disappointed with the level of understanding and appreciation of most students. So few are able to see the tremendous value of this teaching. It is not just Awakening alone which matters but the depth of sensitivity coming from intelligence and the Heart, and this is lacking the most.

As a teacher speaking in the name of Enlightenment I often have to suffer seeker's projections. Some of them look at me with unnatural admiration; some pass their judgements and some just think that I am just a regular guy because I don't project any guru-image. All of them are wrong. I am not God and nothing could be more false than worshipping me. Next, those who have judgements about me are either ignorant or come from an impure intention. And finally those who want to look at me as a fellow to hang out with are simply not sensitive enough to see that I Am Beyond.

I can say that I was blessed. I can say that it was worth it to be alive despite all my suffering along the Path, it has all been worth this absolute total experience of the Now. I have been blessed for I discovered the Purpose, the Meaning and Truth of my existence. I have been blessed for I returned home to the state of unity with the Beloved. Yes, I have been seen by the Divine and embraced by the infinite wisdom and love which entered my life from the Beyond. I have been blessed for I know beyond a doubt that in spite of all the difficulties in human life, there is Only Love.

Now from my future, I can embrace the small child born 38 years ago in his fear and shock of returning to this plain of ignorance. As I guide him towards his Future Fulfilment, I say onto him: It is OK, everything is OK. You are in good hands. The Beloved is with You.

Fig. 1 With Reza 97

Fig. 2 Israel 98

Fig. 3 With Houman Seattle 97

Fig. 4 Houman Seattle 98

Fig. 5 Satsang Pune 98

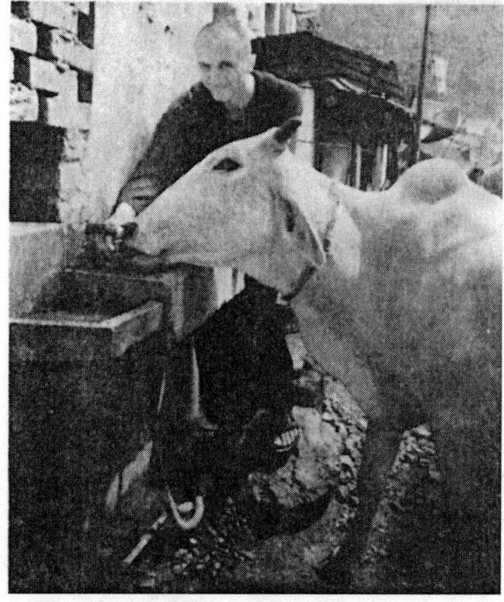

Fig. 6 Rishikesh 99

Fig. 7 Arambol, Goa

Fig. 8 Israel 99

Explanation of Terms

Absolute: The original energy, the Unmanifested, the Unborn. The Centre of Gravity. The Source of manifestation.

Absolute State: The condition of Pure Rest. The dimension where the Soul becomes one with the Absolute, in a conscious way.

Absorption: Samadhi. Rest in Being.

Advaita Vedanta: The Path of "Non-duality." The Mystical assumption that Self-knowledge annihilates the "illusory." in its essence presence of Me. Philosophical interpretation of the enlightened state which denies the presence of Me as being a part of the experience of Self-realisation.

Apperception: The total perception of What Is, within which the impersonal aspect of Self-realisation and the realisation of Me - coexist as one reality.

Awareness: The ability to know. The light of Clarity and the essence of Intelligence.

Being: One of three aspects of the I Am. The ability to rest within. The energy link of an individual being with the Absolute.

Beloved: The Heart of Creation. The power of Love and Intelligence inherent in Creation and Beyond. Divine Mother. The Soul's eternal Parent.

Beyond Polarities: The Eighth State. The stage of Self-realisation where Awareness reaches the condition of complete absorption and motionlessness. The Soul fully merges with the Other Dimension.

Blueprint: The ultimate vision of the Soul's completion. The culmination of the Soul's evolution and her final destiny.

Buddha Mind: Equivalent to the Absolute State. Complete unity with the Original State.

Christ Consciousness: Complete realisation of the Soul. Oneness with the Divine. Enlightenment to the Heart.

Complete Me: The unity of Pure Me and personality.

Complete Meditation: A system of meditation aimed at the awakening of the complete I Am. It is based on the understanding that the I Am, the Inner State of wholeness, is composed of three aspects: Awareness, Being and Heart.

Conscious Me: Intuitive intelligence. A state where Me can partially sense herself apart from the movement of subconsciousness. The ability to give conscious feedback to the experience. In the case of the subconscious Me, the experience refers to the unclear sense of Me, while in the case of the conscious Me - it is the sense of Me which can refer in a conscious way to the experience.

Consciousness: The ability to be "conscious of." A unity of intelligence and Presence. Equivalent to Awareness.

Creation: The cosmic vision of God. The totality of manifestation. The divine play. The apparent reality.

Divine: The Beloved. Universal I AM. Universal ME.

Divine Mother: The Divine Dimension. The Love and Grace of God.

Duality: The experience of separation. The primal polarisation of Existence into the subject-object perception of reality. The basic Two-ness of Creation which enables consciousness to operate.

Dual-non-duality: The Supreme Understanding beyond duality and non-duality, which points to the fact that the realisation of God can become a conscious experience only because of the dual presence of Me (the separation of Me from the Beloved). The state of existence where the universal space of I AM co-exists with the Me that recognises it. Unity of Soul-realisation with Self-realisation.

Dvaita-advaita: Dual-non-duality.

Ego: Self-conscious movement of intelligence based on the inherent sense of Me. The ability of self-referral.

Emptiness: Equivalent of the Absolute. The original state prior to Consciousness. Also Pure Awareness without content: the manifested aspect of Emptiness.

Enlightenment: Awakening to the sense of identity deeper than the personal self. The expansion of the Soul into the Beyond. Meeting of the Soul with her Creator. Many levels of Enlightenment: Enlightenment to the State of Presence, pure awareness; Enlightenment to the Absolute State, beyond awareness; Enlightenment to the Heart; Enlightenment to the Soul. Re-union with the Universal I AM. Oneness with the Beloved.

Exalted State: The Absolute State.

God: The Beloved. The unity of the Absolute and the Divine.

Grace: The loving care of the Beloved embracing the Soul in all aspects of her existence.

Guidance: Conscious presence of the Over-soul. The dimension of Universal Intelligence lovingly guiding the evolution of the Soul.

Heart: The centre of the Soul. The energy centre responsible for the experience of the Divine. The centre of sensitivity and love.

Here: The horizontal reality of time and space. The apparent reality.

Horizontal Reality: The Here. The time-space reality.

I AM: Absolute Subjectivity. The Beloved. The Divine. Universal Intelligence and Love. A transcendental unity of Being, Love and Intelligence.

I Am: The experience of the Universal I AM within the energy system of an individual being. A reflection of Wholeness in the individual Soul. A meeting point of the Soul with the Universal I AM.

Intelligence: The wisdom and creativity of the mind.

Intuitive Intelligence: The faculty to co-create with the thinking process. A meeting point of Me with the subconscious mind. The ego. Conscious feedback from Me to the subconscious mind.

Karma: One of the laws of Creation pointing to the realisation that cause and effect are interconnected.

Koan: A saying of a master which points directly to Truth. A Zen teaching device to stop conceptualisation. Direct pointing to the naked reality perceived without the medium of the mind.

Liberation: Reaching the Absolute State. Complete disidentification with the apparent reality. Freedom from the Here. Different to Transcendence.

Light of Creation: Universal I AM.

Leela: Play of God. The mystery of Creation. The illusion and adventurous character of time-space reality.

Maya: Manifested reality. The play of phenomena. The Here, the environment of the universal subconsciousness. Creation perceived as if in separation from the Creator.

Me: The Soul; the conscious expression of the Soul. The unique angle of perception. The reflection of the Beloved in her individual self-conscious creation. Complete Me: unity of Awareness, Being and Heart. The centre of Me: Heart. The consciousness of Me: mind.

Meditation: The conscious effort to reach I Am. Pure meditation: just being, Non-doing, resting within the I Am.

Mind: Movement of thoughts. The centre of the mind: pure Awareness. Intuitive Intelligence: self-consciousness of the mind. Subconscious mind: impersonal arising of thoughts.

Mystical State: An experience beyond the mind but not centred in the I Am.

Non-abidance: To rest upon "nothing." State of pure Being without referral to objective or subjective reality.

1. **Partial Non-abidance:** rest in the Absolute, to abide in the Unmanifested.
2. **Complete Non-abidance:** pure rest in the Beloved, where the Absolute and the Divine are one.
3. **Transcendental Non-abidance:** Pure Me, beyond the Inner (the Absolute) and the outer (the Creation), rests in the Universal I AM, meets the Beloved.

Non-doing: Pure rest in Being. State of ultimate surrender into the Now.

No-mind: State of consciousness beyond thinking. The State of Presence, a dimension of no-mind. The Absolute State: a deeper dimension of the no-mind. Unity of the State of Presence, the Absolute State and Awakened Heart - represents the deepest dimension of No-mind.

Non-dual Path: The vision of spiritual Awakening which combines the need for practice and evolution with direct insight into the Now.

Now: The vertical reality. The essence of Reality. The Uncreated. The Source of the Here. The Timeless.

Other Dimension: Dimension of the Beloved. The uncreated aspect of the Now.

Over-Soul:

1. The loving expression of the Beloved,
2. The link between the Soul and the Universal Intelligence.
3. The compassionate power of Guidance and Grace.
4. Different families of Souls (having similar evolutionary blueprint) have their own Over-soul.

Personality: The basic structure of identity formed from the physical, emotional and mental bodies. The extension of the Soul in the world.

Prayer: Conscious connection with the Beloved. A deep feeling of unity with the Heart of the Creator.

Psyche: Often the equivalent of personality. A deeper understanding: this part of the Soul which is already manifested but not yet crystallised as personality. Intuitive intelligence.

Pure Me: Fully awakened Me experiencing herself beyond the subconscious mind. A unity of thought-less awareness, pure rest in Being and an awakened Heart. The Soul in her purity experiencing herself beyond the inner and the outer states.

Pure Suffering: Suffering which is not cause by negativity or ignorance but by the fact of being human and being Here.

Real Me: State of Presence. The awareness aspect of the Soul.

Rigpa: State of Presence.

Samadhi: Pure rest in the I AM.

Sat-chit-ananda: The Ultimate Reality. Sat: Being. Chit: Awareness. **Ananda:** Heart.

Satsang: Sitting in the presence of a Self-realised being. Higher meaning: abiding in the I AM.

Self: The I AM. The dimension of Pure Subjectivity. Self-knowingness. The direct experience of Reality without the medium of thought or perception. Pure Consciousness.

Self-conscious Me: The State of Presence. Me fully conscious of itself apart from subconsciousness. Self-awareness. Attention aware of attention. Witnessing consciousness. Centre in the mind.

Shikantaza: Pure meditation. Just sitting. Non-abidance. Non-doing state beyond the personal will.

Soul: A unique taste of the I AM being experienced in its individual manifestation. Pure, sense of Me being centralised in the Heart.

Source: The Absolute. The Uncreated.

Stabilisation: A stage of practice where the experience of the Inner State becomes permanently established. A stage of going beyond practice.

State: A level of evolution:

1. **First State:** Deep Sleep State (dreamless sleep).
2. **Second State:** Dream State.
3. **Waking State:** The ego-consciousness.
4. **Fourth State:** State of Presence (self-awareness).
5. **Fifth State:** Absolute State.
6. **Sixth State:** Enlightenment to the Heart.
7. **Seventh State:** Enlightenment to Me (Soul-realisation).
8. **Eighth State:** Beyond Polarities. Me become one with the Beloved.

State of Presence: Pure Awareness. The centre of the mind. Attention aware of attention, free from objects. The centre of Me in intelligence.

Subconscious Me: Situation where the sense of Me is fully lost in the dream-like activity of the mind. A level of consciousness which is unable to create self-referral. Dream state or day-dreaming. Spontaneous activity of the mind occurring below the level of conscious intelligence.

Subconsciousness: The impersonal movement of intelligence and life, which occurs bellow the conscious level.

Sudden Enlightenment: A non-gradual shift of consciousness into the transcendental state.

Sudden Path: The Non-dual Path. A vision of practice based on the radical insight into the Now.

Transcendence: Beyond Liberation. The state which, apart from the presence of the complete Inner State, encompasses completion in the dimension of Me. The state when the Soul is fulfilled both, in the Inner and in the Outer.

Transmission: Satsang. An event taking place in the presence of a Master, who transmits the experience of Enlightenment through his or her own energy and understanding. A power of Grace coming from the Beyond through a Master in order to bring transformation.

Transparent Me: Enlightenment to Me. The complete Soul-realisation. The unity of Pure Me and the Absolute State.

Turiya: The Fourth State. The State of Presence.

Turiyatitta: Beyond the Fourth State. Various levels of merging into Being from the place of awakened Awareness.

Ultimate Subjectivity: Universal I AM.

Unconsciousness: An astral plane. The bridge between the Universal I AM and the Universal Subconsciousness.

Universal Intelligence: The wisdom of God.

Vertical Reality: The Now. The zero point of existence prior to perception. The dimension of Being.

Witnessing: The presence of self-awareness at the background of the mind. The State of Presence. (Note: not a precise term for it implies duality).

The Family of the Creator

1. **The Beloved:** The unity of the Absolute and the Divine.
2. **The Absolute:** The Being of God, the emptiness aspect of the Ultimate.
3. **Source:** The Absolute, the Uncreated Reality.
4. **The Divine:** The Heart of the Creator, the love of God.
5. **The Divine Mother:** The Divine Dimension, the Grace of God.
6. **The Light of Creation:** The Universal I AM.
7. **Universal Intelligence:** The wisdom of God.
8. **Universal Consciousness:** The infinite ocean of I AM, the mind of God.
9. **I AM:** The totality of the Divine Presence.
10. **Grace:** An aspect of the Divine.
11. **Guidance:** Grace, the guiding quality of the Creator embracing the Soul's journey in time.

The Family of the Soul

1. **Personality:** The basic structure of identity formed from the physical, emotional and mental bodies.
2. **Ego:** The ability for self-referral in the mind.
3. **Subconscious Me:** The sense of Me completely lost in thinking and daydreaming.
4. **Conscious Me:** The ego, the ability to think consciously.
5. **Real Me:** The State of Presence, the state of self-attention, the host of the mind, the Me conscious of herself.
6. **Pure Me:** Pure feeling of Me in the Heart combined with the State of Presence.
7. **Complete Me:** The unity of Pure Me and personality.
8. **Transparent Me:** The unity of Pure Me and the Absolute State.